THE PAINTINGS OF Jakuchū

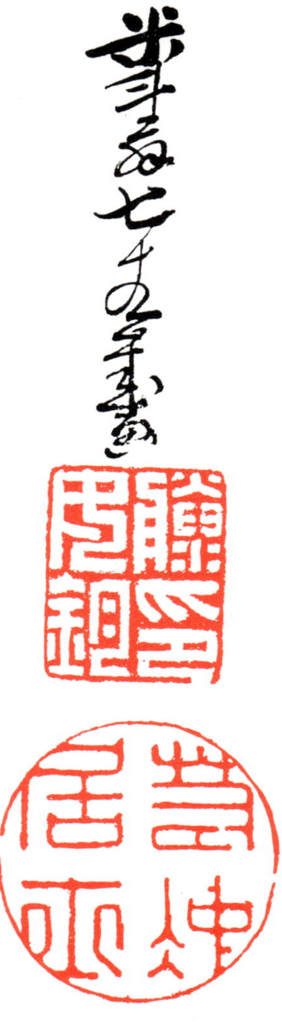

THE PAINTINGS OF Jakuchū

MONEY L. HICKMAN
YASUHIRO SATŌ

The Agency for Cultural Affairs, Tokyo
The Asia Society Galleries, New York
Los Angeles County Museum of Art

Published on the occasion of
THE PAINTINGS OF Jakuchū,
an exhibition organized by
The Agency for Cultural Affairs, Tokyo,
The Asia Society Galleries, New York,
Los Angeles County Museum of Art.

THE ASIA SOCIETY GALLERIES, NEW YORK
October 5, 1989–December 6, 1989

LOS ANGELES COUNTY MUSEUM OF ART
December 21, 1989–February 2, 1990

COVER: *Rooster and Blossoming Plum in Snow* (NO. 13)

First published in the United States of America in 1989
by The Asia Society Galleries

Andrew Pekarik, Director
Osa Brown, Assistant Director, Publisher

Designed by Peter Oldenburg
Photography courtesy of
The Agency for Cultural Affairs, Tokyo, except as noted
Printed and bound by
Toppan Printing Company Ltd., Tokyo, Japan

LIBRARY OF CONGRESS CATALOGUE CARD NUMBER 89-83951
The cloth edition of this book is published in association with Harry N. Abrams, Inc., New York, a Times Mirror Company.

ISBN: 0-87848-070-6 (softcover, TASG)
0-8109-3500-7 (hardcover, Abrams)

First edition

TABLE OF CONTENTS

THIS EXHIBITION AND BOOK
have been made possible by the generous support of

Tobishima Associates, Ltd.

The Stanhope

The Mary Livingston Griggs and Mary Griggs Burke Foundation

National Endowment for the Arts, a United States government agency

Additional support has been provided by

Japan-United States Arts Program of the Asian Cultural Council

The Starr Foundation

The Andrew W. Mellon Foundation

Friends of The Asia Society Galleries

An indemnity has been granted by the
Federal Council on the Arts and Humanities

LENDERS TO THE EXHIBITION

Daikōmyōji Temple, Kyoto
Hiraki Ukiyo-e Foundation, Tokyo
Imperial Household Collection, Tokyo
Kurokawa Institute of Ancient Cultures, Hyōgo Prefecture
Kyoto National Museum
Mampukuji Temple, Kyoto
National Archives of Japan, Tokyo
Private Collections
Rokuonji Temple, Kyoto
Ryōsokuin Temple, Kyoto
Saifukuji Temple, Osaka
Shōkokuji Temple, Kyoto
Sōdōji Temple, Wayakama Prefecture
Tokyo National Museum
Tokyo National University of Fine Arts and Music

FOREWORD

It is with great pleasure that I welcome the opening of this exhibition of the works of Itō Jakuchū, cosponsored by The Asia Society Galleries, the Los Angeles County Museum of Art, and the Agency for Cultural Affairs.

Each year the Agency for Cultural Affairs, in cooperation with a major museum in a country outside Japan, presents an exhibition designed to introduce Japanese culture to the people of that country. The exhibitions in the United States, a country that has an especially close relationship with Japan, have focused on various areas displaying the special characteristics of Japanese art, with the aim of deepening the understanding between the two nations. In recent years, such exhibitions have included *Emaki* (1983), cosponsored with The Asia Society, and *Japanese Ink Painting* (1985), cosponsored with the Los Angeles County Museum of Art. The Agency for Cultural Affairs selected the works and conceived the plan of the present exhibition in accordance with the wishes of The Asia Society Galleries. It is the first time that an overseas exhibition sponsored by the Agency for Cultural Affairs has been devoted entirely to the work of a single artist.

The art of Jakuchū, which is particularly individualistic, even among the variegated expressions of Japanese art, creates a world that is at once realistic and fantastic. It has found enthusiastic admirers among Americans, and I trust that this exhibition will bring many more into contact with the works of Jakuchū so that they will enjoy fully his art's peculiar and enduring charm. At the same time, it is my hope that visitors to the exhibition will consider the nature of Japanese culture during the Edo period, as seen through the world of Jakuchū's art.

In Japan, as in Europe, the eighteenth century was an age of scientific inquiry. Stimulated by curiosity about natural phenomena, numerous scholars and dilettantes observed, recorded, and exchanged a variety of information. Jakuchū's time was also a period in which many intellectuals and artists, in complete disregard of the strict limitations of social stratification upheld by the Tokugawa shogunate, carried on individualistic activities and came close to a free interchange of ideas. These two trends were important in paving the way for Japan's so-called modernization; I think that reflections of them can be seen in the works of Jakuchū.

However, the point to be emphasized above all is that it was an extremely peaceful age that gave rise to Jakuchū's art. Throughout the Edo period, except at the very beginning and the very end, no wars were carried on, either within Japan or abroad, for a period of more than two hundred years. It is surely of great significance for all of us today to appreciate the art encouraged by this long period of peace and to recognize its value.

Finally, I extend heartfelt thanks to Andrew Pekarik, Director of The Asia Society Galleries, to Earl A. Powell III, Director of the Los Angeles County Museum of Art, and to the various members of their staffs, all of whom exerted themselves to the utmost to make this exhibition a reality; and to the Japanese lenders who gladly consented to the public display of their precious works of art.

Hiroshi Ueki

Commissioner General
Agency for Cultural Affairs

THE FINEST JAPANESE art has become increasingly familiar to American audiences thanks to the dedicated work of the Agency for Cultural Affairs. We are very proud to have worked with them on *The Paintings of Jakuchū*, and I thank Mr. Hiroshi Ueki, Commissioner General, for this opportunity. I hope that there will be many more.

When I first proposed to Mr. Nobuyoshi Yamamoto, Councillor on Cultural Properties, then Director, Fine Arts Division, that we collaborate on an exhibition project, we agreed that Jakuchū was a particularly appropriate subject because his paintings are unusually accessible to Western audiences.

I know of this wide appeal from personal experience. While living in Japan in 1971, I attended the great Jakuchū exhibition at the Tokyo National Museum. Although I knew very little about Japanese art at the time, I was moved and excited by the extraordinary intensity and energy that I sensed in Jakuchū's paintings. I was also delighted by the details and juxtapositions that I read as spontaneous touches of humor: the ordinary dove, for example, that appears in the branches of the pine tree to peer at the astonishing white phoenix.

Jakuchū's paintings are visually fascinating because of his mastery of technique and naturalistic abstraction, but the fact that they are based in a deep and penetrating religiosity raises them, in my opinion, above the works of his peers. Jakuchū deserves a more prominent position on the world art stage, and I hope this exhibition will help to focus attention on his work.

We are pleased and honored that the Los Angeles County Museum of Art has agreed to join The Asia Society Galleries in presenting this exhibition. Their interest in Jakuchū's work and commitment to Japanese art are well expressed in their new Pavilion for Japanese Art.

I personally wish to thank Dr. Money Hickman and Mr. Yasuhiro Satō for their work in preparing this exhibition. I owe a deep debt of gratitude to Mr. Nobuyoshi Yamamoto, Councillor on Cultural Properties, and Mr. Akiyoshi Watanabe, Director of Fine Arts Division, who made this project possible and worked with me at every stage. I am very grateful also to Tobishima Associates, Ltd., The Stanhope, the Mary Livingston Griggs and Mary Griggs Burke Foundation, the National Endowment for the Arts, as well as the Asian Cultural Council, The Starr Foundation, The Andrew W. Mellon Foundation, and the Friends of The Asia Society Galleries for the financial support that enabled us to present these paintings. Above all, I wish to thank the lenders who allowed these rare and wonderful paintings to travel to America. This exhibition is a tribute not only to the genius of Jakuchū, but also to the generosity of those who love his art.

ANDREW PEKARIK

Director, The Asia Society Galleries

THE LOS ANGELES County Museum of Art is honored to be the co-presenter of *The Paintings of Itō Jakuchū*. We are deeply grateful to Dr. Andrew Pekarik of The Asia Society Galleries and to Mr. Nobuyoshi Yamamoto of the Agency for Cultural Affairs for inviting us to become the second and final venue of this exhibition. It is particularly fitting that our museum be the co-presenter of the work of Jakuchū, for the Shin'enkan Collection of Japanese painting, a promised gift of Mr. and Mrs. Joe D. Price, has the strongest holdings of paintings by Jakuchū outside of Japan.

In September of 1988 the Los Angeles County Museum of Art opened the Pavilion for Japanese Art. Designed by Bruce Goff and executed by Bart Prince, the Pavilion is the only major structure outside of Japan solely devoted to the display and study of Japanese art. During the course of the Jakuchū exhibition, which will take place in the Ahmanson Building, the works of Jakuchū and his school will be featured in the Pavilion for Japanese Art as a complement to the magnificent exhibition created by The Asia Society Galleries and the Agency for Cultural Affairs. I also wish to thank Robert Singer, Curator of Japanese Art, for his efforts on behalf of the exhibition here in Los Angeles.

EARL A. POWELL III

Director, Los Angeles County Museum of Art

ACKNOWLEDGMENTS

ON BEHALF OF the authors I would like to thank the Itabashi Art Museum, the Osaka Municipal Art Museum, the Shizuoka Prefectural Art Museum, the Tokyo National Institute of Cultural Properties, the Wakayama Prefectural Museum, the publishing firms Kokka-sha and Shibundo, Professor Tsuji Nobuo, and Kodaira Tadao for their help in arranging for photography for the catalogue. I also wish to acknowledge Christine Wirth for her help in typing the original manuscript, as well as Sarah Thompson, Stephanie Wada, Dorothy Wong, Stephen and Francesca Forrest, Todd Harris, and Anat Turbowicz for their assistance in translating the text of the catalogue section. We deeply appreciate the advice and encouragement of Professors Tsuji Nobuo, Kobayashi Tadashi, and John Rosenfield, as well as Joe D. Price, Miyajima Shin'ichi, Watanabe Akiyoshi, and Yamamoto Nobuyoshi.

The successful creation of this book is due to the extraordinary talent and dedication of Osa Brown, who supervised all phases of editing, design, and production.

She was expertly assisted at every stage by Becky Mikalson with the capable support of Kathryn Selig and Merantine Hens. We are indebted to Peter Oldenburg for the wonderful design for the book. Many thanks to Karen Robinson for being the production editor during the initial stages of the book, to Robin Jacobson for editing the text, and to Joanna Ekman for additional editing and proofreading. We are grateful to Mickey Endo of Toppan for seeing the book through production.

The exhibition arrangements have been very skillfully handled by Dana Stein Dince, who also supervised the installation and rotations. We are grateful to Cleo Nichols for undertaking the exhibition design and to David Harvey for designing the graphics.

Andrew Pekarik

Director
The Asia Society Galleries

NOTE ON DATES, AGES, NAMES, AND TRANSLATIONS

Unlike the Western (Gregorian) calendar, which was formulated on the basis of solar calculations, the traditional Japanese civil calendar (following Chinese precedent) was based on the behavior and phases of the moon. Although the basic unit in both systems is the year divided into twelve months, their chronological correspondences vary, and the Japanese lunar calendar had to be intercalated to make it conform to the natural year. Moreover, it did not exactly correspond to the seasons, and from year to year New Year's Day fell anywhere between January 21 and February 19 of the Western calendar.

Therefore, as a matter of convention, references to "months" in this catalogue refer to the Japanese system, and references to a specific year—such as 1716, the year of Jakuchū's birth—are general approximations; no attempt has been made to give exact Western chronological equivalents. Moreover, Japanese history has traditionally involved the use of calendrical eras (*nengo*), which were established and named by the imperial court. Rationales for changing to a new *nengo* included the ascension of a new emperor, the occasion of certain auspicious years of the traditional sexagenary cycle, and the coming to pass of a felicitous or unlucky event. Entries in this catalogue such as "Shōtoku 6 (1716)" reflect this practice.

In general, the traditional way of calculating age in Japan describes an individual as one year old at birth, two at the beginning of the next calendar year, and so forth. Thus, a person's age equals the number of calendar years in which he has lived, and his age is greater by one or two years than it would be by Western calculation. For instance, Jakuchū, who was born in Shōtoku 6 (the general equivalent of the Western year 1716) and died in Kansei 12 (1800), was, by Japanese calculation, eighty-five years old when he died.

By Japanese custom, the family name comes first, followed, according to age and circumstance, by one or more personal, formal, pseudonymous, or lineal appellations, and occasionally a title. Jakuchū's surname was Itō, but there is no record of his childhood name (*yōmei*), personal name (*jitsumyō*), or nickname (*tsushō*). He did use the fancy nom de plume or artist's name (*azana* or *ji*) Keiwa, which was probably conferred on him (perhaps by his learned friend the Buddhist prelate Daiten Kenjō), as well as several distinguishing creative names (*go*) of the sort scholars, writers, and artists of the Edo period generally chose for themselves. The name Jakuchū belongs to this last category, along with Shunkyō (which seems to represent an early affiliation with the artist Ōoka Shumboku), Tobei-ō ("Old Man One-To of Rice") and his studio name, Tobeian ("Hermitage of One-To of Rice"). In addition, during the second half of his life, the artist often signed his name with the suffix *koji*, signifying that he had become a Buddhist lay priest. Nothing is known of the given names of Jakuchū's parents or his siblings (except that the male heads of the family business were all known as Genzaemon), and they can be identified only by their Buddhist posthumous titles (*kaimyō*).

Titles of books and other writings, of works of art, and of personages of noble, military, and ecclesiastical status, as well as passages of poetry and prose, sometimes pose difficulties in translation from Japanese into English, as the Japanese wording often evokes multiple meanings, both literal and poetic. Therefore, succinct translation into English of such titles and passages often can only approximate the original connotation.

Reference: Webb, Herschel, *Research in Japanese Sources: A Guide*, New York and London: Columbia University Press, 1965.

CHAPTER

1

Painting in Kyoto in the Eighteenth Century

During his long and productive career, the Japanese artist Itō Jakuchū produced a substantial corpus of paintings that is much admired for its distinctive beauty and conceptual originality. Jakuchū's life (1716–1800) coincided with a period of remarkable creativity in the history of Japanese painting, and the ancient capital city of Kyoto, where Jakuchū was born and where he pursued his painting, was the most important center of this artistic activity.

In the course of the two and a half centuries conventionally referred to as the Edo period (1615–1868), when Japan was controlled by the Bakufu government of the Tokugawa line of shoguns, prevailing peace and stability stimulated agricultural production and the economy, and encouraged learning and the arts, which flourished with exceptional vigor and variety. The first shogun, Ieyasu (d. 1616), intended to make his newly established seat of government, the city of Edo (present-day Tokyo), not only the military and administrative hub of the country, but also an important economic and cultural center—objectives his successors diligently pursued. Over the decades a massive, moated castle was constructed, and from this center the great city sprawled concentrically, dramatically extending its boundaries. The population grew rapidly; it is estimated to have been well over half a million by 1700. A century later the number of inhabitants had more than doubled, making Edo one of the largest cities in the world.

The residents of this metropolis included members of the Bakufu government, a multitude of administrators, bureaucrats, and functionaries; a garrison of soldiers; the *daimyō* (feudal lords who were, by government edict, compelled to spend extended periods of each year in attendance in Edo under government surveillance) and their retinues of samurai and attendants; and a veritable army of craftsmen, artisans, shopkeepers, laborers, and entrepreneurs who catered to the demands of the military hierarchy. As Edo had little actual industry, it did not become an important entrepôt until a later time. Rather, it was the primary seat of political power and influence in Japan, and its inhabitants were predominantly consumers, not producers. The burgeoning population during the seventeenth and eighteenth centuries stimulated wholesale and retail trade on an unprecedented scale, and enterprising merchants from various provinces came to set up their stores and businesses in the city. This influx was accompanied by a battalion of exchange brokers and opportunistic speculators who played influential roles in finance and trade, some making great fortunes, either through their connection with government undertakings or through their foresight in capitalizing on the logistical needs of the populace.

By contrast, the venerable city of Kyoto, more than three hundred miles to the west-southwest, had been established at the end of the eighth century on a grand scale that emulated the traditional grid system of capital cities in China. As in Chinese precedent, the Imperial Palace and its extensive grounds were located axially in the northern sector of the city, and through the centuries a succession of emperors, attended by their ministers, advisers, and courtiers, reigned ceremonially over the country from its hallowed confines. Kyoto had been the principal metropolis of Japan throughout the Middle Ages—both the seat of the sovereign and the geographical hub of the "Home Provinces," the most populous region of the country. Moreover, the city was the time-honored and influential center of high culture, learning, and the arts in Japan, and many of the most important Buddhist monasteries were situated in and around it. By the early eighteenth century the population of Kyoto had stabilized at about four hundred thousand. A short distance from Kyoto lay Osaka, then Japan's greatest commercial city, which had also grown prodigiously as a result of its dynamic role in the mercantile and financial operations of the country; its population was only a bit smaller than that of Kyoto.

The headquarters of the Ashikaga line of shoguns, who had governed Japan with varying success from the early fourteenth century to the middle of the sixteenth century, was located for much of this period in the Muromachi neighborhood of Kyoto; hence the name of this section is generally used to designate the period between 1392 and 1568. The Muromachi period was characterized by considerable political instability and periodic internecine warfare, the consequences of the Ashikaga shoguns' limited ability to control powerful feudal warriors from the provinces. Ironically, during this difficult and often violent period Zen Buddhism exercised a profound influence on Japanese culture, thought, and the arts.

During the Kamakura period (1185–1336), Zen (Chinese: Ch'an) Buddhism had been brought to Japan by Chinese prelates and their Japanese followers, many of whom had traveled to China to study. The powerful shogun Minamoto Yoritomo and his successors were earnest advocates of Zen philosophy and ritual, and sedulously supported the construction of great monasteries, primarily in the city of Kamakura, where the Bakufu was headquartered, and at various locations in Kyoto, where the ideals, tenets, and religious practices of Zen were assiduously disseminated among the members of the warrior caste.

It was the earnest intention of those who brought Zen to Japan to transmit its wisdom and teachings in their true and authentic forms. This necessarily entailed the acquisition of traditional religious literature, essential canonical materials, and didactic texts—and, of equal ceremonial and inspirational importance, iconographic paintings and calligraphic scrolls. Zen devotees brought paintings from China (which served, in turn, as sources for Japanese painters) that were notable for their diversity: from conventional iconic works drawn from the traditional Buddhist pantheon to portrayals of Bodhidharma (the legendary founder of Ch'an); portraits of eminent priests; depictions of significant incidents or activities, eccentric monks, and other eremitic figures from Zen anecdotal lore; and other subjects, such as landscapes, animals, birds, and plants, which seem to have originated in Chinese secular painting but which had been reinterpreted as evocative religious themes in Zen art. Although color was routinely incorporated into certain of these works, such as the traditional iconic paintings and the portraits of priests, the other subjects were rendered primarily in monochrome ink, with the boundless possibilities of its lines and washes. This challenging expressive means became the chief vehicle among Zen painters in the following centuries.

Zen was a dynamic, influential force in Japan throughout the Middle Ages—from the late thirteenth century until the sixteenth century, by which time its momentum had begun to slow. During the Kamakura and Muromachi periods the great Zen monasteries, with their extensive libraries, archives, and collections of paintings, served as the chief centers of Chinese learning, scholarship, and literary activity; they continued to play this role, albeit with much reduced vigor, in later centuries. Zen painting flourished in these revered institutions, and a number of them, such as the Kenchōji in Kamakura and the Tōfukuji, the Daitokuji, and the Shōkokuji in Kyoto, had their own ateliers, where priest-painters produced iconic pieces that were used in devotional ritual, as well as more intimate, original pieces that embodied the profundities of Zen philosophy and aesthetics in either a didactic or an inspirational way.

Throughout the fifteenth century local hostilities were common, but warfare became widespread during the sixteenth century, when powerful feudal lords maneuvered politically and militarily to increase their domains. Anarchy and social dislocation were endemic until Ōda Nobunaga (1532–1582) and Toyotomi Hideyoshi (1536–1598) defeated most of their enemies and finally brought some stability to the country. The Azuchi-Momoyama period (1568–1615), which takes its name from two splendid castles erected by these men, was characterized by new spirit and vitality in the arts, especially painting; several distinctive painting schools made their appearance during this time. Two years after Hideyoshi's death, his followers assembled their armies to face those of their chief rival, Tokugawa Ieyasu, in the decisive Battle of Sekigahara, in which the former were soundly defeated. The Toyotomi forces made their last stand at Osaka Castle in 1615, and after the fall of this great bastion Ieyasu was finally able to subjugate his remaining adversaries and establish an authoritarian government that was to ensure peace in Japan for two and a half centuries.

The geographical shift of governmental power away from Kyoto and the Home Provinces to the political and administrative headquarters of the Tokugawa Bakufu in Edo was carried out in the early decades of the seventeenth century. However, the dynamic growth of the new metropolis entailed ongoing construction on a monumental scale, which continued well into the latter part of the century.

Like the entrepreneurs and merchants who were drawn to Edo by the promise of profit and prestige, many artists and artisans also came to the city to pursue their various specialties. In the realm of painting, the most prominent example of this circumstance may be seen in the geographical movements of certain artists of the Kanō school. This line of painters is remarkable for its singular role as a prestigious academic school whose history spans almost four centuries; for its multitude of artists; for the continuity of its pictorial traditions and style; and for its unfailing sources of patronage, primarily members of the military caste. Founded in the middle of the Muromachi period by Kanō Masanobu (1434–1530) and established as a major school of painting with close ties to the Ashikaga Bakufu by his son Motonobu (1479–1559), the Kanō school had, by the middle of the sixteenth century, assumed a dominant role in painting in the Kyoto region.

At the hands of the Kanō painters and their successors evolved a distinctive pictorial mode that skillfully synthesized monochrome traditions with styles of the Sung (960–1279) and Yüan (1279–1368) dynasties, and with concepts from Chinese painting of the Che school, which had developed in Chekiang Province during the Ming dynasty (1368–1644). The influence of Che school painting is most obvious in the Kanō painters' polychrome bird-and-flower works, but a broader preoccupation with Chinese anecdotal and popular didactic materials, also apparent in their figural compositions, was a ramification of the traditional prestige of Chinese ethics and ideals among the Buddhist clerics and the military men who patronized the school.

Kanō ateliers flourished in and around Kyoto during the Azuchi-Momoyama period, when masters such as Eitoku (1543–1590) and Sanraku (1559–1635) continued to build on the conceptual precepts of their predecessors, infusing their works with greater dramatic vitality and colorful embellishments in response to the new aesthetics of the period.

Ieyasu's unification of the country early in the seventeenth century and the shift of power from Kyoto to Edo had profound and lasting consequences. The decision of Tan'yū (1602–1674), one of the most versatile and productive of the Kanō artists, to leave Kyoto in order to set up an atelier in Edo is a reflection of the history of the times and is of considerable importance in the evolution of Japanese painting.

Tan'yū was only a youth when, in 1614, he transferred his activities to Edo, but he was subsequently appointed chief official painter of the Tokugawa shogunate, and his atelier, situated in the Kajibashi neighborhood, became the most influential in the city. He not only revitalized the formal style of Kanō Motonobu, but also adopted ink-wash techniques inspired by such Chinese artists as Yü-chien of the Southern Sung dynasty (1127–1279) and the delicate traditional polychrome methods of the Tosa school, thereby reorienting the conceptual objectives of the Kanō school and establishing pictorial and academic standards for his successors. Tan'yū was the foremost painter and arbiter of pictorial taste of his region and period, and he and his numerous followers worked diligently to produce works for feudal houses both in Edo and in the provinces.

Commissions were so numerous and constant that three more Kanō ateliers were established in the following decades, and these workshops continued to produce competent, if not always inspired, paintings for more than two centuries. Although there were signs of creative stagnation by the later decades of the seventeenth century, the prestige that the Edo Kanō style and its subjects carried among the military class guaranteed its longevity and inhibited the development of new schools of painting in the region.

Once Tan'yū and his group had moved to Edo, the Kanō school became divided along geographical lines between the Edo painters and those remaining in Kyoto under the leadership of Sanraku, who had already achieved fame during the Momoyama period because of his work for Hideyoshi. Sansetsu (1589–1651), Sanraku's successor, continued the thematic and stylistic traditions of the line, but he was sometimes eccentric in the choice of his subject matter and had a distinctive, expressive mannerism in his brushwork; these features were passed on to certain artists of his line and appear to have inspired eighteenth-century painters with personal, idiosyncratic styles. Sansetsu's successor Kanō Einō (1631–1697) was a competent artist who is known less for his paintings than for his scholarly interest in the history of painting. Author of the *Honchō Gashi (History of Japanese Painting)*, a pioneering treatise published in 1678, Einō conducted his research in Kyoto on the genealogies, styles, and subject matter of earlier artists simultaneously with Tan'yū's similar investigations in Edo. The latter's influential connections made it possible for him to examine old paintings from various collections, which he industriously sketched and frequently authenticated.

The Kyoto Kanō line was carried on by Eikei (1662–1702), the son of Einō, Eikei's son Eihaku (1687–1764), Eishun (1769–1816), and Eigaku (1790–1867), artists whose chief distinction seems to be that they worked on occasional commissions for the Imperial Court. From the standpoint of numbers and productivity, it is clear that many more artists worked in the busy Edo ateliers than were active in Kyoto. This was especially true from the late seventeenth century on, when the sources of official patronage in Edo continued to grow and the vitality of the Kyoto line was in decline.

Kanō ateliers in both areas, as well as in some locations in the provinces, were also places of training for young painters, thus preserving the conservative approach of the school and propagating its traditional stylistic canons more extensively. With the passing decades this academic training was utilized with greater frequency by artists who wished to profit from the curriculum but had little desire to become part of the school in a formal way. Such men generally went on to carve out careers on their own, sometimes developing personal styles that reflected a new spirit of individual expression characteristic of eighteenth-century painting in Kyoto.

The Kyōhō period (1716–1736) marked a midpoint in the cultural history of the Edo period and a watershed in the evolution of Japanese painting. By the early years of the Kyōhō period, certain influential schools such as the Sōga and Hasegawa—which had flourished during the Momoyama and early Edo periods and had rivaled the Kanō painters in figural, landscape, and bird-and-flower painting—were now moribund, and the last remaining members of the Unkoku school, including Tohan (1635–1724) and Tōkaku, were approaching the end of their careers.

The death of Ogata Kōrin (1658–1716) in the first year of the Kyōhō period serves as a general point of demarcation between the pictorial traditions of the seventeenth century and the new schools and currents of painting that were to emerge in the eighteenth century. Kōrin was one of the most gifted members of that line of artists now known as the Rimpa school, which had its roots in talented men such as Hon'ami Kōetsu (1558–1637) and Tawaraya Sōtatsu (?–c. 1643?), who had exercised a significant influence on the arts of the Momoyama and early Edo periods.

These versatile Kyoto artists worked in a variety of media—lacquer, pottery, textiles, graphic design, calligraphy, and painting—and the distinctive aesthetic that pervades their works, evoking revered native sentiments and traditional aristocratic taste, is quintessentially Japanese. Their unique style ingeniously blended elegant design, spontaneity, and irregular natural forms inspired by the tea ceremony—features that innately appealed to the Imperial Court and to cultivated society in Kyoto. Kōetsu's and Sōtatsu's followers lacked their originality of vision, and the momentum of the school slowed, but it was reinvigorated by Kōrin, who contributed a new boldness and dramatic spirit to its style. After his death, however, the school again declined, although it did regain something of its vitality in the late eighteenth and early nineteenth centuries under eclectic painters such as Sakai Hōitsu (1761–1828) and Suzuki Kiitsu (1796–1858).

The rise of a new line of painters, the Bunjin (also known as Nanga), or "Literati" school, during the early eighteenth century coincides chronologically with the gradual debilitation of the Rimpa school and with the continued decline in the influence of the Kanō school in the Kyoto region. The Bunjin painters were a loose affiliation of artists who drew their inspiration and name from the philosophical ideals of the Chinese Wen-jen (Japanese: Bunjin) painters, whose traditions had much earlier origins. The Wen-jen school had exercised a significant influence on monochrome ink painting of the Sung and Yüan dynasties, which were, in turn, wellsprings for Zen painting of the Kamakura and Muromachi periods.

However, it was not to these early Chinese Literati paintings that the Bunjin artists turned for their stylistic ideas, but to those of less distant times, by such Ming-period masters as Shen Chou, Wen Cheng-ming, and Tung Ch'i-ch'ang, who focused on the landscape as a means of demonstrating their creative ideas. Motivated by the precepts and aesthetics of their Chinese predecessors, the Bunjin artists practiced painting as a means of cultivating character, preserving one's integrity, and maintaining the "amateur" ideal, in which painting was pursued for its own elevating virtues rather than for worldly recognition. This philosophical approach contrasted sharply with the attitudes of established professional schools, such as the Kanō school, and instances of antipathy were not uncommon.

The Wen-jen school had developed into a mature pictorial tradition through the centuries in China; its Japanese offspring grew quickly from this foundation and was soon adopted by pioneer practitioners in various regions. Gion Nankai (1676–1751), Sakaki Hyakusen (1697–1752), and Yanagisawa Kien (1704–1758) are generally credited with having founded the Bunjin school, which underwent its initial development during the Kyōhō period. Wen-jen painters of the Ming period had worked in a variety of personal styles, and the school was therefore eclectic in its pictorial traditions, as reflected in the works of the founders of Bunjin painting. Moreover, knowledge of the styles of their Chinese predecessors reached the Japanese artists in fragmentary and often amorphous form, and it was thus inevitable that their individual works would exhibit considerable diversity. However, a common sense of reverence for Chinese learning and tradition united these men philosophically, and their painting was only one aspect of their sinological pursuits. Thus, Nankai, who headed a school of Confucian learning in Kii Province (present-day Wakayama Prefecture), was a superb calligrapher in several Chinese styles as well as a carver of seals; Hyakusen diligently studied the history of Chinese painting, and the results of his research were published in books such as the *Genmeishin Shōga Jinmeiroku (Index of Calligraphers and Painters of the Yüan, Ming, and Ch'ing Periods)*; and Kien, an accomplished man of letters, was also a serious student of Confucianism and the Chinese tradition of materia medica. Ironically, both Hyakusen and Kien, who criticized Kanō painters for the uninspired formality of their style and their shallow knowledge of Chinese pictorial traditions, received training in the Kanō style before their conversion to Bunjin painting.

Peripatetic travel was integral to the eremitic Literati tradition in China and Japan, as it encouraged communion with nature and contemplation of her varied manifestations in order to promote one's spiritual well-being and aesthetic awareness, as well as to insulate one from the corrupting influences of the vulgar, material world. With the passing of time, this ideal became institutionalized in a practice known as Bunjin-bokkyaku (Literati-ink guest), in which the practitioner traveled about the countryside visiting various local patrons and institutions, where he was conveniently provided with board and other compensations in return for instruction, congenial companionship, or the execution of a commission or other work of art. This tradition not only motivated Literati painters to journey to various regions in order to meet others of their sinological disposition, but it also pragmatically supported their artistic activities. Once established as a behavioral convention, this benevolent practice gradually spread beyond Literati circles, and painters from other artistic traditions adopted it as a means of furthering their careers.

During the Edo period the broad revival of interest in Chinese learning and institutions exercised a profound influence on cultural and political developments. Something of this enthusiasm for Chinese thought was undoubtedly owing to a general convalescence in traditional scholarly activities early in the seventeenth century, after the return of peace and stability to Japan. More important, however, was the decision of the Bakufu to support the study of Confucian precepts and ethics as a philosophical rationale for policy-making and as behavioral ideals for society. Because of this official support, scholars in substantial numbers took up such study, and institutes were later set up in many of the provincial fiefs as well as in Edo, where the traditional annual rites were ceremoniously observed. These institutes were places for indoctrination in the teachings of Chu Hsi, an influential interpreter of Confucian thought who developed his philosophical system during the Sung dynasty; the Bakufu regarded Chu Hsi's teachings as the orthodox branch of Confucian thought. The institutes also served as places of instruction in various aspects of Chinese culture and tradition. Although during the first half of the seventeenth century scholarly research in Confucian thought took place primarily in Kyoto, by the end of the century a great college for Confucian studies had been established in Edo under Bakufu sponsorship and the new capital had become the center of official, orthodox Confucianism in Japan.

The decision by the Bakufu in the 1630s to restrict contacts with the outside world (with the exception of some trade within the port of Nagasaki on the island of Kyushu) effectively isolated Japanese society from any significant cultural interaction or exchange of ideas throughout most of the Edo period. Designed to further reinforce the authoritative control of the Bakufu (and provoked by official fears of the potentially subversive influence of Western politics and ideology), this policy of exclusion introverted and impeded intellectual growth. The Dutch were allowed to maintain a modest trading mission in a small enclave facing Nagasaki's harbor, where their presence served as the sole source of information about the Western world.

Although the visits of Dutch ships and the contents of their cargoes were rigorously supervised by government officials, the more numerous Chinese vessels seem to have been less strictly controlled; communications and trade with China were permitted on a modest scale during the latter seventeenth century and the eighteenth century, and a substantial Chinese settlement developed in Nagasaki as a result. The Chinese primarily traded silk yarns and textiles to Japan, but there was also a market for skins, sugar, minerals, materia medica, and, significantly, books and paintings. In addition, a few Chinese painters occasionally visited Nagasaki, some serving as mentors to native artists who had generally traveled long distances in the hope of receiving instruction from an authentic Chinese specialist.

Among the earliest of these teachers, the Chinese monk I-jan Hsing-jung (Japanese: Itsunen Seiyū; 1601–1668) arrived in Japan in 1645 and took up priestly duties as the abbot of a local temple, the Kōfukuji. I-jan had left China to avoid the widespread hostilities that accompanied the fall of the Ming dynasty. He produced accomplished paintings of figural and Buddhist subjects in a distinctive style that combined Literati pictorial traditions with elements of realism. He founded a line of painters that was one branch of what became known as the Nagasaki school; it included Kawamura Jakushi (1629–1707), Watanabe Shūseki (1639–1707), and Ei Genshō (dates unknown), who was influential in instructing Yanagisawa Kien at a time early in his career when he was shifting away from his Kanō training and searching for a new style.

I-jan was not only responsible for acquainting Japanese painters with a particular Chinese artistic tradition; he also played a central role in introducing a late, syncretic form of Ch'an Buddhism to Japanese soil. Serving as the representative of three temples in Nagasaki, I-jan was instrumental in bringing the Ch'an prelate Yin-yüan Lung-ch'i (Japanese: Ingen Ryūki; 1592–1673) to Japan in 1654. Yin-yüan, like I-jan, was a refugee from the Manchu (Ch'ing) invasion of his homeland in southern China, and he was cordially welcomed to Japan by the retired emperor Gomizuno-ō and the shogun Ietsuna. In 1661 he was provided with a large tract of land at Uji, south of Kyoto, on which he supervised construction of a vast monastery, re-creating in authentic contemporary Chinese form the baroque architectural style and colorful atmosphere of a southern Chinese Ch'an institution. Yin-yüan named the great monastery after the Wan-fu-ssu (Japanese: Mampukuji), the Chinese temple where he had been abbot, and he called his new branch of Ch'an Buddhism Huang-po (Japanese: Ōbaku) after the area in which the Wan-fu-ssu was located, which had been a stronghold of Ch'an religious activities since the ninth century. The Mampukuji was established as the Ōbaku general headquarters, and in the following decades an extensive network of more than four hundred subtemples was erected throughout the country.

All but four of the twenty-two men who followed Yin-yüan as abbots of the Mampukuji were Chinese, and the exotic atmosphere and liturgy of the monastery made it a lodestone for Japanese sinologists, a place to study various aspects of Chinese culture directly from authentic sources. The Mampukuji thus became a vital center of learning, and its convenient location just south of Kyoto, the imperial capital, encouraged many influential figures to make pilgrimages there. The ambience of a splendid, living Chinese religious institution in action, with its foreign monks, language, and regalia, contrasted sharply with that of the other places where one could learn about Chinese religion, thought, and culture: the older Zen temples, with their restrained atmosphere and their austere traditions and architecture, and the Confucian institutes, with their dry academic routines. The Mampukuji was also the principal center for the practice of Sencha, the Chinese form of the tea ceremony, in which the steeping and drinking of tea served as an aesthetic and philosophical ritual for those who revered Chinese Literati traditions.

The great monastery, with its learned monks and rich archival collections, was a wellspring of ideas and inspiration for Japanese Literati painters. Many of the Chinese priests were skilled calligraphers and some were also painters; their influence may be seen not only in the works of Bunjin artists, but also in the paintings by important independent eighteenth-century artists who had no specific school affiliations. Among the numerous Literati painters who frequented the temple were Gion Nankai and Ike Taiga (1723–1776), who executed a number of paintings there, including the celebrated sliding-screen composition of *Five Hundred Arhats*, painted in the 1760s.

During the Kyōhō period several more Chinese painters made the long sea voyage to Nagasaki, where they influenced both the evolution of the Nagasaki school and the early development of Literati painting. I Fu-chiu (also known as I Hai) arrived in 1720 for a ten-month stay and came again for a month in 1730. I Fu-chiu was actually a merchant who had come to pursue his business interests, but he had received a Literati education and was a competent painter in the landscape tradition of Huang Kung-wang (1269–1345) and Ch'a Shih-piao (1615–1698). Shen Nan-p'in (also known as Shen Ch'uan; active mid-eighteenth century), another merchant, sojourned in Nagasaki between 1731 and 1733; he specialized in detailed polychrome renditions of bird-and-flower subjects. His lively, representational depictions captured the imagination of Japanese artists, and he became the fountainhead of a second line of the Nagasaki school, which included such painters as Kumashiro Yūhi (1693–1773), Sō Shiseki (1712/15–1786), and Kakutei Jōkō (1722–1785), an Ōbaku priest who was instrumental in introducing the style of Shen Nan-p'in to the Kyoto-Osaka region in the 1740s.

The three important first-generation painters of the Bunjin school, Gion Nankai, Sakaki Hyakusen, and Yanagisawa Kien, were all inspired by a common body of philosophical tenets inherited from the Wen-jen tradition, but their paintings exhibit considerable diversity in style and approach. The Wen-jen school itself was eclectic in its historical evolution, an admixture of innovative personal styles developed by individual masters whose accomplishments became part of a collective pictorial tradition. Wen-jen artists' expressive motivation was predicated, at least in principle, on the amateur ideal of the cultivated man, for whom painting served as a means of refining and revealing character and philosophical aims. (This was in contrast to the manner of members of the professional academic schools in China, who worked within the parameters of an established style, building and elaborating on a conventional inventory of subjects through the use of prescribed techniques.) The Wen-jen approach encouraged a reverence for the accomplishments of like-minded Literati painters of the past and, more significantly, a reliance on individual creative vision. The diversity of styles exhibited by Nankai, Hyakusen, and Kien also had to do with their fragmented sources of information about the Wen-jen line. Although Chinese paintings, including a number of Literati works, were brought to Nagasaki in substantial numbers by opportunistic Chinese traders over the decades, their quality appears to have been uneven, and works from non-Literati lines, such as the engaging polychrome bird-and-flower paintings that were done by members of local ateliers in Fukien Province (and that were one source of inspiration for the Nagasaki school of painters), undoubtedly predominated. Given these equivocal circumstances, it is understandable that the early Bunjin painters experimented with a variety of Chinese styles and that the results were sometimes blatantly derivative, sometimes reflecting disparate styles with no essential connection to the Chinese Literati school.

The first-generation Bunjin painters appear, in fact, to have been largely self-taught and to have relied less on actual Chinese paintings for their ideas than on another, more readily available source—woodblock-illustrated painters' manuals from China, such as the *Pa-chung Hua-p'u* (Japanese: *Hasshū Gafū* [*Painting Manual of Eight Varieties*], published in the 1620s) and the *Chieh-tzu-yüan Hua-chüan* (Japanese: *Kaishien Gaden* [*Mustard Seed Garden Manual of Painting*], published in its complete form in 1701), two works that were often imported through Nagasaki. Produced by Chinese Literati, these small manuals were an important means by which artists could investigate and simulate the subjects, techniques, and pictorial principles of Wen-jen painting. The manuals were avidly studied by Japanese artists, and demand for them eventually led to reprintings in Japan.

The eight volumes of the *Hasshū Gafū* (reprinted in Japan as early as 1671) encapsulate much of the ambience and aesthetics of the Chinese Literati and their dual preoccupation with literature and painting. They include elaborate prefaces and postscripts, together with extensive sections of poetry written in several traditional forms, but are in large part given over to black-and-white illustrations of typical Literati subjects: plums, bamboo, chrysanthemums, and orchids (traditional pictorial metaphors for ideals of character and behavior); bird-and-flower motifs; compositions in various styles in the fan format; and abbreviated simulations of the works of famous past masters.

The *Kaishien Gaden*, although not reproduced in Japan until 1748, was already widely known in that country in earlier decades. Publication of the Chinese work, which consisted of thirteen "books" arranged in three parts, was begun in 1679 and finished in 1701. The *Kaishien Gaden* was a more comprehensive undertaking than the *Hasshū Gafū*, and it was of greater pragmatic value to Japanese enthusiasts, for it included more instructive data on painting materials, pigments, and brush techniques. Additionally, it contained extensive written and illustrated sections on the history and accomplishments of great Chinese artists of recent and ancient times, and passages devoted to the fundamentals and philosophical premises of Literati painting. The five books of Part 1 deal with landscape painting, the first devoted to general principles and history and a commentary on the appropriate use of colors, the rest to illustrated explanations of the painting of trees, rocks, "people and things" (*jen-wu*) and a further examination of the particulars of landscape portrayal. Part 2 contains four books covering symbolic motifs that had also been addressed in the *Hasshū Gafū*: the orchid, bamboo, plum, and chrysanthemum. The final section of the manual has four books devoted to grasses, insects, flowering plants, and "feathers and fur" (a generic term for animal life in its largest sense).

The contents of these two pedagogical manuals accurately reflect the interests and aesthetics of Wen-jen painters in China and their diligent Bunjin emulators in Japan. However, the influence they exercised on eighteenth-century Japanese painting extended well beyond the confines of Literati art; because of the works' availability, many painters of different persuasions turned to their engaging illustrations.

Earlier, during the second half of the seventeenth century, men such as Kanō Tan'yū, who studiously investigated antique Chinese and Japanese paintings, and Kanō Einō, author of the vanguard study of traditional painting, the *Honchō Gashi*, had established the foundations for art-historical research in Japan. Enthusiasm for antiquarian matters increased in the following decades, and references in the *Hasshū Gafū* and the *Kaishien Gaden* to paintings of celebrated Chinese masters of the past provided additional knowledge of artistic lineages and styles. Moreover, these handy woodblock-printed works also appealed to a growing segment of society, educated and with cultivated aspirations, and certain opportunistic artists produced their own didactic woodblock compendiums, intending them as self-help manuals for those with artistic ambitions. Among the most important of these illustrators were two versatile men trained in the Kanō style, Tachibana Morikuni (1679–1748) and Ōoka Shumboku (1680–1763), both of whom worked in the Osaka-Kyoto area. Characteristically eclectic, their works were assembled for a varied clientele and reproduced a wide range of styles and subject matter from diverse pictorial traditions, both Chinese and Japanese. All of these were printed in plain black ink with one significant exception, Shumboku's beautifully executed polychrome *Minchō Seidō Gaen* (*Ming Dynasty Pictorial Garden of Living Beings*), also known as *Minchō Shiken* (*Ming Dynasty Purple Inkstone*), which was published in 1746.

Given the incomplete and often obscure knowledge of the first-generation Bunjin artists about their Chinese parental line, it is understandable that their painting involved experiments in various styles as well as occasional slavish simulations of works attributed to prestigious past masters. Despite a certain engaging mixture of insecurity and reverence in their approach, their common objective—the search for the authentic sources of their adopted artistic line—unified and inspired their activities. The fact that Nankai, Hyakusen, and Kien each produced numerous monochrome ink paintings of one of the quintessential Literati motifs, the venerable bamboo, with its conventional idealistic associations, demonstrates that they all felt a sense of ideological security in portraying the subject. Moreover, the meticulous facsimiles of woodblock illustrations from the *Hasshū Gafū* in Nankai's oeuvre, along with occasional pictorial references to such prototypes in the works of Hyakusen and Kien, show that they regarded as reliable the artistic credentials of these illustrations.

Nankai's paintings were by-products of his scholarly pursuits, and he was more accomplished as a calligrapher than as a painter. Kien was a competent artist who introduced *shitōga* (finger painting) to the Bunjin repertoire. This Chinese technique, in which the artist eschewed the brush, actually dipping his fingers in ink and creating the image by direct contact with the surface of the paper, went back as far as the T'ang dynasty. It was traditionally associated with eccentric artists such as Wang Mo (active eighth century), who worked in an incisive, spontaneous manner. However, Kien utilized this technique in a more refined manner (as had certain Chinese Literati of the Ming period), and he was apparently attracted to it as an experimental alternative to the stultified conventions of his Kanō-school training. Like Nankai, Kien regarded himself primarily as a student of Chinese thought and culture, viewing painting merely as one of the obligatory pursuits of the cultivated man. Kien seems to have been generous in sharing his knowledge of the history and techniques of Bunjin painting, and he gave much encouragement to Ike Taiga, the most celebrated second-generation practitioner of the Literati school.

Hyakusen, the most creative of the first-generation Bunjin artists, worked primarily in Kyoto and was an influential figure there for more than two decades, cultivating younger Bunjin painters such as Yosa Buson (1716–1783) and Kō Fuyō. Hyakusen came from Nagoya and probably received Kanō-school training early in life, but in Kyoto he came under the influence of Nankai, and one sentimental account has it that Nankai's gift to the promising youth of a copy of the *Kaishien Gaden* convinced him to become a Bunjin painter.

At any rate, Hyakusen was seemingly more single-minded in his devotion to painting than were Nankai and Kien, both of whom came from scholarly samurai backgrounds, for he not only experimented conscientiously with a broad range of styles, but also diligently studied the history and connoisseurship of Chinese painting. Hyakusen's oeuvre is characterized both by many shifts in style, which reflect his ambition to emulate the diverse expressive means of Chinese masters, and by innovative techniques and vision. He experimented with numerous formats in his search for creative possibilities, from diminutive *haiga*, the small, spontaneous ink sketches done in conjunction with haiku, to monumental screen compositions inspired in varying degrees by Chinese ideas.

More personal and idiosyncratic in his approach to painting than Nankai and Kien, Hyakusen came closer to realizing the true artistic objectives of the Literati tradition. A certain ambiguity in the ideological tradition of this school motivated the artist to display through his painting his knowledge of and reverence for the stylistic landmarks of earlier masters, while at the same time using his work as a means of cultivating his character and revealing his essential nature. Too great a disposition by lesser artists toward the first concern routinely resulted in obsequious imitation in the form of mundane, unimaginative works. On the other hand, Hyakusen, a true Literati exemplar, was dedicated to expressing his unique persona in his art, expressing, as do all serious artists, a significant individual point of view. Measured by this criterion, Hyakusen's diverse oeuvre, which evolved from Literati pictorial conventions but interpreted them in a new way, elevated him above his two chief contemporaries, Nankai and Kien. All three men died during the 1750s, thus marking the close of the first period of Bunjin painting.

In contrast to the restless search for roots and direction that pervaded the activities of the first generation, the paintings of Ike Taiga and Yosa Buson, the two men who best exemplify the spirit of the second generation, reveal a more nonchalant accommodation of their pictorial inheritance, which freed them to concentrate more on their individual expressive means. Both men, who pursued their careers primarily in and around Kyoto, developed singular, cohesive styles that utilized established methods in original ways. Taiga experimented with *shitōga* early in his career, but he and Buson most often used the brush to create patterns of dots and textural strokes, also applying ink in puddles and soft washes. Their works are more painterly and accomplished, as well as significantly less dependent on Chinese ideas, than those of the previous generation. Native Japanese taste and aesthetics had clearly become essential influences on both their compositions and their choice of subject matter; their occasional Japanese landscapes were seemingly inspired by renderings of native topographical locations by their predecessor Hyakusen.

The careers of Nankai and Kien more closely reflect the broad ideological conventions of the Literati—those of the cultivated scholarly amateur whose versatile creative activities grew out of a larger reverence for Chinese culture—than does the career of Hyakusen, for whom painting became of paramount importance. The traditional Chinese concept of the principled amateur who remained aloof from worldly esteem and untainted by pecuniary concern had been a hallowed philosophical objective for centuries, but practical circumstances made it an unrealistic goal for most, so it came to be viewed as a conventionalized ideal rather than as a rigid behavioral code. In fact, many of the Wen-jen painters, as well as their Bunjin offspring, earned their livelihood through their painting; although they avoided the stigma of professionalism, they routinely received monetary recompense for their services. The Literati-ink-guest system provided them with a decorous social framework, a circuit wherein they could travel to carry out artistic commissions in return for remuneration. The best examples of this practice were Hyakusen in the first generation of Bunjin painters and Ike Taiga in the second.

Taiga enjoyed displaying his versatile skills, which astonished many of his observers and brought him acclaim. His tendency to exhibit his artistic repertoire and to perform before audiences, his obvious professionalism, and his humble origins all ran counter to the fastidious Literati preconceptions about deportment and training, yet he was, arguably, the most original painter of the Bunjin school.

His chief competitor for this distinction was Buson, who, unlike Taiga, matured gradually, not producing his most characteristic works until he was in his sixties. Buson's paintings are notable for the virtuosity of their ink techniques, the result of his long, diligent experimentation in various manners. They display a range from wild, dramatic brushwork inspired by the distant precedents of the eccentric *i-p'in* (Japanese: *ippin*; untrammeled) painting of the Chinese to softer, more sedate methods of handling the brush that were derived from the followers of Shen Nan-p'in, and to strong lines and tonal harmonies adapted from Ming academic painting of the Che school, which was anathema to the orthodox Literati ideal. Buson's mature brush techniques, with their incisive strokes and saturated washes, are generally more assertive than those of Taiga, which are more precise and calculated, intended to delineate the arrangement of forms within the compositions. The inventive use of materials, such as employment of a satin ground or application of a *gofun* (a gesso made from powdered white shells) base to paper, also reveals Buson's search for unusual effects. Moreover, his success with evocative, atmospheric landscape settings—somber night scenes and snowy panoramas—was the result of his ability to create dramatic highlights and contrasts through his swift, abbreviated brushwork, and these accomplishments are unique in the ink painting of the Edo period.

Although Taiga and Buson were advocates of Literati traditions, they, as well as most of their Bunjin successors, were professional painters who made little pretense of observing the amateur ideal. The oeuvres of both men include large, commissioned screens whose colorful, decorative manner (some even featured bright gold grounds, which would have offended the aesthetics of earlier Chinese masters of the school) demonstrates not only how far these artists had evolved from the orthodox Literati pictorial traditions, but also how original their visions were. Indeed, there is a decided sense of historical irony in the realization that the finest Japanese Literati paintings are, both contextually and aesthetically, the least Chinese in conception and style.

A number of talented Bunjin painters, such as Uragami Gyokudō (1745–1820), Okada Beisanjin (1744–1820), Tanomura Chikuden (1777–1835), and Aoki Mokubei (1767–1833), continued the traditions of the school in the following generations. Although the primary center of Bunjin activities and painting during the eighteenth century was the city of Kyoto, along with the surrounding provinces, later in the century the influence of the school also spread to Edo and beyond that city to the northeast.

Credited with bringing Bunjin painting to Edo, Tani Bunchō (1763–1840), like a number of his predecessors, had studied Kanō-style painting before his conversion to the Literati style. His oeuvre is eclectic, reflecting his studious experiments in various Chinese styles as well as his investigations into Western, scientific methods of rendering perspective, ideas that had reached Japan at an earlier time through the Dutch trading enclave at Nagasaki and through Chinese paintings and prints that had been influenced by European sources. Bunchō was a theorist, an art historian, and an influential teacher under whom more than a hundred men are said to have studied, among them Watanabe Kazan (1793–1841), whose paintings show a greater mastery of Western ideas of chiaroscuro and objective realism than those of his teacher.

From the time of its inception in the Kyōhō period, Bunjin painting flourished for nearly two centuries; a few resolute practitioners were active as recently as the early twentieth century. The school seems to have attracted adherents for a variety of reasons. A pervasive interest in Chinese culture and learning in Japan during the Edo period provided an intellectual and philosophical foundation that lauded cultivated accomplishments and encouraged self-expression. Moreover, the combination of an established yet eclectic artistic tradition and an attitude of deference toward eccentric behavior attracted strong personalities who recognized the pragmatic advantages of a common ideology but were also individualistic in their creative inclinations. At the same time, the concept of the Literati amateur offered a convenient outlet for those whose ethical ideas or background made commercial gain distasteful and who were therefore disinclined to pursue careers as professional artists in established ateliers. Finally, Literati artists' openness to varying points of view and their traditional admiration for eccentric deportment (such as painting or composing poetry while intoxicated) helps to explain the congenial manner in which they were able to mix freely on occasion with artists of other schools and, more significantly, to form close friendships with certain important independent painters of Kyoto, such as Sōga Shōhaku (1730–1781) and Itō Jakuchū.

The second major school of painting that had its inception in Kyoto during the eighteenth century was the Maruyama-Shijō, which made its appearance more than a generation after the Bunjin school and was based on a very different set of concepts. Maruyama Ōkyo (1733–1795), its progenitor, was born to a peasant family either in Kyoto or in the neighboring province of Tamba. Tradition has it that he had no interest in or aptitude for farming and that when he was in the fields he spent his time drawing pictures in the earth with a bamboo stick rather than working. Resigned to his lack of motivation, his parents sent him off to Kyoto, where he was put to work performing menial tasks. However, his desire to be an artist led to his acceptance into the studio of Ishida Yūtei (1721–1786), a painter of the Kanō school who had been trained in the conventional academic style of Tan'yū but who, like most of his colleagues, synthesized traditions of the Kanō, Tosa, and Rimpa schools. Ōkyo began his apprenticeship under Yūtei sometime in his teens, but he also seems to have studied under Watanabe Shikō, a versatile artist who combined Kanō techniques and draftsmanship with decorative elements inspired by Rimpa ideas. Significantly, Shikō also produced sketches and paintings that revealed his interest in the precise representation of natural phenomena, a hallmark of the neoteric method that Ōkyo was to develop in the following years.

A primary interest among eighteenth-century sinologues was the study of *pen-ts'ao hsueh* (Chinese pharmacology; Japanese: *honzōgaku*), the ancient, scholarly discipline of investigating and classifying both mineral and organic materials of all sorts in order to determine how they might be used efficaciously both as materia medica and in the broader contexts of agriculture and industry. This empirical approach to natural compounds, life forms, and products absorbed Japanese intellectuals, causing them to focus their attention on the accurate classification of flora and fauna, and on the hitherto ignored particulars of anatomy. This approach encouraged analytical observation and precise, realistic depiction of specific characteristics that distinguish one form of life from another.

This new intellectual curiosity about natural particulars was also fueled by another source: Western scientific knowledge of medicine, biology, and anatomy, which percolated through the Dutch enclave in Nagasaki in the form of books, diagrams, handwritten accounts, and engravings.

The isolation of Japan from the outside world imposed by the Bakufu merely exacerbated the desire of determined intellectuals to investigate non-indigenous traditions, as is reflected in the search by eighteenth-century Japanese painters for fresh sources of knowledge and inspiration. Furthermore, this search occurred at a time when the Kanō, Rimpa, and Tosa schools had lost some of their creative momentum, so that many painters no longer turned to the work of these established lines for motivation. In the Kyoto region, where the debilitation of the older schools compelled artists to look elsewhere for ideas and affiliations, this situation was more prevalent than it was in Edo, where the prestige and industry of the Kanō ateliers continued to attract students, and new influences had a less immediate impact on painting in general.

Ōkyo's new and distinctive style grew out of the artistic mutability of the period, synthesizing various components drawn from native and foreign sources. His Kanō-school training is revealed in his facile yet formularized brushwork and in his compositions, which utilized large areas of open space in a highly personal manner, focusing the observer's attention on the carefully conceived, rather formally arranged subject matter. The decorative juxtaposition of brilliant colors against backgrounds that were sometimes left plain but were more often enhanced with gold leaf or sprinkled gold flakes demonstrates Ōkyo's debt to his mentor, Shikō. Moreover, the use of vibrant colors combined with scumbled ink washes in gorgeous depictions of peacocks and peonies and of colorfully attired exotic figures from Chinese history and folklore reveals Ōkyo's familiarity with Chinese painting of the Ming and early Ch'ing (1644–1911) dynasties, particularly with the polychrome pieces that were produced by Shen Nan-p'in and by his Japanese followers of the Nagasaki school.

However, the most exceptional aspect of Ōkyo's innovative style was his strong sense of representational realism and his occasional application of Western perspectival concepts. Early in his career, Ōkyo came into contact with Chinese woodblock prints from the Suchow area that were designed to be viewed through optical devices of European origin. Known in Japan as *nozoki karakuri* (trick peep show), these *optiques* utilized a lens and mirror that intensified the illusion of three-dimensional space in the image, which had been organized according to the traditional Western idea of a single vanishing point. Reflecting the seventeenth-century Western infatuation with new technology, these devices were soon introduced to China, where the enterprising natives began to manufacture them. Chinese versions reached Nagasaki in 1718, and they became something of a craze among the bourgeoisie of Kyoto and Edo. The novel effect of deep recession produced by these *optiques* came to the attention of certain painters and woodblock-print designers of the popular Ukiyo-e school in Edo, and they began to integrate perspectival ideas into their works as early as the late 1730s. In subsequent decades other artists, students of Western technology and science such as Hiraga Gennai (1729–1779), Shiba Kōkan (1747–1818), and members of the Akita school of "Western" painters active in the remote northeast region of Akita, also utilized these principles in their paintings, but in a more accomplished manner.

The earliest extant works that can be confidently attributed to Ōkyo's hand are small hand-colored woodblock prints designed for *nozoki karakuri*, which he produced when he was in his mid- or late twenties. According to one tradition Ōkyo was employed by a toy merchant in Kyoto who handled imported *optiques*, and because of the limited number of images available for these devices, the merchant had Ōkyo produce additional designs in order to promote sales. Most of these were thirdhand versions—Japanese copies of Chinese woodblock interpretations of European copperplate engravings—and Ōkyo seems to have worked primarily from Chinese prints produced in the Suchow area, although he also represented familiar Kyoto locations that would have held a special attraction for the local inhabitants. Known as *megane-e* (optical pictures), these unusual images, which employed chiaroscuro techniques and a single vanishing point in order to achieve the illusion of volume and atmospheric distance, had a fresh appeal for Japanese viewers, although the scientific principles behind them were poorly understood. Ōkyo designed *megane-e* for only a short time, but this experience was significant, for the precise arrangement and delineation of form within three-dimensional space through the use of chiaroscuro became one of the distinguishing characteristics of his painting and of the school he founded.

The other innovative feature of Ōkyo's painting is the special sense of realism, of nature carefully observed and studiously assessed for the purpose of depicting flora and fauna with the greatest accuracy of arrangement, posture, and, in particular, anatomical detail. The curriculum in academic Kanō ateliers entailed conscientiously copying the works of accomplished masters and repeatedly rendering prescribed subject matter in order to refine the student's abilities and preserve the conceptual and technical precepts of the school. Ōkyo typically executed an initial sketch and preliminary drawings before he began the final painting, a developmental sequence that seems to reflect his Kanō training under Ishida Yūtei. This calculated process (which has analogies in certain Western academic traditions) was ideally suited to realistic portrayal, for it obliged the painter to assess and refine his work as it evolved, leading to a precise and literal rendering of the subject. Ōkyo's interest in realistic depiction can be seen in his topographical studies, in his depictions of familiar landscape scenes, and especially in his portrayals of animals, birds, fish, and other animate subjects characteristically combined with appropriate flowers and plant forms. Ironically, this obsession with accuracy occasionally worked against the artist's intentions, making his subjects appear rather like those in the zoological drawings of a Western scientific text or like a taxidermist's model, devoid of any enlivened spirit.

There is no denying, however, the facile and accomplished manner in which Ōkyo executed his paintings; his style, sometimes criticized as being flashy and superficial by the Bunjin and other painters of different ideological persuasions, nevertheless held a fascination for the bourgeois society of Kyoto. In fact, the commercial success of the school was such that it produced several branches and lasted until modern times. Ōkyo's career reached its zenith in the last decade of his life, when he carried out ambitious commissions at several important temples in various provinces, at the Kotohiragū shrine in Shikoku, and at the Imperial Palace, assisted in these projects by his followers from the Maruyama school, which had become the most admired professional atelier in the Kyoto area. The paintings that he and his disciples produced in 1790 in connection with the renovation of the Imperial Palace, heretofore the exclusive domain of Kanō and Tosa artists, are dramatic evidence of the influence and prestige of the school at this time. After Ōkyo's death in 1795, his son Ōzui succeeded him as the head of the Maruyama line, and the many talented artists who had trained under Ōkyo responded to this event either by emulating their master's neoteric concepts as faithfully as possible, by endeavoring to bring them to another evolutionary stage, or, as in the case of Nagasawa Rosetsu (1754–1799), by breaking away and creating an expressive style of their own.

Particularly important among those who worked to continue the artistic development of the school, Matsumura Goshun (1752–1811) was able to refine and redirect Ōkyo's stylistic ideas, devising a means of expression notable for its elegance, conceptual virtuosity, and luminous clarity. Goshun came from a family that had resided in Kyoto for four generations, and his residence, situated in the center of the city on Shijō (Fourth Avenue), served as an atelier for his followers. These men trained under him and set up their own workshops nearby on the same street, which accounts for the giving of the name Shijō to the branch of Ōkyo's line that was founded by Goshun.

The progress of Goshun's career reflected the diverse artistic influences and schools that flourished in Kyoto during the eighteenth century. He took up painting initially as an avocation, one of the cultivated activities expected of a young man from an upper-class family, studying briefly under the eclectic master Ōnishi Suigetsu, but he soon became a follower of the celebrated Bunjin painter Yosa Buson, under whom he received instruction both in the writing of haiku and in painting. Goshun absorbed the essentials of Buson's style quickly, and his admiration for the older man's paintings is apparent from his close copies of specific works. A popular celebrity among the wealthy citizens of Kyoto who enjoyed genteel literary and artistic activities, Buson also had extensive contacts with former students and dilettantes in the surrounding provinces. Admiring Goshun's sincerity of character, Buson introduced him to many of these people, and the student, in accordance with the Literati-ink-guest system, traveled about earning a livelihood by visiting well-to-do patrons of literature and painting. Buson instructed Goshun and promoted his interests in this manner from 1772 to 1780, but in 1781 Goshun's wife and father both died, and he seems to have fallen into financial difficulties. As a consequence he moved to Ikeda in Settsu Province (present-day Osaka Prefecture), where he took the tonsure, became a lay priest, and concentrated his efforts on painting, producing a number of fine works in the style of Buson.

Several years after Buson's death in 1783, a gradual stylistic change occurred in Goshun's painting, presumably the result of Ōkyo's influence on Goshun, who in 1787 joined with the older master and a group of his disciples in order to execute a series of compositions on sliding screens at the Daijōji, a temple in what is now Hyōgo Prefecture. In subsequent years, the influence of Ōkyo's style became ever more pronounced in Goshun's works; in 1789 he moved back to Kyoto, taking up residence on Shijō and establishing his atelier there. He diligently studied Ōkyo's methods until the older man died in 1795.

Goshun continued to execute his works within this general framework, but his own artistic predilections grew stronger. His later works show a diminished concern for the detailed delineation of tangible realistic forms, instead manifesting a special impressionistic air of delicacy and translucency that is more evocative, and thus more distinctive. Although the brush techniques and spatial concepts differ, something of Buson's aesthetics and preferences of color seem to have resurfaced in these late works by Goshun.

Nagasawa Rosetsu is thought to have been from a low-ranking family of the warrior class and to have served as a retainer during his early years under feudal lords at Sasayama (in Tamba Province, northwest of Kyoto) and at Yodo (just south of the city). He had already become a member of the Maruyama school by his mid-twenties, however, and was clearly an established artist by the time he was twenty-nine years of age, for his name was included in the section on painters in the 1782 edition of the *Heian Jimbutsushi* (*Directory of Eminent People in Kyoto*). Rosetsu was a man of exceptional talent, and by his late twenties he had mastered the style and techniques of the Maruyama school.

The works he produced in subsequent years demonstrate how he moved away from Ōkyo's conceptual canons and precisely formulated brushwork to a freer, more versatile manner of expression. The first clear signs of this disaffiliation from the formal strictures of the Maruyama style appeared in paintings Rosetsu did when he was in his early thirties. In 1786 he set out from Kyoto on a trip to the southern part of Kii Province (present-day Wakayama Prefecture) in order to carry out painting commissions—which seem to have been negotiated on his behalf by Ōkyo—at several temples in the region. Rosetsu worked industriously on these projects, and within a period of four to five months he had completed compositions on about one hundred eighty panels in three temples, the Sōdōji, the Muryōji, and the Jōjuji. These splendid works constitute one of the great monuments of Edo-period painting, and they demonstrate graphically how Rosetsu had put aside the narrow precepts of the Maruyama school and had conceived an idiosyncratic style that mesmerizes the viewer with its spontaneous brushwork and its daring exploration of spatial arrangements.

The versatile array of brush techniques in these paintings is dazzling, ranging from light, spare, yet elegant linear treatments to broad, wet washes and dynamic tonal contrasts and spatterings, all executed with freedom and confidence. The influence of Ōkyo's realistic formulations is still occasionally to be seen, but those precepts are utilized only where they contribute a novel quality to the gestalt the artist intended. Rosetsu's paintings share the sorts of subject matter that appear in the works of Ōkyo and other Maruyama-school artists, but his interpretation is invariably more personal and interpretive. Thus, Rosetsu depicted elegant Chinese beauties with greater technical élan, imbuing the works with a sensuous, somewhat decadent, and more individualized quality than the static, idealized interpretations of Ōkyo and his followers. Moreover, some of Rosetsu's ink portrayals of traditional Chinese anecdotal subjects show an indebtedness to Bunjin figural works, particularly those of Buson, in which eccentric figures are delineated in restrained, uninflected lines; other works by Rosetsu reflect different Literati means of expression, such as incisive *ippin* ink techniques or the direct use of fingers, fingernails, and sometimes even the palm of the hand for painting.

Rosetsu traveled extensively, producing paintings not only for temples and shrines, but more frequently for wealthy local patrons and dilettantes in the provinces, as in the Literati-ink-guest practice. His reputation as a heavy drinker who sometimes worked while he was inebriated also suggests some Literati influence on his attitude toward painting.

The landscape paintings Rosetsu produced during the last decade of his life show a variety of conceptual approaches. They range from atmospheric depictions of mountains enshrouded in hazy clouds, or mysterious moonlit scenes done in soft, amorphous washes and broad, juxtaposed brush strokes, to smaller, more intimate scenes in which a pervasive mood of fantasy is enlivened by colorful embellishment. Other memorable pieces were done in an abbreviated yet dramatic manner reminiscent of certain impressionistic works of the great English painter J. M. W. Turner (1775–1851). Few stylistic remnants of Ōkyo's realism and calculated spatial arrangements appear in Rosetsu's later paintings. Rather, these works seem to reflect the occasional influence of Literati aesthetics, although Rosetsu's techniques are essentially different from those of Bunjin painters. Yet another expressive approach may be seen in the artist's later group of screen compositions, *Waves* (created for the Shōjūji, a temple in Aichi Prefecture), in which he orchestrated sea currents and breaking waves through the use of repeated lines such as those used earlier and more simply by Ōkyo, but which Rosetsu here brought to a new evolutionary stage. It would be difficult to name another artist of the Edo period whose inventiveness and originality of approach equaled Rosetsu's. Sadly, he died early, at the age of forty-six.

Another eighteenth-century artist whose paintings are much admired for their distinctive brushwork and conceptual originality is Sōga Shōhaku. Shōhaku is thought to have come from a merchant family in Kyoto named Miura and to have studied painting briefly under Takada Keihō (1674–1755), who in turn had studied under Kanō Eikei, the fourth titular head of the Kyoto branch of the Kanō school. The influence of the conventions and precepts of the Kanō curriculum is often evident in Keihō's painting, but his works are enlivened by a greater sense of spontaneity and power. In addition, the eccentricity evident in his choice and portrayal of subject matter is indebted on the one hand to the unorthodox concepts and mannerisms of Sansetsu—the earlier Kanō master of the Kyoto line—and, on the other, to Zen painters of the Muromachi period, who specialized in imaginative ink representations of figural subjects. Keihō worked mainly in Hino, his native town in Omi Province, about fifty miles from Kyoto, but he was fond of the peripatetic life and traveled extensively, making his livelihood by painting works commissioned by local patrons. His oeuvre consists primarily of lively depictions of monks, recluses, and other strange characters from traditional Buddhist and Taoist anecdotal sources, but he also painted landscapes, as well as an occasional dragon or bird-and-flower portrayal.

Shōhaku's tutelage under Keihō probably lasted for only four or five years, but it is clear that the mentor's creative and stylistic inclinations strongly influenced those of the student. This is evinced by the fact that Shōhaku also chose to work almost exclusively in monochrome ink, concentrating on the same sort of eccentric figural subjects and portraying them in a highly personal manner with energetic, expressionistic brush techniques. Fragmentary information about Shōhaku's life and work can be found in various art-historical writings of the late Edo period, as well as in a lively body of oral accounts from the Ise region (where he was active for some years) that were written down and published toward the end of the Meiji period (1868–1912). These materials include laconic comments on the nature or quality of his works, as well as somewhat longer passages that contain observations on his artistic activities but also describe, often with obvious enthusiasm, his unconventional character and colorful behavior. Typically represented as a solitary figure of somewhat indolent, bohemian temperament, Shōhaku spent extended periods of time on the road in search of receptive patrons. Recurrent themes are his penchant for sake and his uproarious exploits while inebriated, a condition he found opportune for his spontaneous, uninhibited manner of painting.

He is described as having delineated some of his eccentric figures by beginning at the toes and finishing with the head and facial features, and as having employed a variety of unusual techniques, such as saturating a rough straw brush with thick, dark ink and literally swabbing the paper with it. On one occasion, when another artist was painting a figure and had paused dilatorily at the midsection, Shōhaku came up from behind, took out a cloth, soaked it in ink, and promptly sketched in the section from the waist down.

Given the unrepressed nature of his own painting, Shōhaku's antipathy for the methodical techniques and literal realism of the Maruyama school is understandable; he is alleged to have said: "If you want a real painting, you must come to see me; if it's only a drawing you're after, you should try Maruyama Mondo [Ōkyo]." On another occasion he took the pompous Kanō-school painter Katsuyama Takushū (?–1788) to task for an obvious inaccuracy in his depiction of the famous floating bridge at Sano and, angered at Takushū's overbearing response, drew his sword and had to be restrained by bystanders. Several delightful stories suggest that Shōhaku and Taiga were congenial acquaintances, but this relationship did not keep Shōhaku from ribbing his friend about his painstakingly slow use of the brush and his meticulous execution of detail in precise dots and carefully formulated strokes.

Thus, Shōhaku emerges from the pastiche of written and oral accounts as a strong individualist, occasionally at loggerheads with the tedious conventions of the world and sometimes inclined to intractability or unpredictable behavior. Measured by conventional standards, Shōhaku may well have been a man of unusual temperament, but seen in the context of eighteenth-century Japanese painting, wherein eccentricity was often viewed as intrinsic to creativity (a view popular in Bunjin circles) and offbeat behavior frequently enhanced, rather than hindered, a painter's image, his personality seems less extreme.

Independent and proud by nature, Shōhaku eschewed affiliation with any of the schools of his own period, choosing rather to identify himself with the Sōga school. This venerable but somewhat obscure line of painters had its origins in the activities of Sōga Dasoku, a monk-artist of the fifteenth century who was associated with the Daitokuji, the renowned Zen monastery in Kyoto. Although the Sōga line was moribund well before Shōhaku's birth, he seems to have had no qualms about referring to himself as the tenth painter in the lineal tradition of Dasoku or about promoting his association with the school through the inscriptions on his paintings. Shōhaku's motivations in this regard seem to have been a paradoxical mixture of the pragmatic and the romantic. The perception in the public mind of kinship between an artist and a prestigious school had its practical advantages—increased status, wider recognition, and the potential for financial gain; Shōhaku was, however, undoubtedly also inspired by a sincere reverence for, and a nostalgic identification with, the past. This circumstance, together with the fact that his subject matter was drawn almost entirely from traditional iconographic sources, led some later commentators to mistake him for a man out of step with his times, a crusty anachronism whose work had no relevance to the innovative spirit pervasive in the best painting of the period. This sort of interpretation tended to focus on the artist's personality and behavior rather than on his creative accomplishments. In point of fact, Shōhaku was very much an avant-garde artist, and his work a direct outgrowth of the heady creative atmosphere that prevailed in the Kyoto area during his time. The distinctive expressionistic quality in his works—his persistent search for unique modes of expression—confirms that he was in the vanguard of contemporary painting.

Itō Jakuchū is customarily grouped by art historians with Rosetsu and Shōhaku. This association may appear arbitrary, for these men had no mutual artistic or ideological affiliation and their distinctive styles were the result of varying traditions and aesthetics. The bond that justifies and gives historical credence to this grouping is the three artists' mutual absorption in plumbing their own creative wellsprings to develop the full potential of their talents and to conceive new means of expression. Although it can be argued that this sort of motivation is common to most serious painters (and certainly to many of the artists mentioned in this essay), its manifestation occurred in particularly compelling forms in the cases of Rosetsu, Shōhaku, and Jakuchū. Scholars have searched for an appropriate descriptive term to encompass the creative approaches of all three men, referring to them as unorthodox, eccentric, and heterodox, but although each of these words is suitable in a particular context, the expression that seems most inclusive and fitting is "individualist." The singular skills and vision that make their idiosyncratic oeuvres so dramatically different from one another also confirm their reputation as three of the most accomplished and original figures in the history of Japanese painting. That they were contemporaries is all the more remarkable, and that ancient Kyoto, the great citadel of Japanese culture, was the center of their activities reaffirms the city's historical role as a fertile source of inspiration for all the arts.

CHAPTER

2

Itō Jakuchū: Biographical Matters

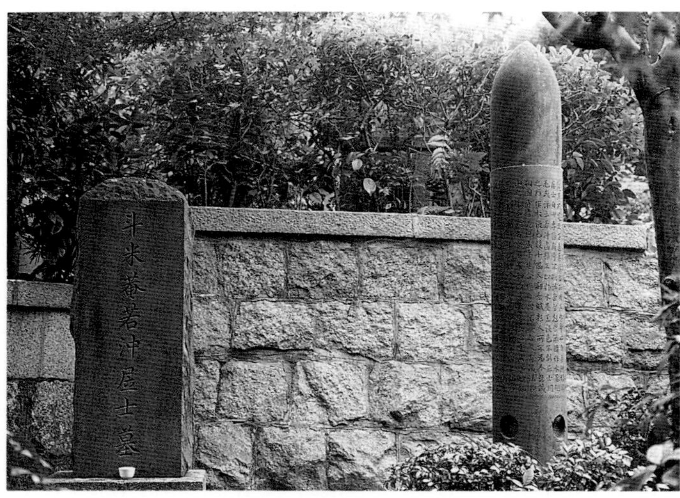

FIG. 1 Brush-shaped stele (right) erected in the Sekihōji in 1833 in honor of Jakuchū. Colophon by Nukina Kaioku (1778–1863).

It is fair to say that the picture of Jakuchū's life preserved in written materials is more accurate and substantive than those of most of the artists of his time—not because the corpus of information is particularly extensive, but rather because it is diverse, generally accurate in detail, and in good portion based on knowledgeable observations of the artist by a close friend.[1] Jakuchū was much respected in artistic circles during the later decades of his protracted career, and it is therefore not surprising that biographical entries on him appear in various traditional art-historical writings of the late Edo period, such as the *Kinsei Itsujin Gashi* (c. 1824) and its later edition, the *Zōhō Kinsei Itsujin Gashi*, as well as the *Gajō Yōryaku* (1831). Other information dealing with Jakuchū's artistic activities and interests is found in the elegant, adulatory inscription (written by the eminent Bunjin painter and Confucian scholar Nukina Kaioku, 1778–1863) incised on a brush-shaped stone monument erected at the Sekihōji temple in 1833 (FIG. 1). A variety of more factual and documentary information—including a number of random entries in the records of the Shōkokuji temple, the deed of gift that had accompanied Jakuchū's presentation of his masterpiece, the *Dōshoku Sai-e* paintings, to that temple, and the burial records of the Itō family—sheds substantial light on the particulars of Jakuchū's life and the evolution of his painting. However, the most comprehensive body of biographical information on Jakuchū and commentary on his works appears in the writings of the artist's friend and benefactor, Daiten Kenjō (1719–1801), the distinguished monk and man of letters from the Shōkokuji monastery who served as Jakuchū's chief biographer. The various materials mentioned above are of value in understanding Jakuchū because they deal with his life and creative efforts from diverse points of view and contexts; their admixture of narrative and detail, general and particular, and historical and personal, presents a balanced and convincing picture of the artist's life.

Itō Jakuchū was born on the eighth day of the Second Month of the sixth year of the Shōtoku calendrical era, which generally corresponds to the year 1716 of the Gregorian calendar. Nothing is known of his early years, not even his childhood name, but the information about his family lineage and relationships that has been preserved is of fundamental importance in understanding both the environment in which he was raised and related circumstances that were to exercise a significant influence on his personality and career as an artist. The Itō family were wholesale greengrocers, an occupation they had pursued in the city of Kyoto for three generations by the time of Jakuchū's birth. The family store, popularly known as the Masugen,[2] was situated in the Nishiki neighborhood, then one of the principal foodstuff markets in the great city, and which continues to perform that role to the present day, although on a much-reduced scale.[3] In Jakuchū's time this marketplace consisted of many specialty shops, most situated along the north and south sides of the small thoroughfare that ran through the middle of the district. Displayed neatly in the open storefronts, a colorful juxtaposition of vegetables, fruits, fowl, fish, and varied delicacies, both fresh and preserved, attracted buyers to the conveniently located market. Appropriately, *nishiki* means "brocade," a word that vividly evokes a sense of the diversity and abundance of the foods displayed.

The Masugen was situated within the Nakauoya-chō section of the quarter, at what is today the southeast corner of the intersection of Nishiki-koji (the pedestrian thoroughfare, running east and west, which bisects the quarter) and Takakura-dōri (the north-south street on the western perimeter of the area). The long, narrow plot of land on which the shop, storage facilities, and living quarters were located measured about six meters by thirty meters, a common layout for traditional merchants' establishments in Kyoto. The Itō family seems to have operated their business at this location for more than two centuries. Although they ultimately lost the shop, sometime during the period of political instability that swept Japan in the 1860s, a greengrocer still operates at the site. Jakuchū's father (Sōsei [posthumous Buddhist name]; 1697?–1738) was the third to own and operate the family business; he was preceded by Jakuchū's grandfather, the second Masugen, who is said to have died in 1710. The first Masugen, who came from Omi, the province just east of Kyoto, is said to have died in 1649 at the age of seventy-seven. This information, to the degree that it can be presumed accurate, attests to the longevity of the family occupation, as well as to the family's essential conservatism. Moreover, their occupational continuity in a single location suggests that they probably led the stable but generally insular life of middle-class merchants, comfortable if not affluent and preoccupied with mercantile routine rather than intellectual or cultural pursuits. Like most members of their class, Jakuchū's father and mother married early; they were only twenty and seventeen years old, respectively, when Jakuchū, their first child, was born. Although Jakuchū's father died in 1738 at the age of forty-two, his mother, Seiju, who was also from Omi, lived on to the advanced age of eighty, passing away in 1779. There appear to have been four siblings, an average number for the times: Jakuchū and his brothers, Sōgan (who was three years younger and painted under the name Hakusai; FIG. 2) and Sōjaku, followed by their sister, Shinjaku.

Despite a lack of information on Jakuchū's early and adolescent years, it may be presumed that, because he was the eldest male offspring, he would have been methodically tutored in the skills necessary for a successful career as a wholesaler: the ability to keep records and handle money, as well as the social proprieties essential to expediting business. Such pragmatic preparation was to prove useful soon enough, for Jakuchū was only twenty-three years old when his father died. This sad event was momentous for Jakuchū, since it compelled him to take up responsibility for operating the family business. Although it is likely that Jakuchū (now the fourth Masugen) devoted himself, at least in the beginning,

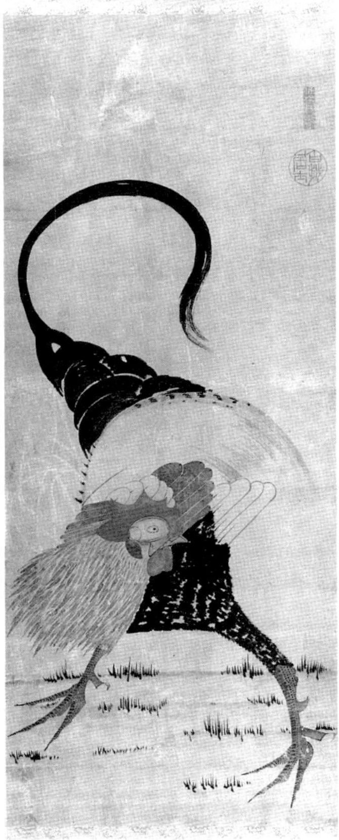

FIG. 2
Hakusai (Sōgan). *Rooster*, n.d.

Los Angeles County Museum of Art, Shin'enkan Collection

to the established routines and mercantile obligations required to further the family enterprise, documentary sources suggest that he was not suited, either in temperament or in personality, to a career as the head of a wholesale business.

Daiten's writings throw some light on this circumstance. A passage in the *Tō Keiwa Gakanoki* (*A Record of the Paintings of Tō Keiwa*, c. 1760) notes:

> When Keiwa [Jakuchū] was small he did not like studying, and was bad at writing characters. Among the multitude of skills and accomplishments, there was not a single one in which he was proficient, except painting. He had no desire to participate in the activities men commonly enjoy, such as singing, sporting with women, or joining in parties and merrymaking. Moreover, he did not aspire to wealth or worldly success, and he was quite oblivious to the luxurious attractions that daily seduce one's eyes and ears in the cities and towns. By nature he was inclined to enjoy solitary pursuits, and he patiently labored day by day to develop his talents and expressive means. In this manner thirty years devoted assiduously to painting passed like a single day.[4]

Although the retiring Jakuchū persevered as head of the family business for about seventeen years, it was undoubtedly a burden for him, and he understandably looked elsewhere for solace from the tedium of shopkeeping. Religion provided him with a convenient refuge from the humdrum, appealing particularly to his introverted, reclusive nature. One incident described in the *Shōsai Hikki*—one of the miscellaneous writings of Hiraga Hakusan (also known as Shōsai; 1745–1805), who knew Jakuchū—brings his emotional dilemma into more immediate focus:

> Jakuchū, the widely known painter, was the head of a wholesale shop in the greengrocers' district in the Takakura neighborhood in Kyoto. Jakuchū was, however, quite reclusive by nature. He led a very solitary life from his youth on, and always had a strong antipathy for mundane, daily routine. On one occasion he went into eremitic seclusion for two years in the deep mountains of Tamba Province, and it was even rumored that he had died from sickness. Moreover, as a result of his absence, the wholesale greengrocery was without a master during this period, and some unscrupulous opportunists got together and tried to take over the business. This caused widespread concern, and three thousand retail peddlers connected with the firm gathered from every direction, and demanded compensation for the inconvenience the affair had caused. Secluded in the mountains, Jakuchū was oblivious of the circumstances. Of course, he had no intention of inconveniencing everyone as a result of his solitary activities, and when he was finally informed of the difficulties he promptly set off, traveling incognito, for the capital city of Edo. Once there, he surreptitiously inserted a letter into the palanquin of one of the Shogun's Council of Elders, respectfully requesting official litigation of the affair. As a result of the ensuing investigation, it became clear that the speculators were to blame for everything, and it was ordered that in the future the wholesale greengrocery was to be administered so that outsiders could not take it over. After this, time passed, things went well, and the business did not change hands.[5]

Nothing is known of where in the mountains of Tamba Jakuchū spent his period of retreat or of how he passed the time there, but he probably did not go simply to escape the routine of work, but rather to find psychological solace in the time-honored Buddhist practice of retiring from temporal entanglements to seek spiritual insight and consolation through meditation and prayer. Indeed, Jakuchū's personality and interests were such that Buddhism, in one context or another, continued to provide him with the emotional environment and inspiration indispensable for both his well-being and his creative activity in subsequent years.

Jakuchū's family temple, where the graves of his parents and other relatives are preserved, is the Hōzōji, a modest enclave located in the Urateramachi, Rokkaku-sagaru district, just a short walk from where the Masugen stood. The Hōzōji, which still ministers to local parishioners, belongs to the Pure Land sect of Buddhism, whose central doctrine of salvation through fervent prayer to the Buddha Amitabha especially appealed to members of the pragmatic merchant class, for whom the promise of easy entry into paradise generally took precedence over the philosophical satisfactions or doctrinal complexities of Buddhism.

Although Jakuchū's early religious training took place within the conventional, prescriptive framework of Pure Land ritual, his curiosity about spiritual matters eventually led him to another realm of Buddhist thought. Sometime in his thirties, he became interested in Zen Buddhism, and this experience was to shape his subsequent life in a profound manner. Jakuchū's friend and confidant Daiten Kenjō was the central figure in the artist's involvement with Zen activities.[6] It is significant that the long lives of Jakuchū (1716–1800) and Daiten (1719–1801) coincided so closely. Their amiable association, which spanned as much as half a century, may also have had its roots in their common origins, as Daiten is thought also to have come from Omi Province, whence Jakuchū's family had come.

Daiten became a Buddhist acolyte when he was ten years old and soon came under the studious influence of the distinguished monk Dokuhō, abbot of the

Jiun'an subtemple of the great Shōkokuji monastery in Kyoto. From the beginning, Daiten showed intellectual promise, and he ultimately became one of the most noted scholar-monks of his time.[7] Daiten was appointed abbot of the Jiun'an in 1746, when he was only twenty-seven years of age, and he served in that capacity until 1759, when he retired to pursue a life of meditation and study. In subsequent years he moved periodically, dedicating himself to the priestly ideal of contemplation and study in seclusion at several hermitages, one situated northeast of Kyoto at Takagamine, another north of the city at Yamabana, and a third southeast of Kyoto, in one of the most venerated centers of the Rinzai Zen tradition, the Tōfukuji monastery. His significant accomplishments in Chinese literary studies were recognized in 1770, when the title Gozan Sekigaku (Eminent Scholar of the Five Mountains) was bestowed on him; he was also appointed a commissioner responsible for overseeing protocol for diplomatic missions visiting from Korea. In later years his official duties in this capacity took him as far as the island of Tsushima, where Korean missions to Japan were welcomed, and also to Edo on various occasions, where he was consulted on matters of diplomacy and interaction between Korea and the Tokugawa government. In 1772, however, Daiten returned to his duties within the hierarchy of the Shōkokuji, and seven years later he became chief abbot of the monastery. After the great conflagration of 1788, which leveled most of the monastery, he assumed a central role in the reconstruction of the compound and also worked diligently to rebuild the temple's archives of Confucian and Buddhist classics and literature. He died in 1801 at the age of eighty-three and was buried in the cemetery of the Jiun'an subtemple of the monastery.

The Shōkokuji, one of the prestigious Gozan (Five Mountains) monasteries of the Rinzai Zen tradition, was an institution in which the study of classic literature and other literary pursuits had been integral activities for centuries, and Daiten, who was a *bungakusō* (literary monk), personified this tradition. He produced several anthologies of writings, poetry, and miscellaneous observations—including the *Sakuhishu* (1761), the *Shōun Seikō* (1775), the *Hokuzen Bunsō* (1792), and the *Hokuzen Shisō* (1793)—which provide evidence of his close relationship with a large number of literati, scholars, and artists of the period.[8]

It is unclear just when Jakuchū began his association with Daiten; a short passage from the "Ketsumei" (FIG. 3), a memorial text by Daiten dealing with Jakuchū that was inscribed on a commemorative

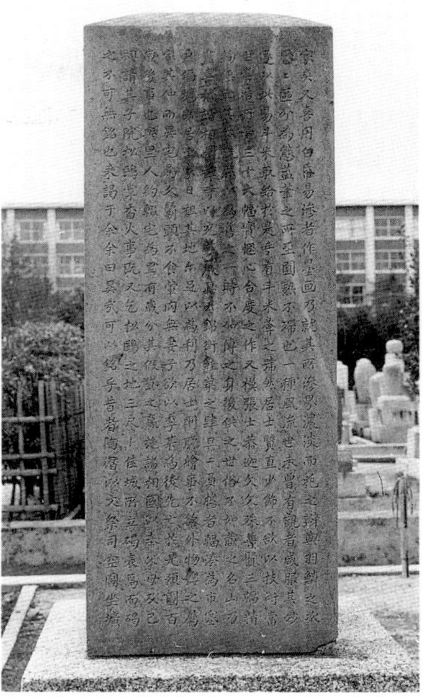

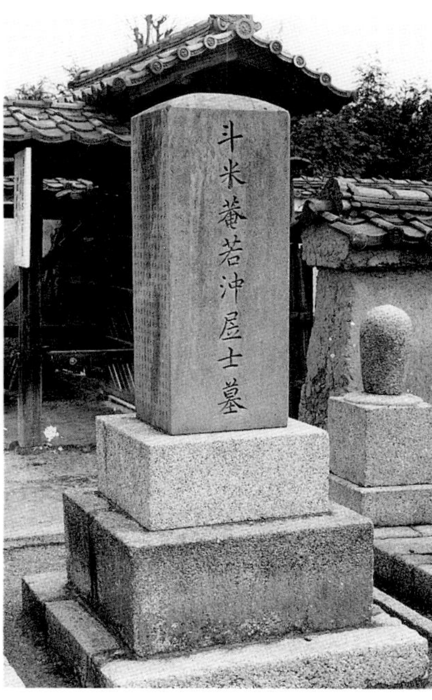

FIG. 3 (Left) Back of the commemorative stele (*juzō*) erected in the Shōkokuji cemetery by Jakuchū in 1766, showing the inscription ("Ketsumei") written by Daiten Kenjō.

FIG. 4 (Right) Commemorative stele (*juzō*) erected in the Shōkokuji cemetery by Jakuchū.

stele (*juzō*) erected by the artist himself in 1766 (FIG. 4), indicates that they had become acquainted either in about 1753 or 1754, when Jakuchū was in his late thirties, or perhaps several years earlier, depending on the interpretation of the rather unspecific wording.[9] The question of when Jakuchū began to use this name, and of how he chose it, is also relevant here. Signatures on some early paintings, in which the name Jakuchū is combined with the Buddhist title *koji* (lay monk), indicate that Jakuchū began to use this distinctive appellation no later than when he was in his late thirties,[10] at a time when he had probably already become associated with Daiten. Professor Akiyama Teruō suggested that Daiten may well have been responsible for conferring the name on his artist friend because of its origin in classical Chinese literature and its philosophical connotation, areas of literary interest to Zen devotees. The term *jakuchū* is composed of two characters that may be translated as "like a void." It originated in the forty-fifth section of an ancient Chinese philosophical text, the *Tao Te Ching* (*Teachings of Tao*, or *The Way*, of Lao-tzu), in which it is part of a four-character phrase that asserts: "The greatest fullness is like a void."[11] This phrase was, in fact, utilized by Daiten in an inscription he wrote for a stone water container dedicated to the

Ōbaku priest and man of letters Baisaō, who was also a friend of Jakuchū's; it would have been familiar in learned Zen circles of the period and was also adopted by at least two Ōbaku monks for their priestly names.[12] Thus, it seems logical for it to have been Daiten who bestowed this appellation on his friend. Moreover, the artist's use, from this time on, of the title *koji* as a suffix to his name indicates that he had become a Buddhist lay monk—that is, he had received the tonsure, given up eating meat, and conscientiously devoted himself to observing the prohibitions of Buddhism and to searching for the path of Zen enlightenment. This development also corresponded chronologically with his final disaffection from the responsibilities and obligations of running the family business. At any rate, after seventeen years, at the age of forty, Jakuchū was finally relieved of this burden, and his younger brother Sōgan took over as the fifth Masugen. In keeping with his vows, Jakuchū appears to have lived as a celibate bachelor throughout his subsequent years. It is impossible to know exactly when he went into retreat and precipitated the controversy over the family business, but this unseemly affair may well have influenced Jakuchū's decision to pass on to his brother the operation of the Masugen.

It is obvious from their long friendship that Jakuchū and Daiten shared many interests, and Daiten seems to have recognized a special sense of religious compassion in Jakuchū. This is illustrated by a brief episode recounted by Daiten in the *Shōun Seikō*: "One day Jakuchū came across some live sparrows which were for sale in the market. He took pity on the birds, which were fated to be roasted on a spit, and he bought a large number of them, taking them back to his house, where he released them in his garden. . . . this expression of pity was like the compassion of one destined to become a Bodhisattva."[13] The freeing of captive birds was a traditional Buddhist practice designed to gain religious merit for the practitioner, but Daiten seems to have regarded Jakuchū's action as a spontaneous expression of compassion for living beings, rather than as an example of self-motivated, conventional ritual. In addition to receiving religious guidance, Jakuchū also greatly benefited from his association with Daiten in his career as a painter.

It is not known exactly when Jakuchū took up painting, but it is thought that he did not start at a particularly early age, unlike his younger contemporary the precocious Maruyama Ōkyo, who showed prodigious artistic talent as a youth. Jakuchū probably began to study painting when he was in his twenties, and this solitary, absorbing pursuit soon became a primary preoccupation, isolating him from the monotonous tedium of daily life. His early activities as an artist are a matter of conjecture. In his "Ketsumei" Daiten noted that Jakuchū had been fond of painting since his youth, cryptically observing that the artist studied under a master from the Kanō school, whom he unfortunately did not identify. Somewhat later, in the *Zoku Shōka Jimbutsushi* (*Noted Calligraphers and Painters, Continued*, 1832), Aoyagi Bunzō noted that Jakuchū worked initially under the artist's name Shunkyō, a circumstance suggesting that he may have received instruction from Ōoka Shumboku, an enterprising artist from Osaka with Kanō-school training, who was particularly interested in Chinese painting of the Sung, Yüan, and Ming periods.[14] This interest led Shumboku to investigate Chinese and Japanese paintings of earlier centuries that had been preserved in Japan; these he copied and reproduced in woodblock-printed books that were intended to cater to the growing number of amateur painters who wished to learn the history and style of earlier artistic schools and pictorial traditions but who had little or no access to original pieces. That many of Jakuchū's works clearly manifest his enthusiasm for paintings of earlier periods and that Shumboku's activities inspired this enthusiasm, either directly or through the younger artist's exposure to his woodblock vade mecums, is a subject that will be considered later in this book, in discussion of the content and style of Jakuchū's paintings.

In the "Ketsumei" Daiten further noted that after a period of working exclusively in the Kanō mode, Jakuchū realized he was mastering only the techniques of this one school, and that he could never surpass Kanō artists in their own (academic) manner.[15] As a result he turned to a different source of inspiration: Chinese painting of the Sung and Yüan periods. Daiten's high position in the Zen hierarchy of the Shōkokuji, as well as his friendship with other Zen clerics and literati, was undoubtedly important to Jakuchū in his study of these works: the great Zen monasteries situated in and around the ancient capital of Kyoto were the chief repositories of important paintings brought back from China and other parts of continental Asia in earlier centuries, and these revered works were assiduously protected and not usually accessible to those lacking the proper introduction or credentials. Jakuchū became familiar with a substantial number of Chinese paintings in his earlier years, and these served as a primary source of inspiration and pictorial ideas for his own creative efforts. Although the original location of certain of these older pieces is unclear, the fact that a good number are still preserved in the Shōkokuji, despite the destruction of fire and the vicissitudes of time, attests to Jakuchū's having been able to study the works thoroughly and make more or less faithful copies of a number of them. There can be little doubt that his friendship with Daiten was essential in facilitating this process. Moreover, the priest not only was an influential figure in religious circles, but also was on good terms with various scholars, men of letters, painters, tea masters, and other men of refinement who were involved in cultural pursuits in the region. It is probable that Jakuchū met a number of these individuals because of his association with Daiten, and that they, in turn, provided new avenues of social interaction and creative ideas for Jakuchū.

Judging from what is known of its holdings in real estate, the Itō family appears to have been at least financially secure, if not well-off, for its merchant status. The incident of Jakuchū's retreat and the level of the subsequent furor over the control of the Masugen also indicate something of the extent of the family business and properties. In addition to the store building itself, there seem to have been two other houses, located close by in the Nishiki neighborhood, as well as a separate residence and studio that belonged to Jakuchū. The location of the studio-residence is not clear, but it may have been southeast of the Nishiki market, at a scenic site on the west bank of the Kamo River, between Shijō and Gojō avenues.[16] The latter structure, which served as an urban retreat and atelier for Jakuchū (who had happily been relieved from his business responsibilities) is said to have been a substantial two-story building that provided several fine views of the city.

In a poetic and topographically somewhat vague passage in the *Sakuhishu*[17] Daiten noted that one could look from this elevated vantage point in various directions, and see the broad expanse of green foliage and hills of Higashiyama to the east; the current of the Kamo River flowing south, past the imposing structure of the Hall of the Great Buddha, surrounded by houses; and what may have been the extensive compound of Nijō Castle to the west. The building was given the evocative name Shin'enkan, whose literary origin—the characters *shin* (heart, mind) and *en* (distant, far)—is a passage in a poem devoted to the pleasures of drinking wine by the celebrated Chinese poet of the fourth century T'ao Yüan-ming (365–427), which reads: "If the heart ranges far, one's spirit follows."[18] There are some differences of interpretation about the significance of this name, but it is generally agreed that the panoramic vistas Jakuchū saw from his retreat provided the basic inspiration and that the term itself incorporates two complementary emotional connotations: the surrounding visual beauty, and the emotional and philosophical response of the viewer, whose spirits were lifted by a sense of freedom from temporal concerns. No rendering in English can replicate the elegant wording of the original language, with its layering of literary and philosophical associations, but the free translation "Villa of the Expansive Spirit" may serve to convey something of the artist's intention.

Jakuchū probably moved to the Shin'enkan sometime in his late thirties, and during his period of residence there he created many of the masterpieces that established his reputation as one of the most revered artists of his time. He was then already an accomplished painter, and three dated works, done when he was forty years old, dramatically demonstrate that he had developed a distinctive style of great originality and refinement. Jakuchū probably began his most ambitious artistic undertaking sometime in 1757, when he was forty-two or forty-three years old. This series of thirty large hanging scrolls, known as the *Dōshoku Sai-e* (*Colorful Realm of Living Beings*; see NO. 14 and FIG. 33), was designed to be hung in two groups, flanking a Buddhist iconic triptych with depictions of Śākyamuni, the historical Buddha, and the Bodhisattvas Manjuśri and Samantabhadra (see NO. 15). Jakuchū worked on this monumental project, one of the most admired works of the Edo period, for close to a decade.

These paintings will be discussed in greater detail later; it is sufficient to note here that they represent an encyclopedic depiction of fauna and flora of various terrestrial, marine, and avian species, a rich inventory of beings of diverse size and appearance. The artist's vision of plants and animals coexisting in an idealized world of peace and harmony clearly was conceived with a deep sense of religious conviction, and it seems to have been intended as a grand, panoramic portrayal of the Buddhist belief in the universal significance and essential unity of all living things.

By early 1761, about three years after Jakuchū had begun the project, he had completed twelve of the scrolls, and in 1765 he presented twenty-four of them, together with the central Buddhist triptych, to the Shōkokuji. The entire set of thirty scrolls (and the triptych) was in the possession of the monastery no later than 1770. When Jakuchū made his magnanimous gift to the monastery in 1765, he included a document of the gift that, because of its elegant literary style, is generally presumed to have been composed by Daiten but clearly expresses Jakuchū's own opinions and circumstances:

I have always devoted myself conscientiously to my painting, and in attempting to render the myriad manifestations of bamboo, trees, birds, and insects, I have collected all kinds of related materials, and, as a consequence [of depicting these], I have become specialized in such subjects. I once viewed the incomparably skilled paintings by Chang Ssu-kung of Śākyamuni, Manjuśri, and Samantabhadra, and I felt inspired to copy these works. So I rendered the three deities in a triptych, and I also did twenty-four polychrome depictions of the realm of living beings. As I had no intention, from the beginning, of producing these paintings for the mundane world, I have presented them to the Shōkokuji monastery in the hope that they will be permanently preserved as revered possessions of the temple. Moreover, I fervently pray that I will be interred in the monastery precincts and rest there even after a century has passed and nothing more than my bones remains. To this end I have humbly offered an insignificant donation to support temple operations, and I hope that this will make it possible that my memory will be observed with candles and incense.[19]

Jakuchū's original motivation (other than religious inspiration) in carrying out this challenging project is not altogether clear, but one event that may well have been influential in his decision to give the set to the Shōkokuji was the sudden death of his youngest brother, Sōjaku, in 1765. Significantly, the document of gift is dated only eleven days after Sōjaku's death. Jakuchū was only fifty years of age at the time, but his brother's demise must have caused him to reflect on his own mortality. Of more fundamental importance, however, was the artist's deep spiritual commitment to Zen Buddhist ideas, which stress the insignificance of temporal activities and view life as a fleeting episode in the process of achieving ultimate enlightenment.

An event that occurred the following month also reflects Jakuchū's focus on his spiritual life in the next world. The artist decided to deed one of the family houses, located at Takakura-dōri, Obiya-chō, to the local neighborhood association with the provision that, after his death, funds would always be available for annual services in his memory. Although Jakuchū's behavior during this period bespeaks an unusual preoccupation with mortality, there is no indication that he felt an impending sense of his own death or even that he was in bad health, and his subsequent years (he lived another three and a half decades) are notable not only for their creative productivity, but also for widespread admiration and acclaim for his painting. He seems, therefore, to have been less preoccupied with the immediate ramifications of memento mori than with the pervasive influence of Buddhism, with its transcendental orientation, in his own activities.

Yet another of Jakuchū's preparations for the next world was his decision to prepare a stele (FIG. 4) for his future grave in the Shōkokuji, although he was only fifty-one years old at the time. In fact, his decision to erect the commemorative stone probably had less to do with the state of his own health than with that of his benefactor, Daiten. As the artist's steadfast acquaintance and an eminent cleric, Daiten was naturally the most appropriate person to compose the memorial text, but although he was three years younger than Jakuchū, Daiten seems to have felt less robust than his friend. As a consequence, he thought that there was little likelihood of his outliving Jakuchū (although he actually did), and that the execution of the stele should not be postponed. The impressive monument (*juzō*), which now stands in the cemetery of the Shōkokuji, was erected in 1766, and the text inscribed on much of its sides and back (the "Ketsumei") serves as one of the basic sources of information about the artist's life and career.[20] Jakuchū was, by this time, a much-admired painter without financial worries, and having his funerary monument completed and in place must have afforded him a reassuring sense of spiritual security, in which he could live out his later years in a contemplative, creative manner.

Although Jakuchū's chief enterprise during his forties and perhaps the first year or two of his fifties was the *Dōshoku Sai-e* series, it is clear that this prodigious task did not monopolize his time. He seems to have worked diligently—at times, perhaps, exclusively—on it, especially in the earlier years, but turned to other projects or paintings from time to time and varied his artistic activities by working in several styles and techniques. The *Dōshoku Sai-e* paintings are notable for their precise brushwork and attention to detail, the splendor and scale of their conception, and the harmony of their polychromatic effects, in which a wide range of pigments—alternately bright and subdued combinations of colors—was skillfully combined into compositions of breathtaking beauty. A small number of other paintings that share these characteristics and are presumed to have been executed during roughly the same period have also been preserved. However, during this time Jakuchū was also producing paintings of a different sort, monochrome pieces that contrast sharply with the artist's polychrome works by virtue of their freer, more exuberant brushwork and their execution with little, if any, color. They depend on expressive means other than color—a variety of ink washes and linear effects—for their visual impact. These paintings belong to the *suiboku* (water and ink) tradition, with its ancient roots in China and Japan. It is not coincidental that Jakuchū's most ambitious *suiboku* project, dating from the period of his work on the *Dōshoku Sai-e* scrolls, was executed for another Zen monastery: the Rokuonji, in the Kitayama area of Kyoto, some distance to the west and north of the Shōkokuji, with which it was closely affiliated. These monochrome works on walls and sliding screens fill five rooms in the Dai-shoin (grand abbot's study) of the temple (NO. 16 and FIGS. 41–44). They were commissioned in 1759 by the priest Ryūmon Shōyū (1734–1800) on the occasion of his appointment as the head abbot when he was only twenty-six years of age. Ryūmon had studied literature under Daiten, and he probably chose Jakuchū to execute the paintings at the recommendation of his mentor.

The artist's creative industry during this time may be observed in his having completed not only this project, but also five of the *Dōshoku Sai-e* scrolls. That Jakuchū worked on both these projects, with their differing styles and techniques, during the same year provides dramatic evidence of his painterly virtuosity. More important, his conception of both series of paintings with great originality and creative vision confirms his reputation as one of the outstanding painters of his century. The colorful *Dōshoku Sai-e* paintings became the object of much attention in the years after they were donated to the Shōkokuji; they attracted a broad spectrum of visitors—scholars and tourists as well as artists and connoisseurs of painting—who came to study and admire them. The scrolls were exhibited at the monastery on special religious occasions, during which they served both as impressive ecclesiastical icons and as eloquent, inspiring examples of the finest painting of the era. Jakuchū occasionally produced other polychrome works in later decades, but he became ever more preoccupied with the challenges of *suiboku* painting, and the largest proportion of his work from the mid-1760s on consists of monochrome pieces.

Unlike many of his contemporaries, the retiring Jakuchū did not travel extensively in search of recreation, inspiration, and patronage or for the purpose of executing artistic commissions. However, he did make one long trip away from Kyoto during the course of his work on the *Dōshoku Sai-e* series in order to carry out another ambitious artistic undertaking. This journey took him to the renowned Kotohiragū shrine on the island of Shikoku in 1764, when he was forty-nine years of age. He was engaged to do a series of paintings on sliding screens in four adjoining rooms of the shrine headquarters. Only portions of the works from one of these rooms have been preserved. These depictions of flowers (FIG. 5), executed in vivid colors and a naturalistic manner, clearly reflect the precedents of the *Dōshoku Sai-e* pieces, but the shrine paintings are somewhat more schematic and decorative, qualities that may represent an artistic accommodation to the layout of the room. Sadly, only fragmentary evidence has survived to document the subject in one of the other rooms; it consisted of a landscape theme, which was rare in Jakuchū's oeuvre.

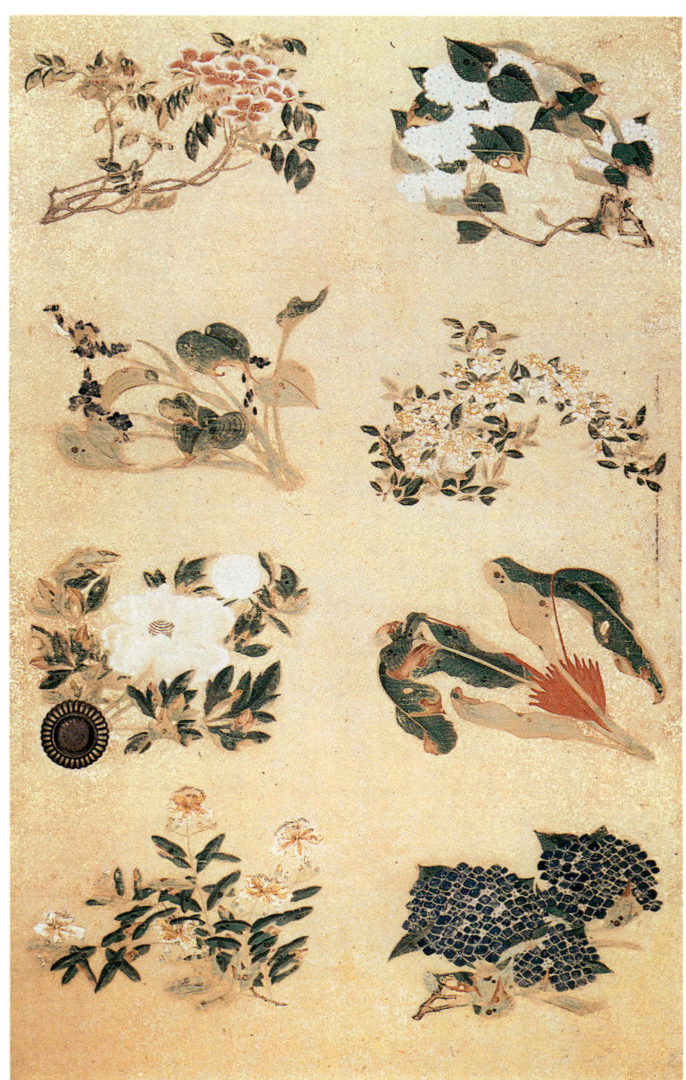

FIG. 5 Detail of screen with depictions of floral motifs, 1764. Kotohiragū shrine, Shikoku

Three years later, in the spring of 1767, Jakuchū and Daiten set out for a brief excursion away from Kyoto. The two companions boarded a modest, flat-bottomed riverboat, and traveled down the Yodo River from Fushimi, then south of Kyoto, to its terminus at Osaka, enjoying the topographical highlights that struck their interest along the way. To commemorate the congenial excursion Jakuchū conceived a landscape composition, based on sketches that he had done during the trip, that was reproduced in woodblock impressions on a long handscroll (FIG. 6). To complement Jakuchū's illustrations, Daiten provided the title—*Jōkyōshū* (*Impromptu Pleasures Afloat*) (FIG. 7)—in his own elegant calligraphy, written in the classical Chinese seal style, along with identifying notations and poetic comments on many of the locations.

It is interesting to note that the special technique of woodblock printing used to reproduce Jakuchū's composition had its origins in China, and Jakuchū seems to have been one of the few Japanese artists of his period to experiment with it. The rare practitioners of this technique preceding Jakuchū in Japan seem to have been Chinese Ōbaku monks who were calligraphy specialists or Japanese sinophiles who were influenced by the monks. This *taku-hanga* (rubbing or intaglio woodblock print) method of reproduction reverses the image and the background in the same manner as do traditional ink rubbings, so that the subjects appear uniformly in white and the background is inked with contrasting values of black or gray or, in rare instances, with light touches of pigment. Jakuchū continued to design compositions utilizing this technique for the next one or two years, producing two exquisite small books in black and white (FIGS. 8, 9) and some superb prints of birds and flowers with colors added (NO. 26).

Some years earlier, Jakuchū had become acquainted, probably through Daiten, with the noted Ōbaku priest Baisaō Kō Yūgai (1675–1763). Baisaō, then in the final years of his life, had long been influential in cultured circles in Kyoto and was an accomplished man of letters; more important, he was one of the foremost practitioners and popular advocates of Sencha, in which steeped, rather than powdered, tea serves as the focus of ritual and reflection. Baisaō, who became eighty-six in 1760, was greatly impressed with Jakuchū's *Dōshoku Sai-e* paintings, and he dedicated a piece of calligraphy composed of seven characters to Jakuchū, extolling his talents: "Enlivened by his hand, his paintings are filled with a mysterious spirit" (FIG. 10).[21] Jakuchū must have savored this praise from one of the most revered elder connoisseurs of taste, and he commemorated the event by having made for his use a special seal with Baisaō's dedication inscribed on it. This seal appropriately appears on one of the most

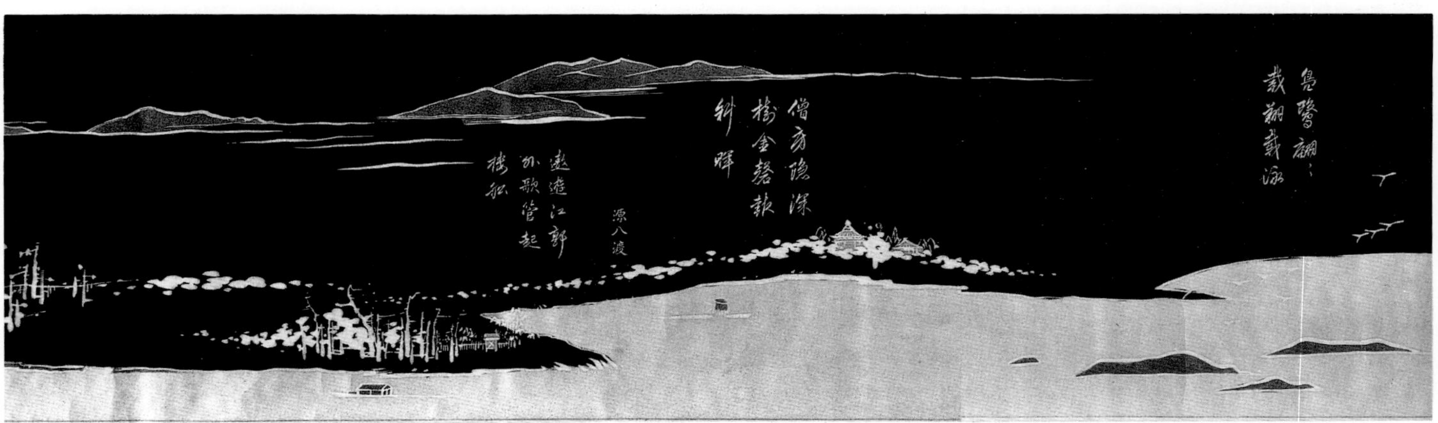

FIG. 6 Section of the *Jōkyōshū (Impromptu Pleasures Afloat)*, 1767.

Museum of Fine Arts, Boston

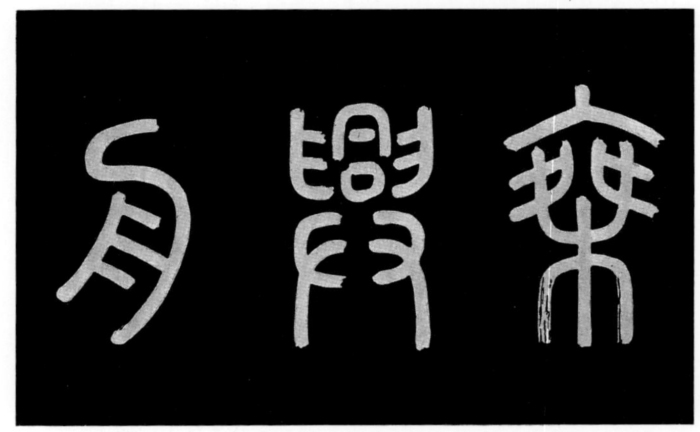

FIG. 7 Daiten Kenjō. Title calligraphy for the *Jōkyōshū (Impromptu Pleasures Afloat)*, 1767.

Museum of Fine Arts, Boston

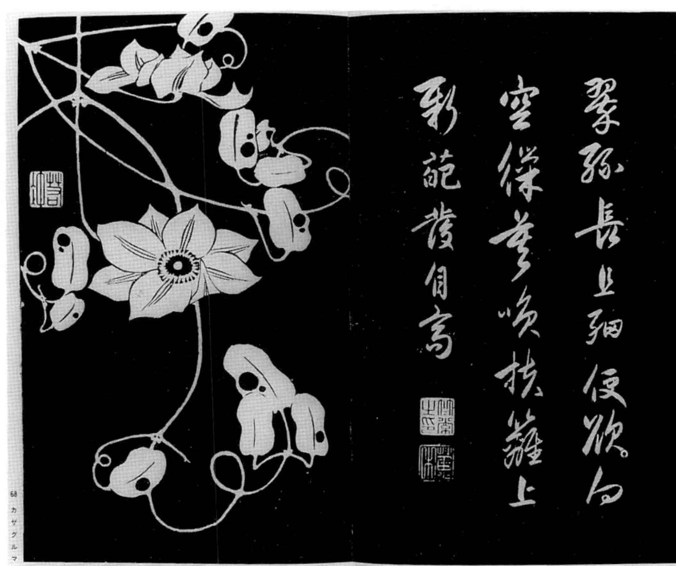

FIG. 8 "Open-flowered Clematis" with poem by Daiten, facing pages from the *Soken Jō (Album of Elegant Designs on a Plain Ground)*, 1768.

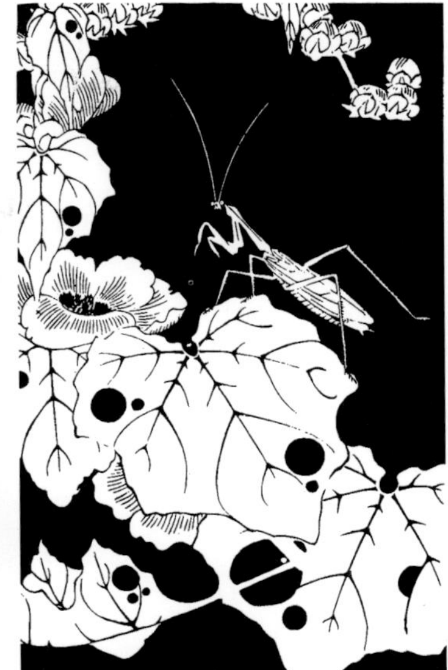

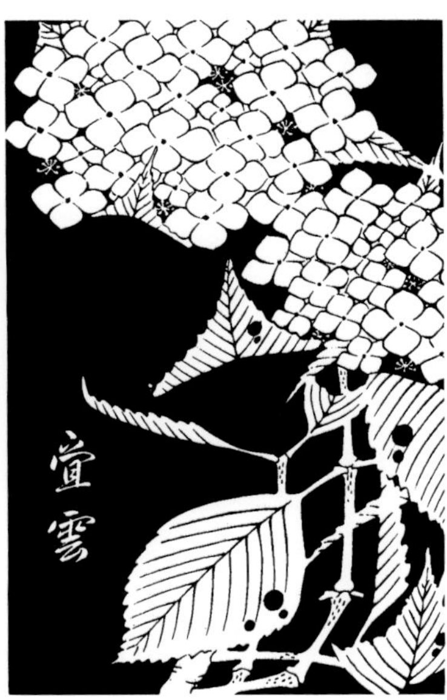

FIG. 9 "Winter Hollyhock and Hydrangea," facing pages from the *Gempo Yōka (Exquisite Flowers from the Mysterious Garden)*, 1768.

exuberant of the *Dōshoku Sai-e* paintings, a highly detailed representation of a pair of small birds in the midst of a cascade of bright peonies (NO. 14.5).

When Baisaō died three years later, Daiten, who had been a disciple and close friend of his for many years, collected his poems and writings and wrote a biography of him called the *Baisaō Gego*. This work, published as a small book, contains a woodblock reproduction of a portrait of Baisaō by Jakuchū (NOS. 18,19); some rare ink portraits on paper (one of them with calligraphy by Daiten) further attest to Jakuchū's admiration for the older man. The *Baisaō Gego* also reproduces a specimen of calligraphy (of a title composed by Baisaō) by the famous Bunjin painter Ike Taiga. Taiga, another prominent figure in the coterie of scholars, intellectuals, artists, and men of refinement who were influential in creative circles in Kyoto at this time, was on congenial terms with Daiten. Jakuchū and Taiga also knew each other, and it is likely that they moved in the same circles and shared a common interest in the transplanted Chinese traditions that flourished in Japan under the auspices of the Ōbaku branch of Zen, with its network of temples administered from headquarters at the Mampukuji. One instance of the gratifying relations between such men appears in the *Shōun Seikō*; Daiten tells of his having been invited, sometime in the spring of 1760 or the following year, by Jakuchū, Taiga, and the Ōbaku priest Mujū (who had served as the editor of the *Baisaō Gego*) to accompany them on genial excursions to the outskirts of Kyoto in order to admire and reflect on the beauties of the plum and

FIG. 10 "Enlivened by his hand, his paintings are filled with a mysterious spirit." Calligraphy by Baisaō Kō Yūgai, 1760.

Imperial Household Collection

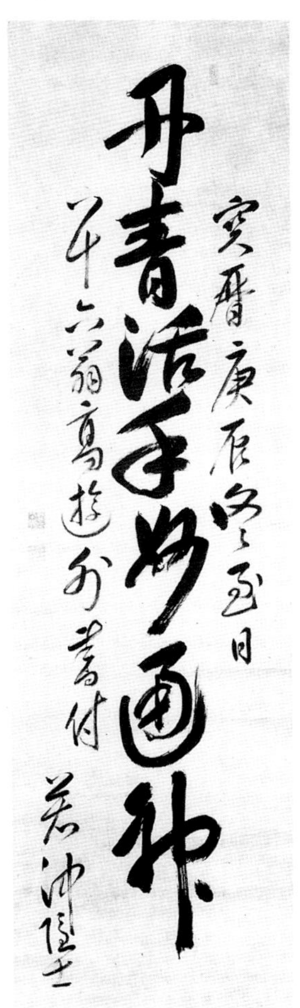

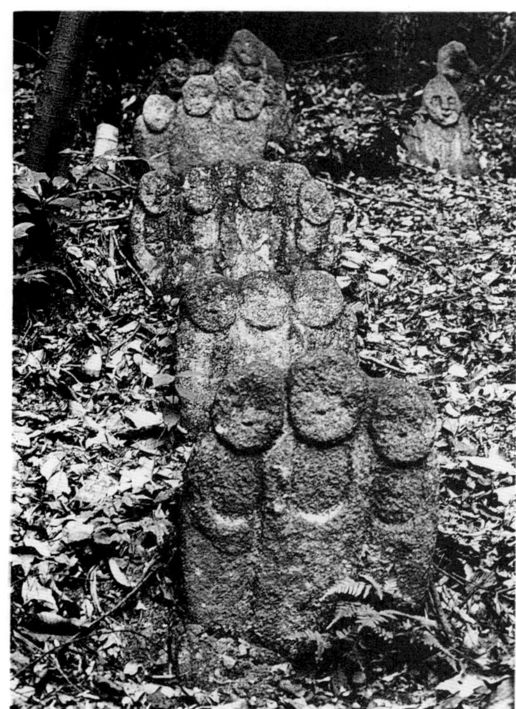
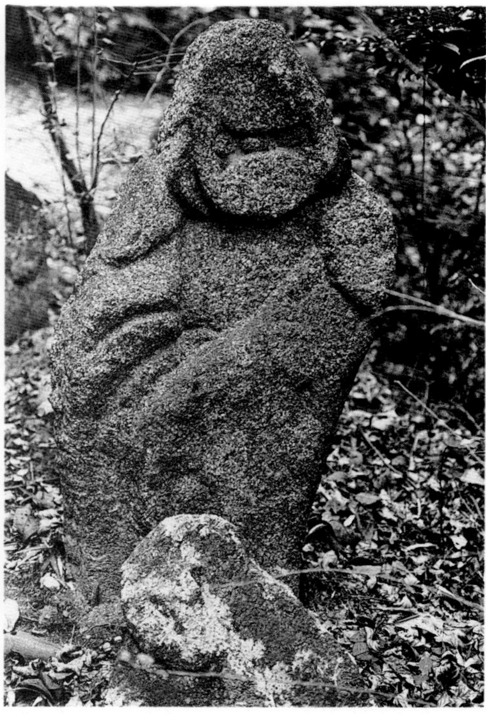

FIG. 11
Sculpture from the *Five Hundred Arhats*, c. 1776–c. 1790s.
Sekihōji, Fukakusa, Kyoto

cherry blossoms.[22] In intimate, relaxed gatherings such as these, the participants enjoyed a stimulating and pleasurable exchange of views about aesthetics, literature, art, and philosophy.

With the completion of the *Dōshoku Sai-e* paintings and their donation to the Shōkokuji, Jakuchū's reputation as one of the foremost artists working in and around Kyoto became widespread. His new status prompted Daiten to travel to the artist's residence in 1767 in order to personally perform the special Buddhist service commemorating the third anniversary of the death of his youngest brother Sōjaku. The following year, Kohen Shōnin, a member of the nobility and bishop of the great Higashi Honganji temple, asked to see the *Dōshoku Sai-e* paintings, and the authorities of the Shōkokuji acceded to this exceptional request, making the entire set available to him for his leisurely study and admiration. It appears that at least one of Jakuchū's large polychrome works had been acquired by the Higashi Honganji as early as 1755, and that by 1757 two or more additional works of this sort had been added to the temple's collection. Kohen was probably not only an enthusiastic admirer, but also a collector of Jakuchū's paintings, arranging to view the *Dōshoku Sai-e* pieces in order to compare them with those he owned, as their execution had been more or less contemporaneous and they had been painted in the same manner. Enthusiasm from such an esteemed audience no doubt further enhanced the artist's already established reputation.

Another indication of Jakuchū's status can be seen in the 1768 edition of the *Heian Jimbutsushi*, in which Jakuchū was ranked third in the artist category, following Ōnishi Suigetsu (a follower of Mochizuki Gyokusen and teacher of Matsumura Goshun) and Maruyama Ōkyo, and preceding the prominent Nanga masters Taiga and Buson. The rankings remained the same in the 1775 and 1782 editions, except that Suigetsu had passed away and all the remaining painters had moved up accordingly, with Jakuchū second only to top-rated Ōkyo.[23] Recognition of Jakuchū as a gifted painter, not only in artistic circles, but also among a broader segment of the population, clearly had its origins in his execution of the *Dōshoku Sai-e* paintings. Because worshipers and other visitors were able to view the scrolls periodically at the Shōkokuji, the works acquired the aura of religious icons in their own right, which further enhanced their renown and attracted a broad spectrum of people to them. Among the more distinguished admirers of the series was Prince Nikkō Jungōgū Kōjun, the third son of Emperor Nakamikado. The prince, who also studied Chinese literature under Daiten, visited the Shōkokuji in 1783, and on this auspicious occasion the entire set of paintings was displayed for his benefit in a spacious room.

In the years following the completion of the *Dōshoku Sai-e* paintings, Jakuchū became increasingly reclusive and ever more absorbed in Zen routine. Ōbaku Zen became the chief focus of his religious life, and he associated with Ōbaku monks from the Mampukuji such as the head abbot Hakujun Shōkō (1695–1776), under whom he received Zen instruction, and Monchū Jōfuku (1739–1829), who

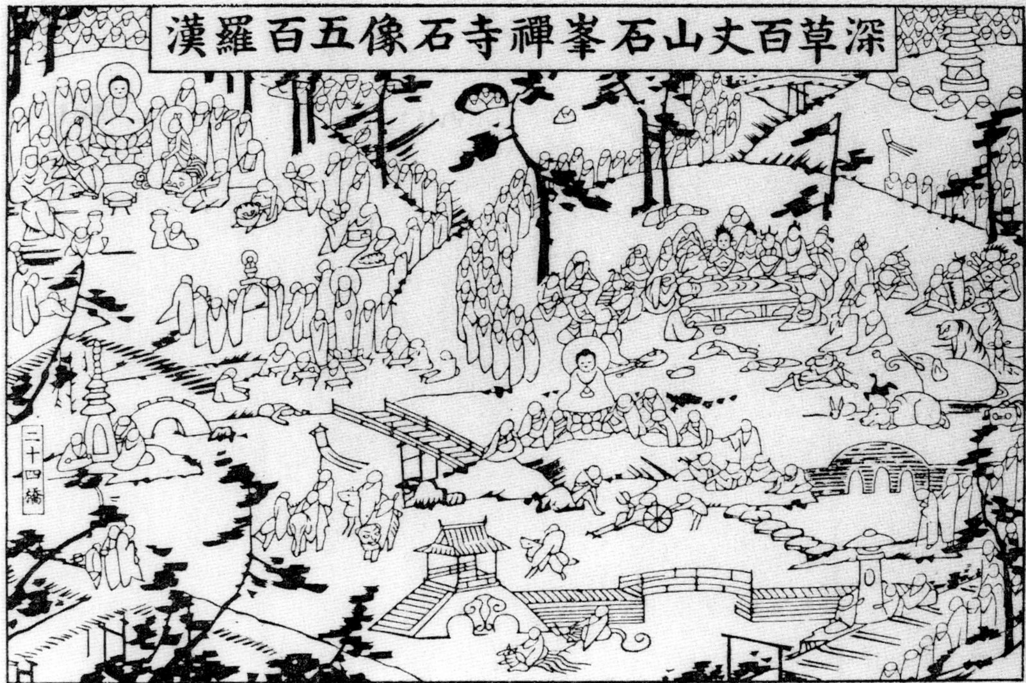

FIG. 12
"The *Five Hundred Arhats* in the Hyakujōzan Sekihōji, Fukakusa." Reproduction of a woodblock print in Takemoto Sekitei, *Sekitei Gadan (Sekitei's Conversations on Painting)*, 1884, after a drawing by Jakuchū.

seems to have been a close friend for an extended period. Monchū studied literature and Rinzai Zen under Daiten at the Shōkokuji, but he subsequently became a follower of Ōbaku Zen, studying under Rai Gan'on, the fifth-generation spiritual descendant of Ingen (Chinese: Yin-yüan Lung-ch'i), who founded the Mampukuji. It is likely that he was also acquainted with the Bunjin painter Gyokuran, as well as her husband, Taiga. Monchū was an accomplished practitioner of Sencha and was known for his knowledge of classical literature and for his seal carving. He served in an administrative capacity at the Shōkokuji for many years, and he was widely known in religious as well as intellectual and artistic circles.

When Jakuchū was about sixty years old, he began an ambitious project that was to preoccupy him for the next six or seven years. A panoramic arrangement of crudely executed stone carvings inspired by traditional Buddhist iconic subjects, it was laid out on a hilly incline behind an Ōbaku temple named the Sekihōji, close to the village of Fukakusa, south of Kyoto. Popularly known simply as the *Five Hundred Arhats*, a title that suggests the multiplicity of the images, the group included significant incidents from the life of the Buddha, as well as depictions of the Arhats and other followers and disciples (FIG. 11). Although Jakuchū was the architect (and financier) of this time-consuming undertaking, it is unlikely that he himself did any of the physical labor, and nothing is known of the actual carvers.

Boulders of various sizes were utilized throughout the project, their natural conformations roughly hewn and carved to create the pieces. The primitive shaping of the stones, which were selected for their existing forms and were modified as little as possible, produced images that are engaging for their naïve directness and eccentric sense of humor. The topographic composition soon became popular with visitors to the Kyoto area, and it is mentioned in such literary works as the *Shōsai Hikki*[24] and the *Gajō Yōryaku*, as well as in popular guides to the ancient capital, such as the *Shūi Miyako Meisho Zue* (*Illustrated Guide to Famous Locations in the Capital*, 1787). Jakuchū conceived this engaging, didactic diorama commemorating the Buddhist faith and its traditional themes as a pious tribute to the chief motivating force in his life. Significantly, the use of rough boulders harmonized with the respect for the integrity of natural forms inherent in Japanese Buddhism. Moreover, some of these shapes and their compositional juxtapositions carried over into Jakuchu's paintings.

Today, the contents and arrangements of the original composition are difficult to reconstruct, for a disastrous earthquake in 1830 did considerable damage, and in the Meiji period, during another low point in the temple's fortunes, certain carvings were carted away, some of them ending up in private gardens. It is, nevertheless, possible to get a general idea of the composition from a woodblock illustration in the *Sekitei Gadan* (*Sekitei's Conversations on Painting*, 1884; see FIG. 12), after a drawing by Jakuchū. This illustration shows the various groups of sculpture set up on the hillside and interlaced with paths and bridges that allowed visitors to move about and closely inspect the works. Recently the remaining stones were set up in an attempt to recreate something of the original arrangement; their subjects include the birth of the Buddha; Bodhisattvas descending to take the soul of a departed believer to paradise; the eighteen Arhats; Śākyamuni preaching; the practice of peripatetic mendicancy; various Arhats meditating in grottoes; the death of the Buddha; and the Sanzu River flowing through the Buddhist hell.

There is little specific biographical information about Jakuchū's activities during his sixties, but he probably spent a substantial amount of time at the Sekihōji. There is, however, no evidence that his interest in painting had waned; on the contrary, he became ever more proficient and versatile, producing some of his finest monochrome works, pieces that resonate with the intuitive spontaneity of Zen thought. In addition, he produced a few polychrome works that demonstrate his progress toward a more abstract, decorative style. Two such works are a painting of a pheasant and a white plum tree[25] and another of a family of monkeys in a blossoming peach tree (FIG. 13).[26] Here again, Jakuchū's close association with and indebtedness to his mentors is apparent, for the first piece contains a colophon by Daiten, and the second, a colophon by the Ōbaku priest Hakujun Shōkō. It is unclear where Jakuchū executed large polychrome pictures of this sort, but most likely he did the majority of them in the spacious surroundings of the Shin'enkan in Kyoto or in one of the remaining family residences in the Nishiki district.

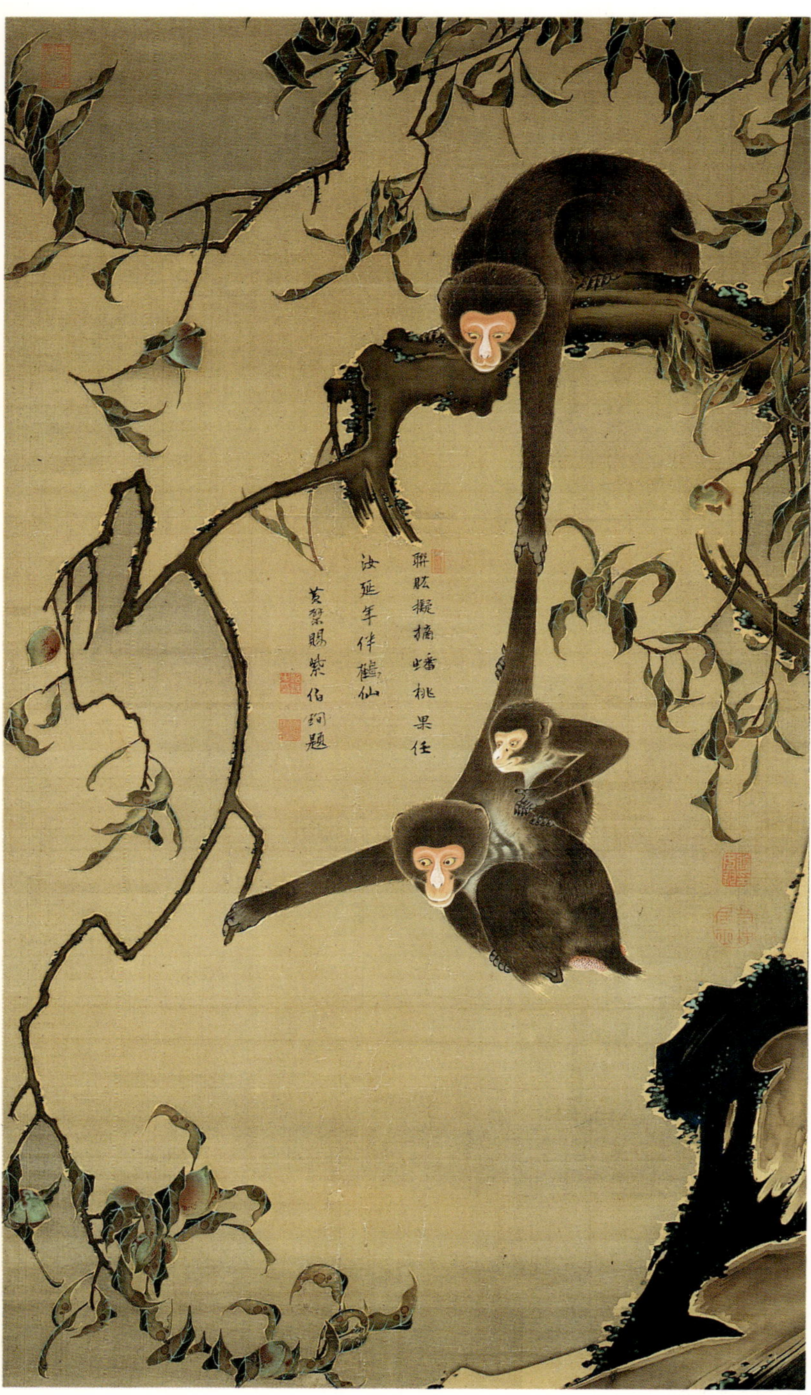

FIG. 13 *Monkeys in a Blossoming Peach Tree*, c. 1772–c. 1776.

Private collection, Hyōgo Prefecture

This portion of Jakuchū's life must have been idyllic, for he lived in a spiritually as well as creatively rewarding manner, pursuing his artistic projects at his leisure, and he was widely recognized as a prominent figure among the community of cultured men in Kyoto. However, when he was seventy-three years of age, a calamity changed his circumstances abruptly and drastically: a fire broke out, devastating the city. It started on the east bank of the Kamo River somewhere below the Shijō Bridge and, fanned by a particularly strong northeast wind, jumped the river, continuing to burn for nearly two days and laying waste to the majority of the city, including the Imperial Palace. The Shin'enkan and the Itō family store, as well as other family-owned structures in the Nishiki neighborhood, were destroyed, presumably along with the family's material resources. To the north, the entire complex of the Shōkokuji monastery, with the single exception of the Hodō (Dharma Hall), was leveled. Most of the Buddhist sculptural images went up in flames, but some of the more easily transported treasures, such as scrolls, paintings, and records—among them the *Dōshoku Sai-e* and its central Buddhist triptych—fortunately escaped destruction.

Until this cataclysm, Jakuchū seems to have been always financially secure, producing paintings essentially for his own artistic and spiritual satisfaction and for the admiration of his friends and acquaintances, but he was now forced to turn to his art for his livelihood. This adversity seems, however, to have stimulated him to greater, more conscientious productivity, and many of his most memorable works were conceived in the following years.

Despite the survival of a substantial number of paintings that Jakuchū produced between his late fifties and his early seventies, there is a puzzling lack of reliable biographical evidence to clarify his activities of this period. It is known that in 1788 he went to visit the noted dilettante and literatus Kimura Kenkadō in Osaka and that in 1790, when he was seventy-five years old, he completed a commission from a rich merchant named Yoshino Yosai Goun to execute a set of sliding screens for the Saifukuji, a temple in Toyonaka, outside Osaka.[27] Jakuchū was probably in residence at this temple for at least half a year, because in addition to the superb screens, he is thought to have produced a number of paintings for residents of the area.

The screens are among his most celebrated creations. The fronts of the six panels consist of bright-colored depictions of animated roosters and hens and of large cactus plants, set off against a rich, unbroken background of gold leaf (FIG. 14); the backs (which faced the inner sanctum of the worship hall) contain a contrasting composition of a dry temple pond in late autumn, with a few lonely lotus blossoms and withered, insect-eaten leaves, rendered in a spare, economical manner in subdued tones of monochrome ink (NO. 35). The lotus is a ubiquitous symbol in Buddhist iconography, but in Jakuchū's unique vision it appears as a metaphor for the evanescence of life and the decay of old age, a theme mirroring the artist's own sentiments in his advancing years.

After completing the Saifukuji screens sometime early in 1790, Jakuchū returned to Kyoto and subsequently executed another set of sliding screens for a room in the Kaihōji (NO. 36), a branch temple of the Mampukuji, located close to the Sekihōji, where the artist had probably taken up residence. Here again, he depicted a family of chickens, but this time in monochrome rather than in color. Compared to the Saifukuji fowl, those in the Kaihōji screens were rendered in a more routine manner, with less spirited brushwork. Jakuchū's apparent decline in creative vigor may have been related to problems with his health, for he seems to have fallen ill after completing this project, and an entry in one of the daily temple records of the Shōkokuji (the *Sankaryō Nikki*) notes that some temple dignitary (perhaps Daiten) made a visit of condolence and prayer to the artist's bedside.[28] Moreover, the records suggest some difference of opinion over the propriety of a high representative of this prestigious monastery's making such a special visit, for Jakuchū, despite his generosity in presenting the *Dōshoku Sai-e* paintings to the temple and his prestige as an artist, still had his origins in the merchant class and was consequently of inferior social status according to traditional Confucian hierarchical prejudices of the time.

Jakuchū had recovered to some degree by the following year and had settled into a comfortable routine at his residence at the Sekihōji. In the *Shōsai Hikki* Hakusan noted:

> He is now living in retirement, and working on the project of the *Five Hundred Arhats*. His set fee for producing a painting is one *to* [eighteen liters; one-tenth of a *koku*] of rice. He has personally designed the layout of the [*Five Hundred Arhats*] project on a hillside to the rear, and the pieces are being installed one at a time. He refers to himself in his signatures as "Beito-ō" [Old Man One *To* of Rice].[29] One *to* brings six *monme* [of silver] on the rice market. This he passes on immediately to the stone carver. Jakuchū produces one fine *soshu* [grass-style or cursive] painting after another for this purpose. His younger sister, who had married but is now a widow, is with Jakuchū. She has brought her child, who lives with them, and the mother has taken Buddhist vows, and is known by the name of Shinjaku. She is fond of composing *waka* poetry, and she makes stone rubbings and sells them. She appears to some to care for Jakuchū as diligently as a wife could. This account was related to me by Matsumoto Hojidō.[30]

Another passage relates how Hakusan, together with a friend from Osaka, made a pleasure trip to Kyoto in 1794 and paid a personal visit to Jakuchū at the Sekihōji:

> Then we went to see the Hyakujōzan Sekihōji. Jakuchū has a residence just at the entrance to the temple, and we talked to him there. There are depictions of lotuses on the sliding screens, done in a manner like that of stone rubbings. They were interesting and very well done. We went out to inspect the *Five Hundred Arhats*. These are shaped at Jakuchū's direction from natural boulders, collected from the mountain, and paths connecting them are gradually being constructed. In addition, Jakuchū is having a new pavilion erected at the entrance to the project. At the left of the temple is Jakuchū's Old Hermitage, and its garden is also

quite rustic and entertaining. His younger sister is known as the nun Shinjaku and the two live together.[31]

These descriptions of the elderly Jakuchū and his attendant sister seem further evidence that the artist spent his old age in a productive manner, under the most pleasant circumstances.

The last concerted project of his long career was carried out, quite appropriately, on behalf of the Sekihōji and consisted of a large number of circular paintings of flowers, trees, and other plants, executed on square panels of wood and installed in the ceiling of the Kannondō (Hall of the Bodhisattva Kannon), a devotional chapel of the temple. During the Meiji period, when strong anti-Buddhist sentiments often made things difficult for Buddhist institutions, the Sekihōji was only one of many temples whose prospects for survival were uncertain. At this time the Sekihōji stopped functioning as a religious center for some years, its precincts were essentially abandoned, a number of the stone sculptures from the *Five Hundred Arhats* were hauled off to other locations by unprincipled opportunists, and the Kannondō fell into disrepair. However, a parishioner of the Shingyōji, a Pure Land temple in Kyoto, was fortunately able to acquire 168 of the ceiling panels, and these were installed in the ceiling of the main worship hall, where they are still preserved. In addition, fifteen other panels ended up in the ceiling of the Okinadō, a small chapel in the Gichūji, a temple in Otsu. At the age of eighty-four, Jakuchū presumably conceived and supervised the execution of the Kannondō ceiling, but he also received substantial help from his coterie of followers in executing the multitude of floral motifs. One of the panels is inscribed with his studio name, Beitoan, along with "age eighty-eight," but he actually died when he was eighty-five years old; the number eighty-eight probably represents Jakuchū's hope that he would live on to that age (*beiju*), which is particularly propitious to the Japanese, who hold longevity in high esteem. It is also thought that he may have meant to express the *bei* (rice) component

FIG. 14 *Cacti and Fowl*, 1790. Saifukuji, Osaka Prefecture

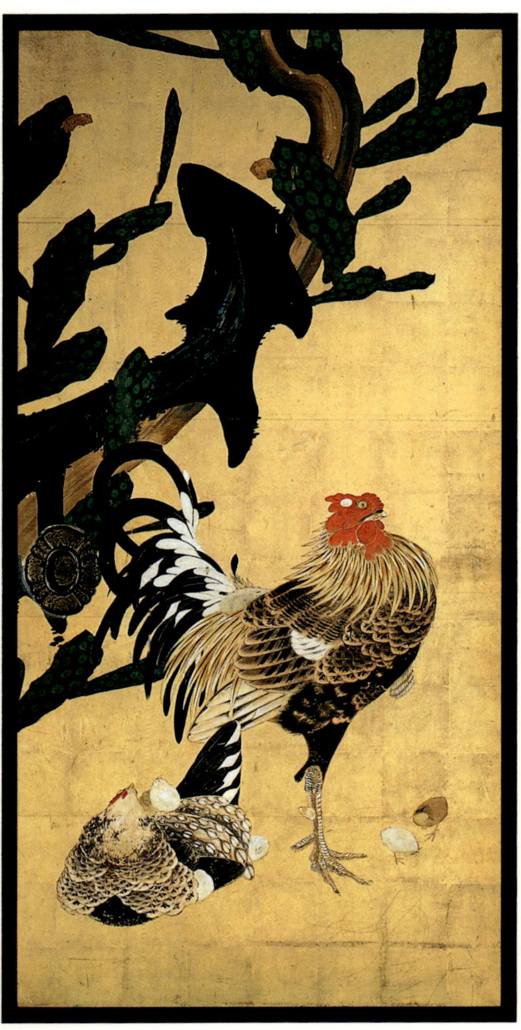

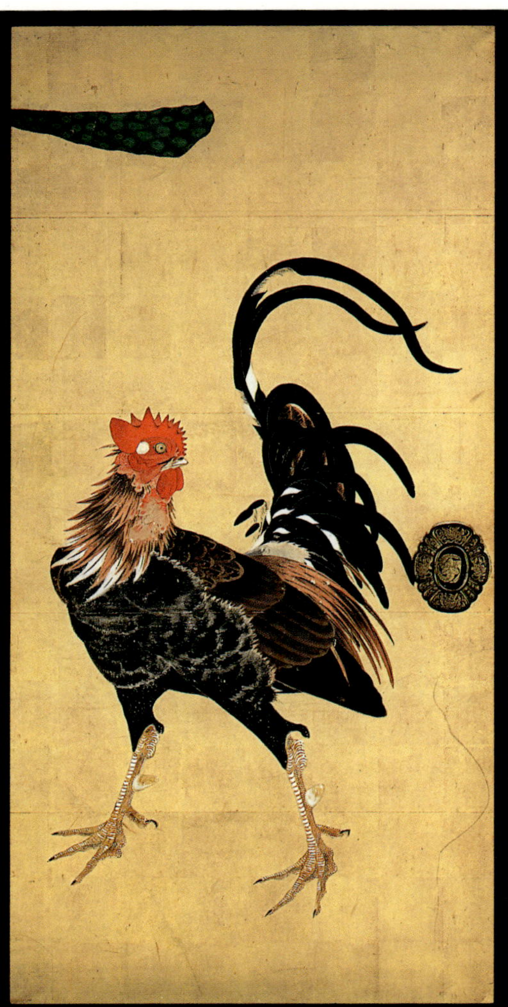

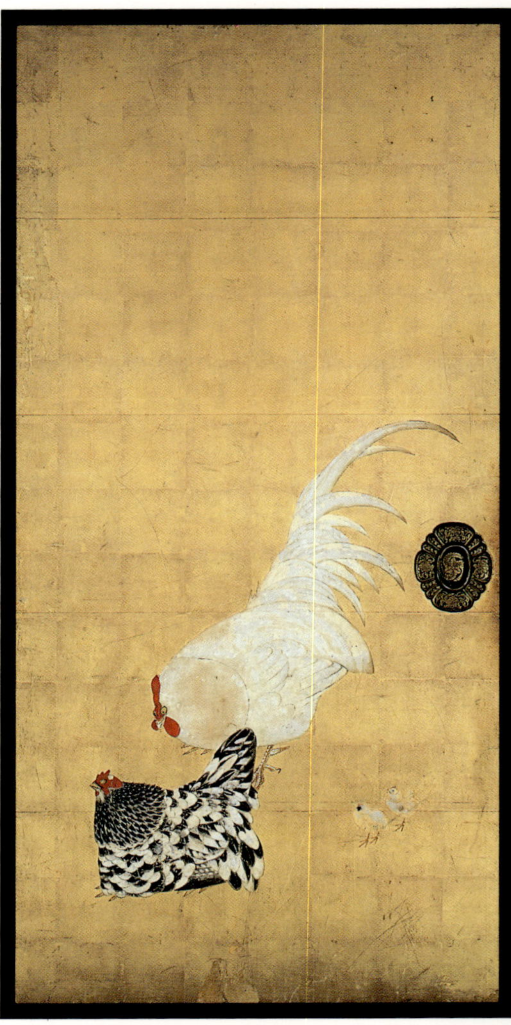

in his studio name, as this is composed of a character that, when written in a slightly modified form, reads vertically as "eight-eight."

In the spring of 1800, commemorative services honoring the twenty-fifth anniversary of the death of Jakuchū's friend the painter Ike Taiga were held at the Sōrinji in the Higashiyama district of Kyoto. A letter of invitation had been delivered to Jakuchū's residence, but the messenger had been informed that Jakuchū was in poor health and could not attend. Jakuchū's death occurred several months later, and funeral services were held at the Sekihōji, where his remains were interred. In addition, services were performed at the Hozōji, the tutelary temple of the Itō family, in Kyoto. An entry in the *Sankaryō Nikki* (which corresponds in date to the traditional Buddhist service commemorating the forty-ninth day after Jakuchū's death) notes that religious rites were also observed at the Rokuonji, which served as a temporary location for religious services of the Shōkokuji, whose main hall of worship had not yet been reconstructed after the great fire of 1788.[32] Two of Jakuchū's relatives, Itō Naoji and Kaneda Chubei, were invited to the services, and Jakuchū's *Śākyamuni Triptych*, accompanied by two of the *Dōshoku Sai-e* paintings, was hung in the central room for the occasion, a practice that was to become an annual custom. It is likely that Daiten was still in passable health and that he officiated at these services for his friend. However, the monk's time was also coming to an end, and he passed away the following year, at the age of eighty-three.

Jakuchū had outlived both of his brothers. As mentioned previously, Sōjaku had died at an early age, and Sōgan, who had relieved Jakuchū of the task of operating the Masugen, had died in 1792 at the age of seventy-four. Other members of the Itō family continued to operate the Masugen in the following decades. After the devastating earthquake in 1830, a descendant named Seibō (1790–1854) worked diligently to restore the composition of the *Five Hundred Arhats*, and he also brought to fruition Jakuchū's

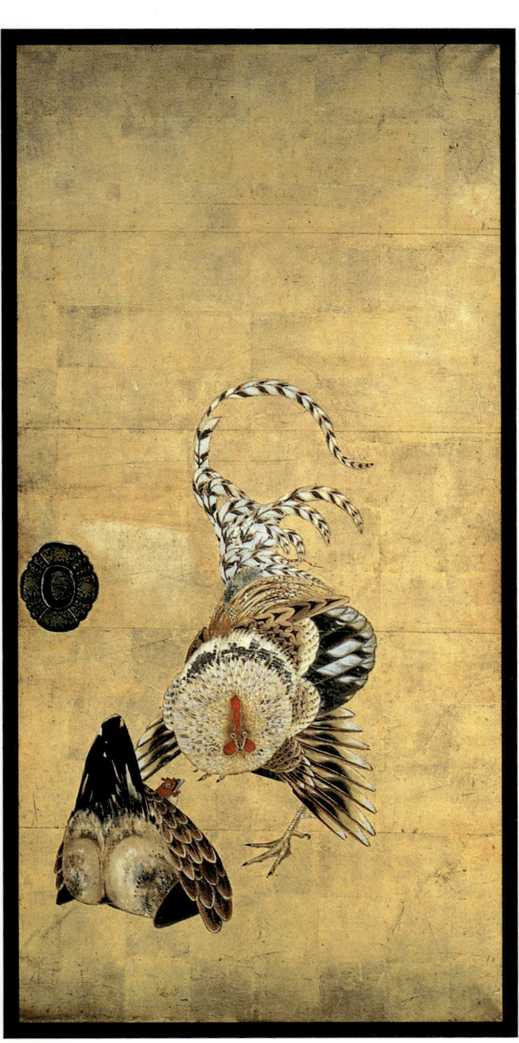

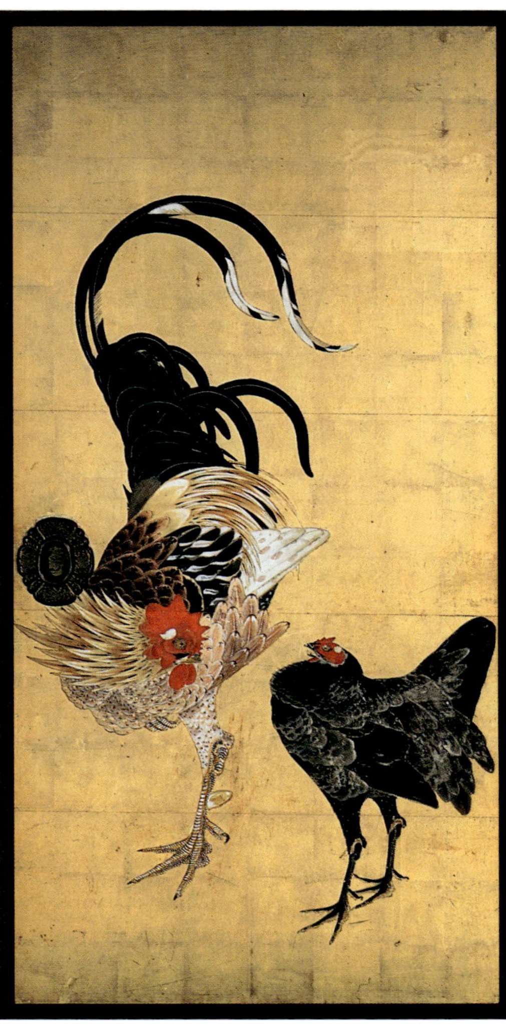

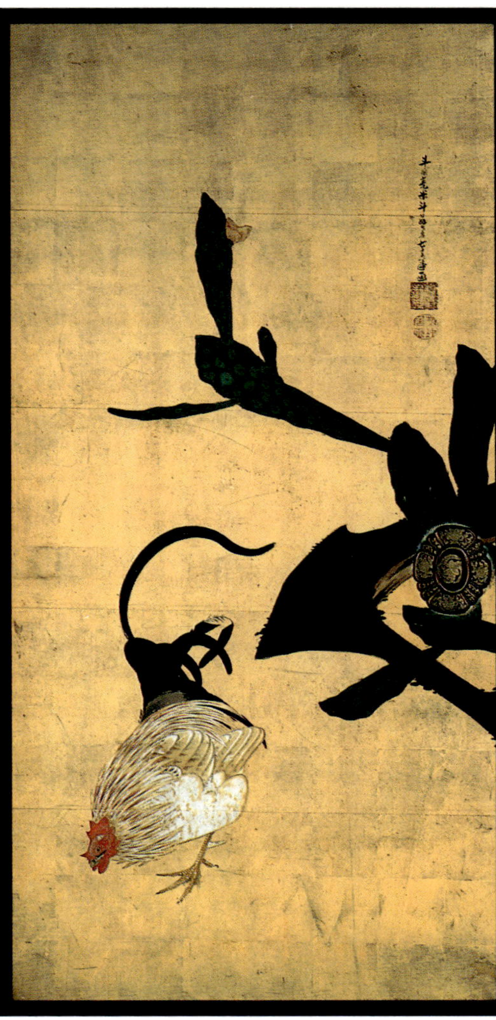

expressed hope that a brush-shaped stele would be erected in his memory at the Sekihōji. No less a personage than the Confucian literatus and Nanga painter Nukina Kaioku was prevailed upon to write the elegant colophon that was incised on the monument (FIG. 1).

After Seibō's death, the fortunes of the Masugen seem to have declined markedly. By 1867, the family residence had been sold and the remaining members of the family had moved to Osaka. Unfortunately, in the process of moving, many of Jakuchū's surviving sketches and preliminary drawings were lost or destroyed. The residence and the management of the Masugen passed into the hands of the Yasui family, who, like the Itō family, were originally from Omi Province. Seibō's daughter had married into the Yasui family, and a descendant continued to operate a grain shop on the other side of the street until recent times, but the business finally failed and the family moved to Kamakura. The present head of the family is now a professor emeritus at Waseda University in Tokyo.

After the great fire of 1788, the Shōkokuji authorities were unable to rebuild the monastery as it had been, and the institution never regained its influential religious status. Fortunately, the governor of Kyoto Prefecture took it upon himself to mediate on behalf of the debilitated monastery, and in 1889 the *Dōshoku Sai-e* paintings were presented to the Imperial Household in return for a substantial donation (10,000 yen) for the maintenance of the temple. This not only placed the paintings safely in the hands of authorities who could properly preserve them, but also guaranteed that they would remain in Japan. In this regard it is interesting to note a passage in the *Sekitei Gadan*: "Recently some foreigners have viewed the paintings and, overwhelmed by admiration for them, have requested that they be allowed to purchase them. The abbot of the temple, however, would not hear of this."[33] The identities of the "foreigners" were not given, but this passage may have been referring to Ernest Fenollosa (1853–1908) or William Sturgis Bigelow (1850–1926), or to both, for they each spent extended periods of time in the Kansai area around Kyoto at about this time, avidly acquiring large collections of paintings. Bigelow's interest in Jakuchū is evident in the extensive collection of the artist's paintings he subsequently presented to the Museum of Fine Arts, Boston, enabling it to be the first museum to show Jakuchū's works outside Japan.

In 1926 the *Dōshoku Sai-e* paintings were displayed in the Tokyo Imperial Museum, where they could be readily admired by the general public for the first time. The resulting enthusiasm both established the great paintings as perennial popular favorites and stimulated the extensive scholarly research on the artist and his works that continues to this day.

CHAPTER

3

Jakuchū's Paintings

It would be gratifying, in the interest of arriving at a more comprehensive and accurate assessment of Jakuchū's artistic evolution, if any evidence existed to throw even the most tentative light on his creative activities during his formative years. No paintings have survived from this initial period, however, and one can only speculate about the reason for this unfortunate circumstance. Perhaps Jakuchū, like other young artists, felt less than satisfied with his initial experiments in pictorial expression and was consequently reluctant to share them with others. Then again, even if he had preserved some of these earlier efforts, they might well have been destroyed in the great fire of 1788, which leveled a large part of Kyoto, including not only the family buildings in the Nishiki market area, but also Jakuchū's studio-retreat, the Shin'enkan, where such paintings might have been stored. Indeed, one can only conjecture about even the most fundamental chronological question—when and under what circumstances did Jakuchū first turn to painting as a source of pleasure and creative expression?—although the previously quoted ambiguous comment by his friend Daiten ("In this manner thirty years devoted assiduously to painting passed like a single day"[1]) might be cautiously interpreted as indicating that Jakuchū began to paint while still in his teens. This void in what is known of the artist's activities during the first decade or so of his career is compounded by the considerable conjecture about his production during his thirties, for the earliest extant paintings that have inscribed dates (of which there are only three) were not produced until he was forty years of age.

Despite this perplexing lacuna, two bits of information would seem to indicate something of Jakuchū's early activities. The first is Daiten's observation that Jakuchū received instruction from an unidentified painter of the Kanō school.[2] Statements that artists received instruction either directly in the traditional style of the Kanō school or from someone who had studied it appear routinely in Japanese art-historical literature and biographies of Japanese painters active from the seventeenth century on, reflecting the fundamental role and widespread influence of the Kanō school in training aspiring painters throughout the Edo period. Its long-standing prestige, its role as an "official" school sanctioned by the tastes and patronage of the ruling military caste, and its established network of ateliers not only in the major metropolitan areas, but also in the provinces, made

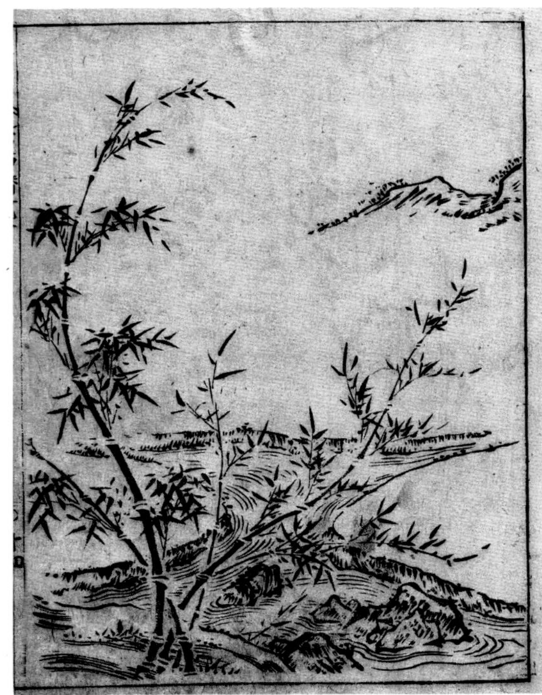

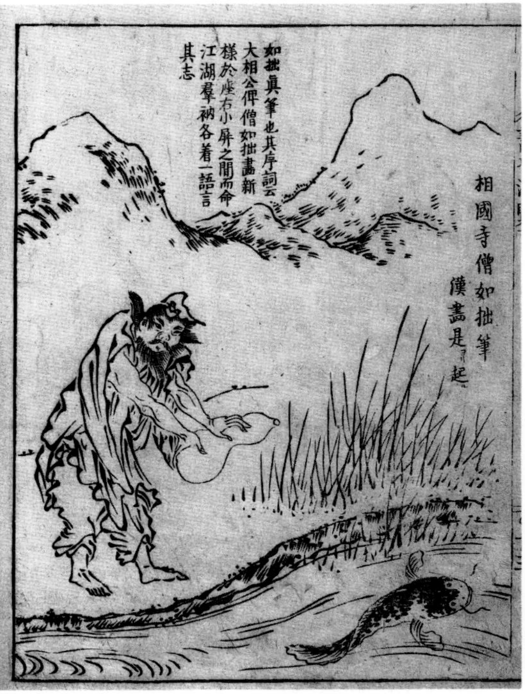

FIG. 15
Ōoka Shumboku. "Hyōnen-zu" ("Catching a Catfish with a Gourd"; after Josetsu), from the *Gakō Senran*, 1740, vol. 1, pp. 13b–14a.

Museum of Fine Arts, Boston

the Kanō school a mecca for generations of young men anxious to acquire a grounding in the discipline and essentials of painting. The basic motivation for most students was not merely to become familiar with the inventory of traditional subjects and codified methods followed by Kanō painters, but to gain acceptance within its prestigious ranks and realize the promise of status and financial reward.

However, a gradual decline occurred in the vitality of the school, and its practitioners seem to have settled into a comfortable reliance on time-honored formulas, becoming less concerned with originality than with the facile emulation of the artistic accomplishments of their predecessors. Because of its customary role in the service of the military caste, the prestige of the school remained high, but membership became a subsidiary concern for young artists (particularly those with idiosyncratic or individualistic tendencies), outweighed by the pragmatic benefits to be gained from the didactic training and structured curriculum.

The pedagogical role of the Kanō school flourished over the years, and many of the important painters of the eighteenth century who established distinctive styles or new schools received their training either in Kanō ateliers or through diligent study of the school's pictorial techniques. This pattern, in which an aspiring painter underwent a period of basic study and subsequently went on to establish a separate creative identity based on a personal artistic vision, is a pervasive characteristic of eighteenth-century Japanese painting, and Itō Jakuchū is an instructive example of this phenomenon.

The second item of significant information about Jakuchū's early career is Aoyagi Bunzō's comment in *Zoku Shōka Jimbutsushi*, that the artist worked under the *gō* (artist's name) Shunkyō.[3] No paintings that bear this signature appear to have been preserved, but it seems likely that the pieces produced while Jakuchū worked under this name were tentative, experimental, and generally indebted to Kanō ideas. Scholars have suggested that the "shun" in Shunkyō indicates that Jakuchū's tutelage during this period involved an older contemporary named Ōoka Shumboku. Shumboku is known primarily for his activities as an artist-entrepreneur who produced a substantial number of woodblock-printed *ehon* (picture books) that catered to a growing popular interest in the history and execution of paintings. Shumboku produced illustrated volumes that dealt not only with the traditions and highlights of native Japanese painting—such as the "Hyōnen-zu", the famous depiction by Josetsu of a man trying to catch a large, slippery catfish using a small gourd with a hole in it (FIG. 15)—but also, in response to a burgeoning Japanese preoccupation with Chinese thought and culture, with selected works of famous Chinese artists and pictorial traditions of the past. Even though Shumboku's knowledge of the evolution of Chinese painting was, at best, imprecise and fragmentary, his efforts were apparently welcomed by an eager clientele from various segments of Japanese society, whose curiosity about Chinese pictorial concepts and methods arose from both intellectual and pragmatic concerns. The books satisfied a desire for knowledge about the history of Chinese painting and its fascinating relationships with certain native Japanese schools and also served as handy pragmatic vade mecums for enterprising amateurs who wished to emulate the spirit, content, and particulars of Chinese painting.

More often than not, it is unclear from what sources Shumboku reproduced his prototypes, and study of the illustrations indicates that he sometimes utilized pieces of questionable authenticity and inferior quality. It has been suggested, in fact, that he was not above fabricating an illustration when no appropriate prototype was at hand. In his defense, however, it must be said that he seems to have worked diligently to assemble relevant materials for his volumes, and that both his general and his specific knowledge of the history of Japanese and Chinese painting must have surpassed that of most of the educated scholar-artists and professionals of his time. That certain of his prototypes for Chinese paintings are suspect, for one reason or another, seems apparent enough in hindsight, but this is symptomatic only of the fragmentary knowledge of the period.

At the same time, it seems that Shumboku did search assiduously for representative pieces—an assertion substantiated by the occasional illustration (FIG. 16) of a fine piece, such as the large pair of Chinese hanging scrolls depicting cranes by Wen Cheng (FIG. 17), an obscure fifteenth-century painter, works that have been carefully preserved in the collection of the Shōkokuji monastery in Kyoto. That Jakuchū was able to study the original paintings, producing some precise copies (FIG. 18), seems more than coincidental. As has been said, the priest Daiten was probably instrumental in making the extensive collection of paintings in the Shōkokuji available to Jakuchū, and the artist was certainly familiar with a number of these revered works, but Shumboku also may have played a significant role in stimulating Jakuchū's interest in Chinese painting. Moreover, Shumboku's interest in this subject was not confined to the works of previous centuries; he also illustrated more recent pieces, such as paintings produced by members of the Nagasaki school and by priest-artists associated with

FIG. 16 Ōoka Shumboku. "Pair of Cranes" (after Wen Cheng), from the *Gakō Senran*, 1740, vol. 1, pp. 17b–18a. Museum of Fine Arts, Boston

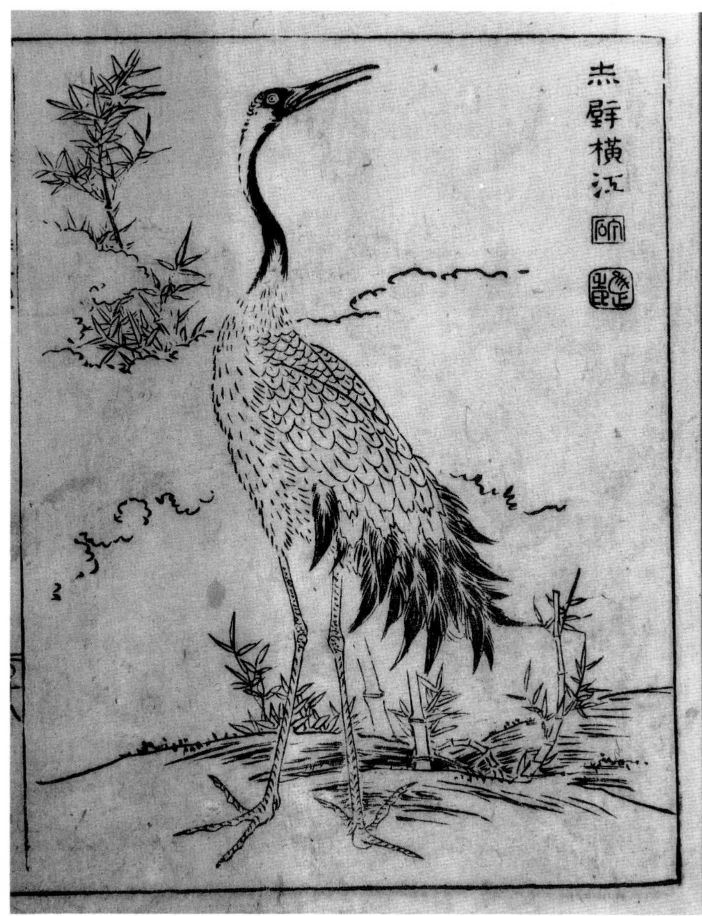

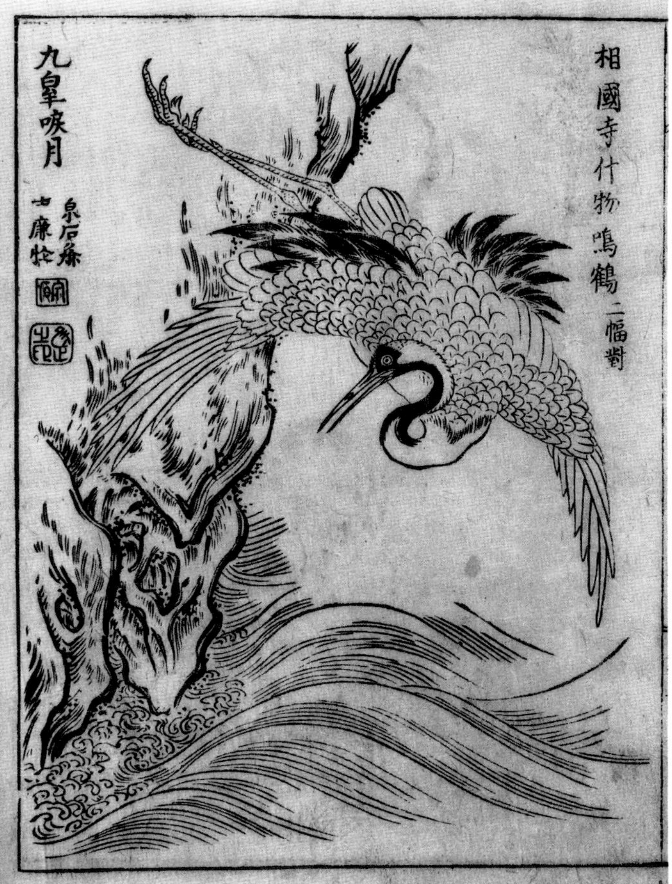

the Ōbaku sect of Zen Buddhism, an important source of spiritual inspiration for Jakuchū.

Little is known of Shumboku's early training, but most accounts, following the lead of the *Koga Bikō* (*Handbook of Classical Painting*, by Asaoka Okisada [1800–1856]),[4] suggest that he was an enterprising, self-taught artist from Osaka. A passage in the *Naniwa Jimbutsushi* (*Noted People of Naniwa [Osaka]*) notes that "he liked painting from the time he was young. He followed the methods of the Kanō school and mastered the secrets of the school without a teacher."[5] Although Shumboku is thought to have been a prolific painter with a long career (he is said to have completed a set of paintings for the Jingoji, a Buddhist temple located at Takao, when he was more than eighty years old), few of his works are known, and scholars have made no concerted effort to track down his paintings.[6] Shumboku's interests extended beyond painting, and he is said to have studied *waka* poetry, music, Noh dancing, and the incense and tea ceremonies. It is quite possible that certain of these activities led to his acquaintance with a member of the nobility, Prince Saga, a connection that may have been instrumental in Shumboku's having been awarded the ranks of Hokkyō (Bridge of the Law) in about 1720 and Hogen (Eye of the Law) in 1735, in recognition of his artistic accomplishments. He did not turn to book illustration until he was middle-

FIG. 17 Wen Cheng (active fifteenth century). *Cranes*, n.d. Shōkokuji, Kyoto

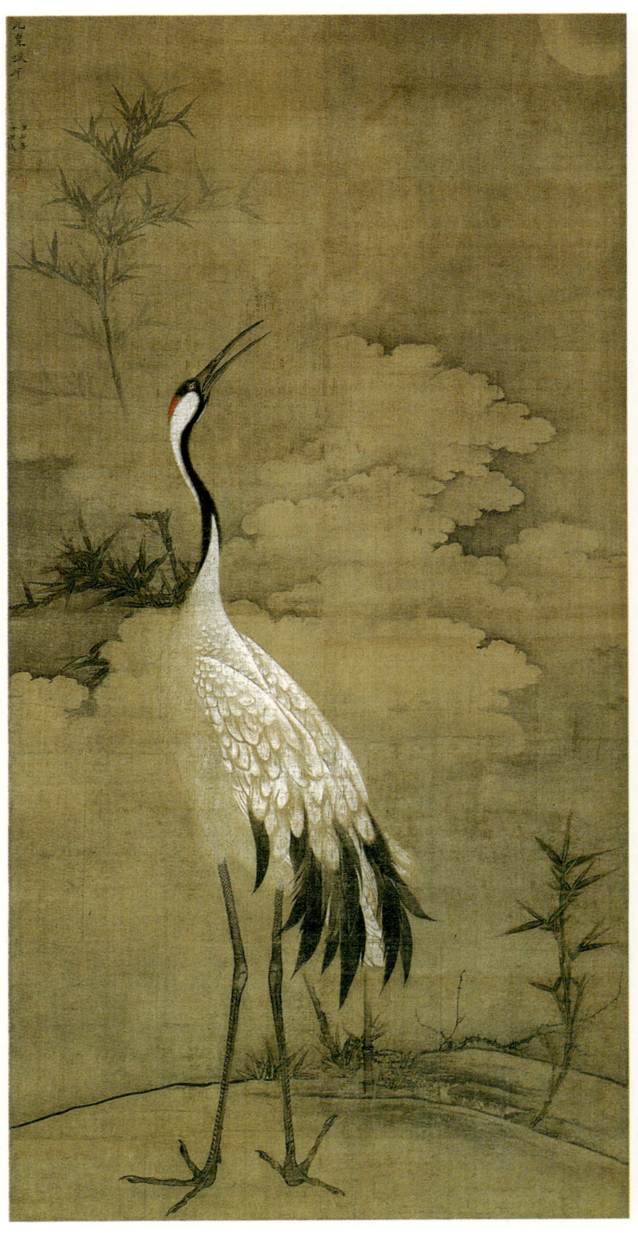

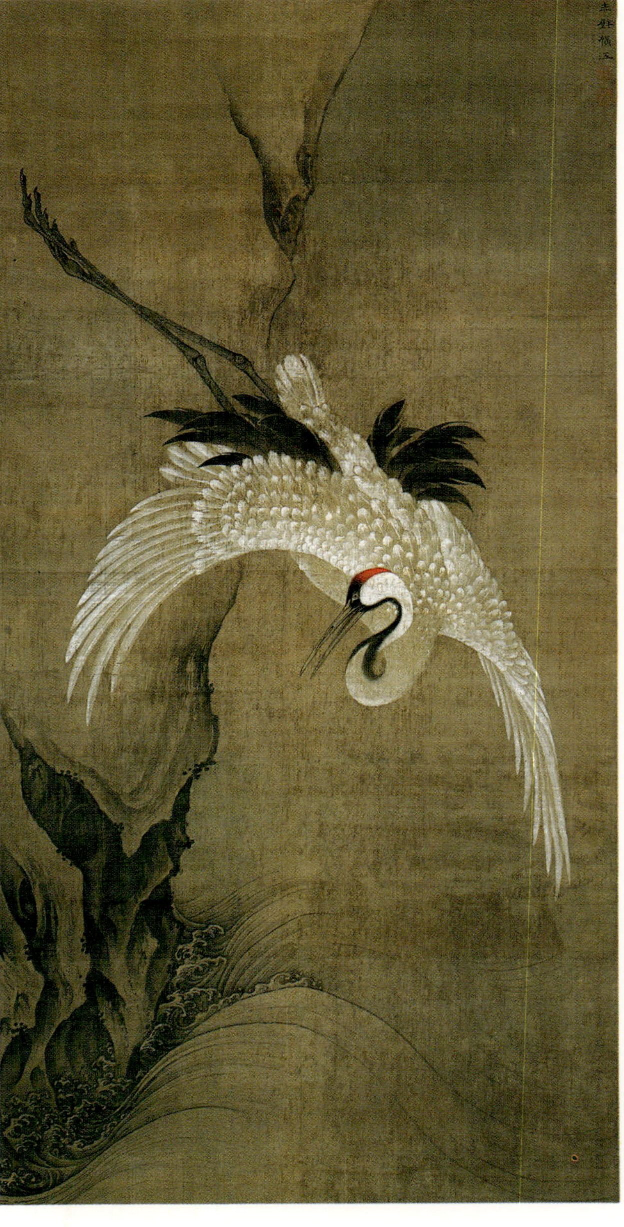

aged; his work in this form dates from 1720 to 1751. Almost all the *ehon* produced during these years were multivolume works with a large number of illustrations, and they undoubtedly required substantial amounts of time to compile and publish. A good deal of diligent scholarly enterprise is apparent in his three large compilations of copies after famous Japanese and Chinese masters, the *Ehon Tekagami* (6 vols., 1720), the *Wakan Meiga-en* (6 vols., 1750), and the *Gashi Kaiyo* (6 vols., 1751), all of which were intended to serve as textbooks for artists. It is indicative of his own training that he treated the Kanō school and its traditions knowledgeably and gave them a prominent place in these volumes.

One compilation of copies among Shumboku's *ehon*, the *Minchō Seidō Gaen* (*Ming Dynasty Pictorial Garden of Living Beings*), is particularly admired. It was originally produced in three volumes in 1746 and is also known as the *Minchō Shiken* (*Ming Dynasty Purple Inkstone*; FIG. 19). Unique among the artist's *ehon*, it was executed in colors, with the subjects rendered in as many as five hues, and was printed with a more extensive inventory of techniques than Shumboku generally used. The compositions, which appear on facing pages, are attributed to various Ming-period artists, such as Wen Cheng-ming, Sun K'o-hung, Tai Wen-chin, Ting Yü-ch'uan, and Wang Wei-lieh. These botanical subjects focus on flowers

FIG. 18 *Cranes*, n.d.

Private collection, Hyōgo Prefecture

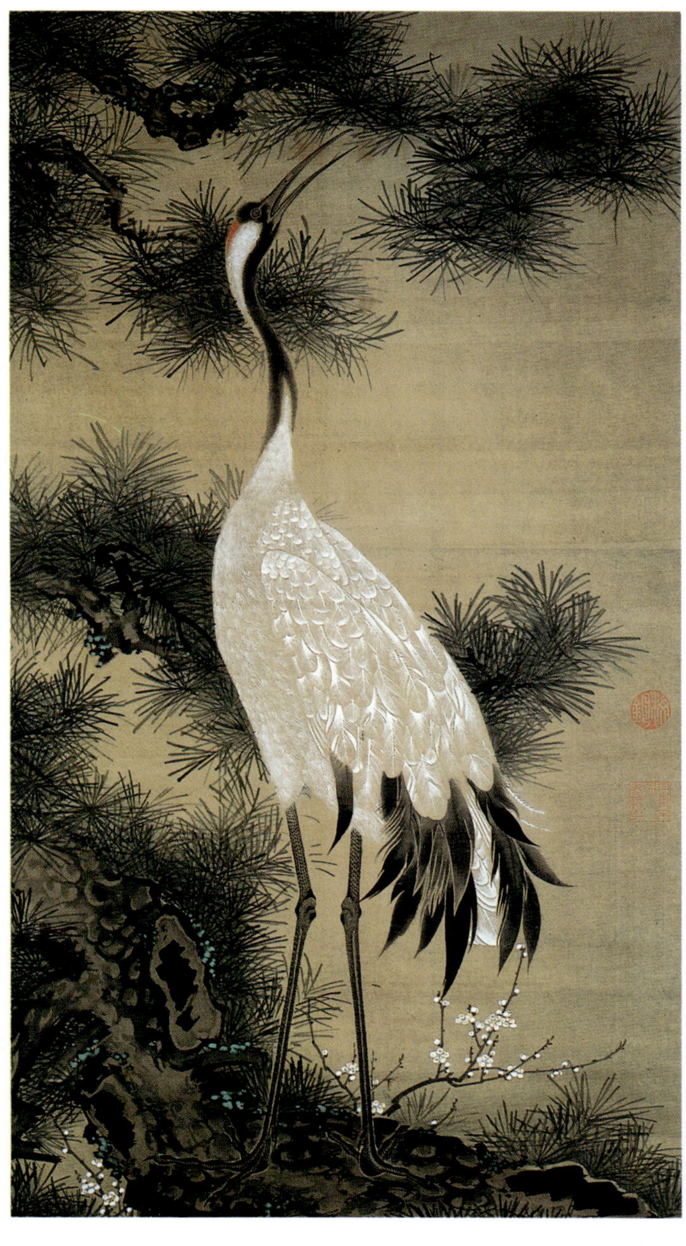

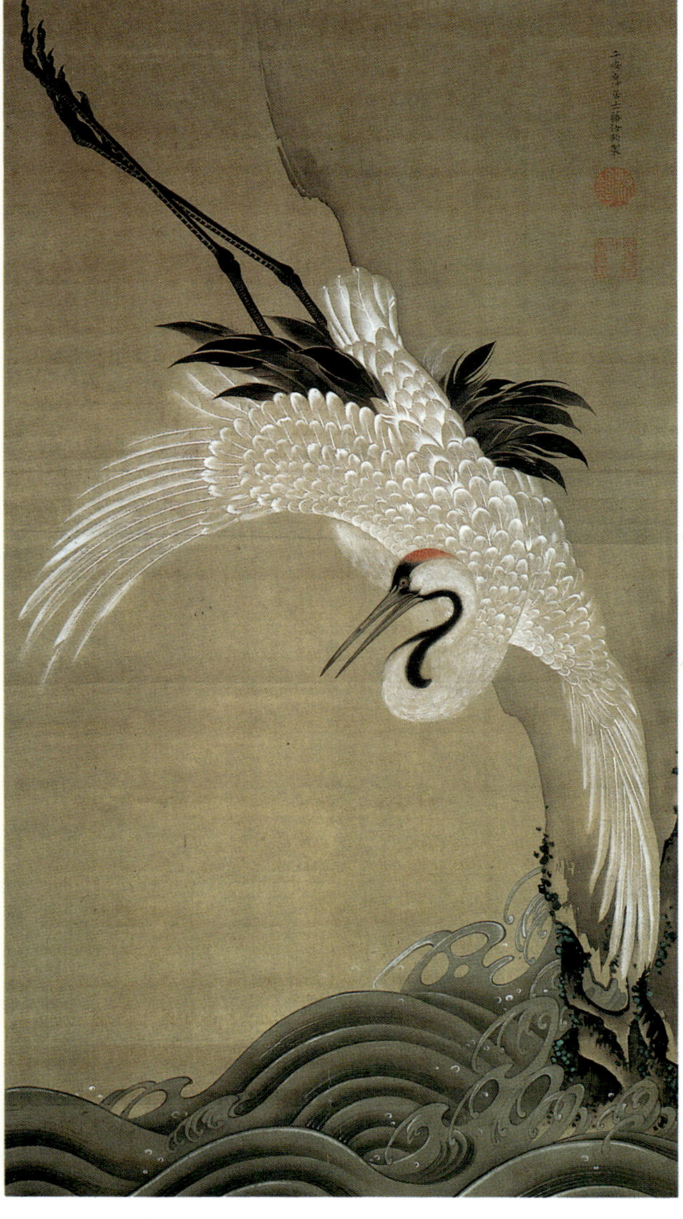

and blossoms, but the compositions also include strangely shaped, often naturally perforated rocks, and a lively cast of insects and marine life, such as shrimps, minnows, and an occasional frog, all organized into charming miniature vignettes of nature. It has been claimed that the general sources of inspiration for the illustrations in the *Minchō Seidō Gaen* were two Chinese woodblock-printed vade mecums for painters, the *Sheng-tung Hua-yüan* (Japanese: *Seidō Gaen*), from which the title of Shumboku's work is borrowed, and the *Chieh-tzu-yüan Hua-chüan*, demonstrating once again Shumboku's preoccupation with, and access to, Chinese pictorial materials.

FIG. 19 Ōoka Shumboku. From the *Minchō Shiken*, 1746. Museum of Fine Arts, Boston

19.1 "Bamboo," vol. 2   19.2 "Grapes," vol. 3

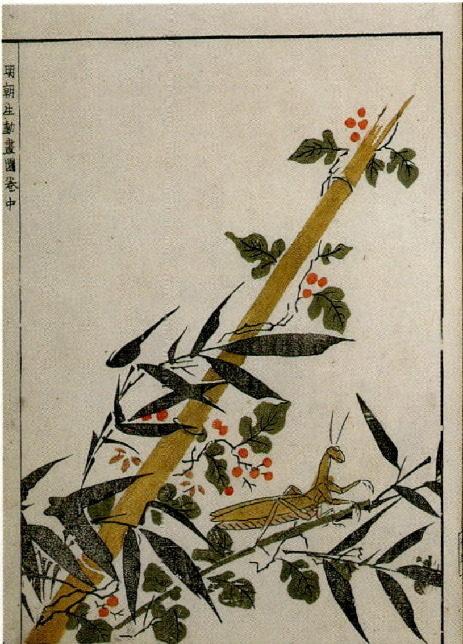

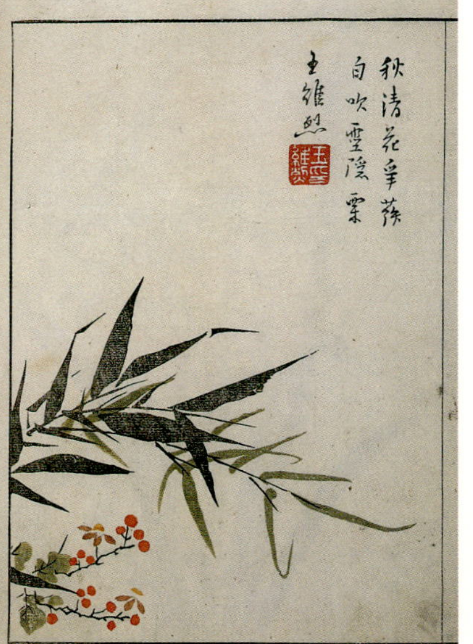

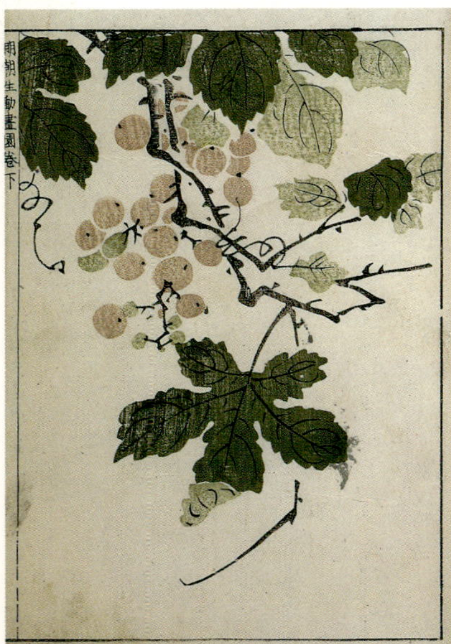

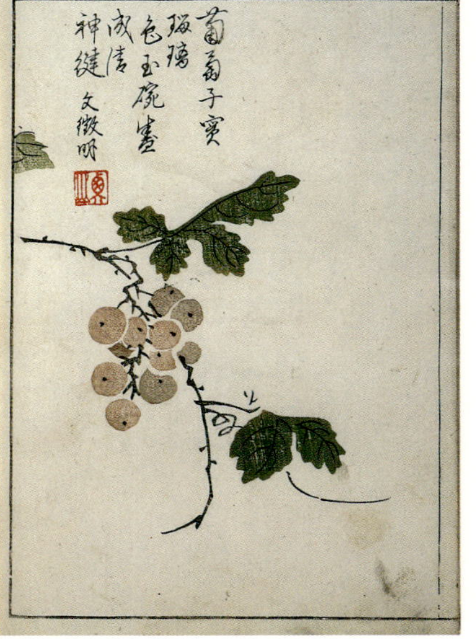

Another facet of Shumboku's interest in these traditions may be seen in the substantial number of illustrations in his *ehon* that are indebted to Chinese stone-rubbing (Japanese: *taku-hon*) techniques and ideas (FIGS. 20, 21). In woodblock-printed illustrations that simulate the appearance of stone rubbings, the conventional manner of printing (in which the lines of pictorial forms stand out in a "positive" manner against a surrounding, lighter background) is reversed: the background itself is rendered in a dark value of ink or color that contrasts with the underlying paper (or a distinctly lighter value of ink or pigment), serving to delineate the subject matter in a "negative" manner. Although the tradition of stone rubbing has a venerable history in China, where stone has been used since ancient times to make commemorative monuments incised with inscriptions and designs, the techniques and cultural aesthetic that inspired stone rubbing as a literary and artistic activity do not seem to have firmly taken root in Japan until the Edo period. At that time stone rubbing was taken up by certain Japanese practitioners of things Chinese, scholars who devoted themselves to the study of Chinese history, literature, philosophy, and science, as well as by artists with related interests who belonged to the transplanted Bunjin school of painting and calligraphy. However, authentic stone rubbing (in which moistened paper is laid over the engraved surface of a stone monument and is subsequently beaten, so that portions of the paper are tamped into the incised concavities and consequently remain untouched when ink is applied over the general surface of the paper) seems never to have attracted more than a minor specialized interest among the Japanese during the Edo period. Woodblock simulations of this reversal process were common in the history of Chinese printing, but this form of printing appears not to have reached Japan until the Edo period, and even then was only experimented with on isolated occasions. Just when this distinctive Chinese block-printing technique actually reached Japan is unclear, but it seems to have been introduced no later than the early decades of the eighteenth century. This process has generally been overlooked by those interested in the evolution of Japanese printing; however, Shumboku was clearly an early practitioner.

Jakuchū was one of the few artists in the period who (in three printed works created in 1767 and 1768 from his compositions) also chose to utilize this unusual process, and the fact that Shumboku's illustrated books contain a substantial number of examples of this type (FIGS. 20, 21) serves to strengthen further the assertion that Jakuchū was, to some degree, familiar with and influenced by Shumboku. Whatever the connection between the two men, any teacher-student relationship would probably have occurred when Jakuchū was beginning his artistic career, perhaps as early as the late 1730s. Shumboku was already in his fifties by this time and was an established figure in artistic circles in the Osaka-Kyoto region. The consistent correspondence between the inventory of subject matter and themes in Shumboku's *ehon* and the selection and range of pictorial materials in Jakuchū's oeuvre is yet another compelling argument for the likelihood of a broader, more general influence on Jakuchū by Shumboku. A comparison of certain designs from Shumboku's *Ramma Zushiki* (1734; FIG. 22) with details in the *Dōshoku Sai-e* scrolls (FIG. 33 and NO. 14) and other paintings by Jakuchū makes this clear. Kimura Kenkadō (1736–1802), the wealthy sake merchant from Osaka, is known to have studied under Shumboku as a youth.[7] A prominent figure in Kansai cultural circles during the second half of the eighteenth century, Kenkadō had a multitude of artistic, scholarly, and antiquarian interests. He was an enthusiastic student of materia medica and botanical matters in the Chinese tradition,[8] a poet and writer, a devoted practitioner of the Sencha form of the tea ceremony, a discriminating collector of rare documents and antiquities, and a versatile painter. As an artist, Kenkadō received varied training, including tutelage in the style of the Kanō school under Shumboku; in traditional Chinese painting under Yanagisawa Kien; under the Nagasaki school painter Kumashiro Yūhi; from the Ōbaku priest Kakutei in the bird-and-flower style of Shen Nan-p'in; and in landscape painting under Ike Taiga. Daiten was Kenkadō's close friend,[9] as was Baisaō,[10] and during his later years, Jakuchū was only one of the many people who routinely made the pilgrimage to visit Kenkadō at his salon-residence in Osaka.[11] Like Jakuchū, Kenkadō is said to have taken no interest in conventional amusements and to have been able to lose himself in studious diversions from early childhood. In his writings, he noted his indebtedness to Shumboku: "From the time I was five or six I was fascinated with painting. Ōoka Shumboku was a noted master of the Kanō school in our era, and for this reason I went to study with him. Shumboku studied the *Mustard Seed Garden Manual of Painting* and copied paintings done by Ming artists, and he reproduced these in a woodblock-colored book of illustrations called the *Minchō Shiken*. It was as a result of seeing this work that I first resolved to try and paint in the Chinese manner."[12]

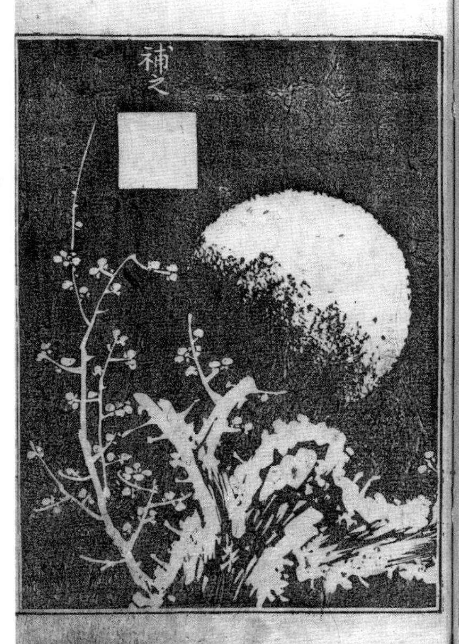
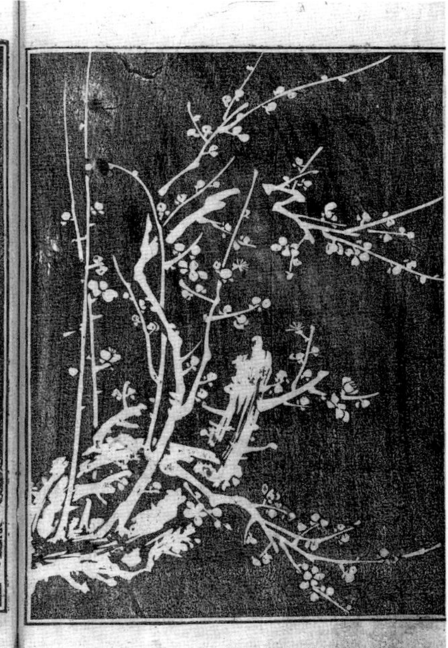

FIG. 20
Ōoka Shumboku. "Plum Blossoms and Moon," from the *Ehon Tekagami*, 1720, vol. 1, pp. 15b–16a.
Museum of Fine Arts, Boston

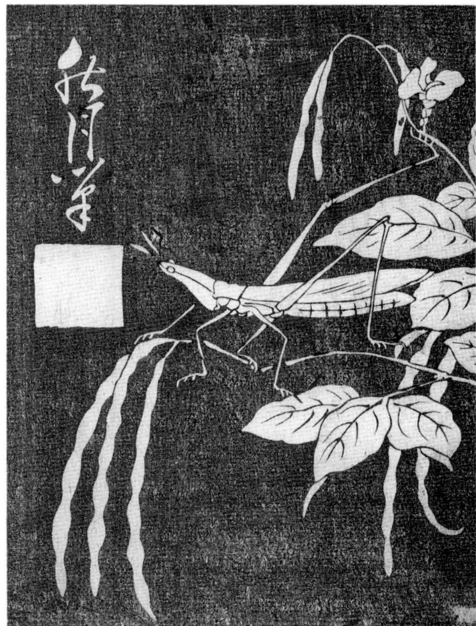

FIG. 21
Ōoka Shumboku. "String Beans and Insect," from the *Ehon Tekagami*, 1720, vol. 4, p. 15b.
Museum of Fine Arts, Boston

As previously mentioned, in his "Ketsumei" Daiten noted: "After Jakuchū had studied the style of the Kanō school under an unidentified master for a period of time, he became aware that even if he gained command of it, he could never surpass Kanō painters in their own academic manner. This realization caused him to turn his attentions to a more promising source of potential inspiration, the investigation of Chinese painting of the Sung and Yüan dynasties."[13] This passage, written when Jakuchū was already middle-aged (and had achieved fame as a result of his

FIG. 22 Ōoka Shumboku. From the *Ramma Zushiki*, 1734.
Museum of Fine Arts, Boston

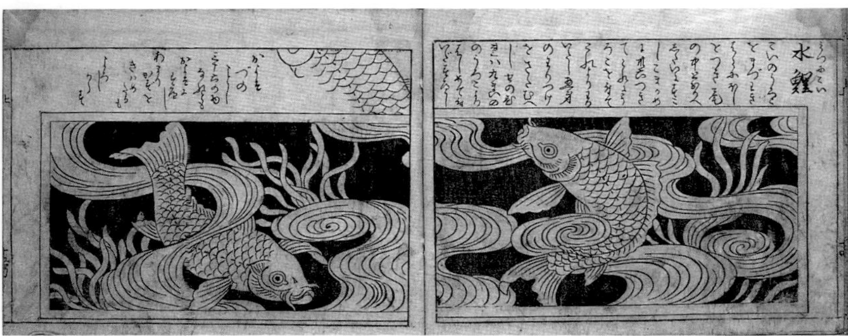

22.1 "Fish and Water Patterns," vol. 2, pp. 5b–6a

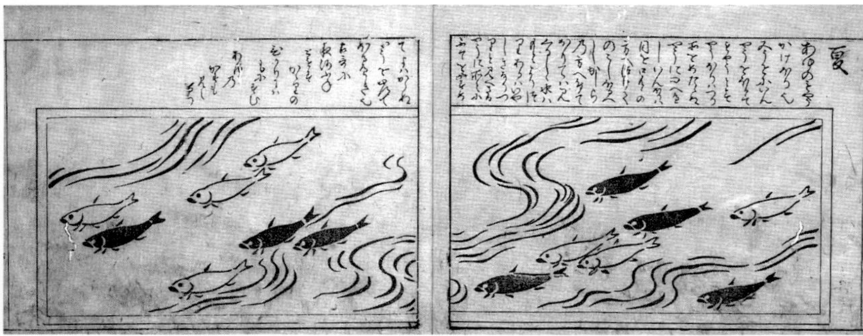

22.2 "Carp and Water Patterns," vol. 1, pp. 14b–15a

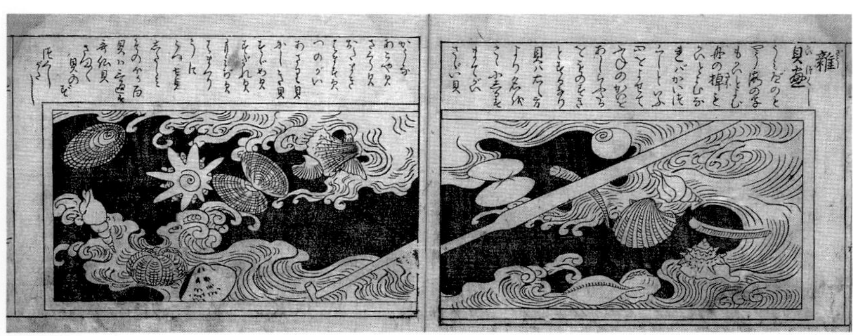

22.3 "Shells and Waves," vol. 1, pp. 6b–7a

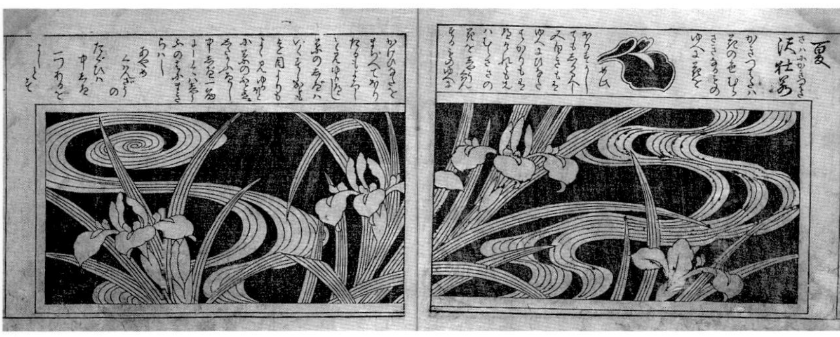

22.4 "Irises and Water Patterns," vol. 1, pp. 2b–3a

Dōshoku Sai-e series and other contemporary polychrome pieces that were often, in varying degrees, inspired by Chinese ideas), does not help in any concrete manner to substantiate the theory of Jakuchū's early tutelage under Shumboku. It does, however, refer to two essential characteristics that seem to tie the men together: the consistent identification in traditional literature of Shumboku as a Kanō master, despite his broader interests; and his preoccupation with the history and characteristics of Chinese painting, particularly bird-and-flower works, combined with his knowledge of where certain pieces of this sort were preserved, which made him a valuable source of information about such materials. Daiten's statement, though vague (probably based on some offhand verbal observation by Jakuchū), does not conflict with the basic premises that it was Shumboku who instructed Jakuchū in the intricacies of the Kanō style and, more important, that Shumboku introduced Jakuchū to certain sources of Chinese pictorial ideas that subsequently encouraged the younger man to pursue an independent career. Moreover, it seems very likely that Jakuchū continued to draw on Shumboku's ideas, notably from the illustrations in his *ehon*, even long after any pedagogical relationship had been terminated. Although the two men may have moved in somewhat different artistic circles in their later years, there seems to be no reason why they might not have run into each other occasionally, for they were active in the same region and Shumboku did not die until 1763, when Jakuchū would have been forty-eight years of age and working industriously to complete the *Dōshoku Sai-e* scrolls.

Despite documentary indications that Jakuchū received schooling in the Kanō manner, there is little explicit evidence of this influence in the corpus of works that is presently available. Tangible manifestations of Kanō influence in Jakuchū's works would probably have been strongest during his early years, when he was working to absorb the particulars of style, brushwork, and conceptual idiosyncracies; however, as noted, no works from this formative period have been preserved. This is not to say that there is a complete absence of vestigial stylistic traces of Jakuchū's training in the mannered forms and conventionalized brushwork of the Kanō school; rather, in his mature works, these elements were skillfully and harmoniously integrated into his own distinctive expressive style, and as a consequence their origins were less apparent.

Professor Tsuji Nobuo of Tokyo University has suggested, however, that a hanging scroll depicting a phoenix may well have been produced when the artist was in his mid-thirties, or perhaps even earlier, and that its brushwork and style indicate the artist's indebtedness to the Kanō school (FIG. 23).[14] This representation of the phoenix is of particular interest, for it differs in some respects from Jakuchū's later paintings of the subject, one of which is NO. 9.

The term *phoenix*, which is routinely used in English sources to describe fantastic birds of this sort, is inadequate, if not indeed misleading, in conveying the significance of the imaginary Chinese avian prototype. The fabulous, mythical bird, most often called by the single generic name *feng-huang* (male-female; Japanese: *hō-ō*) originated in ancient Chinese cosmological traditions. Over the centuries, it acquired a multiplicity of auspicious symbolic associations and metaphorical manifestations that are pervasive in Chinese art, literature, and folklore.[15] It is difficult to generalize about when the phoenix became an iconographically conventionalized artistic motif in Chinese painting, but extant works indicate that it was routinely represented during the Ming period in resplendent polychrome versions and also, on occasion, in monochrome. When and just how this kind of representation of the subject was introduced into Japanese painting is unclear, but it may have occurred sometime during the seventeenth century, for Kanō artists were already representing the motif in large scale on folding screens in the first years of the eighteenth century. Informative examples may be seen in two sets of six-panel folding screens, one by Kanō Tsunenobu (1636–1713) that is thought to have been executed before 1704 (FIG. 24),[16] and another (FIG. 25) by Kanō Juseki Hidenobu (1640–1718).[17] The depictions of phoenixes in these works are undoubtedly based on Chinese prototypes of the Ming period, but the imaginary birds, although iconographically indebted to Chinese models in their anatomical particulars and postures, are nevertheless rendered according to the established artistic conventions and academic style of the Kanō school. This is apparent in a preoccupation with the formal and the decorative that dominates the compositions, and the punctilious quality of the brushwork, with its calculated, impersonal flavor.

FIG. 23 shows a white phoenix in flight, with a red sun behind it, a symbolic association traditional in Chinese depictions of the subject. Comparison of Jakuchū's bird with a similarly fantastic fowl in one screen (FIG. 24) of Tsunenobu's composition is instructive, for it confirms Tsuji's contention of Kanō influence in the piece. The mannered postures of the birds—which are set laterally in space, with their

FIG. 23 *Phoenix and Sun*, n.d.

Museum of Fine Arts, Boston

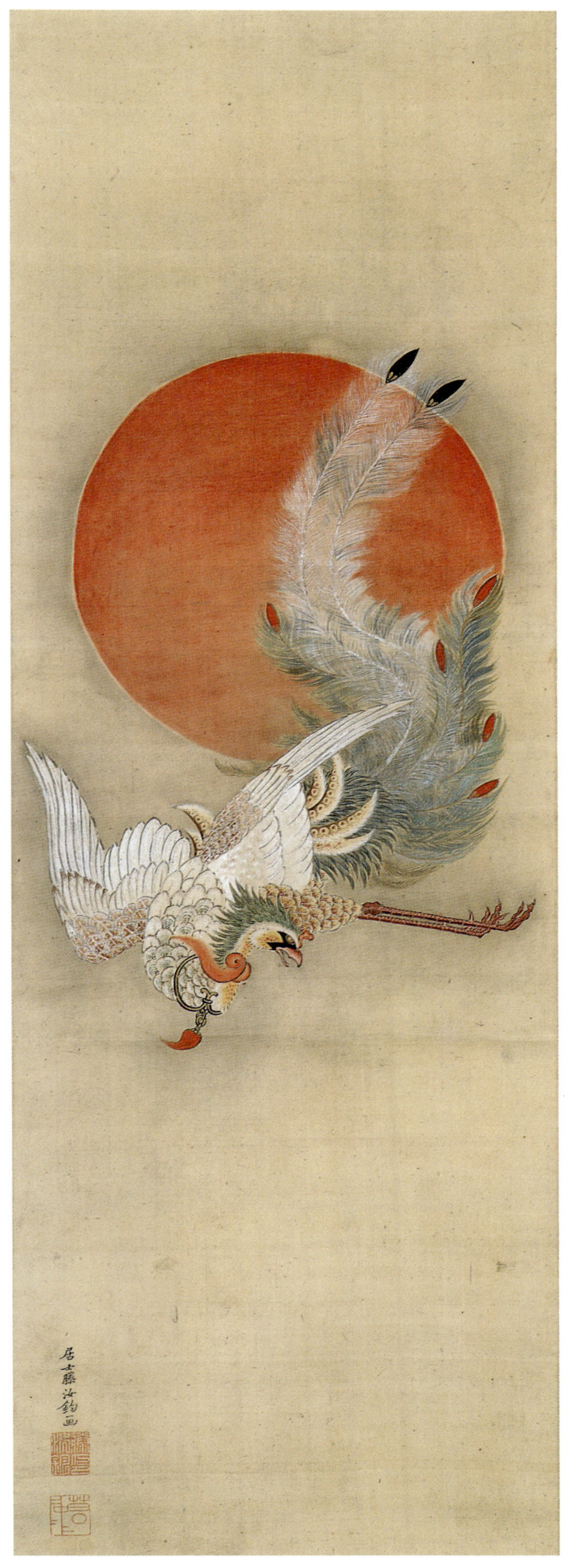

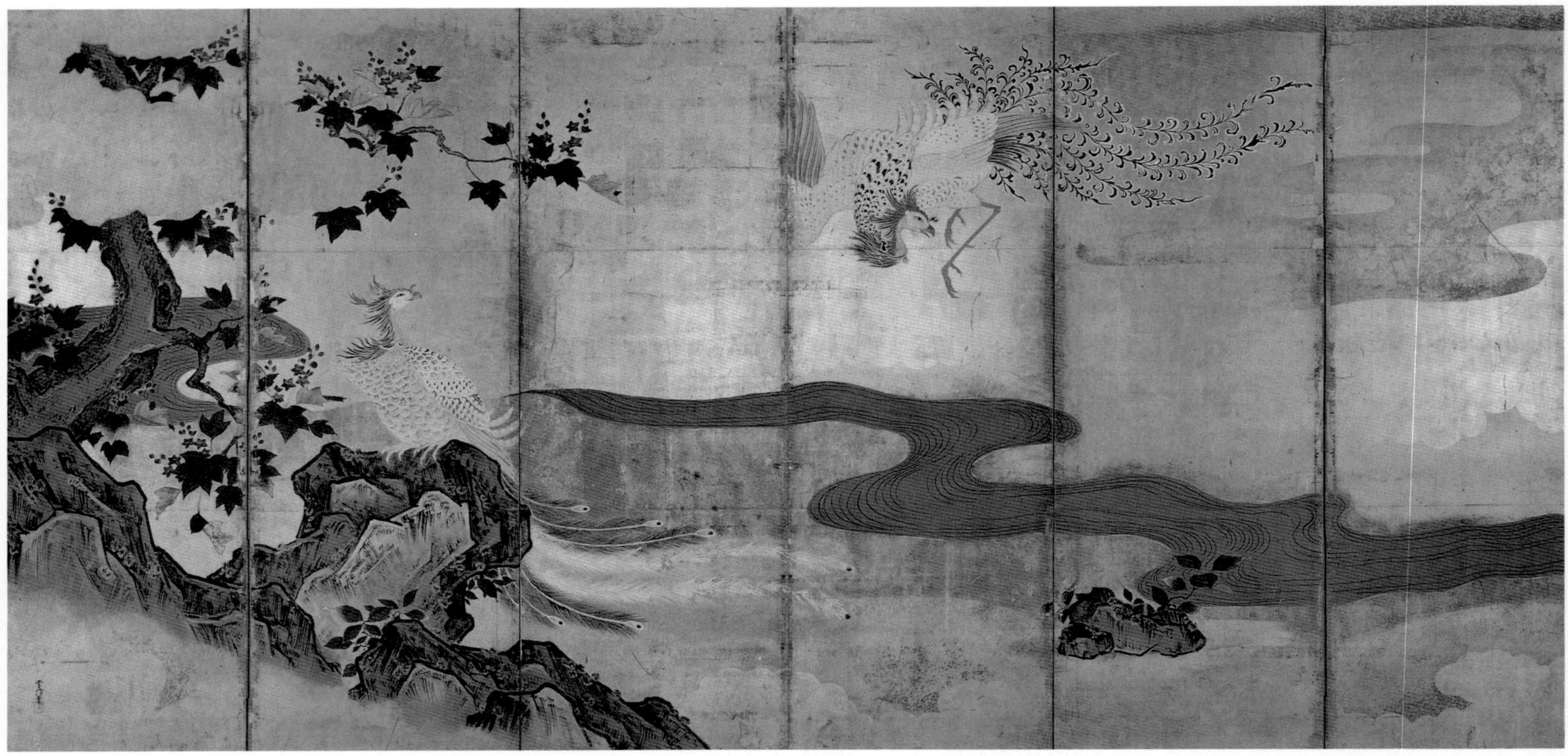

FIG. 24 Kanō Tsunenobu (1636–1713). *Phoenixes* (left-hand screen of a pair of six-panel folding screens).

Tokyo National University of Fine Arts and Music

right wings bent sharply upward and their heads obliquely to their left—are analogous, while the dissimilarities in composition—such as the divergent orientations of the tails—can be explained to some degree by the differing scales and formats of the pieces, one a narrow hanging scroll and the other a spacious, horizontally organized folding screen. The treatment of both birds is flat and patterned, linear and decorative in intention, and lacking in any animating vitality. Contours and defining details are rendered in studied, unmodulated brush strokes, devoid of any enlivening accent. These features demonstrate Jakuchū's early interest in Kanō style and technique, and stand in sharp contrast to the accomplished execution of his later depictions of the subject. A certain ineptitude in the conception of the Boston piece, a sense of preoccupation with details at the expense of the motif as a whole, also supports an early dating.[18]

It is reasonable to assume that during his early forties Jakuchū produced a number of paintings that have survived, including that of the carp (NO. 10). Like the phoenix, this subject has its origins in traditional Chinese painting and was routinely depicted during the Ming period, when it became a popular, standardized motif, more often than not represented according to established pictorial precedents of anatomy and posture. Indebtedness to this sort of prototype is apparent in Jakuchū's painting, and one cannot deny this example's similarities to representations of the carp by members of the Nagasaki school (such as Sō Shiseki),[19] who were instrumental in introducing Chinese pictorial traditions to Japan during the eighteenth century. As in the case of the phoenix, where Jakuchū diligently emulated the stylistic canons of the Kanō masters, here he was inspired by another established artistic tradition, producing a school piece that displays growing technical competence but no promise of the distinctive personal style that was to evolve later.

However, upon examination of three elegant paintings that are very closely related in style and inspiration, it becomes apparent that Jakuchū's years as a studious novice were over. That he had developed into a mature artist, with a distinctive artistic vision and a command of the painter's craft, can be seen in monochrome depictions of kidney-bean vines, insects, and a solitary frog, and of corn plants and sparrows (NO. 3), and a colored representation of snake gourds and insects (NO. 7). Although no dates appear on these pieces, the ink paintings are presumed to be Jakuchū's earliest extant monochrome depictions, produced in the early years of the Hōreki period (1751–1764), perhaps in about 1751 or 1752. The lovely painting of snake gourds and insects, for its part, seems likely to have been produced a year or so later, when the artist was about thirty-eight or thirty-nine years of age. Jakuchū handled the subjects of these pieces with pictorial consistency, despite the differing grounds and pigments—the monochrome pair, with their exquisite ink nuances, was rendered on absorbent, sized paper, and the single scroll, with its precise, naturalistic representations, was done in soft, modulated colors on silk. Although the brush strokes in the monochrome representations are, in certain areas, somewhat freer and less precise, the manner in which the minute details were rendered is almost as meticulous as it is in the silk scroll. These qualities leave the observer with a strong respect for Jakuchū's technical versatility and with the impression that he was equally proficient in both expressive means. Moreover, the artist's superb compositional conception in these pieces provides striking testimony to his creative maturation and originality; an inspired talent for spatial arrangement and the interrelationship of pictorial components underlies these convincing depictions of flora and fauna. The compositions are uniformly and clearly conceived in shallow space, and the engaging natural details, set off against plain backgrounds, draw the observer close and lead him sequentially through the intricacies of the paintings. Notable for their conceptual precision and accuracy, their lively natural forms, and their sophisticated compositions, these pieces serve as artistic prologues to the *Dōshoku Sai-e* series, which was produced in the years immediately following.

Any attempt to reconstruct a more complete picture of Jakuchū's early activities is frustrated by the lack of reliable chronological benchmarks, for the earliest dated works presently available were not produced until 1755, when the artist was forty years of age. During that year, Jakuchū's brother Hakusai had been persuaded to take over the operation of the Masugen, and relieved of this responsibility, Jakuchū was finally free to pursue his own interests and devote his efforts to painting. The year Hōreki 5 (1755) appears in the inscription of three large pieces; these serve as reliable, impressive evidence of the artist's progress. These substantial works on silk exhibit a high degree of technical proficiency and a strong sense of individuality in conception, as well as an instructive diversity of subject matter and a versatility of technique appropriate to the various subjects.

The first of the three, *White Plum Blossoms and Moon* (FIG. 26), is filled with a sense of mysterious, pulsating energy, and the luxuriant blossoms stand

FIG. 25 Kanō Juseki Hidenobu (1640–1718). *Phoenixes* (right-hand screen of a pair of six-panel folding screens).
Private collection, Japan

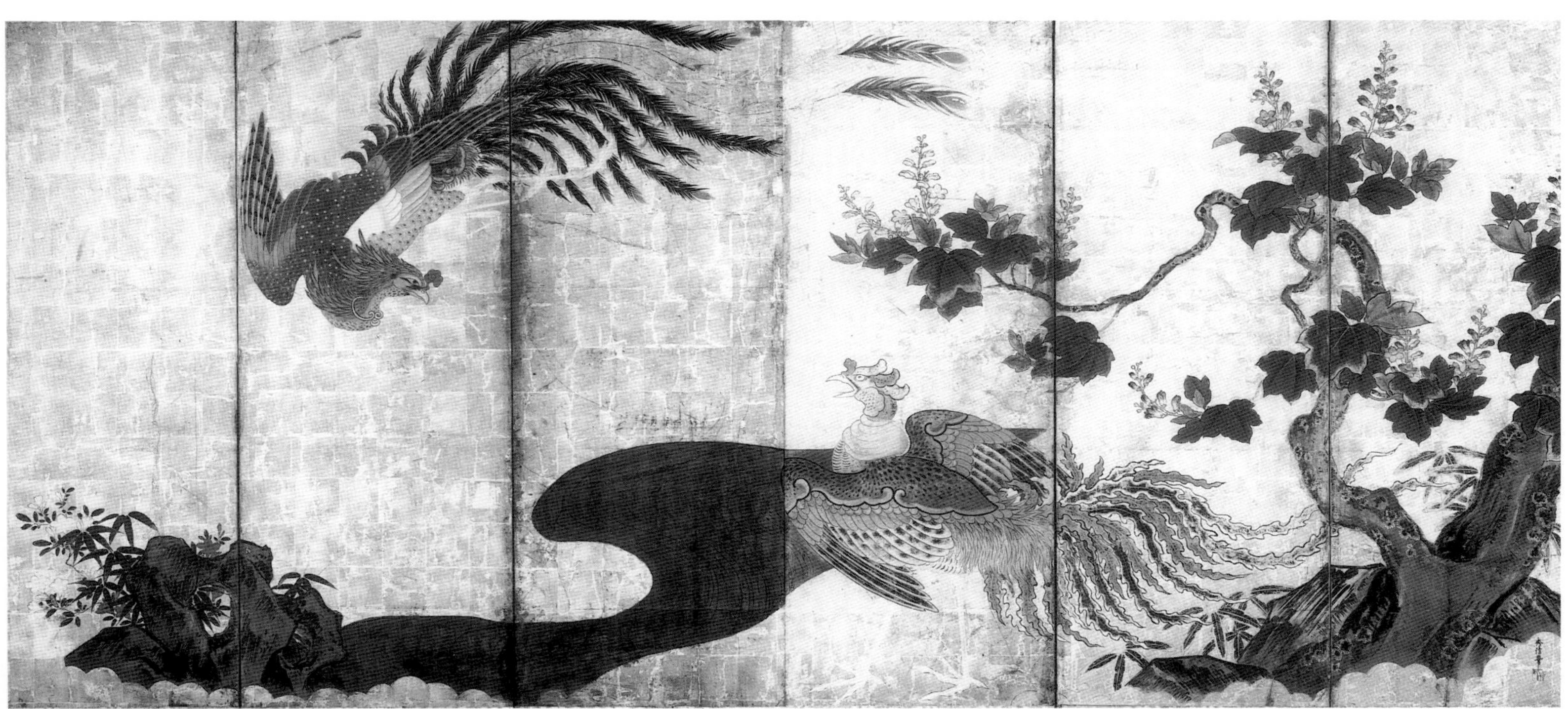

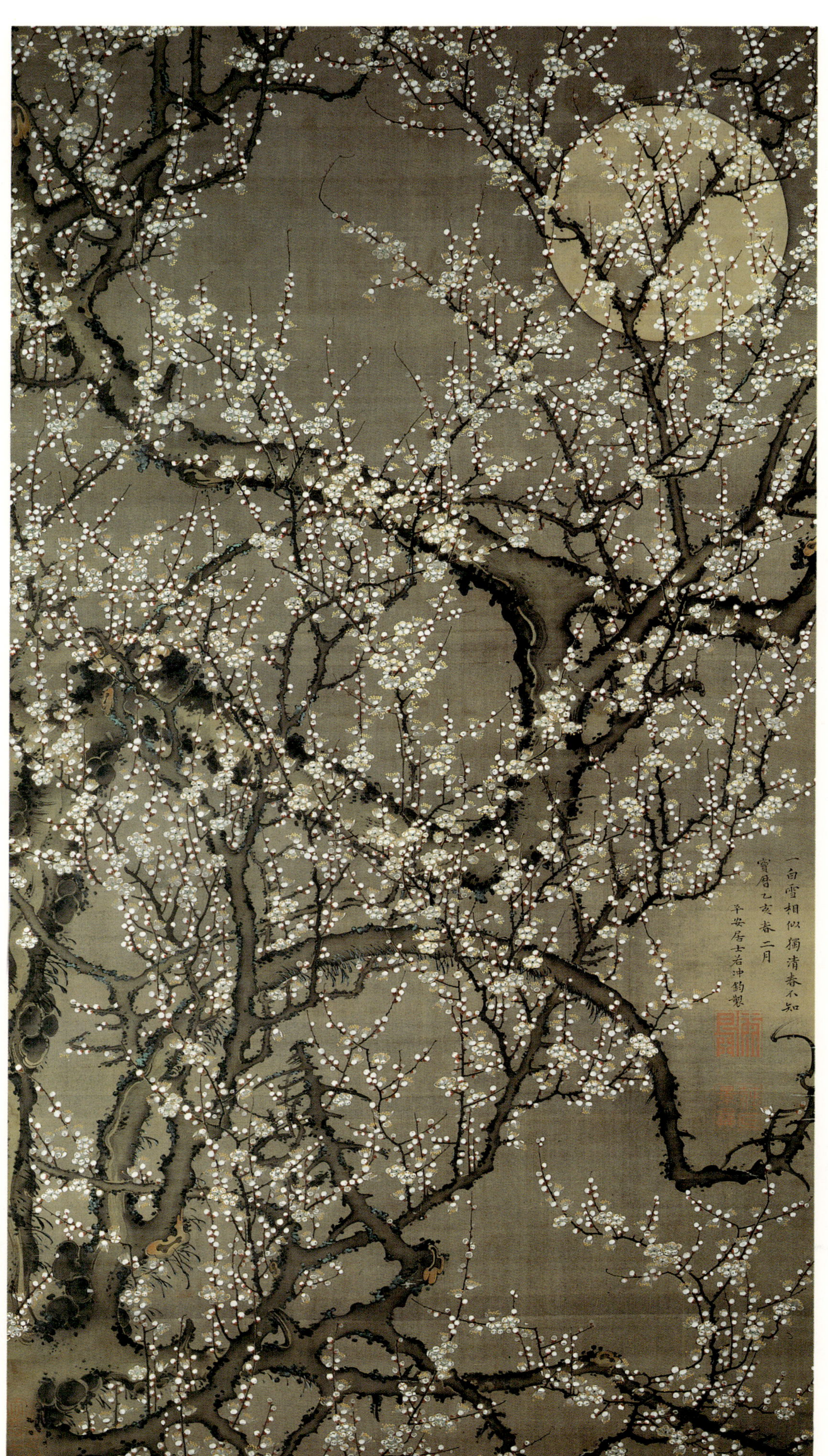

FIG. 26
White Plum Blossoms and Moon, 1755.

Mary and Jackson Burke Collection

out in luminous contrast with the dark, gnarled contours of the ancient tree. Above and behind, shining ethereally against the night sky, is a large full moon. Although the conceptual origins of this traditional monochrome subject go back to Chinese paintings of the Yüan and Ming periods produced by masters such as Wang Mien (1335–c. 1415) and Ch'en Hsien-chang (1428–1500), Jakuchū's interpretation differs from Chinese prototypes in its greater exuberance of mood, its stronger sense of expressive form, and its inventive brushwork. This is the earliest of four paintings of blossoming plums that are closely related in style and period. The second, one of the *Dōshoku Sai-e* series (FIG. 33.6), recapitulates the composition of *White Plum Blossoms and Moon* almost exactly and is clearly a direct copy, thought to have been executed about four years later. The third and fourth plum paintings are very similar in detail and execution, but they differ in their orientation of the tree and they have rocks and flowing water in the foreground. One of these also belongs to the *Dōshoku Sai-e* set and was done in 1758; in it Jakuchū added a group of small birds and deleted the moon (FIG. 33.2). The other belongs to a private collection and may have been painted about 1756.[20] The intimate affinity of these four pieces is established both by the striking consistency of conceptual ideas and uniformity of treatment—they are virtually identical in format and dimension and were executed on identical silk grounds—and by their having been produced all within about five years.

Jakuchū's second dated painting from 1755 is *Pair of Phoenixes and the Rising Sun* (NO. 9), and an inscription on its box indicates that it was presented to the Imperial Household by the Higashi Honganji temple, where, as has been noted, an impressive collection of the artist's works is thought to have been assembled during his lifetime. A work of impressive size, it is the largest known extant hanging scroll on silk devoted to a bird-and-flower theme by Jakuchū. The subject, a pair of fantastic phoenixes on a prominent outcropping of volcanic rock, staring up at the bright morning sun and crowing at it, is, as noted, a quintessential Chinese theme, a traditional favorite among "academic" artists of the Ming period who worked in the bird-and-flower genre.

This interest is further illustrated by two large Ming pieces on silk, the first an unsigned work, *One Hundred Birds*, in which a pair of phoenixes makes up the central compositional focus (FIG. 27),[21] and the second showing five spirited phoenixes strutting on the distinctive rocks under a morning sun (FIG. 28).[22] Although the compositions, pictorial components, and formats of these pieces vary (the first is oriented vertically; the second, horizontally), striking similarities to Jakuchū's painting in the poses of the birds and the details of their richly detailed, colorful plumage clearly indicate that Jakuchū must have been inspired by such pieces. Unfortunately, it is impossible to establish whether either of these particular works

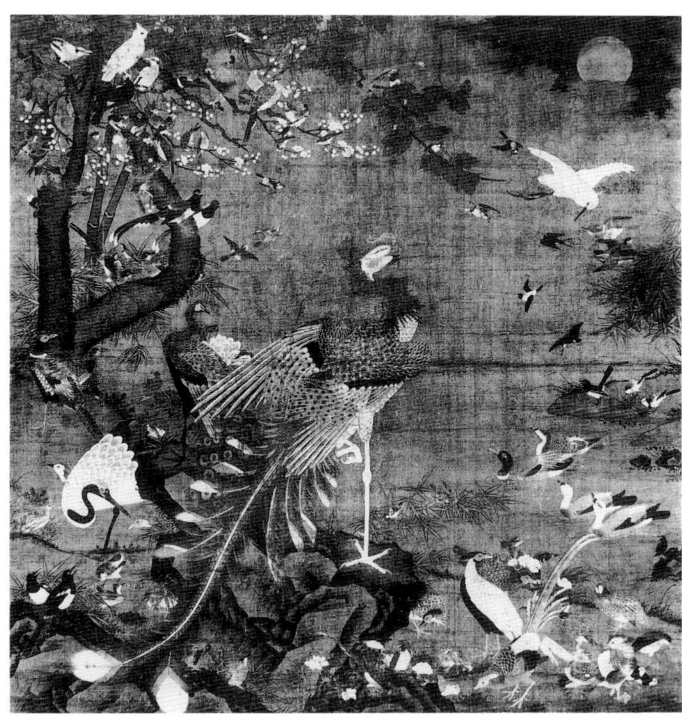

FIG. 27 Anonymous. *One Hundred Birds*, Ming dynasty (fifteenth century?).
Private collection, Japan

FIG. 28 Hsüeh-feng Li I-ho. *Phoenixes under the Morning Sun*, Ming dynasty (fifteenth century).
Present location unknown

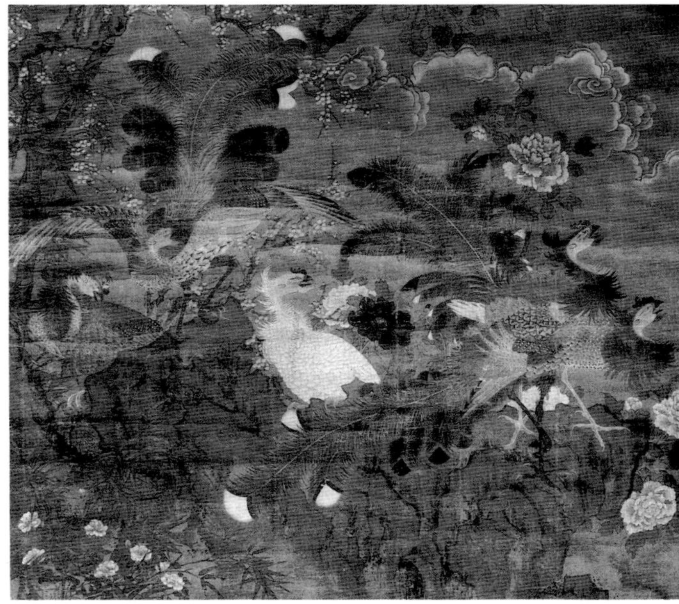

was familiar to Jakuchū, for no records of their location during the eighteenth century seem to exist. However, the second work belonged to Prince Shimazu Tadashige of Tokyo in 1926 (when it was published in the journal *Kokka*), and it apparently survived in his family's detached villa when their castle in Kagoshima was burned in a battle there in 1877. This argues against the possibility that the piece was brought to Japan in recent times and suggests that it was actually a treasured possession in the extensive art collection of the hereditary lords of the Shimazu clan.

The first Ming painting is unsigned, but the second bears the signature of Hsüeh-feng Li I-ho, whose name, together with a few bits of information, appears in the *Koga Bikō*.[23] Because of the fragmentary knowledge of non-native painters in Japan, Li I-ho was assigned to the last categorical section in the *Koga Bikō*, which deals with Korean painters; references to several paintings are included, together with reproductions of signatures and seals. One of the signatures and two of the seals also include the name of the artist's native place, Shang Hang, which is located in the eastern part of Fu-chien Province, and this confirms the Chinese provenance of the painting. Fu-chien was a prolific source for Chinese paintings brought to Japan during the Ming and early Ch'ing periods. Another signature reproduced in the *Koga Bikō*[24] reveals an obvious contextual relationship with the two paintings in question. It reads: "Executed by Hsüeh-feng"; the cursive style of the calligraphy and the details of the strokes correspond closely with the signature on the Li I-ho piece, and a square intaglio seal reading *Hsiao-shan Hou-jen* also appears. A document of authentication written in 1808 by the Kanō painter Isen'in (1775–1828), seventh-generation head of the Kobikicho branch of the Kanō school in Edo, notes that the subject consists of a "pair of phoenixes crowing at the morning sun, two cranes, two wild geese, and a golden oriole, like a plover. . . ."[25]

Investigation of traditional Chinese documentary sources shows that Li I-ho, although known in Japan, was, ironically enough, not famed in his homeland. In fact, there are a number of Chinese artists whose works have been preserved over the centuries in Japan but not in China itself. No precise dating for the two paintings in question here can be established on the basis of documentary materials, but it is unlikely that they were produced any later than the Ming period. The Japanese authors of the articles in which these paintings have been published are of the opinion that they belong to the first part of the period, perhaps the fifteenth century, and were executed in the manner of Lu Chi, a master of the academic Che school. Whatever their dates, their generic and artistic relationship with Jakuchū's piece is undeniable.

Jakuchū's painting of the phoenixes is notable for its elegant detail and for the ingenious manner in which light, luminous colors were juxtaposed with darker components against a subdued background, features inspired by Chinese paintings of the sort just described. At the same time, Jakuchū's work, although reproducing with meticulous fidelity the anatomical particulars copied from a Chinese prototype, also exhibits a greater sophistication in the imaginative resolution of details, together with a distinctive sense of personal vision. The short inscription preceding the artist's signature and date reveals something of his creative motivation:

> Flowers, birds, grasses, and insects each have their own innate spirit. Only after one has actually determined the true nature of this spirit through observation should painting begin. There is, however, no way to actually observe a phoenix's resplendent plumage. So one has no recourse but to rely on existing models in depicting its appearance.[26]

Painting from direct, personal observation of nature was one of Jakuchū's primary concerns during this period, and his attitude was fundamental in the creation of the *Dōshoku Sai-e* series.

The third painting by Jakuchū dated 1755 depicts a tiger (FIG. 29). The brief inscription preceding the date and signature laments the lack of a living model and again emphasizes the artist's dedication to personal observation: "When I paint natural phenomena, depiction is impossible without a true model. As there are no ferocious tigers in this country, I could only imitate [the appearance of] one by copying Mao I's painting."[27] That Jakuchū actually resorted to copying in this particular case is clear, for the work he imitated is extant (FIG. 30). The prototype has been well known for a long time as a treasured possession of the Shōdenji, a temple in the Kamigamo section of Kyoto.[28] Traditionally attributed to the renowned Sung-period Chinese artist Li Kung-mien (also known as Li Kung-lin; c. 1040–1106), it has a dedication written and inscribed on an accompanying document that is attributed to Wang An-shih (1021–1086), but modern scholars consider the piece to be a copy by an anonymous journeyman painter of the Ming period because of its rather mannered and uninspired execution. Comparison with Jakuchū's version demonstrates not only the artist's degree of indebtedness to the earlier work, but also how his own artistic

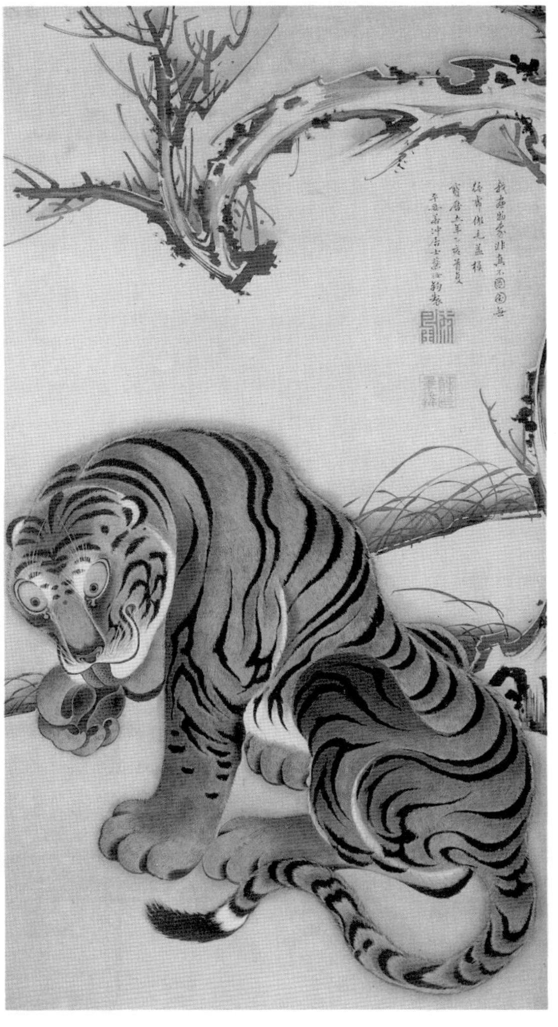

FIG. 29 *Tiger*, 1755.
Los Angeles County Museum of Art, Shin'enkan Collection

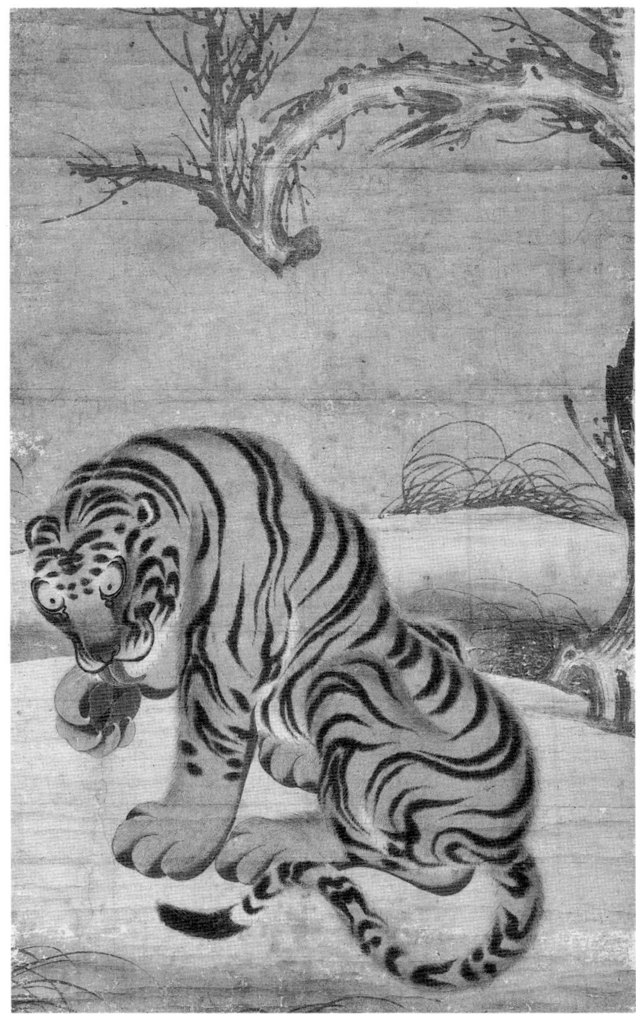

FIG. 30 Anonymous. *Tiger*, Ming period.
Shōdenji, Kyoto

inclinations departed from the original.

Viewed together, the two depictions immediately reveal how much finer Jakuchū's work is. The tiger in the Ming piece is static and inert, but Jakuchū's is filled with animated feline vitality and an assertive presence. The Ming painting exhibits both the measured execution and the deliberate brushwork that are predictable from a lesser talent, whose preoccupation with literal reproduction resulted in a loss of pictorial strength and spontaneity. By contrast, Jakuchū's piece, although faithful to the original in an iconographic sense, is notable for its greater impact, achieved through the elegant use of warm pigments in the tiger's body (creating a convincing impression of sleek fur) and a versatile range of brush strokes, which are both more precise and more lively than any in the prototype. Moreover, Jakuchū modified the format slightly, reducing it in width and tightening the composition and the relationship of its components to make it more coherent and more visually effective. In particular, the artist's skill in executing the monochrome components—the craggy branch at the top, the diagonal ground line with its animated grasses, and the fragment of the base of the tree—clearly demonstrates his innovative means of expression. Jakuchū's creative talents are unmistakable here, for he reversed the usual situation, in which a copy is inherently inferior to its prototype, producing a piece that is superior in all respects to its pictorial parent.

Jakuchū made a second copy of the Ming tiger (No. 28), but he did this one in a looser, less literal manner, entirely in monochrome ink. This work, which belongs to the Rokuonji in Kyoto, is accompanied by a calligraphic hanging scroll with a poem by Daiten, who signed the piece "Baisō," one of his literary names. The artist's inclination to modify composition and reinterpret particulars for his own artistic ends is apparent here, for he eliminated the intermediate ground line and substituted for the overhanging horizontal branch of the pine tree a forceful diagonal bamboo. Several instances like this one, in which Jakuchū produced meticulous, detailed polychrome and freer monochrome versions of the same subject, demonstrate his versatility and training in both pictorial traditions. Moreover, the ability to integrate the polychrome and monochrome traditions harmoniously in large compositions is one of his most striking artistic accomplishments, and this synthesis is an essential feature of the *Dōshoku Sai-e* series, which Jakuchū is thought to have started in about late 1757 or early 1758, close to three years after he completed the three dated paintings described above.

These three paintings function as benchmarks for understanding Jakuchū's artistic evolution. They not only reveal his preoccupation with Chinese prototypes and artistic traditions at the time of their creation, but, more important, demonstrate that he had already developed impressive skills and a distinctive personal vision and manner of execution that set him apart from other painters of the period. These striking works, produced when Jakuchū was approaching middle age, are clearly the result of a protracted period of artistic diligence that probably began more than a decade earlier, in his twenties.

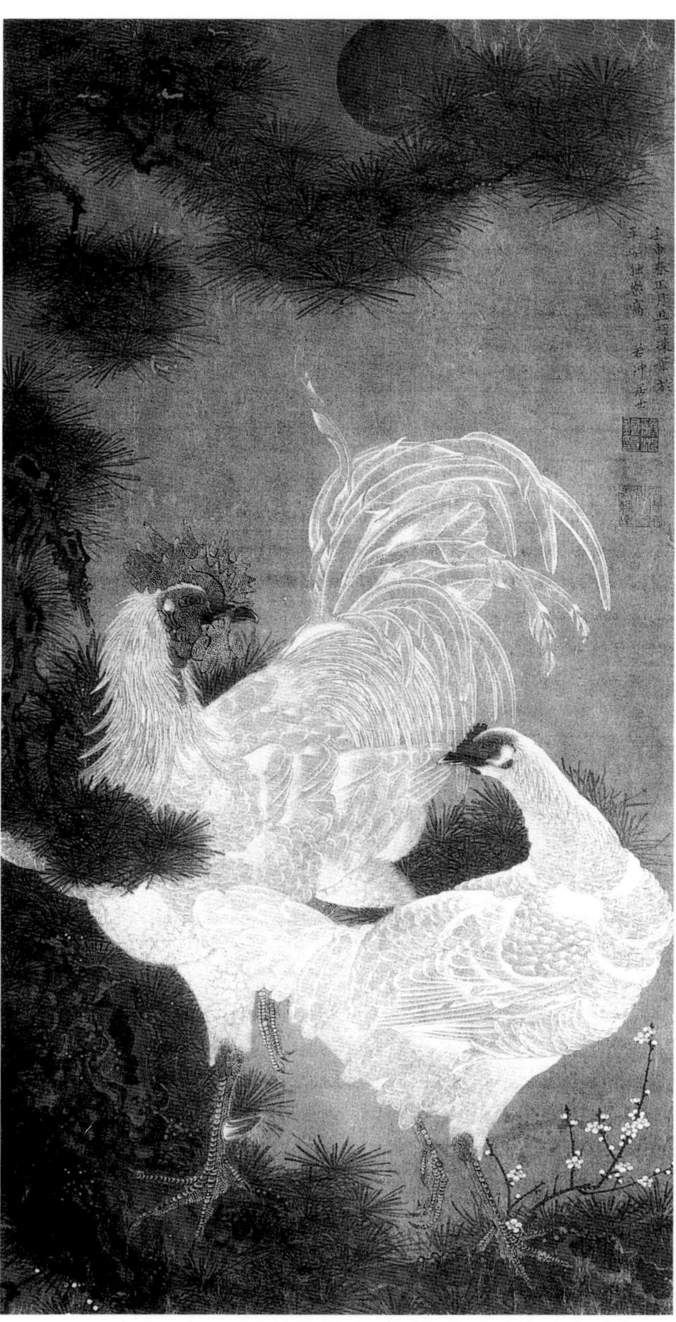

FIG. 31 *White Fowl*, 1752.
Present location unknown

But what of his earlier paintings? One accomplished work executed on silk, with an inscription dating it to 1752 (when the artist was thirty-seven years old), was published in *Kokka* in 1900 (FIG. 31).[29] Unfortunately this fine polychrome piece, which belonged to the Asami family and was sold at auction in 1928, has since disappeared. It depicted a pair of white chickens facing each other on a pine branch, with the morning sun above them. The inscription noted that the piece was produced during the New Year season, at the Dokurakuka (Grotto of Solitary Pleasures), the artist's studio in Kyoto. This is the only known reference to this studio to appear in an inscription. Although the location is unclear, the artist's use of the Dokurakuka seems to have preceded the establishment of his atelier-retreat, the Shin'enkan, and this earlier studio may have been located in one of the Itō family's buildings in the Nishiki neighborhood. The artist signed this painting "Jakuchū koji," and his use of the conventional Buddhist suffix indicates that he had already taken the vows of a Buddhist lay monk by that time. The feathers of the chickens in this elegant painting were rendered in very precise, delicate white strokes, effectively evoking a tangible impression of the light, buoyant quality of feathers as well as delineating the varying sizes and conformations of the individual plumes.

This meticulous and convincing manner of rendering feathers is one of Jakuchū's hallmarks; it appears in a number of works produced when he was in his thirties and forties and is a salient feature of the *Dōshoku Sai-e* series. This painstaking attention to avian anatomy and plumage shows how carefully the artist worked from nature, simulating his animate subjects in all their particulars. Daiten, in the inscription he wrote for Jakuchū's gravestone, described how the artist actually raised a flock of chickens just outside his window and studiously observed them and painted them for some years. Similarly, a brief reference in the *Kinsei Itsujin Gashi* noted that "the origin of his painting style is unclear, and his use of ink and pigments is different from that of other artists. He was skilled in depicting chickens, and 'Jakuchū's fowl,' with their remarkable colors and meticulous details, are widely admired."[30]

The calligraphic style of the inscription on the piece formerly in the Asami collection corresponds closely with the inscriptions on three hanging scrolls that belong to the Sōdōji, a temple in Wakayama Prefecture: a white cockatoo seated on a decorative Chinese perch, done on silk (No. 4),[31] and a pair of ink paintings on paper, one depicting a kidney-bean vine with insects and a frog, and the other, corn stalks and sparrows (No. 3).[32] The similarities in execution, detail, and calligraphic style indicate that these pieces were produced at about the same time; it has been suggested that the cockatoo was done in about 1750 or later, and the ink paintings in about 1751. The painting of the cockatoo, with its white feathers executed in the meticulous manner of the Asami piece, clearly dates from the same period as that piece.

Another fine work on silk that, on the basis of style and pictorial context, belongs chronologically with these two early paintings is a pair of hanging scrolls depicting cranes (FIG. 18); these birds were copied precisely from prototypes by the Ming artist Wen Cheng (FIG. 17), now in the Shōkokuji. According to temple tradition, the Chinese works were brought back from the continent to that monastery by Zekkai Chūshin (1336–1405), renowned *bungakusō* of the Muromachi period. Jakuchū's renditions of the birds (one stands looking upward, the other swoops down in flight toward a precipitous cliff on its left) were done with great exactitude of detail and pose. Each white feather was precisely reproduced, as were other anatomical particulars, such as the red patches on the birds' heads and the black tail plumage and the scales on the legs. Despite this verisimilitude, Jakuchū was inclined to follow his own predilections when it came to composition and to the disposition and treatment of other pictorial components.

The two Chinese paintings, on the other hand, have no compositional interrelationship and, in fact, appear to best advantage when viewed independently, rather than when arbitrarily juxtaposed. Because of their history and subject matter, however, they have traditionally been regarded as a pair, and Jakuchū's versions demonstrate his innovative efforts to resolve this pictorial disparity. In order to accomplish this, he reversed the profile of the cliff in the right-hand painting to parallel the orientation of the crane; he also changed the movement of the waves so they would rebound from the base of the cliff. In the left-hand painting, the artist substituted a gnarled pine for the scattered bamboos in the original, with the base of the pine tree countering the angle of the waves in the companion piece, and added three branches, the uppermost, longest one delineating the composition at the top. These changes effectively interrelate the two works by circumscribing the exterior portions of each painting, bringing the two birds into a more intimate relationship; the position and catenary curve of the lower pine branch, moreover, leads the observer's eye across the left-hand painting and to the graceful, inverted curve of the flying crane's wings in the accompanying piece. The subtle but effective addition of a small branch of flowering plum in the left-hand work, and corresponding white accents on the tips of the convoluted waves on the right, provides a further link.

Comparison of the Chinese pieces with Jakuchū's paintings reveals other significant differences. The Chinese paintings exhibit a pervasive unity in execution and a conceptual consistency in their preoccupation with naturalistic representation, but Jakuchū's works embody a greater variety of artistic ideas, a harmonious combination of anatomical fidelity in the depiction of the cranes and, to varying degrees, departures from a literal view of nature in the handling of the trunk and branches of the pine and in the more arbitrary abstract treatment of the waves. The pine trunk and branches have an idiosyncratic quality, an evocative mixture of naturally inspired forms and expressive brushwork, which is one of the distinguishing characteristics of the artist's style. Jakuchū's rendering of the waves also transcends the conventions of natural form, and his rhythmic linear treatment of the surges and his slow convolutions of breaking water were conceived in a unique expressionistic manner.

Another polychrome painting of this general period is the lovely *Rooster and Bamboo in Snow* (No. 1). The rooster, searching intently for grains or other choice morsels, is a traditional subject in East Asian painting, but this bird's lifelike pose and naturalistic fidelity are highly convincing, and again attest to the artist's careful observation. Moreover, the pleasing balance of darks and lights in the surrounding landscape, with its juxtaposition of heavy, wet snow and dark, angular bamboo stalks, demonstrates Jakuchū's mastery of pictorial techniques, gained from the diligent study of Chinese paintings. This piece is thought to have been created when the artist was in his early thirties, and it is apparent that his style, with its mixture of techniques and components drawn selectively from his earlier training, combined with his own perceptive observation of living models, had already resulted in a mode of representation so accomplished and original in its vision that his works stand above those by any other artists of the period.

In another work by the artist, *Rooster and Blossoming Plum in Snow*, a rooster is depicted in an identical pose, in the same position in the composition (NO. 13). This second work, which belongs to the Ryōsokuin, a subtemple of the Kenninji monastery in Kyoto, also has a snowy setting, but it is noticeably more restrained and slightly narrower. This piece has a single, low ground line and no background components, but *Rooster and Bamboo in Snow* is composed of a series of gently ascending diagonals that mark the successive contours of the weighty snow overlaying blooming chrysanthemums in the foreground and grasses in the upper range of the painting. The snow-laden bamboos, which in *Rooster and Bamboo in Snow* extend above the composition and define its right-hand side, are replaced in the Ryōsokuin piece by an ancient camellia tree that, despite its age, has come into brilliant flower.

Comparing the two works reveals how well the artist was able to dramatically modify the appearance and mood of a basic compositional scheme through the innovative use of components and colors. *Rooster and Bamboo in Snow* is set in late autumn, with its heavy, premature snow a harbinger of the imminent arrival of the dark months of winter. The atmosphere in the Ryōsokuin painting is very different, one of genial anticipation, for here it is late winter, still cold but with the sun's rays growing stronger daily, and with the hardy camellia heralding spring as it blooms against a drab, dormant background. The approach of spring is further confirmed by the presence of a sprightly green bush warbler, perched jauntily on a branch at the top of the painting. The selective use of light, understated colors in the rooster's plumage reinforces the mood of auspicious expectation, even as the vivid colors of the camellias and of the rooster's wattles and comb elegantly imbue the painting with life.

The same signature ("Keiwa") and seals that appear on the first rooster painting also appear on an ink painting in the Shin'enkan Collection (FIG. 32) that is among Jakuchū's earliest extant monochrome works and is presumed to be more or less contemporaneous in execution with the rooster painting. The composition explores the components of a grape vine, a subject that also has its general origins in earlier Chinese painting. Crisp lines, shades, and washes of monochrome ink were innovatively combined to create a work that is striking in its vitality and pictorial diversity. The most likely sources of inspiration for this sort of painting were pieces by journeyman artists of the Ming period that were imported to Japan from the Chekiang area of southern China.

Another of Jakuchū's depictions of grapes (NO. 6) seems more directly indebted to this Chinese tradition, but the Shin'enkan work is engaging precisely because its indebtedness to Chinese ideas is more tenuous, and thus its idiosyncratic composition demonstrates Jakuchū's penchant for expressing his ideas according to his own inclinations. Especially notable, the orientation of the gnarled vine runs counter to the general tradition, in which the vine hangs down from above in a more or less continuous, interrelated manner, as seen in works such as the fine anonymous Ming piece reproduced in *Kokka* 861, and in another done by Wang Liang-ch'en in the Freer Gallery of Art, Washington, D.C. Instead, the twisting, convoluted forms of the vine in the Shin'enkan piece descend from the lower right and then meander upward in stages, departing from the format entirely at one point before reappearing to continue capriciously across the top of the picture plane. Moreover, the composition seems to be a combination of several small pictorial schemes, and the components of the vine, leaves, and grapes are grouped in more or less independent clusters, rather than in the interconnected, flowing manner characteristic of Chinese compositions and of Japanese works closely inspired by them. As such, some other, perhaps smaller pictorial source, such as an illustration from an *ehon* like the grapes in Shumboku's *Minchō Shiken* (FIG. 19), may have inspired the artist to produce the early Shin'enkan piece.

It has already been observed that Jakuchū may have studied during his youth under the Osaka artist Ōoka Shumboku. Shumboku's lineage and position in the history of Japanese painting during the eighteenth century are somewhat ambiguous, for although he is routinely grouped with the Kanō school, his chief

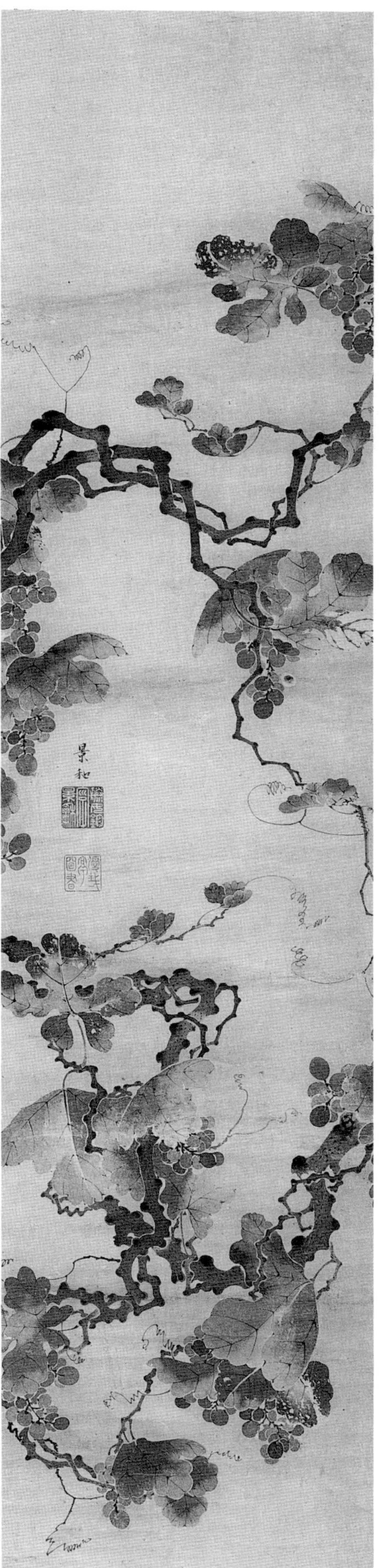

FIG. 32
Grapes, n.d.

Los Angeles County Museum of Art, Shin'enkan Collection

efforts seem to have been devoted not as much to his creativity as a painter as to compiling pictorial materials for his many *ehon*. His motivation is likely to have been not only scholarly, inspired by the search for prototypes from China and Japan, but also pragmatic, for the manuals undoubtedly generated substantial income for him.

The *ehon* compiled by Shumboku and other contemporaries, such as Tachibana Morikuni, also an Osaka artist with Kanō training, are generally of a handy, uniform size. If vertical in form, they measure about 9 to 10½ inches in height and 7 inches in width. A variety of spatial divisions can be seen in their pictorial format. The pages were occasionally subdivided into smaller divisions in order to increase the number of subjects, but by far the most common arrangements consist of one vertically oriented illustration per page or a continuous composition extending horizontally across two facing pages.

A number of the illustrations are miniaturized linear interpretations of noted works in temples or private collections that may not have been easily accessible to view (such as the cranes by Wen Cheng, FIG. 17); others introduced the self-taught artist to a broad range of conventional iconographic subject matter inherited from various artistic lines of earlier centuries, such as bird-and-flower motifs and didactic figural subjects drawn from Chinese (and to a lesser extent Japanese) folklore, mythology, and history. These illustrations, which could be copied by novices or used for reference by more advanced artists, performed a valuable, though as yet not generally recognized, role in the evolution of eighteenth- and nineteenth-century Japanese painting. For example, Sōga Shōhaku occasionally relied on anecdotal figural illustrations from *ehon* for the subject matter in his works. Other painters, most likely including the young Jakuchū, with differing artistic preoccupations and interests, were also inclined to draw on *ehon* illustrations of bird-and-flower subjects for inspiration. A period of tutelage under Shumboku would have provided Jakuchū with knowledge of the actual whereabouts of important Chinese and Japanese paintings while familiarizing him with the subjects compiled in the *ehon*.

As noted, many of the illustrations in the *ehon* consist of a full page (or two) devoted to a given subject; others focused on a portion of some natural form in order to explore its quintessential nature at close range. Illustrations such as these, in which a single entity, such as a plant or animal, monopolizes the work or where a particular detail is represented, are inherently more appropriate to the limited format and small scale of *ehon* than are the constricted linear interpretations of full-size paintings. These intimate illustrations provided the artist with a diverse inventory of exotic and familiar flora and fauna that he could, in turn, combine according to his own proclivities into a larger, more comprehensive composition. This process might be viewed simply as one of pictorial selection and addition, in which compatible components were integrated into more ambitious compositions of larger dimensions. *Ehon* illustrations were emulated by Japanese painters in ways that varied according to their training and experience, and the interpretations range widely from direct copies to more creative depictions that often modified the model considerably, sometimes to a degree that makes it difficult to discern the original pictorial relationship. In general, it seems axiomatic that artists of lesser ability must have felt a sense of security in conforming to the formulas of the past, as opposed to men of true talent, who were inclined to persevere in the exploration of their own unique vision.

Ehon were undoubtedly less relevant to young painters fortunate enough to train in an atelier under the direct supervision of an established master, and who not only received direction, technical guidance, and critical evaluation of their work, but also had immediate access to the pictorial archives of the master and his school, such as working sketches and preliminary ink renderings of masterpieces or of other works that had never reached fruition. For novice artists training in traditions with historic roots and a reputation of artistic accomplishment—such as the Kanō, Rimpa, Maruyama-Shijō, Unkoku, and Ukiyo-e schools—instruction and original materials were conveniently at hand; the curriculum usually consisted of a protracted apprenticeship devoted to repeated copying of prototypes and working sketches, a routine designed to intimately familiarize the neophyte with the styles, subjects, and methods of execution that defined the school and that set it apart as a unique pictorial tradition. For individuals who lacked any formal affiliation or those whose work under an established teacher was only of brief duration, progress in acquiring artistic proficiency necessitated conscientious effort to see famous pieces wherever possible, together with a commitment to refining an expressive vision and means through constant practice. For self-taught artists, *ehon* would have been a valuable source of subjects, conceptual alternatives, and instructive suggestions about painting techniques.

The didactic role of *ehon* must, of course, be viewed within the context of the times. During the seventeenth century, before the appearance of these painting manuals, ateliers tended to evolve in a more exclusive manner, and a significant period of training under a master and the resulting recognition as a member of the school was of primary importance to the career of any aspiring painter. During the eighteenth century, however, new modes of expression made their appearance in Japanese painting. Some were introduced to Japan from abroad, and others were conceived by talented native artists who used their grounding in one of the traditional schools as a foundation for creating distinctive, neoteric styles. The atelier system still flourished (and some new schools were established), but the domination they exercised over the fortunes of individual artists gradually weakened, and this encouraged enterprising individuals to work independently, searching for their own expressive means. This new spirit of innovation and independence is one of the hallmarks of Japanese painting during the eighteenth century, and Jakuchū is only one of a substantial number of gifted artists whose accomplishments distinguish this period as one of the most diverse, original, and expressive in the long history of Japanese art.

A private collection in Osaka includes another unusual hanging scroll thought to have been executed when Jakuchū was in his late thirties (No. 7).[33] The subject, painted in soft green and yellow tones on silk, is a section of a snake-gourd vine in summer, its leaves, tendrils, and attenuated gourds highlighted by the plant's delicate yellow blooms and animated by the presence of a lively cast of insects, each of which moves in and around the plant in its own distinctive manner. This environmental vignette depicts an amiable microcosm in which diminutive forms of life interact harmoniously. This serenity and gentleness is characteristic of Jakuchū's depictions of natural subjects, and it undoubtedly grows out of his own deep commitment to Buddhist beliefs, in which all forms of life are revered for their intrinsic importance in an ideal Buddhist world.

The artist's attention to detail and his preoccupation with depicting the actual, animate appearance of his subjects in a "realistic" manner is of particular interest, for Jakuchū seems to have developed this new "lifelike" mode of representation some years earlier than his younger contemporary Maruyama Ōkyo, who became known for his realistic depictions of living forms. It might also be observed that Ōkyo and his followers of the Maruyama-Shijō school in Kyoto tended, on occasion, to carry this analytical preoccupation too far, and their precise, literal representations often lack the sense of animate presence that is so essential in Jakuchū's works.

Recognition of the significance and beauty of the snake-gourd vine painting is reflected in the history of its owners. It once belonged to the *daimyō* Masuyama Sessai (1754–1819), friend and benefactor of Kimura Kenkadō. A cultured poet and writer, Sessai was also a talented amateur painter with a deep interest in materia medica, and this background must have made contemplating this painting particularly pleasurable for him. The work also belonged to the cultivated collector of paintings from the Echigo area, Imai Takudō, and later to Tomioka Tessai (1837–1924), the noted Bunjin painter from Kyoto.

Jakuchū's artistic reputation was probably already established by the time he was in his thirties, but the broader admiration for his works that evolved during the second half of his life came as a result of his *Dōshoku Sai-e* series (NO. 14 and FIG. 33). As a group, these superb polychrome paintings on silk (each of which measures 143 centimeters in height and about 80 centimeters in width) constitute the most monumental and inspired undertaking of the artist's career, and even though certain other paintings from Jakuchū's hand undoubtedly rival them in sheer beauty and creative originality, the variety of subject matter, exquisite details, and virtuosity of composition of the *Dōshoku Sai-e* scrolls, together with the engaging philosophical premise that pervades and unifies the thirty paintings, distinguish the series as his grandest, most concerted accomplishment.

Liberated from managing the Masugen when he was forty years old, Jakuchū turned enthusiastically to his painting, which he could pursue in the leisurely surroundings of his private atelier-retreat, the Shin'enkan, where most *Dōshoku Sai-e* works are likely to have been conceived. Beginning either in 1757, when he was forty-two years old, or early in 1758, Jakuchū seems to have devoted the better part of a decade to this challenging enterprise, a period during which he also completed at least two other ambitious projects as well as a number of fine individual works. By the beginning of 1761 twelve of the thirty pieces had been finished, and four years later twenty-four of the paintings, together with the iconic central triptych, were presented to the Shōkokuji, together with a document of gift. It was in this deed that the artist

FIG. 33 *Dōshoku Sai-e (Colorful Realm of Living Beings)*, c. 1757–1758—c. 1766–1770. Imperial Household Collection

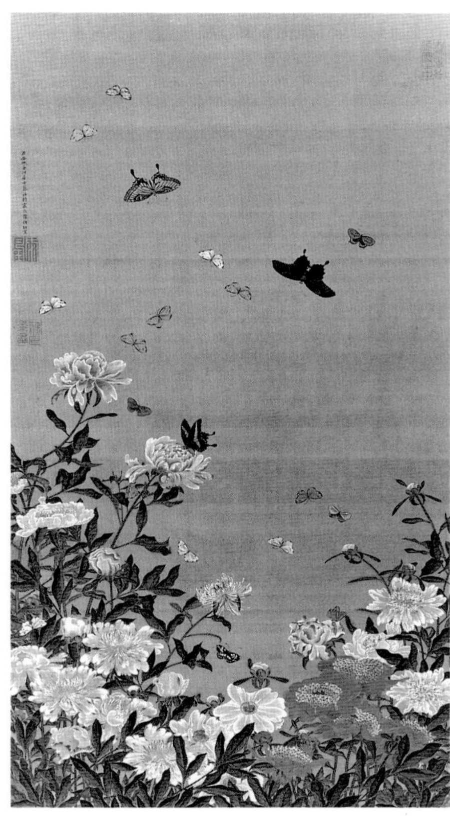

33.1 *Herbaceous Peonies and Butterflies*, c. 1757–1758

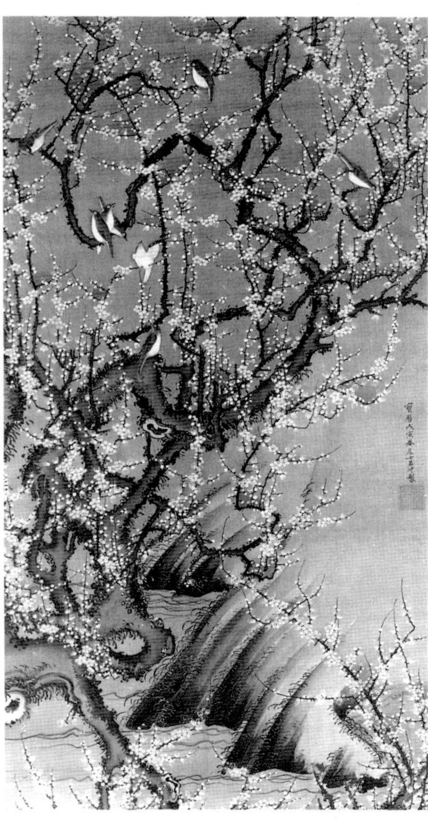

33.2 *Birds in a Blossoming Plum Tree*, 1758

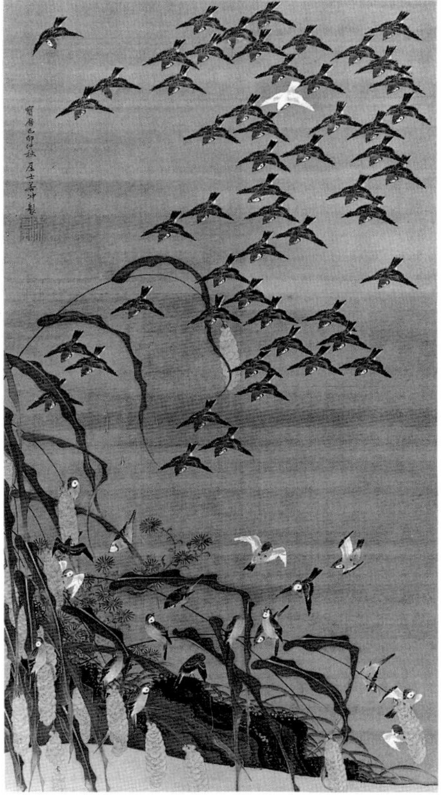

33.3 *Sparrows in Autumn*, 1759

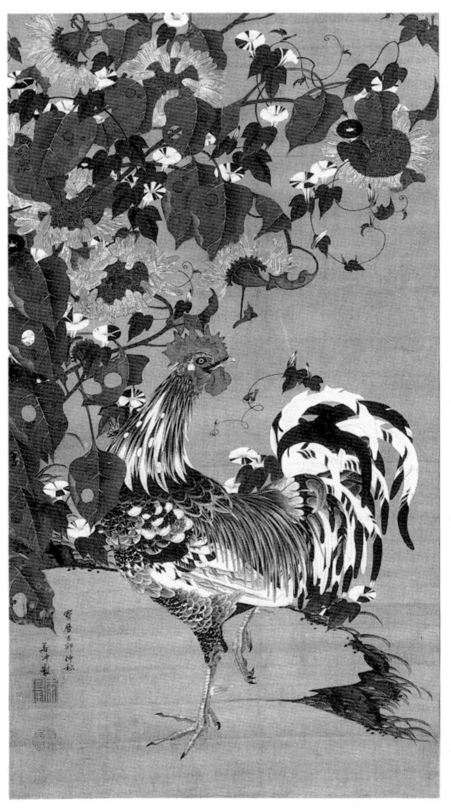

33.4 *Rooster, Sunflowers, and Morning Glories,* 1759

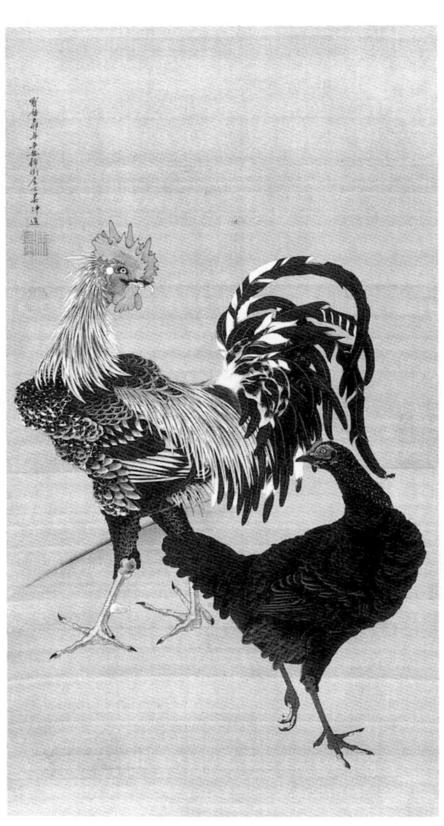

33.5 *Rooster and Hen,* 1759

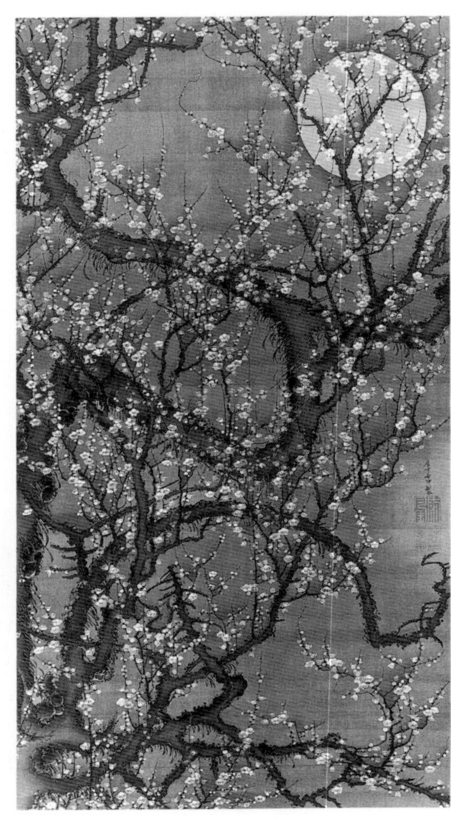

33.6 *Blossoming Plum under the Moon,* c. 1759

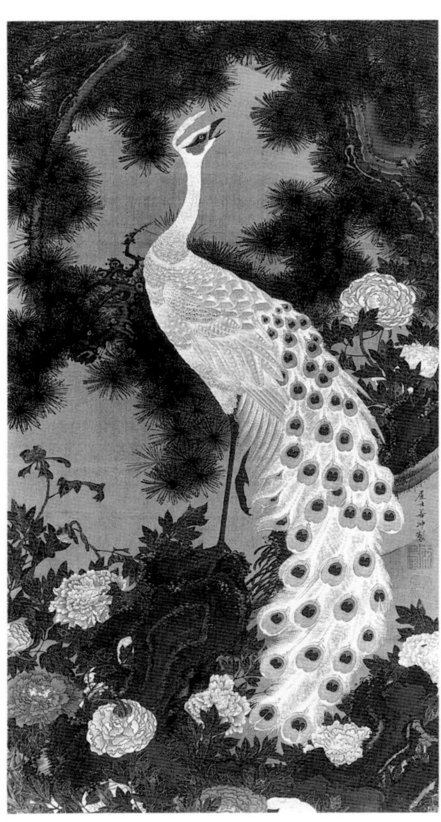

33.7 *White Peacock and Chrysanthemums under a Pine,* n.d.

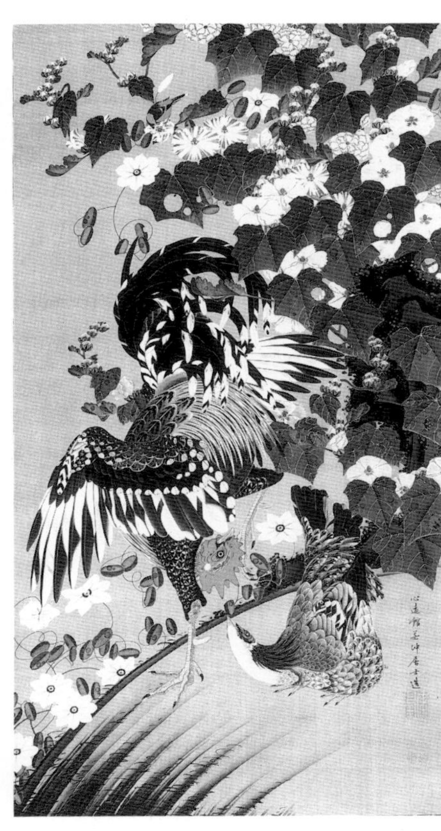

33.8 *Rose Mallows and Fowl,* n.d.

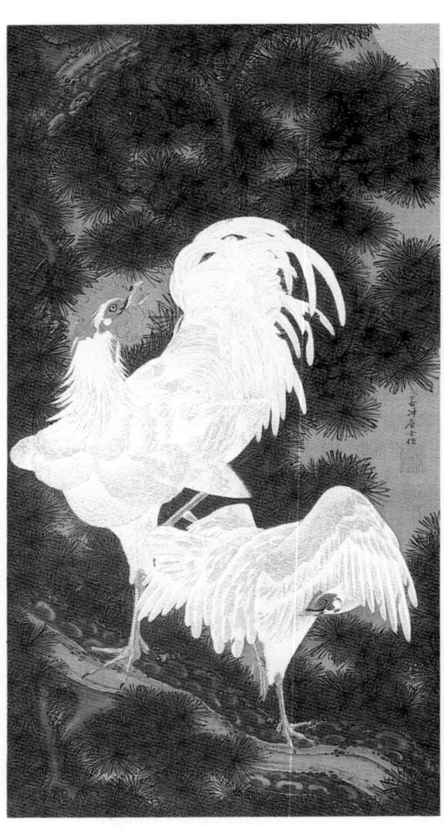

33.9 *Pair of White Fowl and a Pine,* n.d.

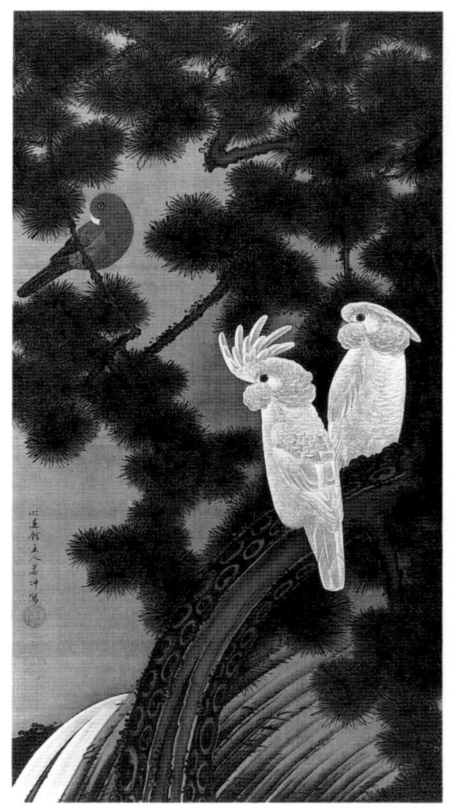

33.10 *Cockatoos in a Pine*, n.d.

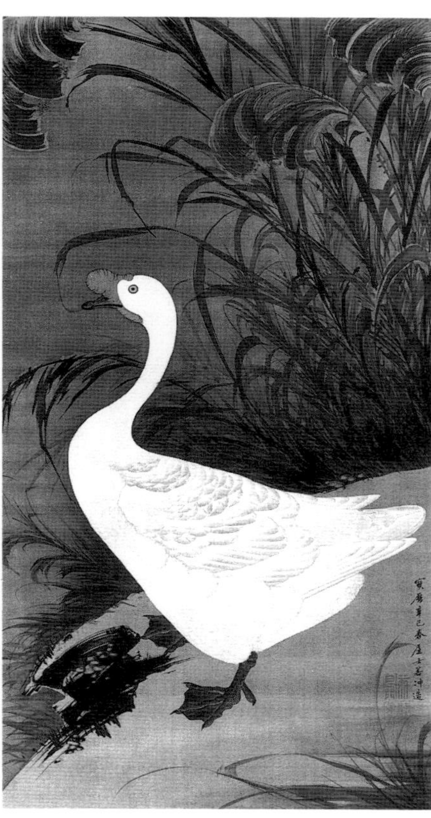

33.11 *White Goose and Reeds*, 1761

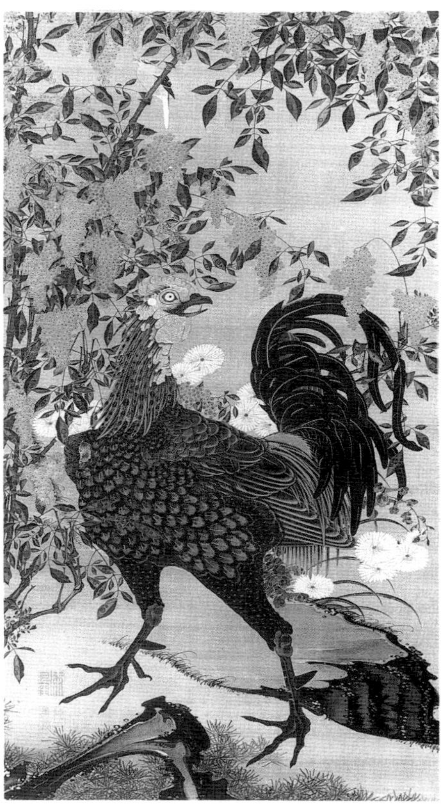

33.12 *Black Rooster and Nandin*, n.d.

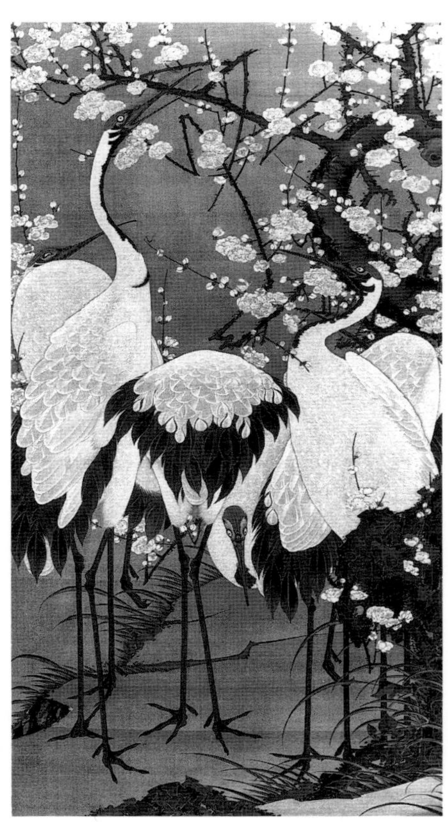

33.13 *Cranes and Blossoming Plums*, n.d.

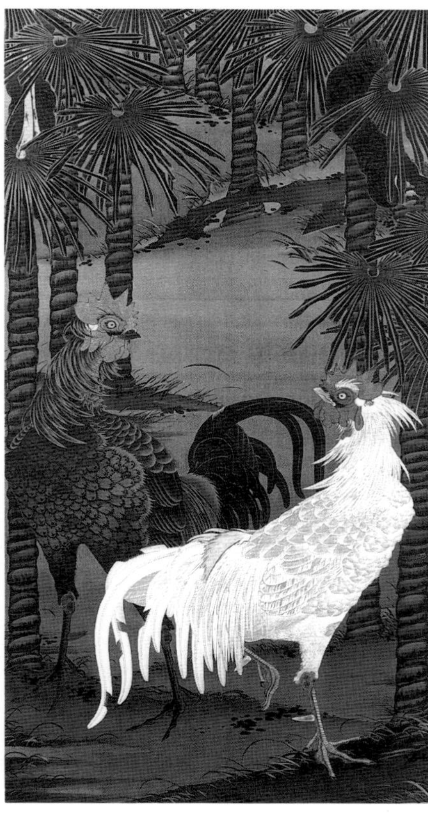

33.14 *Roosters and Hemp Palms*, n.d.

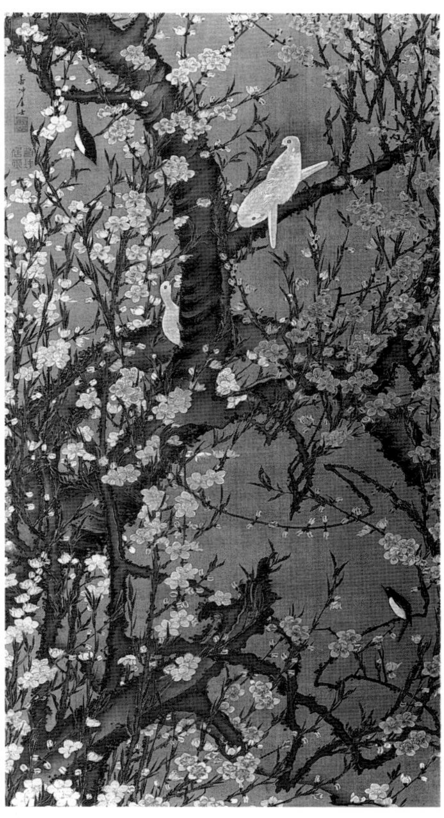

33.15 *Doves in a Blossoming Cherry*, n.d.

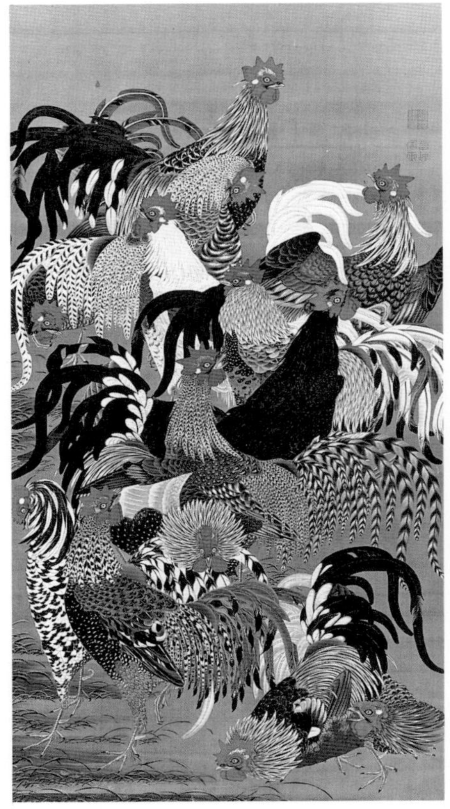

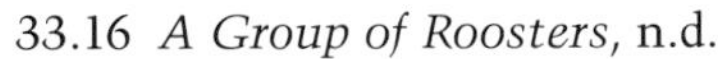

33.16 *A Group of Roosters*, n.d.

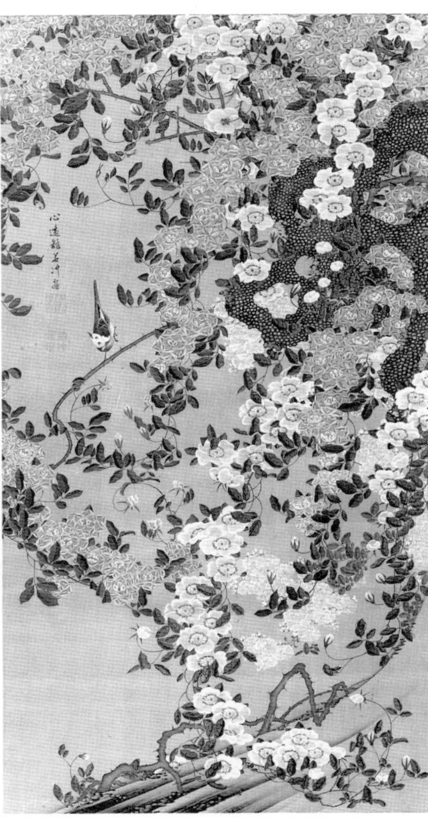

33.17 *Wagtail and Roses*, n.d.

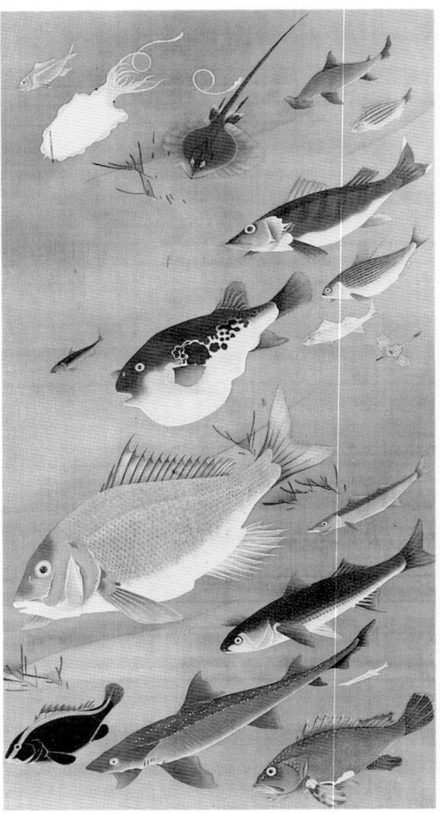

33.18 *Fish and Sea Life*, n.d.

used the title *Dōshoku Sai-e* for the first time. Just when the remaining six scrolls were executed is unclear, but the inscription on a Buddhist mortuary tablet dedicated by Jakuchū to his parents (preserved in the Kaizandō, a chapel of the Shōkokuji), which is dated to the Tenth Month of Meiwa 7 (1770), notes that the triptych and complete set of thirty paintings had already been donated to the temple by this time.[34]

Daiten made his reference to these paintings in about 1760 in the *Tō Keiwa Gakanoki*, noting that "Jakuchū intends to create thirty 'bird-and-flower' paintings and bequeath them to posterity. When fifteen had been completed I [Daiten] gave them titles and recorded the subjects."[35] Three of these works are said to have been done in monochrome ink, and it has been suggested that the artist's initial intention was to create a series in which both polychrome and monochrome works were represented. That all thirty pieces in the final *Dōshoku Sai-e* set were done in color indicates, however, that Jakuchū abandoned this plan, if indeed there ever was one.

The general sequence of their execution was proposed by Professor Akiyama Teruō in 1926, when he published the results of his extensive research on the series, *Gyomotsu Jakuchū Dōshoku Sai-e Sei-ei*,[36] in conjunction with an exhibit at the Tokyo Imperial Museum at Ueno, where, for the first time, the entire series was displayed in a public institution. The subjects are as follows:[37]

1. *Herbaceous Peonies and Butterflies* (FIG. 33.1)
2. *Birds in a Blossoming Plum Tree* (dated Hōreki 8 [1758]; FIG. 33.2)
3. *Mandarin Ducks in Snow* (dated Second Month of Hōreki 9 [1759]; NO. 14.1)
4. *Sparrows in Autumn* (dated Eighth Month of Hōreki 9 [1759]; FIG. 33.3)
5. *Rooster, Sunflowers, and Morning Glories* (dated Eighth Month of Hōreki 9 [1759]; FIG. 33.4)
6. *Hydrangeas and Fowl* (dated autumn of Hōreki 9 [1759]; NO. 14.2)
7. *Rooster and Hen* (dated Hōreki 9 [1759]; FIG. 33.5)
8. *Blossoming Plum under the Moon* (FIG. 33.6)
9. *White Peacock and Chrysanthemums under a Pine* (FIG. 33.7)
10. *Rose Mallows and Fowl* (FIG. 33.8)
11. *Pair of White Fowl and Pine* (FIG. 33.9)
12. *Cockatoos in a Pine* (FIG. 33.10)
13. *White Goose and Reeds* (dated spring of Hōreki 11 [1761]; FIG. 33.11)
14. *Black Rooster and Nandin* (FIG. 33.12)
15. *Cranes and Blossoming Plums* (FIG. 33.13)
16. *Roosters and Hemp Palms* (FIG. 33.14)
17. *Fish in a Lotus Pond* (NO. 14.3)

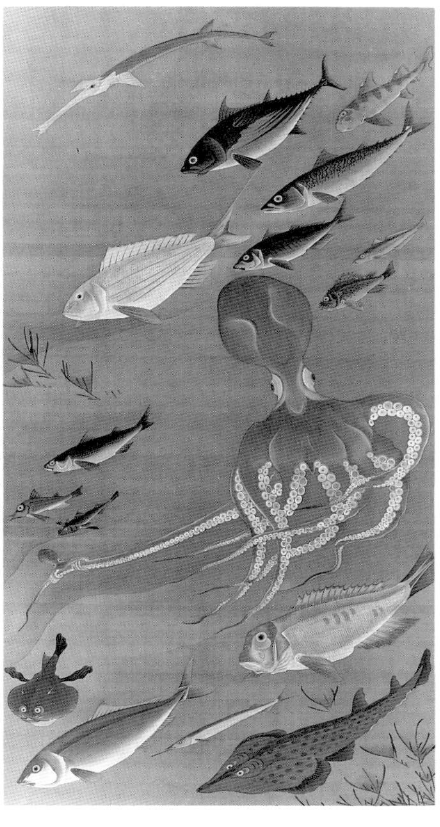

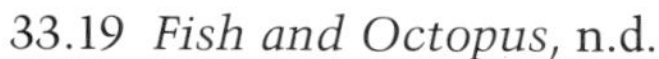

33.19 *Fish and Octopus*, n.d.

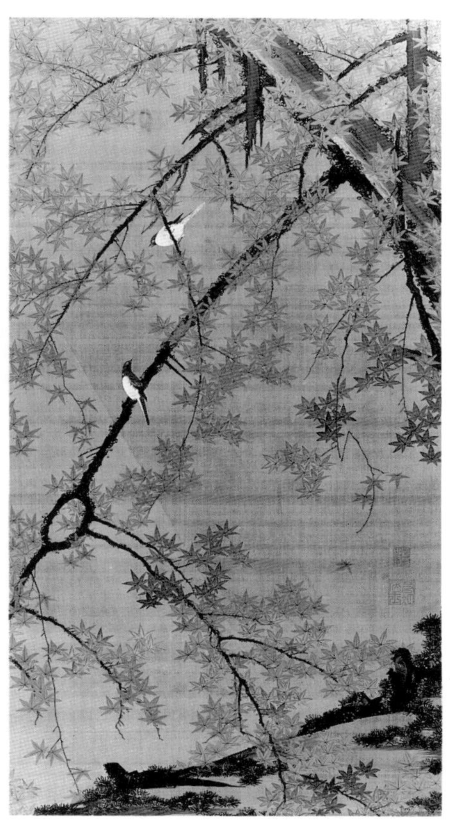

33.20 *Birds and Autumn Maples*, n.d.

18. *Doves in a Blossoming Cherry* (FIG. 33.15)
19. *Golden Pheasants in Snow* (NO. 14.4)
20. *A Group of Roosters* (FIG. 33.16)
21. *Wagtail and Roses* (FIG. 33.17)
22. *Birds and Peonies* (NO. 14.5)
23. *Insects and Reptiles at a Pond* (NO. 14.6)
24. *Shellfish* (NO. 14.7)
25. *White Phoenix and Pine* (NO. 14.8)
26. *Wild Goose and Snow-covered Reeds* (NO. 14.9)
27. *Fish and Sea Life* (FIG. 33.18)
28. *Fish and Octopus* (FIG. 33.19)
29. *Birds and Chrysanthemums by a Stream* (NO. 14.10)
30. *Birds and Autumn Maples* (FIG. 33.20)

The first twelve pieces (of which six are dated in the inscriptions) are thought to be the twelve polychrome pieces mentioned by Daiten and, therefore, to have been executed before the spring of 1761. The first one on the list, because of the similarity of its inscriptions and its calligraphic style to that of other pieces executed between about 1755 and 1757, is presumed to be the first *Dōshoku Sai-e* painting completed.

In summary, Jakuchū probably produced the first twelve paintings in a period of about three years; completed twelve more, together with the central triptych, in the next four to five years; and finished the final six sometime before 1770, perhaps as early as late 1766.[38] Twelve of the paintings, together with the triptych, were displayed in the abbot's quarters of the Shinnyoji subtemple of the Shōkokuji in the spring (Fourth Month) of 1766, by which time the remaining twelve pieces most likely had been completed but as yet had not been backed or mounted. This task was finished in the following months, however, for all twenty-four scrolls were brought out and hung in the central room of the temple for an airing on the twenty-third day of the Sixth Month.

According to the *Sankaryō Nikki* of the Shōkokuji,[39] the triptych and scrolls were displayed in the abbot's quarters on the seventeenth day of the Sixth Month of Meiwa 6 (1769), during the temple's annual Kakusen Memorial ceremony, and in the following years it became customary to hang the scrolls there in order that the many worshipers who attended the services might see them, a practice that must have stimulated both considerable interest in Jakuchū's artistic activities and popular admiration for his works. On these occasions, the triptych was hung on the north side of the Central Chamber, flanked by pictorially related pieces such as the *White Phoenix and Pine* and *White Peacock and Chrysanthemums under a Pine*; *Birds in a Blossoming Plum Tree* and *Blossoming Plum under the Moon*; *Mandarin Ducks in Snow* and *Golden Pheasants in Snow*; or *Wild Goose and Snow-covered Reeds* and *White Goose and Reeds*. Other related pieces were hung sequentially to the east and west, extending laterally into the adjoining Plum and Bamboo chambers. It is not certain that Jakuchū intended to create these contextually related pairs when he began the project, for not all of the pieces match up in such a manner, but he seems to have become interested in this kind of pairing as he moved into the later stages of the protracted enterprise, as evidenced by two late compositions (FIGS. 33.18, 33.19) that deal with various lively denizens of the sea.

Historically, the ceremonial and artistic convention of grouping Japanese Buddhist paintings, with a principal icon flanked by either figural depictions of traditional religious incidents, landscape scenes, or bird-and-flower themes, began in the late Kamakura period, as an outgrowth of the religious practices and philosophical preoccupations of Zen Buddhism.[40] Bilateral arrangements of this sort might consist of the most basic combination of three paintings or of larger combinations dictated by traditional Buddhist iconography, such as a Buddha flanked by Bodhisattvas or other attendants, with other subsidiary figures, such as the Sixteen Arhats, on each side. Moreover, the convention of mixing Buddhist iconic themes with evocative, synecdochic motifs—imaginative landscape settings and idyllic representations of birds, flowers and other living subjects—is a hallmark of Zen imagery.

Jakuchū's grand conception of the *Dōshoku Sai-e* series had its roots in this tradition, but it exceeded any iconographic precedent in terms of grandeur and scale. It seems to have evolved naturally out of his development as an artist, for the subject matter of earlier paintings in the series closely corresponds to that of other works produced in preceding years. For example, two works done in 1755, *White Plum Blossoms and Moon* (FIG. 26) and *Pair of Phoenixes and the Rising Sun* (NO. 9) correspond in subject and style with other early pieces such as the *Mandarin Ducks and Snow-covered Reeds* at the Shin'enkan (FIG. 34) and its larger companion work (NO. 11).[41] Indeed, some of the initial group of twelve may have been finished before the project actually began to take form in the artist's mind. Once it did, Jakuchū's deep piety and his desire to create an artistic monument of lasting significance provided the motivation necessary to bring the challenging project to fruition. It may be significant that there is a total of thirty-three paintings in the triptych and *Dōshoku Sai-e* series, for this number is of traditional importance in Buddhist thought: the Bodhisattva Kannon has thirty-three transcendental manifestations, and worship of this popular compassionate deity was widespread during the Edo period. On the other hand, as the project took shape, Jakuchū may have felt that he could not adequately express its profound theme—the harmonious interaction of diverse life forms in an ideal Buddhist universe[42]—in fewer than thirty scrolls.

Jakuchū's concern for depicting a variety of nature's inhabitants, each in its indigenous environment, was matched by his diligence in having included an equally broad sampling of trees, flowers, plants, and grasses and in having integrated these components into compositions that properly represent all the seasons. Conversely, it is also apparent that Jakuchū's selection was arbitrary, reflecting the subject matter he deemed appropriate, and that certain forms of life were excluded. Although his oeuvre does include occasional depictions of dogs (NO. 43), monkeys (FIG. 13), and tigers (FIG. 29 and NO. 28), these were doubtless inspired by Chinese pictorial precedents, and they represent departures from his main interests. However, even Jakuchū's rare portrayals of such creatures as hawks betray no sign of belligerence or ferocity—a phenomenon that reflects the artist's amiable personality and compassionate attitude toward the world.

No subject is more closely identified with Jakuchū's painting than his colorful representations of chickens. The artist depicted fowl throughout his career; nevertheless, his creative fascination with their variety, their lively movements, and their gorgeous plumage reached its greatest intensity when he was in his thirties and forties. During this period, he produced his most detailed, impressive representations of them, utilizing a broad, rich palette and working with great precision on silk. The appearance of such subjects in the *Dōshoku Sai-e* sheds light on the manner in which the series evolved, on how the artist's ideas shifted as the philosophical premise underlying the project emerged. Seven of the paintings represent either single chickens or pairs; another, a tour-de-force piece, depicts thirteen spirited birds. Significantly, there are five representations among the first twelve paintings, only three among the second twelve, and none among the last six, revealing a stronger preoccupation with fowl during the initial years of the project; a gradual, perhaps reluctant shifting away from the subject during the next five years, and the necessity, in the final six works, of expanding the range of subjects in order to express more fully the underlying Buddhist theme. The final depiction of thirteen of these sprightly birds in a single composition implies an ambivalence on Jakuchū's part; perhaps the painting was the artist's attempt at an inclusive, pragmatic solution (within the framework of the series) to his having to set aside a cherished subject in favor of other motifs.

In regard to the evolution of the *Dōshoku Sai-e* series, the earlier representations appear more closely dependent on pictorial precedent or tradition, but the later pieces exhibit a greater independence of conception as well as a greater refinement in execution and compositional complexity. As he worked in succession on these large paintings, the artist discovered new, more ingenious means of expressing spatial relationships and variations in scale and arrangement. Of equal importance, he refined further his ability to represent flora and fauna in a tangible, convincing manner, and the later compositions vibrate with a lyrical sense of life and activity.

The technical considerations involved in producing extensive compositions on silk using delicate, water-soluble pigments are formidable. Compositional modifications and repainting are precluded by the unforgiving materials, and although preliminary sketches are likely to have been made, the compositional schemes and arrangement of pictorial components had to be clearly conceived in the artist's mind before he took up his brush. Jakuchū's exceptional skill in the use of *gofun* as an undercoating for the pigments was an essential ingredient in his expressive use of color, with its rich subtleties, exuberant chromatics, and pervasive luminosity—a combination of characteristics that makes these works unique among Japanese polychrome paintings of the eighteenth century. The contents of Baisaō's calligraphy (FIG. 10) written in admiration of the *Dōshoku Sai-e* scrolls are worth restating here: "Enlivened by his hand, his paintings are filled with a mysterious spirit."

As previously noted, the large central triptych had its iconographic origins in traditional Buddhist imagery, and the artist based these paintings on specific prototypes; in his document of dedication he observed that he had "scrupulously copied them from the ingenious and unique triptych of Śākyamuni, Manjuśri, and Samantabhadra painted by Chang Ssu-kung." Chinese documentary sources on traditional painting unfortunately make no mention of this artist, but his name does appear in the late-fifteenth-century Japanese compilation the *Kundaikan Sōchōki*,[43] where depictions of "figural subjects and Buddhist and Amitabha representations" are listed under his name;[44] these categories suggest that Chang Ssu-kung may indeed have been a specialist in orthodox Buddhist devotional painting.

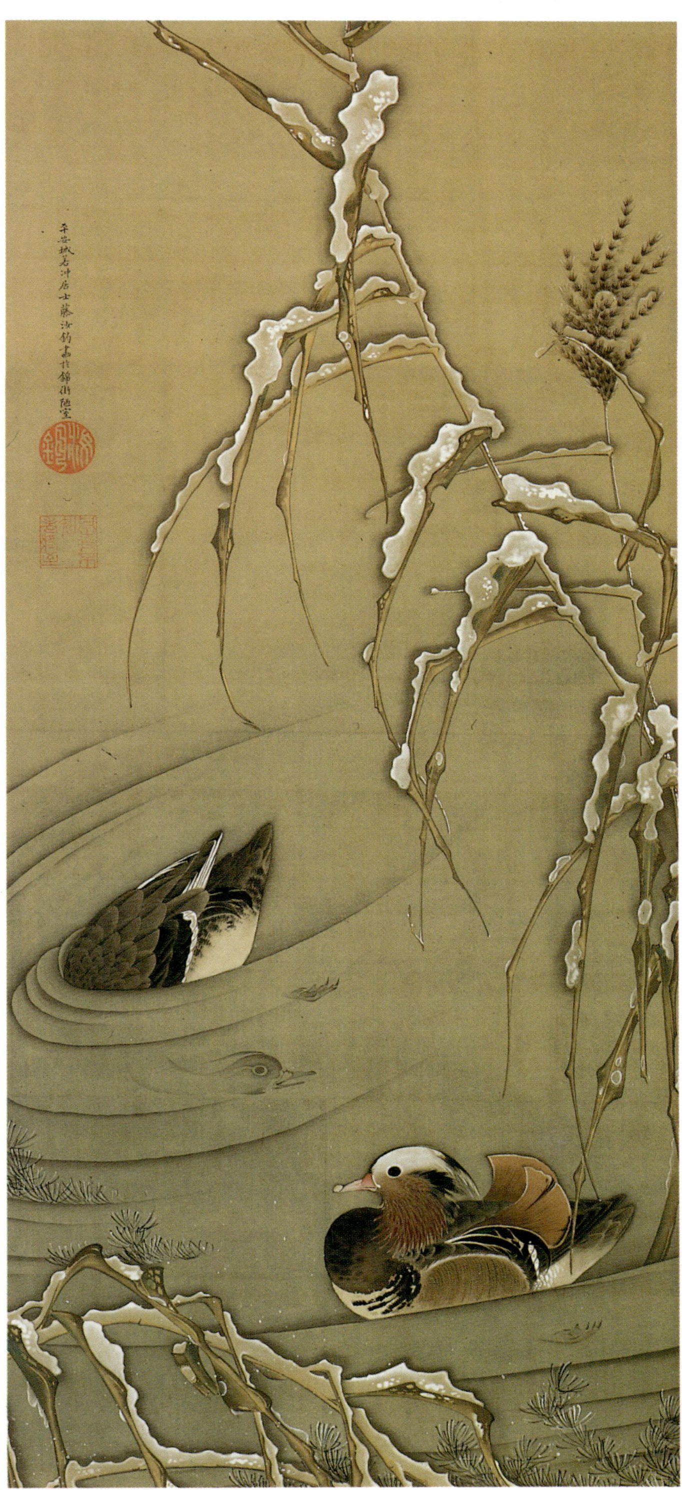

FIG. 34 *Mandarin Ducks and Snow-covered Reeds*, n.d.

Los Angeles County Museum of Art, Shin'enkan Collection

Temple collections in various regions of Japan contain a number of iconic works that have traditionally been attributed to this enigmatic artist, but none of these are signed, so their true authorship remains to be established. In the case of these and other similar Buddhist paintings, future study will likely reveal that such traditions often have their origins in that convenient deterministic process in which a venerated icon was attributed to a revered master of the remote past, out of either calculated or ingenuous motives, consequently heightening the prestige of the piece as a work of art and an object of worship.

Given the long-standing prestige of Chinese Buddhist traditions in Japanese ecclesiastical circles, it is not surprising that paintings of this sort have routinely been identified in Japanese accounts as being of Chinese provenance. Modern scholarly opinion is inclined (as in the case of the tiger painting FIG. 30) to assign such pieces to the Ming period, rather than to accept older, reverential traditions that often dated such paintings back even further, to the Yüan, the Sung, or occasionally even the T'ang period. Some specialists who have in recent years turned their attention to this body of iconic painting have observed that the execution of some of these pieces varied somewhat from that of representative Ming iconic pieces, suggesting for them a related lineage but a separate provenance. The central piece in Jakuchū's triptych, which depicts Śākyamuni enthroned, is another example of this kind of derivation. It is clear from Jakuchū's statement, quoted above, that he based his triptych on a specific prototype, which he conscientiously attempted to simulate in its particulars. No intact set of three paintings that might have served as the artist's source of inspiration is presently known, but judging from his reverential tone, he must have been deeply impressed by the original paintings. The fact that he did not trouble to identify the location of these works suggests that they were well known, and that he had the opportunity to meticulously copy them (a task that must have required considerable time) indicates that they probably belonged to a monastery in his native Kyoto, perhaps even the Shōkokuji itself, where Daiten's influence would have been valuable to the artist in gaining protracted access to the pieces.

Large, impressive Korean Buddhist icons of the Koryō period (918–1392) have been preserved in some numbers, principally in Japan, and they are among the finest religious paintings produced in the Far East. They are admired for their rich, luminous colors, intricate gold details, and linear accents, all of which contribute to an ethereal appearance that facilitates the worshiper's focus on transcendent matters.[45]

The Cleveland Museum of Art has recently acquired a painting that clarifies the origins of Jakuchū's triptych (FIG. 35). In all likelihood, this painting served as his prototype for the central image of Śākyamuni. The correspondence in proportions and details is striking, and close examination of the iconographic particulars reveals that Jakuchū's work is remarkably faithful to the original.[46] The source of the Cleveland piece is unclear, but it was recently acquired in Japan and is said to have been traditionally associated with the mysterious Chang Ssu-kung. Unfortunately, no flanking pieces have as yet come to light. Interestingly, the Cleveland piece was actually of Korean rather than Chinese manufacture, and it dates back to the Koryō period, probably the early fourteenth century. The painting exhibits several characteristics of Koryō Buddhist imagery that were faithfully simulated in Jakuchū's piece,[47] including the strict frontality of the enthroned deity, the precisely bilateral composition, and the insistently flat, nonvolumetric treatment, in which elaborate, patterned details and elegant juxtapositions of color are the primary concerns and the icon is rendered as a shimmering, abstract presence.

Despite Jakuchū's painstaking attention to accurately reproducing detail, his painting of Śākyamuni is essentially different in appearance from the Koryō prototype and others of its kind. It was, to begin with, intended as a literal rendition of the original, and this preoccupation with iconographic verisimilitude caused the artist to delineate details and contours in deliberate, constrained brush strokes—in contrast to the special life and character and the distinctive linear treatment of the flanking *Dōshoku Sai-e* paintings. In the choice and application of pigments, the differences in the two paintings are even more apparent. The appearance of any piece of the antiquity of the Cleveland work would inevitably have changed, owing to loss of pigment, chemical deterioration, and fading, and it is reasonable to assume that Jakuchū, faced with the challenge of trying to simulate an ancient painting, would have given some thought to recreating its original appearance.[48] However, the rich, ethereal quality characteristic of Koryō works is absent in Jakuchū's painting, and he applied the pigments in a flat, patterned manner that lacks the contrasts, highlights, and soft nuances of color characteristic of the earlier Korean pieces. Jakuchū's most notable departure from the original lies in his choice of pigments. Here, the viewer may sense the artist's impatience with the iconographic restrictions of the task and his desire to express his own creative

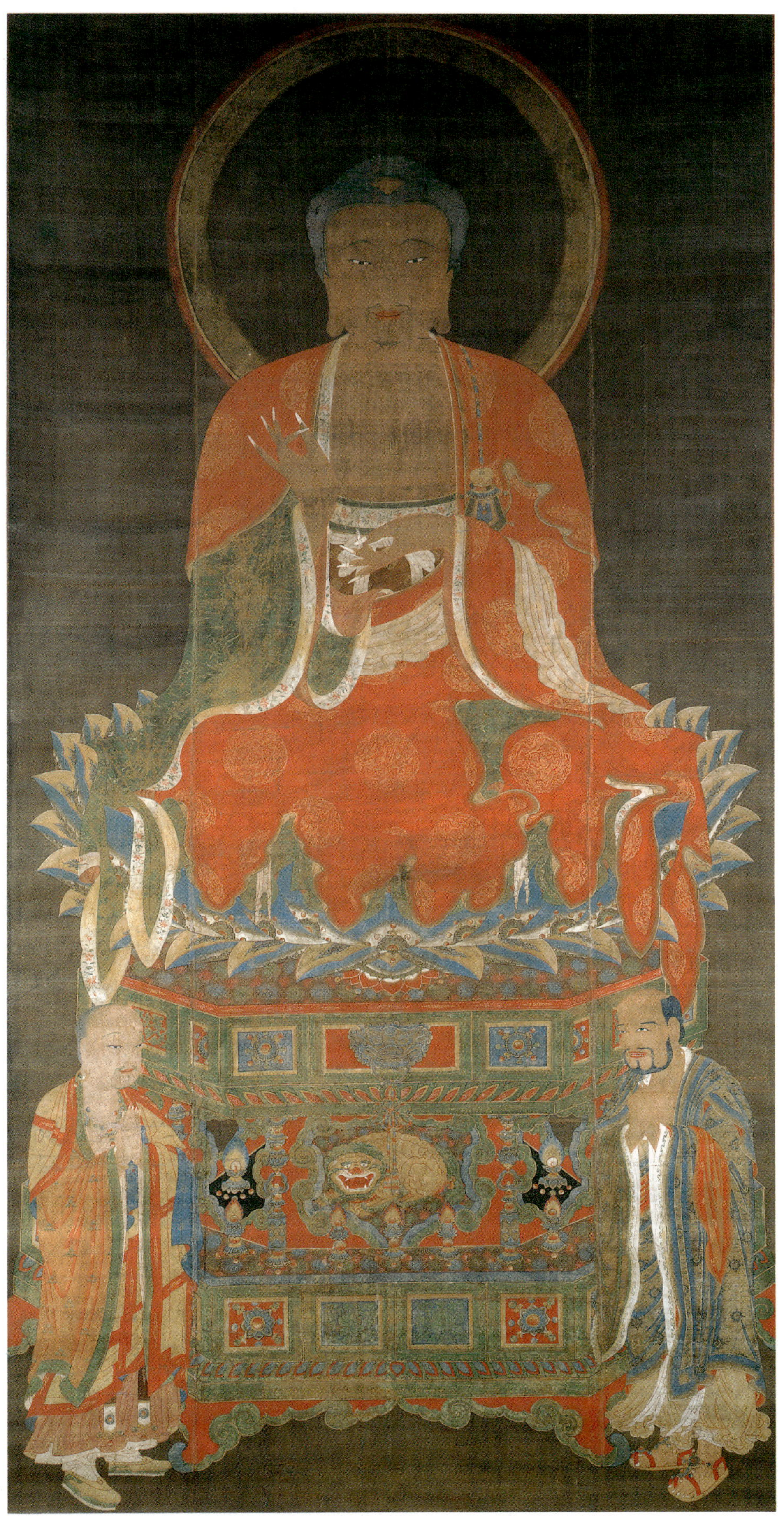

FIG. 35
Śākyamuni and Two Attendants,
Koryō period, Korea, c. 1300.
Cleveland Museum of Art

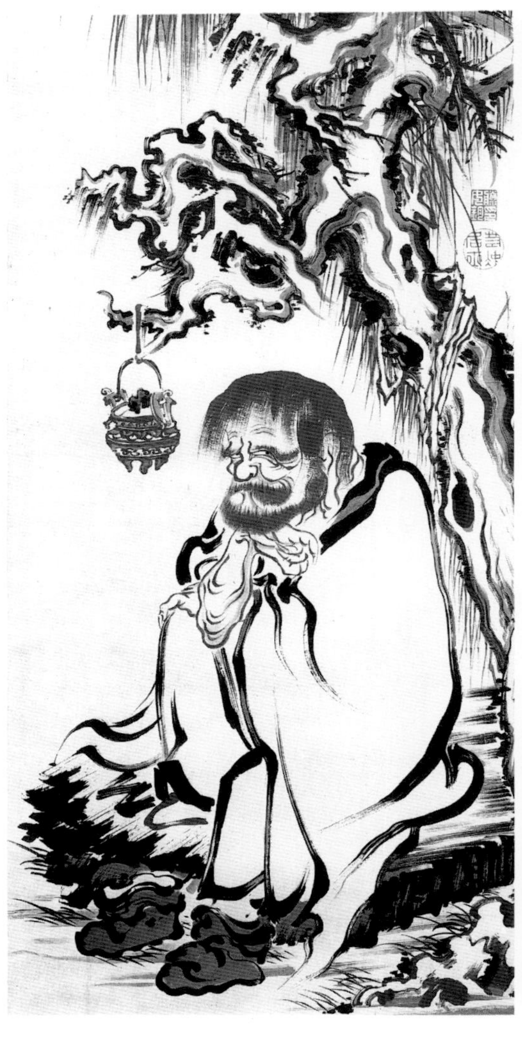

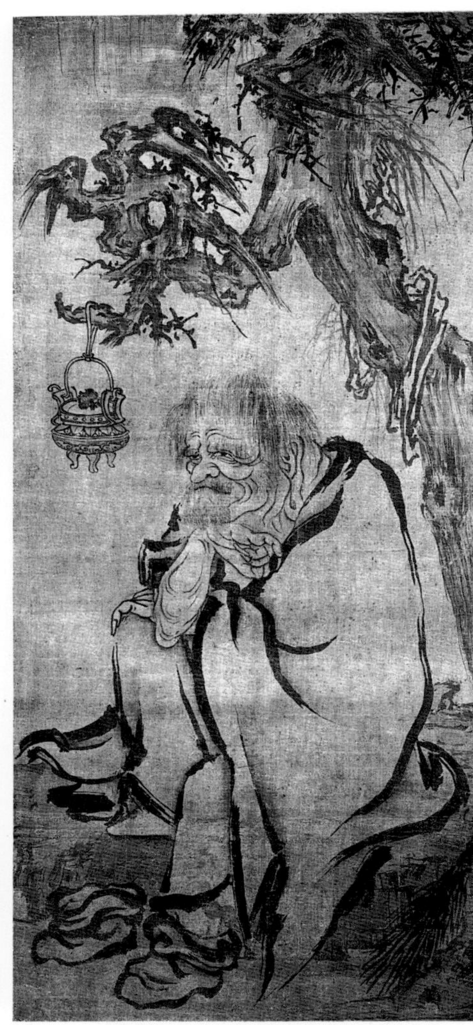

FIG. 36
Arhat, n.d.
Museum of Fine Arts, Boston

FIG. 37
Anonymous. *Zengetsu Daishi*, fourteenth century.
Fujita Museum, Osaka

inclinations, concerns that led him not only to utilize a greater range and variety of colors, such as pinks and light blues and greens, but also to combine and juxtapose pigments according to his unique predilections. Jakuchū conceived the iconic triptych as a devotional linchpin for his grand composition of thirty-three works. Ironically, the spectator's attention is invariably drawn away from his thematic centerpiece by the wonderful mandala of flora and fauna that extends out on each side, demonstrating that the *Dōshoku Sai-e* works are unmistakably creative accomplishments of a higher and more original order.

In light of Jakuchū's devotion to Buddhist ideals and ritual, his association with many influential ecclesiastical figures, and his apparent success in gaining access to old paintings in temple collections, it is not surprising that he occasionally turned his hand to a variety of other traditional Buddhist subjects. A set of monochrome paintings with depictions of the *Sixteen Arhats*, acquired in Japan in the 1880s by William Sturgis Bigelow and now in the Museum of Fine Arts, Boston, again illustrates the artist's interest in copying such works. It is not clear where the pieces that served as Jakuchū's models were located originally, but three apparent prototypes have been preserved in the Fujita Museum, Osaka.[49] A comparison of one of Jakuchū's copies (FIG. 36) with its likely parent (an anonymous Chinese work of the Yüan period, FIG. 37) reveals a predictable indebtedness to pictorial precedent in regard to details but a significantly different inventory of idiosyncratic brushwork of the sort that is unique to Jakuchū.

In addition to the Arhat representations, the Museum of Fine Arts, Boston, has a pair of paintings depicting the Bodhisattvas Manjuśri and Samantabhadra (Japanese: Monju, Fugen), which were also acquired by Bigelow in the 1880s (FIG. 38). These two works are close monochrome copies of the left- and right-hand paintings of the celebrated polychrome triptych in the Tōfukuji monastery in Kyoto, a revered work of art traditionally attributed by the temple to Wu Tao-hsüan (also known as Wu Tao-tzu; active c. 720–760), a legendary Chinese master of the T'ang dynasty. However, like the tiger painting pre-

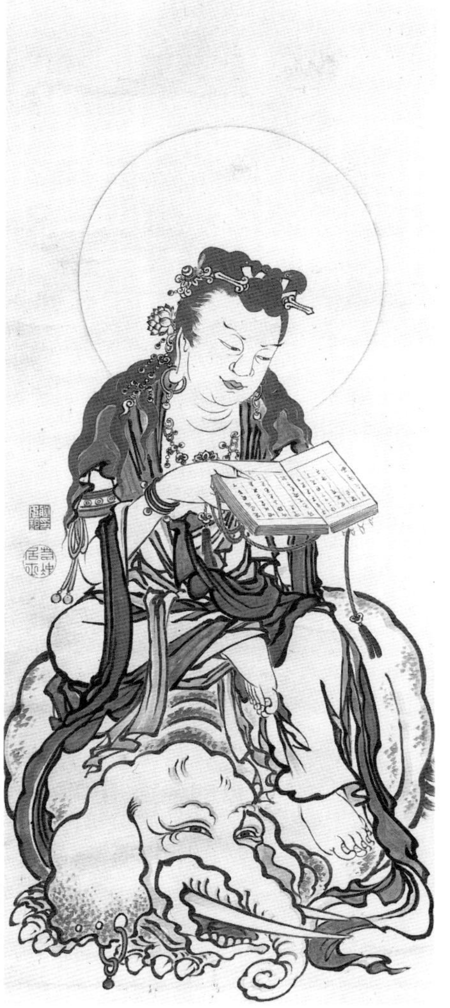
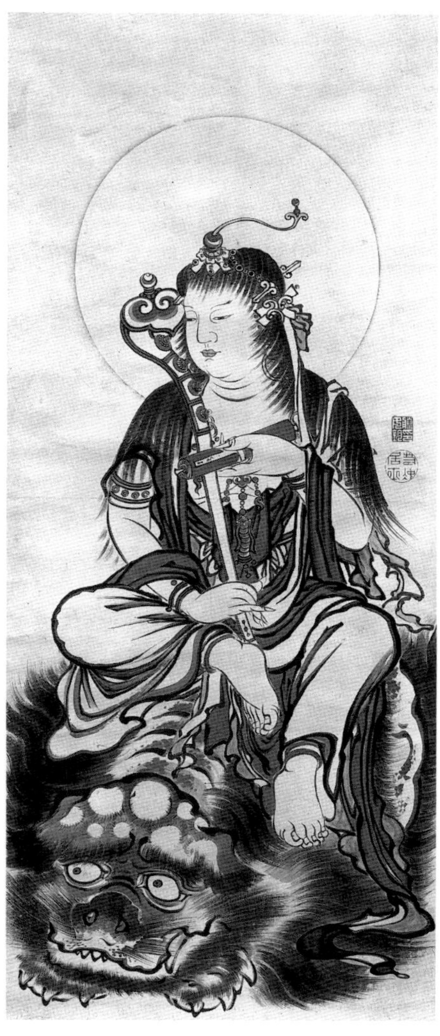

FIG. 38
The Bodhisattvas Manjuśri and Samantabhadra (Manjuśri, right; Samantabhadra, left), n.d.

Museum of Fine Arts, Boston

viously described, the Tōfukuji triptych is now generally thought to be an anonymous workshop piece from a later time, in this case, the Southern Sung period. One of the most celebrated icons in Japanese history, this triptych has been copied by native artists since medieval times, and it is no wonder that Jakuchū produced his own versions. The artist undoubtedly also did a representation of the central image of the seated Śākyamuni, although this work does not appear to have been preserved. Although there is no evidence to confirm the thesis, it is possible that the Bodhisattva paintings and the *Sixteen Arhats* originally constituted a single set,[50] as there are traditional iconographic precedents in Buddhist painting for such a combination. Moreover, the fact that the Bodhisattva paintings were executed in monochrome on *gasenshi* (a soft, absorbent Japanese paper that was a favorite of Jakuchū's and that he regularly utilized for monochrome compositions) may indicate that the artist wished them to be consistent in execution and materials with the Arhat pieces, which are analogous in their brushwork and medium—unlike the Tōfukuji pieces, which were done on silk in polychrome.

According to Buddhist tradition, Śākyamuni, the historical Buddha, resolved to renounce the vulgar world and isolate himself in the mountains in order to fast and meditate, in the hope of achieving enlightenment.[51] After following these practices in the wilderness for six years, he realized that the path of asceticism and mortification would not lead him to his goal, so he gave up his protracted retreat and returned to the world of human affairs, weary and emaciated, to seek another means of achieving his spiritual objective. The theme "Śākyamuni Returning from the Mountains" has a long history in Zen painting, going back at least as far as the Northern Sung period (960–1127) in China, and it was familiar in Japanese Zen monasteries by the early years of the Kamakura period.[52] Revered as a biographical event from the Buddha's spiritual career, the subject was traditionally depicted in a less hieratic and more human form than the more conventionalized iconic themes and was sometimes rendered in colors, but more often in monochrome ink. Fine depictions dating from medieval times that have been preserved in Japanese temples attest to the popularity of the subject among Zen devotees.[53] Jakuchū's interpretation of this motif (FIG. 39) was obviously inspired by such precedents, but unlike the artist's works described above, which are replications of specific iconic prototypes,[54] this painting appears to be a generalized interpretation.

Although Jakuchū's handling of the robe, with its leisurely, parallel curvilinear patterns, has a tenuous connection with Chinese pictorial traditions, the artist's unique, mannered treatment, with its slow, repeated passages, demonstrates his persevering search for original expressive means. This distinctive manner of depicting robes (which is also occasionally seen in the rendering of other compositional components in other paintings) is rare in Jakuchū's pieces on silk, although it is common in his paintings on paper. As noted, Jakuchū produced both color and monochrome versions of tigers (FIG. 29 and NO. 28), and this is also true for the painting *Śākyamuni Returning from the Mountains*: an impressive version in ink monochrome on *gasenshi* can be found in a private Japanese collection (FIG. 40). Surprisingly, despite the differing natures of the grounds of the color and monochrome versions, and their dissimilar reactions to an ink-laden brush, the paintings correspond closely in their linear particulars.

FIG. 41
Cranes and Pines (detail), 1759.
Ninoma (Second Chamber), Rokuonji, Kyoto

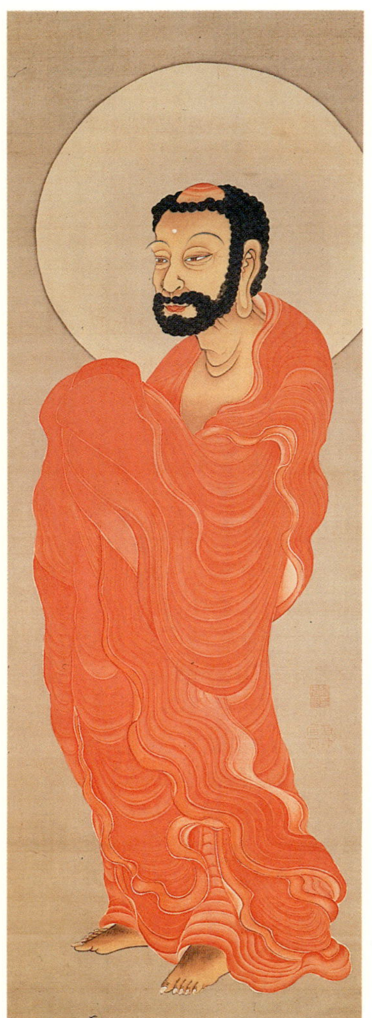

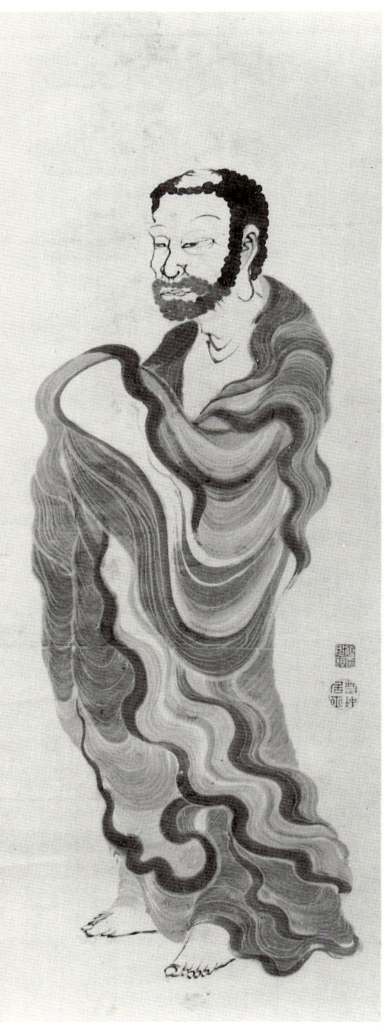

FIG. 39 *Śākyamuni Returning from the Mountains*, n.d.
Private collection, Hyōgo Prefecture

FIG. 40 *Śākyamuni Returning from the Mountains*, n.d.
Private collection, Hyōgo Prefecture

The same sort of soft, repeated curvilinear strokes may be seen in Jakuchū's depiction of another popular traditional Zen motif, *Bodhidharma Crossing the Yangtze on a Reed* (NO. 20).[55] Here again, the ground is *gasenshi*, whose special absorbent qualities the artist utilized to create a distinctive pattern of evocative brush strokes.

Jakuchū's interest in depicting traditional Buddhist iconic subjects in a more or less literal and faithful manner apparently began in about his fiftieth year (when the Śākyamuni triptych was presented to the Shōkokuji) and extended into his sixties. He continued to represent Buddhist subjects in the following years, but shifted his attentions away from fixed iconographic types, with their creative restrictions,

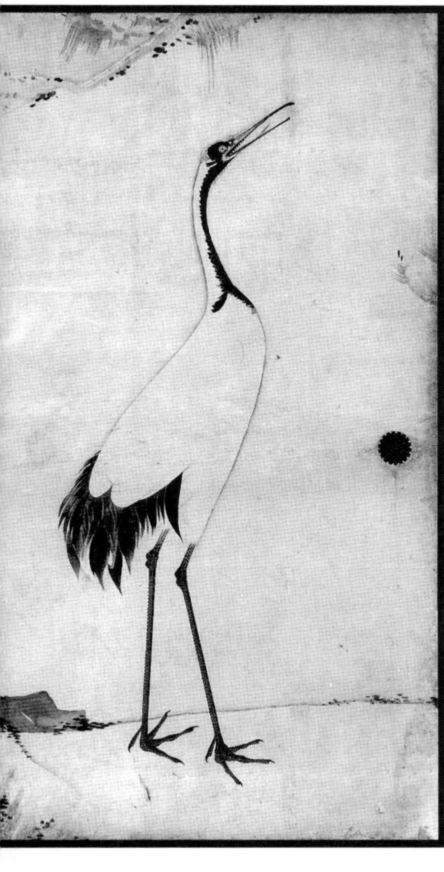
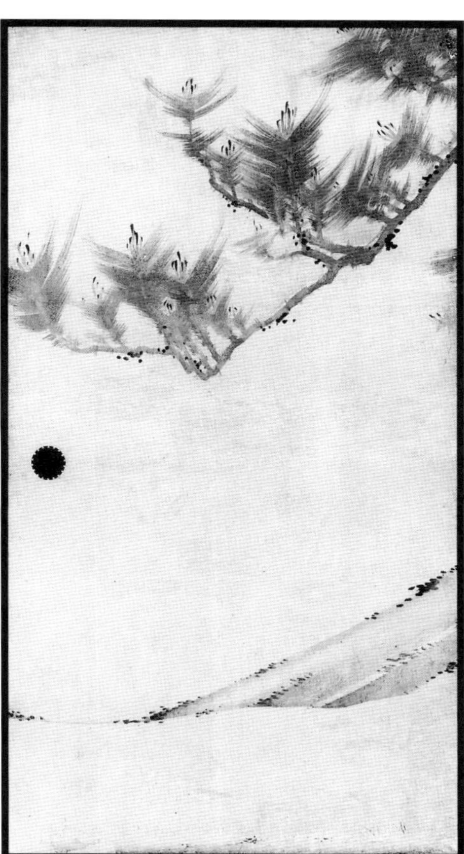
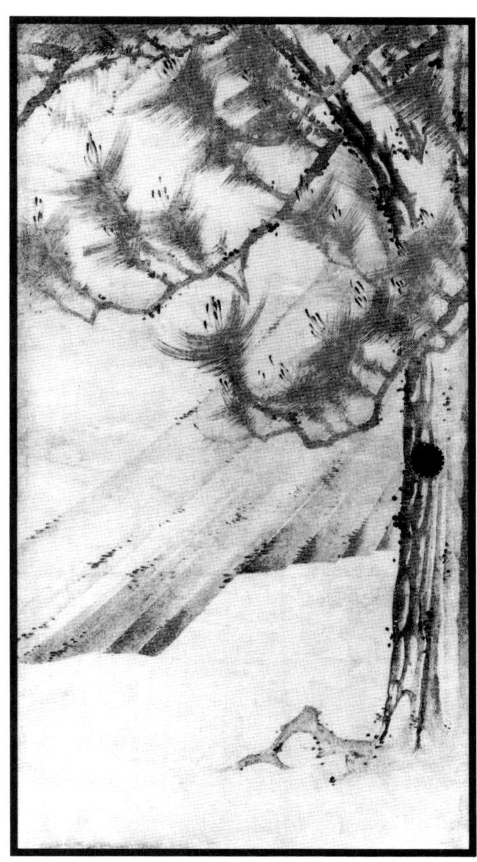

and toward more personal and inventive images, utilizing the challenging expressive potential of monochrome ink.

In 1759, while Jakuchū was working industriously on the first group of *Dōshoku Sai-e* paintings, he determined to undertake another challenging project, a large series of monochrome compositions on sliding screens and wall panels for the Rokuonji, the famous Rinzai Zen temple. Like the Shōkokuji, the Rokuonji had been founded in the late fourteenth century by the Ashikaga Shogun Yoshimitsu. The Rokuonji paintings, which include some works on sliding screens and others affixed to walls, were created to embellish five rooms in the Dai-shoin. This structure had been erected about eighty years earlier, during the Empō period (1673–1681) but seems not to have had any screen paintings commissioned for it until 1759, when the priest Ryūmon Shōyū engaged Jakuchū to produce works for all five rooms. Of the five rooms in the Dai-shoin that contain Jakuchū's paintings, three are arranged from west to east: the Ichinoma (First Chamber), with compositions of grape vines on the walls of the Chigaidana (shelved alcove) and the Tokonoma alcoves, and on the northern wall (all at the western end of the room), as well as on sliding screens (NOS. 16.1, 16.2); the Ninoma (Second Chamber), with compositions of cranes and pines on sliding screens (NOS. 16.3, 16.4 and FIG. 41); and the Sannoma (Third Chamber), with compositions of banana trees and rocks under the moon on the wall of the Tokonoma on the east (FIG. 42), and of banana trees and *haha-chō* (black birds) on sliding screens (FIG. 43). The other two rooms extend laterally to the south: the Yonnoma (Fourth Chamber), with depictions of chickens and chrysanthemums, and of begonias on sliding screens (NOS. 16.5, 16.6); and the Sayanoma (Narrow Chamber), with depictions of bamboos (NOS. 16.7, 16.8).

The grape composition on the four screens in the First Chamber is much admired for its ingenious spatial conceptions and for the innovative qualities of its brushwork. Comparison with the two ink paintings from the Sōdōji (NO. 3) done about seven years earlier reveals how the artist had continued to experiment with techniques and materials. In the earlier paintings the brushwork and methods of utilizing ink are more closely indebted to traditional techniques by virtue of their delicate accents, precise lines, and formularized shaded washes; in addition, anatomical accuracy was a central preoccupation, as it continued to be in the polychrome *Dōshoku Sai-e* pieces. By contrast, the Rokuonji grape paintings demonstrate the artist's evolution of a new expressive means utilizing the soft, absorbent qualities of *gasenshi*; on this paper, ink washes tend to gradually expand and diffuse, and to dry more slowly than on other papers traditionally used for painting. Jakuchū exploited this characteristic for his own purposes by initially brushing in broader components (such as the grape leaves in this composition) with watery ink washes, and then, while the paper was still moist, lightly adding the fine, animating details (such as the veins and imperfections of the leaves, and other natural minutiae) using a thin brush saturated with darker ink. In addition, he deliberately dropped ink directly onto certain areas of the still-moist paper, creating small, contrasting circular areas that effectively simulate the insect-eaten portions of leaves. Even though fidelity to the literal forms of nature preoccupied Jakuchū less here than in the Sōdōji paintings, his new technique (and his inspired conception) created an even more convincing impression of the essence, the innate life, of the plant. It is likely that Jakuchū's idea of decorating an entire room with grape vines had no precedent, and in any case it demonstrated the artist's inventiveness and imagination.

Two separate compositions depict cranes and pine trees in the Second Chamber; each of four screen panels contains a single crane and a yellow pine. Tsuji Nobuo has suggested the likelihood that for these works Jakuchū was inspired directly by Wen Cheng's crane paintings, preserved in the Shōkokuji (FIG. 17);[56] the general similarity in pose and anatomical details of the standing cranes, with their necks and heads arched upward at an oblique angle, seems to bear this out. Both paintings are enlivened by light yet incisive brushwork and are filled with a compelling sense of space enveloping the inventive representations of natural forms. Jakuchū's idiosyncratic handling of the pine trees, with their mannered bark and contours, and the distinctive treatment of the pine needles are unique, as are the evocative yet spare methods with which the ground lines and rock forms were executed. The artist ingeniously created a persuasive impression of stiff, spiky pine needles by using a thin flat brush (*hake*), applying the ink sparingly and quickly before it had a chance to sink into the paper and become blurred. A passage from Daiten's *Tō Keiwa Gakanoki* apparently refers to this innovation: "He renders the pine needles entirely with *hake*, and this is a remarkable new idea."[57]

The handling of the cranes in the Rokuonji paintings contrasts with the detailed, naturalistic representations in the *Dōshoku Sai-e*; the former were executed concisely and economically, with a minimum of natural detail—a conceptual approach that exemplifies the expressive means and aesthetics of Zen-inspired monochrome painting. The date on the extreme left of the composition on the east side of the chamber (FIG. 41) reveals that the piece was completed in 1759; the artist signed the piece "Koji Jakuchū" (Buddhist Layman Jakuchū), noting in the inscription: "In the path between the pines, I look down and then gaze upward; enlightenment comes to me, and my heart is in the heavens."

On the east wall of the Third Chamber, the dramatic depiction of a large, luxuriant banana tree (which stands about two meters high) under a bright full moon (FIG. 42) shows another aspect of the artist's passion for exploiting the expressive potential of monochrome ink. The brushwork in the leaves ranges from heavy, dark passages executed with quick, insistent parallel strokes to contrasting areas, where the leaves were delineated in light, soft, nebulous strokes that are hardly visible. These extremes, repeated in the rock forms and ground contours, balance and enliven the composition, which is filled with a mysterious aura of infinite space and with

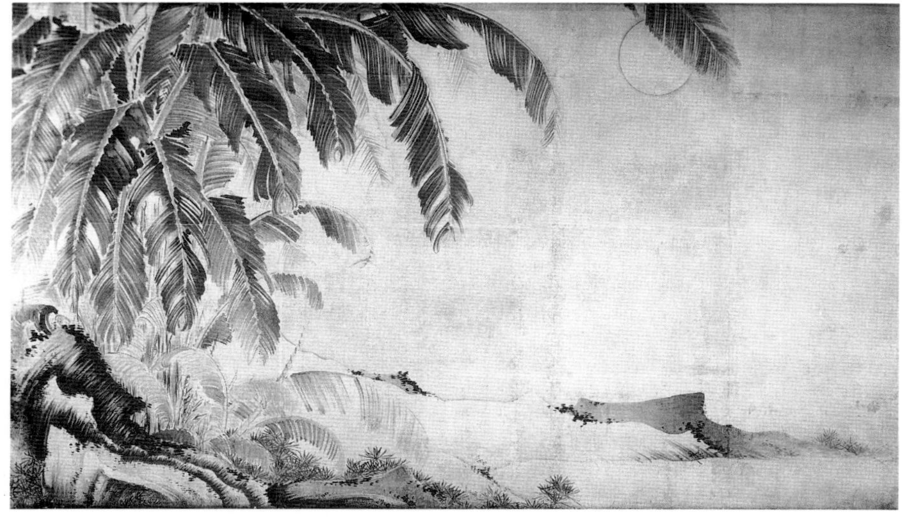

FIG. 42
Banana Trees and Rocks under the Moon, 1759.

Sannoma (Third Chamber), Tokonoma (alcove), Rokuonji, Kyoto

FIG. 43 *Banana Trees and* Haha-chō (detail), 1759. Sannoma (Third Chamber), Rokuonji, Kyoto

pictorial diversity. The original manner in which Jakuchū injected the abbreviated extremity of a banana leaf at the top, partially overlapping the moon, further heightens the work's enigmatic atmosphere.

Facing this composition and running perpendicular to it on the right are two four-panel compositions with *haha-chō* and banana leaves, subjects frequently depicted by Kumashiro Yūhi and other members of the Nagasaki school who drew their inspiration from the style of Shen Nan-p'in. The brushwork in two of the panels, which show a jaunty bird perched atop a bizarre rock, with two banana fronds extending diagonally to the right (FIG. 43), provides further evidence of the artist's creative evolution and growing inventory of idiosyncratic expressive means. Here, the economy of compositional components, the incisive execution, and the innovative combination of abbreviated forms set against blank space attest to Jakuchū's superb command of monochromatic ink painting.

Two four-panel sets of screens face each other on the north and south sides of the Fourth Chamber: *Cock and Chrysanthemums* and *Begonias* (NOS. 16.5, 16.6). The latter piece is also very personal in conception, with soft forms of the plants concentrated along the very bottom of the screens, in what is compositionally a reversed, more restrained version of the grape-vine painting in the First Chamber, in

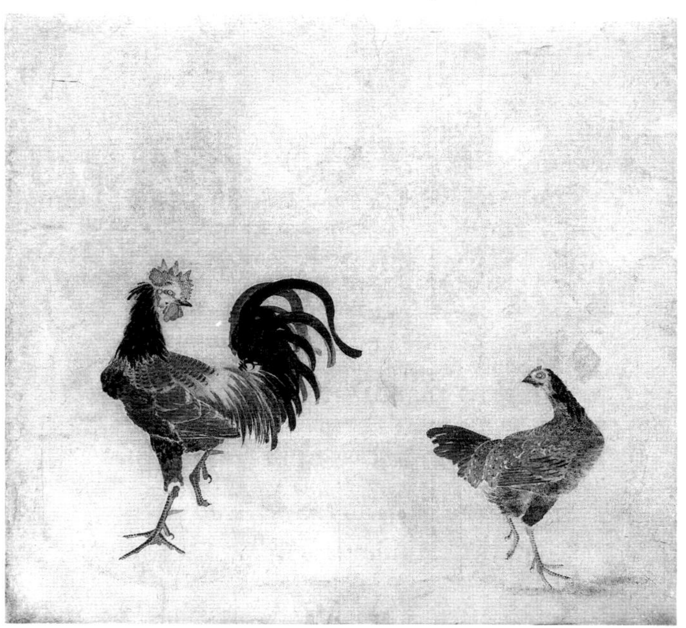

FIG. 44 *Chickens*, 1759.
Yonnoma (Fourth Chamber), Rokuonji, Kyoto

which all the components are grouped along the top of the screens. The east wall of the Fourth Chamber also has a depiction of a cock and hen (FIG. 44), done in small, precise, soft brush strokes that very effectively emulate the essential quality of birds' feathers. Each bird stands on one leg and turns back to look at the other; interestingly, the poses of subjects in one of the

Dōshoku Sai-e paintings (FIG. 33.5) are virtually identical, but the limitations of format in the latter piece necessitated a more intimate arrangement.

The screens in the Narrow Chamber present the spectator with yet another strikingly original conception; these bamboos have no equivalent in Japanese painting (NOS. 16.7, 16.8). Here Jakuchū created graphic, abstract forms, with emphatic yet rhythmic lines representing the stalks and concentrated groupings of wet, staccato brush imprints representing the leaves. Conceptual innovation necessitated a departure from the literal forms in this work, but the artist captured the unique nature of his subject, nonetheless.

The Rokuonji paintings, which have been designated "Important Cultural Properties" by the Japanese government, constitute an impressive monument to the artist's originality at a time in his career when his ideas and expressive methods had evolved to a level at which his works stood apart from those of all his contemporaries. This is equally true for the *Dōshoku Sai-e* paintings, and these two superb accomplishments, the artist's most ambitious in vision, scale, and number, demonstrate his unique virtuosity in two great pictorial traditions: polychrome painting on silk, with its lyrical warmth and precision, and monochrome painting on paper, with its greater evocative power and expressive potential. That Jakuchū was able to concurrently produce magnificent paintings in both genres, with their disparate aesthetic premises, methods, and techniques, is remarkable. Moreover, the fact that within one year the artist produced the entire set of the Rokuonji paintings, at least five of the meticulous, time-consuming *Dōshoku Sai-e* paintings, and other works indicates that his physical resources as well as his creative abilities were then at their peak.

As noted, certain elements of the artist's style, brushwork, and subject matter are common to the *Dōshoku Sai-e* and the Rokuonji paintings. With the *Dōshoku Sai-e* pieces the artist conceived compositions on a large scale, combining a great variety of subject matter within their generous vertical formats, without the limitations of earlier, smaller polychrome pieces on silk, such as the lovely depiction of snake gourds and insects (NO. 7). Similarly, the screens and walls in the Rokuonji provided him with a broad, challenging expanse of paper surfaces on which to work out novel compositional schemes and to develop an extensive inventory of neoteric ink techniques. Freed from the fetters of lesser scale and format, Jakuchū could work in an expansive, uninhibited manner, and these paintings feature some of the painter's most original spatial arrangements.

Historically, the *Dōshoku Sai-e* paintings marked a high point in the artist's interest in rendering subject matter "naturalistically" and meticulously in color on silk. Although he occasionally turned to polychrome in later years, he shifted chiefly to monochrome ink painting sometime in his late fifties and continued to work productively in this medium for the rest of his life.

Two works that Jakuchū produced soon after he completed the Rokuonji paintings illustrate his continuing investigation of the expressive possibilities of monochromatic ink. The first piece, a large hanging scroll, with its solitary crane standing discreetly on the trunk of a yellow pine (NO. 21), is closely affiliated with the screen compositions in the Second Chamber of the Dai-shoin. At the same time, they are significantly different in conception. Whereas the Rokuonji paintings are infused with a soft, mysterious atmosphere, the hanging scroll is invigorated by emphatic brushwork. The Rokuonji cranes, although depicted in a spare, abbreviated manner, still convey to the viewer a sense of the birds' natural movement and appearance; however, in the hanging scroll, the artist reduced the crane to a graphic abstract form that is merely a compositional component in his dynamic spatial arrangement. He obviously based the dramatic handling of the pine tree and its needles in the scroll on pictorial precedents in the Rokuonji pieces but carried them out here more forcefully and incisively, in his evolution away from the literal depiction of nature and toward a more painterly, abstract manner of representation in his monochromatic works.

Moreover, Jakuchū adapted certain brush treatments from his ink paintings and selectively introduced them into *Dōshoku Sai-e* pieces that he was completing at about the same time. Thus, for example, in the painting of a pair of white fowl perched in a pine tree under the sun (FIG. 33.9), he treated the trunk and bark of the tree in a mannered, conceptualized way that relates directly to this same feature in the hanging scroll.

An even more distinctive kind of brushwork appears in a pair of six-panel folding screens done when Jakuchū was forty-five years of age (NO. 17). Here, the imagery is more elliptical than ever; birds, trees, flowers, and plants of the four seasons were rendered in an expeditious and cursive manner that marked a new phase in the artist's progress. The mesmerizing power of the images takes precedence over the subjects themselves, and the viewer recognizes their natural forms only as an afterthought. Because of the rapid yet sure manner of execution, the artist must have had to envision the compositions clearly before he took up his brush. However, the diverse and innovative use of ink balances the dark, assertive brushwork with elegant details that soften and harmonize the images. The artist exploited the unique qualities of *gasenshi* with obvious facility, but he concentrated on creating images chiefly through the use of dark, viscous ink, which he applied with a dry brush in order to minimize the soft, nebulous forms that occur with a water-saturated brush.

Although Jakuchū's versatility of technique is impressive in its own right, in these works his control of expressive line and wash in unique compositional schemes is of greater significance. As in the case of the hanging scroll described above, something of the rough, spontaneous use of ink in these screens seems to have been selectively utilized in a *Dōshoku Sai-e* piece: the abbreviated handling of the reeds in the composition with a white goose (FIG. 33.11), which was produced about six months later, corresponds closely with brushwork in the screens.

Two monochrome hanging scrolls, produced in the following years, attest to Jakuchū's continuing efforts to expand the range of his technique and his concepts. The first is of a section of a banana plant, its flaccid leaves weathered and split by the elements (NO. 29). The artist conceived and executed the varied contours and forms of the battered leaves with considerable ingenuity; his distinctive soft, parallel brush strokes convey both the configurations of the dilapidated leaves and the strength of the wind that moves them. Jakuchū's versatility allowed him not only to capture the essential qualities and vulnerable circumstances of the plant, but also to synthesize these features into a powerful symbol of evanescence. A seven-character quatrain, composed by Daiten and written in the calligraphic manner of Chao Tzu-ang (also known as Chao Meng-fu; 1254–1322) accompanies the banana painting.

The second scroll, which was probably done during the artist's mid-fifties, shows a sprightly kingfisher perched on a reed (NO. 30). Executed in an abbreviated manner with wet brushwork on *gasenshi*, this charming work is notable for its evocative mood, and its subject and small scale suggest that it was intended for use in connection with the tea ceremony. The handling of brush and ink is reminiscent of certain Chinese works done during the Ming and Ch'ing periods in the *i p'in* manner by artists such as the individualist Pa-ta Shan-jen. Above the image is a poem by Daiten, written in Chinese in two seven-character lines.

Jakuchū's interest in monochrome interpretations of traditional iconographic subjects seems to have been strongest in the middle of his career. Sometime during his fifties this interest took on an additional dimension, and he moved beyond his largely literal depictions of established Buddhist pictorial parody.[58] This development not only demonstrates his continuing efforts to broaden his conceptual parameters, but also provides insights into another aspect of his personality: his wry sense of humor and his pleasure in representing his subjects in a highly personal, whimsical, and ironic manner. These are manifestations of the artist's deepening interest in Zen ideas, of which such humor is an essential component, and this quality can be seen in two of his most original paintings, a pair of hanging scrolls representing two of the legendary Zen eccentrics, Gama and Tekkai (NO. 24) and his memorable reinterpretation of the Parinirvāna of the Buddha (NO. 32).

Gama (Chinese: Hsia-mo) and Tekkai (Chinese: T'ieh-kuai) are two of the large group of mysterious "immortals" or "transcendents" that had their genesis in ancient Chinese popular religious beliefs of combined Taoist and Buddhist origin and that later assumed a significant role in Zen imagery. The identifying characteristics of these strange, eremitic figures known as *sennin* (Chinese: *hsien-jen*) are their unorthodox, eccentric behavior and their possession of various supernatural powers. Gama, who characteristically holds a peach, which symbolizes immortality, takes his name from the fact that his constant companion was a three-legged toad; Tekkai, who walks with the aid of a rustic staff, is celebrated for his startling ability to project his life essence out of his mouth and into space in a diminutive version of himself. Extant representations, such as the fine depictions of the two *sennin* by the Chinese painter Yen Hui (active in the second half of the thirteenth century) preserved in the Chion'in temple in Kyoto, go back as far as the late Southern Sung or early Yüan period. Gama and Tekkai, who came to be portrayed together as a fixed theme, were typically depicted in full figural form as grotesque but likable eccentrics, and this precedent was generally perpetuated in Edo-period representations, such as the engaging interpretation by Jakuchū's celebrated contemporary from Kyoto Sōga Shōhaku (FIG. 45).

Although Shōhaku's portrayals, with their bizarre poses and expressions, and their energizing, dynamic brushwork, achieved a new level of innovative interpretation, Jakuchū's versions were unique, and they extended the bounds of conceptual originality even further. Compositionally, both of Jakuchū's paintings were conceived so that the spectator's gaze inexorably proceeds from bottom to top as a result both of the orientation and upward thrusts of the soft, dark brush strokes at the base of the paintings, and of the orientations of the heads: Tekkai's head is tilted at a grotesque angle, his open mouth extending upward toward his spirit, which freely levitates far beyond the tip of his twisted staff; Gama's head, his unkempt hair encircling the tonsured area of his scalp, is surmounted by the delicately balanced figure of a dancing frog, who stares resolutely toward the top of the tall, narrow composition.

Traditional representations of the Parinirvāna, one of the most dramatic and universal of Buddhist iconic images, show Śākyamuni, the historical Buddha, recumbent on his death bier and surrounded by a grief-stricken throng of disciples, Arhats, Bodhisattvas, and various members of the animal kingdom as he is about to enter the ultimate stage of Nirvāna. Śākyamuni is invariably depicted lying on his right side, facing west, on a resplendent bier between two groups of four *śāla* trees, while his mother, the lady Māyā, sorrowfully descends from the Tuśita Heaven on a celestial cloud for a final farewell.[59] Jakuchū's *Vegetable Parinirvāna* (No. 32) is unique in the pictorial history of this great theme, for the artist chose to depart from established precedent and substituted vegetables and fruits for the traditional iconographic components. Although he retained the essential arrangement of the original composition, he replaced the mourners with more than fifty varieties of vegetables and fruits, each portrayed with unerring accuracy. Śākyamuni is represented by a giant Japanese white radish prostrate on a farmer's coarse basket, the *śāla* trees have been replaced by two groups of corn stalks, and lady Māyā is symbolized by a single citron at the top of the left-hand group. Arranged around the giant radish, in general accordance with the traditional composition, are the diverse forms of vegetables and fruits, which seem to express compassion by dutifully attending the final Nirvāna of the recumbent radish.

Although no documentary evidence exists to explain the artist's motivation and intent in producing this enigmatic work, certain assumptions seem justified. To begin with, the piece is notably taller (more than 1.8 meters in height) than his other monochrome works, suggesting that it was produced in connection with some significant event in his life. Second, the sense of parody seems intended less to amuse than to enlighten; this is not to deny the droll, whimsical atmosphere that pervades the work, but rather to suggest a deeper, more compassionate sentiment. The ambience of high drama and grief that characterizes traditional representations is absent here, replaced by a levity that attests to the artist's pleasure in portraying the life force common to all sentient forms.

The painting is a treasured possession of the Seiganji in Kyoto, a temple of the Nishi Honganji branch of Pure Land Buddhism. The Hōzōji, the mortuary temple of the Itō family, is a satellite temple of the Seiganji, and it has recently been suggested that Jakuchū may originally have painted the piece in commemoration of the death in 1794 of his brother Hakusai and later presented it to the Seiganji.[60] Considering the style and details of the painting, however, it seems more likely that he created it in memory of his mother, who died in 1779. In any event, it is particularly appropriate that the artist chose vegetables and fruits for his interpretation of the subject, given his family background, especially his long experience as master of the family's greengrocery. His intimate familiarity with fresh produce inspired him not only to depict the varied forms with fidelity, but also to imbue them with a palpable animation. This is consistent with the Buddhist conviction that inspired Jakuchū to produce the *Dōshoku Sai-e* paintings: that the Buddha nature (Busshō) is universal and pervades all sentient beings, making them all important to the harmonious balance and continuity of life.

Two works produced during his sixties further evince Jakuchū's perennial experimentation with ink and his search for unusual subject matter. The first is his spirited depiction of a tiger and bamboo, which is paired with a poetic passage composed and inscribed by Daiten (No. 28). The painting is, as observed, a rather freely adapted version of the artist's earlier polychrome copy of a Chinese work of the Ming period (FIG. 29; Shin'enkan Collection), done when he was forty years of age. The monochrome tiger, thought to have been done about a decade later, demonstrates how Jakuchū's style had developed, for the animal was executed in a more lively and imaginative manner than was its predecessor. Moreover, the dramatic portrayal of the contorted bamboo, with its wind-filled leaves, though clearly indebted in concept and brushwork to the bamboo composition in the Rokuonji (Nos. 16.7, 16.8), had evolved to another expressive level, even more abstract and abbreviated.

The second work is a representation of the *Five Hundred Arhats* (No. 27), executed when Jakuchū was industriously working on the ambitious sculptural project devoted to the same subject at the Sekihōji temple. The painting shows the multitude of Arhats, crossing the ocean in a leisurely fashion, on a traditional variety of eccentrically animated beasts (such as elephants, deer, tigers, and dragons) or on

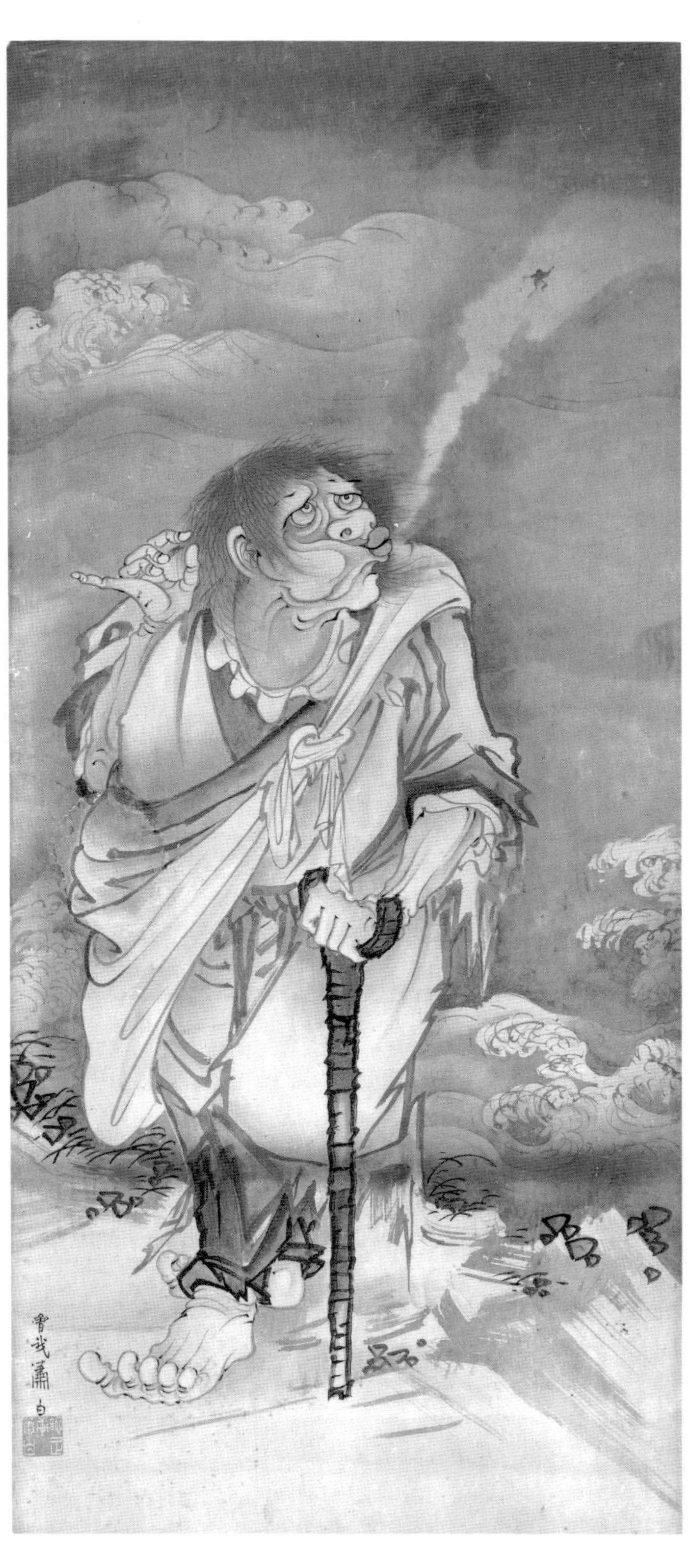

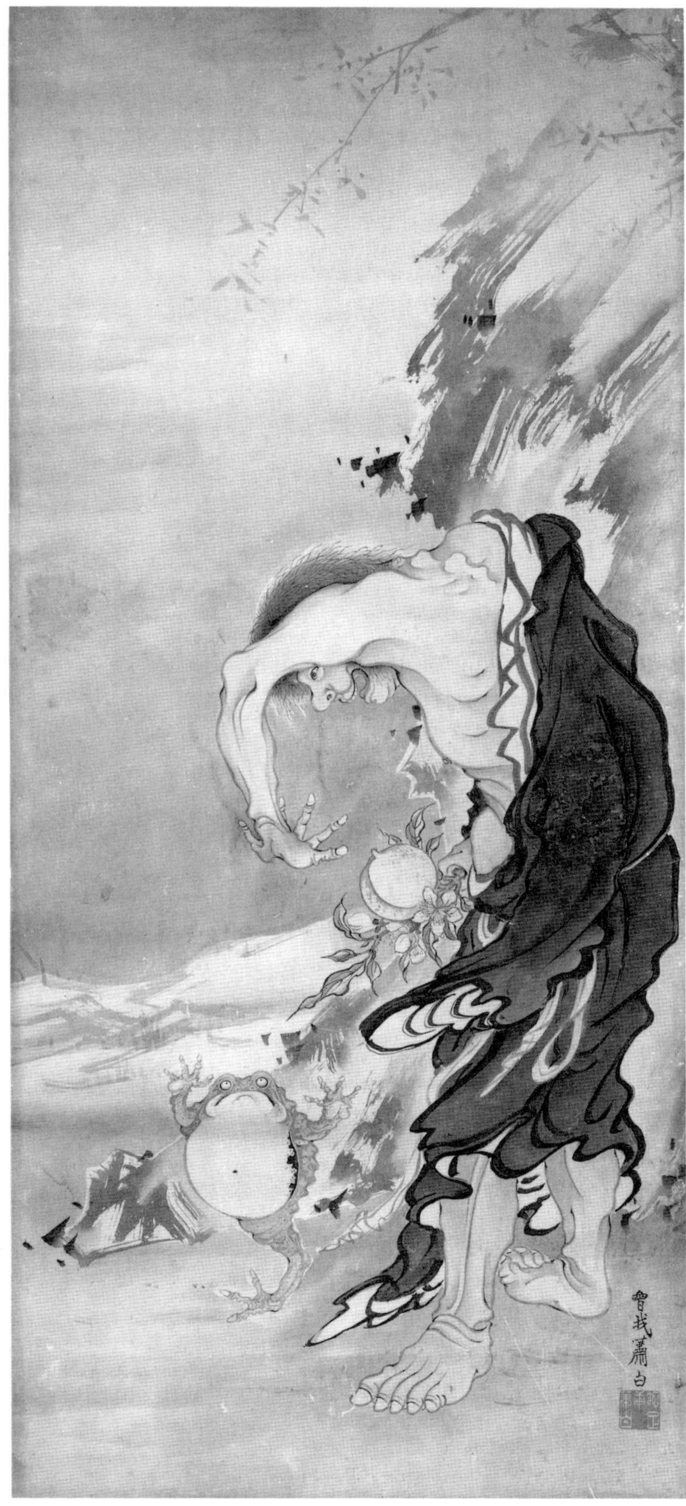

FIG. 45 Sōga Shōhaku. *The Transcendents Gama and Tekkai* (Gama, right; Tekkai, left), n.d.

Museum of Fine Arts, Boston

foot, as they gesticulate and congenially converse. One lively figure at the top points toward the distant clouds, where another throng of Arhats may be seen. Although the work is modest in size, the artist painstakingly individualized each of the miniature figures in this fanciful, quixotic world, and just as the tiger painting above demonstrates a freer, more spontaneous dimension in Jakuchū's painting, the *Five Hundred Arhats* shows how skilled and precise his brushwork could be. Each one of the amiable companions is worthy of the observer's attention, for each is distinguished by some amusing mannerism, posture, or expression, and as the viewer's eyes wander through the composition, perusing these figures brings him into intimate contact with Jakuchū's fertile, creative mind. After the Sekihōji sculpture had finally been completed and properly set in place, Jakuchū did a drawing of the composition, which was subsequently published in a woodblock-printed illustration (see FIG. 12). This portrayal corresponds with the painting in various particulars of layout and detail; it is intended to lead the viewer sequentially from one unconventional iconic group to another—a process that could be experienced by visiting the Sekihōji.

As mentioned, the leisurely boating excursion down the Yodo River that Jakuchū and Daiten made in the spring of 1767 inspired the artist to produce the continuous composition that was subsequently reproduced in a distinctive manner known as *taku-hanga*, a technique that had been utilized on occasion by Jakuchū's presumed mentor Ōoka Shumboku. The printed handscroll was given the title *Jōkyōshū* by Daiten, who inscribed the three characters in the archaic "seal" style (FIG. 7) and added elegant poetic notations on topographical and man-made features depicted in the scroll (FIG. 6).

Jakuchū seems to have been intrigued by the *taku-hanga* process and continued to conceive works in this manner, such as two exquisite small monochrome books, the *Soken Jō* (*Album of Elegant Designs on a Plain Ground*; FIG. 8), produced in the winter of 1767–68, and the *Gempo Yōka* (*Exquisite Flowers from the Mysterious Garden*; FIG. 9), produced in the Third Month of 1768, as well as the superb series of bird-and-flower designs produced three years later, the *Kachō-zu (Birds and Flowers*; NO. 26), in which pigments were utilized.

The fact that no dated paintings seem to exist from this span of about four years suggests that Jakuchū devoted his efforts during this period primarily to producing *taku-hanga* works. Moreover, considering his productivity in the preceding years—the large, detailed polychrome *Dōshoku Sai-e* works, as well as the extensive screen and wall paintings done for the Rokuonji in 1759 and for the Kotohiragū shrine in 1764, all paintings of large scale—it is not unreasonable to presume that Jakuchū was tired of such projects and glad to turn his creative efforts to a different scale, format, and technique.

The *Jōkyōshū* handscroll is made up of ten sheets of paper totaling more than 11.3 meters in length. Although documentary evidence indicates that a landscape composition was originally included among the screen and wall paintings produced for the Kotohiragū shrine in 1764, this composition unfortunately no longer exists, so the *Jōkyōshū* scroll is the only substantial pictorial evidence of Jakuchū's rare excursions into the landscape genre. In accordance with the *taku-hanga* process, the subject matter was delineated in white and two shades of gray, with a contrasting black background. In addition, the darker shade of gray was skillfully blended into selected areas of the lighter gray, a process that resulted in a unique atmospheric quality, a kind of abstracted chiaroscuro employed primarily for pictorial emphasis rather than to suggest volume or specific topographical features.

The downstream journey from Fushimi to Osaka took about half a day; the return required a full day. In the scroll, Jakuchū chose to place features such as small towns, ferry crossings, temples, shrines, and a castle some distance apart, and these were interspersed with Daiten's Chinese-style couplets, providing the viewer not only with a depiction of the points of interest along both banks, together with elegant poetic commentary, but also with a tangible sense of the time consumed in making the round-trip journey. Other details, such as boats of various sizes, a farmer with an ox, and gangs of coolies in raincoats laboriously pulling their vessels upriver, contribute to the unhurried sense of lateral movement and continuity. The composition was skillfully conceived to draw the viewer into a pleasant, imaginary participation in the trip, and this ability to stimulate the viewer's mind and emotions as he is led through an innovative arrangement of space was, as observed earlier, one of the artist's special talents.

As an experiment in landscape composition, the *Jōkyōshū* stands somewhat apart from the main body of Jakuchū's oeuvre. The river excursion obviously provided the basic inspiration for this piece, but Jakuchū may also have been influenced by his talented contemporary from Kyoto Maruyama Ōkyo. Ōkyo had, two years earlier, created a long scroll in color in which the river and the topographical features on its eastern bank were precisely depicted, although this work was schematically different from the *Jōkyōshū*.[61]

The two diminutive *taku-hanga* books produced soon afterward are technically less sophisticated, executed entirely in black and white.[62] The *Gempo Yōka* consists of forty-eight single-page designs (depicting flowers, plants, insects, and reptiles) with titles by Daiten. Thirty-six pictures of similar subjects, each depicted on two facing pages, appear in the *Soken Jō*, accompanied by Chinese five-character quatrains composed by Daiten and executed in his distinctive calligraphy. The designs in these books are notable for their vitality and graphic strength and serve as an inventory of many of Jakuchū's subjects drawn from nature, for the majority of these intimate, close-up designs reappeared, essentially unchanged, in the artist's paintings, particularly the *Dōshoku Sai-e*, in which they were portrayed in larger scale and in more complete natural form.[63] In his preface to the *Soken Jō*, Daiten calls the book *Soken Sekisatsu*, perhaps an alternate title. The postscript of the book gives the name of the block carver, Se Keisen, and identifies the Junshōji, a Kyoto temple, as the owner of the blocks. Jakuchū's younger contemporary Sakai Hōitsu (1761–1828), of the Rimpa school, had access to a copy of the *Gempo Yōka* and was inspired by its bold, evocative designs, for he copied ten of the illustrations, embellishing them with colors and refined naturalistic details, sometime in the years after Jakuchū's death.[64]

Jakuchū's use of the unusual *taku-hanga* techniques demonstrates, once again, his continuing search for expressive ideas and methods; the exquisite polychrome prints he produced about three years later mark the final step in this development. Daiten's intimate involvement in the production of the *Jōkyōshū* scroll and the illustrated books is apparent from the presence of his poems and calligraphy in those works, and he undoubtedly took a special interest in *taku-hanga* printing because of its indebtedness to Chinese traditions. Daiten may well have inspired Jakuchū to further his experiments with *taku-hanga* through the use of pigments in the series of six looseleaf bird-and-flower prints that appeared in 1771.

In "A Frivolous Poem Inspired by Edo Pictures" from his *Shōun Seikō* (vol. 3, 1775), Daiten clearly refers to the characteristic prints produced in Edo known as Ukiyo-e (Pictures of the Floating World), expressing his admiration for the quintessential figures of women and actors in these prints, "which nowadays are done with great skill, and are quite beautiful."[65] The prints Daiten refers to may well be Nishiki-e (Brocade Pictures), the new, full-color prints made with an expanded number of single-color blocks, a technological breakthrough made in 1765 by Suzuki Harunobu (1724–1770) and several of his colleagues. Daiten's poem is apparently the earliest documentary evidence of a Kyoto resident being aware of Nishiki-e, which at this time were produced exclusively in Edo, a considerable distance away. Daiten may have seen such prints during one of his trips to Edo on government business. At any rate, he is likely to have brought to Jakuchū's attention these new full-color prints, with their evocative images.

If such innovative works did indeed inspire Jakuchū, however, the appeal would have been their skillfully printed juxtapositions of color rather than their subject matter, for he devoted his own color prints entirely to the same sorts of subjects found in his paintings: a white cockatoo, a Chinese pheasant, and several parakeets with blossoming plums, bamboo, and other trees whose leaves he characteristically depicted with round spots representing the damage caused by mildew or insects. Moreover, the *Minchō Seidō Gaen*, Ōoka Shumboku's influential woodblock-printed reproductions of Chinese paintings, had been published in 1746, and this work must have been familiar to Jakuchū, who used some of Shumboku's unusual printing techniques, such as pigments applied to blocks and then partially wiped away before printing to create a kind of bleeding or fading; sprayed pigments (*fuki-bokashi*); and intaglio reversal printing, in which linear details are defined by the uninked, rather than the inked, areas.

A variety of exotic birds, all of them believed to be species imported from China or Southeast Asia, are depicted in Jakuchū's prints, and most, if not all, of them also appear in the artist's paintings. Thus, the golden pheasant in one print (No. 26.4) can be seen in more elegant form in one of the earlier *Dōshoku Sai-e* paintings (No. 14.4) as well as in another painting (in a private collection in Tokyo) from about the same time or soon after the print was produced. Another familiar subject found in Jakuchū's prints, the white cockatoo on a colorful, ornate Chinese perch with miniature flower-shaped food receptacles (No. 26.6), had been previously depicted by the artist in at least three paintings on silk, including the Sōdōji piece (No. 4) and another (FIG. 46). Jakuchū is presumed to have carefully supervised the production of the prints, but he must have relied on the expertise of a printing specialist, as he undoubtedly had in the case of the *Jōkyōshū* scroll and the two books. Despite the anonymity of this master printer, he was obviously quite skilled, for these works stand out as superb accomplishments in the history of woodblock printing in Japan. Inexplicably, Jakuchū, who was fifty-six years of age at the time, chose not to continue producing woodblock designs, and the six colored looseleaf prints mark the end of his creative interest in this medium.

In the following years, Jakuchū occasionally produced works in color, such as the lovely *Chinese Pheasant on a Blossoming Plum Tree.*[66] He continued to expand his expressive means, as in the exotic panel with a depiction of a *White Elephant and Other Beasts* (NO. 31).

Jakuchū's exquisitely detailed, multihued painting of a Chinese pheasant, with its rich, tapestry-like treatment of the bird's feathers, bears no date, but it is assumed, on stylistic grounds, to have been produced between sometime in the artist's late fifties and his early sixties (c. 1770–1780). During this decade Jakuchū created few such hanging scrolls; both this painting and another large, fine work on silk, *Monkeys in a Blossoming Peach Tree* (c. 1772–1776; FIG. 13), stand out as rare and instructive examples of the artist's polychrome work of the period.

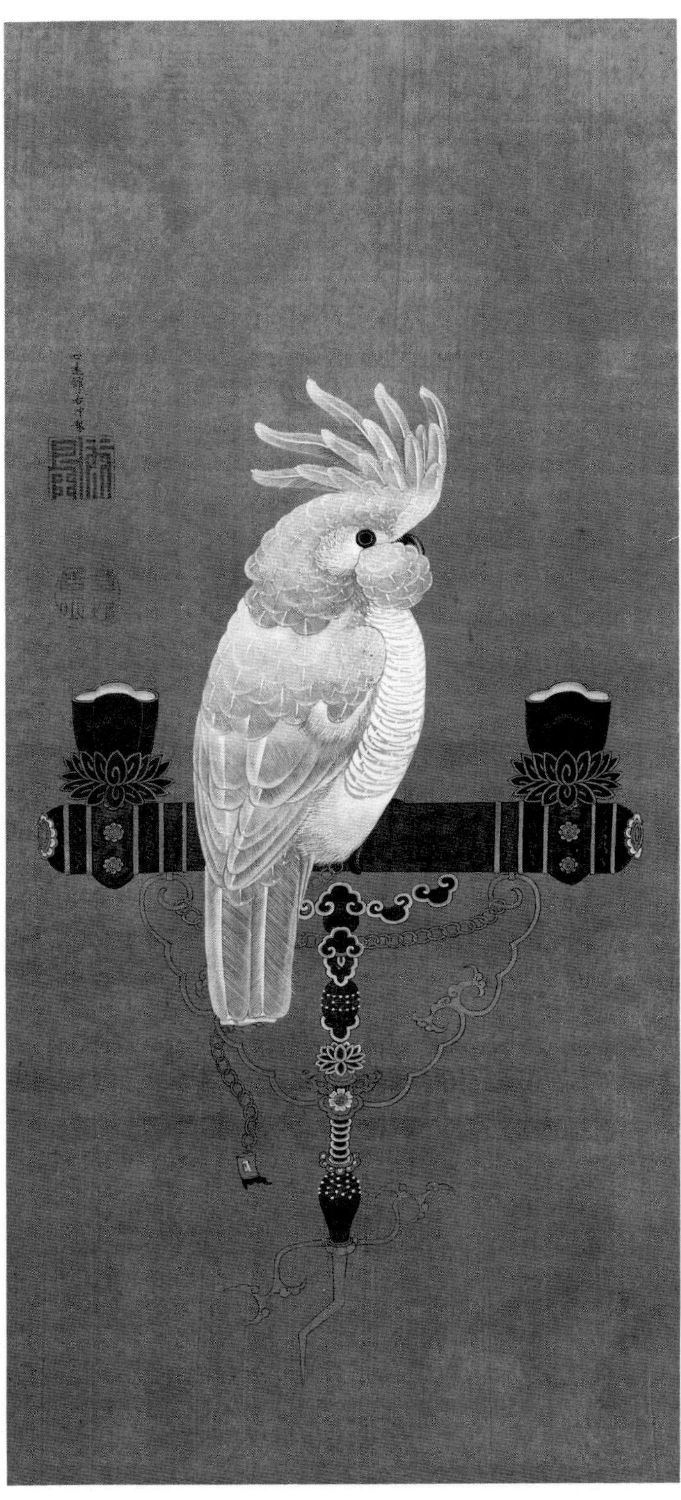

FIG. 46 *Cockatoo*, c. 1755–1757.
Museum of Fine Arts, Boston

Sitting alertly on the truncated section of an ancient, gnarled plum, the gorgeous pheasant dominates the composition by virtue of its brilliant colors and central location, and its animated presence is heightened further by the subdued background of plain silk. Surrounding the bird are a variety of eccentric, innovative tree forms: the attenuated limbs and the assertive trunk, which terminates in a bizarre combination of concavities and excrescences, as well as the extraordinary decayed remnant of the tree in the foreground; these dark, dynamic shapes vitalize the composition and focus the viewer's attention on the vivacious bird. The somber, taut forms of the tree are softened and balanced by the bright, contrasting pigments of delicate, ethereal plum blossoms and luxuriant camellias in the foreground. A very similar Chinese pheasant appears in one of the *Dōshoku Sai-e* paintings, *Golden Pheasants in Snow* (NO. 14.4), which was produced sometime during the first half of the 1760s, perhaps a decade earlier than the painting under discussion here. The earlier piece is filled with exuberant activity, its dark background showing through the foliage, snow, and flowers only in certain areas. Pervading the composition is a vivid sense of life, the result of an elaborate series of dense patterns that the artist composed, using minutely detailed natural forms. The later painting was, by contrast, conceived with a greater clarity and economy of means. Its mood is lighter and more precise, its brushwork more innovative, and its use of natural forms more radical.

The most extreme manifestation of Jakuchū's diligent search for inspiration in various styles and techniques is his singular panel painting, *White Elephant and Other Beasts* (NO. 31). Only the front half of the elephant appears in this panel, suggesting that the composition is incomplete in its present form and that it originally had at least one more panel. Conceptually less a painting than a mosaic, this unusual piece consists of a uniform grid of small squares that were individually filled with diverse colors in order to create a composition of graphic patterns and reticulated details. The source of inspiration for this peculiar technique is a matter of speculation. Considering the state of the arts and related technology in Kyoto during Jakuchū's time, perhaps the most promising area for comparative investigation is textile manufacture, for the modular uniformity of weaving suggests a superficial similarity. The fact that Kyoto was the traditional center for the production of the finest and most intricate textiles in Japan may have guided Jakuchū's inquiring mind in that direction and may have stimulated his curiosity about weaving techniques. At any rate Jakuchū's interest in this mode of depiction appears to have been short-lived, as this piece appears to be the only authentic example of the several done in this manner.

Another category of Jakuchū's polychrome works consists of his paintings of miniature molded clay figures known as Fushimi Ningyō (Fushimi dolls) because they were manufactured and sold at the Fushimi Inari shrine (NOS. 33, 34). One of the most influential and well-patronized Shinto shrines in Japan, the Fushimi Inari is situated only a short distance south of the Sekihōji, where, it seems, Jakuchū began the *Five Hundred Arhats* sculptural project about 1776, spent considerable time during this period, and resided during the last decade of his life.

The small, humorous Fushimi dolls, traditionally purchased by visitors to the shrine as inexpensive mementos of their pilgrimages, are characterized by their childlike shapes and decoration. They represent various subjects, such as a white fox, the legendary messenger of the shrine deity; a seated "peacock child," or young boy, dressed in colorful ritual clothing; a taciturn, patient ox; and, most frequently, Hotei, the popular deity of prosperity, a bald, rotund standing figure dressed in a coarse robe. Hotei symbolizes the contentment and happiness that prosperity brings, and his corpulence and congenial expression convey these attributes. The naïve quality of these figures, which are embellished with basic pigments sometimes mixed with mica or metal particles, have endeared them to the general populace over the centuries, and it is easy to see how Jakuchū would have been attracted to their unpretentious forms and colors.

The artist may have begun to depict Fushimi dolls in his paintings as early as his late forties, but they became one of his favorite themes during his sixties, when he was busy with the panoramic sculptural project at the Sekihōji, and he continued to produce paintings of them in significant numbers during his later years. The stones used for the *Five Hundred Arhats* were carved in a direct, primitive manner that utilized their natural conformations to a large degree in delineating the various figures, resulting in forms with a striking mixture of the primitive, eccentric, and naïve. The correspondences in shape between these stone carvings and Jakuchū's paintings of Fushimi dolls are more than coincidental; both reveal the artist's continuing conceptual pleasure in the abstract, schematic arrangement of pure form. The artist closely juxtaposed multiple depictions of Hotei, usually seven in number, in a vertical, curvilinear arrangement that closely paralleled the stone compositions, particularly the processions of Arhats in the upper-middle section of the Sekihōji sculpture (see FIG. 11).

Jakuchū's sixties and early seventies constituted a productive yet idyllic period, when he was able to pursue his painting free from distractions or difficulties. Entries in the *Heian Jimbutsushi* show that he was one of the most respected artists in the Kyoto region, and his painting probably brought him a reasonable income. The *Five Hundred Arhats*, begun when he was sixty-one years of age, occupied him for a decade or more. Although it is likely that he spent a substantial portion of his personal funds to bring the project to completion, the health and profitability of the family business safeguarded him from any financial concerns. However, the great fire of 1788 seems to have left Jakuchū and his relatives impoverished, making it imperative for him to support himself.

This seems to have motivated him to search for income-generating commissions such as the set of screen paintings he created for the Saifukuji in 1790. This project, completed when he was seventy-five years old, allowed him to use his highly developed skills in both polychrome and monochrome painting in the production of two compositions that are among his finest artistic accomplishments.

The combination of fowl and sections of giant cacti

in the *Cacti and Fowl* screens (FIG. 14) is highly unusual. Cacti of this size were not native to Japan, but several are said to have been imported in 1670. The artist may actually have been able to see a living example,[67] perhaps in Osaka, where Yoshino Kansai, the rich merchant who commissioned the screens, did a flourishing business in patent medicines, many of which were concocted from exotic materia medica imported from China and other regions of Asia. However, Jakuchū reduced the scale of the cacti in his composition, for the actual variety is about thirty to forty percent larger. The bizarre blue shapes intermingled with the cacti are also quite unusual, and the ambiguity in their conformation makes it difficult to determine whether Jakuchū intended them as stylized organic forms or highly mannered, attenuated rock formations. These recondite components introduce a sense of mystery into the composition and reinforce the exotic mood evoked by the plant. Also atypical is Jakuchū's choice of a plain gold background for the composition and of strong, bright pigments for the cactus forms and the dark blue shapes intertwined with them. Investigation of the paper covered by the *hikite* (hand pulls) has revealed that originally the blue and green pigments as well as the gold surface were significantly brighter.

These features, together with the stylized treatment of the cacti, and the portrayal of the fowl in a patterned, decorative manner against the uninterrupted expanse of gold, indicate that Jakuchū was familiar with and influenced by the stylistic ideas of the Rimpa school. This venerable line of artists, which had its origin in Kyoto in the late sixteenth century and was distinguished by a series of gifted masters such as Kōetsu, Sōtatsu, and Kōrin, who died the year Jakuchū was born, continued to exercise a significant influence on painting, crafts, and design throughout the eighteenth and early nineteenth centuries. A strong yet discerning disposition toward bright colors and graphic design, expressed in a highly decorative, flat, and stylized manner and organized into orderly yet abstract compositions, typifies the tradition of this school, seen in such works as Sōtatsu's depiction of *Bugaku Dancers* in the Daigoji and Kōrin's *Irises*, which once belonged to the Nishi Honganji. The influence of this school may be seen occasionally in earlier works by Jakuchū, such as two of the later *Dōshoku Sai-e* pieces, *Shellfish* (NO. 14.7) and *Birds and Chrysanthemums by a Stream* (NO. 14.10), and certain designs in the two *taku-hanga* books, the *Soken Jō* and *Gempo Yōka*. As noted, a later member of the Rimpa school, Sakai Hōitsu, reversed this indebtedness by copying ten of the illustrations during the early nineteenth century (see note 64).

The very precise compositional scheme in the *Cacti and Fowl* screens consists of a series of fowl, either singly or in pairs, skillfully arranged in each panel, with an abbreviated section of cactus at either end. The birds are placed and posed to interact with their neighbors in adjoining panels, leading the viewer's eyes back and forth through this carefully calculated pictorial scheme. The tour de force handling of the details demonstrates the artist's inventory of brush techniques and his skill in combining colors and pictorial effects. The minutest particulars were carried out with clarity and precision, revealing the lovely complexity of the bird's plumage, juxtaposed against the reflected glow of the solid gold background. Psychologically, the dazzle of the gold encourages the spectator to admire the elegant spatial relationships from a distance even as mesmerizing details invite him to observe the lively antics of the chickens from an intimate vantage point.

In Jakuchū's earlier depictions of birds, such as the roosters in paintings from the private collection in Osaka (NO. 1) and the Ryōsokuin (NO. 13), both executed three to four decades earlier, the birds are more anatomically accurate and naturalistic in appearance but seem calculatedly posed and situated, treated essentially as merely another component in the composition. The birds in the Saifukuji screens are, by contrast, more clearly the products of the artist's imagination, their proportions and details modified to suit his artistic intentions. Despite the elegant arabesques of the tail feathers, their basic shapes are simplified, reduced to geometric forms. Still, paradoxically, their graphic richness and their eccentric postures and expressions imbue them with a heightened sense of vitality that is notably absent in the earlier examples. Moreover, the observer's interest is stimulated further by the exaggerated scale of the roosters, which are larger than life size in comparison to the reduced cacti. Jakuchū made these superb screens at the height of his creative powers, when he was confident in the originality of his compositional scheme and drew freely on his accumulated experience and skills to produce a superb work of great artistic importance.

The continuous composition *Lotus Pond* (NO. 35), formerly attached to the reverse side of the screens, is antithetical to *Cacti and Fowl* in both mood and execution. Low in the foreground, the edge of a pond was rendered in a spare, economical manner, and scattered across this bleak landscape are the solitary remnants of several lotuses and a few clumps of lichens and grass. It is late autumn, and the senescent lotuses are in their final decline, ravaged by insects and debilitated by the passage of time. A pervasive sense of desolation is achieved through the images of the decaying plants as well as the use of soft, monochrome washes and the meticulous, dry brushwork of the details. For this conception, the artist drew on ideas and techniques already present in his work at least thirty years earlier.

A general prototype for this unusual composition, in which all the components are compressed at the bottom, can be seen in the *Begonias* screens (Nos. 16.5, 16.6) from the Rokuonji, which were completed in 1759, when Jakuchū was forty-four years of age. However, the spatial implications of the two works are quite different. The *Begonias* are flat or "two-dimensional" in feeling, leaving the observer with a sense of the large area of blank space above the flowers as essentially vertical and neutral. In the *Lotus Pond*, however, the subtle sequential arrangement of the plants gradually leads the observer's eye and mind deep into an abstract space unconstrained by the bounds of physical reality. Then again, Jakuchū's meticulous use of lines and washes has stylistic precedents in his intimate portrayals of subjects such as *Snake Gourds and Insects* (No. 7) and *Corn Plants and Kidney-bean Vines* (No. 3), which were probably executed when the artist was in his late thirties.

Despite the correspondences in the careful delineation of detail, however, the forms of the *Lotus Pond* were conceived in a more personal and painterly manner, and they serve less as convincing naturalistic features than as eloquent metaphors for old age and physical decline. In fact, it seems reasonable to assume that the painting was intended to express the artist's advanced age and psychological state at the time. He was seventy-five years old, and his financial circumstances had made it necessary for him to leave his comfortable situation in Kyoto and to travel to Osaka to work on the commission. In addition, after he had completed the screens and returned to the Sekihōji, he fell ill, and he may have had some premonition of failing health or declining vitality while he was working on the Saifukuji project, as suggested by the mood of gloom and enervation that infuses the lotus painting.

Once back in his comfortable hermitage at the Sekihōji but before he became ill, Jakuchū began painting a set of four sliding screens and wall panel paintings for the Kaihōji, another Ōbaku temple close by (No. 36). The monochrome depictions of chickens are very similar to the polychrome birds in the Saifukuji composition, although they were treated in a somewhat more cursive and abstract manner. Perhaps Jakuchū, fatigued from his extended labors away from home and not in the best of health, determined that his most pragmatic approach to the Kaihōji project would be to follow the compositional and stylistic precedents of the Saifukuji screens, which would still have been fresh in his mind; he may simply not have been prepared to come up with a new conception. The fact that the brushwork in the Kaihōji screens seems somewhat tentative, repetitive, and formularized supports this theory.

Jakuchū apparently spent the last decade of his life in comfortable seclusion in the Sekihōji. Although he may have left occasionally for short excursions nearby, he seems to have had no interest in traveling away from Kyoto, and he must have devoted himself conscientiously to his painting, for a number of pieces from this period are extant. In the congenial confines of his atelier, his needs diligently attended to by his sister, he worked to refine his expressive means, attracting a group of followers who took names derived from his own, such as Jakuen, Ichū, and Shochū; under his supervision, they strove to emulate his ideas and methods.

Jakuchū's painting during this period is characterized by his ever-greater interest in the expressive potential of monochrome ink, but he still occasionally produced polychrome works. The delicate colors in the ethereal *Cockscomb and Mantis* (No. 37) stand out luminously against the ink wash on a silk background. The precise, rather dry, and carefully calculated delineation of the cockscomb obviously corresponds in style with the *Lotus Pond*, which was done a year earlier. Although adapted for color, this treatment is essentially monochrome ink technique, as are the methods in which the grasses and contours of the bank were handled. Although certain components in the mantis painting are highly detailed, the basic composition is almost geometric in its simplicity, and it reveals the conceptual clarity of a mature, experienced painter.

During this decade Jakuchū continued to produce Fushimi-doll paintings in color, and the number of such works preserved indicates not only that he took pleasure in their endless possibilities for abstract compositional schemes, but also that these amusing pieces struck a responsive chord in the emotions of the local populace. Jakuchū painted pieces in this lively genre up to the end of his life, as evidenced by the fine *Seven Hoteis* in the Shin'enkan Collection,[68] which was done in his eighty-fifth year.

The most ambitious polychrome project of

Jakuchū's last years was his rendering of the ceiling panels for the Kannondō chapel within the precincts of the Sekihōji. This consisted of 168 depictions of flowers and plants, in individual circular formats (32.6 centimeters in diameter) on flat wooden panels, which were installed in the gridlike structure of the ceiling. Because of its scope, this project must have taken some months to complete, and it was probably carried out either in 1799 or in 1800, the last year of the artist's life. Each painting shows a representative portion of a flower or plant and is therefore intended as a "vignette," much the same as the illustrations in Jakuchū's *taku-hanga* books done three decades earlier. There are, indeed, many close correspondences in style and subject, although the panel depictions are simpler and lack the animated presences of the insects, reptiles, and birds in the book illustrations. At the same time, both were conceived to portray the varied forms and beauty of nature essential to the idealized Buddhist view of the universe. Jakuchū's interest in monochrome ink techniques is apparent in his handling of the subjects on the panels, for although pigments play an important role in distinguishing the appearance of each plant and flower, the details are rather abbreviated and cursive. Furthermore, the artist used varying shades of black and gray ink to depict many of the particulars, and he left the wood in the background plain. In addition, the influence of the Rimpa style of painting is apparent in the flat, decorative treatment of the subjects. The aged Jakuchū probably received both logistical and artistic assistance from his several followers in bringing this project to completion.

The engaging *One Hundred Dogs* (No. 43) was an unusual choice of subject for the artist, as was his earlier depiction of monkeys (FIG. 13), and the former is one of his last works in color. Here, for some as yet unexplained reason, the painter has given his age as eighty-six. Speckled, multicolored dogs of Chinese origin were often portrayed by Japanese artists who worked in the stylistic tradition of Shen Nan-p'in, the influential Chinese painter who came to Nagasaki in 1731 and taught there for two years before returning to China. As observed previously, the bright, colorful style of this artist, whose naturalistic bird-and-flower subjects were much admired in Japan, seems to have come to the attention of Jakuchū early in his career, influencing pieces executed when he was in his thirties, such as *Peonies and Lilies* (No. 2), as well as *One Hundred Dogs*, which was executed close to five decades later. Jakuchū depicted the frolicking dogs in a precise but nonrealistic manner, and his abstract, schematic groupings of similar module-like forms are more complex than, but essentially similar to, his arrangement of the stone sculpture in the Sekihōji and of the components in the Fushimi-doll paintings. The individual dogs were charmingly portrayed, but the subject is likely to have been unfamiliar to Jakuchū, and rather than attempting to emphasize their canine personalities, he chose to depict them in a flat, decorative manner and to concentrate on the graphic potential of their varied colors, shades, and coat patterns.

Although a certain number of fine pieces in color, such as the Saifukuji screens, with their sprightly fowl set against a gold background, were produced in the later decades of Jakuchū's life, his most intense period of interest in the expressive possibilities of color occurred during the middle of his career, when he was devoting his creative energies to the *Dōshoku Sai-e* paintings. The artist's earliest extant paintings already reveal his talent for assimilating the essential features of both polychrome and monochrome techniques and for synthesizing them in a distinctive, original manner, but as the decades passed, monochrome painting, with its challenging brush techniques and aesthetic ideas, became the dominant motivating force in his art. This is borne out not only by the growing number of monochrome works he produced, but also by the influence on his color pieces of his monochrome painting techniques and brushwork.

Jakuchū's depiction of a skull abandoned in a desolate field (No. 38) was painted quickly and directly in a graphic, dramatic manner to create a strong, evocative image. Done when the artist was seventy-nine years of age, it is the spontaneous product of his imagination, and his having eschewed the literal in favor of a symbolic abstraction increases the visual impact of the painting and fixes it in the viewer's memory. The subject succinctly expresses the world-weariness and memento mori that also infuse the *Lotus Pond* (No. 35), done four years earlier. At the same time, it betokens a disconcerting irony eventually faced by many great painters—that of having their physical resources fail while their powers of conception are at their most lucid and imaginative.

Two works compiled when Jakuchū was eighty-one years of age exhibit the artist's continued experimentation with varying approaches to monochrome expression. The first, depicting two roosters and a hen (No. 39), was carried out with a number of brush techniques and contrasting ink values. Its graphic strength and compositional structure are complemented by a harmonious mixture of emphatic brushwork, light, feathery touches, and the animated, skittish quality of the birds. Here again, the artist's skills in selecting appropriate calligraphic strokes, innovative washes, and the salient features of the birds' postures and attitudes, while avoiding realistic anatomical details, imbued the chickens with a sense of irrepressible vitality.

For the second work, a pair of six-panel screens (No. 40), Jakuchū chose an even more abbreviated and conceptualized approach, portraying in separate panels twelve extraordinarily prodigious vegetables, so large that several extend beyond the lateral boundaries of their formats. Although this work corresponds somewhat in style and genre with the earlier *Vegetable Parinirvāna* (No. 32), the artist's intention here is more radical, for not only were the vegetables magnified many times beyond their original sizes, but they were also rendered in a remarkably spare manner that reduced each to its most basic form and particulars. Pictorial embellishment and superfluous details are entirely absent here. Each image is a creative and technical tour de force, first lucidly conceived in the artist's mind and then confidently reproduced in a direct, spontaneous manner, with strong, continuous brush strokes and soft, wet washes on absorbent paper. This late work is a concise example of the expressive ideal in ink painting: the direct pictorial realization of conceptual inspiration, unencumbered by calculation or sequential process, an artistic accomplishment that has its religious equivalent in the moment of enlightenment in Zen.

Jakuchū was concerned here with the delineation of simple yet unusual and provocative shapes and with their arrangement within the formats of each panel—a process that, in terms of modern painting, certainly qualifies the work as an abstract composition. However, these are not only evocative graphic images, but also convincing shorthand symbols of the essence of each outsize vegetable; they therefore demonstrate the artist's allegiance to a fundamental ideal in East Asian painting, that of revealing the underlying nature of the subject.

Although Jakuchū portrayed on several occasions Baisaō, the Ōbaku monk and practitioner of the Chinese tea ceremony, his depiction of Hoan Jōei (No. 41) seems to be the only other extant example of his rare attempts at portraiture. Jōei (1722–1796) was a somewhat younger contemporary of Jakuchū's, a distinguished Ōbaku prelate and the twenty-third Bishop of the Mampukuji. It is reasonable to presume that Jakuchū was motivated to depict Baisaō because of his admiration for and friendship with the older man. Although no existing evidence substantiates a similar relationship between Jakuchū and Jōei, it seems likely that Jakuchū was prompted to portray him for similar reasons. The artist's years of residence at the Sekihōji and his various endeavors on behalf of the Ōbaku temple make it likely that the two were on congenial terms. Jakuchū's portrait of Jōei—which belongs to the traditional Zen pictorial genre known as *chinsō*, a form of commemorative portrait of a revered monk that was customarily handed down to a close disciple[69]—denotes an attitude of respect on the part of the artist for the sitter.

As is conventional in *chinsō* portraiture, Jōei is shown seated on a coarse rush mat, turned slightly to the left, holding the *kyōsaku* (an implement of the Zen instructor). *Chinsō* were intended to be insightful depictions not only of the revered sitter's actual features, but also of his personality and enlightened nature; successful examples are therefore a synthesis of physical and psychological realism, and the artist's primary intent is to concentrate the observer's attention on the face of the subject.

Jakuchū worked conscientiously to capture the essential appearance and innate spirituality of Jōei, but he was apparently working in an unfamiliar and difficult genre, and his creative orientation and style at this late date were basically antithetical to representational depiction. Thus the priest's face suffers from a preoccupation with literal details, and the artist's excessive reliance on delicate, uninflected contour lines resulted in an overmannered quality. The treatment of the body underneath the robe was also less than successful, and the delineation of Jōei's right shoulder seems awkward and incomplete. These comments must, however, be considered in light of certain pictorial and stylistic conventions of *chinsō* done by painters associated with the Ōbaku sect, in which these characteristics are often to be seen. Jakuchū obviously felt more confident when it came to handling the robes, which were done in the quick, incisive strokes and schematized structure that constitute the hallmark of his late monochrome painting.

The superb painting of an eagle poised momentarily above rough, breaking waves (FIG. 47) in the Shin'enkan Collection stands as a final, dramatic statement of Jakuchū's accomplishments in this challenging medium. Signed "age eighty-five," this may well be his last ink painting that can be accurately dated. Although the size and forceful presence of the venerable bird impress the viewer, there is also something tentative in its pose and diffident in its attitude that suggests the bird is a pictorial metaphor, symbolic of the elderly, world-weary artist himself. As noted, in Jakuchū's benevolent view of the natural world, the Buddhist ideal of harmonious interaction

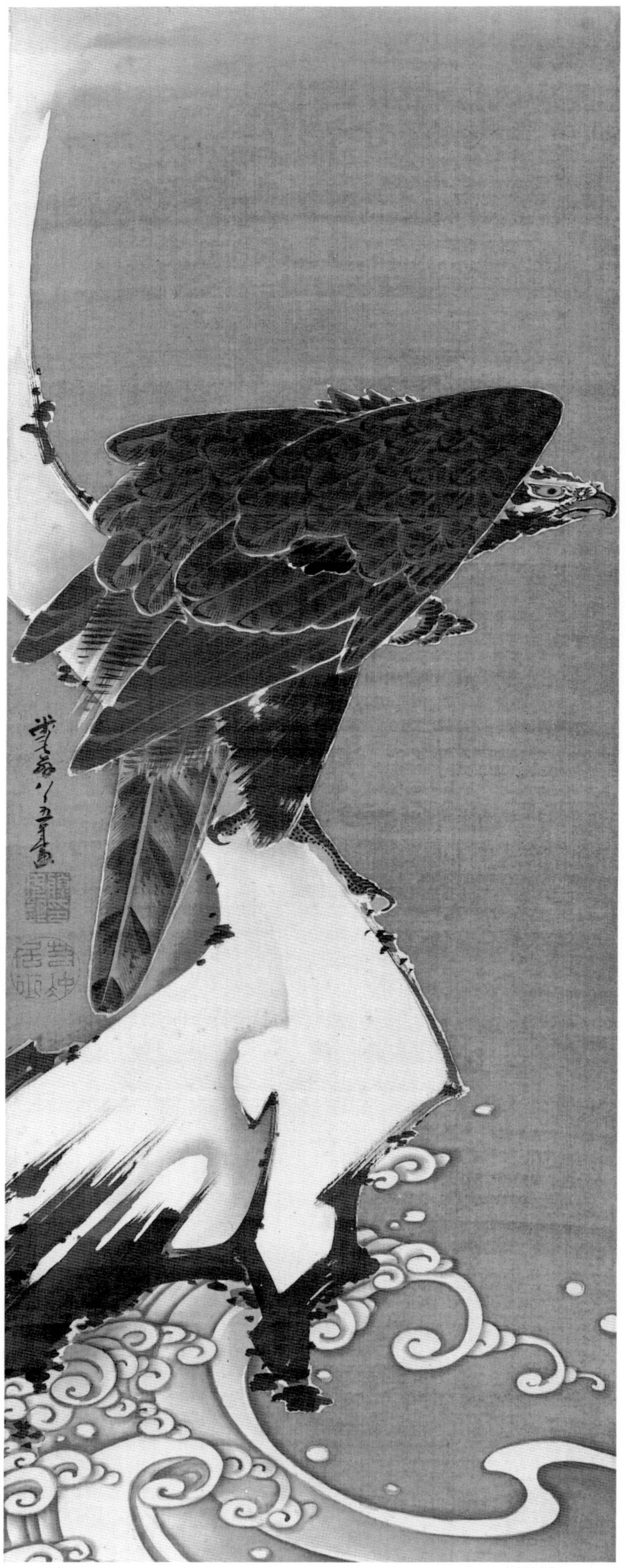

among living beings prevailed and the more violent manifestations of animal behavior were fastidiously ignored. Even in the case of such a fierce bird, the artist's portrayal is more reserved than assertive, in sharp contrast to the traditional depictions of hawks and eagles by members of the Kanō school or to the more ferocious and intimidating interpretations by Jakuchū's gifted contemporary Sōga Shōhaku.

Nevertheless, Jakuchū's compositional conception is striking in its strength and originality. The jagged, overhanging cliff, conceived in assertive diagonal thrusts and rendered in thick, dark ink, combined with the asymmetrical composition and the dramatic contrasts of dark and light, invigorates the whole painting. The chief structural elements, a series of abstract triangular forms of various sizes and orientations, are juxtaposed in an interlocking manner that is, in turn, enriched and diversified through a virtuosic demonstration of innovative ink treatments and embellishments of brushwork. The imaginative rendering of the waves breaking with tentacle-like tips can be seen in a formative manifestation in one of the *Dōshoku Sai-e* paintings, *Shellfish* (No. 14.7), but this lacks the coherence and graphic strength of the later treatment. The special concern for design and decorative elaboration in these wave forms clearly signifies Jakuchū's awareness of the stylistic canons of the Rimpa school, also an influence in works such as the *Dōshoku Sai-e* painting *Birds and Chrysanthemums by a Stream* (No. 14.10). In its clarity of conception and adroit execution, this superb work

FIG. 47 *Eagle on a Cliff above Waves*, n.d.

Los Angeles County Museum of Art, Shin'enkan Collection

serves not only as a final testament to Jakuchū's creative activities over a period of some six decades, but also as an illustration of the unique synthesis of his accumulated pictorial experience and evolution, which set him apart from other artists of his time and distinguish him as one of the most original and illustrious talents in the history of Japanese painting.

When Jakuchū died in 1800, all of his peers who had pioneered new styles or significantly influenced painting in the Kyoto-Osaka region had already died: Shōhaku in 1781, Buson in 1783, Ōkyo in 1795, and Rosetsu in 1799. Although Jakuchū's conceptions and stylistic ideas were diligently emulated by a small group of followers who seem to have worked under his guidance at the Sekihōji—men such as Jakuen (FIGS. 48, 49), Ichū, Daichū, and Shochū, who are known only through their competent but largely uninspired interpretations of Jakuchū's models—none of these artists had the energy or vision to establish an artistic line or to build on the achievements of their mentor.

Nevertheless, the collective memory of Jakuchū's unique accomplishments remained very much alive in Kyoto, as the periodic display of the *Dōshoku Sai-e* series along with its central iconic triptych continued to serve as a source of religious and aesthetic inspiration for the local populace. Artists of various backgrounds, filled with enthusiasm for Jakuchū's compelling originality, contemplated his paintings reverently in the hope that some small motivating spark of the master's genius might be intuitively transmitted to them.

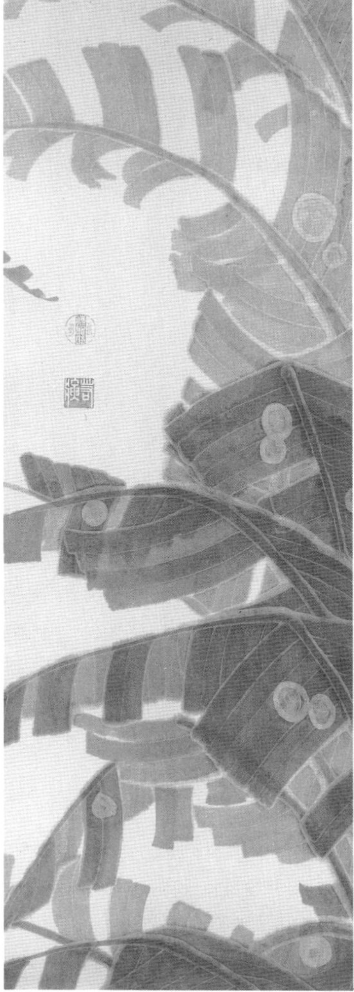

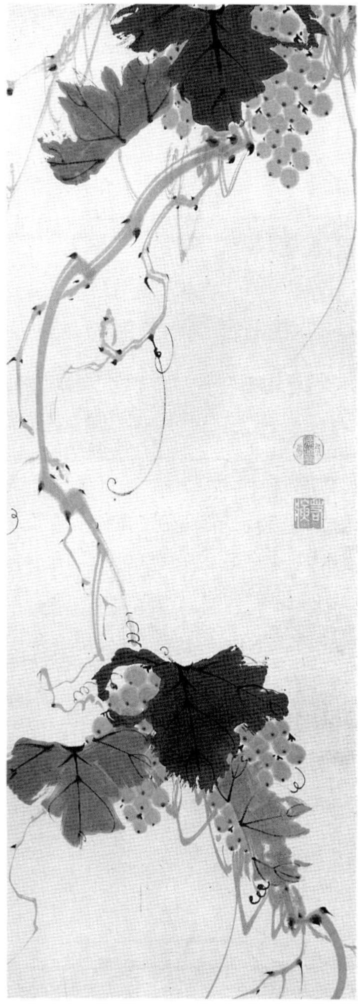

FIG. 48 Jakuen. *Banana Leaves*, n.d.

Los Angeles County Museum of Art, Shin'enkan Collection

FIG. 49 Jakuen. *Grapes*, n.d.

Los Angeles County Museum of Art, Shin'enkan Collection

Catalogue

1 *Rooster and Bamboo in Snow*

Second half of the 1740s

Colors on paper, hanging scroll
114.2 × 61.9 cm
Signature: *Keiwa*

SEALS:
square intaglio: *Tō Jokin azana Keiwa*
square relief: *Yūkatei Tosho*
Private collection, Osaka Prefecture

In this painting a single rooster searches for food in the snow in a bamboo grove, and a hearty chrysanthemum, partially covered by snow, blooms nearby. Roosters had been the subject of paintings in China and Japan for many centuries. Traditionally they were portrayed not simply as components in larger compositional schemes, but as the central focus of attention. For this reason this painting, with its large scale and its precisely rendered details of all compositional components, marked a new tendency in the handling of the subject in Japan. It is thought that Jakuchū was inspired by the bird-and-flower depictions of the Chinese painter Shen Nan-p'in (also known as Shen Ch'uan; Japanese: Chin Nampin), who came to Nagasaki in 1731. Motivated by the idea of using the rooster as a subject in his painting, Jakuchū not only worked to master artistic techniques for portraying the anatomy and feathers, but also focused his attention on painting realistically by observing actual fowl.

It seems unlikely that this work was intended just as a pictorial representation of a rooster. A Chinese painting in the Tokyo National Museum, *Rooster in Bamboo* (FIG. 50), by the Chinese Ch'an (Zen) priest Lo Ch'uang (active late thirteenth century), provides an interesting comparison. In this work, the rooster stares intently toward the east just as the first dim light of sunrise appears, and its expectant posture seems to be symbolic of the Buddhist devotee's fervent desire to proclaim to the world that he has grasped the eternal truth of his faith through spiritual enlightenment. In addition, in China the rooster was traditionally thought to possess the "Five Virtues"[1]—namely, literary accomplishment, martial spirit, courage, virtue, and loyalty—and Lo Ch'uang used the phrase "Concealing the Five Virtues" in his inscription. Consequently, in paintings such as this one the rooster can be understood to embody human characteristics.

This sort of imagery was also passed down in Zen culture in Japan. Thus, upon perusing a painting of a rooster (perhaps from Jakuchū's hand), Daiten Kenjō (1719–1801), the Zen priest who was a close friend of the artist's, composed a poem that appears in his poetic anthology the *Shōun Seikō*:

> His head lowered, he drinks and feeds;
> who can compare with him in the "Five
> Virtues."
> Night passes, and with morning
> the sun rising in the east;
> all appears in his crow.[2]

The rooster in Jakuchū's painting, like the one in Lo Ch'uang's, seems to have some metaphorical significance, to express some human trait. Both the bamboo and the chrysanthemum growing by the rooster symbolize the noble-mindedness of the Kunshi (Chinese: Chun-tzu), the traditional ideal man of superior virtue, and these plants were, as a consequence, two favorite subjects among Literati painters in China as far back as the Sung dynasty (960–1279). Perhaps Jakuchū's rooster, isolated from the vulgar world and withstanding the rigors of wind and snow, symbolizes the solitary seeker of truth searching for the proper path, confident of his own abilities. Perhaps it is even a pictorial metaphor for Jakuchū himself.

Jakuchū executed both the complex scheme of the bamboo stalks and the abbreviated curvilinear contours of the layered snow in his distinctive manner. In 1751 the pioneer master of the Literati style, Sakaki Hyakusen (1697–1752), was engaged to execute a series of paintings on sliding screens (now in the Suhara Collection, Nara Prefecture) in which he delineated fallen snow in unusual curvilinear contours and perforations; from this source, with its roots in Chinese painting, Jakuchū developed his even more radical expressive means for portraying snow. The styles of the inscription and seals on this painting correspond closely with those on the painting of grapes (FIG. 32) in the Shin'enkan Collection, and these two scrolls are among Jakuchū's earliest extant works.

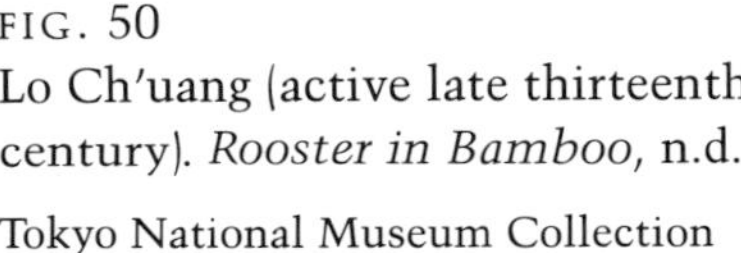

FIG. 50
Lo Ch'uang (active late thirteenth century). *Rooster in Bamboo*, n.d.

Tokyo National Museum Collection

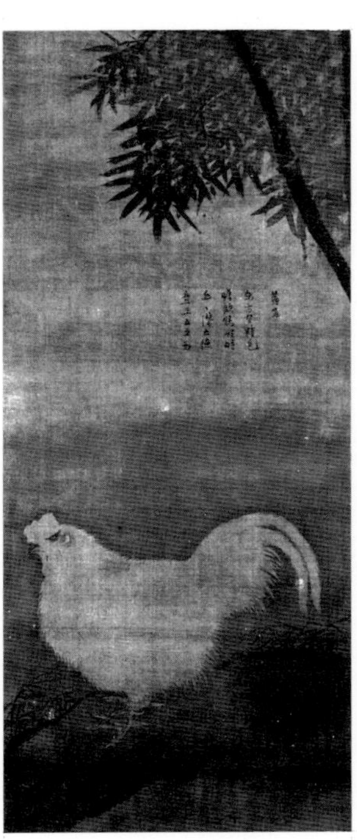

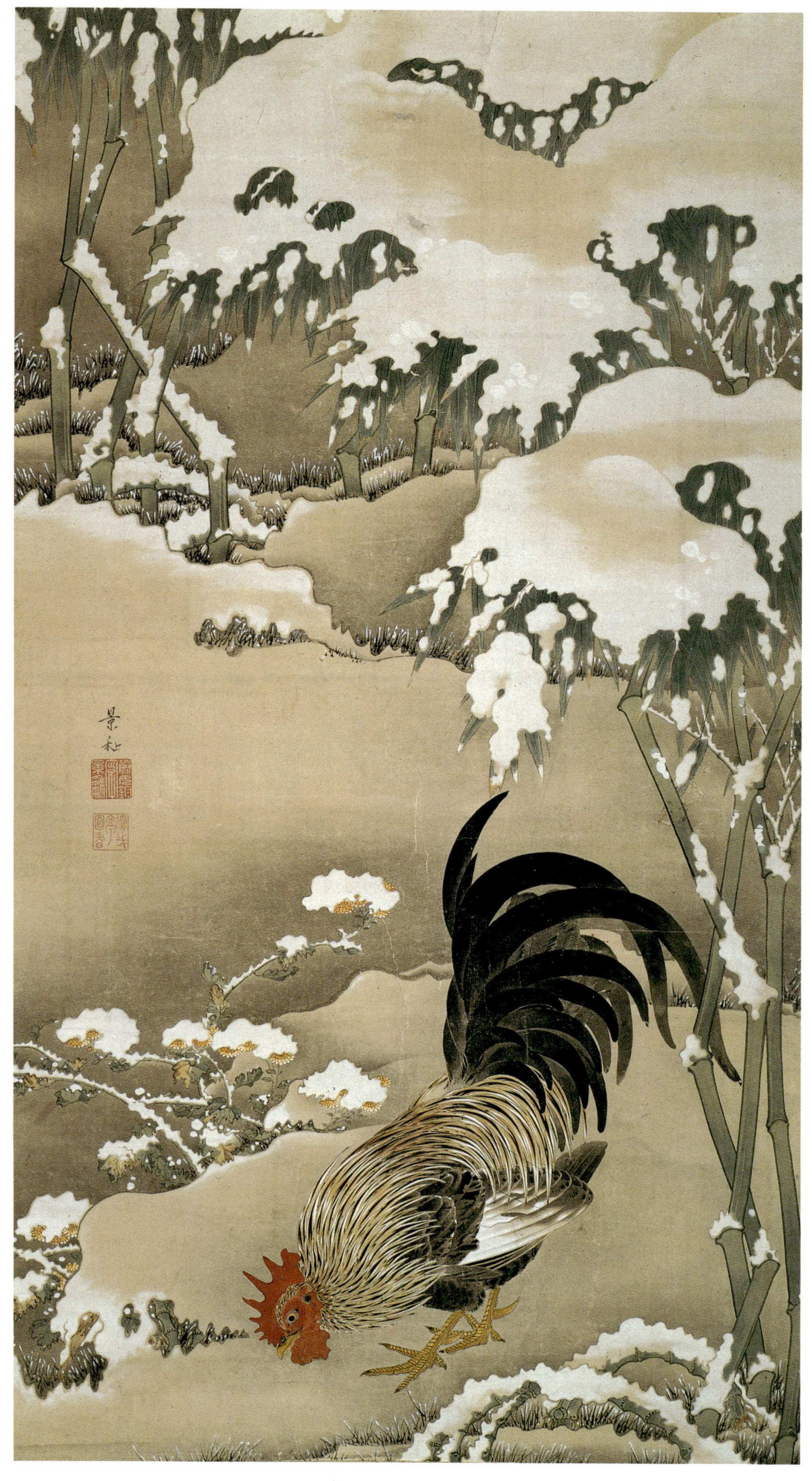
景和

2 *Peonies and Lilies*

Mid-1750s

Colors on silk, pair of hanging scrolls
121.5 × 75.5 cm (each scroll)
Signature (on *Lilies*): *Made by Jakuchū koji, Tō Jokin, of Heian* [Kyoto]

SEALS (on both paintings):
square intaglio: *Tō Jokin azana Keiwa*
square relief: *Yūkatei Tosho*
Private collection, Kanagawa Prefecture

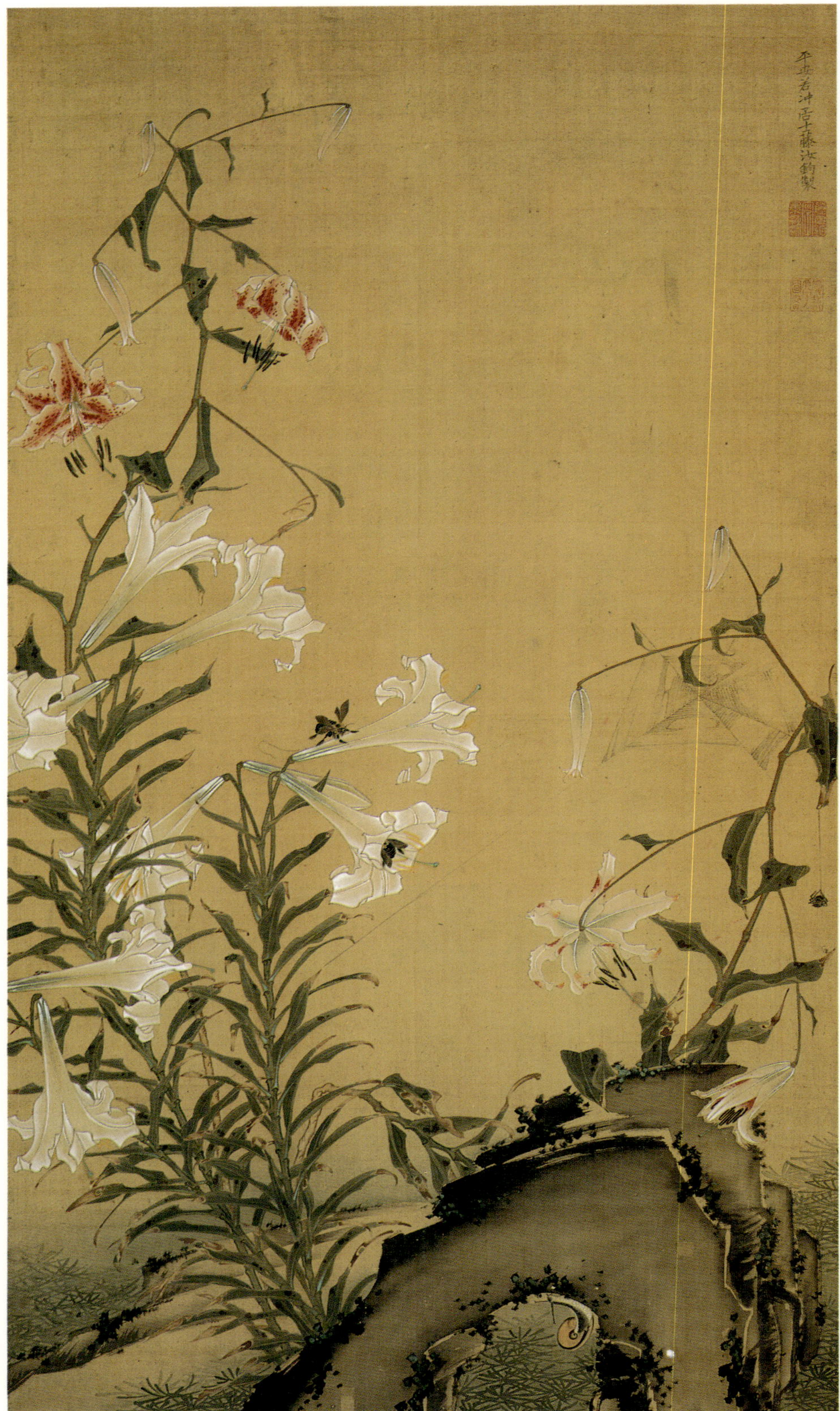

The minutely detailed style of bird-and-flower painting brought to Nagasaki by Shen Nan-p'in was introduced to the Kyoto-Osaka area by Kakutei Jōkō (1722–1785). Kakutei was a priest of the Shōfukuji in Nagasaki; this temple of the Ōbaku branch of Zen was established in Japan by the Ming priest Yin-yüan Lung-ch'i (Japanese: Ingen Ryūki; 1592–1673), who arrived in Japan in 1654. By 1747 Kakutei had moved to Osaka, where he taught painting to the noted connoisseur Kimura Kenkadō (1736–1802) and became a close friend of the Bunjin painter Ike Taiga (1723–1776). Jakuchū was probably also part of this congenial circle, although this contention has not been substantiated. He painted the present diptych in the manner of Shen Nan-p'in—a style he had absorbed through his contact with Kakutei.

No works by Kakutei can be cited as direct models for these paintings, however. Jakuchū undoubtedly derived such features as the shapes of the petals and the convoluted leaves from the style of Shen Nan-p'in. In *Peonies*, the spherical forms of the flowers and the modeling of the perforated Chinese *t'ai-hu* (Japanese: *taiko*) rocks resemble elements and techniques that can be seen in works by Kakutei in the Kobe Municipal Art Museum and in other collections. The rocks in *Lilies*, which display a rougher touch than those in *Peonies*, can also be related to components in Kakutei's ink paintings. To judge from the calligraphic style of the signature and the choice of seals, Jakuchū painted this diptych when he was in his mid-forties, under the influence of Kakutei.

Jakuchū executed the narrow brush strokes carefully and the applied colors precisely, yet for the most part these elements do not generate the illusion of reality present in the artist's later works, but instead produce hard, flat shapes. Nevertheless, even amid the ineptitude of these immature works, the first signs of Jakuchū's style are unmistakable, particularly in the holes in the rocks and in the blemishes on the fallen leaves and flower parts. These paintings are extremely important in

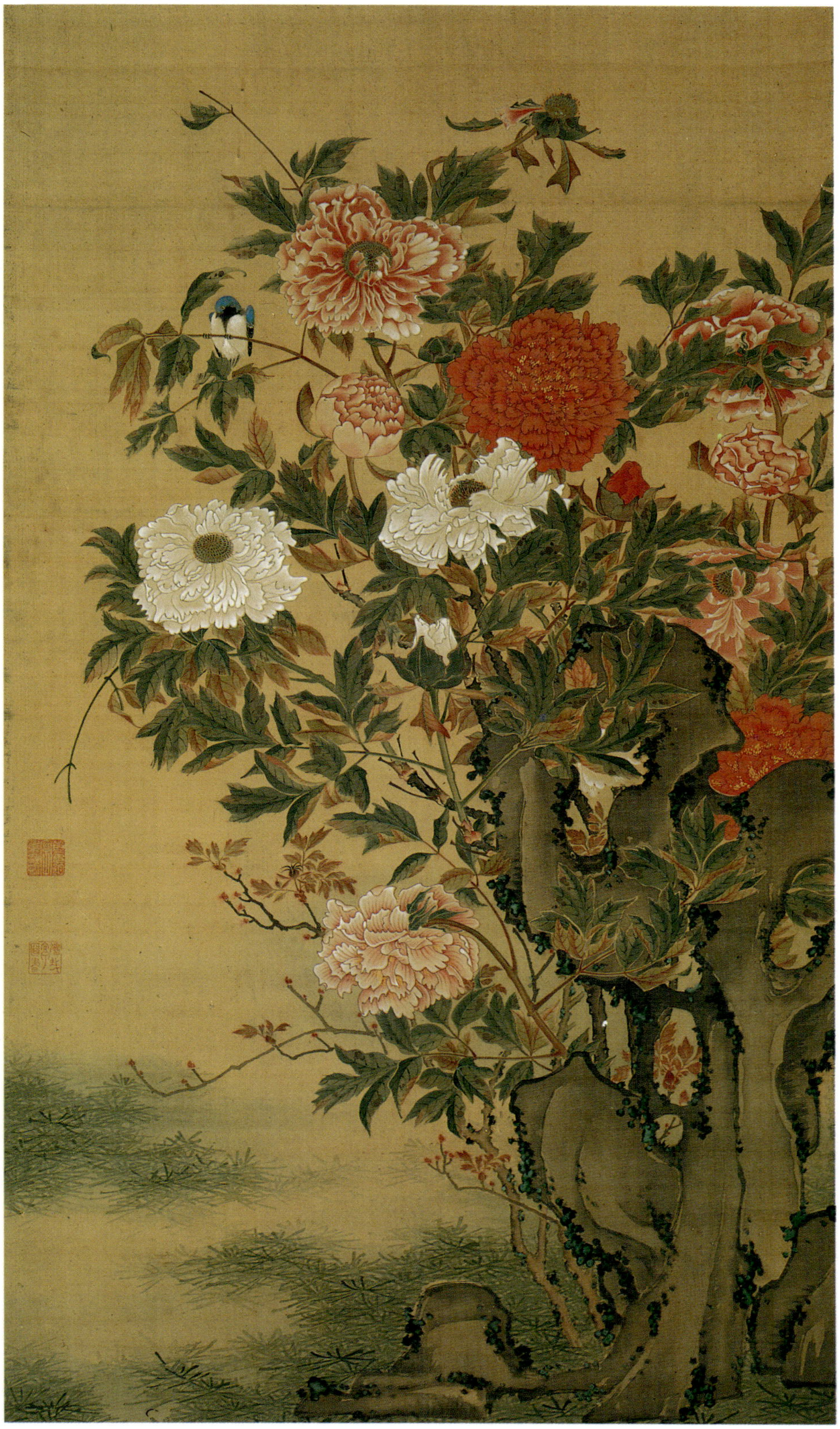

FIG. 51
Lilies, n.d.
Location uncertain

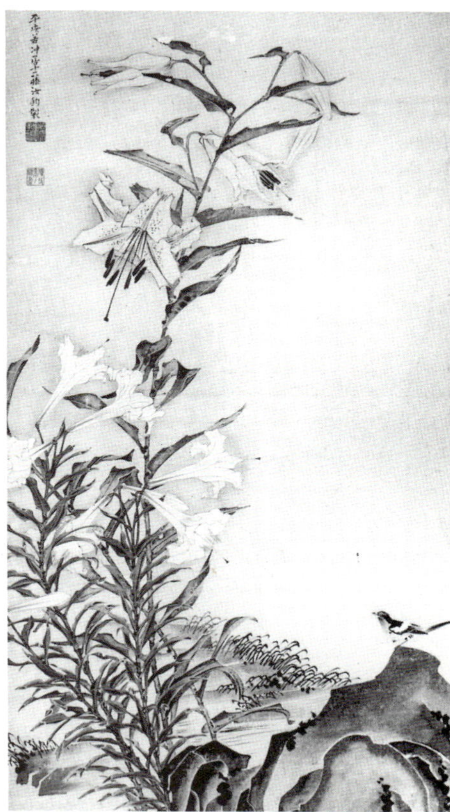

the evolution of the artist's distinctive style.

Jakuchū did an ink painting (now known only from a photograph in the archives of the Tokyo National Cultural Properties Research Institute, FIG. 51) that had almost exactly the same composition as *Lilies*. Unfortunately, no information regarding this painting was recorded, and it is unclear whether or not the work itself is extant.

Inside the lid of the box in which the paintings are kept is a piece of paper that reads: "Mr. Shibusawa, Furukawa, Tsukiji"; this seems to refer to Shibusawa Eiichi (1840–1931), a leading industrialist of modern Japan and, apparently, a former owner of the scrolls. The diptych, an important example of Jakuchū's early work, had never appeared in sale records or any other publications before 1984, when it was introduced to the world in *Geijutsu Shinchō*.[3] It has not yet been exhibited in Japan and is on display for the first time ever in the exhibition that this catalogue accompanies.

3 *Corn Plants and Kidney-bean Vines*

Mid-1750s

Ink on paper, pair of hanging scrolls
143.4 × 71.5 cm (each scroll)
Signature (on both): *Made by Jakuchū of Heian* [Kyoto]

SEALS (on both):
square intaglio: *Tō Jokin azana Keiwa*
square relief: *Yūkatei Tosho*
Sōdōji, Wakayama Prefecture

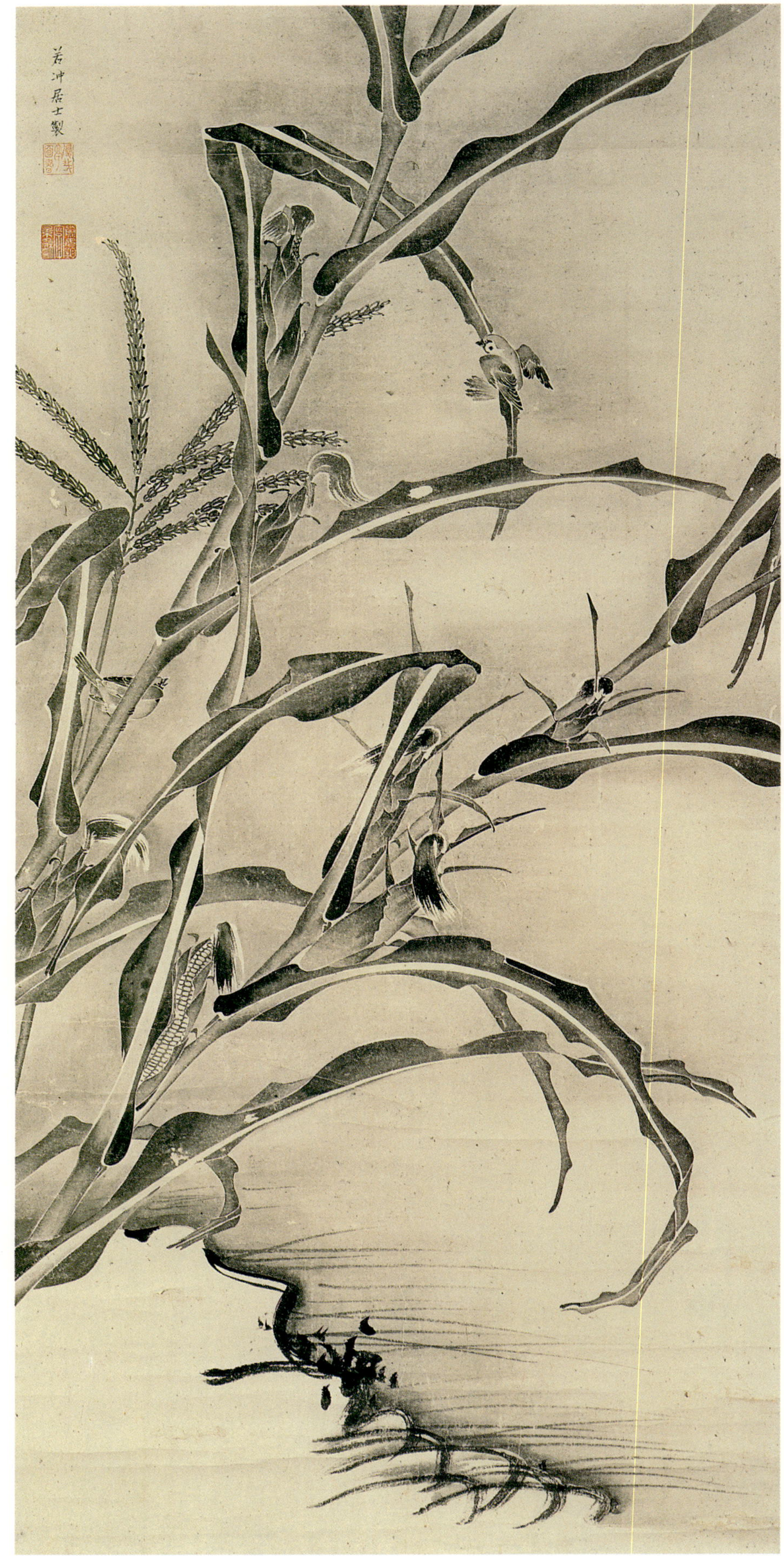

The right-hand scroll of this pair shows bean vines with two grasshoppers and a toad; the left-hand scroll depicts corn plants and two sparrows. These works belong to the lineage of plant-and-insect paintings made in the P'i-ling region of China (present-day Wu-chin County, Kiangsu Province). This genre, established during the late T'ang dynasty (618–907) through the Five Dynasties (907–960), about the first half of the tenth century, featured arrangements of grasses, flowers, vegetables, and fruits, together with insects, such as butterflies or mantises, and small animals, such as lizards and frogs. From the time of the Northern Sung dynasty (960–1127), the making of such paintings continued as a tradition in the P'i-ling area; and a number of works from the Yüan (1279–1368) and Ming (1368–1644) dynasties were imported into Japan. Jakuchū would probably have been able to see some of these and to study them.

The plant-and-insect genre includes works both in color and in ink, and there is little distinction in the techniques used in the two mediums. Even in the case of ink paintings, artists did not wield the brush freely; rather, they created highly crafted works, as if converting a minutely detailed color painting directly into a monochrome version. Various works, such as *Grapes* (anonymous; Tokyo National Museum), demonstrate this process: the application of ink wash around the outer edges of the

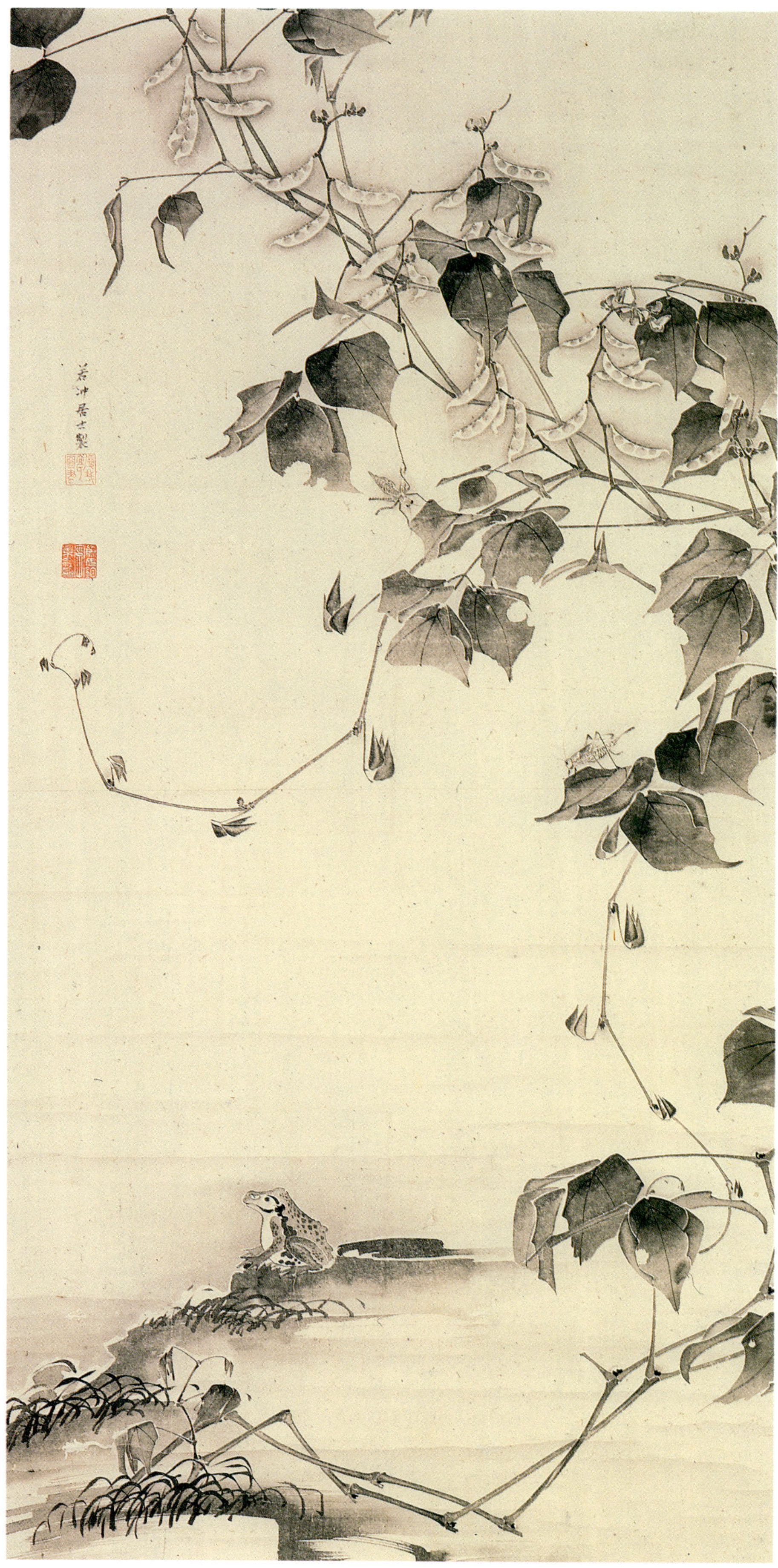

bean pods, defining the contours of the beans with shading in light ink and leaving the pods themselves white; and the use of a paper pattern to paint the veins of the corn leaves into pointed shapes.

No specific plant-and-insect paintings can be identified as the source of the present diptych, but Jakuchū clearly employed the special characteristics of P'i-ling painting in, for example, the stiffened shapes of the bean leaves, which look almost as if they were attached to thin iron plates—a result of the artist's application of the ink in flat washes and of his acute consciousness of the forms. However, the conventional techniques of the P'i-ling school took on a new life when they were seen through the naïve eyes of the Kyoto artist. The plants bend, twist, and overlap in a collection of near-abstract shapes, yet they have a biological rhythm that excites the eye of the viewer. No other artist either before or after Jakuchū produced this kind of image from the worn-out style of P'i-ling painting.

The Sōdōji, which owns both this diptych and *White Cockatoo* (No. 4), is a temple of the Tōfukuji school of the Rinzai Zen sect, and the temple is known for its *fusuma* (sliding-screen) paintings by Nagasawa Rosetsu (1754–1799). It is unclear through what connection the temple came to have these early works by Jakuchū.

4 *White Cockatoo*

c. 1750(?)

Colors on silk, hanging scroll
83.6 × 42.7 cm
Signature: *Made by Jakuchū koji Tō Jokin of Heian* [Kyoto]

SEALS:
square intaglio: *Jakuchū koji*
square relief: *Jokin*; *Tansei wa rōshō ni itaru o shirazu*
Sōdōji, Wakayama Prefecture

Jakuchū painted at least four hanging scrolls of a white cockatoo on an elaborate perch (one of which is in the Museum of Fine Arts, Boston; FIG. 46). To judge by the signature and technique, the present painting seems to be the earliest among them.

In addition to extant works and those known through photographs, another painting of the same type was described in a poem by Minagawa Kien (1734–1807), a Confucian scholar and Bunjin painter in Kyoto. Anthologized in *Kien Shishū* (*Collected Poems of Kien*, 1792), the poem entitled "A White Cockatoo Painted by Jakuchū" shows how Jakuchū's paintings of this subject were appreciated during his own time:

> Mr. Itō, who lives in the southern part of Kyoto, endows his paintings of plants and animals with spirituality. Yesterday, a certain person who knows that I like paintings in brilliant colors took some silk for painting to this superb artist and requested a work from him. In the finished painting of a cockatoo, the feathers are neatly arranged, and the white of the wings is so bright that they seem about to move. There is divinity contained in it, which shines through from the back. The golden ring and the colored perch support the dark blue feet; the green lotus blossoms offer water in jewel-like cups. The cockatoo raises its crest and turns its eye to the side. It seems to be recalling how it once perched on a tree in Lungshan [a mountain in Lung County, Shensi Province, China]. Bound by a long chain to a vermilion stand, surely it must be feeling resentment. What words are contained in the beautiful beak? Ah, this is truly superb technique. It is like the skill that created the painting in the story of Chao Yen of the T'ang dynasty, who poured wine on a painting of a beautiful woman and pulled out the beauty named Chen-chen. Who knows whether we may not some day hear the words of this cockatoo.[4]

The phrase "lives in the southern part of Kyoto" indicated that Jakuchū painted the work to which the poem refers in his last years, when he was living in seclusion in Fukakusa; nevertheless, this painting seems to have been of the same type as the four early works of cockatoos. It is of great interest that, as implied by the poem, the artist painted the detailed work in less than a single day. Kien's own attitude toward the painting is also noteworthy: not only did he express surprise at its realism, but he also introduced emotion by anthropomorphizing the bird. This attitude was not limited to Kien. Once, Daiten Kenjō had seen an imported parrot on display at the Gion Festival and had written a poem (in *Sakuhishū*) in which he expressed pity for the parrot, which was kept in captivity far from its home in the southern seas. Jakuchū himself may have seen a bird displayed in this way and have felt emotions similar to Daiten's.

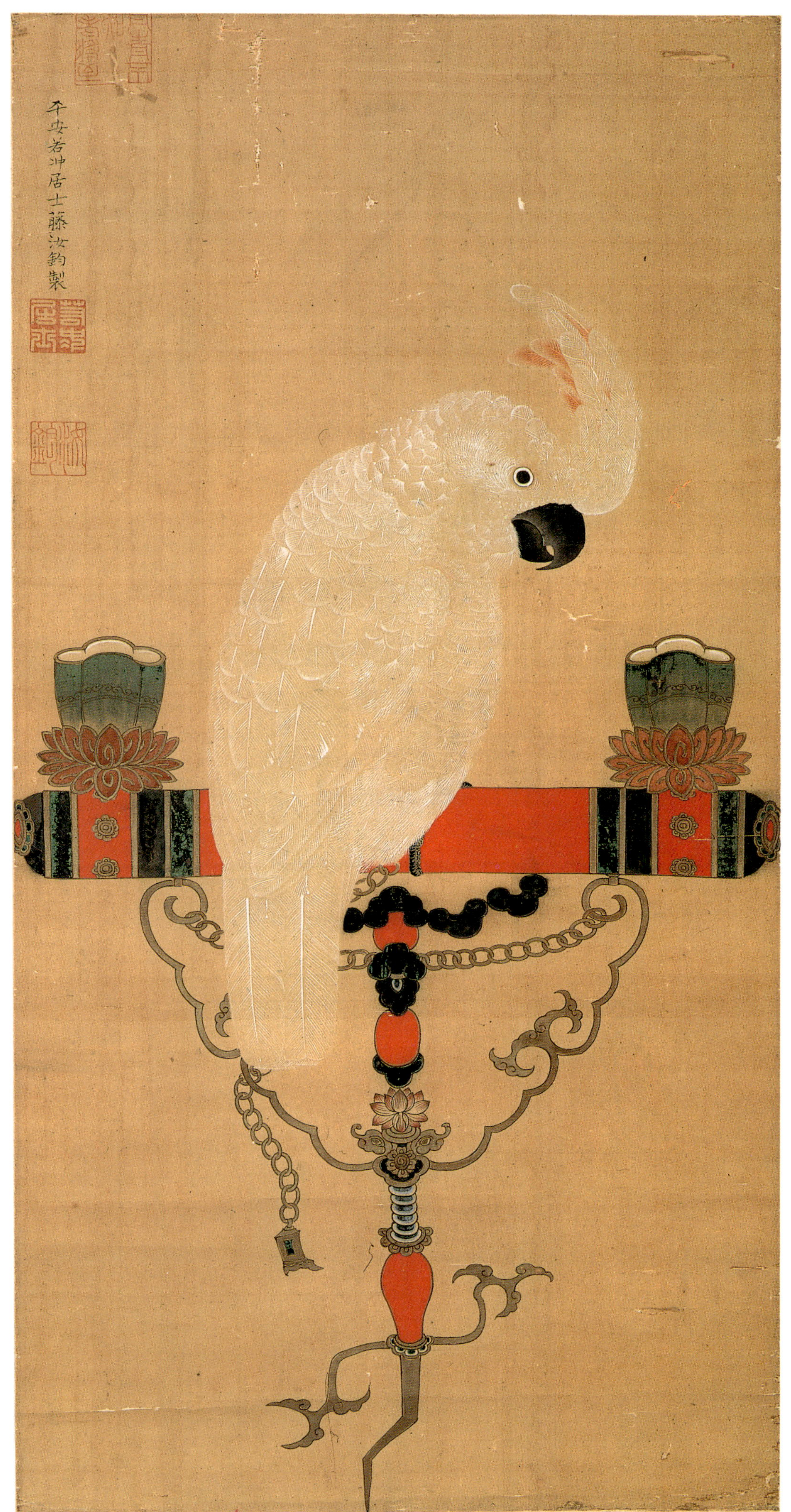
平安若冲居士藤汝鈞製

5 *Willow Kannon*

(*Yoryū Kannon*)

n.d.

Colors on silk, hanging scroll
129.2 × 61.8 cm

SEAL:
round relief: *Jakuchū koji*
Private collection, Hyōgo Prefecture

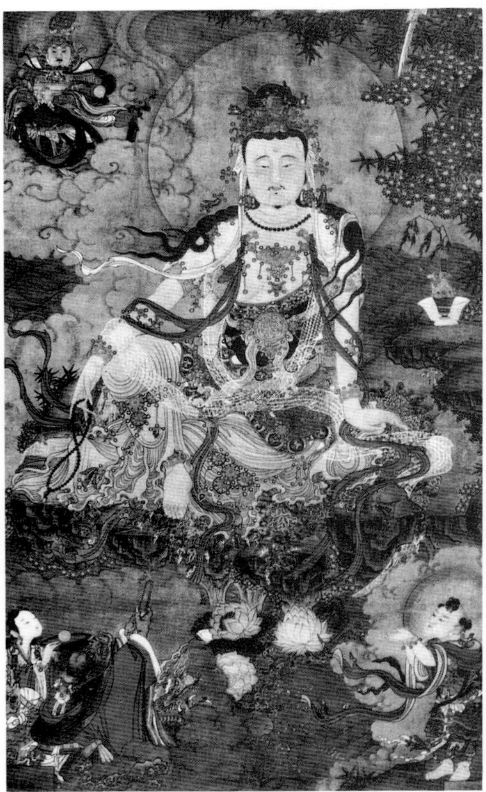

FIG. 52
"Willow Kannon," n.d., from the *Gaen Shūei*.

Infinite compassion and an unfailing dedication to the salvation of all sentient beings are the distinguishing attributes of Kannon (Sanskrit: Avalokiteśvara), the most widely venerated Bodhisattva of Mahayana Buddhism. The idea that Kannon could appear in various guises in different locales in order to accomplish salvation gave rise to the concept of the "Thirty-three Manifestations of Kannon," of which the "Willow Kannon" is one.

With a large halo behind the head and wearing a white robe, Kannon sits with crossed legs on a rock at the edge of the water. To the right is a vase containing a willow branch. The lotus blossoms and the coral in the water and the bamboo growing behind show that the setting is the sacred cavern on Mount Potalaka, the island-mountain paradise where Kannon resides. The figure standing on a rock at the lower right is Sudhana (Japanese: Zenzai Dōji), who received instruction first from the Bodhisattva Manjuśri (see NO. 15) and then from a succession of fifty-three wise and holy beings. Finally, guided by the Bodhisattva Samantabhadra (see NO. 15), Sudhana gained enlightenment, or entry into the realm of universal truth. During his pilgrimage, he visited Kannon at Mount Potalaka. At the lower left of the painting are the Dragon King and an attendant offering a jewel to Kannon; at the upper left is one of the protective deities of the sky, the swift-footed Skanda.

In Japan many paintings of this subject have survived that were produced in Korea during the Koryō period (918–1392). Almost all exhibit the same iconographic features and are similar in their manner of execution, as shown in three works in the Daitokuji, a monastery in Kyoto.

This painting appears to be related to a Koryō image of Willow Kannon, but, when compared to actual surviving examples, it displays significant differences. Of the extant Koryō works, a painting in the Yamato Bunkakan is the closest to Jakuchū's in its depiction of the figures of Kannon and Sudhana, although differences clearly indicate that it could not have served as the immediate prototype. (According to Ariga Yoshitaka, a painting of similar composition resides in a temple in Saga Prefecture,[5] but this subject remains to be studied.) Professor Tsuji Nobuo of Tokyo University has pointed out close correspondences in a painting in the *Gaen Shūei* (FIG. 52), which indicate that the prototype for Jakuchū's work may have been a *Willow Kannon* identical in basic composition, but with additional components that reflect beliefs of folk religion.[6] Nevertheless, the artist of the painting recorded in the *Gaen Shūei Shūei* used the techniques typical of Buddhist paintings of the Koryō period to depict translucent garments and minutely detailed decorative patterns, whereas Jakuchū treated these elements so summarily that there is much room for speculation as to the nature of the model for his work. Indeed, the artist may have based his work on a mass-produced popular painting or print.

The present painting was published in *Kokka*.[7] Upon reexamination in light of current research, it cannot be identified with certainty as a genuine work by Jakuchū. The round relief seal reading *Jakuchū koji* is not precisely the same as the standard impressions of the phrase. The brushwork is somewhat tentative, and the shading on the rocks and clouds was not skillfully executed. However, it seems certain that, at the very least, this painting is based on one from Jakuchū's hand, and the stiffness may simply have been owing to a combination of the style of the original model and the fact that it was copied from an early piece by Jakuchū. It is included here as an example of the various types of Buddhist paintings created by Jakuchū.

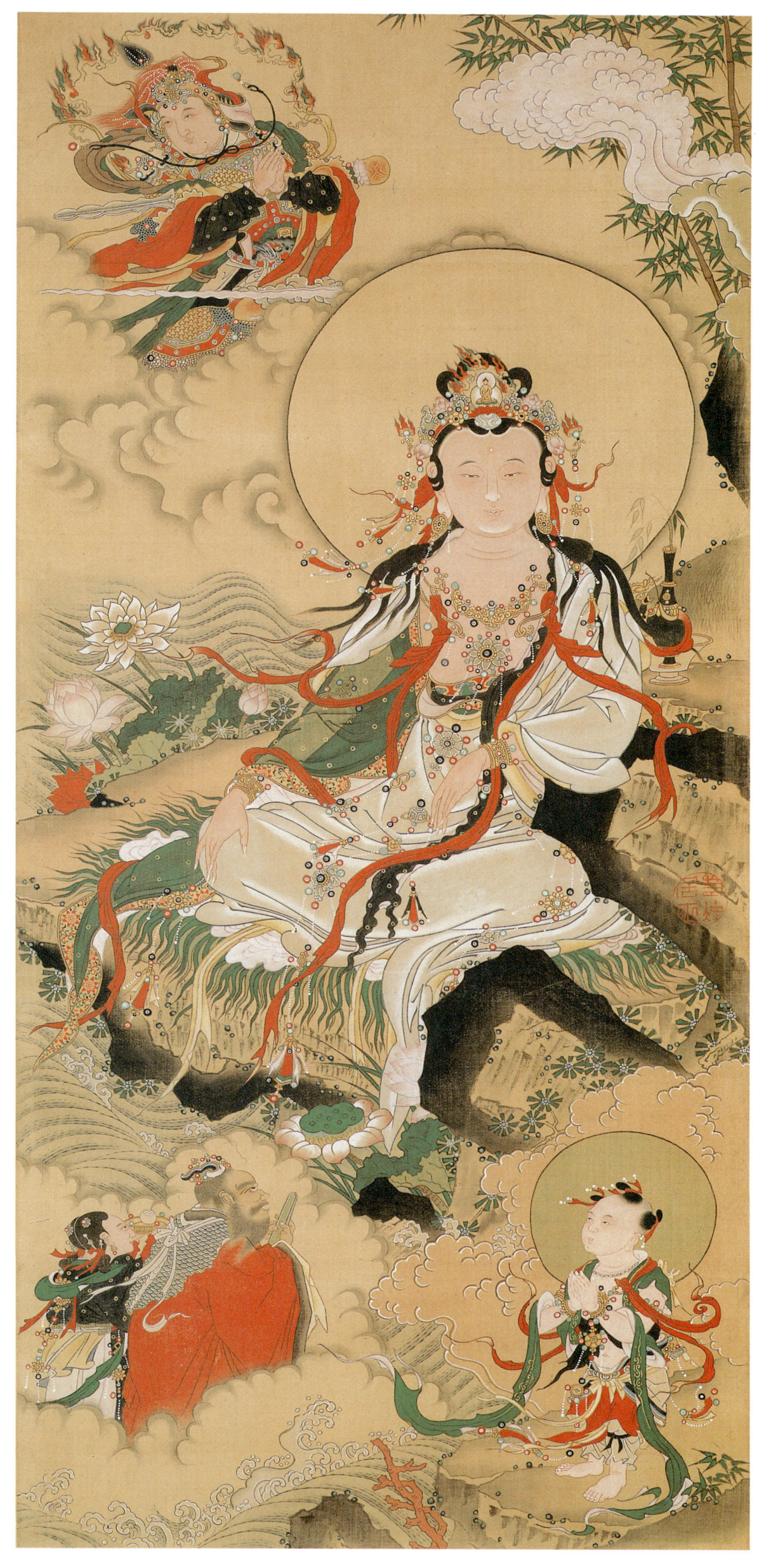

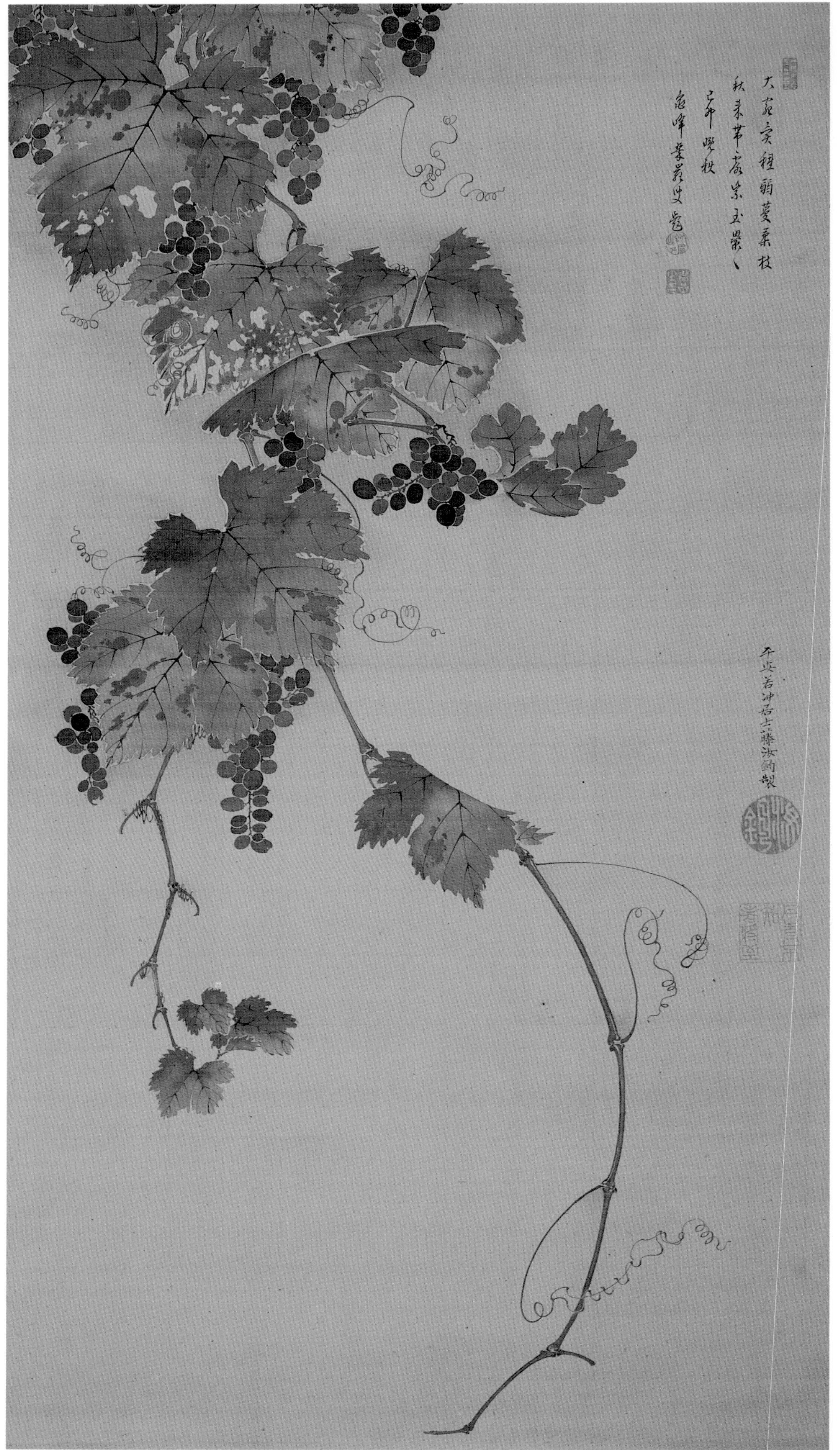

6 *Grapes*

c. 1753–1754

Ink on silk, hanging scroll
99 × 57 cm
Signature: *Heian Jakuchū koji Tō-Jokin-sei*
Inscription:
Singular variety of grape, with supple tendrils and soft vines. With the coming of autumn it is tinged with dew, heavy with grapes like purple jewels.
Written by Kihō Suigan

SEALS:
round intaglio: *Jokin*
square relief: *Tansei wa rōshō ni itaru o shirazu*
Private collection, Tokyo

According to one tradition, the Chinese painter Jih Kuan (active during the late years of the Southern Sung dynasty [1127–1279] and the early part of the Yüan dynasty) was the first artist to depict grapes in monochrome ink. From documentary references as well as pictorial evidence (such as his painting of grapes of 1291, now in the collection of the Hamazawa Industrial Corporation, Nagano Prefecture), it is clear that Jih Kuan's grape compositions were conceived and executed in accordance with the stylistic tradition of the Literati school known as "ink play" or "ink diversion" (Japanese: *bokugi*).

The intention of artists working in this way was not to reproduce the subject realistically, but rather to simplify it, rendering it in a combination of brush strokes that ranged from the slow and dilatory to the lively and assertive, and that were innovative in their changes of orientations. By these and other idiosyncratic means, such as sprinkling ink on the painting with the hand itself, artists sought to express their creative originality and essential spirit. *Bokugi* was introduced to Japan as early as the fourteenth century, when the Zen priest Ue Guan produced paintings in this manner.

By contrast, certain Chinese artists of the Yüan period developed a method of depicting grapes in a more detailed manner, also combining colors with ink. *Grapes*, a painting in the Tokyo National Museum that is thought to have been painted in the P'i-ling region, illustrates this mode of execution. Then again, a painting of grapes by Wei Tuan (a man of whom little is known, but who is thought to have been active during the Yüan period) that was displayed in the exhibition "Arts of the Sung and Yüan" at the Osaka Municipal Art Museum in 1978 has none of the stylistic characteristics of the *bokugi* tradition, but is rather the product of a professional workshop artist who worked in a conservative, technical manner. Later, during the Ming period, there was a growing tendency, exemplified by numerous pieces, to depict grapes in monochrome. A work by Wang Liang-ch'en in the Freer Gallery of Art, Washington, D.C., and an anonymous piece reproduced in *Kokka* 861[8] are examples of this trend. Depictions of grapes in this style served, in turn, as the basic source of pictorial inspiration for men such as Guan, during the Muromachi period (1392–1568), and Jakuchū, during the Edo period (1603–1868), both of whom produced exquisite examples.

The present painting is somewhat more realistic in depiction than the grape composition in the Shin'enkan Collection (FIG. 32), and the careful rendering of the spotted, insect-eaten leaves and of the delicate tendrils attests to Jakuchū's close observation of the subject. His conception differs completely from the *bokugi* style, not only in expressing the distinctive vision and strength of the artist, but also in revealing something of the spiritual wellsprings that inspired his art.

The inscription, which is dated to 1759, was conceived by Kenshō (also known as Kihō) Suigan, a priest from the Tenryūji, a temple of the Rinzai branch of Zen Buddhism. If the painting was executed in the same year the inscription was added, it would have been concurrent with Jakuchū's work on the monochrome compositions in the Rokuonji (NO. 16), but this is not likely. After studying the style of the work and that of its signature, Professor Tsuji Nobuo has convincingly stated that the painting must have been done several years earlier.[9]

7 *Snake Gourds and Insects*

c. 1753–1754

Colors on silk, hanging scroll
111.5 × 48.2 cm
Signature: *Heian Jakuchū-sei*

SEALS:
round intaglio: *Jokin*
square relief: *Tansei wa rōshō ni itaru o shirazu*
Private collection, Osaka

In this painting, the yellow flowers of the snake-gourd plant, which bloom in late summer and early fall, appear together with some of the characteristic insects and reptiles of the season: a snail, two varieties of crickets, a cabbage butterfly, two green caterpillars, a praying mantis, a katydid, a dragonfly, two varieties of green frogs, and a grasshopper. It is unclear whether snake gourds were ever portrayed in any of the Chinese paintings devoted to "grasses and insects," but bamboo and insects are depicted in a Yüan-period piece in the Tokyo National Museum, and melons appear in many works, such as a painting of insects and melon by the Ming-period master Lü Ching-fu (Nezu Art Museum, Tokyo); it is thought that portrayals of insects and snake gourds developed out of this tradition.

In the present work, the method of representing the ridges in the gourds with minute broken lines, the finely detailed treatment of the leaves, and the shapes of the flowers may have been inspired by an illustration in a woodblock-printed album. Moreover, the use of pigments to create shaded areas seems reminiscent of Western chiaroscuro techniques; this characteristic also may be an indication that the artist was trying to emulate a woodblock illustration. However, no such prototype has yet come to light, so this thesis remains unproven. Even if such a prototype were found, it is likely that the bold, innovative manner in which Jakuchū handled the snake-gourd plant was attributable to his idiosyncratic conception.

Among the characteristic components in the pictorial inventory of this piece are flowers, vines, seedpods, whirlpool-like tendrils that thrust upward in opposition to gravity, and leaves spotted with insect-eaten holes, together with the diminutive forms of insects and frogs. The insects depicted here appear in almost identical forms in the *Dōshoku Sai-e* painting *Insects and Reptiles at a Pond* (NO. 14.6), which was done about ten years later and is a veritable teeming garden of flourishing insects. However, in *Snake Gourds and Insects* this crowded, vibrant atmosphere is not present. Rather, Jakuchū here depicted a more subdued sense of the insect world, an atmosphere of tranquility; this charming, understated quality is a characteristic feature of his early works.

Tomioka Tessai (1837–1924), the famous Literati painter of recent times, wrote three documents that now accompany *Snake Gourds and Insects*, and he also did the distinctive calligraphy on the box in which the painting is stored. One of the documents, written to Imai Takudō, an ardent art collector from Echigo Province, describes how Tessai, who considered the painting to be a masterpiece, strongly recommended that Takudō acquire it. Another document states that the painting once belonged to Masuyama Sessai (1754–1819), the provincial lord of the Nagashima region in Ise Province (present-day Mie Prefecture), who did accomplished bird-and-flower paintings in the style of Shen Nan-p'in. One of Sessai's representative pieces, an album now in the Tokyo National Museum, includes detailed depictions of various kinds of insects, and it is easy to imagine how fond he was of Jakuchū's painting. Sessai was also a friend of both Daiten Kenjō and Kimura Kenkadō. In 1790, when Kenkadō was punished by the government for distilling too much sake, Sessai arranged to have him exiled to Ise, where Kenkadō lived for some years before he was finally allowed to return to Osaka. Perhaps Jakuchū's painting came into Sessai's possession as a result of this network of friends and acquaintances.

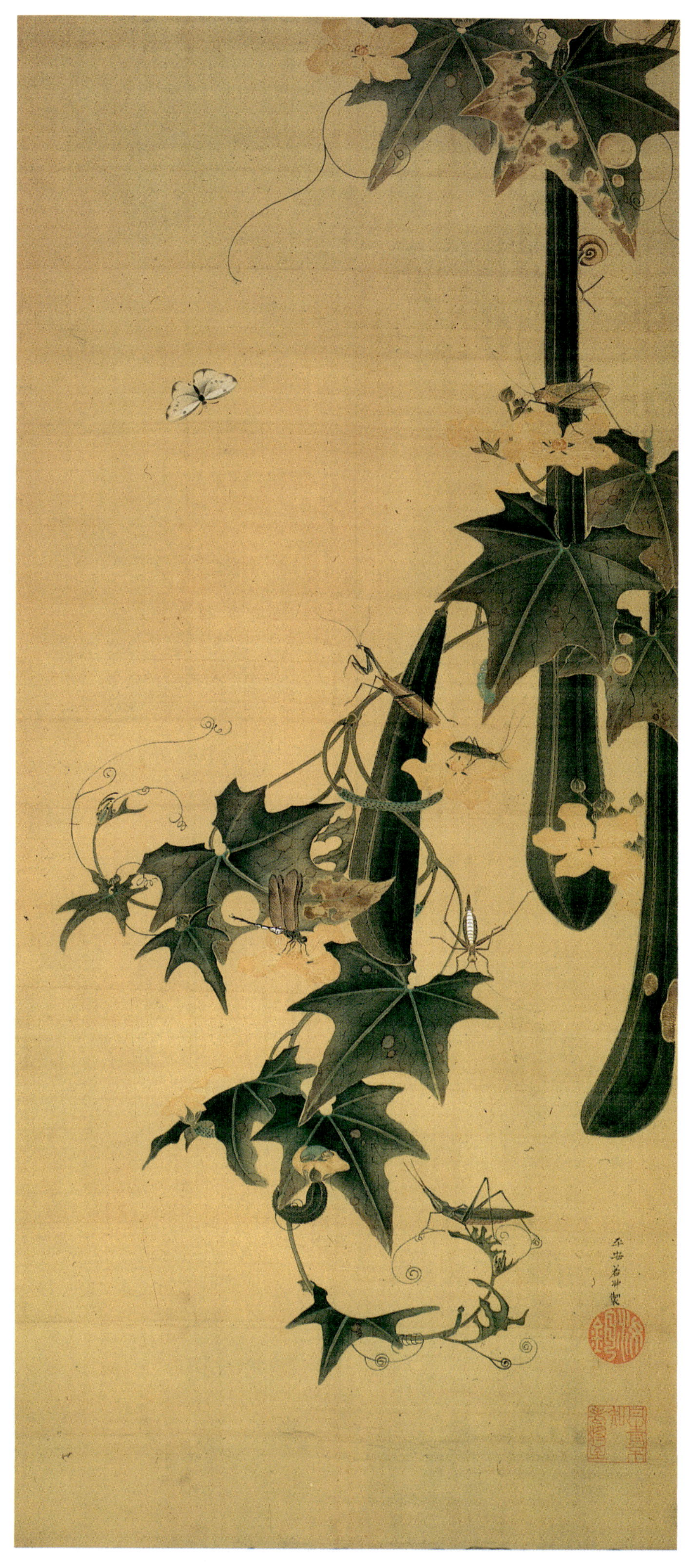
平安若冲製

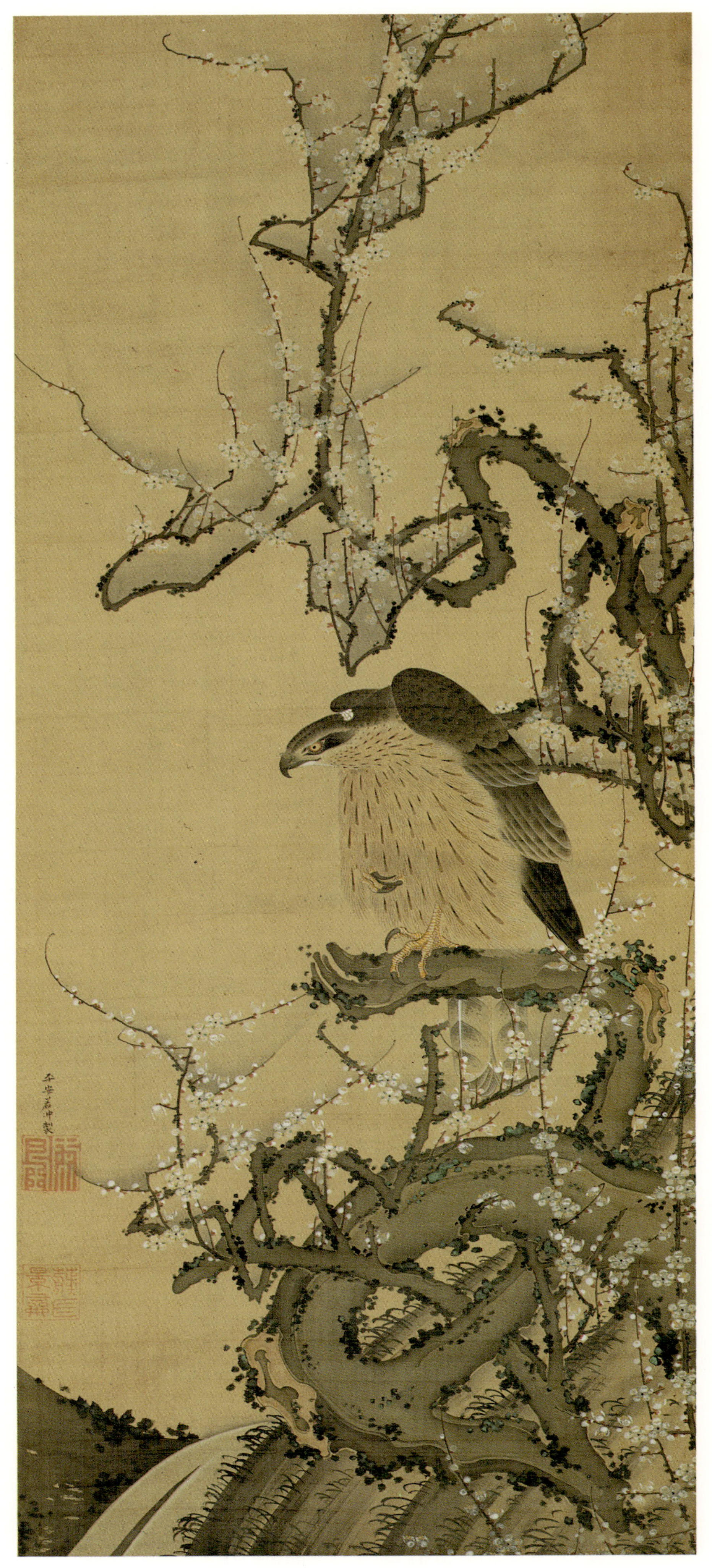
平安若冲製

8 *Hawk in a Blossoming Plum Tree*

c. 1753–1754

Colors on silk, hanging scroll
120.5 × 54.7 cm
Signature: *Heian Jakuchū-sei*

SEALS:
square intaglio: *Jokin*
square relief: *Tō-shi Keiwa*
Private collection, Osaka

Jakuchū here depicted a single hawk resting on the remnants of a large branch bent horizontally like a natural perch, in a bizarre plum tree. With its twisted, contorted trunk and limbs, the tree has no equivalent in nature. To the rear is a small hill, and in front of it a small stream flows.

The figure of the bird here is virtually identical to one that appears in a folding screen with depictions of hawks and other birds by the renowned master of the Momoyama period (1568–1603) Kanō Sanraku (1559–1635), which is now in the collection of Keiichirō Nishimura of Shiga Prefecture. Jakuchū's hawk differs only in the treatment of the details of the breast feathers. The Sanraku screen formerly belonged to the Nishi Honganji, a monastery in Kyoto, and it is altogether possible that Jakuchū had a chance to see it there. Other depictions of hawks such as this one exist, so it is possible that Jakuchū was inspired by another work, but there can be no doubt that his prototype was a painting done by an artist of the Kanō school.

Daiten's inscription ("Ketsumei") on the stone monument that Jakuchū had erected in the Shōkokuji (FIG. 3) notes that, at the beginning of his career, the artist studied Kanō methods of painting, but it is difficult to discern any clear evidence of the distinctive style and brushwork of the school in his other extant works. The hawk depicted here is unusual in Jakuchū's oeuvre because it clearly preserves Kanō stylistic precedents. In this pictorial tradition, which extended from the Muromachi period into the early Edo period, hawks, tigers, and other impressive beasts were periodically depicted as symbolic manifestations of the power of the military class.

Although inherited as a theme from the past, Jakuchū's hawk was painted during the eighteenth century, when Japan was at peace, and so is likely to have had a different significance. Perhaps it is simplest to regard the bird as a covert symbol of a lonely, eremitic artist who was confined in a skillfully contrived environment of his own making. Thus, the painting can be viewed as a reflection of Jakuchū's state of mind at a time when he was inclined to isolate himself from the demands and obligations of society.

There is no way to determine what sort of Chinese painting Jakuchū studied in order to create the unique blend of painting methods evident in the plum tree, with its wonderful forms and its combination of pigments and ink rendering the branches. If we compare this tree to those in such works as *White Plum Blossoms and Moon*, dated to 1755 (FIG. 26) and *Birds in a Blossoming Plum Tree*, dated to 1758, from the *Dōshoku Sai-e* series (FIG. 33.2), the sense of form and volume here is much flatter, and the light ink wash between the limbs was added only to one section of the background, indicating that the work is an early one. The handling of the plum, arched mound of earth, and flowing water becomes refined in later works.

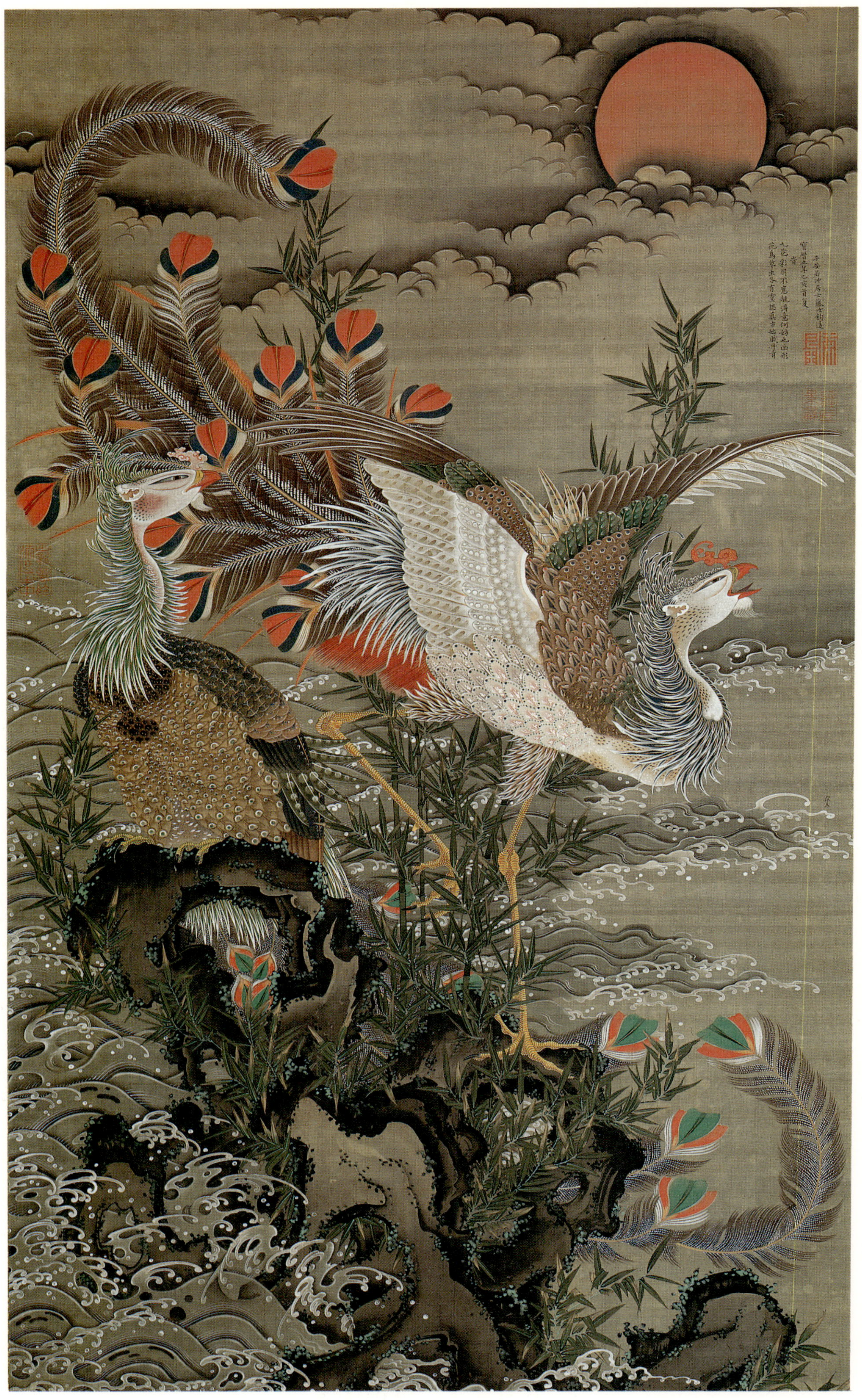

9 *Pair of Phoenixes and the Rising Sun*

1755

Colors on silk, hanging scroll
185.5 × 113.8 cm
Inscription and signature:
Flowers, birds, grasses, and insects each have their own innate spirit. Only after one has actually determined the true nature of this spirit through observation should painting begin. There is, however, no way to actually observe a phoenix's resplendent plumage. So it may be portrayed freely, with no hindrance to the imagination. Hōreki 5 [cyclical signs; 1755], *Shuka* [Fourth Month] *Heian* [Kyoto]—*Jakuchū koji Tō Jokin-zō*

SEALS:
square intaglio: *Jokin*
square relief: *Tō Keiwa-in*
vertical rectangular relief: *Shin'i o hatto no uchi ni idasu*
Imperial Household Collection

The *hō-ō* (phoenix) is an imaginary sacred Chinese bird that appears on bronze ritual vessels of the Shang (c. 1600–c. 1100 B.C.) and Chou (c. 1100–256 B.C.) dynasties and subsequently has been widely used as an artistic motif in the architecture, crafts, and painting of East Asia. This legendary bird is said to dwell in paulownia trees, to eat bamboo seeds, and to have feathers of five colors. Revered as the king of the avian world, the phoenix is attended by a retinue of birds of all varieties. Its celestial presence is thought to be revealed when a sage of great religious significance is born into the world, and this propitious symbolic association seems to be the reason for the popularity of the phoenix as an artistic motif.

The phrase on the vertical rectangular relief seal, *Shin'i o hatto no uchi ni idasu* (A new concept departing from established precedent), is one used by Su Shih (1036–1101), a literatus of the Northern Sung period, in reference to the legendary painter of the T'ang period Wu Tao-hsuan (also known as Wu Tao-tzu; active c. 720–760), and Jakuchū impressed the same seal on *White Plum Blossoms and Moon* (FIG. 26) and on *Herbaceous Peonies and Butterflies* (FIG. 33.1), one of the *Dōshoku Sai-e* paintings. The style of the present painting clearly indicates that its particulars were copied quite faithfully from a Chinese prototype, but that it incorporates a new conceptual attitude.

Because of his close affiliation with the Shōkokuji, the artist is likely to have seen there an ink depiction of a phoenix standing on a tree trunk and gazing at the sun, done by the Chinese academic artist Lin Liang (active late fifteenth to early sixteenth century). Although the subjects show certain general similarities, Jakuchū's painting is quite different in conception and style, and the Chinese work seems not to have served as a source of pictorial ideas for him in any way.

Rather, it seems that he drew his inspiration directly from a Chinese painting of a different sort, such as *Phoenixes under the Morning Sun* by Hsüeh-feng Li I-ho (published in *Kokka*;[10] FIG. 28) and the anonymous *One Hundred Birds* (published in *Kokka*;[11] FIG. 27). However, the "new concept" to which the seal in the present work makes reference is what distinguishes Jakuchū's piece from such Chinese models. In some areas the handling of color in the male's feathers differs noticeably from that in the female's, and various details of the plumage not only are exceptionally beautiful as designs, but also far exceed the prototypical Chinese works in the precise, crisp execution of their particulars. Moreover, the delicate, tentacle-like, attenuated forms of the miniature wave crests surpass, in their innovative mannerism, anything of this sort in Chinese or Korean painting, again demonstrating the artist's highly refined aesthetic sensitivity.

The inscription on this painting, together with the contextually related inscription on the painting of a tiger produced in the same year (Shin'enkan Collection; FIG. 29), provides instructive insights into Jakuchū's creative preoccupations at this time in his career, when he was forty years of age. The phrase *i o ete* at the end of the inscription is somewhat ambiguous and has been interpreted in two ways: either as "draw on one's own [creative] imagination" or, as above, "freely, with no hindrance to the imagination." The first interpretation arises from the artist's practice of actually painting flora and fauna from direct observation and experience and his being forced, in the case of an imaginary bird, to portray the subject purely from his imagination. The second suggests that there are no impediments restricting the free exercise of the imagination. However, it should also be noted that the painter Yosa Buson (1716–1783) mentioned in one of his letters that he had "extensively utilized the style of Chinese painters" in two landscapes he had recently completed,[12] and the phrase *i o ete* also appears in those two works. It may well be, therefore, that Jakuchū used this phrase in his inscription to acknowledge that he had, in this case, emulated the style of another painting (such as one of the two Chinese pieces mentioned above).

The inscription on the box in which this painting has been preserved indicates that it was presented to the Imperial Household by the Higashi Honganji monastery in Kyoto.

10 *Carp*

c. 1754–1756

Colors on silk, hanging scroll
106.2 × 48.1 cm
Signature: *Heian Jakuchū-sei*

SEALS:
square relief: *Jokin*
square intaglio: *Jakuchū koji*
Tokyo National University of Fine Arts and Music

In one category of Chinese painting, that of fish and water plants, fish swimming in shallow water were depicted together with duckweed or similar forms of marine plants. Documentary sources suggest that this subject was first depicted by Hsü Ch'ung-szu, an artist active during the early part of the Northern Sung period.[13] In such paintings, contour lines were kept to a minimum and combinations of dark and light pigments and ink were used to portray the scales and other details of the fish. This technique, which was particularly suited to such representations and seems to have been handed down from the Sung period to the present without any significant stylistic modification, resulted in the production of many paintings with essentially identical methods of execution.

Although depictions of fish and water plants were also produced in Japan during the Muromachi period, the motivation to portray the subject during Jakuchū's time clearly reflects the introduction into Japan of stimulating stylistic ideas by painters of the school of Shen Nan-p'in. Although no depictions of carp by Shen Nan-p'in himself are known, there are examples by Kumashiro Yūhi (1693–1773), who studied briefly under the master; by Sō Shiseki (1712/15–1786), who studied under Yūhi; by Ringan (also known as Shorin-sanjin; ?–1792), another follower of Yūhi; and of Katsu Jagyoku (also known as Jagyoku-sanjin; 1734–1780), who studied under Kakutei, yet another disciple of Yūhi—and a distinctive, detailed manner of treating the scales of the fish is common to all of these paintings. Thus it appears that this subject category, in which carp were depicted in a skillful, "boneless" manner, must have been a part of Shen Nan-p'in's artistic repertoire and must have been revived by members of his school, who added a decorative treatment.

Katsu Jagyoku was an artist from Osaka whose activities as a painter demonstrate how this subject, as part of the style of the school of Shen Nan-p'in, was brought from Nagasaki to the Osaka-Kyoto area and subsequently introduced to Edo. That Katsu Jagyoku himself was known as Ri-ō (Old Man Carp) attests to his special interest in the subject, and that the carp was also a favorite subject of Maruyama Ōkyo (1733–1795) and his followers is further evidence of the popularity of this fish as a pictorial theme in the Kansai area. Depictions of fish and water plants were more or less prescribed by pictorial precedent, and the influence of this stylistically confined tradition may be seen in Jakuchū's painting of the subject, which is less innovative and less pictorially interesting than his other works.

This is not to say that some of Jakuchū's ideas are not present in the painting. He carefully orchestrated the orientation of the fish and the grasses from the lower right up and toward the left, and this arrangement, together with his extension of the plant outward in a flattened manner, like an image in a kaleidoscope, resulted in a distinctive composition. He depicted the fish in shallow space, and the dorsal fin, which he executed with delicate parallel brush strokes, looks like a piece of bent fabric and is devoid of any sense of anatomical reality. Moreover, the fish whiskers, which in a real carp extend backward from its mouth, are shown here originating from the nostrils on its snout, as on a catfish, and the constricted eyes focus on the bubbles emanating from its mouth. Jakuchū's sense of levity and his occasional touches of ornamental embellishment in the brushwork serve to set this piece apart from the usual banal representations of the subject.

One, square relief, seal reads *Jokin*, and no other instance of its use is known. The painting was purchased for the Tokyo National University in 1889.

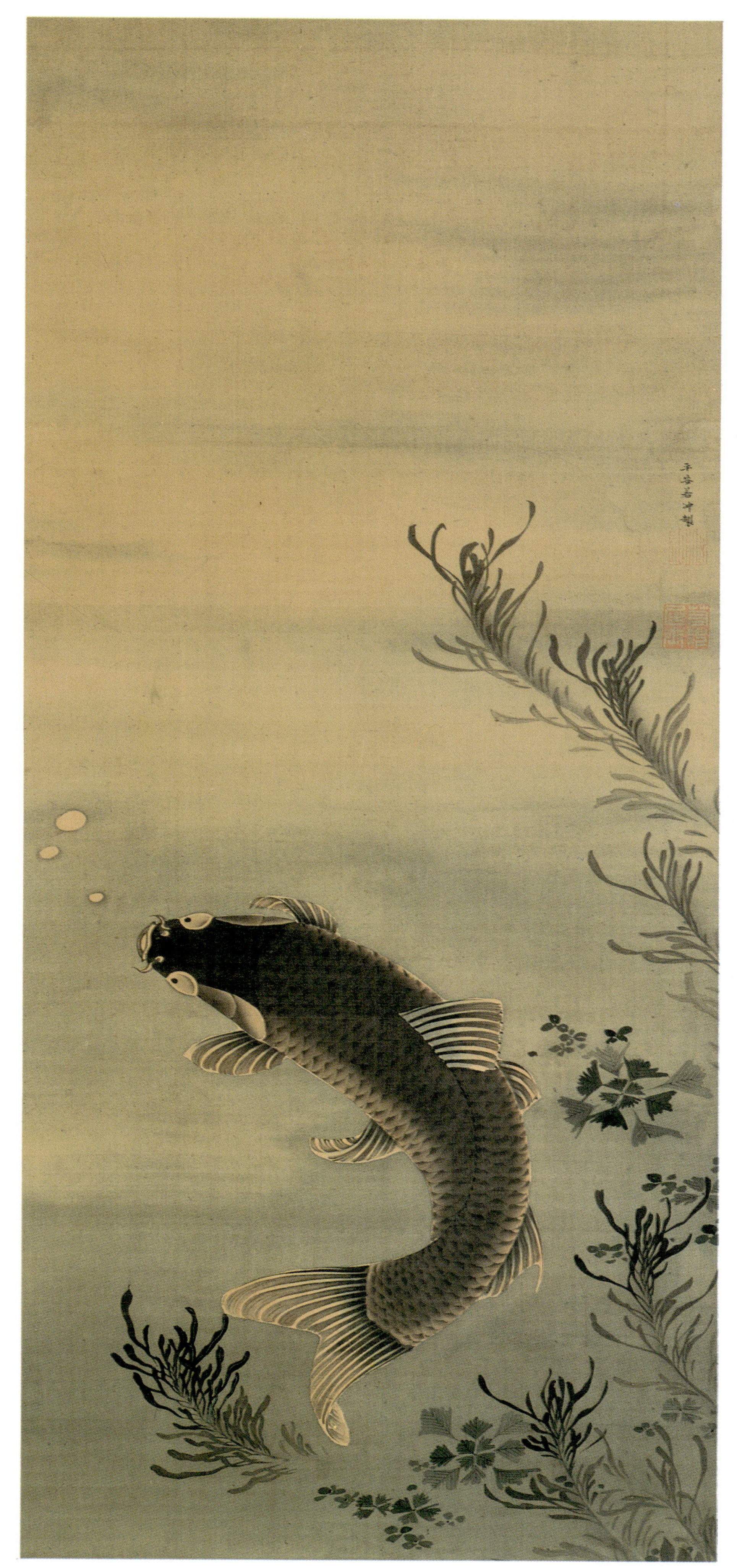
平安若冲製

11 *Blossoming Plum and Mandarin Ducks in Snow*

c. 1756–1757

Colors on silk, hanging scroll
139 × 93.3 cm
Inscription:
Painted by Jakuchū koji, Tō Jokin, of Heian-jō [Kyoto] *at the humble studio in the Nishiki* [Brocade] *neighborhood*

SEALS:
round relief: *Jakuchū koji*
square intaglio: *Tō Jokin azana Keiwa*
Private collection, Tokyo
Important Art Object

There seems no doubt that this superb work is indebted in several respects to the traditions of bird-and-flower painting that flourished in China during the Ming and Ch'ing (1644–1911) dynasties: the subject itself; the composition and handling of the flowers, trees, and small birds; the methods of shading and rendering feathers; and the traditional manner of utilizing pigments and ink to define forms, as in this portrayal of mandarin ducks, in which the above-water portions of the birds were done in colors and the underwater portions delineated in ink. Although it is difficult to find stylistic prototypes in Chinese painting for other aspects of the work—such as the way adjacent areas have been painted into the background in a colloidal manner and overlaid with white pigment in order to give the impression of layered snow, and dark ink has been applied in short, parallel brush strokes at the edges of profile lines to create an impression of shadowing on rocks and trees—the possibility cannot be ruled out. However, even if a Chinese painting exists that is close enough in its details to have served as a prototype, the combination of features in Jakuchū's piece, the individualistic manner in which he handled these components, and the striking way he utilized them for his own expressive purposes confirm the artistic quality of the piece.

The application of a thin wash to the background and the manner of simulating layered snow by leaving sections of the silk unpainted are techniques typical among painters of the school of Shen Nan-p'in. But Jakuchū defined contours with meandering, curvilinear lines, utilizing these lines in an extravagant way to create many of the forms in the composition, a feature he developed himself. Furthermore, he left the snow and flowers partially transparent, and treated features that should have a substantial appearance, such as the large tree trunk, in a flat, non-volumetric manner, with the delicate limbs appearing only as silhouettes. Similarly, the rocks have little sense of solidity and the boundary between the shore and the surface of the water is nebulous. As a consequence, there is a great deal of ambiguity in the vague interrelationship of delineation and ground in the painting. The ground (those areas painted with washes or pigments) overlaps regularly into the delineated areas (those executed with line), so that each interacts with the other. Moreover, the sinuous line used to delineate the accumulated snow has a special rhythmic vitality not present in similar works by other artists. This type of line, which Jakuchū employed to portray a variety of elements—such as the narcissus, rocks, shoreline, concentric movement of the water, and camellia blossoms — fills the entire composition with a uniform pictorial rhythm. The retreat from strict realism evident in the flat treatment of some components is offset by a mysterious life force that pervades the painting.

This evocative work, with its distinctive conceptual and stylistic qualities, constitutes nothing less than a new type of bird-and-flower painting in Japan, leading the viewer on into the dazzling, heady world of the *Dōshoku Sai-e* paintings (NO. 14 and FIG. 33). One of the most creative of the artist's early pieces, the lovely work shown here is directly related in its subject, technique, and elegance to those magnificent scrolls. Still, the sense of heightened contrast in forms, colors, and pigments in the *Dōshoku Sai-e* paintings is less apparent in the present painting. Moreover, the creatures depicted here are more tranquil and less assertive than their counterparts in the great series, and the lively yet mannered conventions of brushwork that characterize the *Dōshoku Sai-e* paintings are largely absent in this earlier work.

Here, Jakuchū chose his colors in a deliberate, calculated manner and executed the painting with notable precision. The ducks are surrounded by evocative curvilinear lines that seem to expand and subtly harmonize with similar forms; the color scheme, which relies primarily on lovely intermediate hues, evokes a sense of pleasure in the observer. However, the sharp, spiky contours of the plum branches, on which the accumulated snow apparently seems to melt away, have a tense, unsettling quality. Furthermore, the male and female ducks, usually depicted close to one another as a traditional symbol of conjugal harmony, are here situated some distance apart in an artificial, contrived manner, and this placement may cause the viewer to feel a vague sense of uneasiness.

This piece was formerly in the possession of the Higashi Honganji monastery.

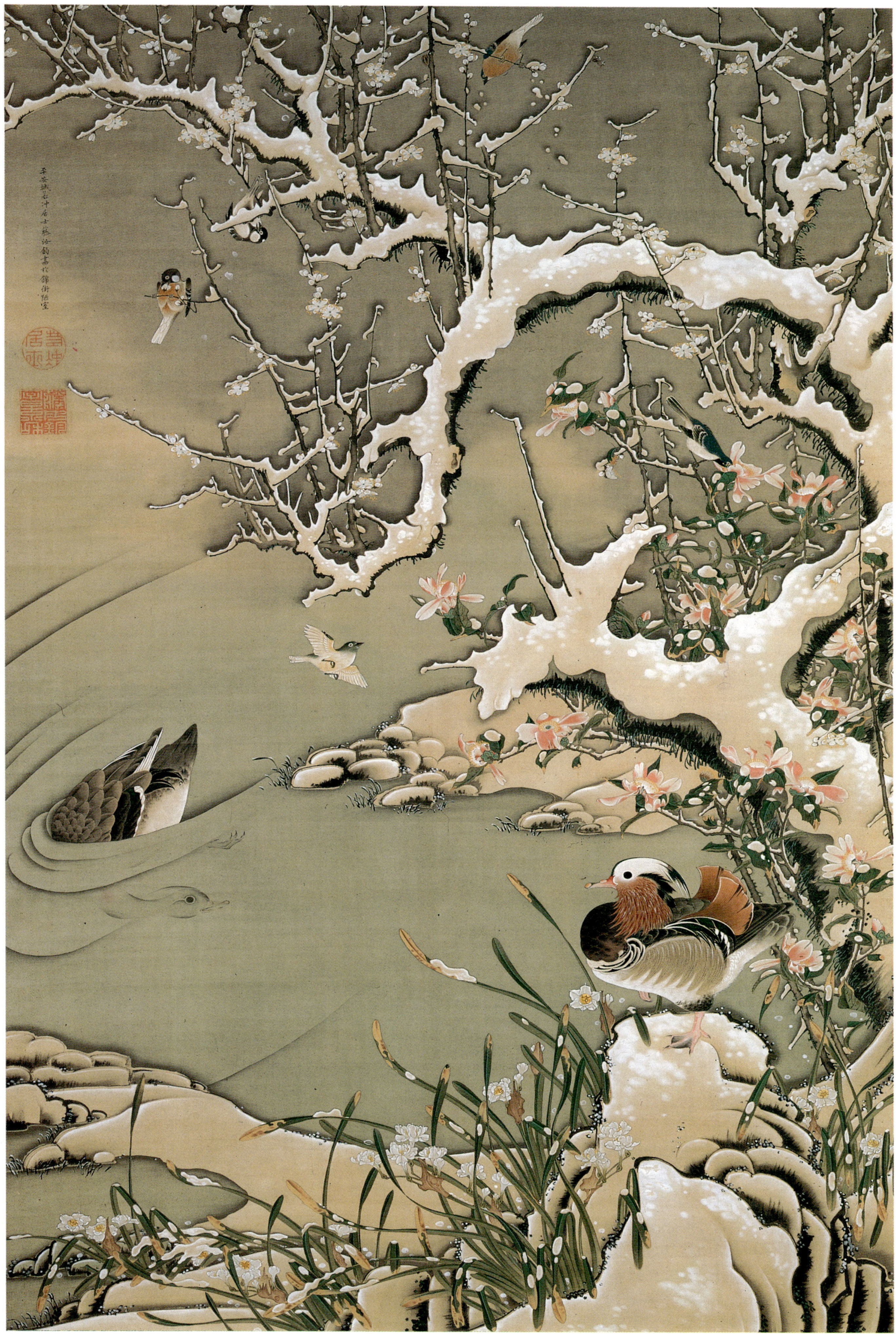

12 *Iris and Wagtail*

c. 1756–1757

Colors on silk, hanging scroll
40.6 × 57.0 cm
Signature: *Shin'enkan Jakuchū-sei*

SEALS:
square intaglio: *Tō Jokin-in*
square relief: *Jakuchū koji*
Private collection

The custom of using paintings as one of the essential elements in the tea ceremony—whereby an appropriate hanging scroll is displayed in the Tokonoma (alcove) of the tea chamber for the enjoyment and admiration of the participants—goes back to the Muromachi period and continues to the present day; the tradition has had a significant influence on the history of painting criticism and aesthetics in Japan. Even this small work by Jakuchū, which would otherwise appear to be far removed from the characteristic tastes of practitioners of the tea ceremony, would not have been without appeal to those circles, and must have been intentionally created for such use.

Although iris and wagtail at the water's edge was a conventionalized subject in Japanese painting, Jakuchū's interpretation inevitably reflects his own artistic inclinations. The languorous iris, which grows close to the water, is reminiscent of some submarine flower in its gentle, curvilinear stems and leaves, and it seems to float weightlessly in the upper-middle section of the composition. The artist used gold pigment along the shoreline. He delicately rendered the blue and purple flower petals in dark and light shades, skillfully blended in various ways. He used greens of varying intensities to the left and right of the delicately precise, light green strokes of the veins that run up the leaves and rendered the ends of the leaves in brown, with round speckles in reddish purple. He bent and overlapped some of the leaves, showing both the front and back surfaces. Jakuchū depicted the feathers of the wagtail in precise detail, but in contrast intentionally executed the contours of the rocks and areas of moss in a rougher manner. He used a light shade of blue for the surface of the water and carried out the pattern of the water's movement in ink that he lightly shaded on one side.

Although the subject of this painting is conventional, its composition and execution are notable for their intricacy. A pronounced sense that the innate complexities of natural shapes were literally reproduced distinguishes Jakuchū's oeuvre and sets it apart from paintings by members of the Kanō and Rimpa schools. The artist combined this quality with a preoccupation with innovative, original shapes, and his tendency to search for beauty in forms and patterns is one of the significant characteristics of his painting. Even in this small work, these features are superbly realized.

The compositional scheme of this work seems to have been inspired by *Blossoming Plum and Mandarin Ducks in Snow* (NO. 11), for there are close pictorial parallels between the lines and orientation of the plants in the lower part of the composition and the shoreline radiating from the corner; the curvilinear shapes of the daffodil and iris leaves; the postures of the ducks and the wagtail; and the handling of the rocks and the water. It would appear that Jakuchū conceived both paintings in the same manner, just as *Rooster and Blossoming Plum in Snow* (NO. 13) and *Mandarin Ducks and Snow-covered Reeds* (FIG. 34) correspond to *Mandarin Ducks in Snow* from the *Dōshoku Sai-e* set (NO. 14.1).

The square intaglio seal, which reads *Tō Jokin-in*, is very unusual, but it was also used in a portrayal of Baisaō by Jakuchū that has an inscription by Daiten.[14] The present painting was originally owned by Kimura Kenkadō, who in 1794 presented it to a Mr. Tsuda.

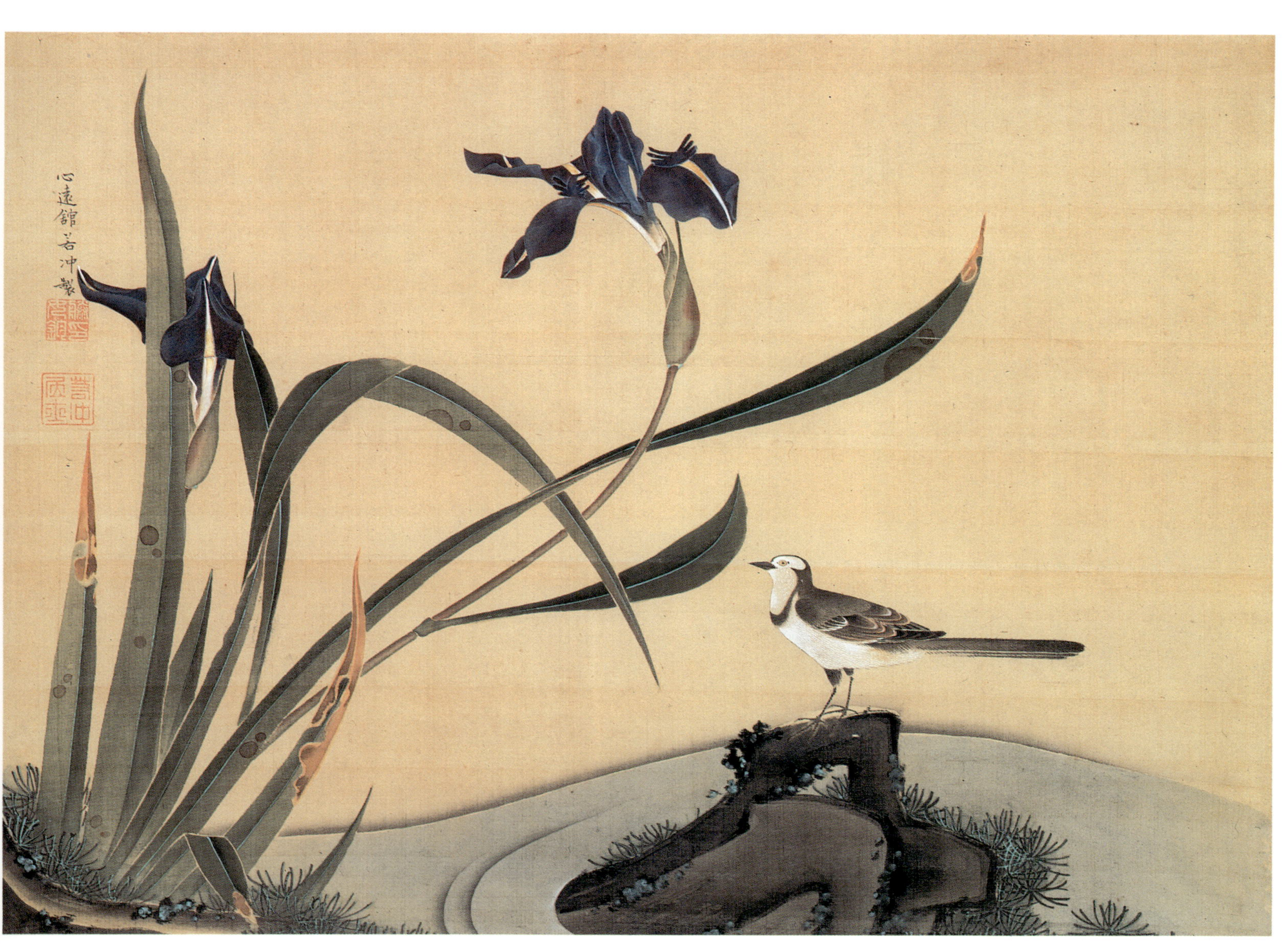
心遠館若冲製

13 *Rooster and Blossoming Plum in Snow*

c. 1756–1757

Colors on silk, hanging scroll
113.5 × 56.4 cm
Inscription:
Painted by Jakuchū koji, Tō Jokin, of Heian-jō [Kyoto] *at the humble studio in the Nishiki* [Brocade] *neighborhood*

SEALS:
round intaglio: *Jokin*
square relief: *Tansei wa rōshō ni itaru o shirazu*
Ryōsokuin, Kyoto

Comparison of this painting with the similar snow scene *Blossoming Plum and Mandarin Ducks in Snow* (No. 11) shows that the backgrounds were treated in the same manner. The curved trunk of the plum tree here has the same jagged, abbreviated form as that in the other painting, and a single bush warbler is also perched precariously on a thin, diagonal branch at the top. Although fewer in number, peonies and narcissus also appear, while the waterline has been reduced in size and simplified. Jakuchū abbreviated the composition and delineated details of the lower section of the plum tree in a somewhat different manner, but it is nevertheless clear that *Blossoming Plum and Mandarin Ducks in Snow* served as his direct source of inspiration for this work. Moreover, the rooster here is virtually identical in pose and form with a bird depicted against a similar background in an earlier painting (No. 1).

The present work is, therefore, instructive concerning Jakuchū's compositional ideas. In this case, the artist apparently did not take his subjects directly from nature; rather, he selected motifs from existing paintings, modifying and recombining them in accordance with his conceptual preferences.

This painting demonstrates the extent of Jakuchū's skill in creating compositional designs. The limbs of the plum tree were conceived in a triangular scheme, with the sort of precise placement reminiscent of a Japanese flower arrangement, and the red peony bloom in the center of the composition draws the viewer's attention, standing out in the otherwise spare use of color. Jakuchū's innovative conceptual ability is also apparent in his treatment of ground contours and rocks: he retained the natural qualities of these elements, while at the same time abstracting their forms. In addition, the depiction of the rooster, whose vermilion comb resonates with the red hue of the peony above him, not only serves as a metaphorical reference to admired traits of human character, but is also an intimate, pleasing image in its own right.

The Ryōsokuin is a subtemple of the Kenninji monastery in Kyoto. According to the interpretation of the current abbot, an inscription on the box in which the painting has been preserved indicates that the work was acquired by an earlier abbot late in the Edo period.

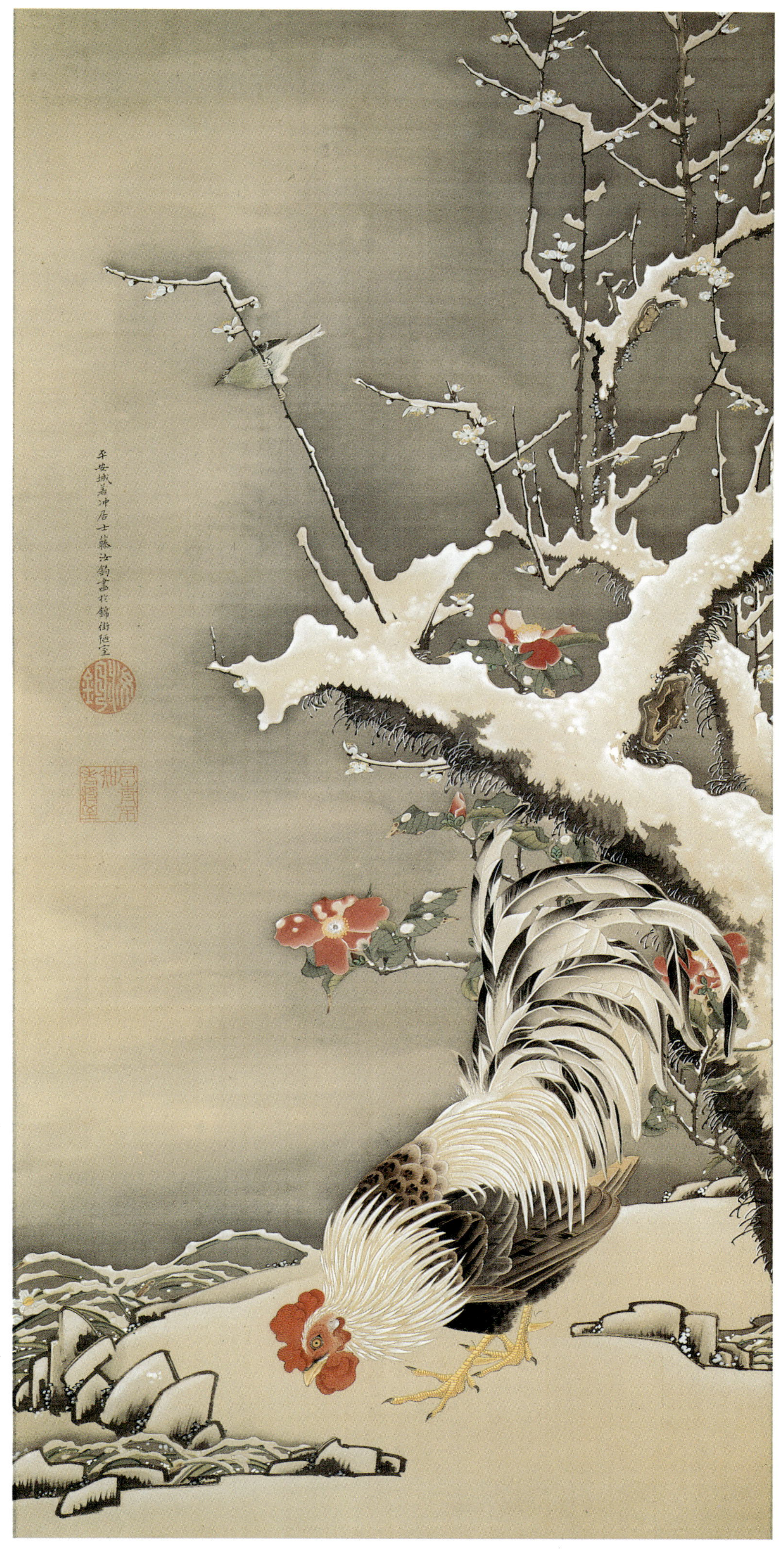
平安城若冲居士藤汝鈞畫於錦街陋室

14 *Dōshoku Sai-e*

(Colorful Realm of Living Beings)

c. 1757–1758—c. 1766–1770

Colors on silk, 10 hanging scrolls
142.5 × 79.5 cm (each scroll)
Imperial Household Collection

The thirty scrolls of the *Dōshoku Sai-e* were executed by Jakuchū when he was in his forties and early fifties. In the *Tō Keiwa Gakanoki* (*A Record of the Paintings of Tō Keiwa*, c. 1760) Daiten Kenjō noted: "Jakuchū is producing thirty paintings of birds and flowers to pass on to posterity, and he already has fifteen completed."[15] Daiten also included the poetic titles he had written for each of the artist's pieces and described their subjects. Among these were three no-longer-extant monochrome works, but the remaining twelve titles and subjects clearly relate to specific pieces from the *Dōshoku Sai-e* series. This list constitutes the first documentary record of the famous paintings. In it Daiten praised the works, noting how finely Jakuchū had conceived them and how skillfully he had captured the innate vitality of his subjects, rendering them in fine detail combined with rough brushwork in order to express completely the inner essence and external form of each. Daiten also quoted the artist:

> The things that are called paintings today are nothing more than representations of representations, and I have yet to see a case in which a painting has been done of an animate being. And artists think only of selling their works on the merit of their technique; but there are, as yet, no works in which the technique is of a surpassing nature. It is only in these respects that I am different in my aspirations from others.[16]

Daiten noted, in addition, that

> Jakuchū has no other talent or ambition in the mundane world, wishing only to perfect his painting, desirous of nothing in the wide world other than to concentrate his efforts on the imaginary realm of painting. . . . For this reason he has been able to portray the forms of his subjects superbly in his paintings, and to reveal their underlying spirits successfully, creating ingenious compositions and utilizing charming, evocative colors in a manner that the ordinary, mediocre artisan-painter can never hope to equal.[17]

Finally Daiten observed, in words that reflect a religious attitude, that he hoped others would be as determined as Jakuchū, in order to be successful in their various enterprises.[18]

The next recorded reference to the *Dōshoku Sai-e* scrolls appears in Jakuchū's deed of gift (now preserved in the Imperial Household Collection), dated the last day of the Ninth Month of 1765, in which the artist presented his paintings to the Shōkokuji, the great Zen monastery in Kyoto. In this document he wrote:

> I concentrate on painting almost every day, trying to depict lovely flowers and trees, and the forms of birds and insects. I have gathered examples of many kinds of subject matter, and have developed the skills of a master. I have studied the triptych by Chang Ssu-kung of the Buddha Śākyamuni and the Bodhisattvas Manjuśri and Samantabhadra, admired their incomparable skill of execution, and aspired to copy them. This I did, depicting each of the deities in a separate hanging scroll, as well as completing twenty-four of the *Dōshoku Sai-e* set. Frivolous motives and the desire for worldly acclaim have played no part in this undertaking. I have humbly donated all the paintings to the Shōkokuji in the hope that they will always be utilized as objects of solemn reverence.[19]

Jakuchū concluded that he hoped to be interred in the cemetery of the Shōkokuji after his death and that he intended to provide the funds for this purpose.[20] Jakuchū made his great gift when he had completed the Śākyamuni triptych (No. 15), the initial group of twelve *Dōshoku Sai-e* scrolls mentioned in the *Tō Keiwa Gakanoki*, and twelve more scrolls, but before he had finished the last six. His timing of the gift appears to have been influenced by the death of Sōjaku, his youngest brother, a few days earlier, on the nineteenth day of the same month. The loss of his immediate familial successor must have left him with doubts about his own future.

The section of the records of the Shōkokuji that deals with the year 1766 includes an entry stating that only twenty-four of the *Dōshoku Sai-e* paintings had as yet been completed, but, in his inscription ("Ketsumei") on the gravestone (*juzō*) that Jakuchū had erected on his behalf in the Eleventh Month of the year, Daiten noted that "he painted thirty large scrolls."[21] It may be, therefore, that the final six paintings had been donated to the temple by this time.

The various documentary materials that related the details and nature of the *Dōshoku Sai-e* project indicate that from the beginning Jakuchū intended to create a set of thirty paintings of bird-and-flower subjects, but this number does not seem to relate to any used in Buddhist tradition. Nothing in Daiten's account implies that these paintings have any connection with Buddhism. Both the deed of gift and the inscription on the gravestone consistently mention the *Dōshoku Sai-e* before the Śākyamuni triptych and make no attempt to relate the works. Thus, it must be presumed that the *Dōshoku Sai-e* series was originally conceived as an independent group to be admired solely for its aesthetic merits and that it was

14.1

Mandarin Ducks in Snow

1759

Signature and date: *Hōreki* [cyclical signs, 1759], *chūshun* [mid-spring, Second Month] *Jakuchū koji-sei*

SEALS:
square intaglio: *Tō Jokin azana Keiwa*
round relief: *Jakuchū koji*

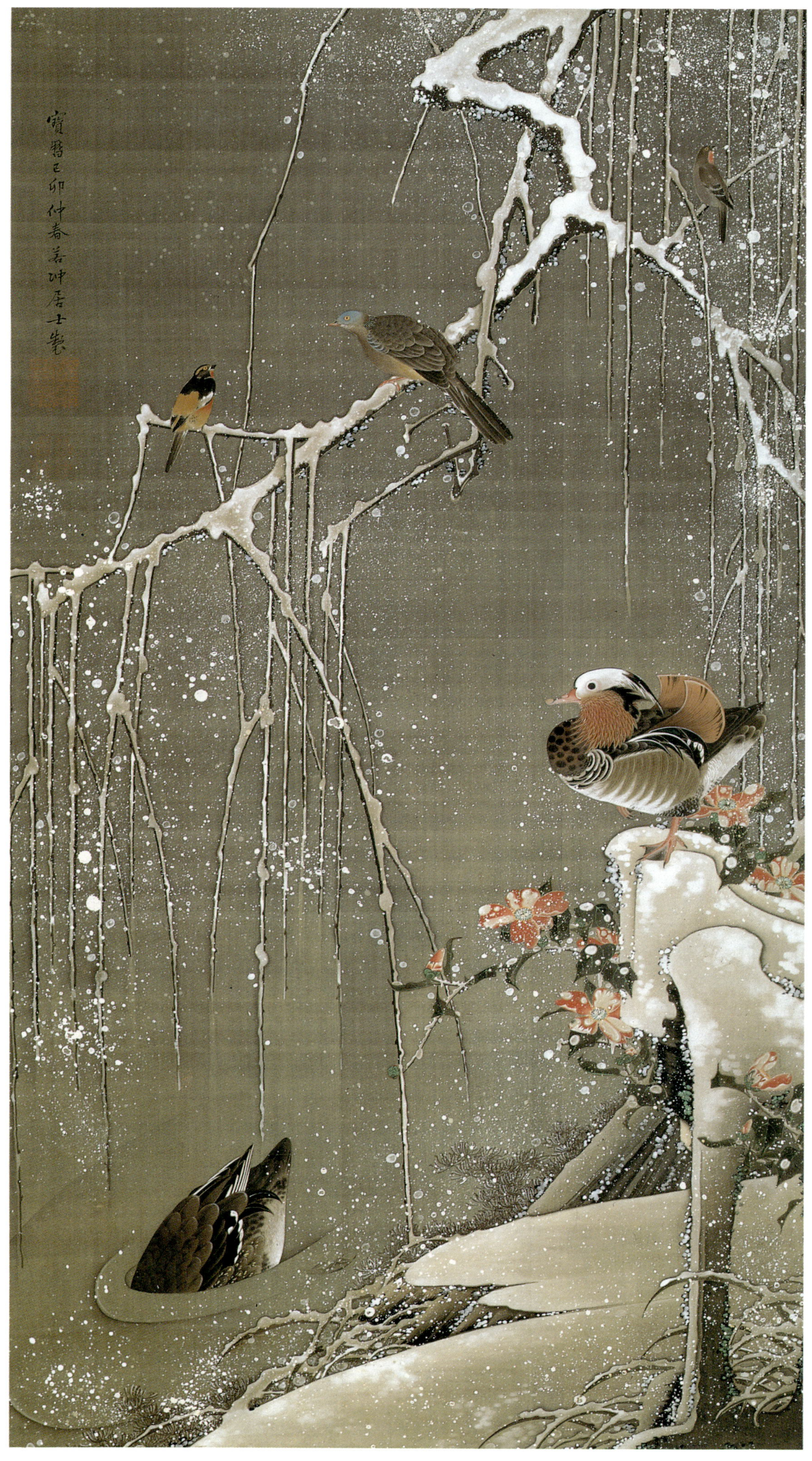
寶暦己卯仲春若冲居士寫

not designed to express some Buddhist concept in combination with the iconic triptych, which was created specifically for religious veneration.

According to the artist himself, he only wished to portray the forms of all kinds of living beings, not in the superficial manner of works produced for the popular market, but by utilizing his most advanced skills. It is likely that Jakuchū decided to donate these works to the Shōkokuji because of Daiten's intimate relationship to that temple and so that the paintings would be preserved for posterity. Conceivably, it was Daiten who thought of combining the triptych with the other scrolls and of donating them all as a unit. When the paintings were first hung in the Shōkokuji, the triptych was placed in the center and the *Dōshoku Sai-e* scrolls were situated to the left and right; this precedent was followed thereafter in public displays during the annual religious observances on the seventeenth day of the Sixth Month. This sort of tradition would probably not have evolved if Jakuchū had donated the *Dōshoku Sai-e* scrolls without the triptych. Only after the practice of combining the paintings had become a tradition was the *Dōshoku Sai-e* series used in the religious activities of the Shōkokuji, allowing visitors to admire the works frequently. Daiten was also likely to have established this practice.

Nevertheless, it seems premature to conclude that the combination of the *Dōshoku Sai-e* paintings and the triptych was carried out simply for artistic reasons. Even if Jakuchū had intended the *Dōshoku Sai-e* scrolls to have religious significance, neither he nor those around him would necessarily have recorded this objective. The diverse creatures and plants portrayed in the thirty scrolls may have been meant to symbolize all of the beings of the universe listening to Śākyamuni, who was depicted in the central triptych delivering his sermon on the Buddha nature in every living thing, but this theory cannot as yet be corroborated.

In all thirty paintings of the *Dōshoku Sai-e* set, Jakuchū depicted flora and fauna in minute detail using pigments with a glue binder on silk grounds. Ten scrolls from this monumental series are reproduced here. *Mandarin Ducks in Snow* recapitulates the composition of the somewhat larger *Blossoming Plum and Mandarin Ducks in Snow* (NO. 11). According to Professor Tsuji Nobuo, the concept of the drooping, snow-covered willow branches seems to have been based on the painting *Herons and Snow-covered Willows* of the Yüan period, which is in the Nishi Honganji collection.[22] The geometric precision of the willow branches and the rock forms, combined with the skillful use of sprayed *gofun* (white pigment), unforgettably evokes the cold of winter at the edge of a pond, as well as a pervasive sense of transitory beauty.

Hydrangeas and Fowl is very close in content and composition to the earlier painting of the same subject in the Shin'enkan Collection (FIG. 53), but the hydrangeas here are even more luxuriant. The ethereal clouds resemble flower blossoms, with each petal having been executed individually without outline and with narrow, unpainted areas of the underlying silk serving as delicate lines of demarcation—all beautifully expressing the dense, lush quality of the blooms. The plumage and dramatic poses of the rooster and hen are more accomplished than those in the earlier Shin'enkan piece, and the rooster's comb is superbly detailed.

The conceptual inspiration behind *Fish in a Lotus Pond* probably came from a Chinese depiction of the subject, but the unique, evocative sense of space here is unlike any in Chinese painting. The departure from the actual

14.2

Hydrangeas and Fowl

1759

Signature and date: *Hōreki*, [cyclical signs, 1759], *chūshū* [mid-autumn, Eighth Month], *Jakuchū-sei*

SEALS:
square intaglio: *Jokin*
square relief: *Jakuchū koji*

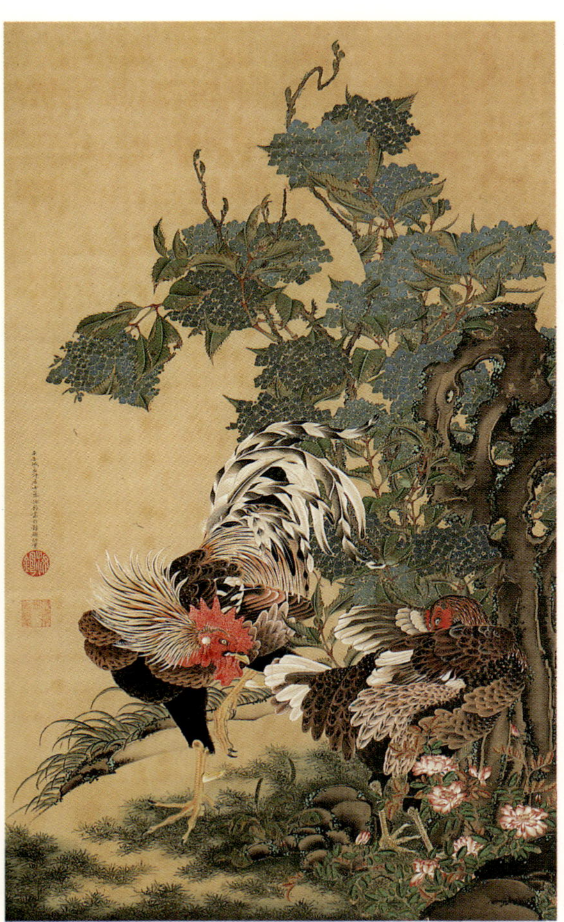

FIG. 53
Rooster, Hen, and Hydrangea, n.d.

Los Angeles County Museum of Art, Shin'enkan Collection

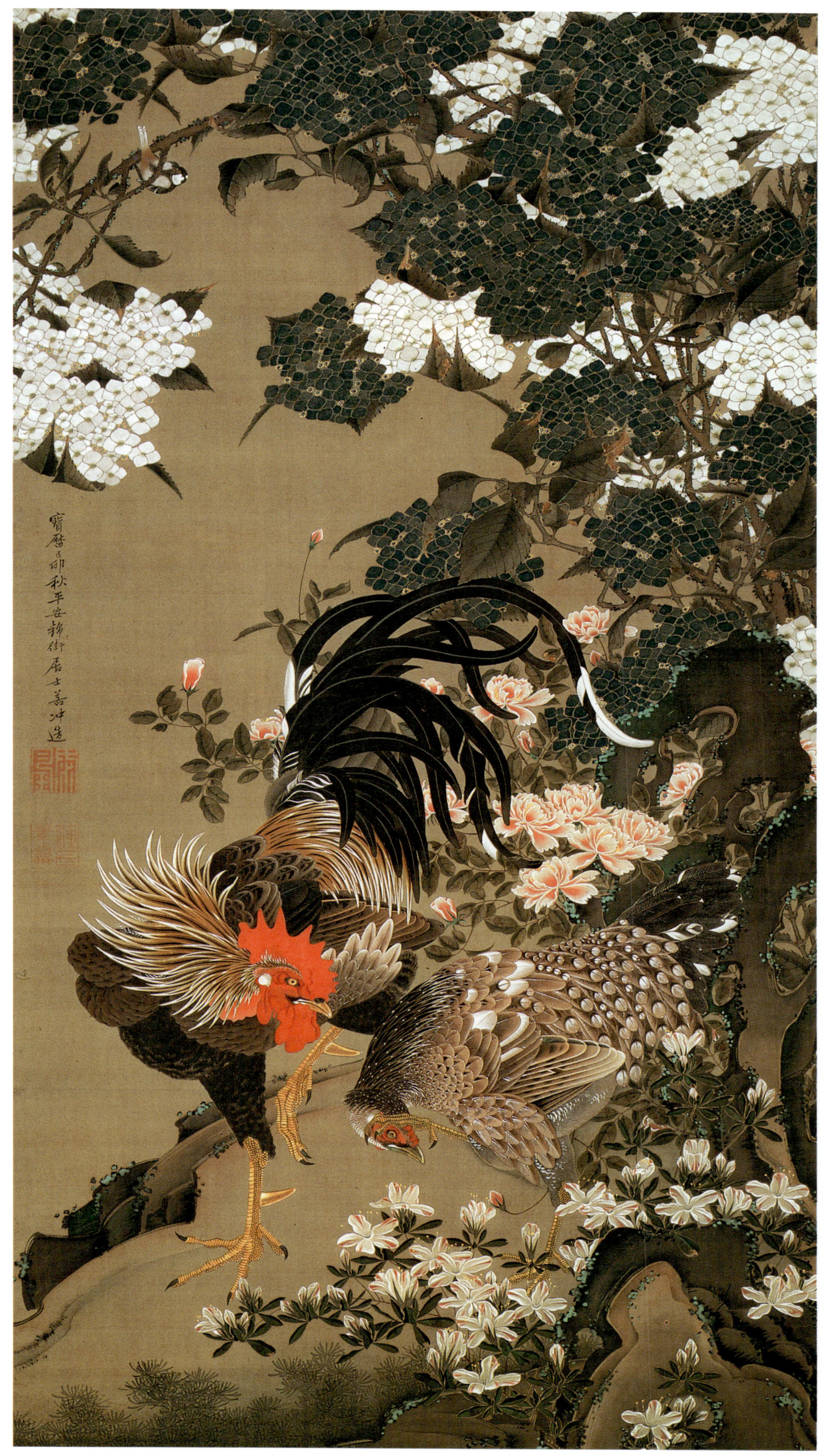
寶暦己卯秋平安錦街居士若冲造

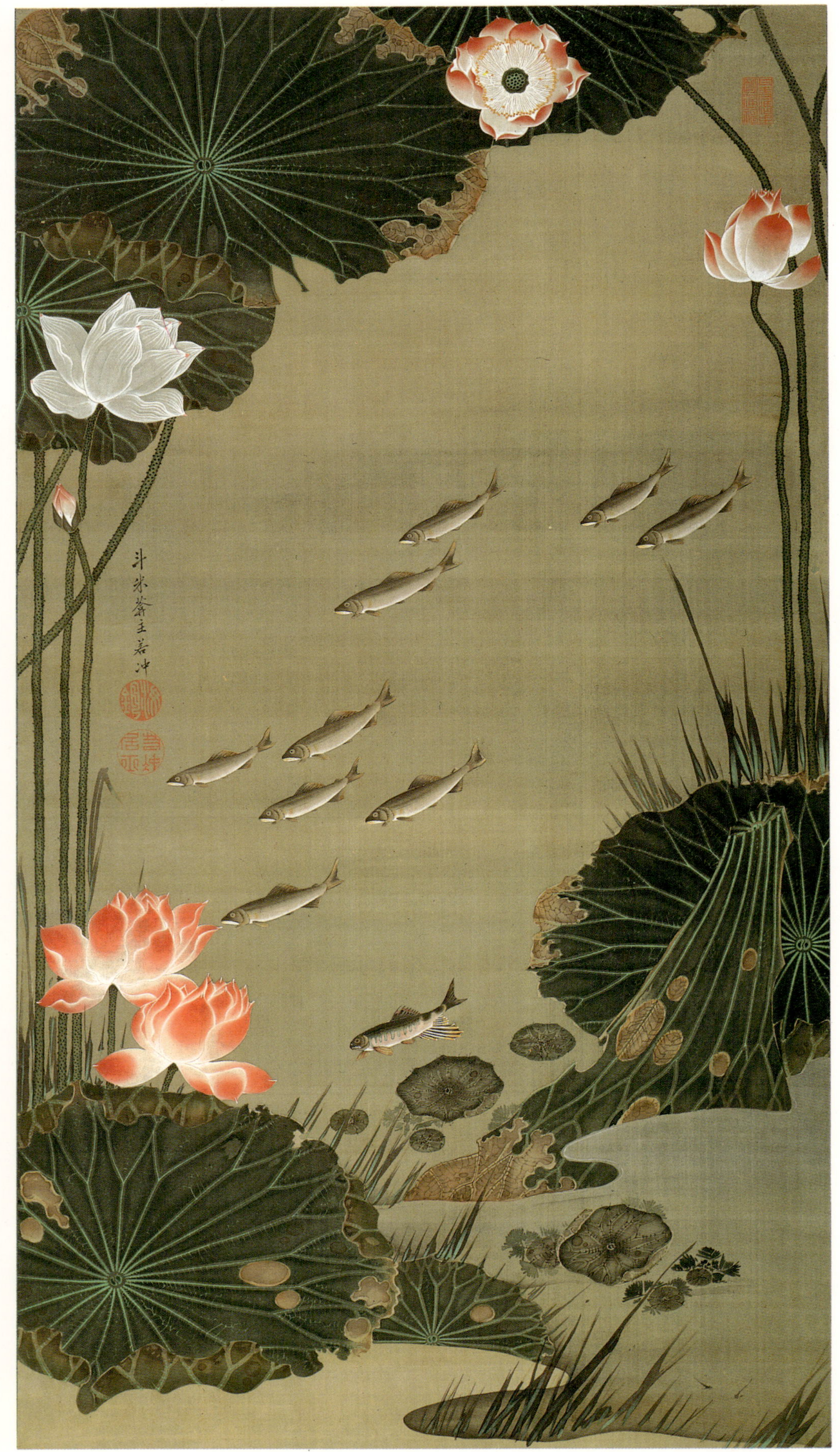

relationships in nature and the arbitrary rearrangement of compositional elements in imaginative groupings or locations are spatial conceptions peculiar to Jakuchū.

Golden Pheasants in Snow is notable for its rich complexity. It is interesting to note how meticulously Jakuchū applied the pigments. If the areas sprayed with *gofun* were to be removed, it would become apparent that they were carefully separated from adjoining areas of pigment: nowhere does the *gofun* overlap the green pigment used for foliage. This sort of precise, individual delineation of each area is also apparent in the cryptomeria boughs, covered with snow executed in complex, curvilinear lines, and in the lovely petals of the flowers. The impact of this sublime, dramatic painting is breathtaking.

Birds and Peonies is the most extreme example in the *Dōshoku Sai-e* of the artist's progressive tendency to fill

14.3

Fish in a Lotus Pond

c. 1761–1765

Signature: *Tobeian-shu Jakuchū*

SEALS:
round intaglio: *Jokin*
round relief: *Jakuchū koji*
vertical rectangular relief: *Tansei kasshu no myō kami ni tsūzu*

the format with subject matter to the degree that the background almost disappears. This characteristic, occasionally found in Chinese painting, occurs in late Edo period works of the Kanō school, suggesting that Jakuchū was also influenced by imported paintings.

Insects and Reptiles at a Pond represents the development on a larger scale of themes in earlier works, such as *Snake Gourds and Insects* (NO. 7), which appear to be based on paintings of the "grasses and insects" genre produced in Kiangsu Province in China. Jakuchū depicted each of the diverse creatures and plant forms meticulously and accurately, enlivening the composition with eccentric rendering of details such as the convoluted tendrils of the gourd plants and the gourd at the lower left, which looks like the profile of a demon's face.

Shellfish depicts more than a hundred kinds of these marine creatures strewn

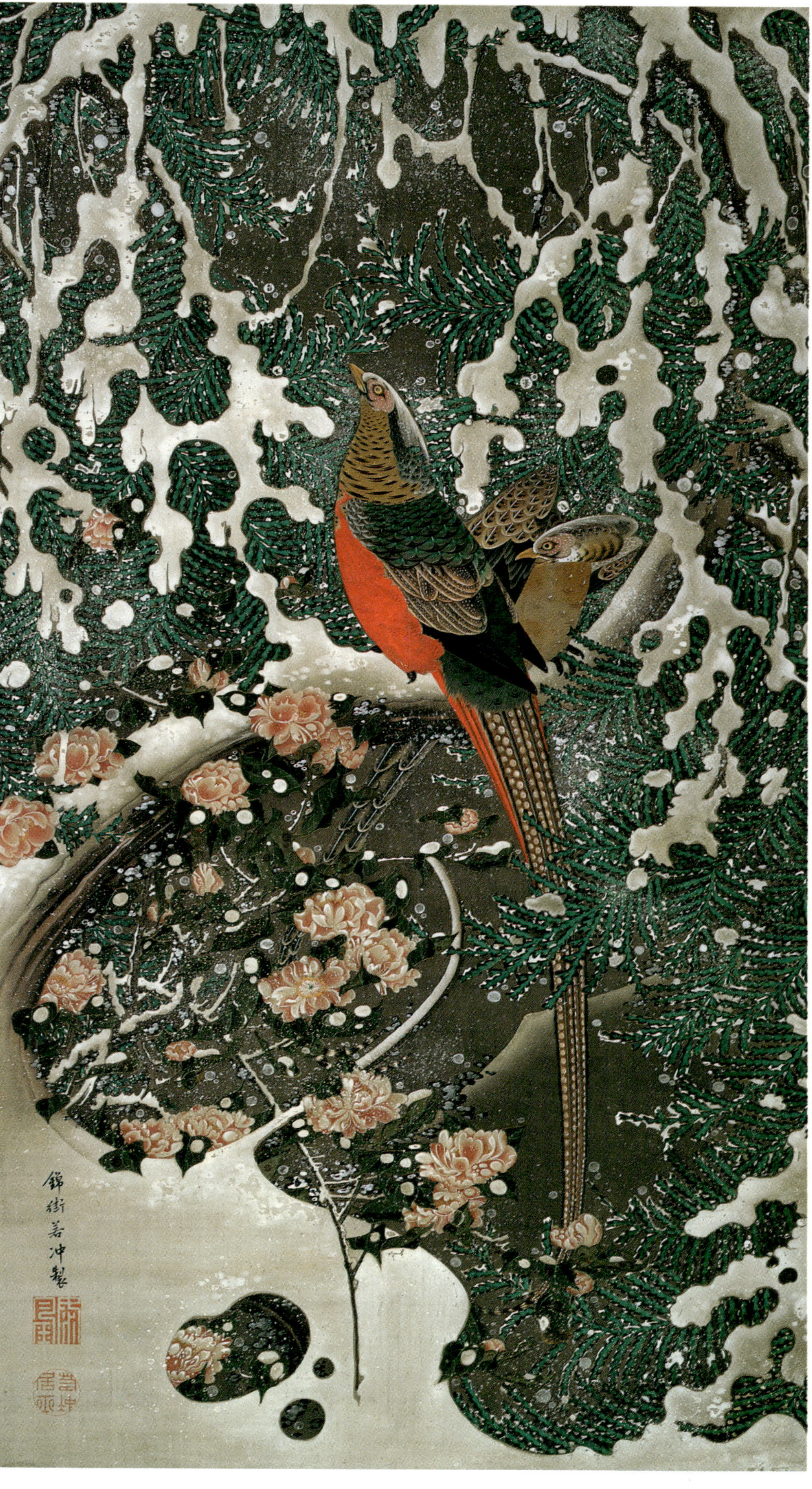

14.4

Golden Pheasants in Snow

c. 1761–1765

Signature: *Nishiki-machi Jakuchū-sei*

SEALS:
square intaglio: *Jokin*
round relief: *Jakuchū koji*

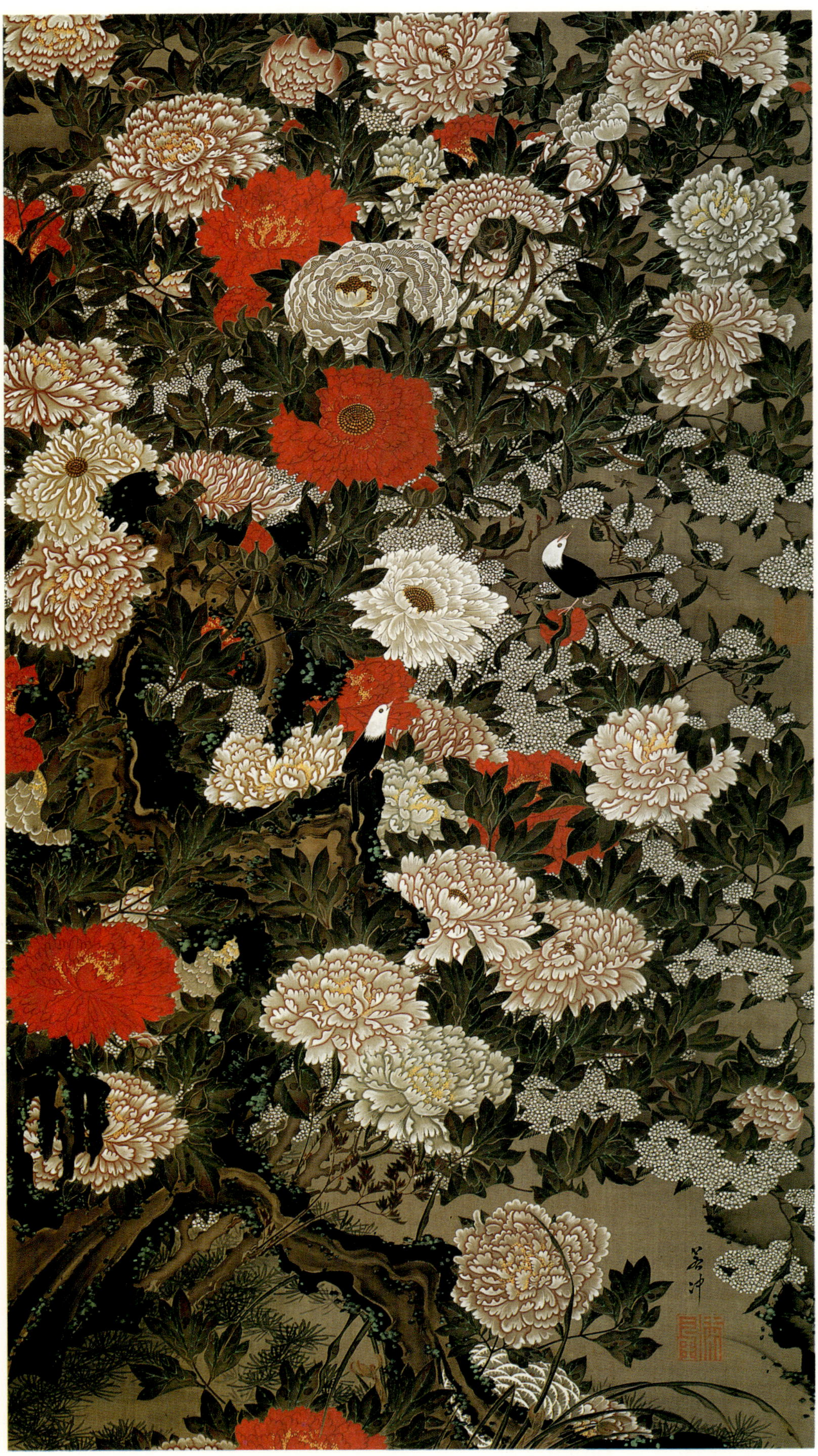

across a sandy area of seashore. Although the shells were rendered accurately, some have a peculiar, deformed quality, and one flat specimen in the middle right (an area where some details have a surreal, membranous quality reminiscent of works by Salvador Dalí [1904–1988]) is humorously demonic in its appearance. Moreover, the odd rock form at the lower right, with its multiple eroded perforations, and the attenuated, tendril-like tip of the miniature stream that passes behind it seem to evoke the image of a skull with a projecting tongue. Fantastic rivulets meander arbitrarily across the surface of the sand, like animated tentacles, giving the composition a dreamlike, otherworldly quality that is not easily forgotten.

The pose and conformation of the white, male bird in *White Phoenix and Pine* simulates almost exactly the appearance of the multicolored bird in an

14.5

Birds and Peonies

c. 1761–1765

Signature: *Jakuchū*

SEALS:
square intaglio: *Jokin*
vertical rectangular relief: *Tansei kasshu no myō kami ni tsūzu*

earlier depiction of the subject (No. 9). Jakuchū rendered the feathers with great delicacy, using *gofun* over a thin wash of gold, a technique that imbued the bird with a sense of lightness and luminosity. For emphasis, he added small, precise touches of red to the white on the comb, the beak, and the heart-shaped tips of the long tail feathers, which thereby assume a sense of graceful motion. The captivating quality of this mythological image attests to Jakuchū's imaginative powers as well as to his superlative technical ability.

The large, solitary bird in *Wild Goose and Snow-covered Reeds* flies directly down toward the frozen surface of a lake; this unusual compositional conception may be indebted to some Chinese prototype. Although Jakuchū did other, similar depictions of dry reeds under snow, the quality of this portrayal is exceptional. The snow is shown

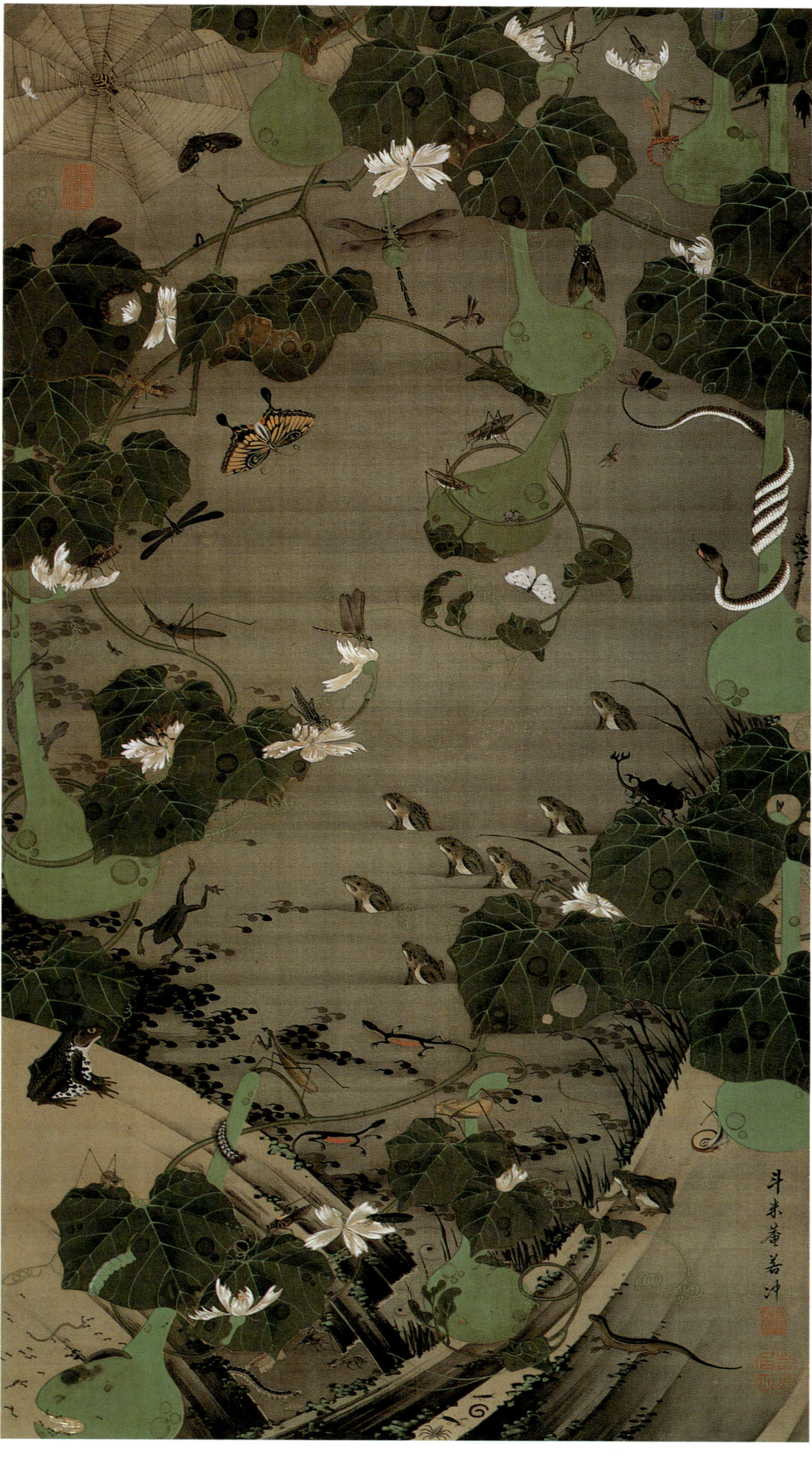

14.6

Insects and Reptiles at a Pond

c. 1761–1765

Signature: *Tobeian Jakuchū*

SEALS:
square intaglio: *Tō Jokin-in*
round relief: *Jakuchū koji*
vertical rectangular relief: *Tansei kasshu no myō kami ni tsūzu*

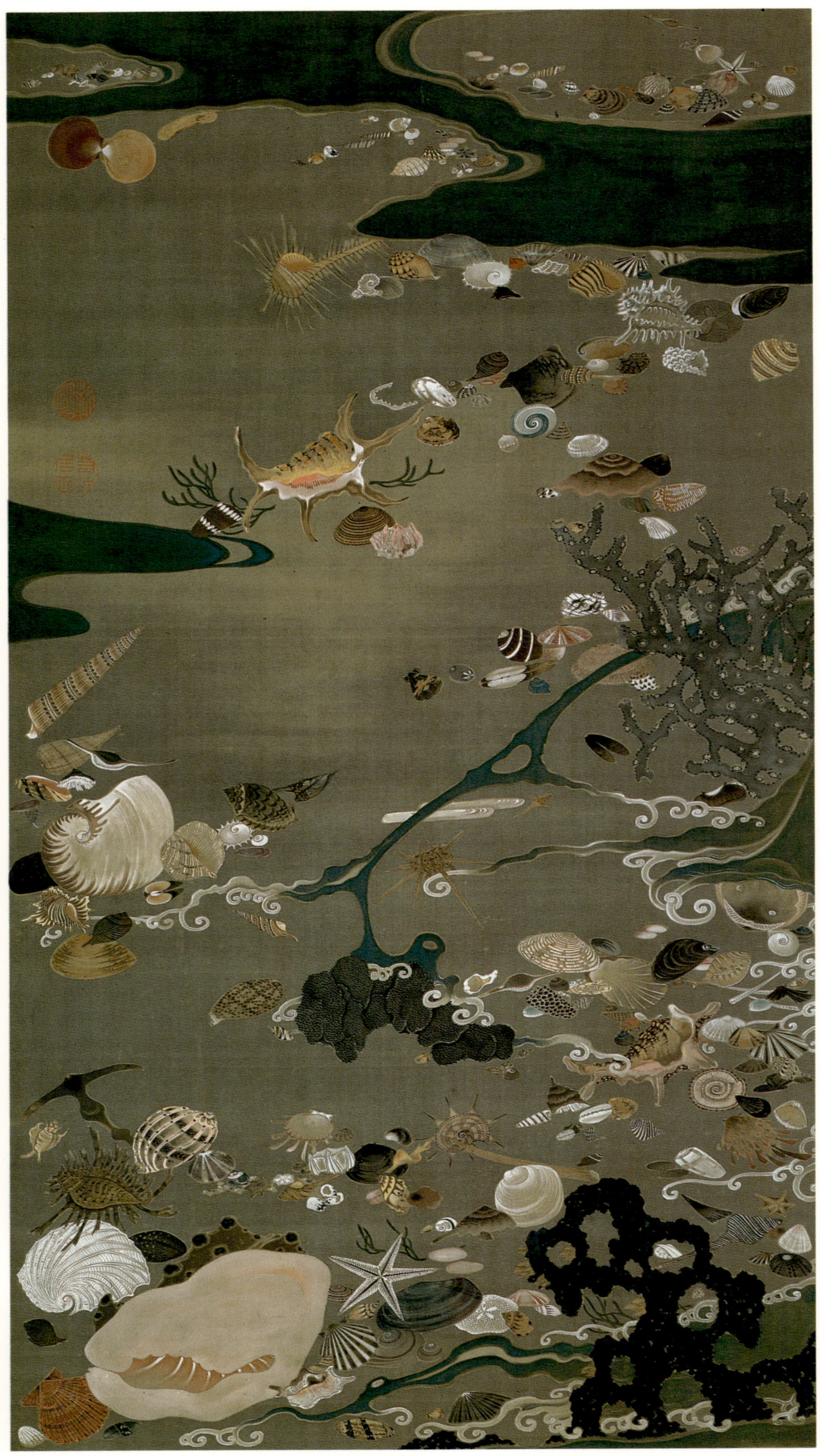

partially melted, effectively transmitting to the viewer a tangible sense of its cold yet slushy nature. As in *Mandarin Ducks in Snow*, the artist gave the sky a very thin wash of monochrome ink and the water a very subtle, light wash of green, but his skill was such that the transition between the two is indistinguishable.

Birds and Chrysanthemums by a Stream not only reflects the various influences from Chinese painting found in other works in the *Dōshoku Sai-e* series, but also contains pictorial motifs—such as flowing water—borrowed from painting and craft designs of the Rimpa school master Ōgata Kōrin (1658–1716), who died the same year Jakuchū was born. The question-mark shape of the chrysanthemum plant floating above the stream is similar in conformation to the cryptomeria in *Mandarin Ducks in Snow*. The dark leaves and stem of the chrysanthemum,

14.7

Shellfish

c. 1761–1765

SEALS:
round intaglio: *Jokin*
round relief: *Jakuchū koji*

which terminates in the large, fluffy petals of the blossoms, re-created the large, arabesque curve of the tree trunk.

Before Jakuchū's execution of the *Dōshoku Sai-e* scrolls, a project so comprehensive had never been attempted in Japanese painting, nor has it been since. However, Jakuchū's great accomplishment is significant for other reasons as well. In East Asia realistic polychrome portrayals of birds and flowers reached their highest achievement in China during the Sung period. Jakuchū studied later works, of the Yüan, Ming, and Ch'ing periods, when painting had gradually lost its natural realism and had evolved in style into a mannered, conceptualized expression. Jakuchū, for his part, revived pictorial motifs of this later sort, but he portrayed them in a strongly individual manner, imbuing them with a new kind of vitality. Jakuchū's polychrome bird-and-flower paintings are distinguished by his ability

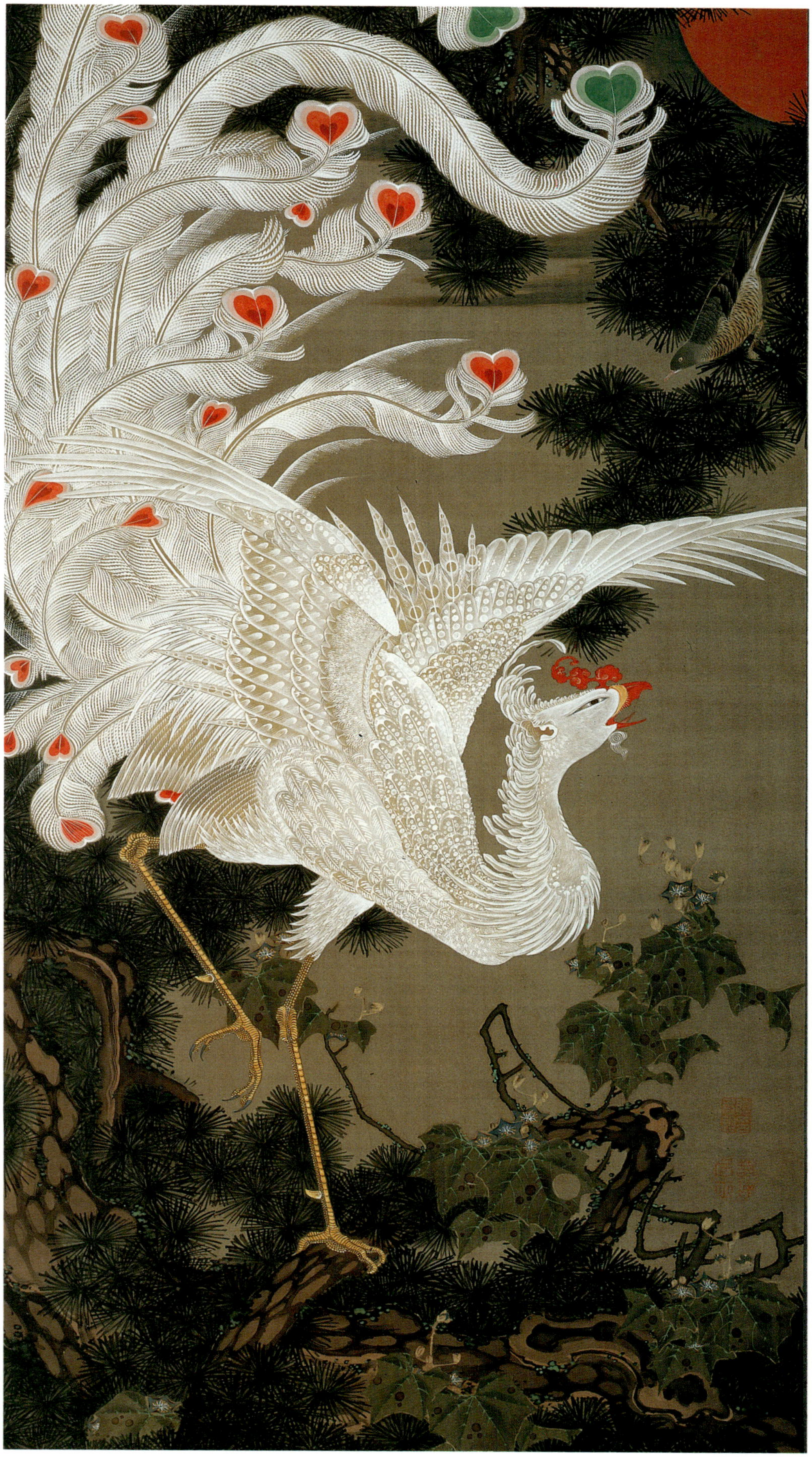

14.8

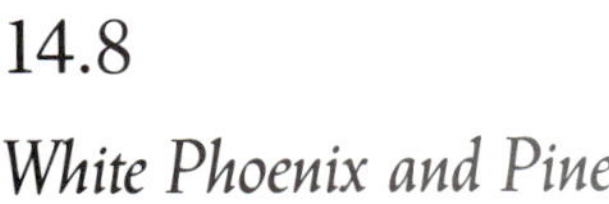

White Phoenix and Pine

c. 1765–1766

SEALS:
square intaglio: *Tō Jokin-in*
round relief: *Jakuchū koji*

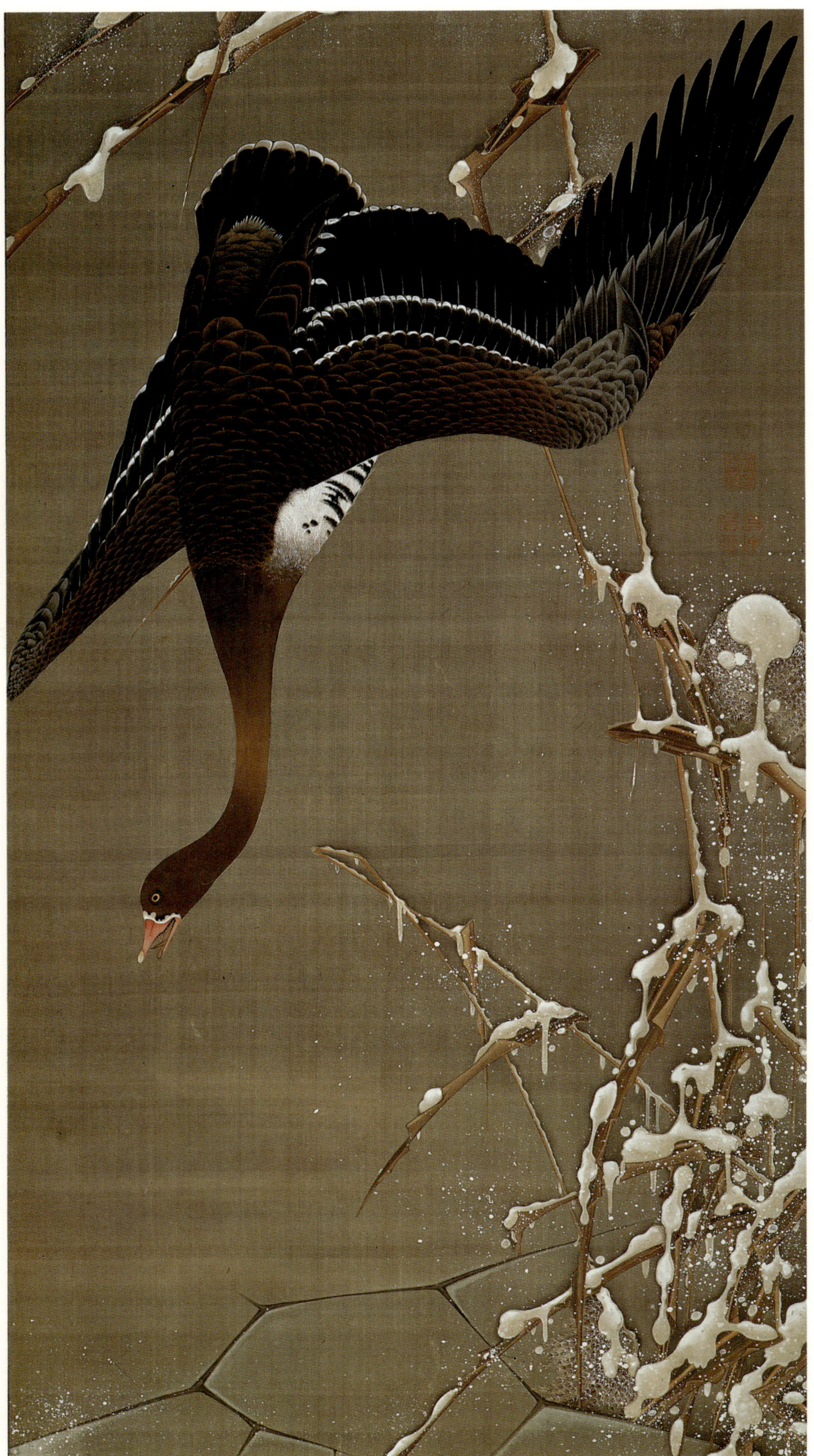

to render his subjects precisely and objectively, at the same time projecting his personal experience and sensitivity into their compositional fabric.

Thus, for instance, in *Mandarin Ducks in Snow*, Jakuchū situated the female, half-submerged in the water searching for food, below the needle-like projections of the willow branches, but placed the diffident male alone on a rock above, possibly an expression of the artist's lifelong bachelorhood and his ambivalent feelings about the opposite sex. Similarly, in *Golden Pheasants in Snow*, the strange, much-perforated patterns of snow could be symbolic of the uneven course of, and adverse events in, his personal life. On

14.9

Wild Goose and Snow-covered Reeds

c. 1765–1766

SEALS:
square intaglio: *Tō Jokin-in*
round relief: *Jakuchū koji*

the basis of their seals, six paintings in the series are thought to have been completed after the death of Jakuchū's brother Sōjaku. The bird in *White Phoenix and Pine* may be a manifestation of the artist's concern for his brother's happiness in paradise; the precipitous descent of the huge, dark bird in *Wild Goose and Snow-covered Reeds*, which flies down through the reeds like an outsize sickle, may be a pictorial metaphor for the emotional stress and instability he experienced following the death of a loved one. It is this sort of highly individualistic expressive means that gives Jakuchū's *Dōshoku Sai-e* series its profound significance in the annals of art history.

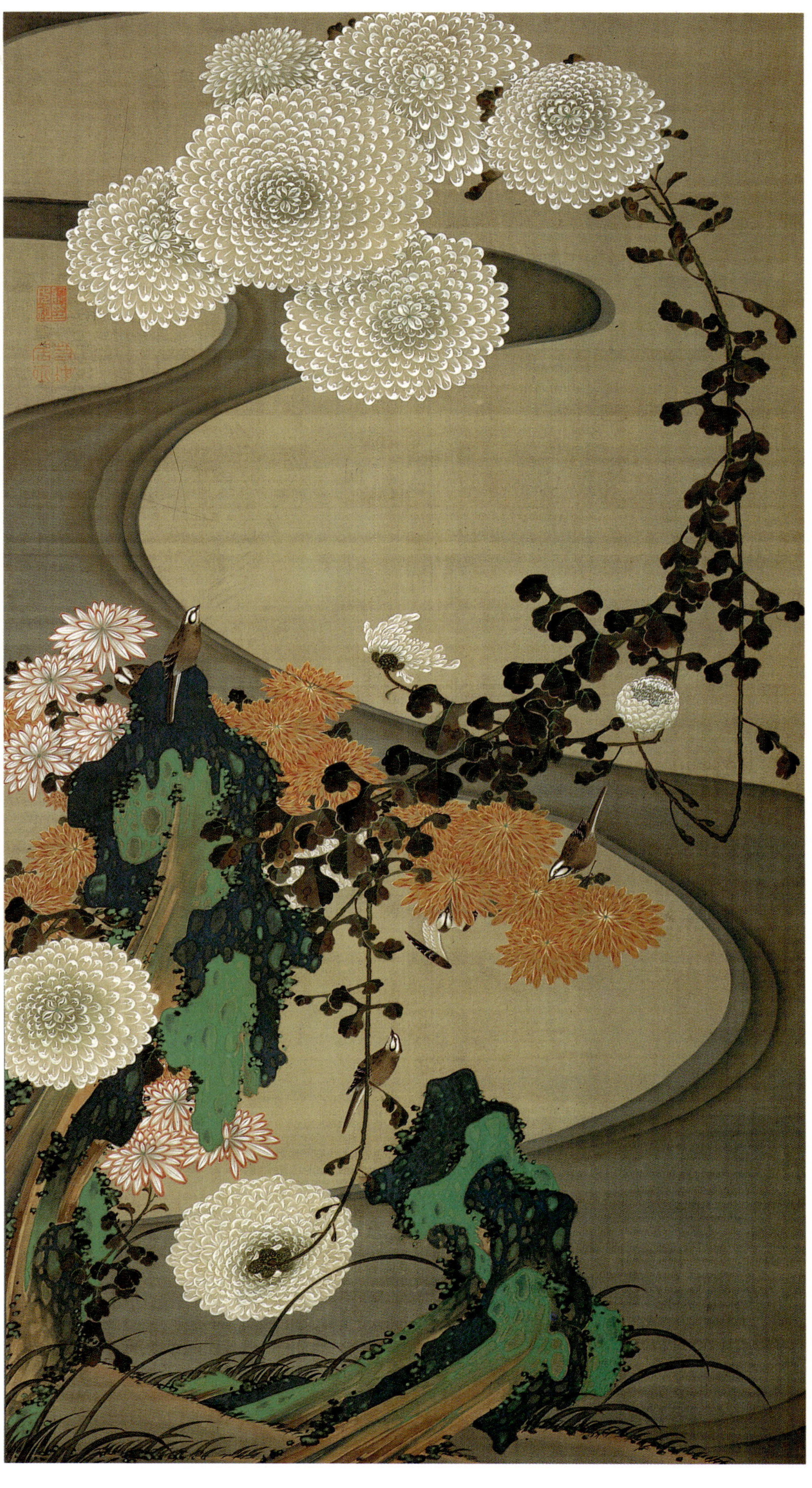

14.10

Birds and Chrysanthemums by a Stream

c. 1765–1766

SEALS:
square intaglio: *Tō Jokin-in*
round relief: *Jakuchū koji*

15 *The Buddha Śākyamuni Flanked by the Bodhisattvas Manjuśri and Samantabhadra*

c. first half of the 1760s

Colors on silk, three hanging scrolls
210.3 × 111.3 cm (each scroll)
Signature (on all three scrolls):
Copied by Tō Jokin Shinshuku of Heian [Kyoto]

SEALS (on all three scrolls):
square intaglio: *Jokin*
square relief: *Tōshi Keiwa*
Shōkokuji, Kyoto

In this triptych, Śākyamuni, the founder of Buddhism, is flanked by two Bodhisattvas: Manjuśri, who symbolizes wisdom and insight (right), and Samantabhadra, the deity of Universal Virtue, who represents the pragmatic aspect of Śākyamuni's teaching (left). This iconographic combination is common in Buddhism; but Jakuchū's images, with their attendant figures and their numerous ornaments, are somewhat unusual in appearance.

In 1765, Jakuchū donated this triptych and twenty-four of the *Dōshoku Sai-e* scrolls (NO. 14) to the Shōkokuji. In his dedication, he stated that the triptych had been copied from an original by Chang Ssu-kung. That artist's name is not recorded in Chinese documentary sources on painting, but he is mentioned in a Japanese work of the Muromachi period, the *Kundaikan Sōchōki*, as a Sung-dynasty artist who specialized in depictions of figural subjects and Buddhist images;[23] no further information about him appears anywhere. Korean Buddhist paintings of the Koryō period have frequently been attributed in Japanese sources to Chang Ssu-kung, and it is more than likely that a Koryō Buddhist painting served as the model for Jakuchū's triptych, with its techniques and motifs characteristic of such works: the dense coloring, emphasizing red and green, and the extensive use of gold pigment; the exquisite decorative gold patterns on the red robe of Śākyamuni; and the minutely detailed ornamentation of the hexagonal pedestal, upon which rests the lotus throne of the deity.

In recent years, a painting has come to light (FIG. 35) that is thought to have been the model for the central scroll. After coming into the Tokyo art market, this painting of Śākyamuni was acquired by the Cleveland Museum of Art in 1981. Rumor at the time had it that the painting came from a temple in Nara, and it is unclear whether the flanking paintings of Manjuśri and Samantabhadra are extant. Although Jakuchū's copy is extremely faithful to the original, which is considered to be a work of the late Koryō period, it also displays differing expressive tendencies.

Jakuchū departed from the style of the Cleveland painting in several respects: because the artist copied the details with uniform density, the subtle relationships between the whole and its parts suffered, and the forms, although minutely detailed, were flattened. He extended the robe of Śākyamuni so that it hangs over the left and right sides of

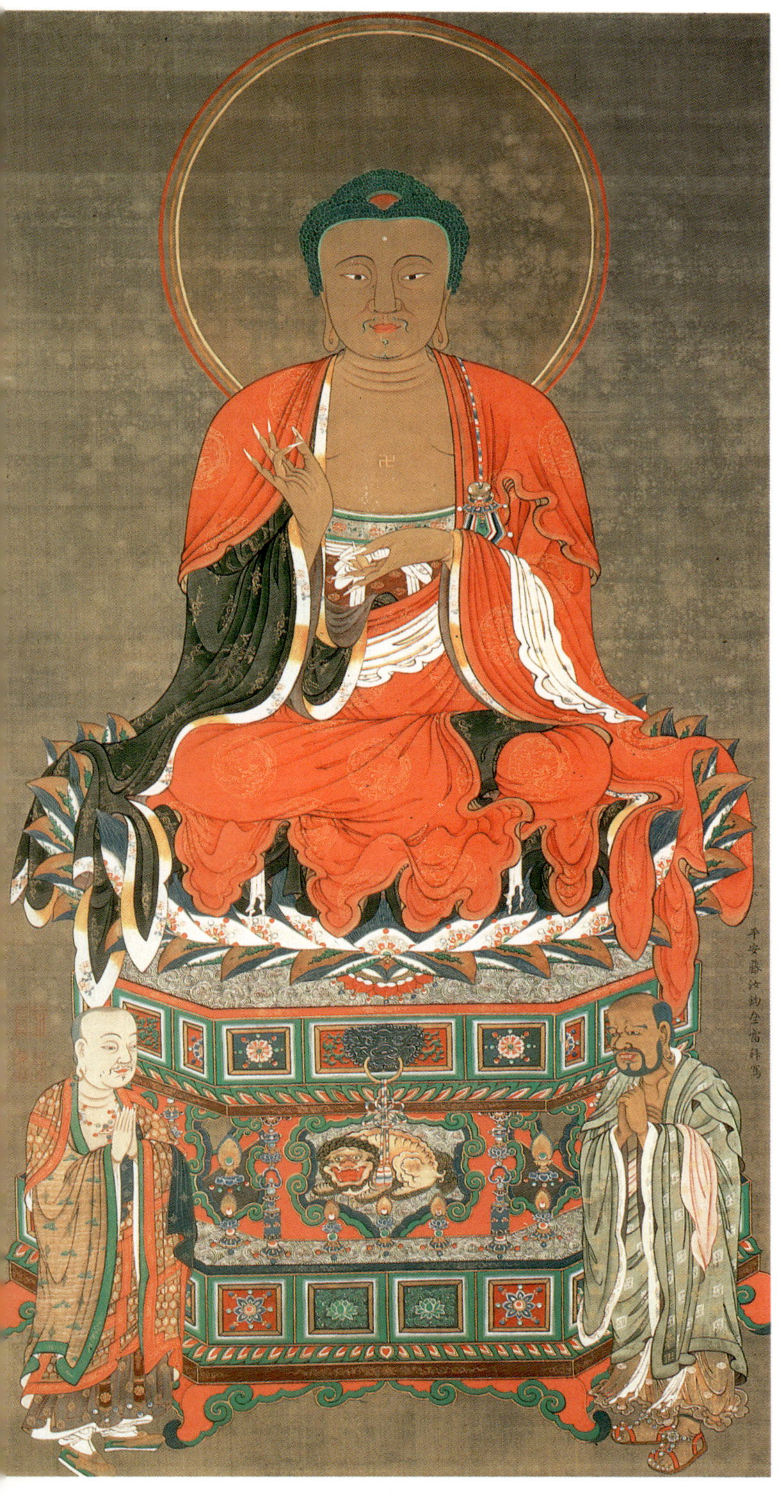

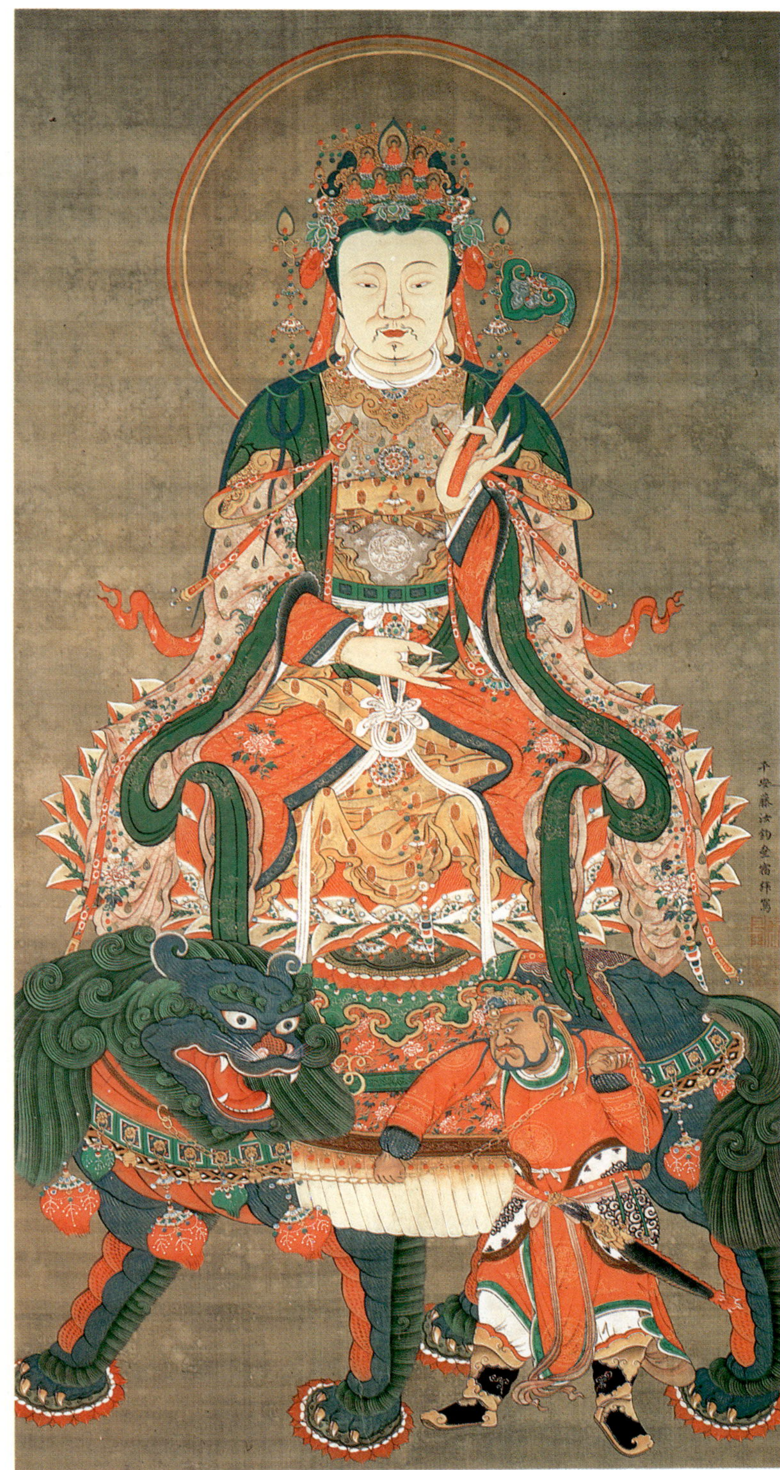

the lotus pedestal. He emphasized the lines of the garment more strongly, creating the undulating movement peculiar to his style. Finally, he used bright, intense colors throughout the painting (except for some restraint in gold pigment of the decorative pattern), creating strong contrasts. These characteristics can also be seen in Jakuchū's polychrome bird-and-flower paintings, and like these, his Buddhist paintings went beyond their models to harbor an entirely different expressive force.

The signature is written in precise brush strokes appropriate to a Buddhist painting. The calligraphic style is similar to that of Jakuchū's document of dedication, indicating that the paintings were probably completed not long before they were donated to the temple. The name Shinshuku (Chinese: Shen Hsiu) refers to one of the Twenty-eight Lunar Mansions, constellations that marked divisions of the sky in ancient Chinese astronomy, and it is equivalent to part of the Western constellation of Orion. Each of these twenty-eight constellations was associated with an animal, and the creature corresponding to Shinshuku was the monkey. Following Chinese precedent, it became customary in Japan to use a twelve-year calendrical cycle in which a different animal was associated with each year. Under this system Jakuchū was born in the year of the monkey, which may explain his choice of Shinshuku for the signature. There are no other examples of its use in his work.

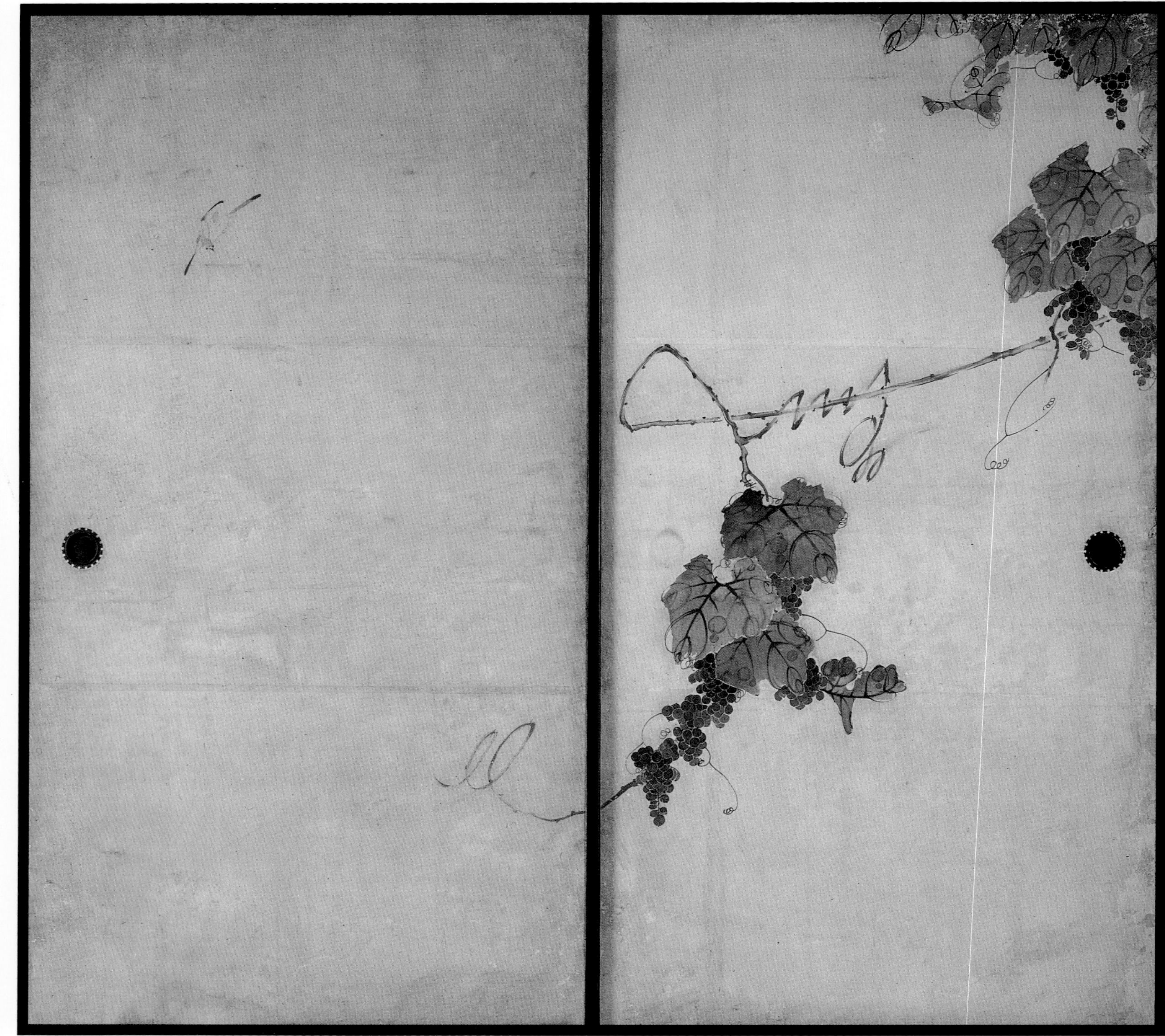

16.1

16 *Grape Vines; Cranes and Pines; Begonias;* and *Bamboo*

1759

Ink on paper, sixteen sliding-screen panels
168.3 × 93 cm (each panel)

SEALS (on FIG. 41):
square relief: *Jokin*
round intaglio: *Jakuchū koji*
square intaglio: *Tō-shi Keiwa*
Rokuonji, Kyoto
Important Cultural Properties

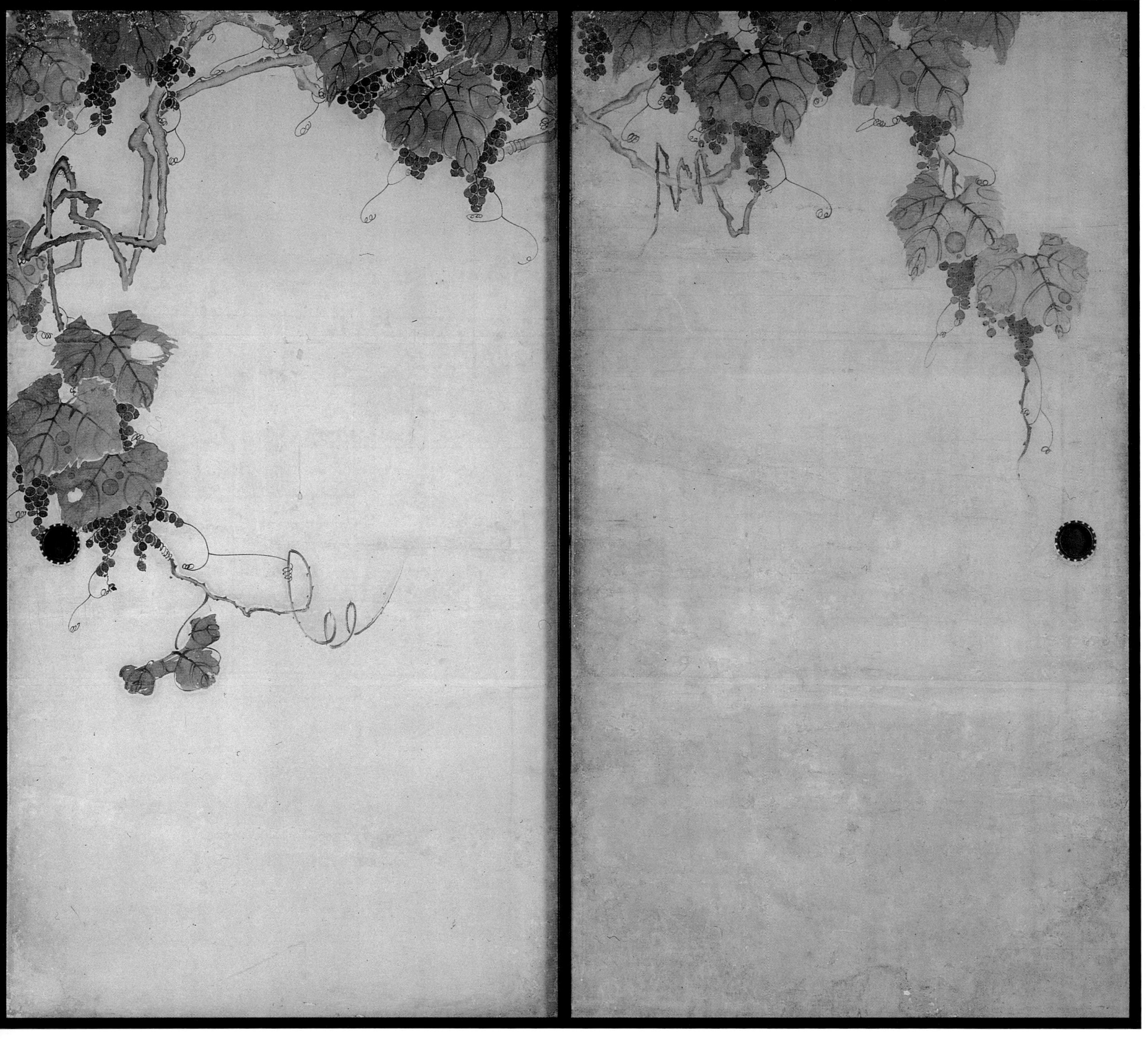

16.2

Jakuchū produced fifty monochrome screen and wall panel paintings for the Dai-shoin, the grand abbot's study of the Rokuonji. All have since been removed from the building that initially housed them and are now in the Jōtenkaku Museum of the Shōkokuji, where until recently they have been displayed in five rooms that recreate the L-shaped conformation of the original building, in which three chambers were laid out in a line from west to east, and two more extended perpendicularly to the south. The sequence of subject matter in these rooms is first room, *Grape Vines*; second room, *Cranes and Pines*; third room, *Banana Trees and* Haha-chō; fourth room, *Cock and Chrysanthemums, Chickens*, and *Begonias*; and fifth room, *Bamboo*. The first room also originally had paintings on walls behind the Chiga idana (shelved alcove) and the Tokonoma (alcove), and on an adjacent wall; the second room had a painting behind the Tokonoma; and the fourth room had a painting on a section of one wall. All of the other paintings were executed on the panels of sliding screens.

The paintings in the exhibition consist of four sets of continuous compositions on four-panel screens—one each from the first, second, fourth, and fifth

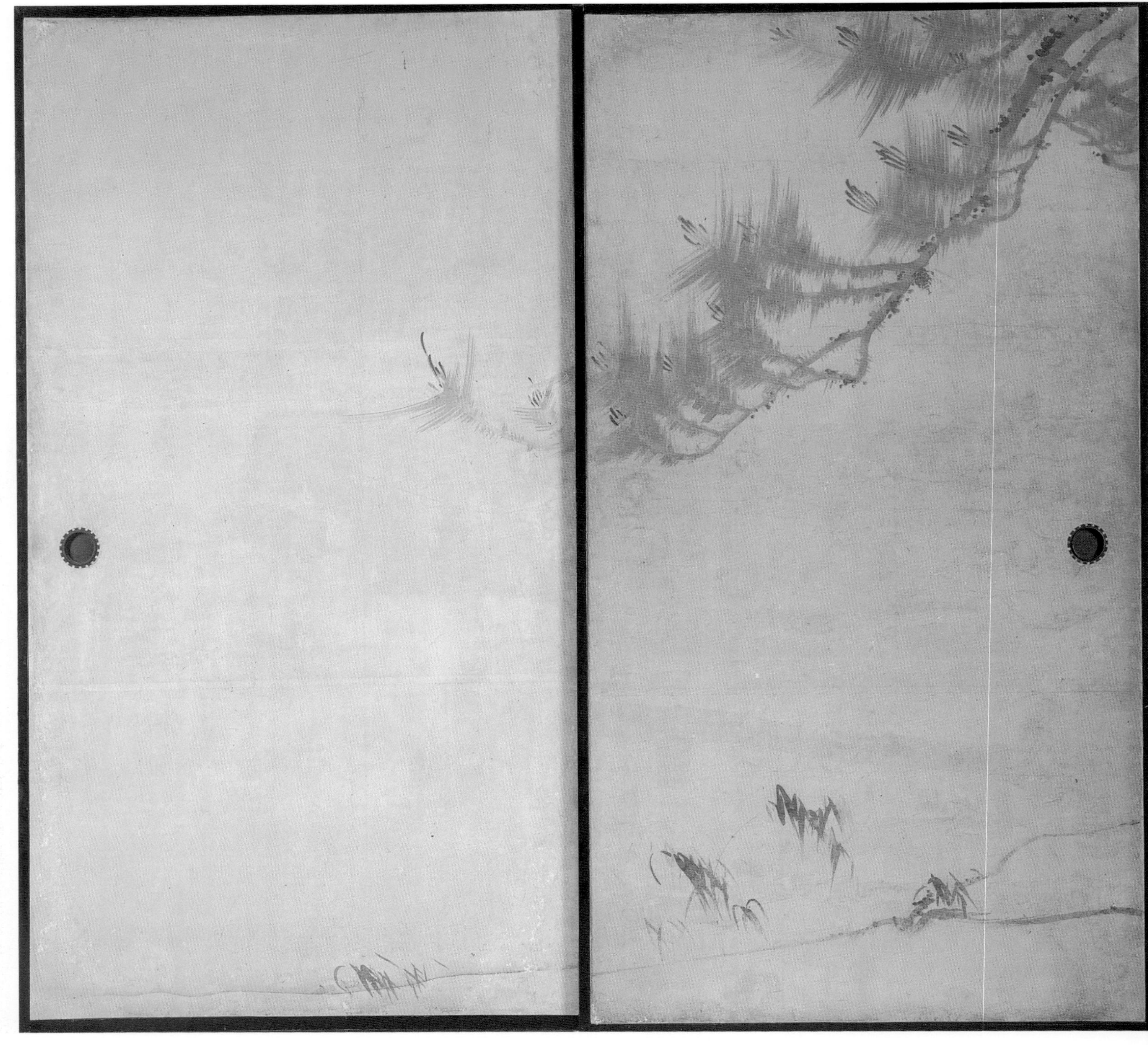

16.3

rooms. Of the two four-panel compositions with cranes and pines in the second room, the work originally on the west side of the room has been chosen in preference to the painting on the east side (FIG. 41). The inscription, date, and signature at the extreme left of the latter work attest to the paintings' having been completed in 1759: "In the path between the pines, I look down and then gaze upward; enlightenment comes to me, and my heart is in the heavens. Hōreki 9 (1759), [Tenth Month], Koji Jakuchū-zō." The Dai-shoin was erected during the Empō period (1673–1681), but no screen paintings seem to have been done for the temple until 1759, when Ryūmon Shōyū (1734–1800) became the abbot of the Rokuonji.

Ryūmon had studied literature under Jakuchū's friend Daiten, and the artist presumably was given the opportunity to create these paintings when Ryūmon took up his new position, although the circumstances are not entirely clear. One indication that Ryūmon admired Jakuchū's abilities, however, appears in the abbot's collected poetry, the *Meikō Yōkō* (vol. 3),[24] in a work about a painting by Jakuchū of a chicken perched on top of a well. In the compositions in this room, two cranes look

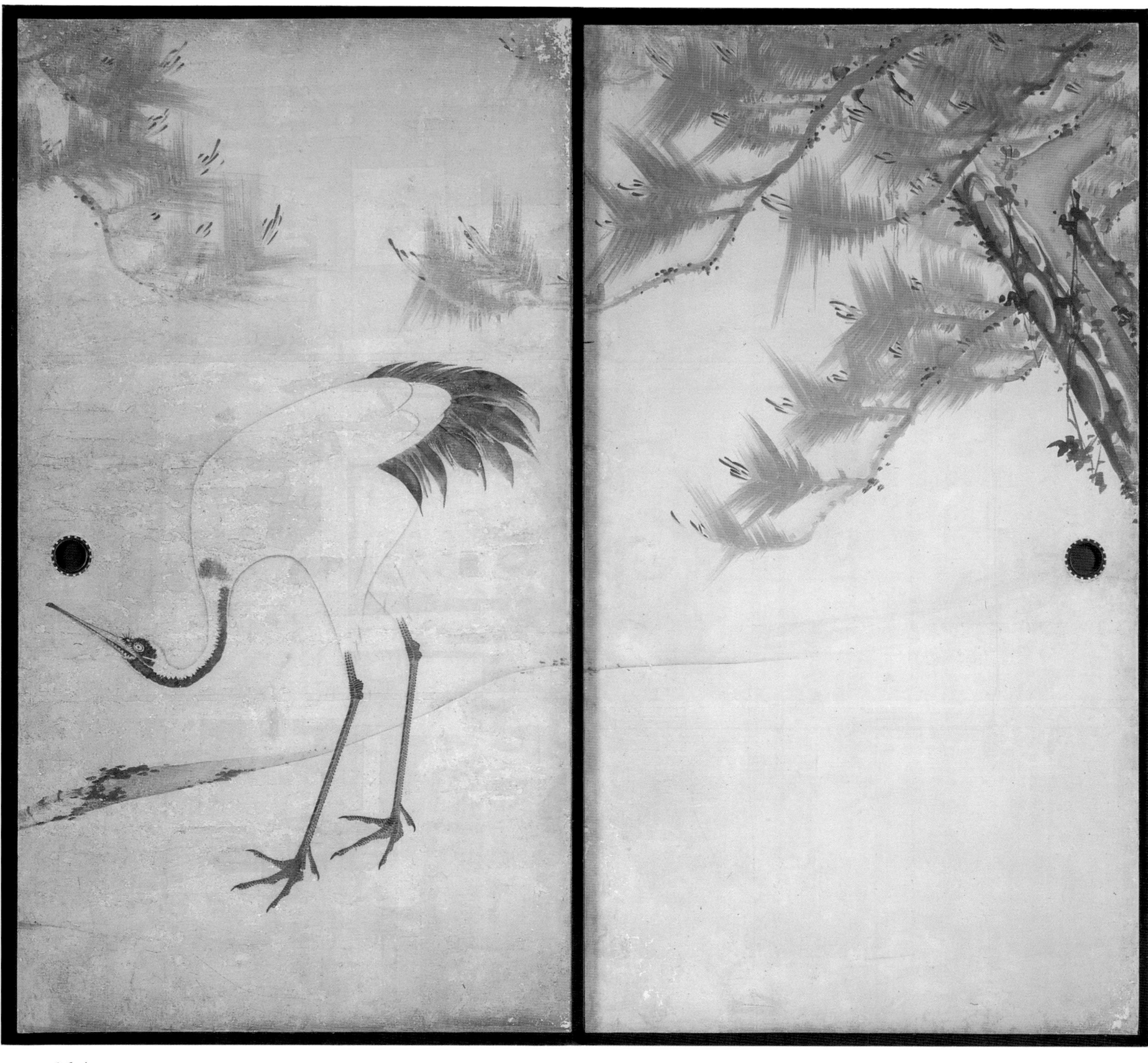

16.4

up through the branches of the pines, and it has been suggested that the term *mei-shin* (literally, bright heart), in the inscription, is a metaphor for the moon. The painting on the wall in the Tokonoma of the third room (FIG. 42) does have a full moon floating in the sky between the banana leaves; thus it has also been suggested that all of the paintings in the Dai-shoin are actually night scenes infused with the light of the moon. However, no instance of the term *mei-shin*'s having been used to represent the moon has been substantiated. Furthermore, since most birds are not active at night, common sense would indicate that this imaginative theory is unfounded. The concept of transcending the bewildering circumstances of mundane life in the search for spiritual truth is one of the basic premises in Buddhism; it seems reasonable to interpret the evocative posture of the two cranes here as a pictorial metaphor for this profound message.

In the Rokuonji paintings,[25] there are frequent instances in which Jakuchū geometrically arranged and oriented pictorial components, such as the branches of trees and rock forms, to lead the viewer's attention diagonally down from upper right to lower left. The grape-vine compositions reveal this

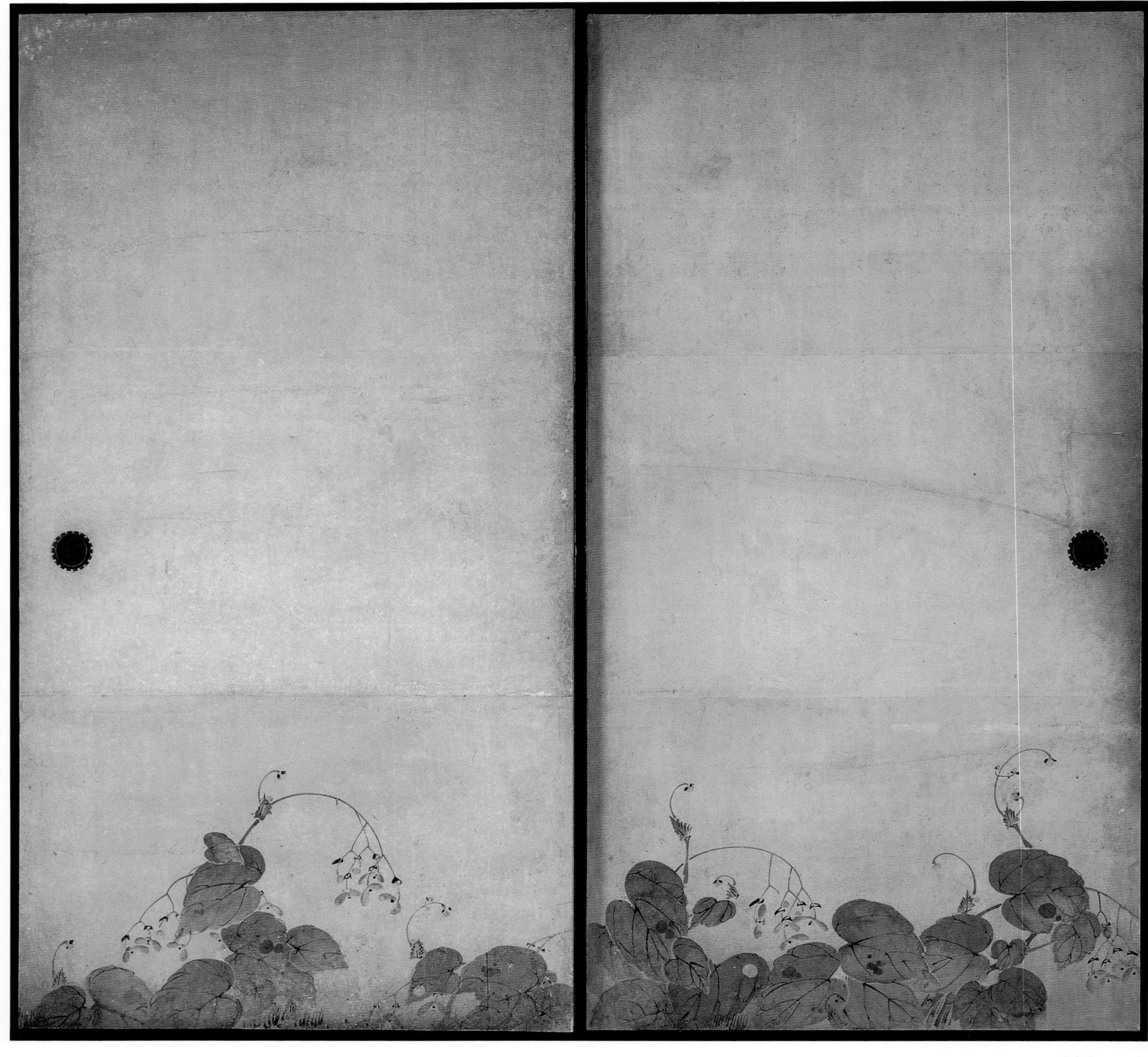

16.5

tendency, and so do even minute details, such as the representation of a small bird. At the same time, the artist treated both the tendrils of the vines, with their circular conformations and jagged shapes, and the runners, with their convoluted extremities, in a lively decorative manner that might be described as "abstracted nature," making manifest the sense of innate life unique to his art.

The Rokuonji portrayals show an indebtedness to Chinese monochrome traditions similar to that displayed in the artist's earlier works (see Nos. 3, 6), but the pieces here are much freer and have more creative energy. Thus, Jakuchū did not precisely confine the leaves of the grape vines by their outlines; he spread the soft washes beyond them and added the structural details of the leaves quickly, but surely added in dark ink before the underlying wash dried. To this, he skillfully added circular areas portraying the stains and insect-eaten areas of the leaves in both dark and light ink. He rendered the grapes individually, in a most convincing manner that utilizes complementary dark and light washes.

Cranes and Pines also has a geometrical structure, but its compositions go far beyond being simple designs.

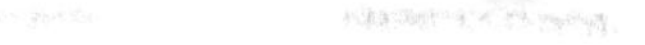

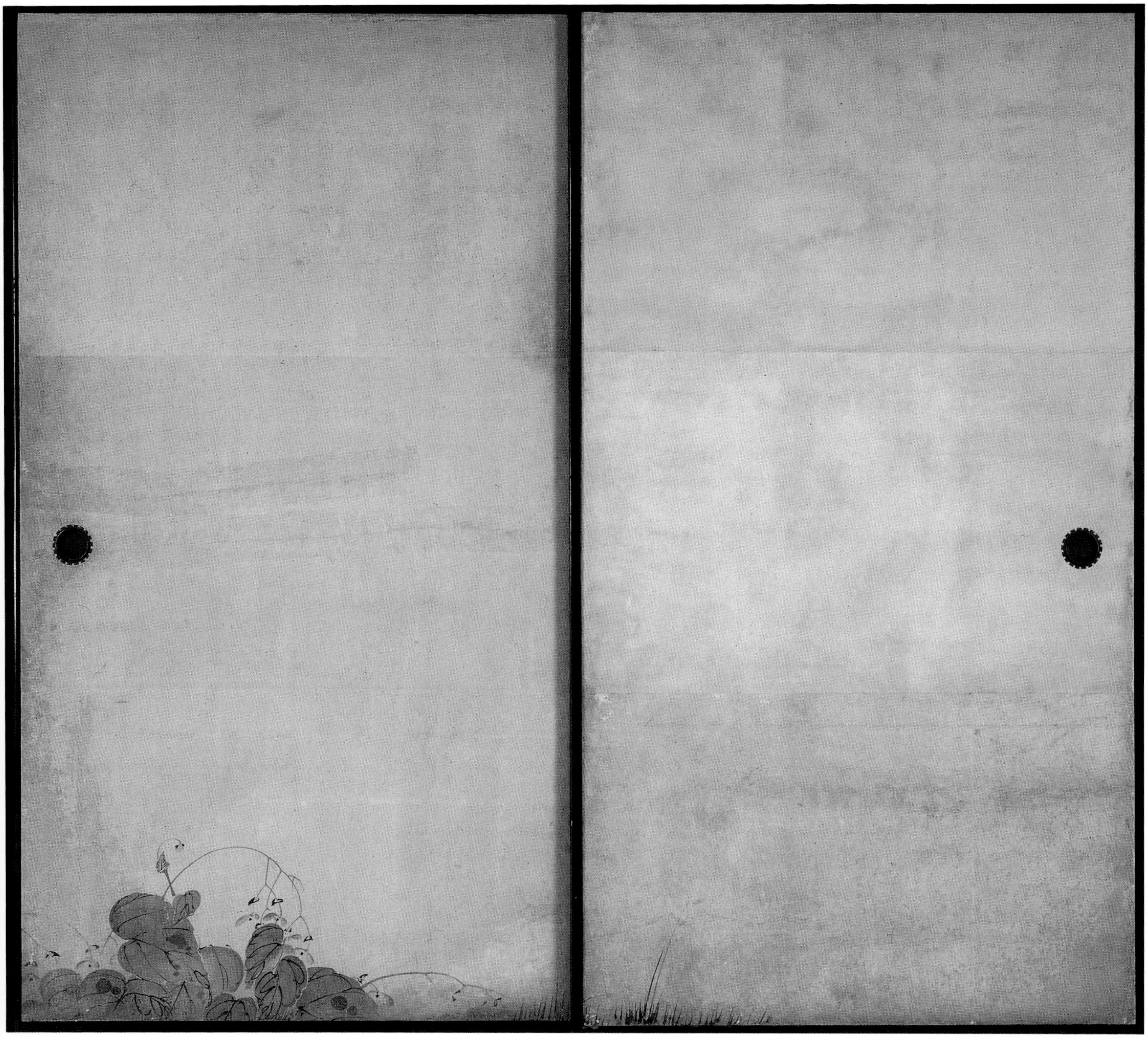

16.6

Here, the pine branches give a distinctive life to the paintings; Jakuchū rendered them with a narrow *hake*, or flat brush. According to Daiten (in his *Tō Keiwa Gakanoki*), the artist had completed three monochrome works, together with the first group of *Dōshoku Sai-e* scrolls, by about 1760, and the author described one of these ink paintings as "a disconcerted owl in a pine tree, surrounded by eleven crows, [a composition] in which a *hake* has been used to brush in all the pine needles, [displaying] an impressive new conceptual means."[26] *White Cockatoo and Pine* (Museum of Fine Arts, Boston; FIG. 54), which is presumed to have been done between about 1755 and 1757, provides in the dramatic handling of its pine needles another tangible example of this innovative technique.

If the explanation by Professor Toda Teisuke of Tokyo University can be enlarged here, the conformations of the pines and the manner of their representation may have been inspired by the portrayal of the withered tree in the painting of a monkey that is one of the flanking segments of Mu Ch'i's (?— c. 1274–1279) great triptych, the *Bodhisattva Kannon* (also flanked by a representation of a crane), one of the most revered treasures of the great Zen

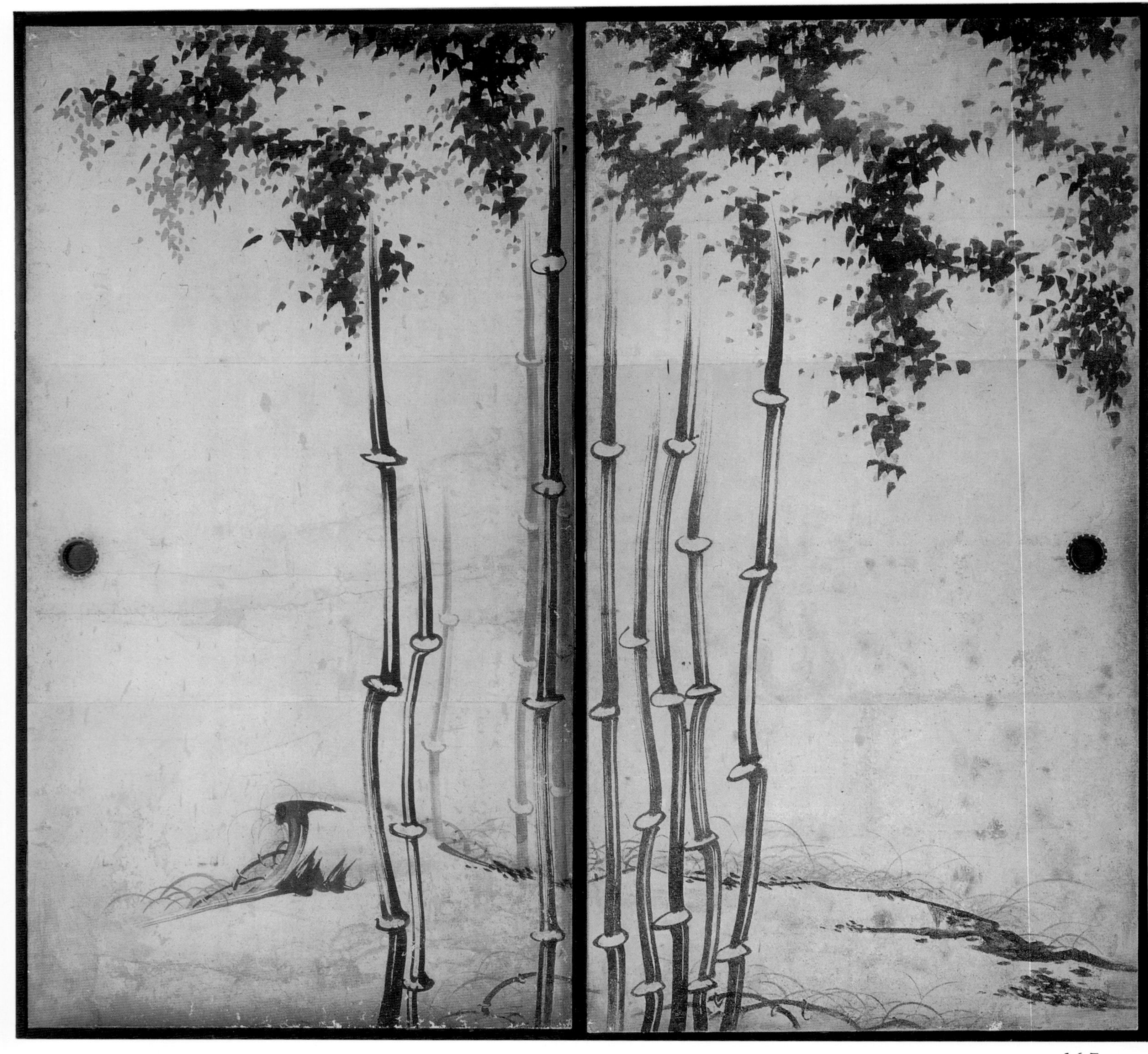

16.7

monastery Daitokuji in Kyoto. The portrayal of the crane, which stands on an incline and stares up at the sky in this triptych, may also have influenced Jakuchū.[27] Even if these suggestions have validity, however, it should be emphasized that Jakuchū gave his pines a highly individualistic graphic treatment; in the case of the cranes—whose exterior contours he executed in fine, uninflected lines, whose forms he floated in space, and whose dark and light pictorial components he clearly differentiated—the expressive means belong to an entirely different realm than that of Mu Ch'i, who portrayed the subjects in a more representational, more realistic manner.

Begonias is notable for its exceptional amount of empty white space; for the blooming flowers situated across the bottom of the work; and for the soft tendrils of the plants, which lean back, emphasizing this extremely low compositional conception. This scheme contrasts with the ideas that characterize the *Dōshoku Sai-e* scrolls, produced at the same time, works in which the varied subject matter generally filled the vertical space. The artist's realistic treatment of the begonias in the present painting also contrasts with his depictions of the plant in later

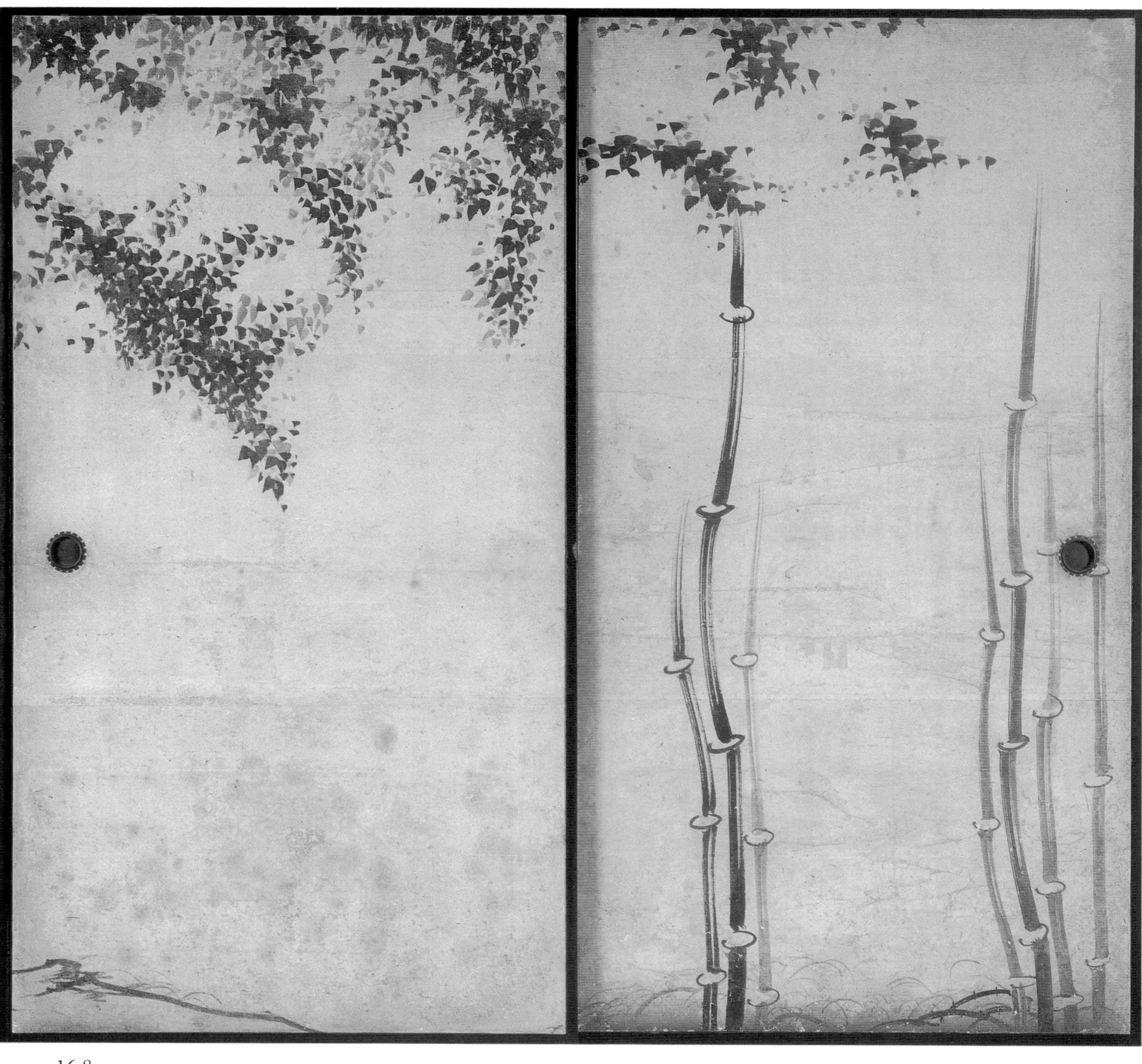

16.8

folding screens, in which he isolated the subjects in independent formats and portrayed them in a more mannered, abstract style.

Jakuchū's representation of bamboos is particularly innovative. He seems to have executed the individual stalks simultaneously with two brushes, and their parallel strokes rise in a rhythmic sequence and ultimately disappear into blank space, as if fading out in the hot, shimmering air of summer. The exaggerated circular forms of the nodes serve as strong visual accents, and the artist depicted leaves, with their distinctive triangular accents of brushwork, in various dark and light tones, conveying the sense of the soft, effusive sunlight typical of bamboo groves.

Professor Tsuji Nobuo thinks that Jakuchū may have freely adapted this method of depicting bamboo from some Chinese album of woodblock-printed illustrations of the late Ming or early Ch'ing period, such as the *Pa-chung Hua-p'u* (Japanese: *Hasshū Gafū*; *Painting Manual of Eight Varieties*) or the *Chieh-tzu-yüan Hua-chüan* (Japanese: *Kaishien Gaden*; *Mustard Seed Garden Manual of Painting*).[28] However, Professor Toda has recently suggested that although Jakuchū may have been influenced by such illustrations, he would also have been familiar with the method Mu Ch'i used in portraying bamboo in the painting of a crane in his famous triptych.[29] Mu Ch'i's handling of bamboo in that painting is said to be unique in the history of Chinese painting in that he represented the stalks and leaves individually and precisely, with a variety of dark and light washes, and faded out the tops of the stalks into blank space. Thus it seems likely enough that Jakuchū was influenced in his distinctive execution of bamboo by details in the Chinese painting.

In an attempt to demonstrate the influence on Jakuchū of pictorial ideas from sources other than woodblock album illustrations, it also seems appropriate to point out how the monochrome painting of Kakutei (see FIG. 55) reveals these models. Even in comparing the depiction of bamboo in these works, it should be considered how radically different the cranes in Jakuchū's screen composition are from those in Mu Ch'i's portrayal. The Chinese piece is notable for its naturalistic representation, with its enveloping atmosphere of light and air; Jakuchū's work is highly personal in its expressive means and has a diverting sense of levity.

However much Jakuchū's fertile imagination may have been inspired by Mu Ch'i's triptych (a work of great religious significance), the relationship should not be viewed simply as an example of clever artistic innovation, for it may well have occurred for a more profound reason. Jakuchū had moved beyond the bounds of established pictorial tradition and, in the case of the Rokuonji paintings, had infused the compositions with a special sense of serenity and transcendence appropriate to the refined world of Zen thought; in the process, he had also expressed his admiration for Mu Ch'i's accomplishments by boldly deriving his inspiration from them.

FIG. 54
White Cockatoo and Pine, n.d.

Museum of Fine Arts, Boston

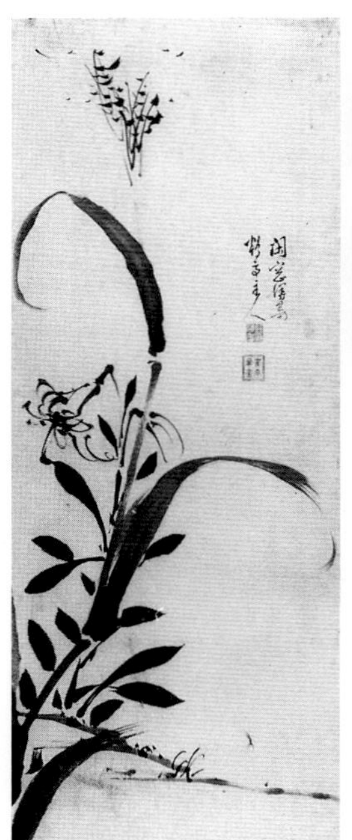
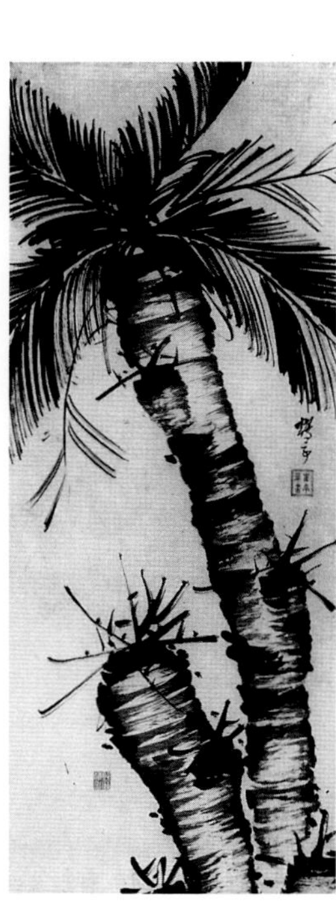
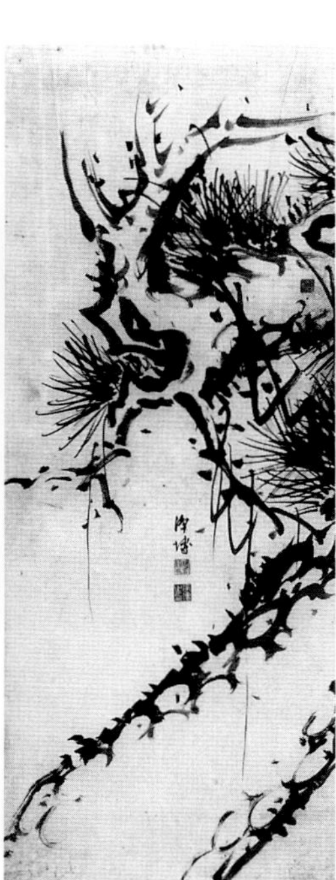
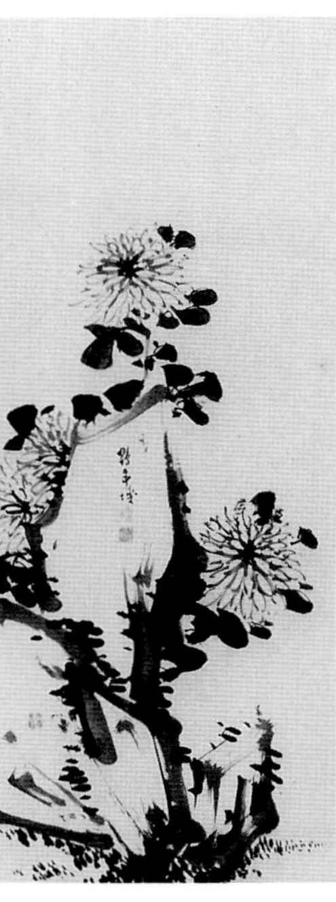
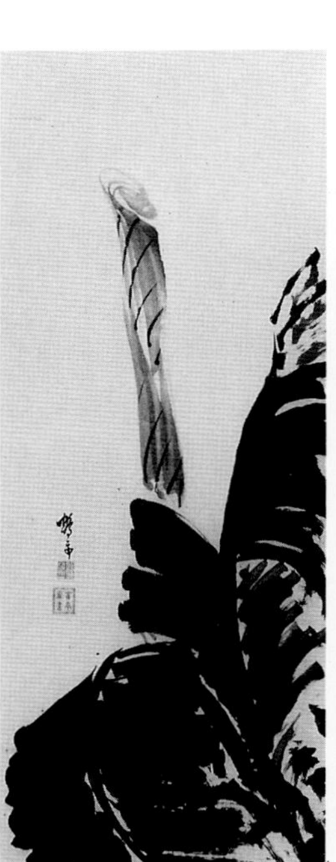
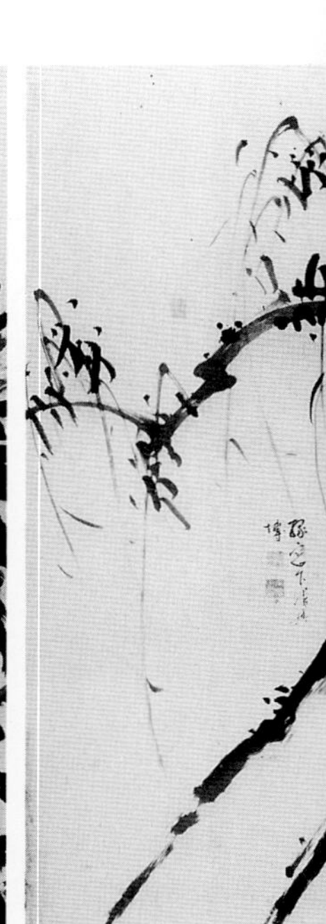

FIG. 55
Kakutei Jōkō (1721–1785). *Flowers and Plants of the Four Seasons*, n.d.

Location uncertain

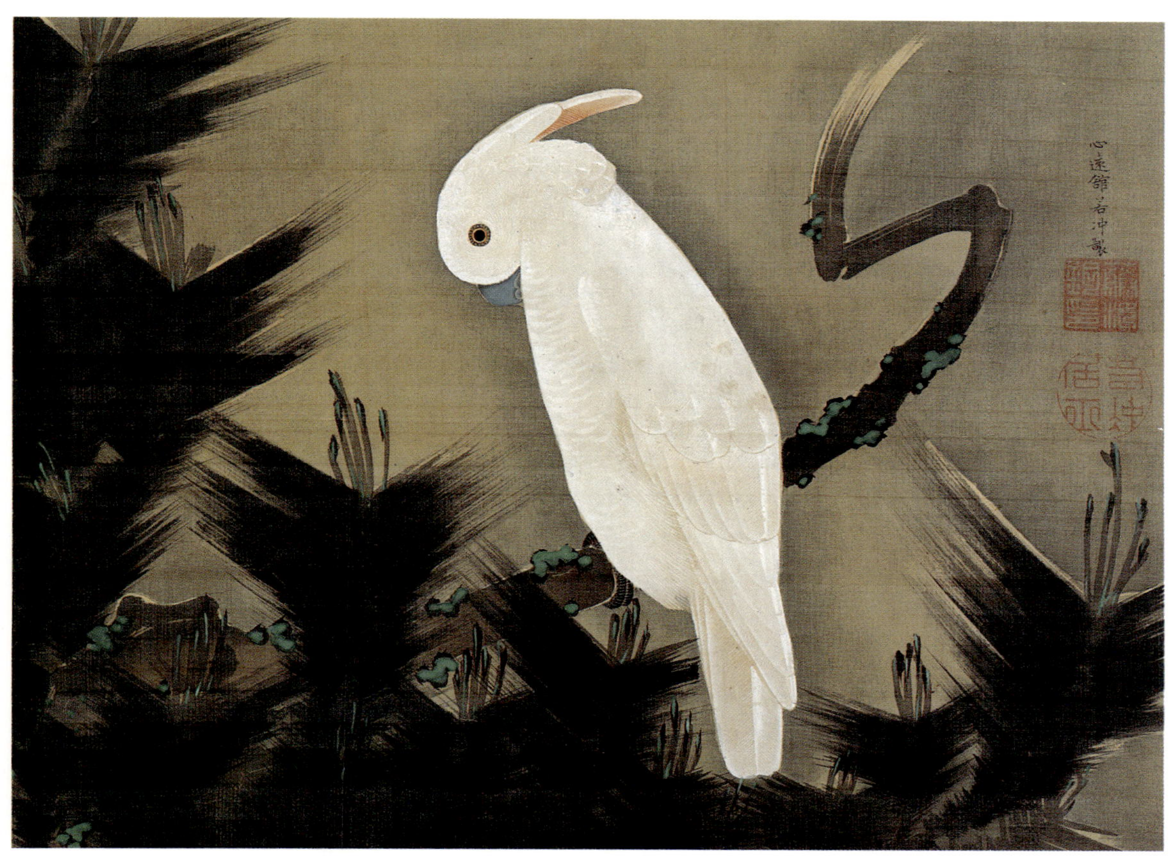

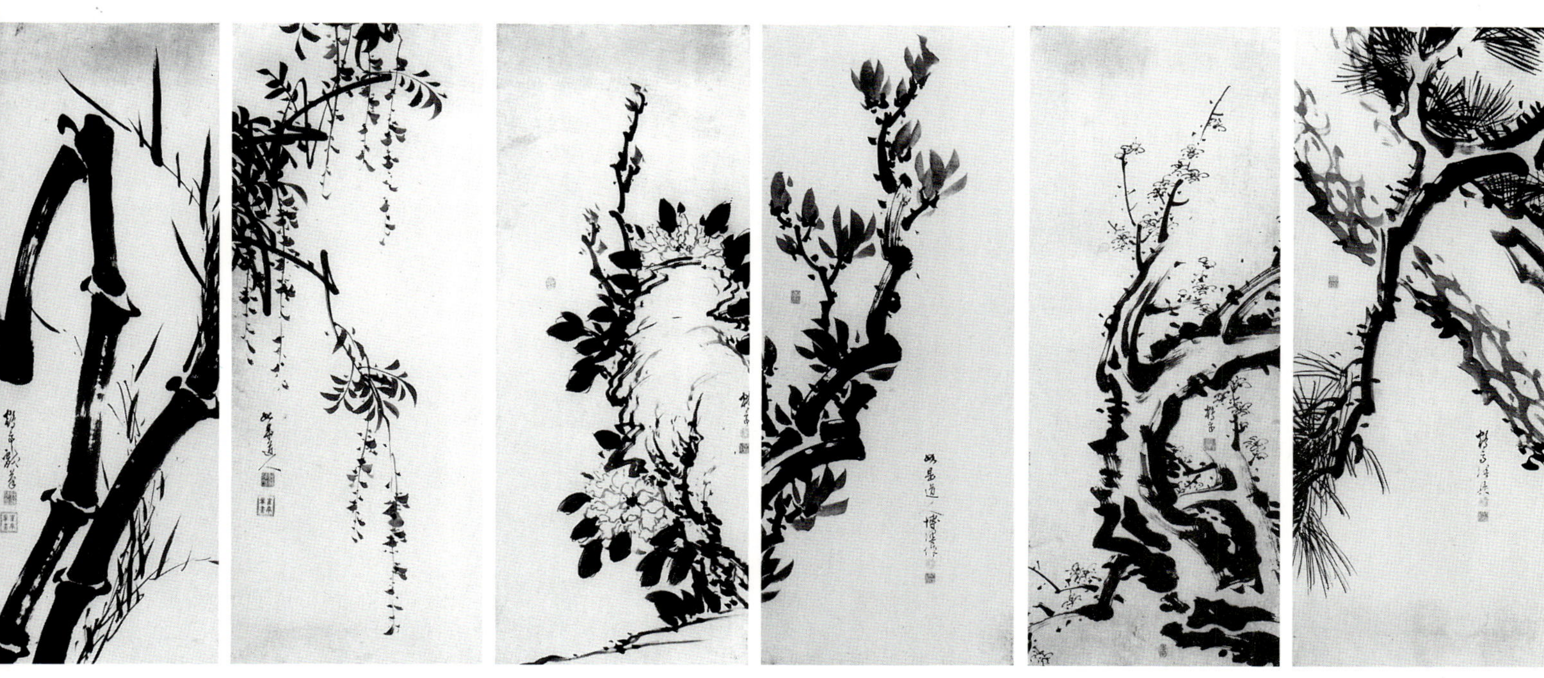

17 *Flowers, Birds, and Vegetables*

1760

Ink on paper, pair of six-panel folding screens (independent paintings on individual panels)
134.8 × 50 cm (each painting)
Inscription:
Painted by Tō Jakuchū at the Shin'enkan, Hōreki 10 [1760], mid-autumn [Eighth Month]

SEALS:
elongated square intaglio: *Tō Jokin-in*
round relief: *Jakuchū koji*
Private collection, Hyōgo Prefecture

The depiction in monochrome ink of various sorts of natural subjects, such as flowers, birds, animals, fruits, and vegetables, has a venerable history in China. Such depictions may be seen in the work of the Ming Literati artist Shen Chou (1427–1509)—who was inspired by ink paintings of flowers, fruits, and vegetables done by the celebrated thirteenth-century master Mu Ch'i—and by later works of such Ming and Ch'ing artists as Hsü Wei, Pa-ta Shan-jen (also known as Chu Ta; 1626–1705), and the "Eight Eccentrics of Yangchou." This genre was, in essence, affiliated with the Literati painting tradition, but the method of depiction evolved in its own way, depending on quick washes and innovative brushwork rather than the use of carefully executed dots and lines. Jakuchū was clearly one of the most important pioneers of this genre in

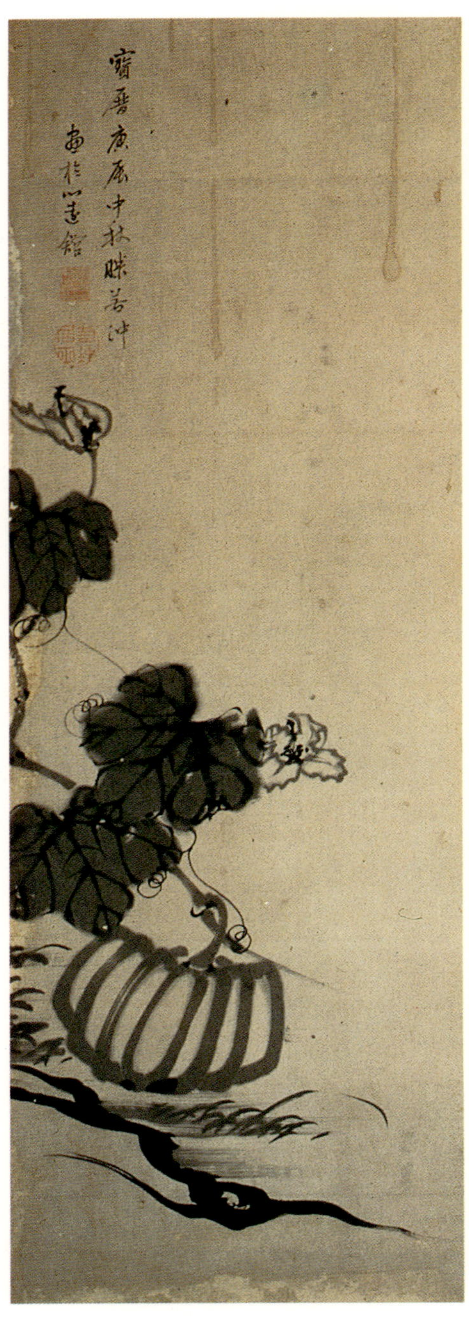

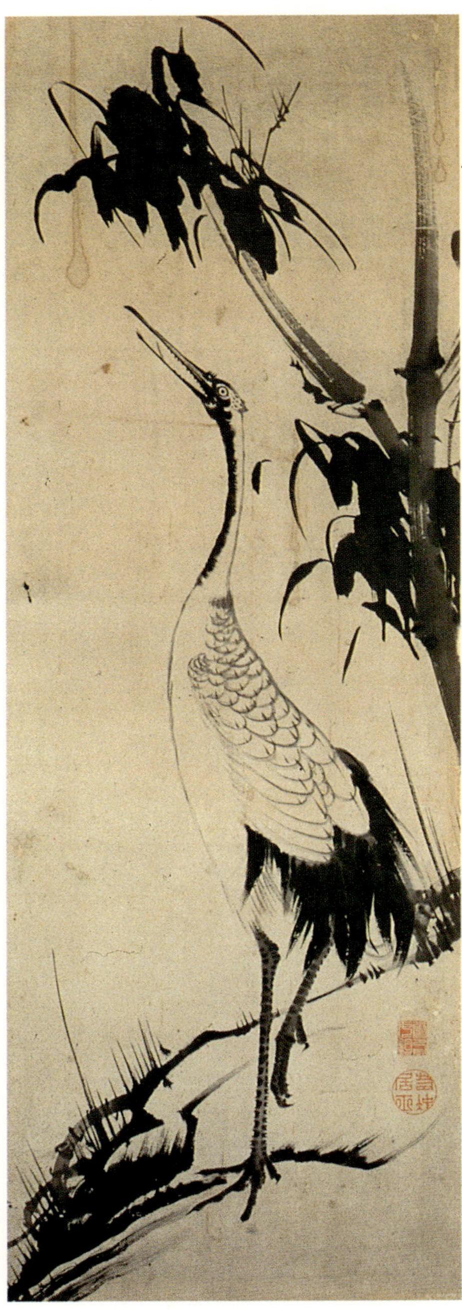

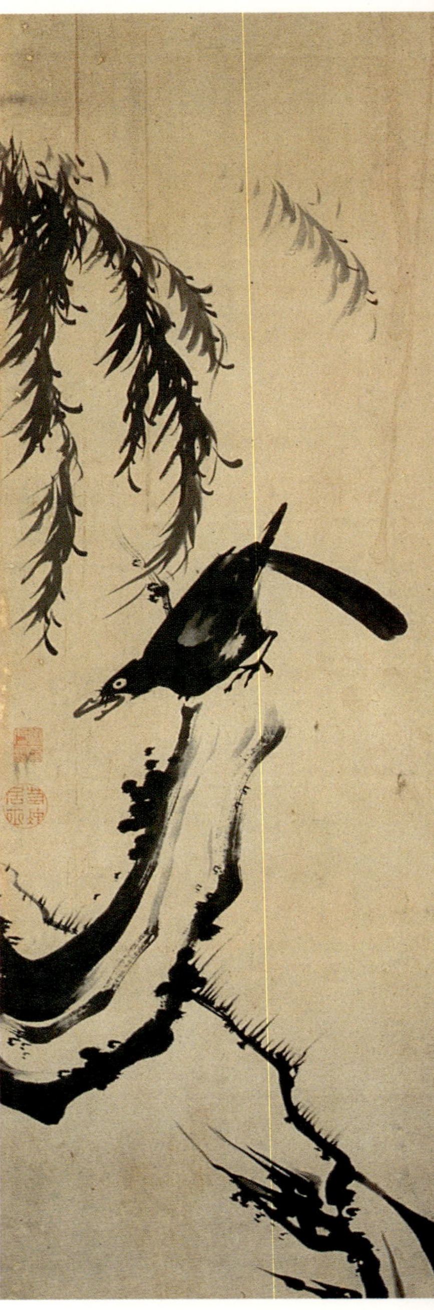

Japan, and the date that appears on this set of screens indicates that it was one of his early experiments in this manner.

The subjects portrayed in the screen below are (from the right) blossoming plum, small bird in a pine, rooster and wisteria, crow and willow, crane and bamboo, and squash; and in the screen on the next page, they are lotus, begonias, chrysanthemums, mandarin duck in reeds, narcissus, and hawk perched on an oak branch. The sequence of flora was arranged in accordance with the four seasons.

The archives of the Tokyo National Cultural Properties Research Institute contain photographs of a pair of six-panel folding screens of paintings of flowers and trees of the four seasons by the priest-painter Kakutei (FIG. 55). These photographs were taken in 1941, and a comment on the accompanying card notes that the screens belonged to a private collection in Tōyama Prefecture at that time, but it is unclear whether these pieces are still in existence. Works of this sort probably served as a source for Jakuchū's paintings in this manner.

Kakutei executed his scenes entirely in ink on paper, and the subjects, which he depicted independently (as did Jakuchū) are pine, blossoming plum,

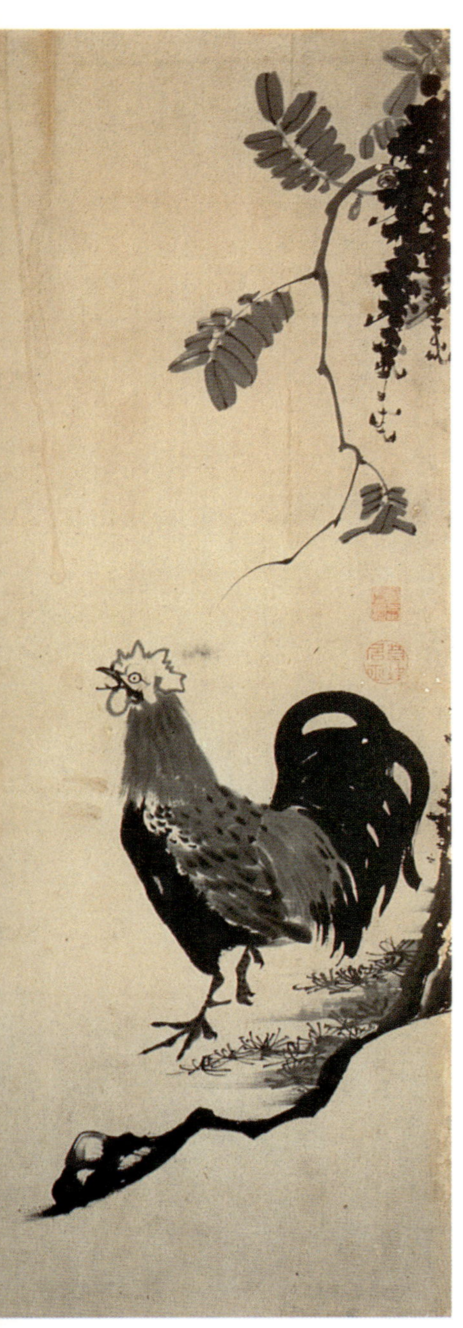

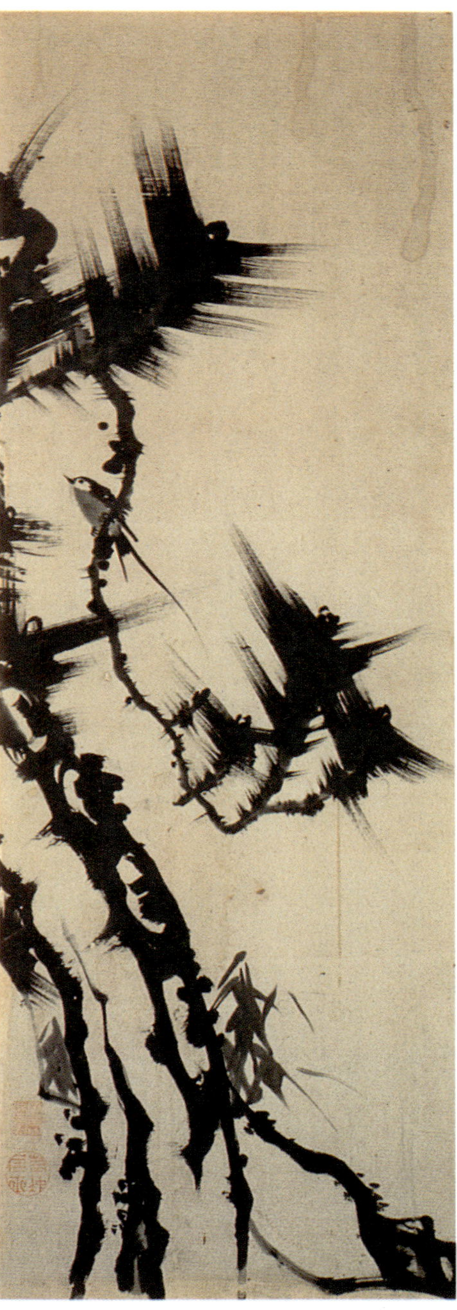

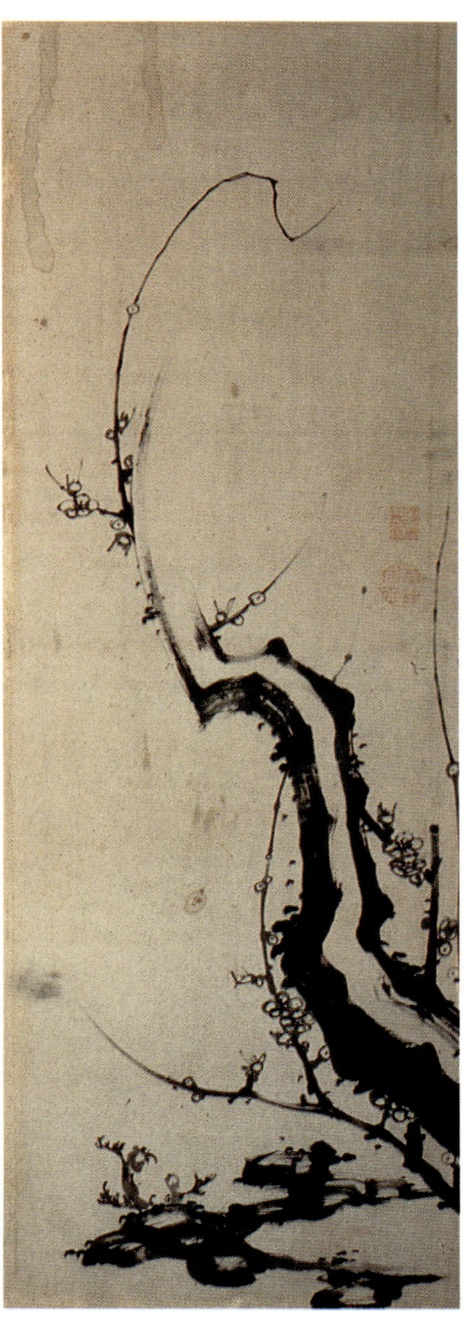

magnolia, peony, wisteria, and bamboo on one screen; and willow, banana tree, chrysanthemum, pine, palm, and lily on the other. A portion of the inscription contains the painter's name Nyoze Dojin, which Kakutei used early in his career. The last known work on which he used this name is a piece produced in 1760; it is therefore presumed that the screens by Kakutei reproduced here were done before that year, and thus predate Jakuchū's screens.

The two artists' screens resemble each other in many respects. Both were conceived as twelve individual monochrome depictions and were devoted to plants and trees of the four seasons. In each, the trunk of the pine tree is cut off laterally by the edges of the format and the branches extend down diagonally, one of them curving back up near its end. Second, the trunks of both plums emerge from the lower right-hand corner of the composition, and a branch extends up into the center. In both works the stalks of the bamboo were done with a *hake* (flat brush), and they disappear into empty space at the top. Finally, there is the similarity in the treatment of certain details such as rough, curved contours and angular forms, which were rendered with a large brush, saturated with thick ink. There seems little doubt that Jakuchū was inspired to carry out his screens in this new style of monochrome ink painting

17

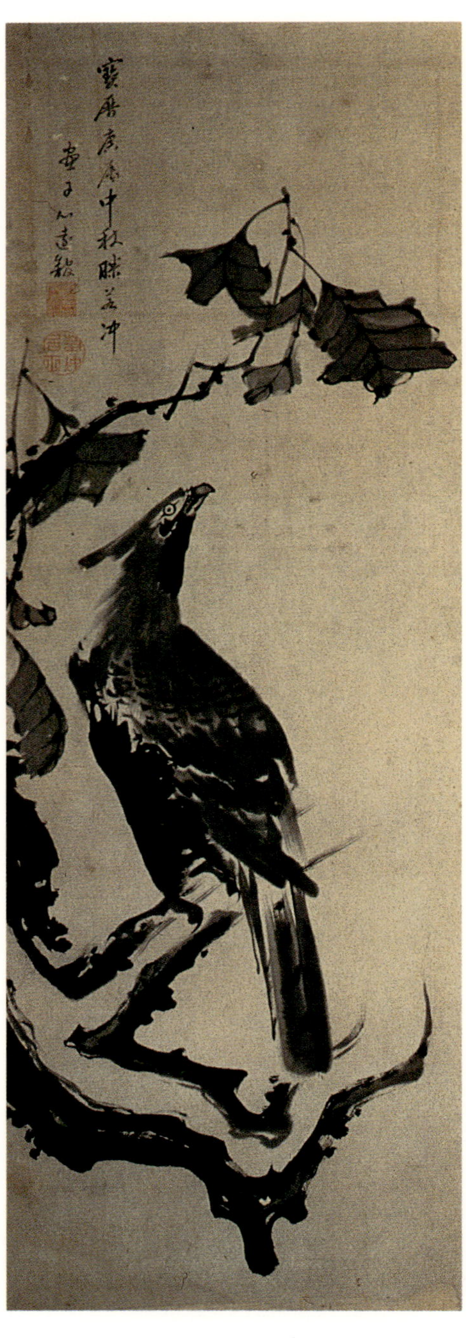

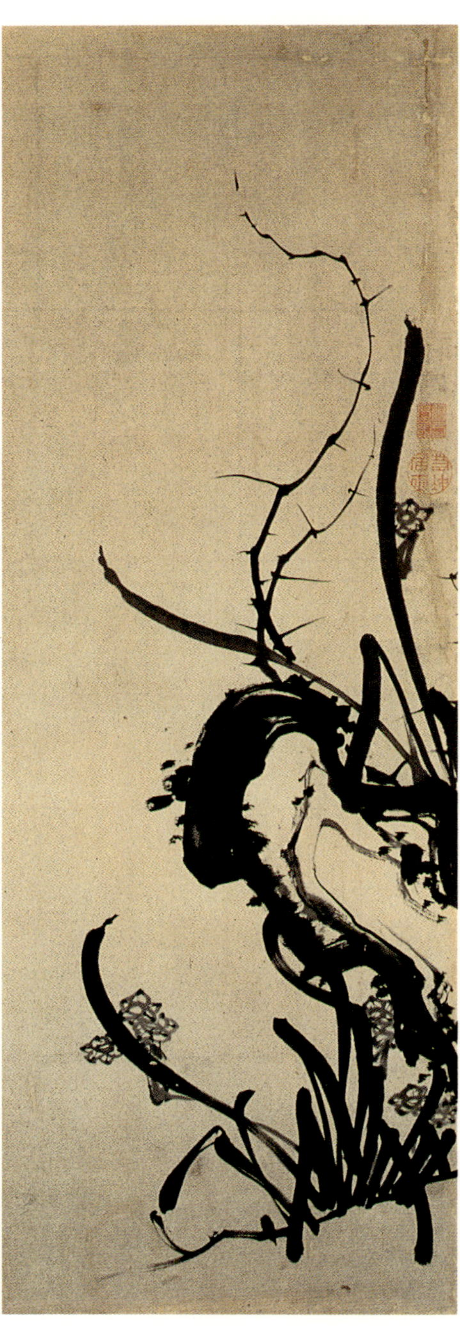

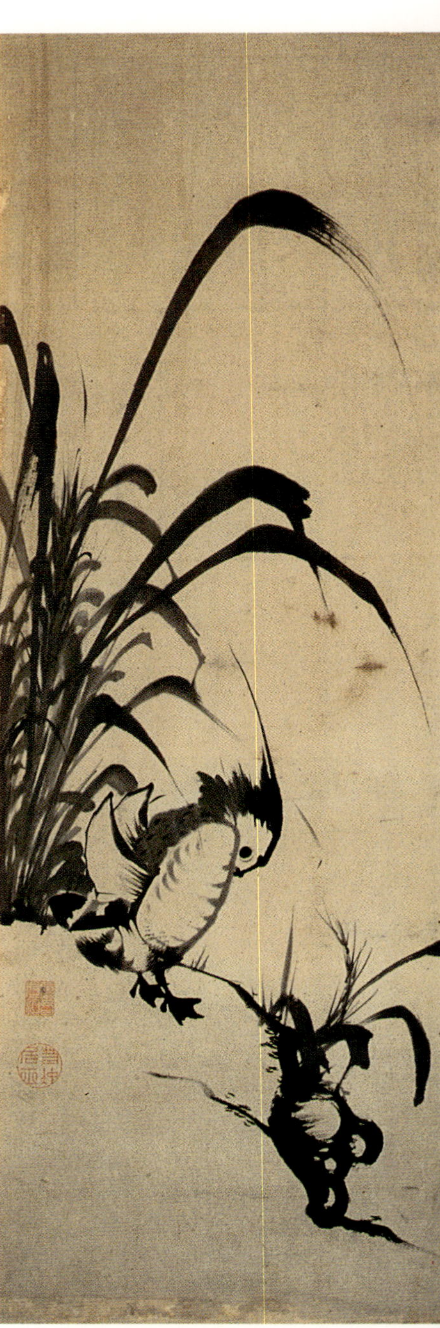

developed by Kakutei. It appears that Jakuchū's sharp, angular brush strokes were not his own innovation, but were indebted in large part to Kakutei's distinctive style.

In one respect, however, Jakuchū's screen compositions are significantly different from Kakutei's: they were executed on *gasenshi*, a type of paper noted for its soft, absorbent qualities and used even today for calligraphy and painting. *Gasenshi* reacts in a distinctive way when washes are brushed into juxtaposed areas, for the exterior contours do not blur and the edges of each area, when dry, retain a subtle, gray outline. Jakuchū skillfully utilized this quality when he rendered the individual feathers of a chicken or the separate petals of a chrysanthemum. This innovation influenced the subsequent history of monochrome painting.

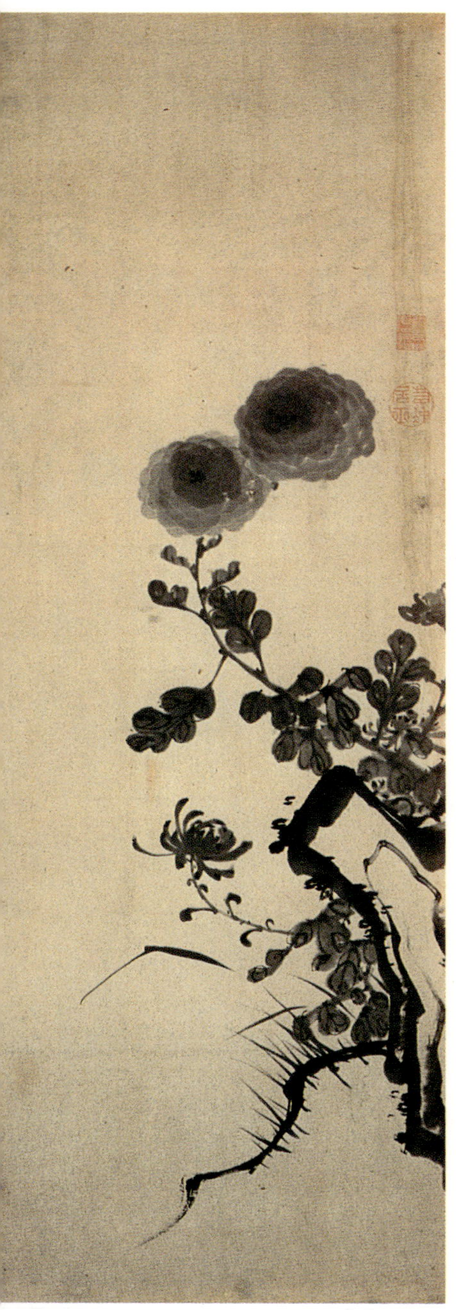

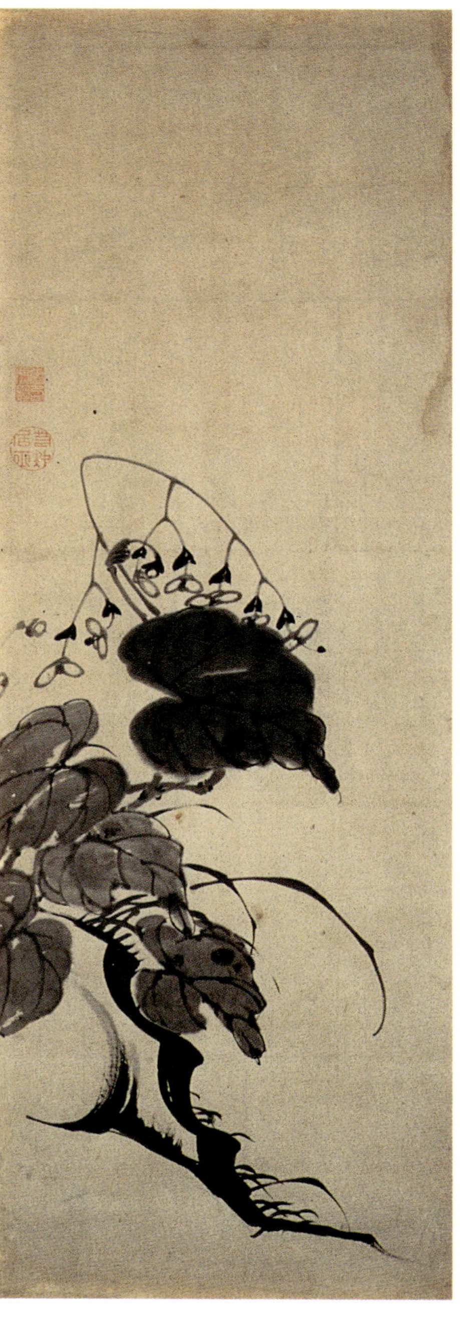

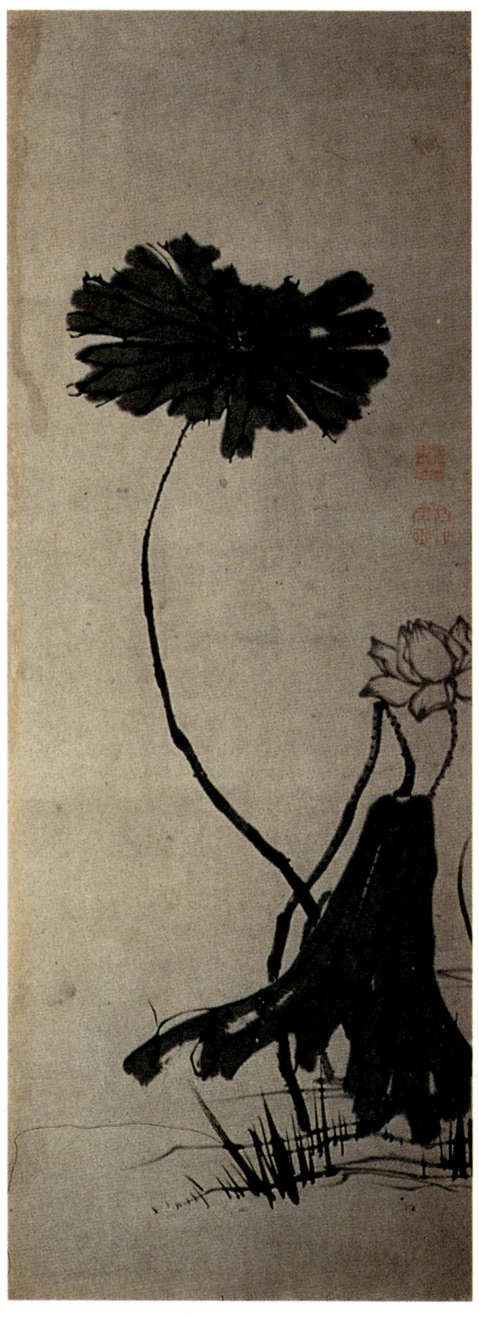

18, 19 *Pages from two versions of the Baisaō Gego*

(Woodblock-printed books)

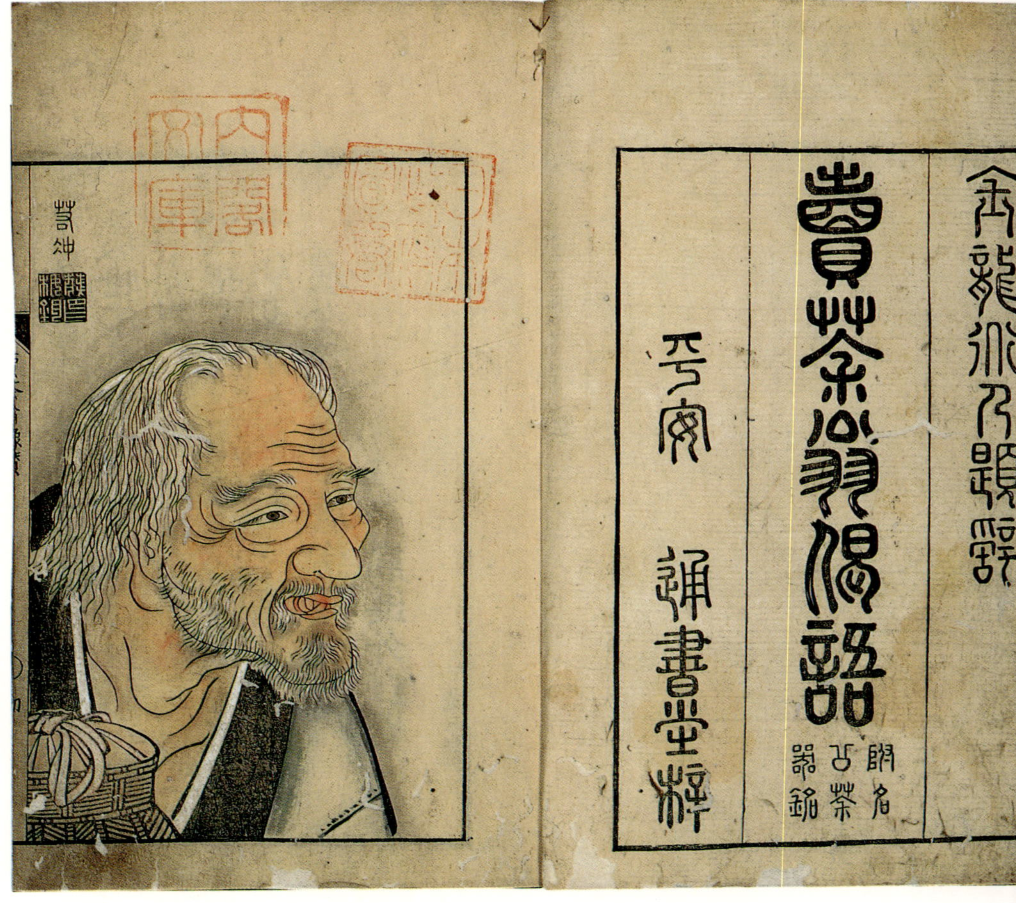

18

1763

27.7 × 17.5 cm
Title-page inscription:
Preface by Kinryū dojin, [the] *Baisaō Gego with an appendix on* [Baisaō's] *tea-ceremony implements, Kyoto, published by Tsūshodō.*
National Archives of Japan, Tokyo

Baisaō Kō Yūgai (1675–1763) was the eccentric Zen priest responsible for establishing Sencha, the Chinese form of the tea ceremony, in Japan. Born in Hizen Province (present-day Saga Prefecture), he became a monk of the Ōbaku branch of Zen under the direction of Gerin Doryū, taking the priestly name Gekkai Genshō. Later, as a mendicant priest, he traveled to Kyoto, Edo, and the Tōhoku region, pursuing the ideals of Buddhism. In about 1735, he set up a simple shop close to the Kamo River in Kyoto, where he made a livelihood brewing tea for the common people. Occasionally he carried his tea utensils to popular Buddhist temples, such as the Tōfukuji, the Sanjūsangendō, and the Hall of the Great Buddha at the Hōkōji, or to other noted places nearby, where he accepted a modest fee in return for preparing tea. Appropriately he took the *gō* Baisaō, which means "Old Man Who Sells Tea." In a tract entitled the *Taigen Kyaku-shi*, he explained his point of view:

> When one observes the priests of today, one notices that, although they live in temples, their hearts are given over almost entirely to activities of the secular world. I dislike those whose hearts are concerned only with utilitarian concerns. Although I can't lead a life such as those of the men of high virtue of ancient times, I can at least brew tea and sell it to the common people who pass by. Selling tea in this manner is considered a humble occupation by most people. But that which others view as humble I view as being worthy of esteem.[30]

Baisaō put his priestly responsibilities behind him and devoted himself to selling tea, and soon a circle of intellectuals and artists of the time were drawn to him. Among these men were the Confucian scholar Uno Meika (1698–1745) and his students Akutagawa Tankyū (1710–1785) and Daiten Kenjō; the poets Katayama Hokkai (1723–1790) and Rikunyo (1734–1810); the dilettante Kimura Kenkadō; and the artist Ike Taiga (1723–1776), along with many other leading members of the world of arts and letters in eighteenth-century Kyoto and Osaka, all of whom were influenced by Baisaō's teachings in some way. Recently the scholars Takahashi Hiromi and Kano Hiroyuki have proposed the likelihood that Baisaō's ideas exercised a significant influence on Jakuchū's philosophical and spiritual development, and they have concluded that aspects of Jakuchū's humble, eremitic way of life were probably based on Baisaō's behavior.[31]

Daiten was probably responsible for introducing Jakuchū to Baisaō. One winter day in 1760, Baisaō, who had seen and admired Jakuchū's paintings, sent the artist a piece of calligraphy reading: "Enlivened by his hand, his paintings are filled with a mysterious spirit" (FIG. 10). Jakuchū seems to have been deeply affected by this expression of the older man's esteem, and he had a seal made with the phrase inscribed on it. Looking at this example of Baisaō's calligraphy, which now belongs to the Imperial Household Collection, the viewer can imagine how proud Jakuchū must have been when he presented it, together with his *Dōshoku Sai-e* paintings, to the Shōkokuji. Jakuchū did several portraits of Baisaō, and although a number of other artists, ranging from Sakaki Hyakusen to Tomioka Tessai, also painted the priest, Jakuchū's pictures stand out from the rest for their

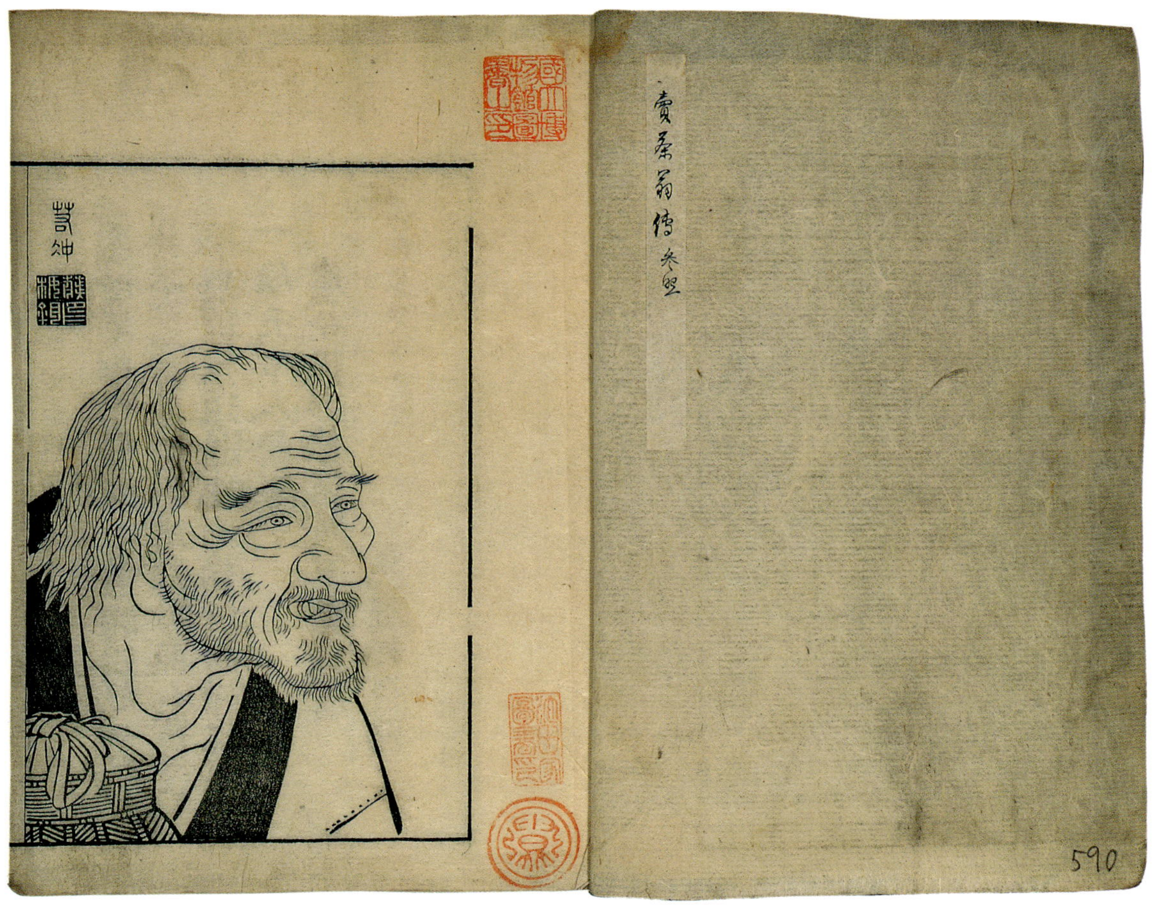

19

n.d.

26.4 × 18.8 cm
Tokyo National Museum

strength of expression. Among these, the portrayal in the *Baisaō Gego* is noted and widely admired for its realistic treatment.

The *Baisaō Gego* is a compilation of poems and other writings in Chinese that Baisaō used to propagate Zen teachings and doctrine in an easily comprehensible manner when he traveled about selling tea. The Ōbaku priest Baizan and the Tendai priest Kinryū-dōjin (also known as Keiyū, 1712–1782), both of whom specialized in Chinese poetry, decided to publish these materials, which they had compiled from a scroll in the possession of Baisaō's follower Mujū, along with other writings gathered by Mujū's senior Daiyū. The compilation appeared in the Seventh Month of 1763, the same month in which Baisaō died; it was published in Kyoto by the Tsūshodō, a firm operated by Ogawa Gembei. In the first edition (No. 18) Jakuchū's portrait is opposite the title page, on which Baisaō's title, in calligraphy by Ike Taiga, appears. A preface by Kinryū-dōjin is next, followed by a biography of Baisaō written by Daiten. The inclusion of this section by the renowned Buddhist prelate must have played a significant role in the broad propagation of Baisaō's teachings. The text of the *Gego* consists of 101 selections from Baisaō's writings and an epilogue by his follower Daichō. There is also an appendix, composed of twenty poems by Daiten and others, devoted to individual Sencha implements used by Baisaō (which gives the special names of these implements), as well as another epilogue, this one by Baizan.

In the later edition, Kinryū-dōjin's preface and Baizan's epilogue were deleted. The edition in the Tokyo National Museum (No. 19) has no title page, and it is unclear just when it was published.

Jakuchū's interpretation of Baisaō is a fine example of portraiture, certainly reflecting the true appearance of the sitter. In this bust portrait, Baisaō is wearing a *kakushōe* (traditional Taoist garment) and carrying a *teiran* (portable container for tea implements). With his slovenly hair and unkempt beard, his much-wrinkled features and sunken cheeks, and with but a single tooth visible in his mouth, Baisaō is portrayed here with all the characteristics typical of a man approaching ninety years of age. Strangely, it is not the inner, spiritual nobility of the old man, dressed in the garb of a mendicant priest, that draws the viewer's attention, but the keen, insightful quality of his eyes. Jakuchū's interest in and admiration for the free-spirited old man is revealed in the expressive portrait.

The artist's name and his square intaglio seal *Tō Jokin* appear at the upper left. This same seal appears on works such as the handscroll *Vegetables and Insects* and the hanging scroll *Horse-beans and Insects*, both of which date to 1792,[32] and on *Portrait of Hoan Jōei* (No. 41).

In the unusual example in the National Archives of Japan (No. 18) colors were painted in with a brush. Although this was competently done, it seems to have been the effort of an amateur and does not appear to have had any connection with Jakuchū.

20 *Bodhidharma Crossing the Yangtze on a Reed*

c. 1760–1765

Ink on paper, hanging scroll
98.2 × 28.8 cm
Inscription and signature:
Enduring heat and cold, he sailed for three years across the sea and, in the Kingdom of Liang Bodhidharma, had an audience with the emperor Wu. "Who are you, here in my presence?" asked the emperor. Bodhidharma replied, "I know not." On whose behalf had Bodhidharma suffered hardship to come to Chin-ling?—Murasakino-on'son biku Dokuan Jō hai-sho.

SEALS:
square intaglio: *Tō Jokin-in*
round relief: *Jakuchū koji*
Private collection, Tokyo

The legendary monk Bodhidharma is traditionally credited with having introduced the teachings of Zen to China from India, and he is said to have arrived in Kuang-chou in about A.D. 520 for the purpose of propagating the faith. Bodhidharma met with the first emperor of the Liang dynasty Liang Wu-ti (460–549) at his capital in Chin-ling, where they had a dialogue in which Bodhidharma attempted to explain the essential principles of Zen thought to the emperor. But Wu-ti was unable to comprehend the esoteric teachings, and Bodhidharma departed surreptitiously from the Kingdom of Liang, crossed the Yangtze River, and proceeded north, eventually reaching the capital of the Northern Wei dynasty, Lo-yang.

The painting under discussion here shows the eremitic patriarch Bodhidharma standing on the abbreviated section of reed, which mysteriously enabled him to cross the river. Although the origin of this artistic motif is unclear, it is thought to have evolved from the iconic representations of Arhats crossing the sea. Many Chinese and Japanese Zen paintings show Bodhidharma moving ceremoniously across the surface of the river on his diminutive section of reed.

The technique used to delineate the robe here is a characteristic of Jakuchū's work and can also be seen in the screens of *Flowers, Birds, and Vegetables* (NO. 17) completed in 1760. This technique involved painting washes in juxtaposed areas on *gasenshi*, resulting in a line that remained, delineating the washes, after the ink had dried. It appears that, for the present painting, the artist was not yet accustomed to working in this manner—which involved making sequential strokes with a long-tipped brush in order to simulate folds of material—as the washes are not uniform in their application and the manner in which they spread is inconsistent. Nevertheless, it is necessary to acknowledge Jakuchū's desire to incorporate a new expressive brush technique in his depiction of a traditional subject. This demonstrates the artist's continued efforts to expand the innovative means in his artistic repertoire. In a painting in a private collection in Hyōgo Prefecture, *Śākyamuni Returning from the Mountains* (FIG. 39), the depiction of the figure closely resembles Jakuchū's portrayal of Bodhidharma; the folds of the robes were treated in the same wavelike fashion, and it seems likely that the painting of Śākyamuni, which had its pictorial origins in Buddhist paintings produced in China by professional workshop artists, served as the immediate source of inspiration for Jakuchū's work.

The inscription is by Dokuan Sōjō, a priest associated with the Zenrakuji, a Zen temple in the city of Sakai. Dokuan's name appears in the *Zoku Naniwakyō yūroku* (a guide to noted people in the Osaka area, 1823), and in the *Sakai Jimbutsushi* (*Record of Personages from Sakai*, 1851), which gives his *azana* (nickname) and describes him as an accomplished calligrapher, although it provides nothing of his personal history.[33] The contents of the inscription were adapted from a passage in the famous *Pi-yen-lu* (Japanese: *Hekigan Roku*; *Green Cliff Record*), a collection of 100 strange Zen stories accompanied by abstruse commentaries and verse, which was compiled in China in the early twelfth century.[34] In his signature Dokuan called himself Murasakino-on'son (Distant Offspring of Murasakino), and as the term *murasakino* here referred to the Daitokuji, the great Zen monastery located in the Murasaki area of Kyoto, it would appear that Dokuan had at one time pursued his religious training at that institution.

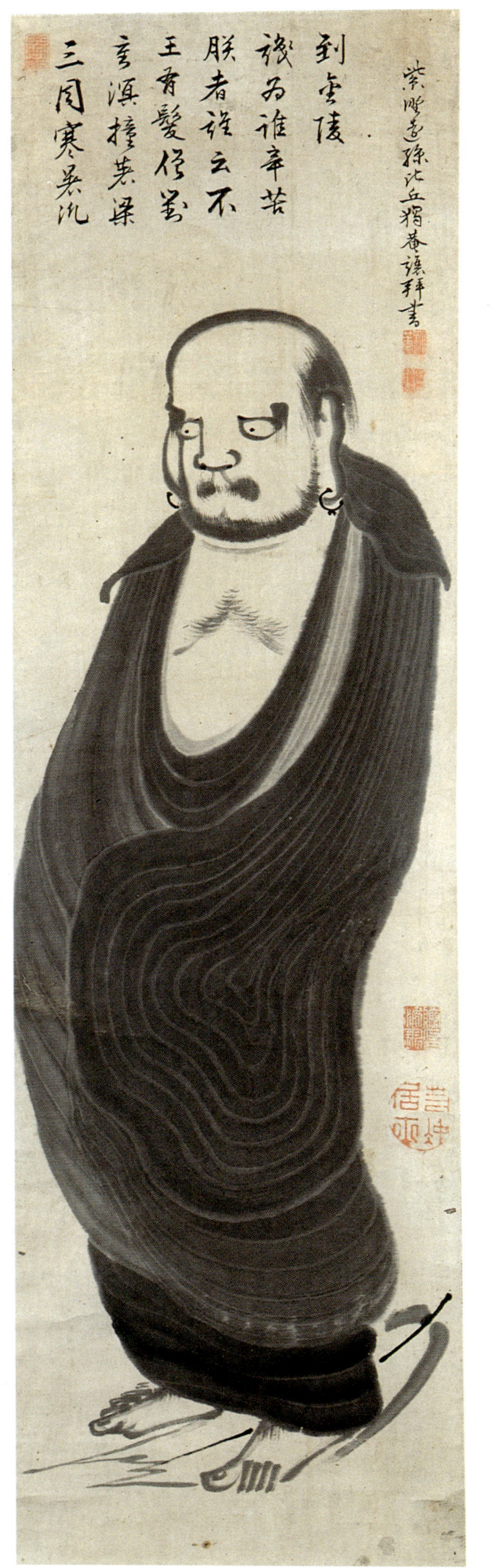

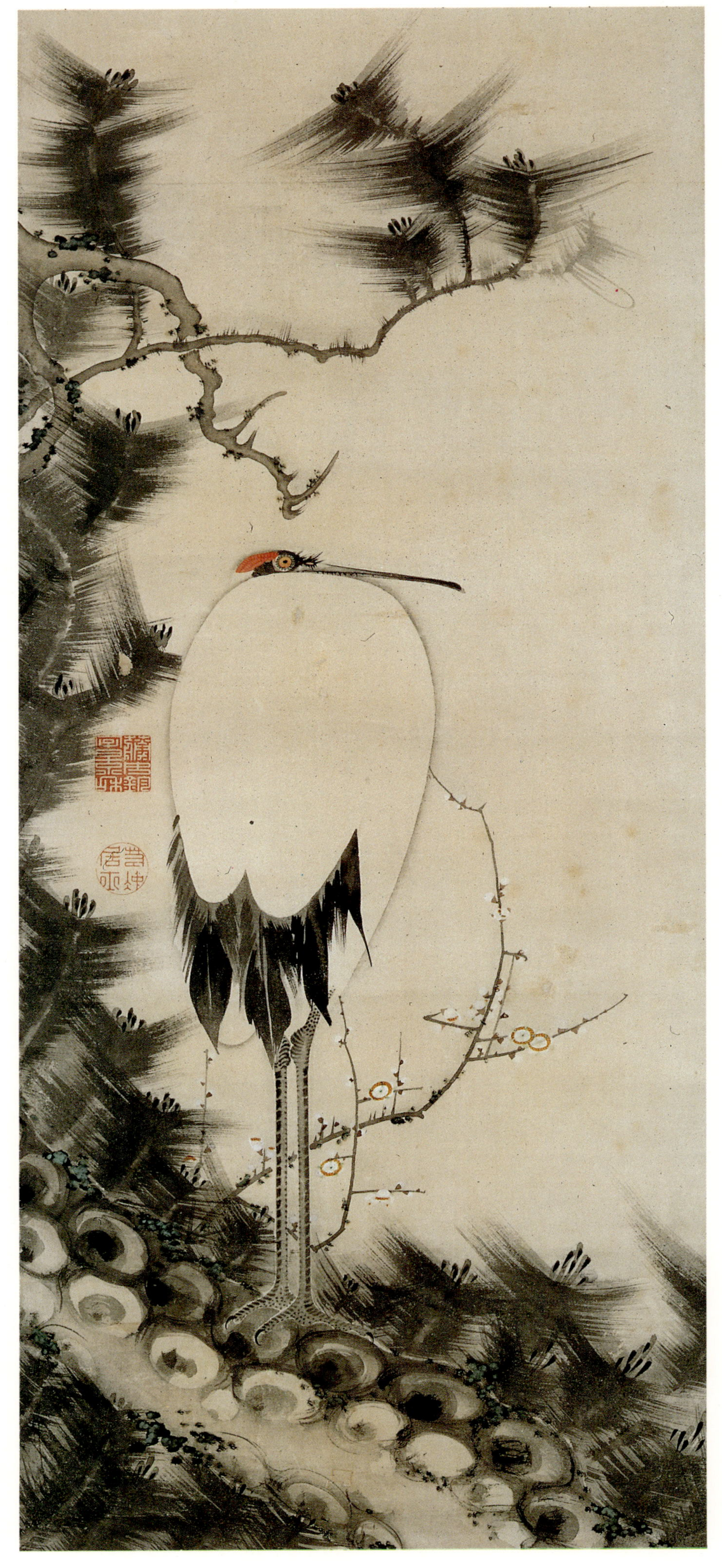

21 *Pine, Plum, and Crane*

First half of the 1760s

Ink and light colors on paper, hanging scroll
136.9 × 61 cm

SEALS:
square intaglio: *Tō Jokin azana Keiwa*
round relief: *Jakuchū koji*
Tokyo National Museum

One of the Chinese works that Jakuchū is thought to have copied in the course of his studies is *Pair of Cranes on a Pine*, a polychrome painting that belongs to the Daiun'in, a temple in Kyoto; this work was done by Ch'en Po-chung, an artist who was active during the Ming period and is said to have been a gifted painter. Although this piece is not particularly impressive, Jakuchū seems to have studied it very conscientiously. Thus, *White Fowl* (FIG. 31; reproduced in *Kokka*),[35] which the artist painted in 1752, is clearly indebted to Ch'en Po-chung's work in its compositional scheme.

The piece shown here was also inspired by compositional aspects of Ch'en's painting in the placement and conformation of the pine trunk and branches, and in the branch of flowering plum, which is situated in the same location. However, Jakuchū's work is basically in monochrome (although it has a few light touches of color), and the style and manner of depiction are quite different.

In most ink paintings the external aspects of the subject are not treated in detail, with forms rendered in an abbreviated and arbitrary manner, and there is an emphasis on individual expressive means in the movement of brush. Jakuchū executed the pine here in conformance with these principles, and his handling of the pine needles exhibits the same brushwork characteristics as those in the Rokuonji screens (NO. 16) and in the pair of six-panel folding screens of *Flowers, Birds, and Vegetables* completed in 1760 (NO. 17). In addition, the wirelike branch of blossoming plum is much longer and more attenuated here than in Ch'en Po-chung's painting. The cranes, which stand against plain backgrounds in both works, are similar in their somewhat elongated, elliptical bodies, which seem to float independently in space. The handling of the crane in Jakuchū's work clearly had its inspiration in his monochrome depictions of these birds in the Dai-shoin of the Rokuonji (NO. 16.4; FIG. 41) done in 1759.

The artist's treatment here of the crane, with its body reduced to an ellipse, had evolved from the naturalism of his earlier works to the abstraction of pure form. Jakuchū clearly intended to create an evocative graphic contrast between the neat, systematic depiction of the crane and the nervous, energetic treatment of the pine tree and plum. Restrained touches of pigment—red ochre on the trunk and limbs of the pine, white and yellow on the plum blossoms, and vermilion on the bird's head—serve as local accents, and the touches of yellow are particularly effective.

This painting was donated to the Tokyo National Museum in 1978 by the Uematsu family of Shizuoka Prefecture. During the Edo period the Uematsus were provincial samurai who lived near the thoroughfare that leads through Hara-no-shuku, one of the towns situated along the Tōkaidō (the main road that connected Edo with Kyoto) that supplied lodgings to travelers. The family members were enthusiastic art collectors, and many celebrated personalities seem to have visited their residence at the foot of Mount Fuji; one of the heads of the family went to Kyoto, where he studied under Maruyama Ōkyo, from whom he received the artist's name Ōrei. As a result of this relationship, many paintings, sketches, and documents of the Maruyama school were preserved by the family. Moreover, the Zen priest Shikyō (1723–1787), who had studied under the celebrated priest-painter Hakuin (1685–1769) and who stayed for a time with the Uematsu family, and became the abbot of the Kaifukuin, a subtemple of the Myōshinji monastery in Kyoto; as a result, the family also acquired paintings by artists such as Sōga Shōhaku (1730–1781) and Ike Taiga, who were, to some degree, influenced by Zen. Although it is unclear whether Jakuchū was connected in any way with either Hakuin or Shikyō, it seems possible that Shikyō played a role in the acquisition by the Uematsu family of Jakuchū's painting.

22 *Rain Dragon*

First half of the 1760s

Ink on paper, hanging scroll
130.5 × 53 cm

SEALS:
square intaglio: *Tō Jokin-in*
square relief: *Jakuchū koji*
Private collection, Akita Prefecture

The dragon, like the phoenix, is an imaginary sacred beast with origins in ancient China. Living in water, rising up to the heavens, and causing clouds to form and rain to fall are all aspects of its divine nature. As early as the Shang and Chou dynasties, the dragon was being portrayed in the shape of a reptile in designs on bronze artifacts, and by the Han dynasty it had taken the form in which it is known today—with two horns sprouting from its head, scales covering its long body, and a dorsal fin running down its back to its tail. Beginning with the inception of ink painting in the T'ang dynasty, dragons were a popular theme in Chinese art, and artists who specialized in the subject, such as Ch'en Jung, appeared at the end of the Southern Sung dynasty.

In Japan, too, many painters created monochrome depictions of dragons. From the Muromachi to the Momoyama period, dragons were generally depicted as daring, valorous creatures (except in the sixteenth-century paintings of the artist Sesson Shūkei), but in the Edo period a tendency to give the dragon an ironic or humorous expression, as in the works of Iwasa Matabei (1578–1650) and Kanō Sansetsu (1590–1651), became noticeable. This is a manifestation of the spirit of the Edo period, when parodies of classical models, in painting as well as literature and theater, were enjoyed. In the painting of the mid-Edo period, when Jakuchū was active, this tendency became striking; the expression and style of dragons portrayed by Sōga Shōhaku and Nagasawa Rosetsu overflow with a sense of the comical. The present work by Jakuchū was painted in the same vein.

Here the dragon faces directly forward, with mouth open wide. Its eyes are rolled heavenward, and it has a pug nose. Its body, which extends beyond the edge of the picture, is shaped like a question mark. The dragon's countenance is inappropriate for that of a sacred beast and resembles the face of Bodhidharma in Jakuchū's *Red-robed Daruma* (Powers Collection). Such eccentric depiction of features is thought to have its roots in Sōga Shōhaku's paintings. One such prototype is recognizable in the figure's face in Shōhaku's *Demoness and Windblown Willow* (Tokyo National University of Fine Arts and Music; c. 1760). It seems likely that Jakuchū, recognizing the amusing quality of the ugly and strange characters first drawn by Shōhaku, wanted to add that element to his own pictures.

Jakuchū painted the horns and winglike appendages on the legs in an abbreviated fashion, but the degree of detail indicates that he intended the piece to be more than simply a cartoon. Not only did he delineate the back and the belly with light and dark tones of ink, but he also carefully painted the scales that cover the body one at a time, using his own special ink-painting technique, which took advantage of the absorbent nature of *gasenshi*. The result is a truly unique image of a dragon, richly amusing and full of strange eccentricities.

Of the seals Jakuchū used on his paintings, the square intaglio *Tō Jokin-in* is among the most common. If, as it is assumed, this work dates to the first half of the 1760s, then it is among the first paintings on which he used this seal. The square relief seal *Jakuchū koji* also appears on *Birds and Autumn Maples* (FIG. 33.20), the last painting in the *Dōshoku Sai-e* series.

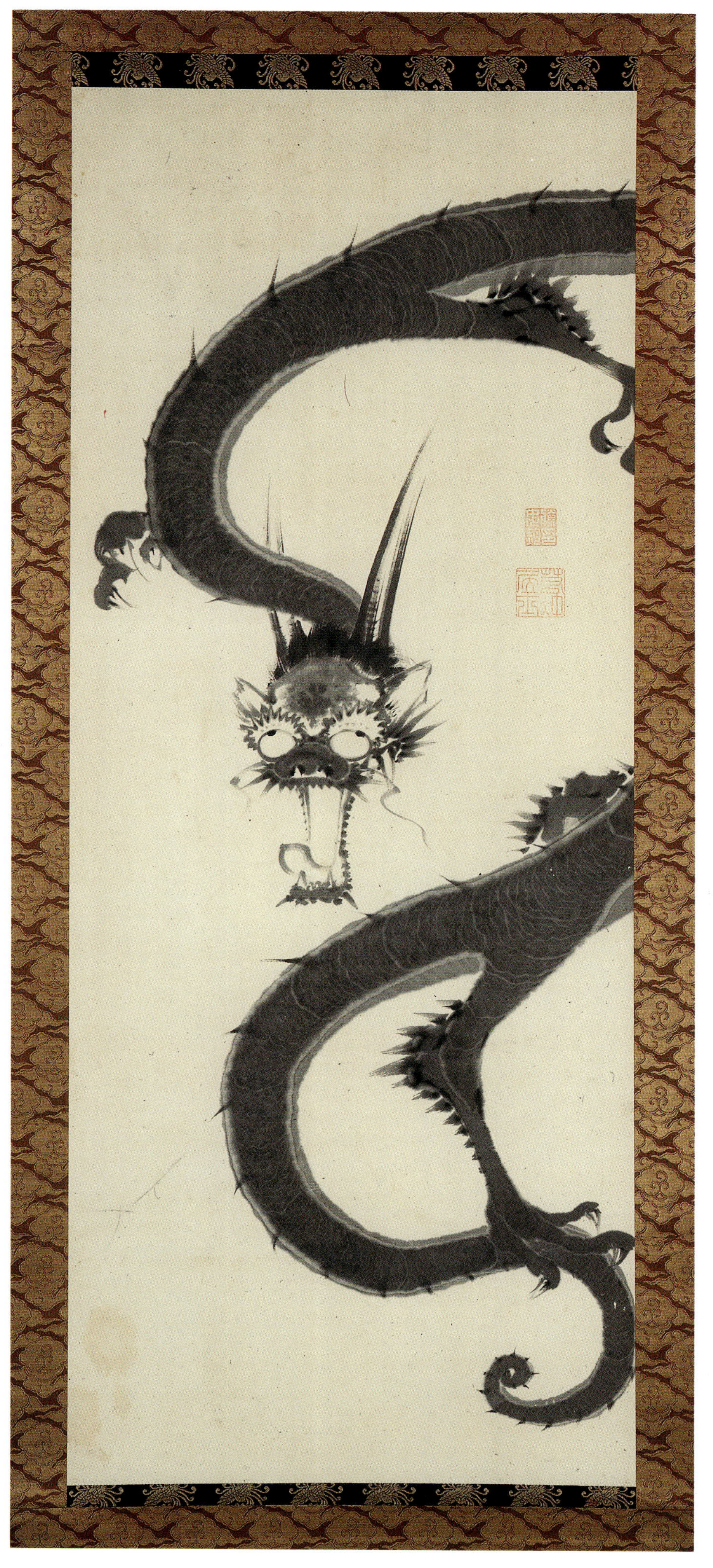

23 *Gourd and Peonies*

First half of the 1760s

Ink on paper, pair of hanging scrolls
114.5 × 46.0 cm
Signatures: *by Jakuchū* (on *Gourd*); *Karaetsu* [Sanskrit: Kulapati: Head of a Clan] *Jakuchū* (on *Peonies*)
Inscriptions:
see below

SEALS (on both paintings):
square intaglio: *Tō Jokin azana Keiwa*
round relief: *Jakuchū koji*
Private collection, Osaka Prefecture

Although the gourd and peony motifs in the colorful *Dōshoku Sai-e* pieces (NO. 14) are notable for their complex execution, the monochrome hanging scrolls shown here are much simpler in their handling of the same forms; the pair was intended as an exercise in the complementary potentials of dark and light in composition. In the gourd and its leaves in one scroll and the peonies and the butterfly in the other, dark ink tones contrast dramatically with the white paper. The present pair of scrolls is probably close in date and intention to Jakuchū's work of 1761 depicting the Zen eccentrics *Kanzan and Jittoku* (Gitter Collection), done essentially in black and white, where the two recluses have been reduced to merely a triangle and an oval. In depicting plants and animals, Jakuchū devised a unique form of ink painting, which combined a sense of levity with a strong feeling for design. The rough, dark touches of ink that enliven the forms of the peonies and the boulder continue the stylistic features of the artist's folding screens (NO. 17) influenced by Kakutei, but these elements nevertheless have been arranged carefully in the design. Indeed, the sharp black-and-white contrasts in these paintings exhibit very little use of ink gradation in the delineation of form. The striking portrayals of the gourd leaves and the peony petals, for which Jakuchū used the blurring effect of ink on *gasenshi*, show a high degree of technical accomplishment, and the clever way in which he revealed the soft nature of the subject matter is also impressive.

The inscription on *Gourd* is by Keishū Dōrin (1714–1794), the 221st abbot of the Tenryūji. It reads:

> A strange apparition descends from the sky. Its body is slim; its head is big. Perhaps it is an act of vengeance from heaven. From above their heads a fist comes down—it will strike those mediocre souls who do not follow the Buddhist Way. This is something to fear! But it is best not to try to flee. Ha, ha, ha. There is no need to fear. If you look closely at it, you will see that in fact it is just a gourd. The lazy, ascetic monk Itō (Hole in the Robe).

The inscription on *Peonies* is by the Ōbaku priest and literatus Musen Jōzen (1693–1764). Jōzen was the eighth-generation priest of the Jikishi-an, a temple in the Saga district of Kyoto. He seems to have been introduced to Daiten Kenjō by another Ōbaku monk, and he also wrote inscriptions for *Kanzan and Jittoku* and five or six of Jakuchū's other works. The inscription for *Peonies* reads:

> Let not your heart be seized by ostentatious color alone. Why is it spring that you praise and honor? If in teaching Lu Hsuan you show this flower, the butterfly's dream, too, will perhaps be able to break out of the Wheel of Delusion. Composed by "Old Man Tangai (Red Cliff)."

The peony is a symbol of wealth and honor, but the Zen priest did not acknowledge this in his inscription. Lu Hsuan was a high-ranking official in China during the T'ang dynasty. He converted to Zen Buddhism and studied under the priest Nan Ch'uan P'u Yuan. On one occasion, he asked about the Zen statement "Heaven, earth, and I have the same origin; the Ten Thousand Things and I have one body." Nan Ch'uan pointed to a flower in the garden and said: "Look at this flower. Flower and man, dreamlike, resemble each other"[36] (*Hekigan Roku*; see NO. 20). He explained that the truth about which Lu Hsuan asked was evident in the flower, that everything in heaven and earth has the same original form, which becomes both the Ten Thousand Things and the self when it comes into being. Chuang-tzu, the famous philosopher of the Warring States period in China (fourth century B.C.) told of dreaming he had become a butterfly and not knowing whether he was Chuang-tzu, who became a butterfly in the dream, or a butterfly, who became Chuang-tzu in the dream. Because the scroll depicted both flowers and a butterfly, Musen combined these two traditions—of Lu Hsuan and Chuang-tzu—in his poem. The year of his death, 1764, provides the latest possible date for these contrasting scrolls.

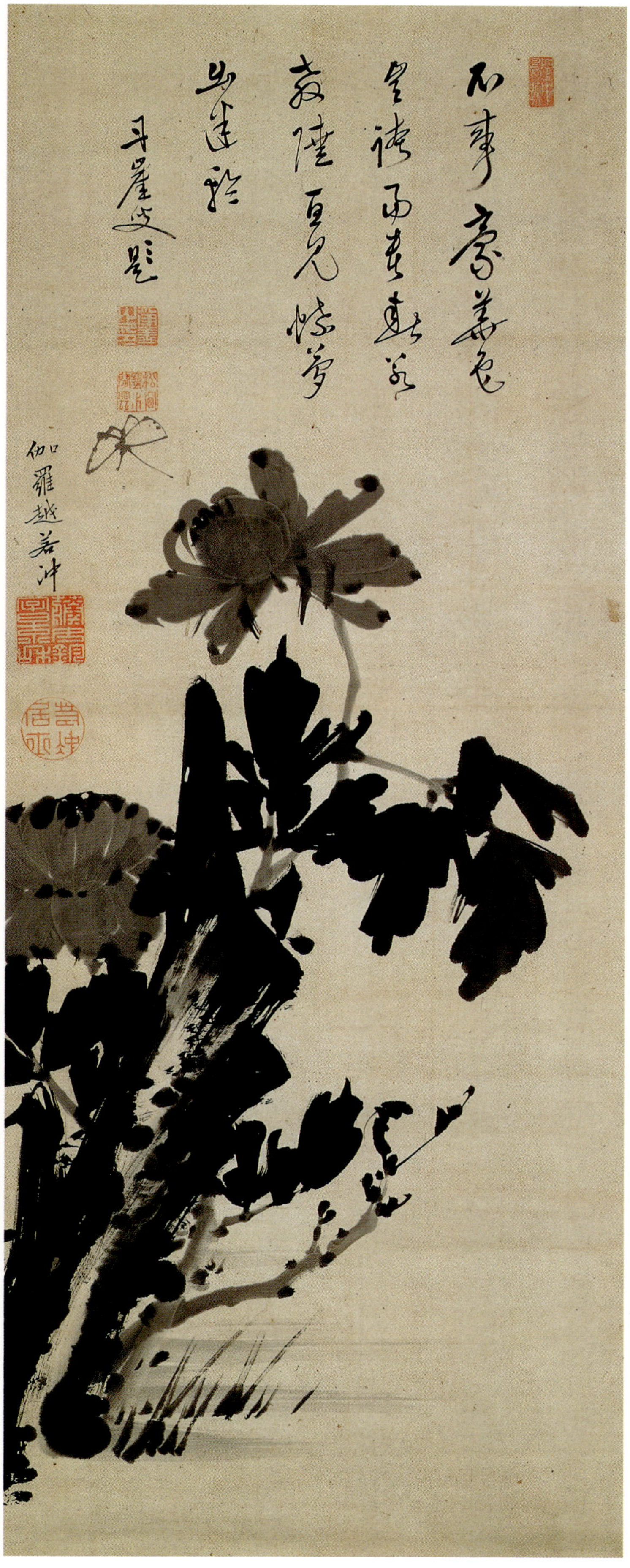

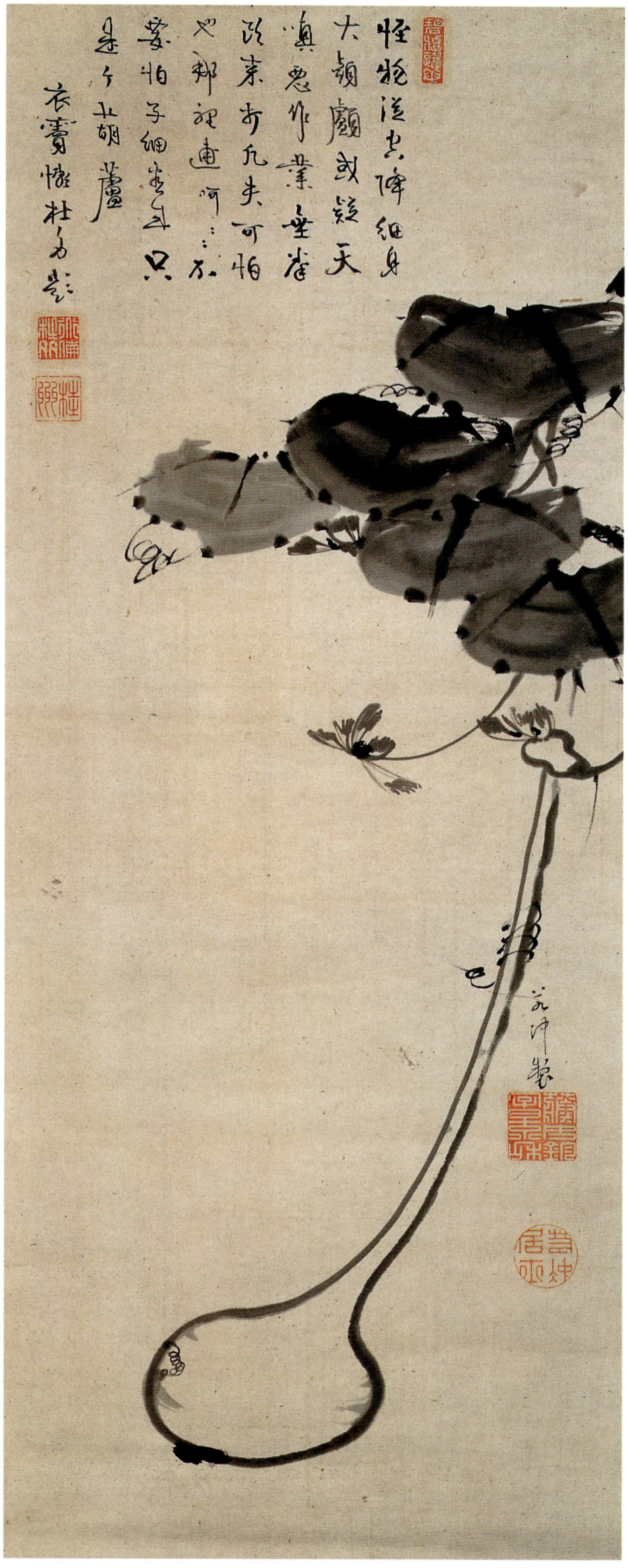

伽羅越若冲

若冲製

24 *The Two Transcendents Gama and Tekkai*

1760s

Ink on paper, pair of hanging scrolls
102.5 × 29.6 cm (each scroll)
Inscriptions:
see below

SEALS (on both pieces):
square intaglio: *Tō Jokin-in*
round relief: *Jakuchū koji*
Private collection, Kyoto

These two eccentric figures belong to a group of mysterious *sennin* (immortals or transcendents). They had their genesis in the popular religious beliefs of Taoist origin that evolved in China in early times.

Gama-sennin lived in the Kingdom of Wu during the period of the "Three Kingdoms" (third century A.D.), and his proper name was Ko Hsüan. He was celebrated for his many miraculous abilities, one of which involved his constant companion, a strange, three-legged toad, who followed his commands.

Tekkai-sennin's actual name was Ri Tekkai (Chinese: Li T'ieh-kuai). According to one tradition, he decided one day to visit Lao-tzu (the founder of Taoism), leaving his physical body behind and proceeding to Mount Hua (a high mountain in Shensi Province) in his spiritual form. Tekkai held a ceremony at the time of his departure, and he made his disciple promise that his body would be burned if his spirit did not return within seven days. However, the disciple's mother died, and possibly as a consequence of the ensuing confusion, Tekkai's body was burned on the sixth day. When Tekkai's spirit returned on the seventh day, it was compelled to take up residence in the body of a person who had died of starvation. As a result, he is said to have walked with a limp, using a staff, and to have been bizarre and unsightly in appearance.

It seems that the earliest extant representations of these two waggish eremites are those in the superb pair of works by the Chinese painter Yen Hui (active second half of the thirteenth century) that is preserved in the Chion'in, a noted temple in Kyoto. Yen Hui graphically depicted the weird appearances of the transcendents in his celebrated works and the influence of these pieces on Japanese painters was significant. The monk-painter Minchō (1351–1431) made copies of these paintings, which are still preserved in the Zen monastery where he worked, the Tōfukuji in Kyoto. Kanō Tan'yū (1602–1674) also produced somewhat simplified copies, which are now in the Nanzenji in Kyoto. Sesson's depiction (Tokyo National Museum) seems to be based on a different iconographic source and is a more humorous interpretation, showing Gama dancing with the three-legged toad.

Jakuchū carried this tendency much further, and his pieces are notable for their unique, infectious humor. Tekkai looks directly upward, his mouth pursed as he projects his spirit out into space, his chin directly before the observer's eyes. It is possible that the inspiration behind the conception may have been a work such as Ōgata Kōrin's *Hotei Kicking a Ball*, in which the deity balances on one leg atop his large, round sack, while looking upward at the small ball that he has just kicked into the air. Kōrin's tall, narrow ink painting, which is arranged in a similarly frontal manner, shows several compositional similarities to Jakuchū's piece. Jakuchū's Gama holds a "peach of immortality" in his right hand, while the three-legged toad dances on one leg atop the immortal's head (which, with its round, bald spot and shaggy hair, is reminiscent of the head of the *kappa*, a mythological Japanese water creature). Jakuchū rendered the bodies of the two transcendents in the elliptic forms he frequently favored, and the dark, incisive brush strokes are so powerful that they seem to cut through the surface of the paper. He handled the robes in a linear manner, similar to that characteristically used by Ōbaku priest-artists in their figural depictions, which harmonizes well with the ingenious deformation of shapes in the composition.

The inscription on the Tekkai painting, done by the Shingon priest Sennan Jakushō (whose name was included in both the scholar and calligrapher sections of the 1768 edition of the *Heian Jimbutsushi*), reads: "His flesh exposed to the elements for many long years, he has entered the worlds of inaction and quietude. Blowing his spirit out into space, his days are spent pleasantly in diversions in the immortal realm where no one grows old. Sennan-sō."

The inscription on the painting of Gama was done by the Ōbaku priest Gessen Jōtan (?–1769), the second abbot of the Kaiunzan Hozōji, a temple in the Narutaki area of Kyoto. Jōtan, like Monchū Jōfuku (see No. 44), was a practitioner of the Sencha form of the tea ceremony who trained under Baisaō (see Nos. 18, 19). The inscription reads: "Having lost his body, he was forced to inhabit the corpse of one who had died of starvation. This was not his original body, of course. [But] how could people be aware of this?" The poem clearly refers to Tekkai, rather than to Gama. Gessen Jōtan's death in 1769 provides a terminus ad quem for the paintings.

Before these works came into the possession of the present owners, they belonged to the Yasui family, relatives of the Itō family who carried on the operation of the family store in Kyoto during the nineteenth century and who preserved various materials relating to Jakuchū.

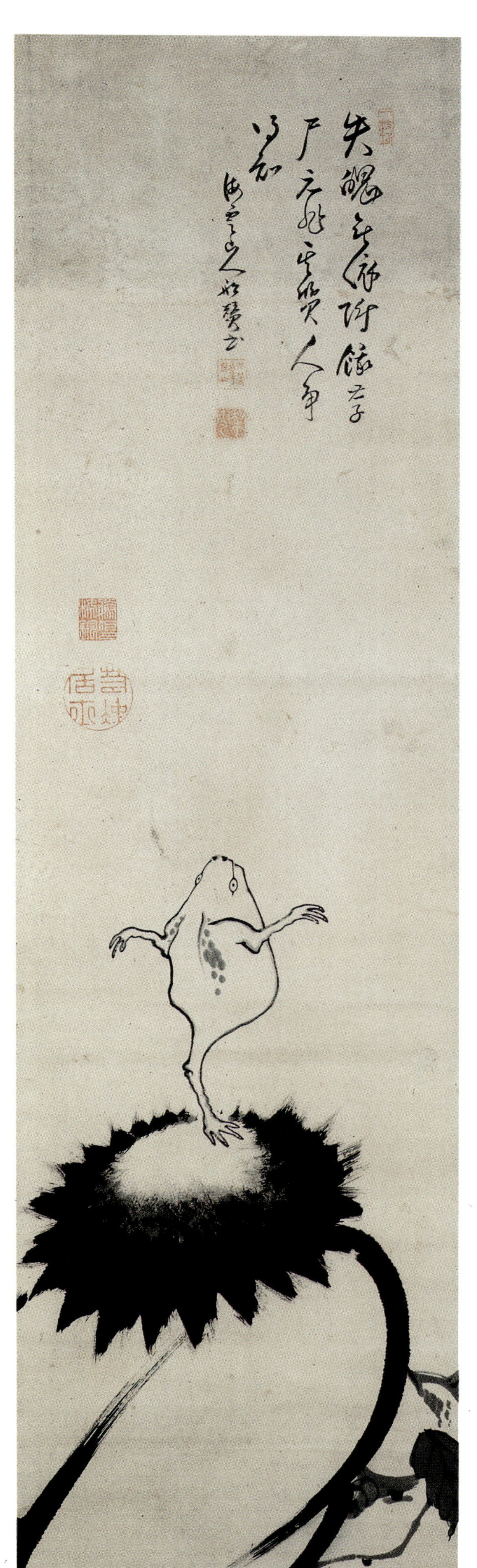

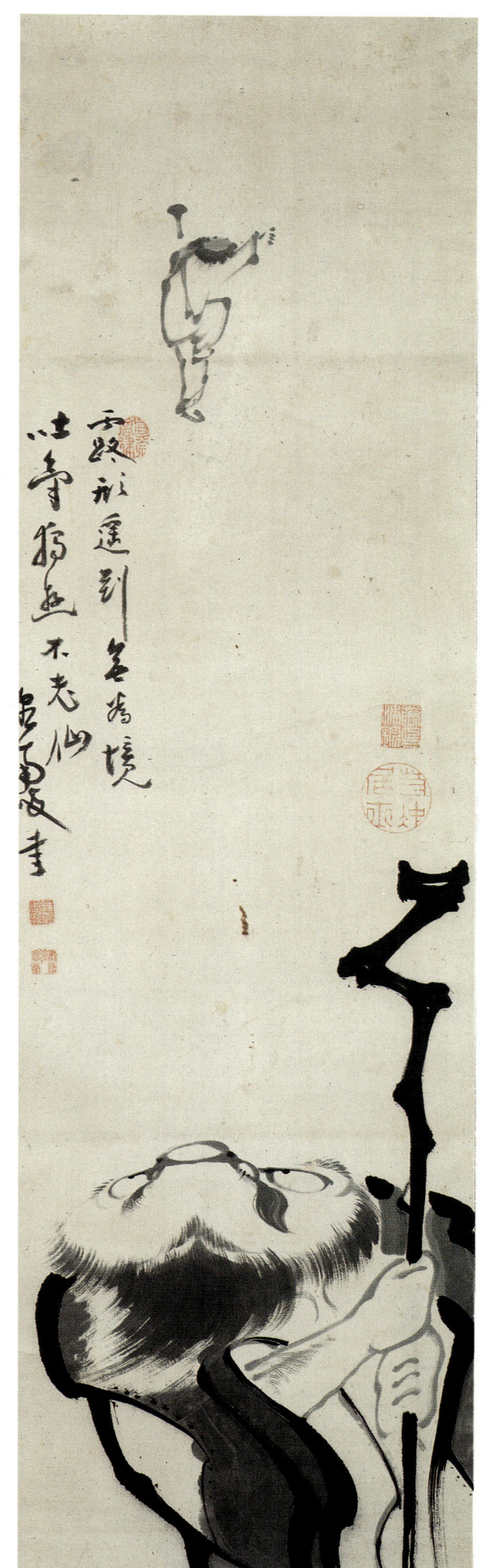

25 *Chickens*

c. 1760s

Ink on paper, two-panel folding screen (independent compositions)
139.4 × 62.4 cm (each painting)

SEALS:
square intaglio: *Tō Jokin-in*
round relief: *Jakuchū koji*
Kurokawa Institute of Ancient Cultures, Hyōgo Prefecture

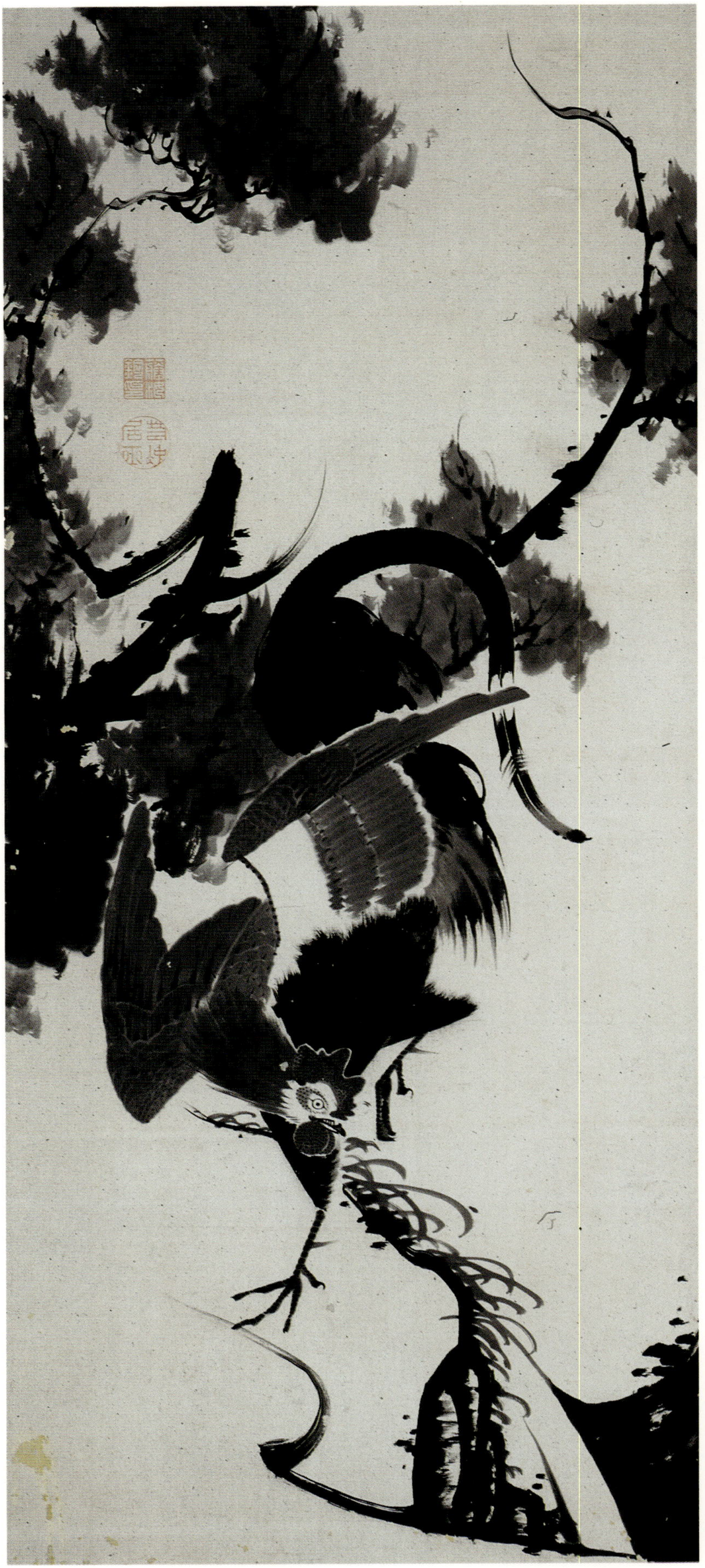

Interestingly, the same motifs that Jakuchū represented in color also appear frequently in his ink compositions. Among the pieces that fall into this category are those of the chickens in the Rokuonji Dai-shoin screens (see NO. 16), the bamboo and tiger (NO. 28), the lotuses (NO. 35), and the carp (NO. 42)—as well as certain of the motifs in flower, bird, and vegetable screens (NO. 17).

The largest number of such paintings are depictions of chickens, Jakuchū's favorite subject. However, not until the 1760s did the artist develop proficiency in the peculiarly expressive qualities of ink (which differ fundamentally from polychrome painting techniques) in his fascinating representations of fowl. Thus, for instance, a depiction of a pair of chickens completed in 1759 (FIG. 44) and a representation of a rooster and wisteria dated 1760 (NO. 17) both convince the viewer that they faithfully simulate prototypes done in color. It seems likely that the artist first produced detailed polychrome versions, which he subsequently reproduced in a literal manner in monochrome. However, one depiction of a rooster and chrysanthemum in the Dai-shoin screens shows an immature quality in its brushwork and a constrained, abbreviated treatment of the form of the rooster; this manner of depicting fowl stylistically presages Jakuchū's later, more mature interpretations of the subject in ink.

The present screen, with its independent panels, is one of Jakuchū's finest pieces including monochrome depictions of chickens. Daiten's inscription ("Ketsumei"; FIG. 3) on the commem-

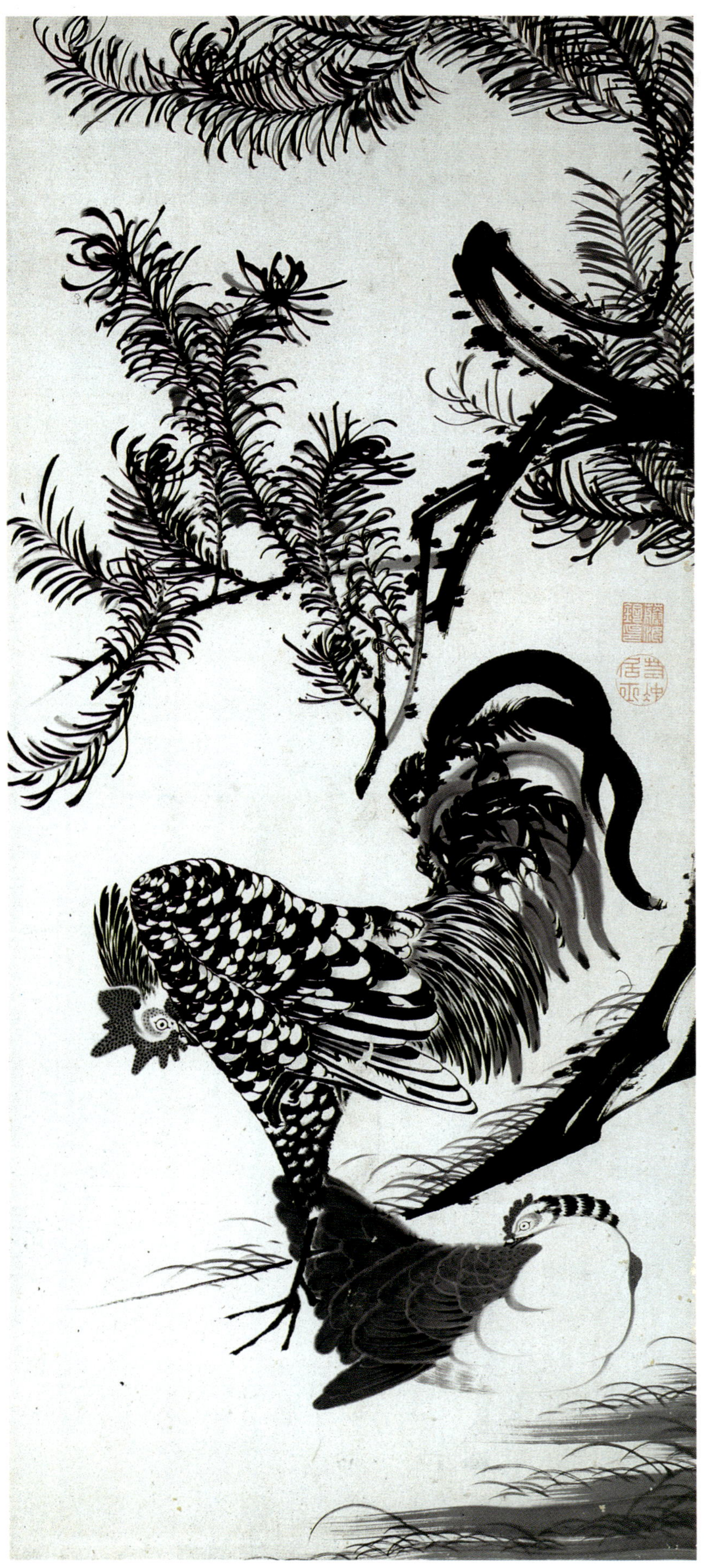

orative stele (*juzō*; FIG. 4) erected in 1766 on Jakuchū's behalf in the Shōkokuji describes the history of Jakuchū's artistic activities:

> Moreover, he executed ink compositions on [gasenshi(?), the absorbent] white paper that blotted and blurred easily. Areas of dark and light were achieved by the use of [juxtaposed tonal variations of] blurred ink; patterns and details, such as flower petals, feathers, and the scales of fish were delineated with great skill. This kind of elegant ink technique was completely unknown until this time, and observers were filled with wonder and admiration![37]

The feathers on the chickens in the present screen, painted in this exquisite technique, are just the sort to which Daiten referred. The screen is also of interest for a feature that appears elsewhere in the artist's ink representations of chickens. Each of the splendidly conceived roosters is poised momentarily on one leg. One is shown standing under a miscanthus tree in the right-hand composition; the same sort of bird, a mottled black-and-white rooster, appears at the lower left of *A Group of Roosters* (*Dōshoku Sai-e*; FIG. 33.16). The close similarities in these two works indicate that they were probably executed at about the same time, and the accurate anatomical depiction of the details of the monochrome version is in every way equal to that of the polychrome, making it clear that the former portrayal is based on observation of an actual bird. Precisely represented in black, white, and an intermediate tone of gray, this bird has a convincing sense of buoyancy in its plumage, and its captivating form stands out dramatically in a lovely, monochrome arabesque.

26 *Kachō-zu*

(Birds and Flowers)

1771

Hand colored on paper, six woodblock prints
Hiraki Ukiyo-e Foundation, Tokyo

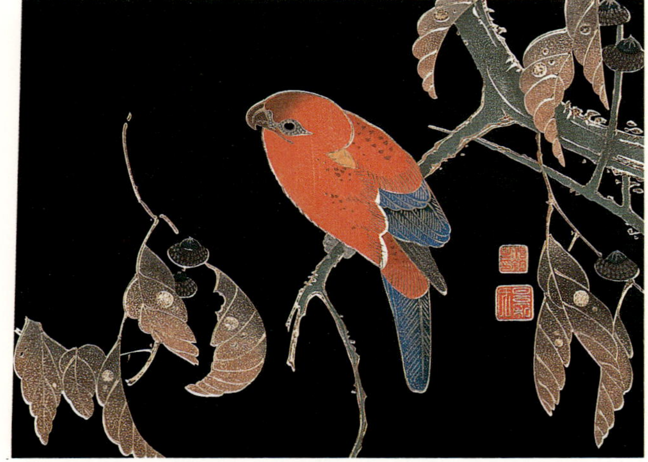

26.1

Parakeet in an Oak Tree

24.7 × 33.4 cm

SEALS:
square relief: *Jokin-no-in*
square intaglio: *Keiwa-shi*

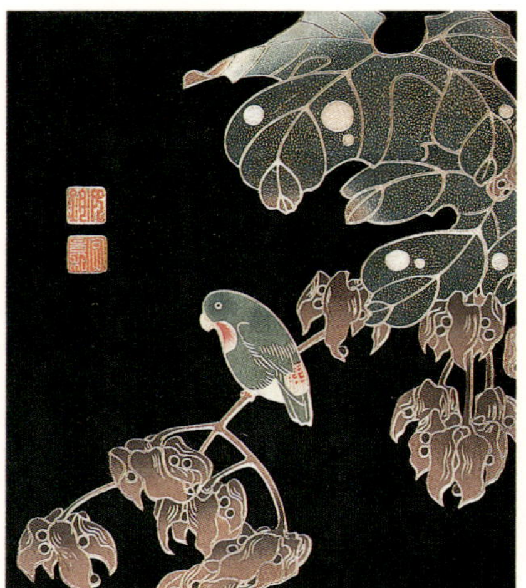

26.2

Satōchō (Parakeet) in a Chinese Parasol Tree

27.2 × 24 cm

SEALS:
square relief: *Jokin*
square intaglio: *Ji Keiwa*

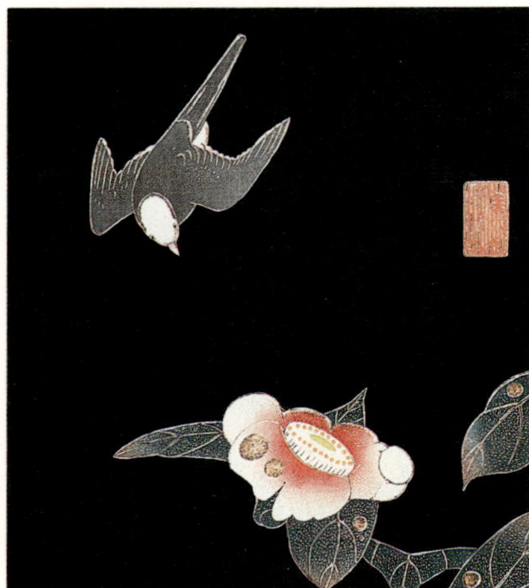

26.3

"White-head" and Camellias

23 × 21 cm

SEAL:
rectangular intaglio: *Tō-in*

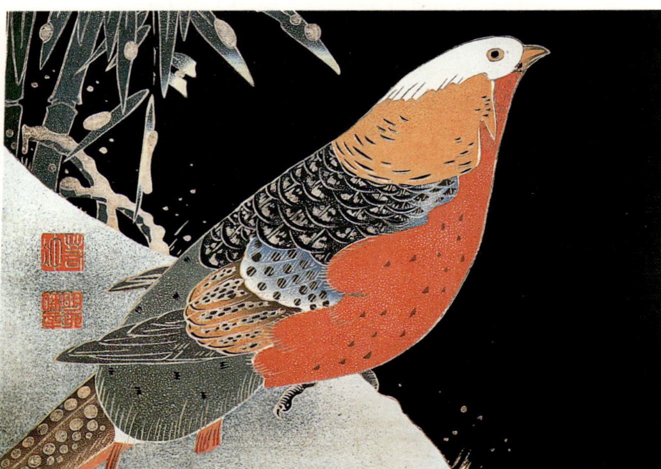

26.4

Golden Pheasant and Bamboo in Snow

25.2 × 36.7 cm

SEALS:
square intaglio: *Jakuchū*
square relief: *Meiwa kanato no u* [Meiwa 8; 1771]

In addition to his painting and sculpture, Jakuchū produced designs for several woodblock printing projects. Although his accomplishments in this area are overshadowed by the more familiar color prints known as Ukiyo-e (Pictures of the Floating World), they nevertheless constitute a unique and undeniable achievement in the history of Japanese woodblock printing.

In 1765 the Ukiyo-e artist Suzuki Harunobu (1724–1770) and men who worked with him in Edo developed the first full-color woodblock prints, or Nishiki-e (Brocade Pictures). In these a substantial number of pigments were printed sequentially, each with an individual color block, and this ushered in a new era of technical accomplishment in the history of woodblock printing in Japan. Daiten Kenjō was probably one of the earliest intellectuals from Kyoto to become aware of these lovely new polychrome prints, and it seems more than likely that Jakuchū became familiar with them as a result of his association with Daiten.

Jakuchū created the woodblock designs for at least four works: a handscroll, the *Jōkyōshū* (*Impromptu Pleasures Afloat*), 1767 (FIG. 6); two softbound books, the *Gempo Yōka* (*Exquisite Flowers from the Mysterious Garden*), 1768 (FIG. 9), and the *Soken Jō* (*Album of Elegant Designs on a Plain Ground*), 1768 (FIG. 8); and a set of prints, the *Kachō-zu*.

The three other woodblock works were done in an unusual manner resembling *taku-hon*, the traditional rubbing technique in which moistened paper is applied to the surface of a stone or metal object and tamped down into the concavities, so that the incised designs or inscriptions on the objects are transferred to the paper when ink is applied

26.5

Parakeet and Roses

25.5 × 34.5 cm

SEALS:
Sequential square intaglios: *Jo* and *kin*

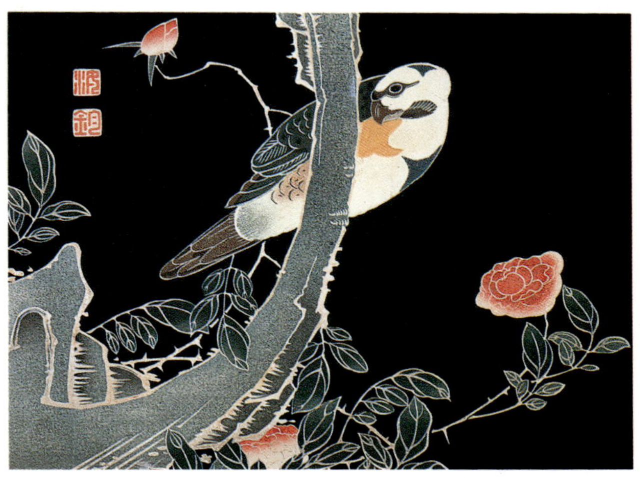

26.6

White Cockatoo on a Chinese Perch

26.5 cm (diameter)

SEALS:
round relief: *Jokin*
square relief: *Jakuchū koji*

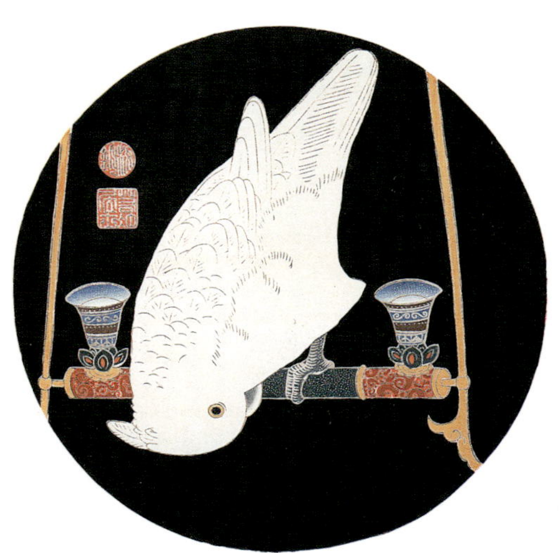

to its surface. Because of this similarity, the scholar Aimi Kōu coined the term *taku-hanga* (rubbing print) to describe the novel woodblock technique used in the three works.[38] In a process opposite to that of traditional woodblock printing, the initial drawing is applied directly to the block (rather than reversed) and the pictorial elements of the design (rather than the background) are carved out. When the carved block has been completed, a sheet of paper is laid across it, and ink applied to the exterior surface. As a result, the designs appear in the uninked portions of the paper, and the inked background has a dark, shining quality. According to Professor Nakano Mitsutoshi, a specialist in the literature of the Edo period, Jakuchū's works (including his book designs) are the finest examples of the *taku-hanga* technique from either his own period or afterward.[39]

The six prints included here have the same sort of black, lacquerlike background, but as Professor Kobayashi Tadashi of Gakushūin University has pointed out, the back of the paper shows that a *baren* (rubbing implement used in making Ukiyo-e prints) was employed, differentiating these works somewhat from those made by the *taku-hanga* method.[40] It seems, therefore, that Jakuchū reproduced the black ground here simply to simulate the pictorial effect of the *taku-hanga* process.

He precisely cut designs for each of the colored areas out of sheets of stiff paper and applied the pigments to the print within these cut-out portions with a brush by the *kappazuri* technique, a type of stenciling. This technique was traditionally favored in the Kyoto-Osaka region, and with it Jakuchū was able to produce exceptional works that were quite different from Nishiki-e. Jakuchū himself probably was responsible for his designs' distinctive beauty, which resulted from their elegant colors. The prints were done with superb skill, with harmonious dark and light variations in pigment, and with small areas carefully sprayed white and purple.

A connection between Jakuchū's techniques and the methods used in lacquer and textile design seems likely. The six prints shown here are also related to Jakuchū's painting in the skillful portrayal of the substance of things; in the use of rich, polychrome colors to depict bird-and-flower subjects; and in the use of opaque colors to give a sense of volume to an arrangement of flat motifs (an experimental tendency of the later *Dōshoku Sai-e* pieces).

Only a few examples of the *Jōkyōshū*, the *Gempō Yōka*, and the *Soken Jō* have been preserved in collections in Japan, America, and Europe. The colored woodblock prints of the *Kachō-zu* are even more rare, and the Hiraki Ukiyo-e Foundation is the only place where a complete set of six prints is known to be preserved. In 1897, facsimile reproductions of these prints were produced; fortunately the owner of the originals also has a set of these facsimiles, and when comparing the two groups, the viewer can see an obvious difference in quality.

27 *Five Hundred Arhats*

c. 1765–1775

Ink on paper, hanging scroll
47.0 × 62.3 cm

SEALS:
square intaglio: *Tō Jokin-in*
round relief: *Jakuchū koji*
Private collection, Hyōgo Prefecture

An Arhat is a Buddhist sage who has successfully undergone austerities, has entered the realm of enlightenment, and is therefore universally revered. When the Buddha passed into Nirvāna, he ordered sixteen of the Arhats to preserve the Dharma (Buddhist law) and to labor on behalf of all living beings. Based on the scriptural account of this occurrence, faith in the Sixteen Arhats became widespread during the T'ang dynasty in China. Although the scriptural sources for the Five Hundred Arhats are unclear, it is evident that, beginning in the latter part of the T'ang era, faith in them became widespread.

According to the *Shūi Miyako Meisho Zue* (*Illustrated Guide to Famous Locations in the Capital*), Jakuchū began working on his stone sculpture project, the *Five Hundred Arhats*, in about 1776 at the Sekihōji, an Ōbaku temple in Fukakusa, in the Kyoto area.[41] In 1790, according to a passage in Takemoto Sekitei's work, *Sekitei Gadan* (*Sekitei's Conversations on Painting*, 1884), Jakuchū made a sketch showing the layout for the group of figures, which depicts various events in Śākyamuni's life.[42] The original sketch has been lost, but today visitors to the temple can buy woodblock prints (see FIG. 12) made from a block carved in 1918 based on the original sketch.

Although there are certain similarities between the sketch from the Sekihōji and the painting, it appears that the relationship with the stone sculptures reflects only one aspect of the motivation behind the painting.

A unique feature of the composition here is that all of the Arhats are depicted "crossing the sea." Of the many works that show this theme, no others are known where all the figures are depicted in this activity. A work of the Yüan period in the Freer Gallery of Art, Washington, D.C., does show all five hundred on one scroll, but those crossing the sea make up only a small number of them. It is likely that the inspiration behind Jakuchū's conception was Ike Taiga's celebrated set of paintings on sliding screens in the Mampukuji, the Ōbaku headquarters.[43]

Taiga, like Jakuchū, had close connections with the Ōbaku branch of Zen, and between 1770 and 1771 he executed a series of paintings on walls and screens in the Mampukuji, including his depiction of West Lake (Seiko-zu) in the eastern abbot's quarters. Among these compositions (which have since been mounted as twenty-nine hanging scrolls), the eight works that portray the Five Hundred Arhats were made as free adaptations of the handscroll version (also preserved in the Mampukuji) attributed to the Yüan artist Wang Chen-p'eng. Particularly noteworthy are the four panels of Taiga's work depicting Arhats crossing the sea, which was originally on the western side of the room; this panel includes a small group of figures riding the clouds, and the composition, like Jakuchū's, is oriented diagonally from the upper right down to the lower left. Jakuchū probably saw this work in situ at the Mampukuji and was influenced by it.

In contrast to typical portrayals of Arhats, which emphasize bizarre physiognomy, the facial expressions of Jakuchū's figures are uniformly happy and innocent. His conception could even be described as naïve, but it resulted in a pure and charming quality. These differences in expressive manner are precisely what distinguish the work and relate it to Taiga's Arhat pictures. In this regard, perhaps there is justification for the idea that the two painters' fundamental faith in Buddhist ideals inspired similar attitudes.

When he was seventy-seven years of age, Unge, who was a monk of the Higashi Honganji temple and a friend of such artists as Aoki Mokubei (1767–1833), Tanomura Chikuden (1777–1835), and Rai San'yo (1781–1832), made the inscription for the box in which this scroll was preserved.

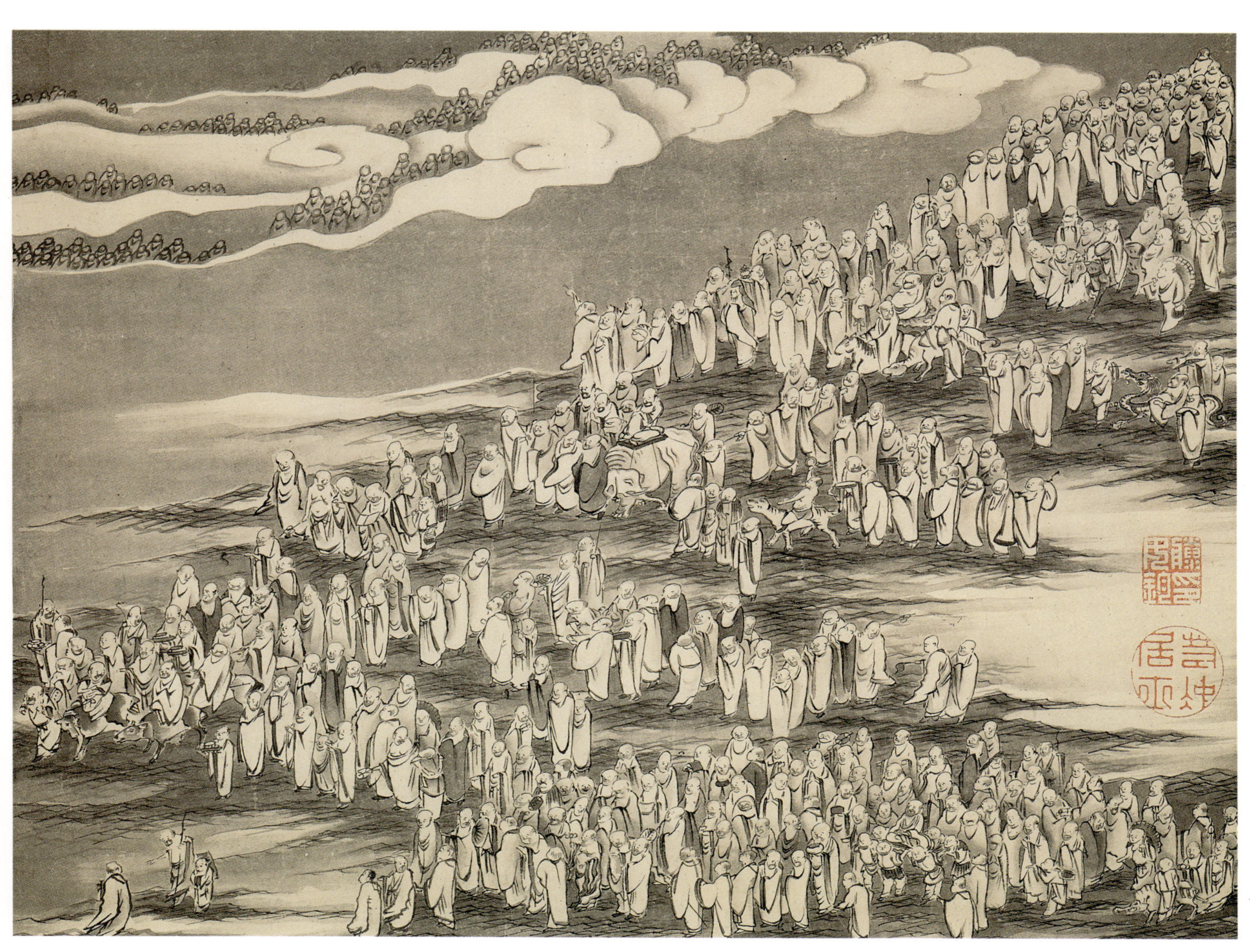

28 *Bamboo and Tiger*

Second half of the 1760s–first half of the 1770s

Ink on paper, two hanging scrolls
151 × 69 cm
Inscription:
see below

SEALS:
square intaglio: *Tō Jokin-in*
round relief: *Jakuchū koji*
Rokuonji, Kyoto

In 1755 Jakuchū produced his polychrome *Tiger* (Shin'enkan Collection; FIG. 29), copying the prototypical Chinese painting (FIG. 30) in the Shōdenji, a temple in Kyoto. In the inscription on his painting Jakuchū wrote: "When I paint natural phenomena, depiction is impossible without a true model. As there are no ferocious tigers in this country, I could only imitate the appearance of one by copying Mao I's painting." The Shōdenji painting to which he referred is thought to be by a professional painter of the Ming dynasty, although Jakuchū apparently believed it to be the work of Mao I, the Southern Sung expert in "running-animal" pictures. Jakuchū's forthright copy seems to possess a life force surpassing that of the original.

The monochrome painting under discussion here, done in much the same style as Jakuchū's polychrome work in the Shin'enkan, was also based on the Shōdenji work. The tiger has fewer stripes; these Jakuchū rendered with dark ink, and he did the rest of the tiger's fur in lighter tones that captured its flow—a deft transformation from the artist's finely wrought works in color to the medium of monochrome ink. Here the background is bamboo, rather than a withered tree, but vestiges of the withered tree from the Shōdenji work appear in the way in which the curved bamboo trunk projects into the picture from the right-hand side and in the composition of the bamboo leaves, which hang down over the tiger's head. Jakuchū's method of rendering the

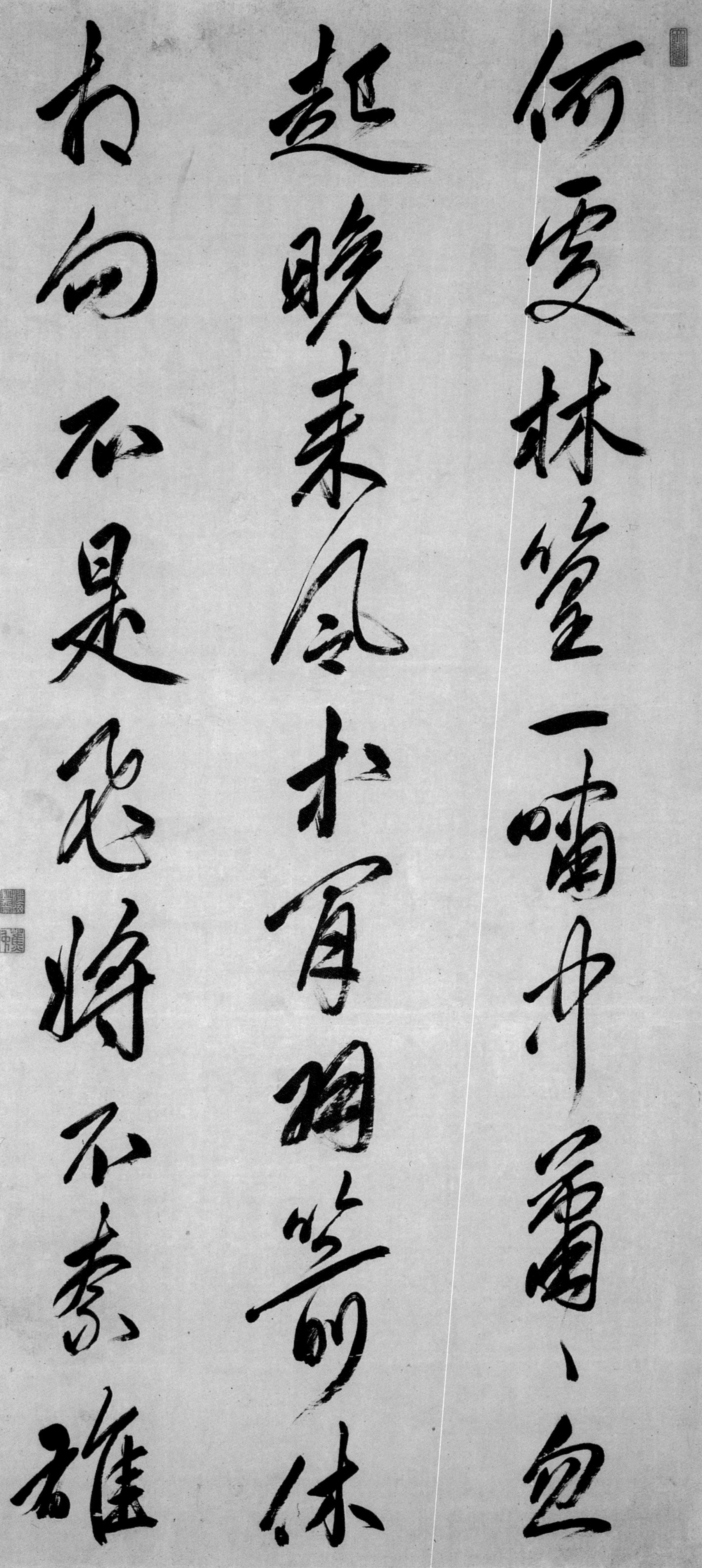

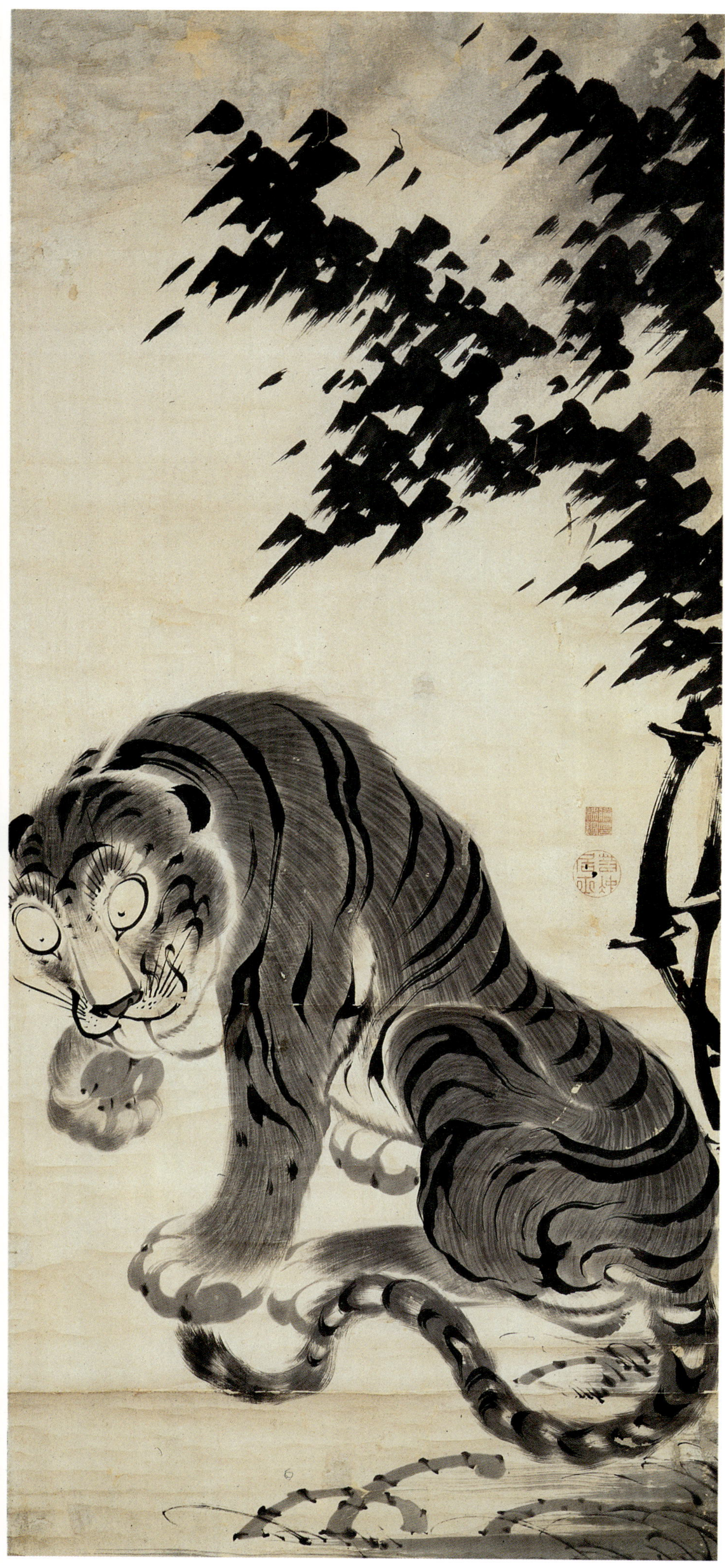

bamboo is close to that of his screen composition in the Rokuonji (No. 16.7, 16.8) however, the bamboo leaves in the painting show strong movement toward the lower left, representing the wind that blows in the bamboo grove.

A scroll with a heptasyllabic quatrain by Daiten accompanies the painting:

What bamboo grove is this?
The tiger roars
And instantly the evening wind comes
whistling
Give it up! You who foolishly face the tiger
now
Arrow ready in your hand
For surely only a surpassing general
Could bring this virile tiger down

The inscription is recorded in Daiten's *Shōun Seikō* (vol. 5), indicating that the picture dates from no later than 1775, when the collection of Chinese poetry was published.[44]

At the beginning of his "Note on a Tiger Painting" in the *Hokuzen Bunsō*, Daiten wrote: "In our country there are no tigers; one can see them only in pictures. These pictures are copied from earlier pictures; no one ever inspects a real tiger to see if he has done it correctly. All these pictures of tigers look like nothing but oversized cats."[45] Doubtless it was this sort of opinion that stimulated Jakuchū to produce his polychrome *Tiger*. However, Daiten's inscription does not convey as deep a sense of emotion as that he felt upon seeing a Korean painting of a tiger, mentioned in the reference above. (Tigers were native to Korea, and Korean painters traditionally specialized in their depiction.)

29 *Banana Plant*

Second half of the 1760s–first half of the 1770s

Ink on paper, two hanging scrolls
152.5 × 68.6 cm (each scroll)
Colophon: see below

SEALS:
square intaglio: *Tō Jokin-in*
round relief: *Jakuchū koji*
Daikōmyōji, Kyoto Prefecture

In 1759 Jakuchū painted compositions of banana plants in monochrome ink in the Third Chamber of the Dai-shoin of the Rokuonji. Among these, the section on the southern side, *Banana Trees and* Haha-chō (FIG. 43), provided the prototype for the composition and technique of the present painting. Jakuchū laid out the banana plant and the rock along an oblique line stretching from the upper right to the lower left, executing the leaves in a series of parallel strokes with a narrow, flat brush (*hake*) and creating the contours of the peculiar rock in dark ink. The eccentric rock, shaped with assertive, deep black ink, seems to have been inspired by the ink paintings of Kakutei Jōkō, and it adds a dramatic accent to the design. Jakuchū concentrated the oblique lines and arcs in a narrower picture plane that those in the Rokuonji work and portrayed more graphically the wind-battered banana tree. The banana leaves, here painted in parallel lines and a more crowded fashion than in the Rokuonji screens, also contribute drama, and his clever technique of preserving white spaces between the brush strokes convincingly simulates the veins of the leaves. Jakuchū skillfully executed the backs of the leaves in a lighter tone of ink than that he used for the fronts.

Although the artist thus effectively evoked the appearance of nature, he only went so far in portraying things realistically. This quality of selective realism helps to distinguish Jakuchū's works from those of his imitators, such as Jakuen's *Banana Leaves* in the Shin'enkan Collection (FIG. 49), which is more mannered and lacks vitality.

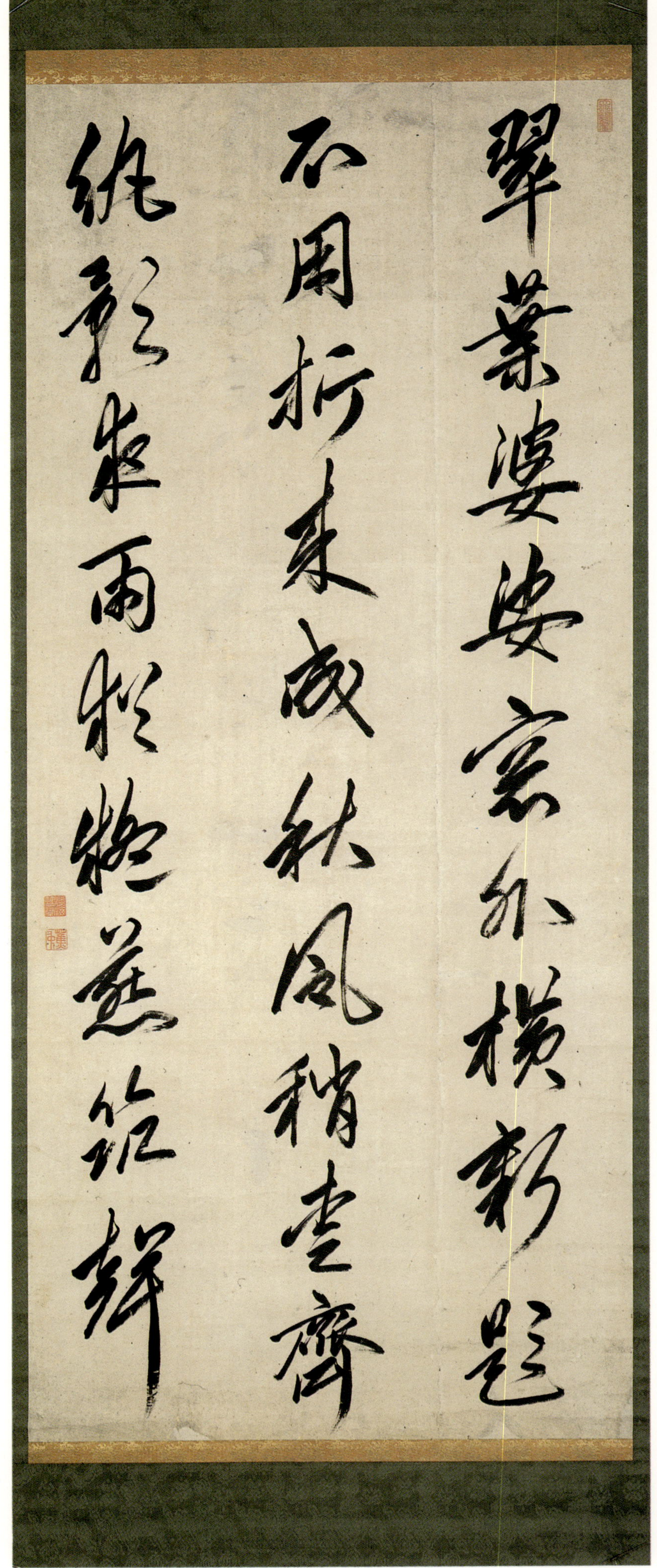

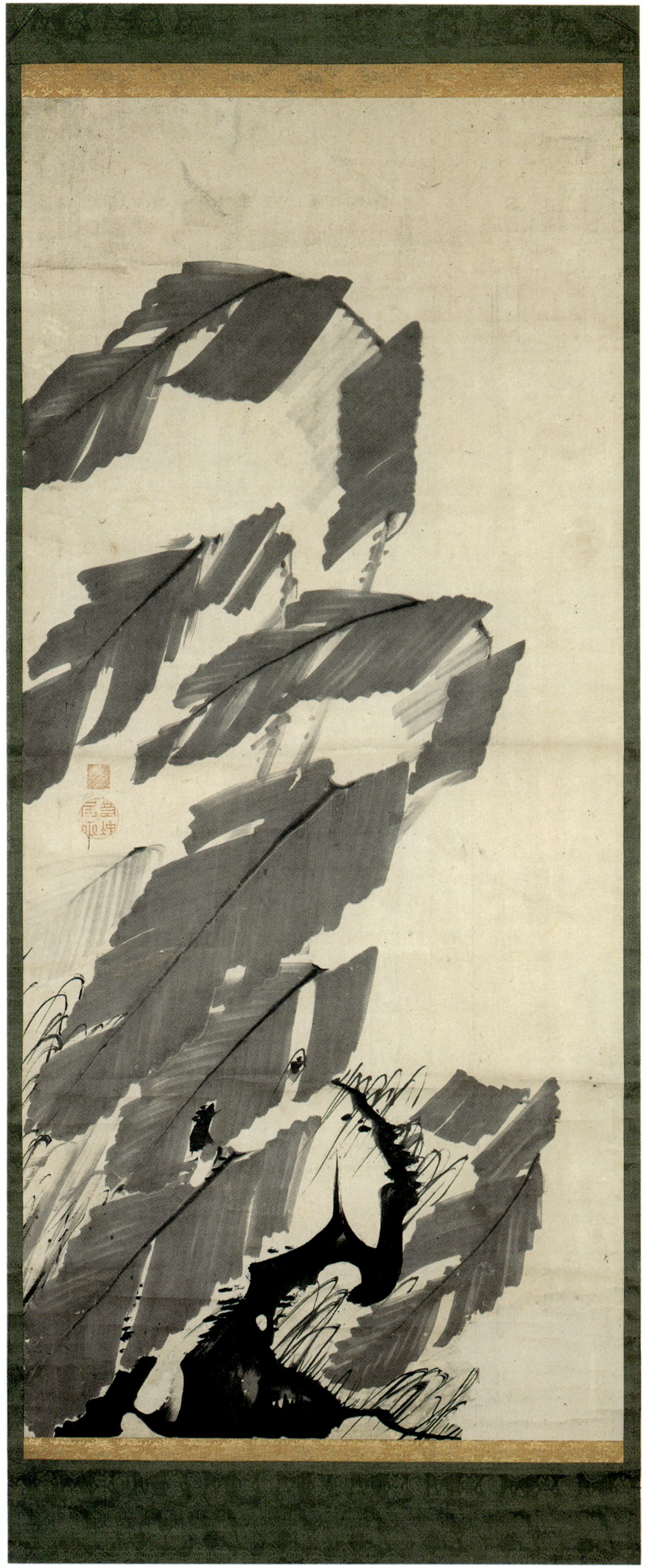

As is the case with *Bamboo and Tiger* (No. 28), a scroll with a heptasyllabic quatrain (composed and calligraphed by Daiten) accompanies the painting:

Green banana leaves outside my window
  tremble, rustling
I will not break them to write verses anew
How lovely are the wind-swayed autumn
  shadows
they cast upon the white silk windows of my
  study
The night rain falling on them is like the
  sound
of the lute played at a banquet[46]

In China the banana plant is widely cultivated, and in Japan it is grown on the premises of temples, although it is not popular in household gardens because its big leaves have a barren, forlorn appearance when torn by autumn winds. In the texts of Buddhist sutras, the banana plant is a metaphor for ephemeral things, and this association was common among Zen monks of the Muromachi period, who added verses to pieces such as *Banana Plant in the Night Rain* (dated to 1419; collection of the Agency for Cultural Affairs). Daiten's inscription was inspired by the literary tradition of such verses.

The present inscription, like the one for *Bamboo and Tiger*, is included in Daiten's *Shōun Seikō* (vol. 5), indicating that the painting was done sometime before 1775.[47] Furthermore, this poem appears in the anthology just after the one for *Bamboo and Tiger*. This documentation lends support to Professor Kobayashi Tadashi's suggestion that the paired poem-picture formats of these two paintings (which are of similar dimensions) were intentional.[48]

The Daikōmyōji is a subtemple located within the precincts of the Shōkokuji.

30 *Tasseled Reeds and Kingfisher*

Late 1760s–early 1770s

Ink on paper, hanging scroll
114.0 × 30.0 cm
Inscription:
see below

SEALS:
square intaglio: *Tō Jokin-in*
round relief: *Jakuchū koji*
Daikōmyōji, Kyoto Prefecture

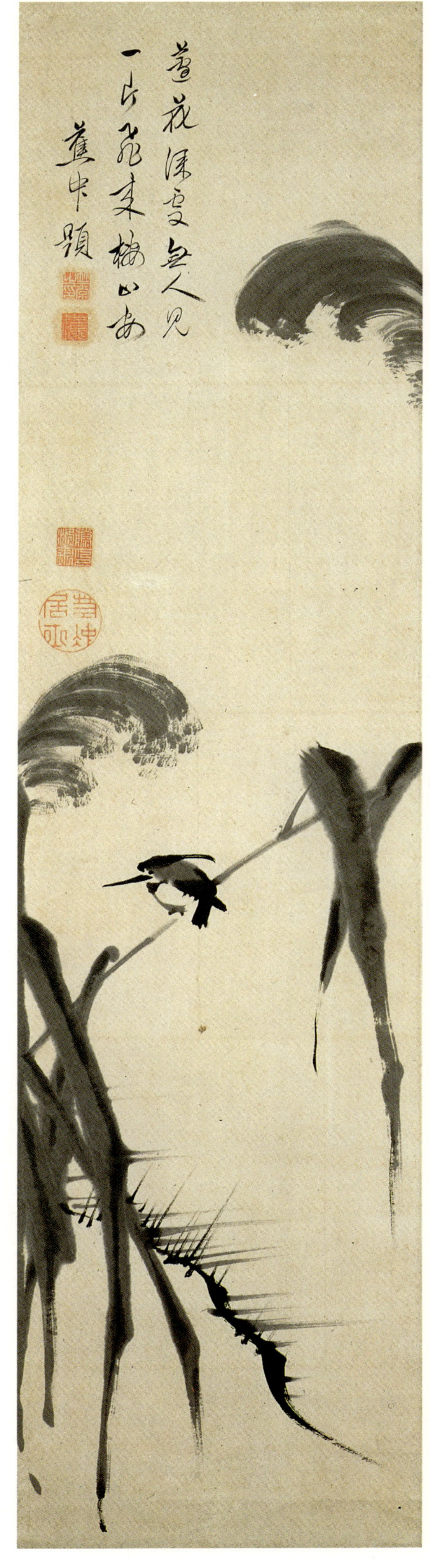

In this work, Jakuchū represented the shore and the grasses with a dark line of ink running diagonally downward from the lower left with the intersecting diagonal brush strokes; he depicted the surface of the water in pale, horizontal lines. The reed stalks and leaves, though few in number, overlap each other, and the method by which the artist painted this simple subject gave the painting an intricate quality. He sketched in the shapes with pale ink, onto which he selectively added dark ink before the first layer had dried, causing blurring; then he added small, abbreviated brush strokes to the tips of the reeds. The reed tassel at the upper right enters from beyond the picture plane, its shape acting in concert with the tassel on the left. Painted mainly with rough, dry brush strokes, the tassels evoke a feeling of lightness, delicacy, and extended space. A kingfisher sits alertly on a reed stalk that cuts diagonally across the picture, his form unerringly captured in a few brief strokes. This small, somewhat abbreviated work reveals quite well the distinctive features of Jakuchū's ink painting and is notable for its mood of tranquility.

Professor Tsuji Nobuo has pointed out the similarity between the style of this type of monochrome ink painting by Jakuchū and that of works of the early Ch'ing painter Pa-ta Shan-jen and has suggested that, even if Jakuchū did not have access to actual paintings by this Chinese master, he may well have known works that had a close stylistic link to them.[49] This hypothesis remains to be proven, but at least in the case of *Tasseled Reeds and Kingfisher*, the more relevant question seems to be one of its relationship to the style of Mu Ch'i (the superb painter of the Southern Sung period): Jakuchū probably would have known pictures in the style of Mu Ch'i rather than works actually done by him. For instance, Jakuchū may have seen a painting such as *Withered Reeds and Kingfisher* (MOA Museum, Shizuoka Prefecture), which bears the seals of Mu Ch'i and Zen'a, in a Zen temple where this type of ink painting had been cherished. Characteristics of the painting shown here seem more closely related to works done (probably in Japan) in the tradition of Mu Ch'i than to those in the tradition of Pa-ta Shan-jen: the motif of a kingfisher resting on a reed that cuts diagonally across the picture plane; the use of areas of white space in the composition; and the handling of details such as the kingfisher's face. Japanese artists reinterpreted and utilized Mu Ch'i's style in accordance with native tastes; thus the elegant and refined aspects were favored, and something of the original strength of expression was lost. Jakuchū added his individualistic ink-painting techniques to this derivative style, thus saving the present piece from being a minor work. Daiten's inscription reads:

The tassels of the reeds bloom there
In secluded depths never perused by man
A solitary kingfisher comes flying and stops there
Where it rests peacefully

According to a statement recorded on the mounting, this piece was formerly kept in the storehouse of the Gyōsuian, a subtemple within the precincts of the Shōkokuji.

31 *White Elephant and Other Beasts*

c. 1770–early 1780s

Ink and light colors on paper, panel
122.9 × 73.1 cm

SEALS:
square intaglio: *Tō Jokin-in*
round relief: *Jakuchū koji*
rectangular relief: *Senga zeppitsu*
Private collection, Hyōgo Prefecture

A depiction of the front half of a seated white elephant, a waggish squirrel firmly grasping its elevated trunk, dominates the composition in this panel. Surrounding the elephant are a variety of real and imaginary creatures: a weasel in front; a bear and two long-armed monkeys to the side; and a deer and a dragon in the rear. Behind the monkeys is a strange-shaped rock resembling calcite crystals, and in the background is a stylized pattern of flowing water common to paintings of the Rimpa school. Jakuchū imprinted three seals on separate sections of paper and affixed them to the surface of the painting.

The artist executed the painting in a very strange manner, as if engaging in some modern experiment in expressive imagery. Apparently he first divided the surface of the paper vertically and horizontally with a series of straight, light ink lines about nine millimeters apart, creating a uniform series of approximately six thousand small squares across the entire surface of the paper. Over this he applied a thin coating of white pigment. Then he filled in the squares one by one with a thin, gray wash, using a darker gray to fill in the upper left-hand corner of each square with an even smaller square. Finally, he delineated the contours of the individual components with light colors on top of the tile-like prepared ground. That Jakuchū was fond of working in a precise manner with geometrically conceived forms is apparent in his experiments with expressive forms in monochrome painting. The specific impetus for his working in this bizarre manner is entirely unclear, however.

The owner of the piece has pointed out that it had at one time been in *makuri* (unmounted) form and that a sheet of paper attached to the back contained an inscription, reading "Kōkinsha Itō Genzaemon," which was written by someone other than Jakuchū. The three-character term *kōkinsha* appears to be an abbreviated name for the Itō family house, located in the Nishiki market area where Jakuchū was born: Taka *kō*-kura (street), Nishiki *kin*-koji (lane), and *sha* (house). Genzaemon was the traditional name of the owner and manager of the Masuya, the family's greengrocery. Thus, this painting was probably once owned by Jakuchū's descendants. The present owner says that the piece was once mounted on one panel of a two-panel folding screen but was later mounted as a single panel.

Professor Kobayashi Tadashi was the first scholar to publish this piece, and he presumed that the pair of six-panel folding screens in the Shin'enkan Collection, executed in the same manner but having no inscription or signature, were also authentic pieces.[50] However, it is difficult to support the contention that the Shin'enkan screens were actually from Jakuchū's hand. The flora and fauna in those screens are different in their essential conformations from such subject matter in authenticated works. The pigments, moreover, have a raw, hard quality, and the gray areas within the individual squares were poorly executed. On the basis of a comparison with the present panel painting, it also appears that neither the Shin'enkan screens nor a single six-panel folding screen in the Shizuoka Prefectural Art Museum (which has a similar subject and manner of execution) are authentic; rather, they seem to be works that simulated the conceptions and techniques developed by Jakuchū. It is thought that these copies were produced sometime in the nineteenth century, during the last years of the Edo period or the early years of the Meiji period (1868–1912), rather than during the eighteenth century.

Another example of similar subject matter and techniques was reproduced in the catalogue *Rinkō Kinen Meika Hizōhin Tenrankai Zuroku* (1933); this eight-panel folding screen with depictions of Śākyamuni and the Sixteen Arhats, at that time in the Osaka Municipal Museum, unfortunately no longer seems to be extant.[51]

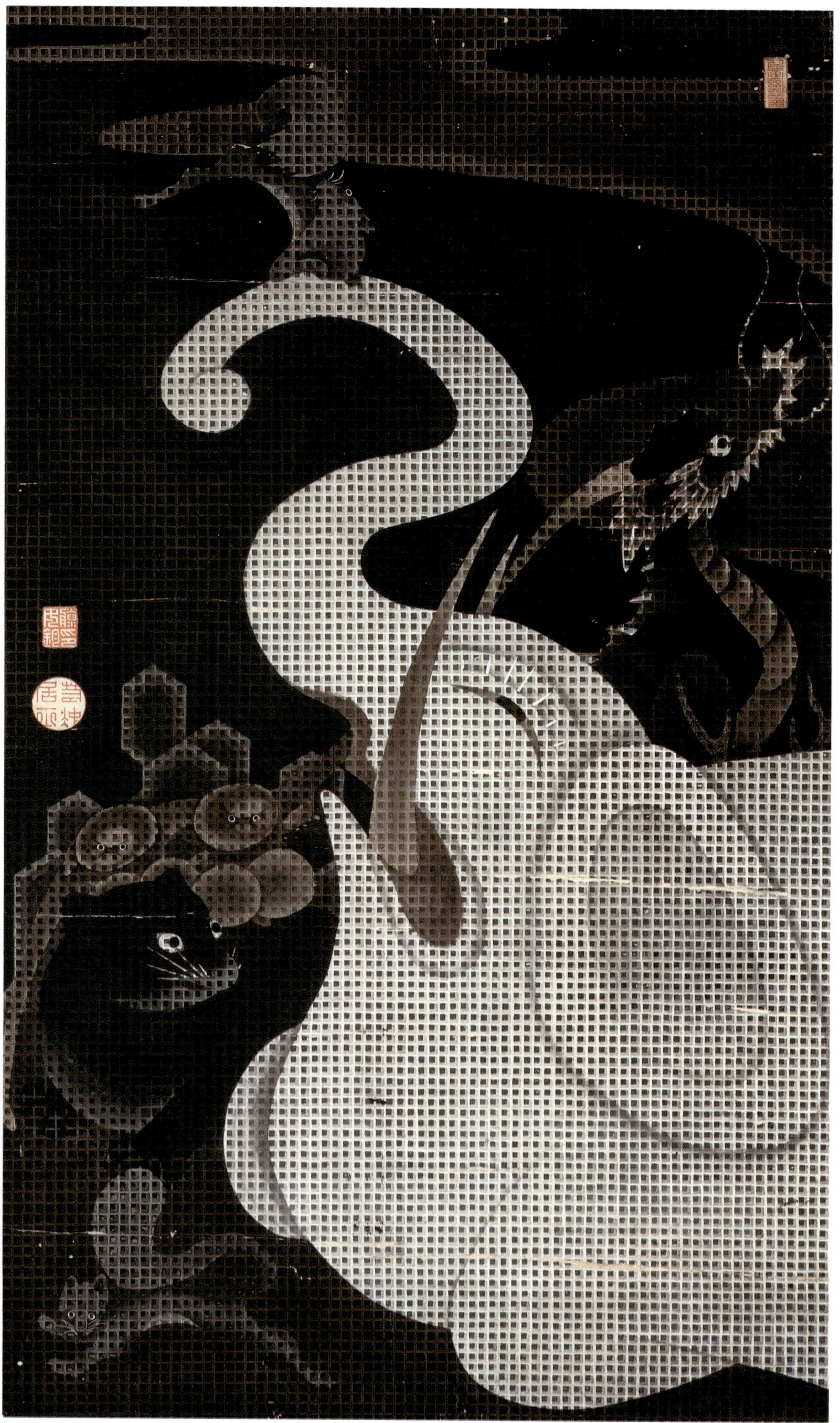

32 *Vegetable Parinirvāna*

c. 1780

Ink on paper, hanging scroll
181.7 × 96.1 cm

SEALS:
square intaglio: *Tō Jokin-in*
round relief: *Jakuchū koji*
Kyoto National Museum

Śākyamuni, the historical Buddha, traveled to various regions of India with his disciples and preached his faith until the end of his life, when he fell ill and on his death bier achieved ultimate enlightenment. In Kuśinăgara, in northern India, at a location close to a river where two *śāla* trees stood, a bier was prepared for him. After he had responded to his disciples' questions for the final time, he lay down on his right side, with his head oriented toward the north, and expired in the middle of the night. It is said that, at his death, all living beings cried with grief, their lamentations echoing everywhere, and the *śāla* trees flanking the bier turned white. Traditional pictorial and sculptural representations of this dramatic scene were done in great numbers in East Asia. In Japan many examples have been preserved, the oldest being a monumental painting (anonymous, 1086) that belongs to the Kongōbuji, the great monastery on Mount Koya in Wakayama Prefecture.

In Jakuchū's humorous and fantastic Parinirvāna scene, an unusual parody of the traditional theme, vegetables and fruits have gathered for the Buddha's final departure from this world. The artist replaced Śākyamuni with a giant Japanese radish (*daikon*), the jeweled bier with a farmer's coarse woven basket, and the *śāla* trees with corn stalks. As pictorial metaphors for the throng of grieving Bodhisattvas, disciples, members of the laity, and representatives of the animal world present at the Buddha's death, he chose the peach, turnip, citron, two kinds of chestnuts, eggplant, lotus, three kinds of melons, pear, garden pea, two kinds of cherries, squash, corn, horsetail, lily bulb, ginger, arrowhead, two kinds of mushrooms, red pepper, two kinds of persimmons, ginger yam, cucumber, gourd, and bamboo shoot. In the upper left he rendered a single quince, apparently to represent Lady Māyā, the Buddha's mother, descended from her realm in paradise.

In conventional icons depicting the Parinirvāna, the Buddha's head is situated to the left, and Jakuchū carefully simulated this precedent in the orientation of the upper portion of the giant radish, including the green leaves. Similarly, the *śāla* trees were traditionally depicted with eight trunks each, and Jakuchū replaced them with an equal number of corn stalks. This careful fidelity to the iconographic particulars of the prototype—replacing the original components with familiar objects—is an approach to parody common in various cultures and historical periods.

As a result of his years of experience as the proprietor of a wholesale greengrocery, Jakuchū was intimately familiar with all kinds of fruits and vegetables, and he was therefore able to accurately depict each variety in the composition, with an obvious knowledge of its individual characteristics. Vegetables and fruits are not usually thought of as animate beings, but as rendered by Jakuchū's evocative brush, they seem to peer up at the giant radish symbolizing the Buddha and to prostrate themselves in lamentation, crowding closely about their spiritual leader. The viewer cannot help feeling that the artist intended much more than a simple parody and that he actually expressed an eloquent message of religious devotion and sincerity. Despite the precision in execution, the brushwork shows no sense of hesitation, and the complementary tones of ink were beautifully modulated. Jakuchū began to paint in ink on *gasenshi* as early as 1760, and the *Vegetable Parinirvāna*, done two decades later, represents his ultimate refinement in the use of this material.

Professor Yoshiaki Shimizu of Princeton University has pointed out various aspects of cultural history relating to this work, observing that it reflects the concept that the Buddha nature (Busshō) is present even in trees and plants, a traditional idea in Buddhism; that the *daikon* symbolizes the frugal, homely nature of the Buddhist monk's meager fare; that this vegetable became a frequent subject in ink monochrome painting; and that depictions of it, such as the painting attributed to Mu Ch'i, became objects of aesthetic contemplation in the tea ceremony during the Middle Ages in Japan. Professor Shimizu has also suggested that Jakuchū probably painted his work after the death of his younger brother Hakusai in 1792. According to Shimizu's interpretation, the *Vegetable Parinirvāna* signified both Hakusai's death and the end of the wholesale greengrocery, which Jakuchū had turned over to his brother many years earlier.[52] However, there are difficulties with this contention. First, the style of the painting does not seem to substantiate a dating of the piece to Jakuchū's last years. Moreover, Hakusai's son inherited the wholesale greengrocery, and he continued its operation.

Nevertheless, the hypothesis that the piece was produced as the result of the death of a family member is worth pursuing. Jakuchū seems to have created a number of other works in honor of his family. It is possible that his gift of the paintings in the *Dōshoku Sai-e* (NO. 14 and FIG. 33) and the Śākyamuni triptych (NO. 15)—totaling thirty-three—was intentionally timed to coincide with the rites of the thirty-third anniversary of the death of his father, which were observed in 1770. The inscription on a Buddhist ancestral tablet that Jakuchū had installed in the Shōkokuji (Tenth Month of 1770) notes: "The three paintings of the Śākyamuni triptych and the thirty paintings of the *Dōshoku Sai-e* have all been donated to the Shōkokuji."[53] If the correspondence in these numbers was more than coincidental, this plan may have been a motivating factor in Jakuchū's carrying

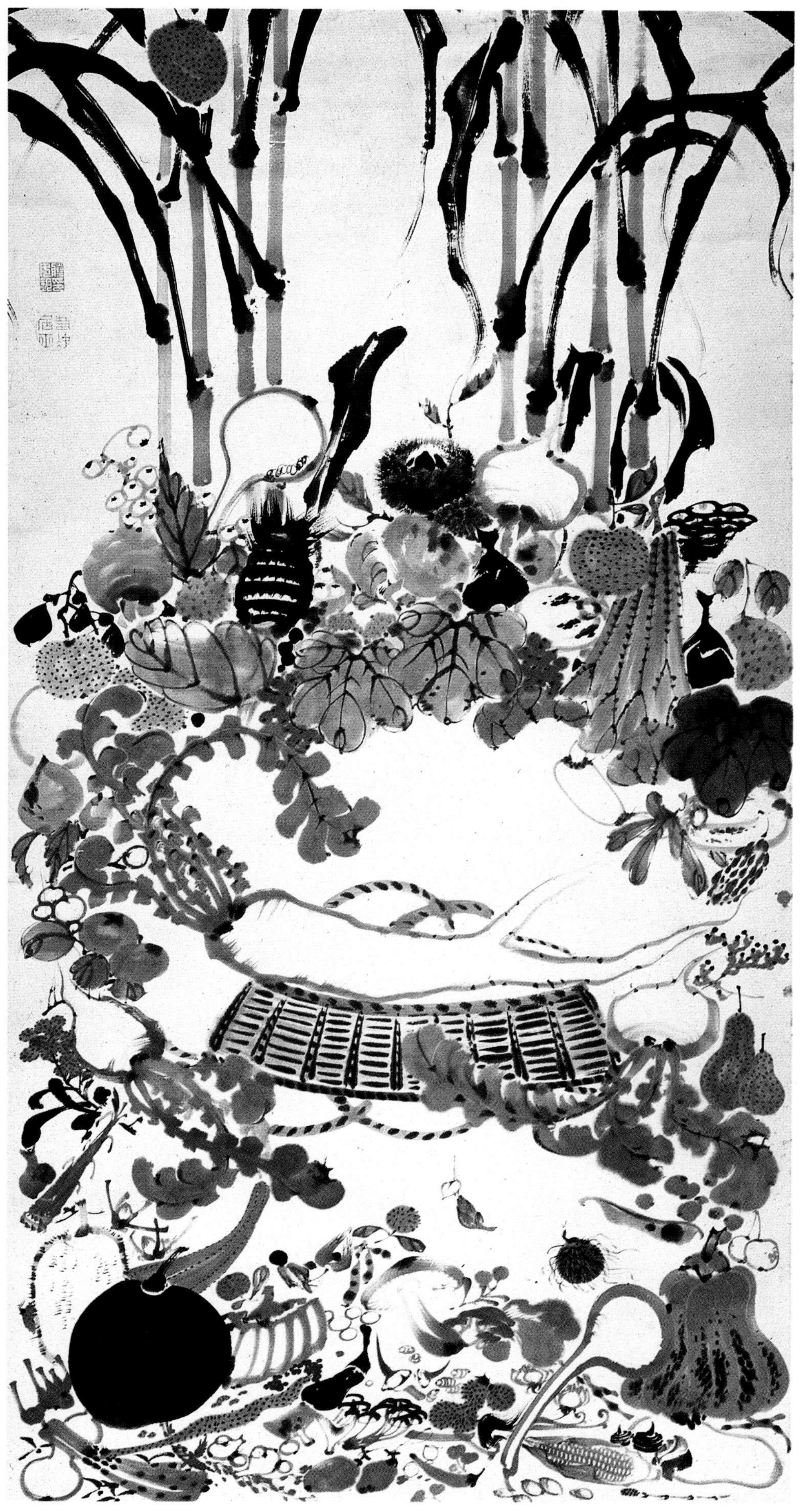

out the protracted project.

The view that the vegetables and fruit in the *Vegetable Parinirvāna* were intended as a metaphor for the Itō family's greengrocery seems plausible enough. The piece therefore may well have been executed in honor of a relative. In light of the painting's style, it would appear that the death of Jakuchū's mother is the only event likely to have motivated the artist to create this work.

In support of this thesis, Hayashi Susumu of the Yamato Bunkakan has made two observations. First, the bifurcated form of the *daikon* suggests a woman. In Europe as well as China, vegetables with a bifurcated shape from time to time have been regarded as representations of procreation and fertility and, by association, as covert symbols of the female sex. Furthermore, the *daikon* is recumbent on a basket, bringing to mind the goddess from Japanese mythology described in the ancient *Kojiki* as having performed an erotic dance while crouching on top of a bucket, thereby luring the sun goddess out of a cave where she had hidden herself. It may also be pointed out that during the Edo period a bifurcated *daikon* was customarily used as a religious offering to Daikokuten, the god who brought riches, and that Jakuchū probably not only intended for the painting to commemorate his deceased mother, but also hoped that her entry into paradise would bring prosperity to the family business.[54] In general, it seems likely that the artist was trying to express devotion for his parents, even though he no longer had any affiliation with the family business. Thus, there may well have been several motivations behind the *Vegetable Parinirvāna*.

The painting was formerly in the possession of the Seiganji, a temple of the Pure Land sect of Buddhism in Kyoto. Professor Shimizu has suggested the possibility that the painting was presented to the Seiganji by the Hōzōji, the tutelary temple of the Itō family.[55]

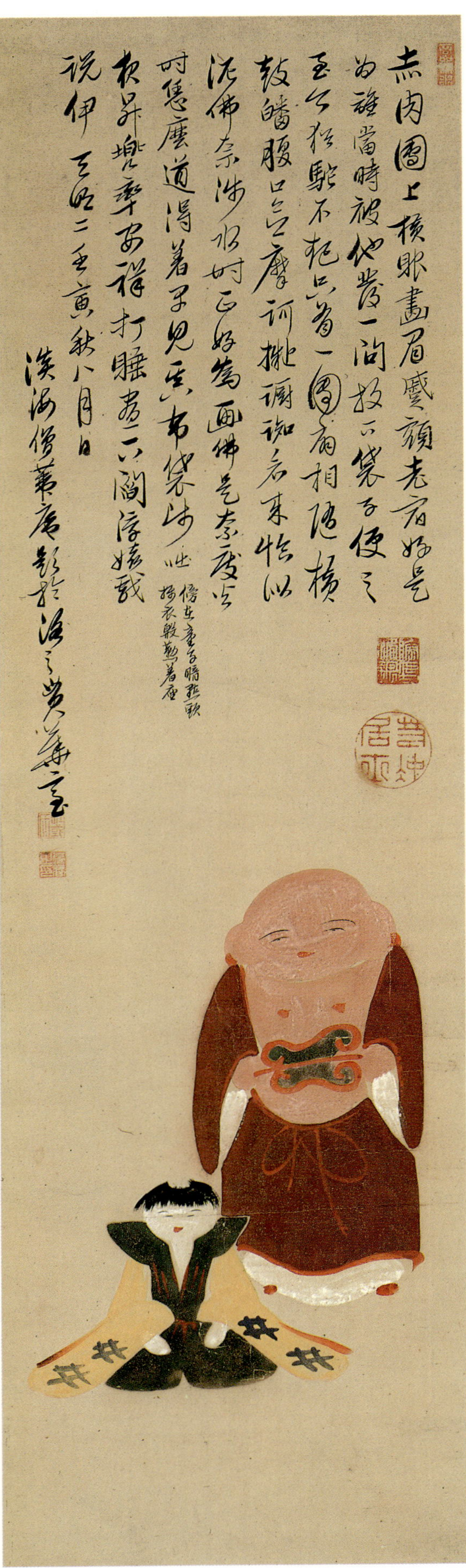

33 *Fushimi Ningyō*

(*Hotei with a Young Attendant*)

1782

Colors on paper, hanging scroll
93.6 × 28.5 cm
Inscription:
see below

SEALS:
square intaglio: *Tō Jokin-in*
round relief: *Jakuchū koji*
Private collection, Osaka Prefecture

34 *Fushimi Ningyō*

(*Inari Fox*)

c. late 1790s

Colors on paper, hanging scroll
103.8 × 29.6 cm
Inscription:
see below

SEALS:
square intaglio: *Tō Jokin-in*
round relief: *Jakuchū koji*
Private collection, Tokyo

Fushimi Ningyō are clay dolls made in Fushimi, in the southeastern part of present-day Kyoto. Their origins are unclear, but the earliest specimens probably date to the seventeenth century. It appears that they were first sold as souvenirs in the town that grew up next to Fushimi Castle and at the famous Fushimi Inari shrine, situated nearby. They became popular throughout Japan, stimulating the production of clay dolls in different regions of the country. Fushimi Ningyō achieved their greatest popularity during the nineteenth century, toward the end of the Edo period. Production has declined since that time, and it is said that nowadays only one workshop maintains this traditional craft.

The dolls are molded in clay and fired in kilns, and then embellished with *gofun* (white pigment) and inexpensive mineral pigments. Their main characteristic is an endearing simplicity and directness of form and color. They are made in hundreds of shapes, but the most frequently depicted is that of the portly Hotei, the popular god of prosperity and good fortune, and almost all of the Fushimi Ningyō that Jakuchū depicted were representations of this humorous subject.

Jakuchū generally did not use outlines in his depictions of these dolls, instead portraying the figures with areas of color and curvilinear brush strokes in order to create an impression of roundness. He skillfully combined pigments with mica or gold powder to simulate flesh tones and gave the facial expressions of the dolls an animated yet ingenuous quality that reflects the emotions of the anonymous craftsmen who produced them. Two of Jakuchū's finest paintings of Fushimi dolls are included here, one a rare portrayal of Hotei with a young attendant and the other a unique work depicting a fox.

Thought to have been a Chinese monk of the early tenth century, Hotei lived an itinerant life, carrying all his belongings in a voluminous hemp bag hung over his long staff. A popular subject in Zen ink painting, this eccentric figure was characteristically portrayed with a wrinkled brow and a large abdomen. In Japanese folk belief, Hotei became one of the Seven Gods of good fortune and happiness, and he was therefore often depicted with a happy demeanor. However, the long colophon written above Jakuchū's painting gives a rather strained Buddhist interpretation to the cheerful-looking doll:

On the red flesh are eyebrows painted like long, narrow eyes. His face is that of an old monk with a wrinkled brow. On whose behalf does he repeatedly appear in this familiar form? On one occasion someone took the opportunity of asking him a single question, and he proceeded to put down all of his possessions and tried to explain simply, saying that he was like a camel who was unable to get up on his feet [as he had not yet attained enlightenment]. Hotei has a single, round fan with him, and his great belly extends out like a big drum. While chanting the *Mahaprajna-paramita* sutra, if one hesitates and concentrates only on the characters, it is just like meditating on a Buddha made of clay. What does he do when he must cross a river? He is only a painted Buddha, so this is easily accomplished. How does he cross over fire? [According to the *Hekigan Roku*] this is possible by means of a path. Seen in the morning, it was truly Hotei who scolded one. [Next to Hotei there is a young boy with black hair. He is dressed in formal attire and sits politely.] At night Hotei ascends to the Tuśita Heaven [where the Bodhisattva Maitreya resides], and sleeps peacefully. In the day time he descends to the worlds of men, diverting himself and preaching the Buddhist Law. Inscribed at the Kanka studio, Kyoto, on a day of the Eighth Month of Temmei 2 [1782] by I'an, a monk from Omi [present-day Shiga Prefecture].

According to passages in the *Hekigan Roku* (see No. 20), "Buddha made of clay cannot cross a river" and "a wooden Buddha cannot pass through fire."[56] However, as all natural phenomena contain the Buddha nature, there is no reason to cross over water or pass through fire; this concept seems to be reflected in the colophon. The inscriber's seals read: *Kokoku shi* and *Enshun no in*, perhaps indicating that he was the Ōbaku monk Enshun from Kōkoku (Omi Province). This obscure monk is known only from a single reference in a Buddhist document dated to 1756.[57]

The second painting (right) shows a fox and two clay bells. The fox is the messenger of Inari-myōjin, the deity of grains, who is worshiped at Inari shrines throughout Japan. Fushimi is home to the headquarters of Inari worship, and this fact accounts for the popularity of Fushimi fox dolls. The *Koeki Kokusan-ko* (a study of local products, published from 1830 to 1844) contains illustrations of such clay foxes. The fox in this painting holds the key to a storehouse (or granary) in its mouth and sits on a *koban* (a round gold coin used during the Edo period), and these two objects represent wishes for fortune and happiness. The reddish brown pigment at the end of the fox's tail represents fire, an indication of the divine nature of the animal. The clay bell, originally used for exorcising evil, is a traditional toy sold in Fushimi.[58]

The inscription, a haiku, reads: "The selling of clay dolls [at the Fushimi Inari shrine] at the *hatsuuma* market heralds the blossoms of spring." The first phrase of this poem, *ara kane no* (unrefined gold), is a *makura-kotoba* (pillow phrase) also referring to clay, the material of the dolls. *Kigo* refers to the heavenly and earthly branches of the day in the traditional calendar; it is the first (*hatsu*) horse (*uma*) day in the Second Month (this year it fell on a day of *tsuchinoto-uma*), on which day festivals were held at Inari shrines all over the country, the one in Fushimi being particularly large in scale. At bazaars held at the shrines and along the streets, Fushimi dolls were (and are still) sold as souvenirs. The name of the haiku poet was recorded in the *Haika taikei zu* (1838);[59] her gō (nom de plume) was Wasen, and her name is known to have been Machi from the inscription on this painting. Wasen Machi's husband, Ishida Fusen (1720–1776), was also a haiku poet. Wasen probably became a nun after her husband's death; it is not clear when she died. Although she wrote this haiku at the age of seventy-seven, the painting itself is unfortunately not dated.

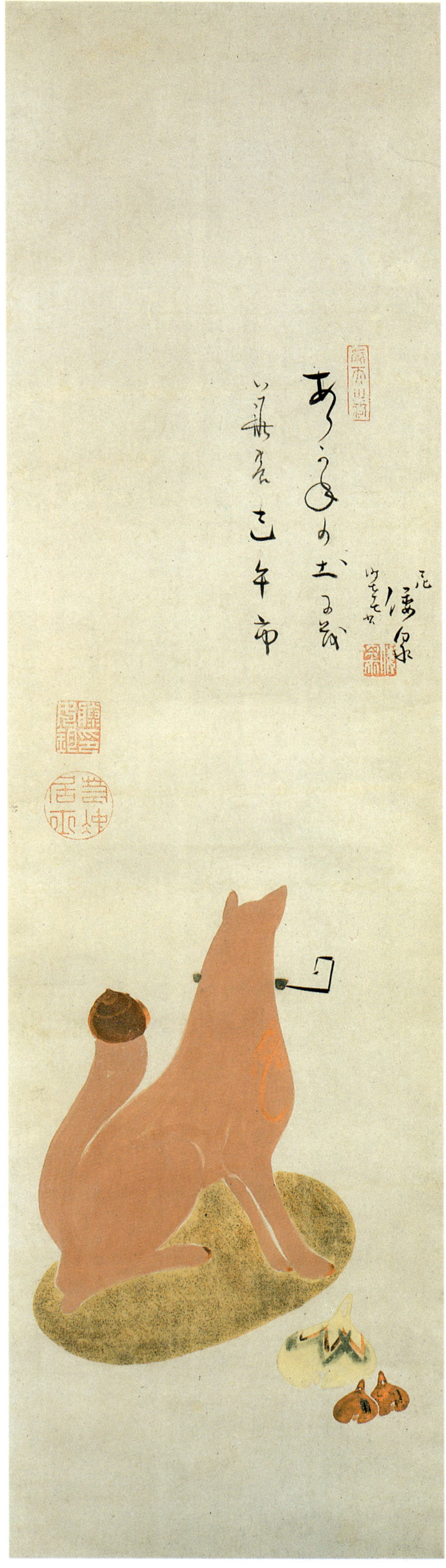

35 *Lotus Pond*

1790

Ink on paper, six hanging scrolls
195.0 × 89.5 cm (each scroll)

SEALS:
square intaglio: *Tō Jokin azana Keiwa*
square intaglio: *Tō Jokin-in*
round relief: *Jakuchū koji*
Saifukuji, Osaka Prefecture

Cacti and Fowl (FIG. 14), done in colors on a gold ground and bearing the signature of the artist and the age of seventy-five, was painted on the outer side of the six sliding-screen panels that separated the outer area of the main hall of the Saifukuji (a temple of the Jōdo Shin sect in Toyonaka City, Osaka Prefecture), from the inner sanctum, where the Buddhist images were kept. *Lotus Pond* was executed on the inner (or more sacred) side of the same sliding screens, but during repairs to *Cacti and Fowl* between 1928 and 1930, the monochrome ink paintings shown here were remounted as six hanging scrolls, and the upper half of the third scroll from the left was restored with new paper.

The great fire that burned down more than half the city of Kyoto in 1788 deprived Jakuchū of his home and atelier. Later that year, Jakuchū paid two visits to Kimura Kenkadō in Osaka, perhaps deciding to take up residence in the area for a while. According to the records of the Saifukuji, the parishioner Yoshino Goun, a wholesaler of materia medica, became Jakuchū's patron and commissioned these *fusuma* paintings from him.

The lotus has long been a symbol of Buddhism in India, China, and Japan, and Buddhist tradition has it that human beings who go to the paradise of the Pure Land after their deaths will be reborn there on lotuses blossoming in a pond. Deities seated on lotus thrones appear frequently in Buddhist painting

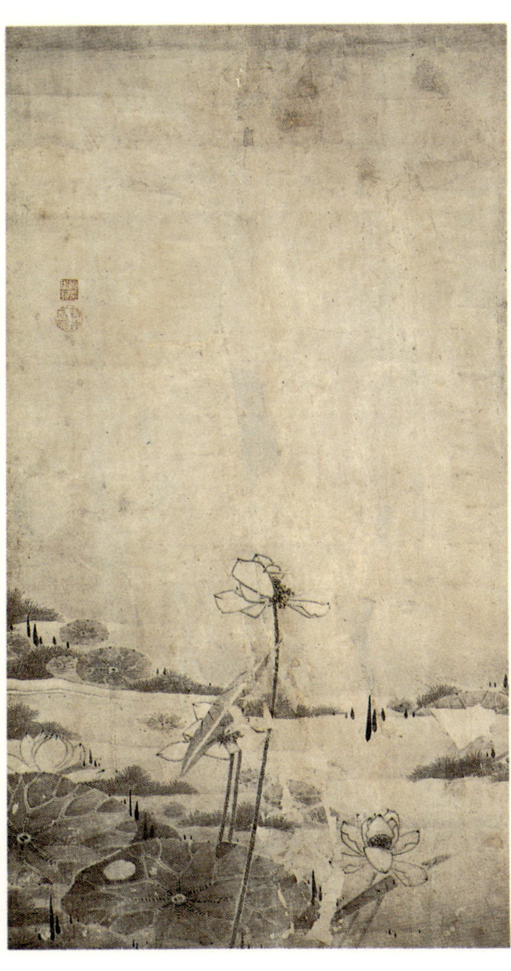
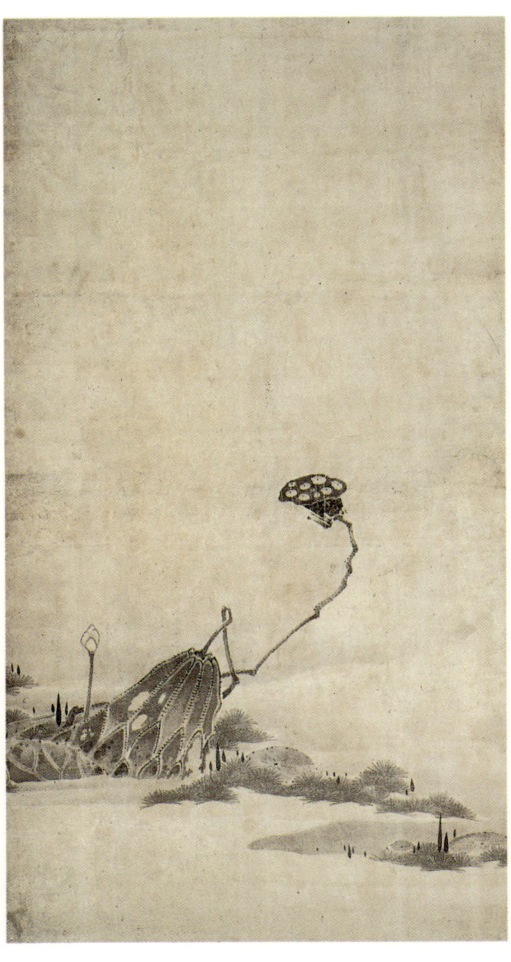

and decorative arts, as do other lotus motifs, and lotus paintings are common in Buddhist chapels. In keeping with this tradition, Jakuchū's paintings of the subject reveal a world of tranquility well suited to a Buddhist sanctuary, with lotuses in all stages of development—buds, half-open blossoms, flowers in full bloom, and centers from which the petals have fallen—thus echoing Buddhist teachings of the transience of life. Jakuchū probably learned this means of expressing the passage of time from Chinese paintings of lotus ponds and waterfowl.

The artist delineated the petals in angular, light outlines of ink and then went over them with darker ink. He emphasized the tips with short, incisive lines and rendered the turned-up edges of the leaves in light ink, with shading toward the edges. He divided the leaves into mosaic-like sections of dark ink painted over a light ground, and in the radial interstices between the dark areas he created lines of an intermediate intensity to represent the veins of the leaves, following these with short, dark, parallel strokes. He left unpainted the holes eaten through the leaves by insects.

Jakuchū revived the precise style of his early works, in which he had been influenced by paintings of "grasses and insects" from the P'i-ling area of Kiangsu in southern China (see Nos. 3, 6), in order to produce this group of pieces in ink, which are unique in the history of lotus painting. The artist probably turned to this style for personal reasons, and the entire work conveys a deep feeling of loneliness. The leaves, with their insect holes and wedge-shaped tears, are pitifully broken, as in a metaphorical portrait of a patient with a degenerative disease. The destruction of the aged artist's home must have had a devastating impact on him, very possibly accounting for this imagined landscape, which is evocative of some desolate planet.

A work entitled *Landscape*, painted in ink during the same year, is also kept at the Saifukuji.

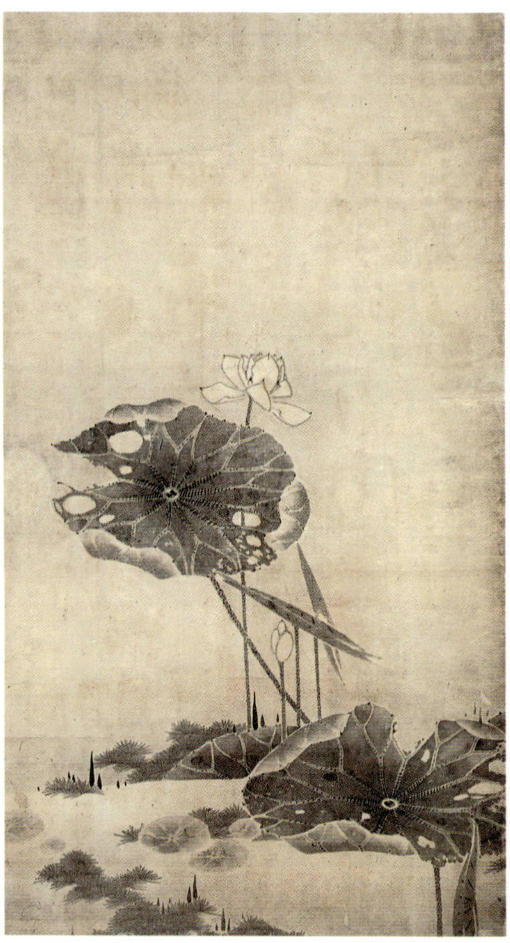

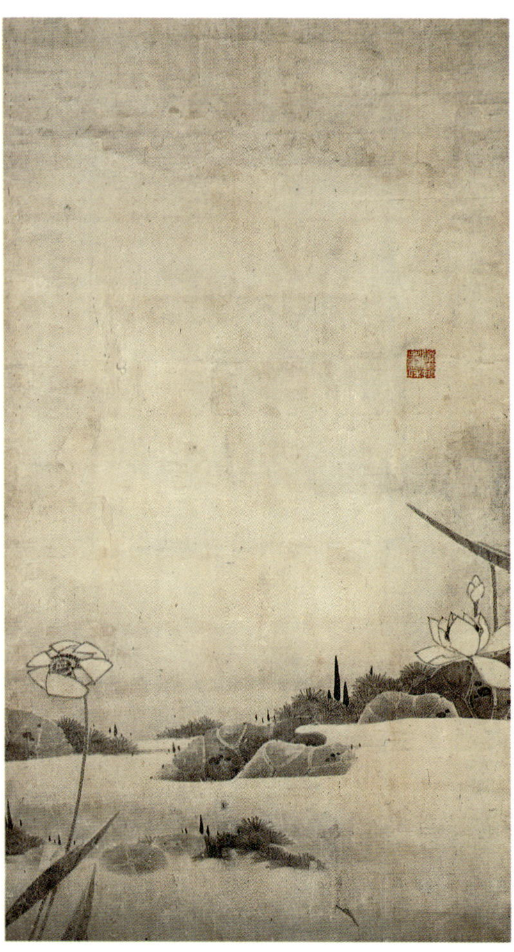

36 *Roosters and Hens*

1790

Ink on paper, one wall panel and four sliding-screen panels
Wall panel: 176.5 × 179.0 cm
Sliding-screen panels: 176.5 × 91.0 cm (each)
Signature: *Painted by Old Man Beito in his seventy-fifth year*

SEALS:
square intaglio: *Tō Jokin-in*
round relief: *Jakuchū koji*
Kyoto National Museum

The paintings shown here came from a set of works created for the Kaihōji, an Ōbaku temple in Fushimi. It included two panels attached to the walls of a Tokonoma, six panels attached to *fusuma* sliding screens, and one panel attached to another wall. The first two panels were mounted in the Tokonoma on the southern side of the eastern wall of the abbot's quarters, but since they did not fill the space, it is thought that there once must have been another section between them. To the left of the Tokonoma, two of the sliding-screen panels continued the composition. They were connected directly to the north wall of the abbot's quarters, which was decorated with the works shown here — the other wall panel and the remaining four sliding screens. A signature on the wall panel indicates that Jakuchū did the paintings in 1790, the same year that he did the sliding screens at the Saifukuji (see NO. 35 and FIG. 14).

Roosters and Hens is the only surviving example of monochrome wall and screen paintings from Jakuchū's last years. In 1787 Jakuchū painted sliding screens, thought also to have been done in ink, for the principal room of the new residence of Prince Shinjin (1768–1805) at the Myōhōin, but they were lost in the fire of 1788. The prince's diary relates that, before placing the commission, he had Jakuchū deliver twelve paintings of chickens for him to view and that it took the artist only a week to paint the commissioned screens.[60]

The present panels have certain features in common with the polychrome *Cacti and Fowl* at the Saifukuji (FIG. 14) that transcend the difference in medium. They all share the concept of an entire composition composed almost entirely of roosters, hens, and chicks; the shapes and poses of the birds; the detailed rendition of the feathers; and the atmosphere of intimacy. These points of correspondence suggest that Jakuchū used in his polychrome paintings the expressive techniques and the forms of the chickens that he had perfected in his ink paintings, clearly manifesting his awareness during this period of the qualities and advantages of ink versus those of color.

Despite the similarity of both subject matter and expressive method, the chickens here are somewhat less lively than those in the Saifukuji works—probably a reflection of the state of the artist's health. The records of the Shōkokuji note that during the Sixth Month of 1790, Jakuchū was very ill and that there was a discussion of sending someone from the temple to visit him.

The Kaihōji was founded by Chu-an Ching-yin (Japanese: Jikuan Jōin; 1699–1765), the thirteenth head of Mampukuji. The Sekihōji, where Jakuchū spent his last years, is located nearby and belongs to the same Ōbaku sect—circumstances that probably led to the creation of the paintings. The panels were purchased by the Kyoto National Museum from the Kaihōji and were repaired by the museum.

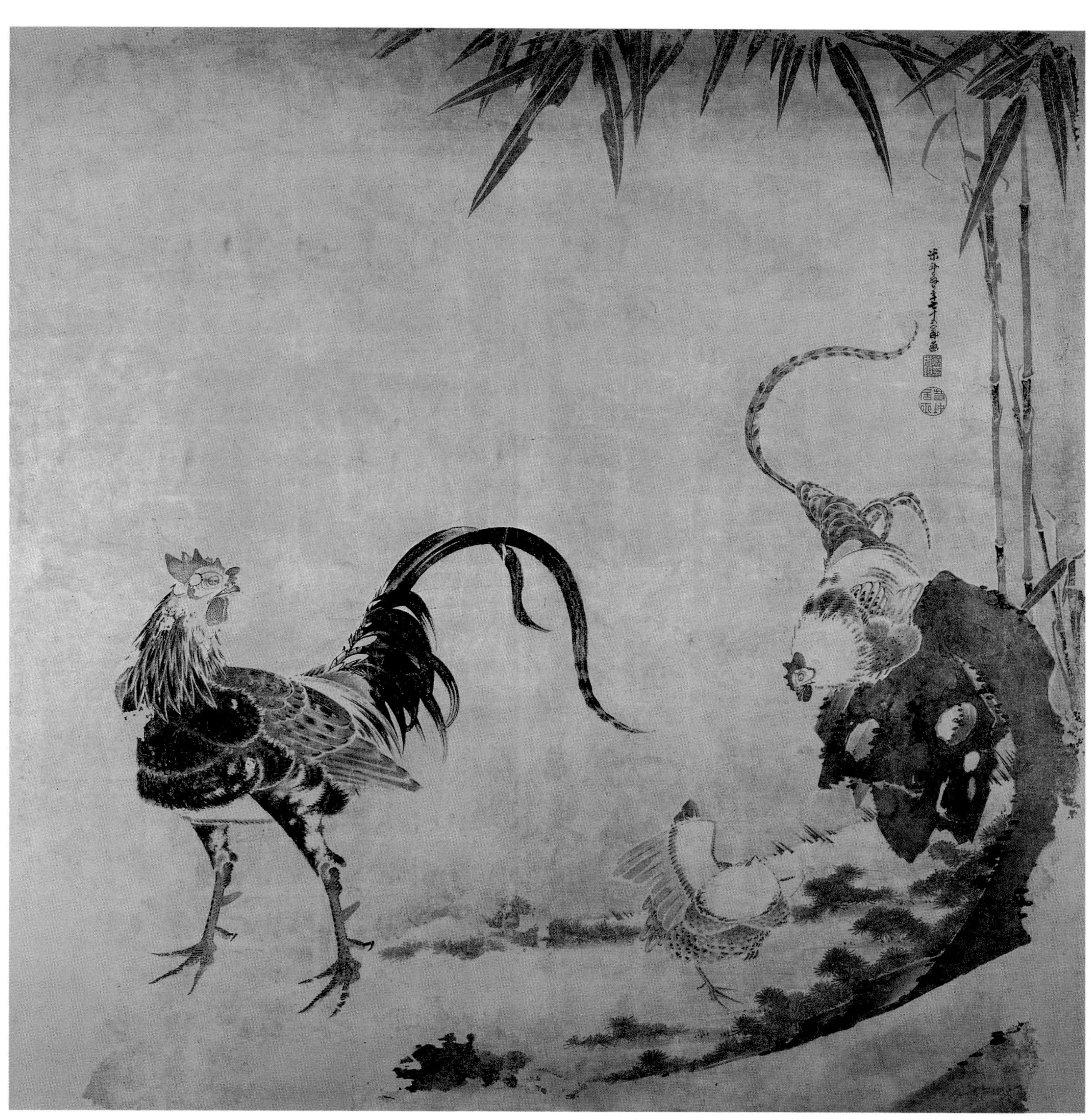

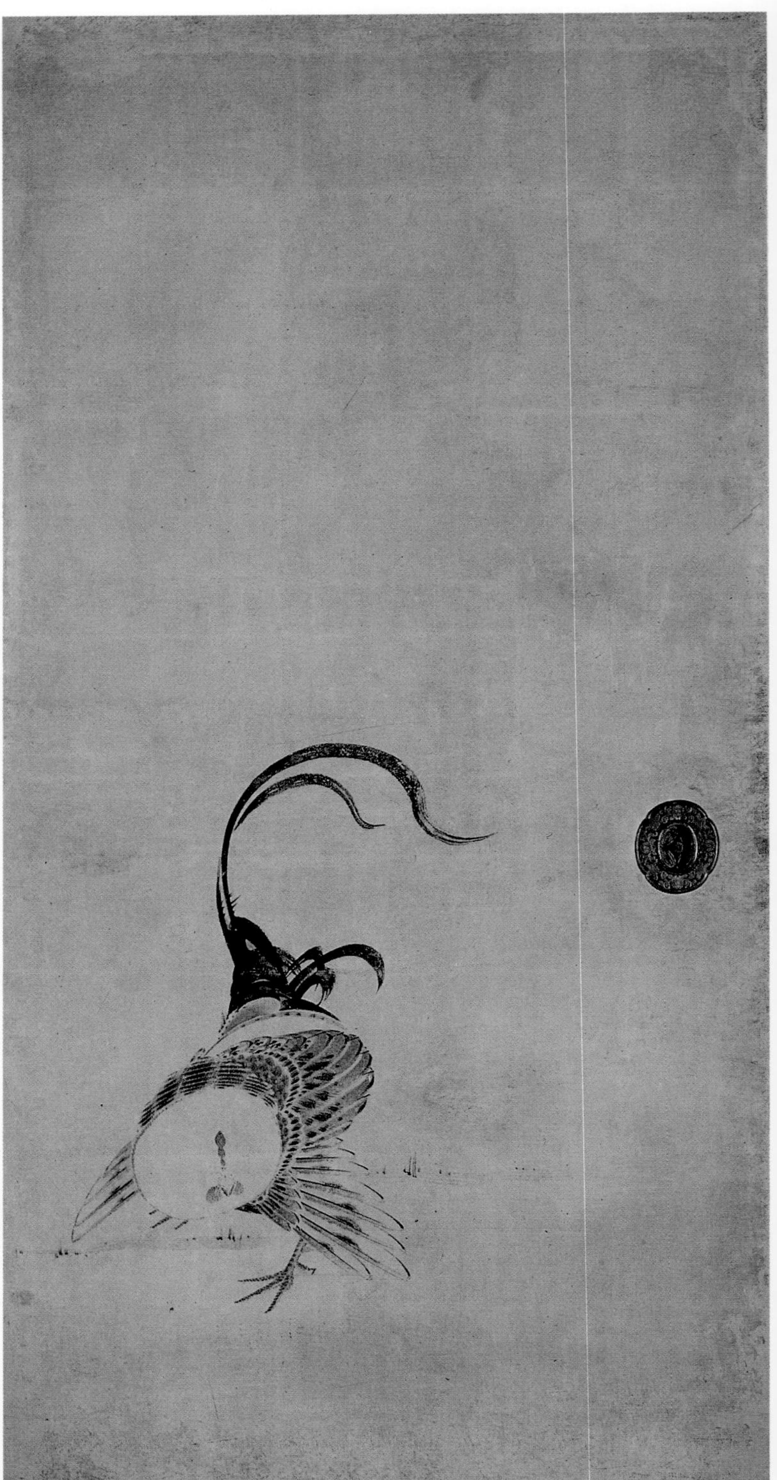

36

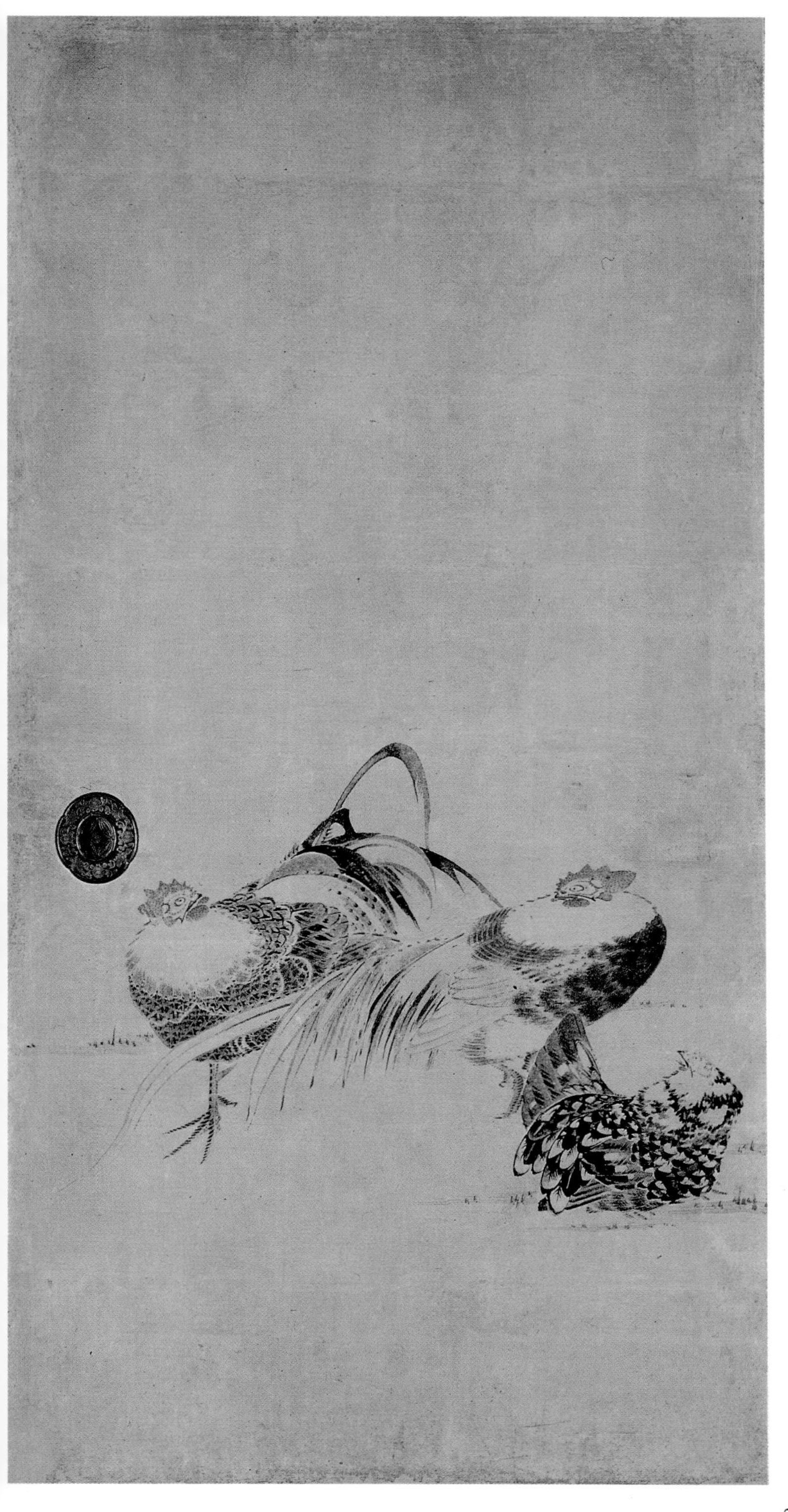

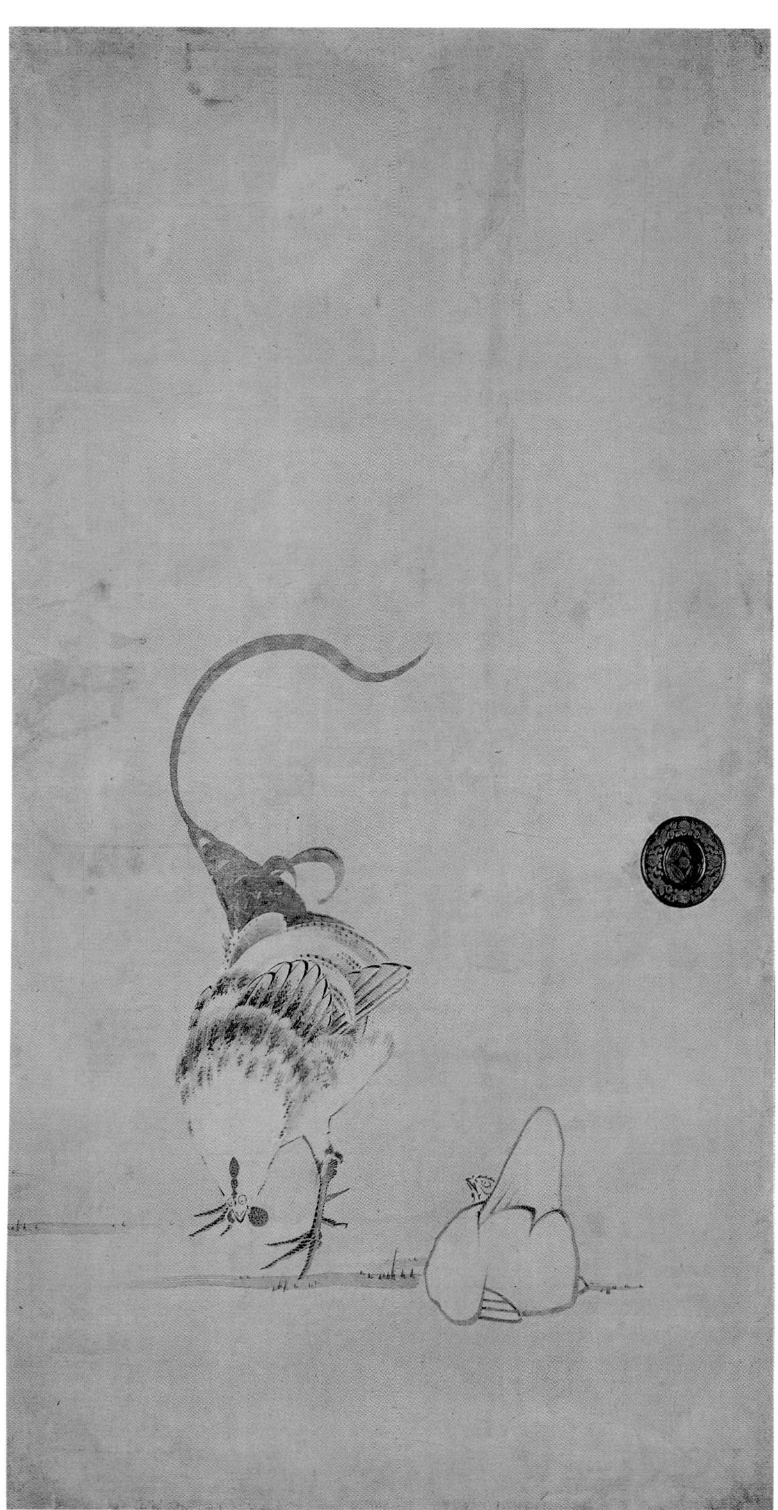

36

37 *Cockscomb and Mantis*

1791

Colors on silk, hanging scroll
103.1 × 55.5 cm
Signature: *Painted by Old Man Beito in his seventy-sixth year*
Colophons: see below

SEALS:
square intaglio: *Tō Jokin-in*
square relief: *Jakuchū koji*
Private collection, Kyoto Prefecture

The plant known in English as the cockscomb, which blossoms in summer and fall and whose flowers resemble the comb of a rooster, is known in Japanese as *niwatori no atama* (chicken's head). Jakuchū painted the stalk of the cockscomb turning and twisting at acute angles, with shockingly bright red and yellow blossoms at its tip. The purple and green of the stem have a strange, flowing motion, like a decorative pattern in running ink; the leaves are separate from the stem and arranged in peculiar shapes. The blue ink wash that covers the entire background, stopping precisely at the outlines of the forms, flattens the sky. After the *Dōshoku Sai-e* scrolls (NO. 14), Jakuchū painted only a few polychrome works on silk grounds, including *White Plum and Golden Pheasant* (private collection, Tokyo), *Monkeys in a Blossoming Peach Tree* (private collection, Hyōgo Prefecture; FIG. 13), and the present painting, but these pieces show that his creative power in this medium had by no means been exhausted. These works continue the style of the later *Dōshoku Sai-e* scrolls, sharing their arrangement of motifs in very shallow space, as if they were on a flat surface.

The fire of 1788 not only undermined Jakuchū's health, but shook the economic foundations of his life. In 1765, the year the artist had donated twenty-seven paintings (twenty-four of the *Dōshoku Sai-e* series as well as the Śākyamuni triptych) to the Shōkokuji, a three-way contract had been drawn up among him, his neighborhood organization, and the Shōkokuji. It stated that after Jakuchū died, the house in which he lived was to be turned over to the neighborhood and that, in return, it was to pay for memorial services at the Shōkokuji on every anniversary of his death. In 1791, however, as a result of Jakuchū's extreme economic distress in the aftermath of the fire, it became necessary to dissolve the contract (as noted in the records of the Shōkokuji). In this painting, the image of the mantis brandishing his pincers at the empty sky seems to be a metaphor for the penniless Jakuchū.

The colophon written by Keishū Dōrin, the same person who had inscribed the earlier *Gourd* (NO. 23), reads: "How beautiful is the cockscomb crowned in red. The mantis loves it and will not leave its side. Written by the ascetic priest Gabi Kei [shū]." The research of Takeda Kōichi and others has shown that, in addition to his contribution to these two paintings, Keishū also wrote a colophon for Jakuchū's *Skull* (Rinkōji, Tokyo).[61]

The present owners of the painting, the Teramura family, are descended from Teramura Hyakuchi (1748–1835), a wholesale haberdasher who studied poetry under Yosa Buson (1716–1783) and contributed to his economic support. Their collection is known for its many examples of Buson's painting and calligraphy; it also includes a few works by other artists from Kyoto.

Among the panels of *Flowers and Grasses* that Jakuchū painted in his final years for the ceiling of the Kannon hall at the Sekihōji (168 of which today decorate the ceiling of the Shingyōji) is one depicting a cockscomb of the same shape as that in the present painting.

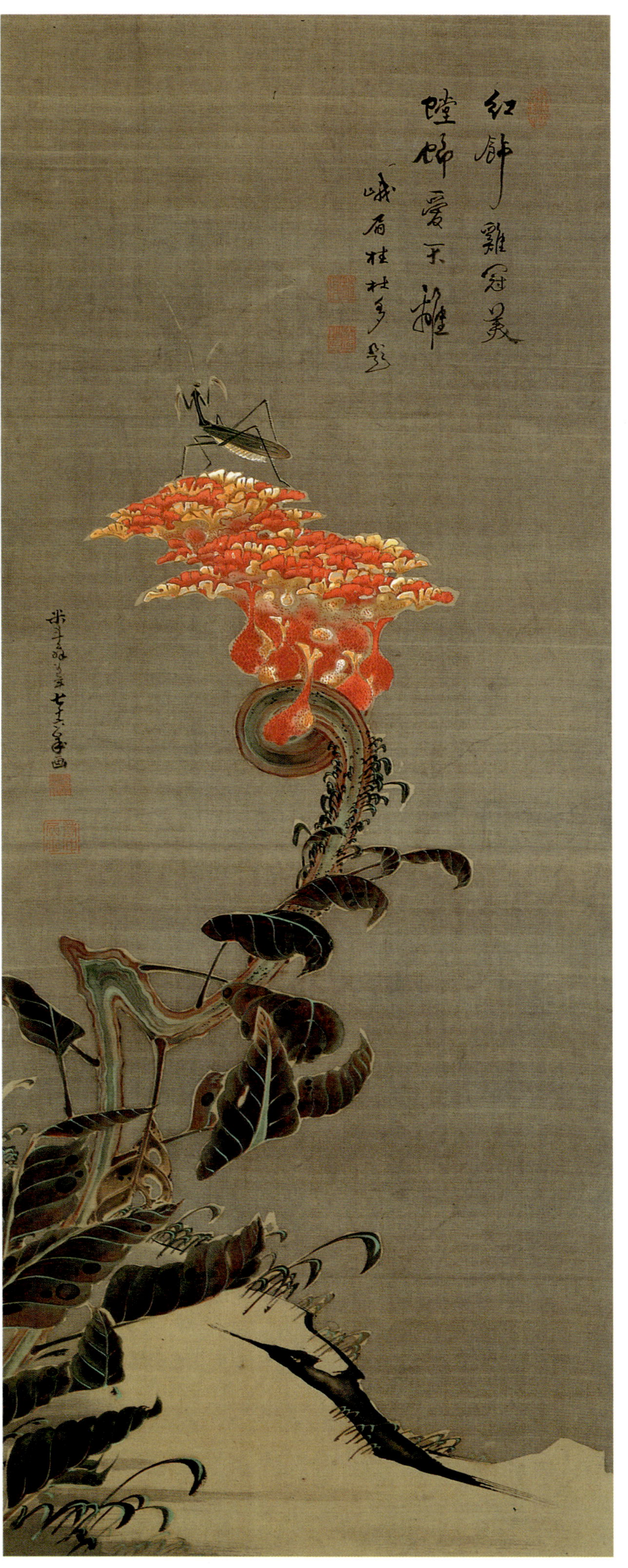

38 *Weathered Skull*

1794

Ink on paper, hanging scroll
100.8 × 58.3 cm
Signature: *Painted by Old Man Beito, age seventy-nine*
Colophon: see below

SEALS:
square intaglio: *Tō Jokin-in*
round relief: *Jakuchū koji*
Saifukuji, Osaka Prefecture

This painting depicts human bones lying in an open field, exposed to the elements. Its theme, memento mori—the evanescence of this world, the ephemerality of life—is in accordance with Buddhist teaching. Three other works by Jakuchū depicting the same subject are: a hanging scroll painted in *gofun*, with an inscription by Keishū Dōrin (Rinkōji, Tokyo); a scroll with an inscription by a Zen monk, executed in the same manner as the work under discussion here (Muryōji, Wakayama Prefecture); and a hanging scroll with an inscription by Baisaō (known only from a photograph in the collection of Tanimura Tameumi; present location unknown). The third piece is presumed to have been done in the same manner as the present work, but it may have been executed in the *taku-hanga* technique (see No. 26).

The idea of painting the ground in black and representing the bones with sections of uninked paper, as seen here, was probably inspired by the reversal process of *taku-hanga* printing. In the year 1794, when Jakuchū painted this work, Hiraga Shōsai (1745–1805), a writer of Chinese verse (*kanshi*), visited the painter's house just outside the gate of the Sekihōji. He listened to Jakuchū's tales and admired the lotuses he had painted on sliding screens in the manner of a stone rubbing, noting in the *Shōsai Hikki* (vol. 3): "He is fond of unusual things."[62] The lotus composition, which no longer exists, was formerly thought to have been an ink painting done in a style similar to that of *Lotus Pond* in the Saifukuji (No. 35). Since, in a stone rubbing, the image is created by rubbing the paper into the crevices of a stele or other stone or metal object, the Sekihōji work was probably an ink painting that simulated a *taku-hanga* print, with the subject in white and the background in black. Even when he was in his late seventies, Jakuchū was attempting such novel projects.

The *taku-hanga* concept was very well suited to the theme of *Weathered Skull*. The black holes in the skull, which has been bleached white by the sun and weathered by the wind and rain, evoke a sense of nothingness. Both the Rinkōji scroll and the one known only from its photograph show a preoccupation with anatomical accuracy, as does the *Picture of a Skull* (in the Daijōji, Hyōgo Prefecture) by Maruyama Ōkyo, but the present work reveals no interest in literal detail. Instead, the rough brush strokes depicting the grassy ground add an air of desolation.

Written by Edo-period poet Kagawa Kageki (1768–1834), the verse attached to Jakuchū's painting reads:

Never darkening,
constantly it shines, this moon—
and if it is so
there will surely be no one
that sleeps through the night of this world.

This poem is one of a pair that appears under the topic "Moon" in the Autumn section of Kageki's anthology *Keien Isshi* (*A Branch from the Katsura-tree Garden*, 1830).[63] Whether or not the calligraphy is by Kageki himself is still to be decided by the specialists, but the inscription clearly was not attached to the painting from the start, as Kageki was not appointed to the vice-governorship of Nagato (the office given in the inscription) until 1803, three years after Jakuchū's death. This painting was probably executed in Kyoto and then sent to Osaka for some unknown reason.

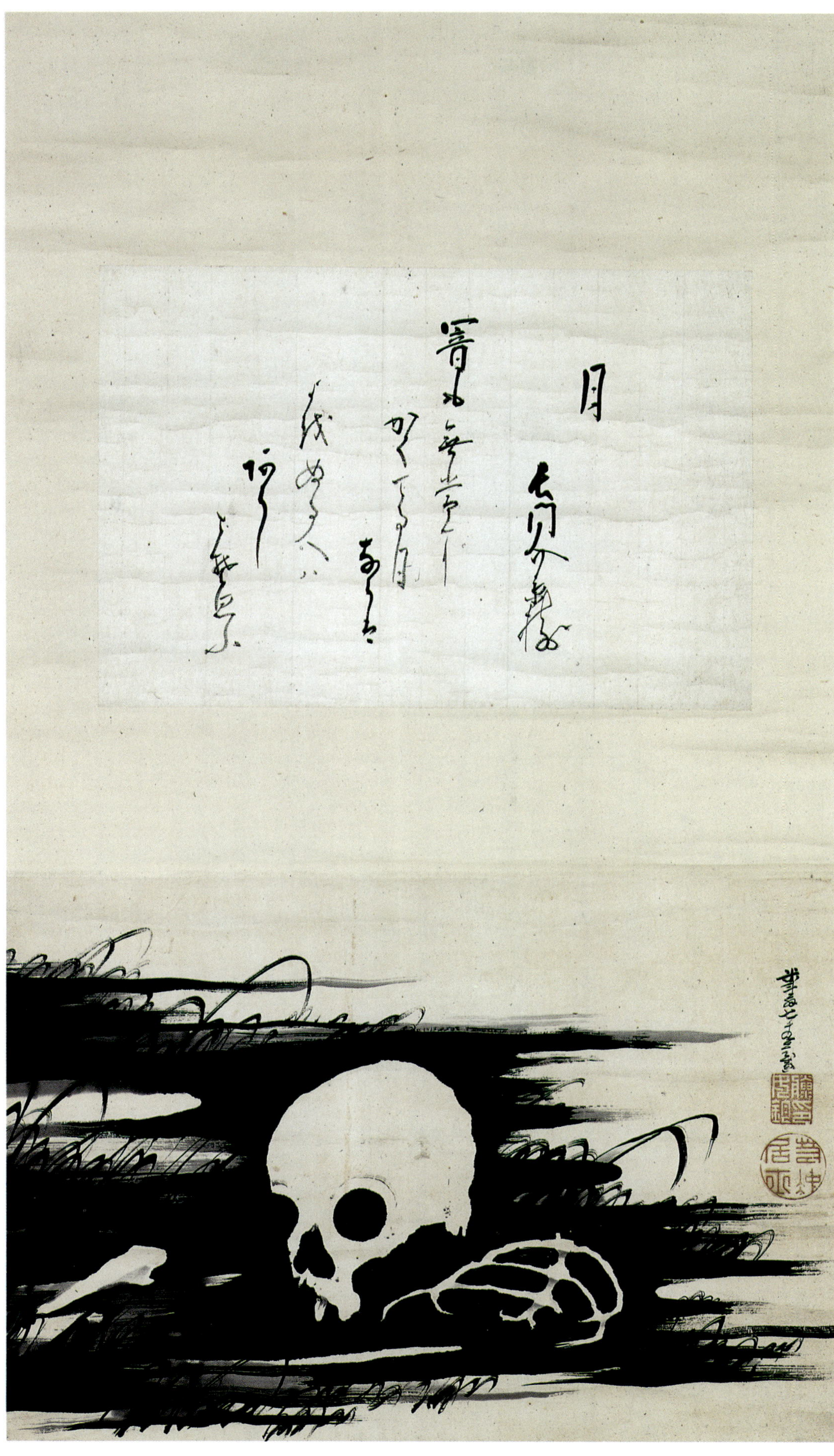

39 *Two Roosters and a Hen*

1796

Ink on paper, hanging scroll
143.5 × 52.5 cm
Inscription:
Painted by Old Man Beito, age eighty-one

SEALS:
square intaglio: *Tō Jokin-in*
round relief: *Jakuchū koji*
Private collection, Osaka Prefecture

Here Jakuchū created a lively image of two roosters and a hen. The rooster standing on the edge of a slope with one leg raised is stylistically almost identical to the rooster in the artist's *Well Bucket and Rooster* (Yamato Bunkakan, Nara Prefecture), which he painted in 1795. Those two scrolls, along with *Chickens*, a pair of six-panel folding screens painted in 1797 (private collection, Hyōgo Prefecture), provide criteria for judging the ink paintings of fowl that Jakuchū did in his later years.

It seems that in the artist's later years his followers would paint pictures emulating his designs and would affix his seals to these works. Thus, even when the seals are genuine, it is difficult to assert unequivocally that a late work was by Jakuchū himself. (The only documentary reference to Jakuchū's disciples, except for extant works on which appear the names of such followers as Jakuen, Ichū, Shochū, Taichū, and others, is an entry dated 1787 in the diary of Prince Shinjin noting that he granted permission to four of Jakuchū's disciples to witness the airing of various works of art kept in the storehouse of the Myōhōin.)[64] Professor Kobayashi Tadashi is the first scholar to have taken up the question of such paintings produced in Jakuchū's atelier.[65] During the Edo period this sort of studio work was quite normal and was not regarded as improper in any way, but nowadays issues such as an artist's individual style are taken very seriously, making it necessary to distinguish between works by masters and those of their disciples.

The fowl in this scroll, overflowing with vitality, are unmistakably from the artist's hand, but works in which the brushwork is weak and the birds' forms are less inventive must have been painted by other artists. The chickens represented here have a unified, coherent quality, a supple sense of underlying structure. Jakuchū painted their plumage with a strong, tactile sensitivity and a deft touch, in contrasting tones of ink.

The two seals imprinted on this work are the ones most common both on Jakuchū's own paintings and on pieces from his studio. In the *Dōshoku Sai-e* scrolls (NO. 14) and in *Rain Dragon* (NO. 22) the square intaglio seal *Tō Jokin-in* is not damaged, but impressions on later works, such as *Śākyamuni Returning from the Mountains* (private collection, Hyōgo Prefecture; FIG. 39) and *Blossoming Plum and Golden Pheasant* (private collection, Tokyo), show some damage to the lower right-hand side of the seal. Again, in the case of *Monkeys in a Blossoming Peach Tree* (private collection, Hyōgo Prefecture; FIG. 13)—which, thanks to the inscription of the Ōbaku priest Hakujun Shōkō (1695–1776), is datable to the period between 1772 and 1776—there is slight additional damage to the upper left-hand, upper right-hand, and lower left-hand portions of the seal. The round relief seal *Jakuchū koji* showed damage from the outset near the center of the left-hand side of its outline; in the *Five Hundred Arhats* (NO. 27) and in *Vegetable Parinirvāna* (NO. 32), there is damage near the center of the right-hand side of the outline as well. These subtle changes in the condition of seals provide substantial assistance in estimating the dates of works and in deciding issues of authenticity.

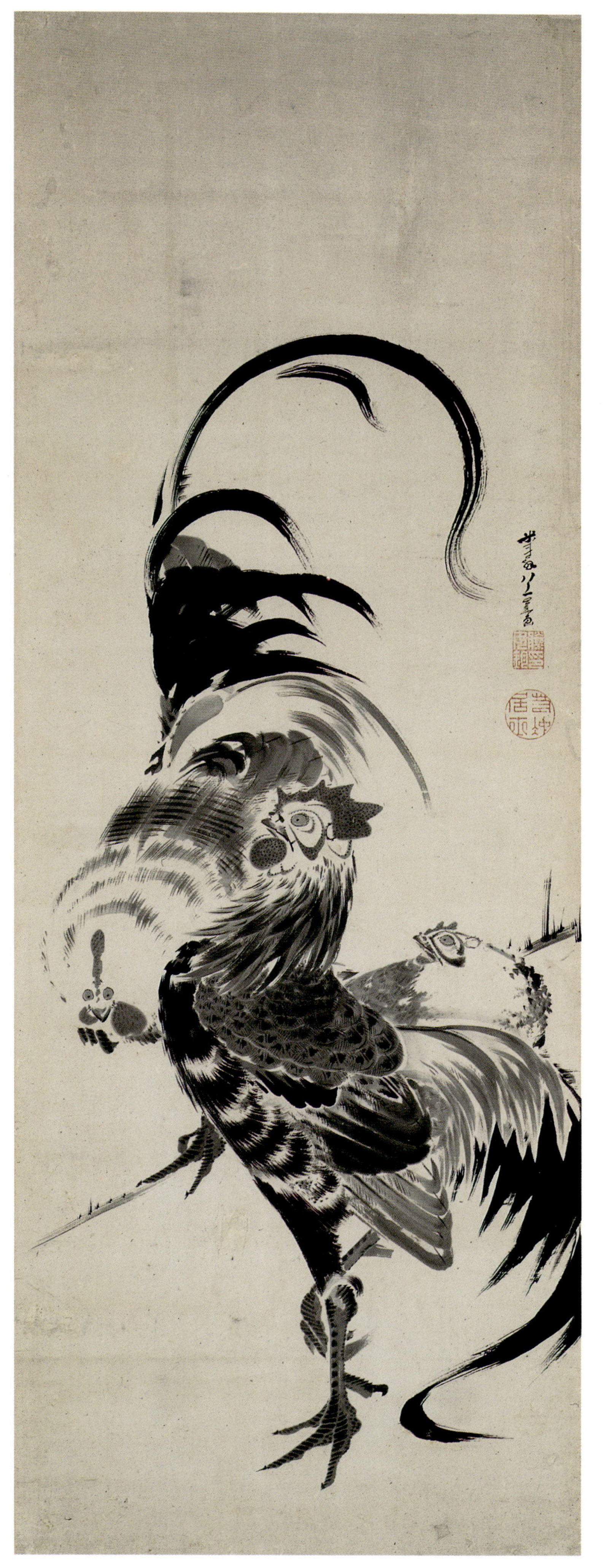

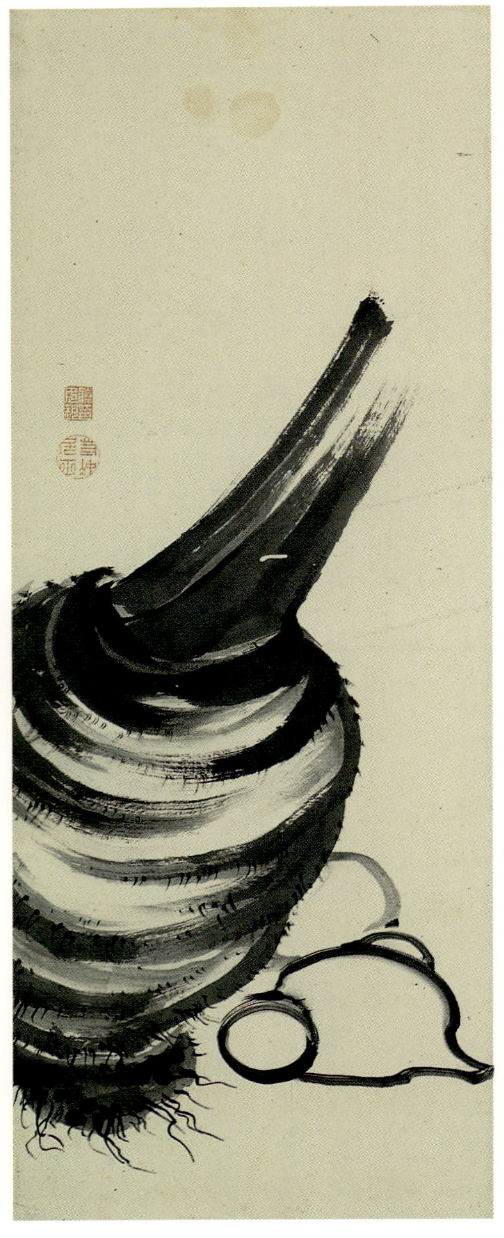
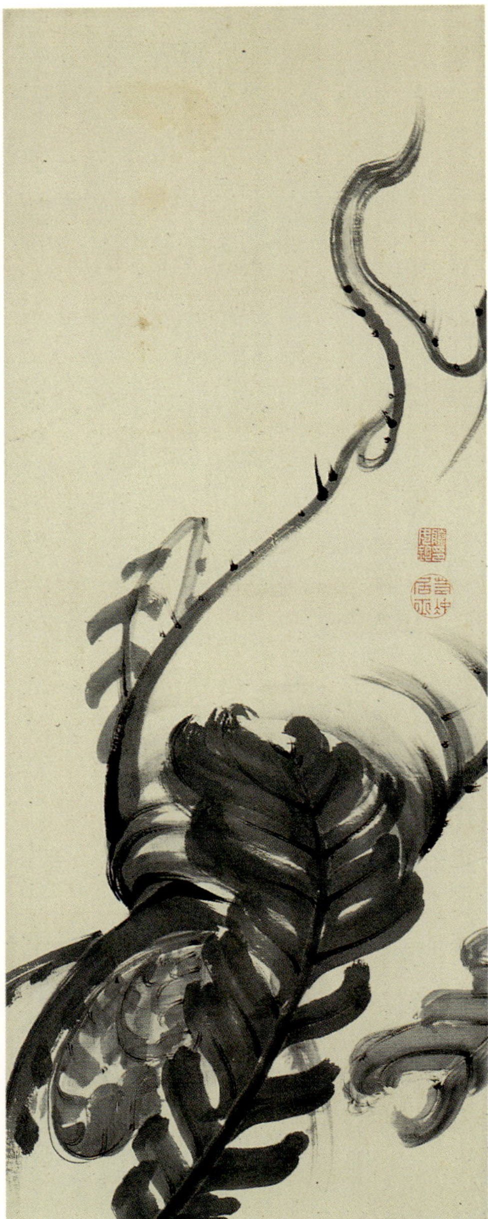
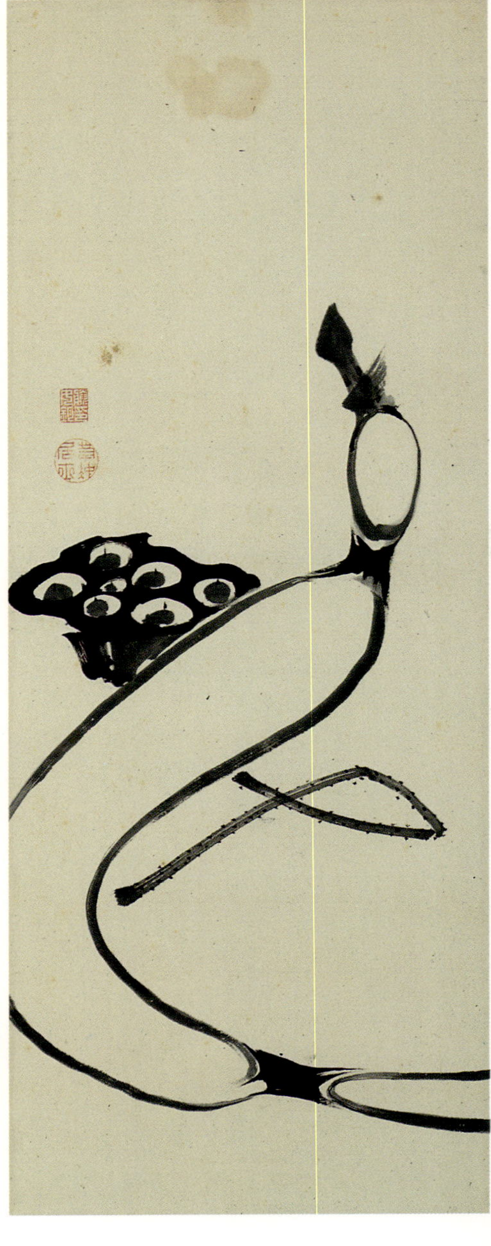

40 *Vegetables*

1796

Ink on paper (independent compositions on each panel), pair of six-panel folding screens
124.0 × 33.3 cm (each)
Signature: *Painted by Beitoan at age eighty-one*

SEALS:
square intaglio: *Tō Jokin*
round relief: *Jakuchū koji*
Private collection, Hyōgo Prefecture

The screen above of this pair depicts (from right to left) pea pods, turnip, melons, lotus root, *daikon*, and taro root; the screen on the next pages depicts eggplants, *matsutake* mushroom, squash, arrowheads, yam, and winter melon. In both screens, each vegetable occupies an entire panel. Jakuchū abandoned his meticulous technique here, delineating the subjects with rough brush strokes. Unlike the forms of vegetables he had depicted in such earlier works as *Vegetable Parinirvāna* (NO. 32) and *Vegetables and Insects* (handscroll, 1792),[66] those in the present screens demonstrate the resurgence of Jakuchū's artistic vigor as he entered his eighties. Furthermore, the artists Sōga Shōhaku and Nagasawa Rosetsu, who were also active in the Kyoto area, frequently created compositions in which they boldly enlarged their subjects, and it is possible that Jakuchū was influenced by such works.

The screens are accompanied by a document of provenance. Although it contains some dubious points, such as giving 1884 as the date for the memorial service of 1885 (see NO. 45), this record is of much interest. It reads as follows:

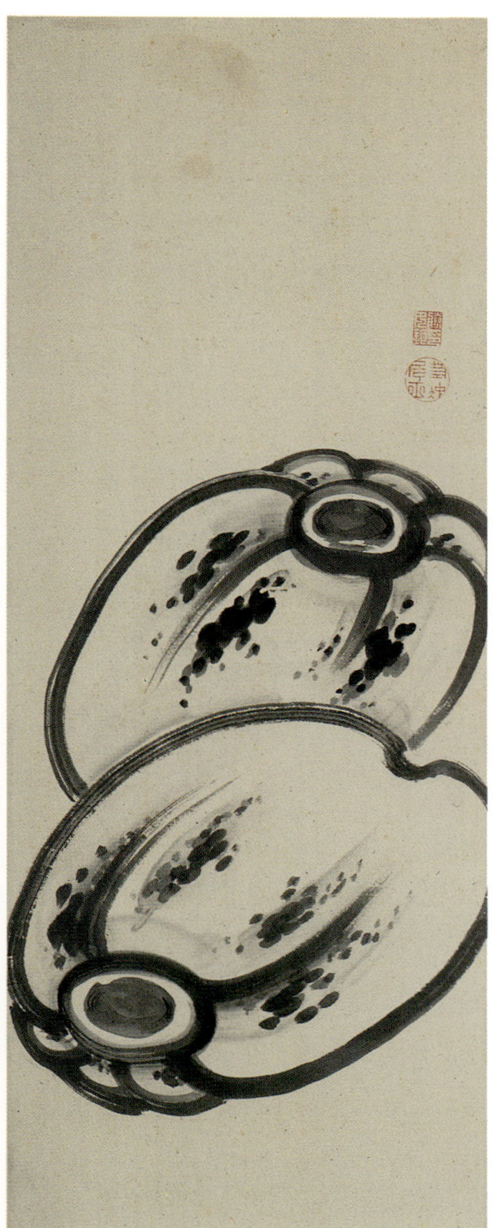

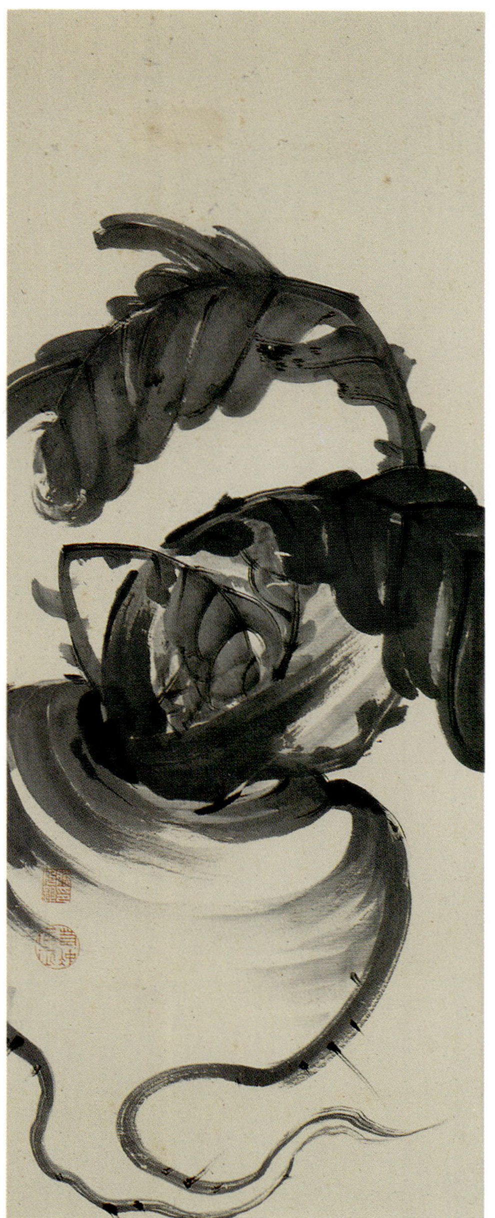

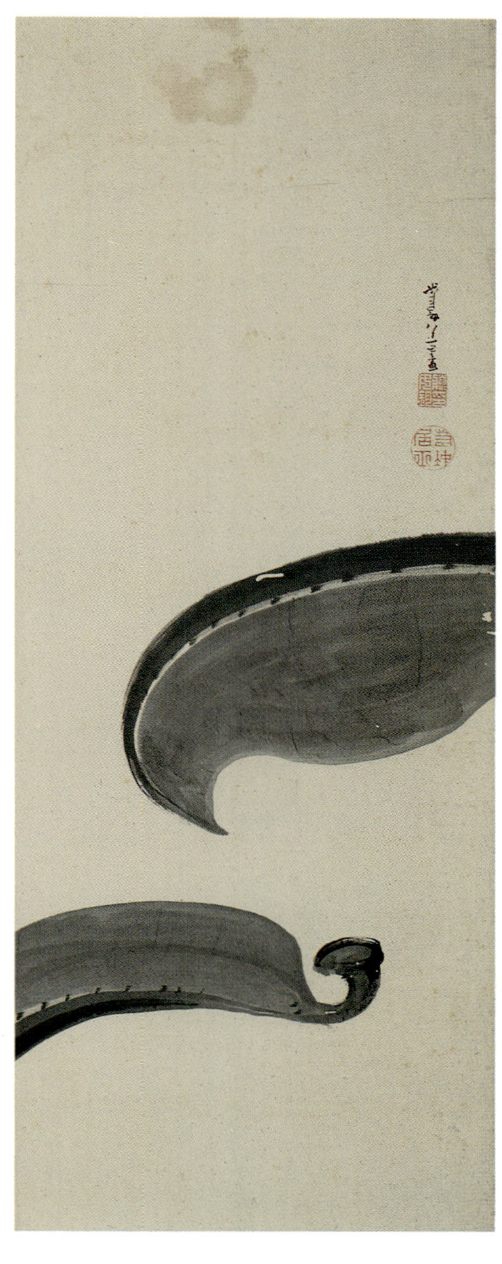

These twelve paintings are the monochrome works of the master Jakuchū, a monk of the Sekihōji at Hyakujōzan in Fukakusa, Kyoto. Mr. Takeuchi Shinzō, the grandfather of Mr. Takeuchi Yoshishige, received them as a gift of friendship from Jakuchū. In the summer of 1798, Katsuno, a wealthy gentleman from Osaka, built a Kannon hall at the Sekihōji. Takeuchi Shinzō made substantial donations to the completion of this hall. When the construction was completed, all of the necessary Buddhist altar objects and utensils for the reception of guests were provided. Jakuchū was overjoyed, and he produced these screens, which show his unique, eccentric means of expression, as a way of demonstrating his admiration and indebtedness to Takeuchi Shinzō. Shinzō admired and cherished these paintings, but owing to the press of business he never managed to have them mounted. In this unmounted state they were passed down to his grandson Yoshishige, who also kept them for his private pleasure and seldom showed them to anyone, a state of affairs that continued, until April 1884. In that year [sic], on the occasion of the eighty-fifth anniversary of Jakuchū's death, a commemorative celebration was held at the Shōkokuji, and some dozens of monochrome works by him were displayed freely to the public. These screens were among those exhibited, and they were greatly admired. In March 1886, on the occasion of the fiftieth anniversary of Shinzō's death, they were made into a pair of folding screens and were shown to many visitors. In addition, I was asked to write about their history. I think of the many decades that have passed with the paintings safely stored in Yoshishige's storehouse. They have suffered no deterioration and have not been damaged by insects; their pristine appearance has been preserved just as it was. It is apparent how well the paintings were cared for. A man of old once said: "Even without seeing the man himself, if one looks at something that the man has treasured, it is like seeing the man himself." Clearly, Yoshishige's feeling for these works, and the manner in which he regarded them, is somehow different from the interest that other viewers feel toward them. Written on February 11, 1887. Shakuan Sawada Toshinori.

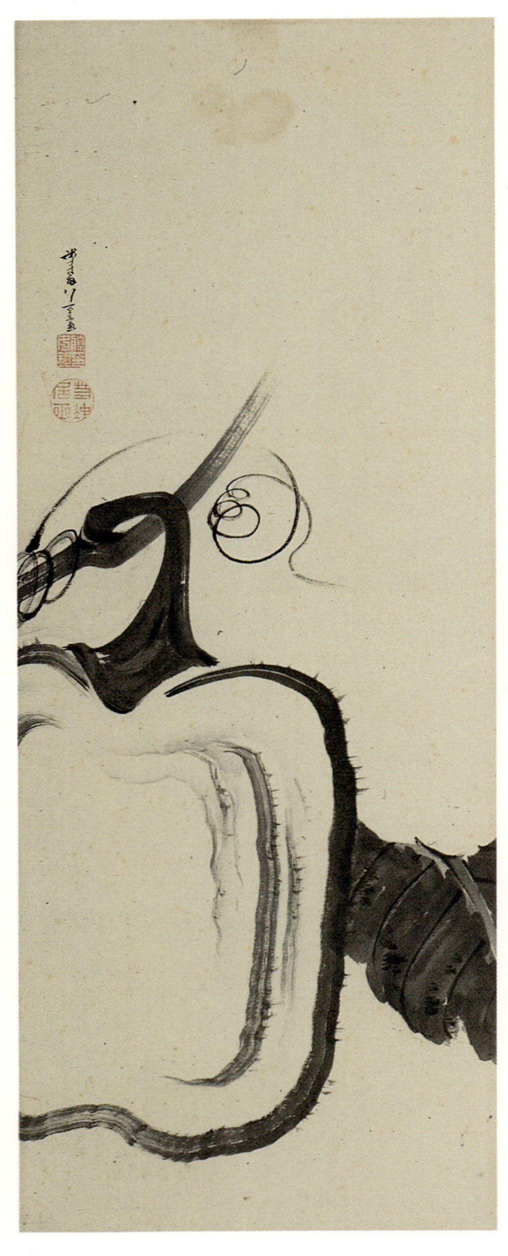

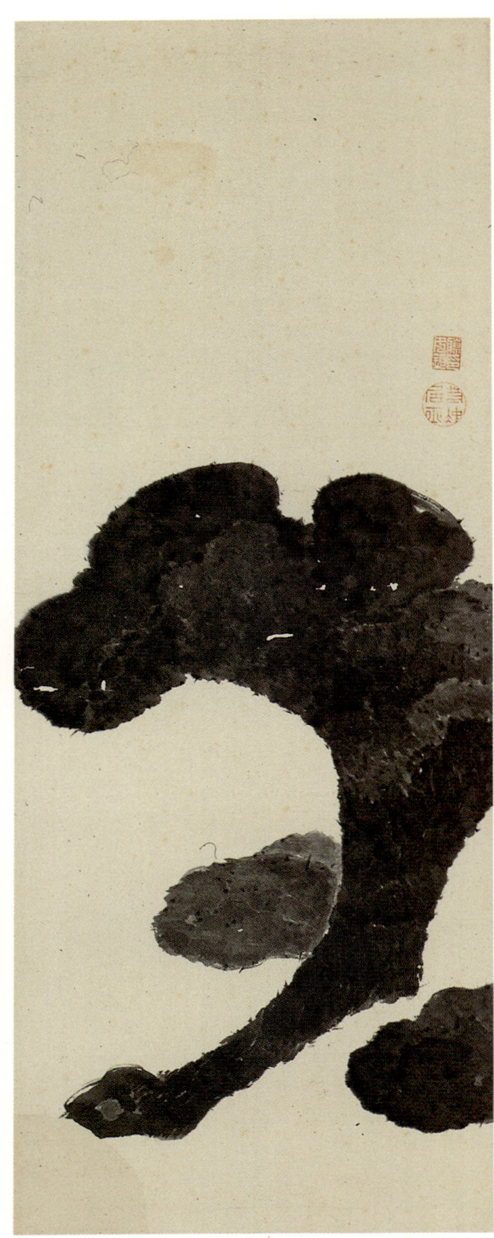

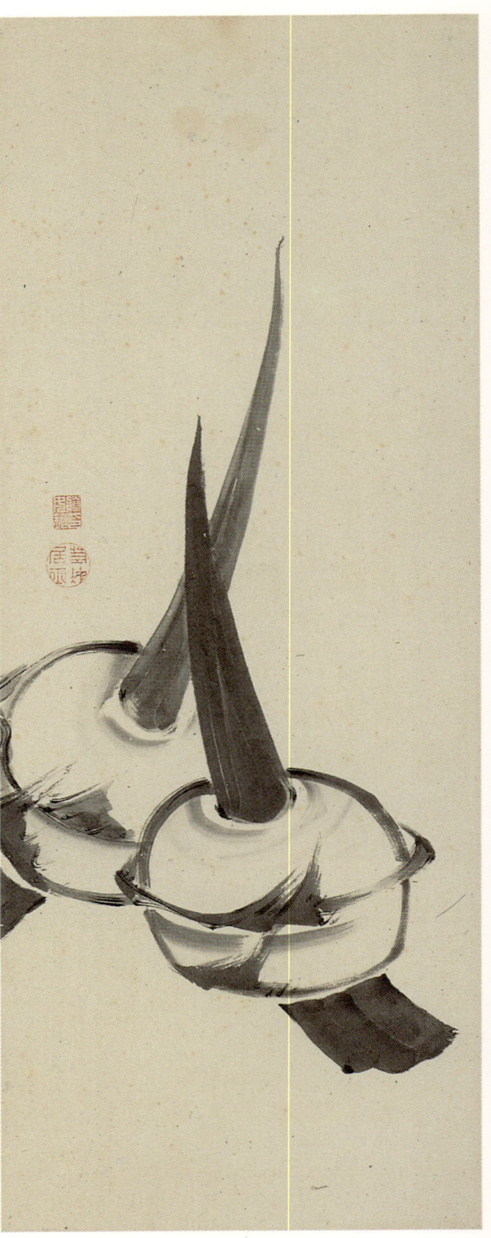

40

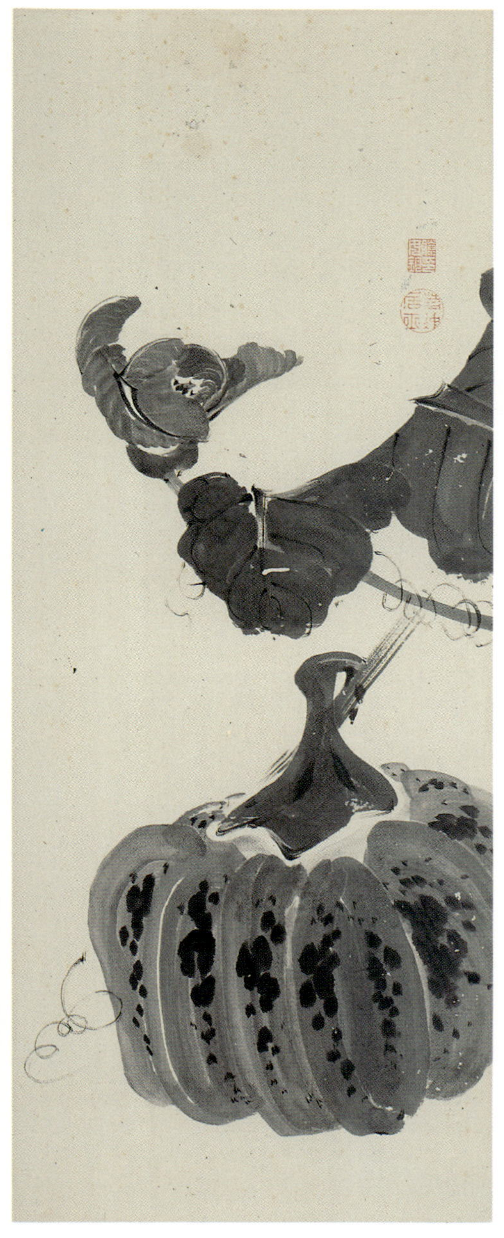
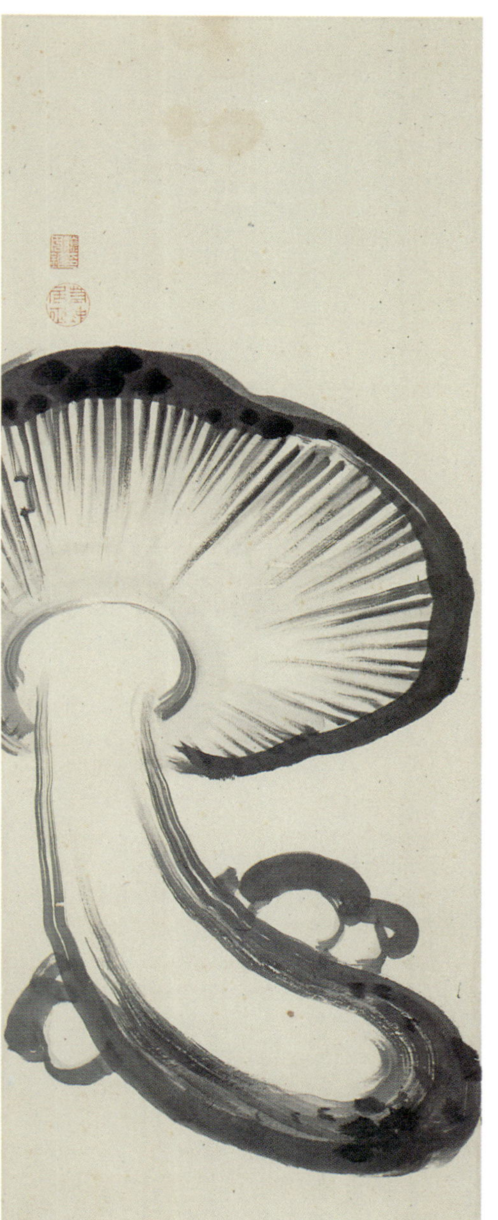
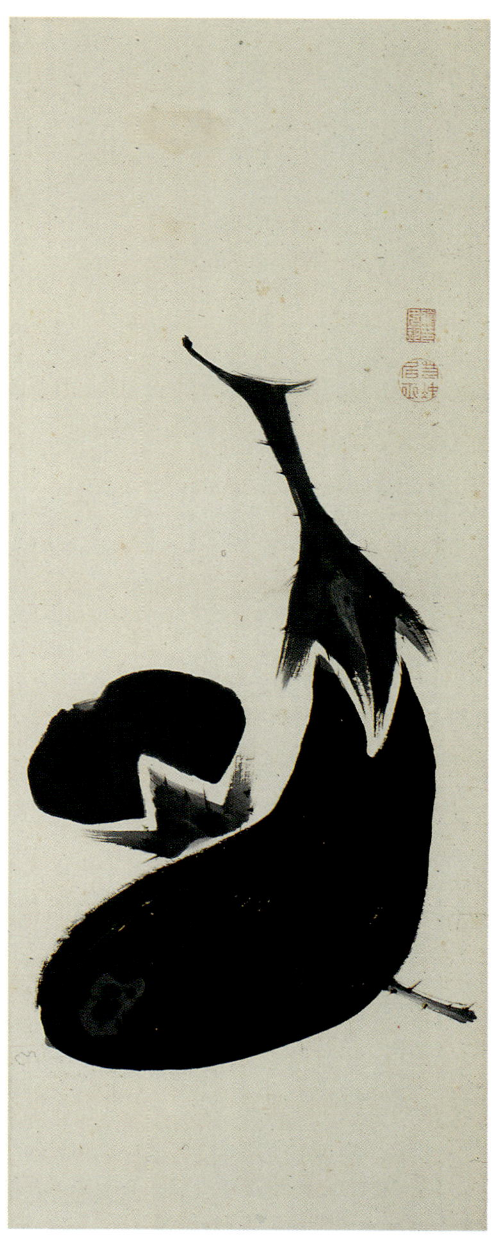

40

41 *Portrait of Hoan Jōei*

1797

Ink on silk, hanging scroll
170.0 × 80.5 cm
Signature: *Painted by Old Man Beito, age eighty-two*
Colophon: see below

SEALS:
square intaglio: *Tō Jokin*
square relief: *Jakuchū koji*
Mampukuji, Kyoto Prefecture

Hoan Jōei (1722–1796) was the twenty-third abbot of the Mampukuji. Jakuchū depicted him here in three-quarter profile, seated on a round mat and holding a *kyōsaku* (an oak stick used to hit the shoulders of meditating Zen monks in order to prevent drowsing or to admonish lapses in concentration). The artist delineated the facial features with shading in minute detail, but he roughly sketched in the body, clothed in a priest's robe, with ink lines of varying thickness. In fact, he so abbreviated the hands that they are barely recognizable. Into the area surrounding the figure, he painted a blue ink wash.

Paintings of the *chinsō* genre—commemorative portraits of Zen priests passed on to disciples—were generally done in color in a realistic style; in particular, the Ōbaku sect traditionally made realistic, heavily colored portraits based in style on shading and coloring methods that incorporated Western techniques. The manner of painting in the present piece, done entirely in monochrome ink and rather roughly executed, is unusual in Zen portraiture.

Neverthless, this portrait undoubtedly has a close relationship with some aspects of the Ōbaku painting tradition. For instance, Jakuchū's work has obvious similarities to portraits by the late Ming artist Ch'en Hsien (active 1634–1654) depicting Śākyamuni, Bodhisattvas, Avalokiteśvara, and thirty-three Ch'an patriarchs (inscribed by Yin-yüan Lung-ch'i in an album at the Mampukuji). Clearly Jakuchū based his portrait of Hoan on the style and composition of such figure paintings, and shortcomings in representing the volume of the shoulders and the garment can be explained by the artist's excessive adherence to this method of depiction. Jakuchū, who worked in a representational manner for his portrait of Baisaō (NOS. 18, 19), was certainly capable of producing a more realistic portrayal. That he chose not to do so for the present work, but rather to create such a clumsy yet forthright portrait, may reflect a deliberate attempt to express the independent, forceful character of Hoan (who on one occasion was punished by temple officials) calligraphic, linear movement far removed from physical realism of the body.

Although most colophons were written after a painting was completed, in the case of this work the events occurred in the reverse order. The colophon was written one year before Hoan's death, and the portrait was painted two years later (when Jakuchū was eighty-two years of age). The colophon reads:

To serve at many temples; to propagate the good plans learned there, acknowledging that one is capable of committing every sort of indiscretion, and revealing frankly in one's face the sense of embarrassment in one's heart; to rectify the confused [Buddhist] lineages of the old rules, and to correct the bad sects of the present day in accordance with rules established in the past; to dedicate body and mind to the mundane world; to vow to the Dragon King [the protector of the Law] to serve without resting; [such was my ideal, but] alas, I have grown old. The years pass quickly. Though I struggle to assert my meager will, my remaining days are short. It is lamentable indeed. Tenth Month of 1795, written under the southern window of the Kanrodō [Hall of Sweet Dew; abbot's residence] by Hoan [Jō]ei, twenty-third abbot of the Mampukuji.[67]

〻下
偶書于甘露堂南窓
本山二十三主肯庵英自題
日短焉 嘆 乙酉年上冬
不住堤〻吾望矣争且適足寸表〻
之彝派其子心於華莉擔龍云〻
未満面〻肩改正古規之亂統肖度仁他
住山數處宜〻歟徽猷[illegible]滑弥天白華窓

42 *Carp*

1798

Ink on paper, hanging scroll
103.2 × 30.6 cm
Signature: *Painted by Old Man Beito at age eighty-three*

SEALS:
square intaglio: *Tō Jokin-in*
round relief: *Jakuchū koji*
Private collection, Osaka Prefecture

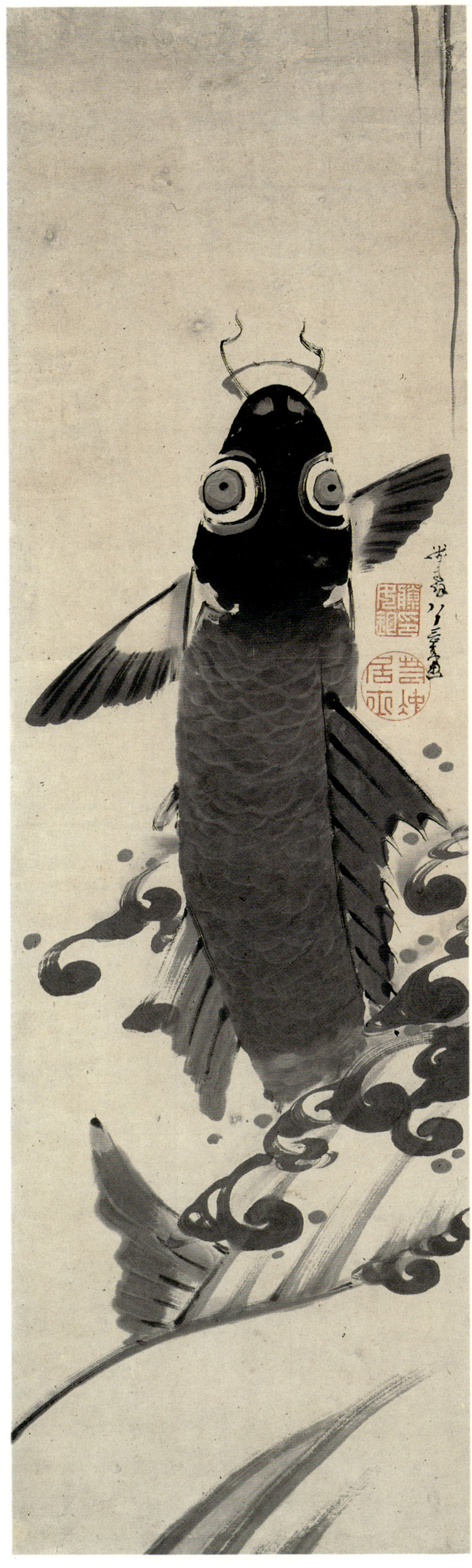

Lung-men (Dragon Gate) is a mountain located in China between Ho-chin County in Shansi Province and Han-ch'eng County in Shensi Province. Because of the falls at this point in the Yellow River, it would be extremely difficult for a fish to swim upstream: thus it was said that any fish that succeeded in doing so would turn into a dragon (see NO. 22). On the basis of this story, which was recorded in the *Hou Han Shu* (*History of the Later Han Dynasty*), the expression "going up Lung-men" came to mean "striving to improve one's position in life."[68] With its auspicious connotations, a painting of a carp ascending a waterfall was likely to be given as a gift to a person hoping for success.

This theme, which was also depicted by artists of the Nan-p'in and Maruyama-Shijō schools, was utilized by Jakuchū in the present painting as a means of displaying the distinctively shaped breaking wave forms unique to his style. Two years earlier, the artist had painted a carp of the same type, which is recorded in a sale catalogue (see list below). The carp in that painting, which rises through the stream, wrapping the water around its body like a garment, has greater strength and originality than the present work. Although the brushwork in this example is less vital, the work nevertheless is probably by Jakuchū himself.

The works of Jakuchū's later years include many whose date is known by virtue of the artist's age having been recorded on them. Those presently known, including some whose current whereabouts are uncertain, are listed below:

Cacti and Fowl, 1790 (sliding screens, colors on gold-leafed paper; FIG. 14)
Lotus Pond, 1790 (NO. 35)
Landscape, 1790. Saifukuji, Osaka Prefecture (hanging scroll, ink on paper)
Roosters and Hens, 1790 (NO. 36)
Cockscomb and Mantis, 1791 (NO. 37)
Vegetables and Insects, 1792. Recorded in Kyoto 1927 (handscroll, colors on silk)
Horse-beans and Insects, 1792. Recorded in Kyoto 1927; Satō 1987, pl. 117 (hanging scroll, colors on silk)
Grapes, Rooster, and Hen, 1792. Metropolitan Museum of Art, New York (hanging scroll, colors on silk)
Grapes and Fowl, 1792. Recorded in Tamura sale catalogue, March 1929 (hanging scroll, colors on silk)
Fushimi Dolls, 1792. Recorded in Viscount Niwa sale catalogue, Oct. 1919 (hanging scroll, colors on silk)
Six Poets, 1793. Private collection, Aichi Prefecture (hanging scroll, ink on paper)
Chrysanthemums, 1793. Fogg Art Museum, Harvard University, Cambridge, Mass. (hanging scroll, colors on silk)
Weathered Skull, 1794 (NO. 38)
Well Bucket and Fowl, 1795. Yamato Bunkakan, Nara Prefecture (ink on paper)
Han Shan and Shih Te, 1795. Private collection, Akita Prefecture (hanging scroll, ink on paper)
Chrysanthemums, 1795. Private collection, Osaka Prefecture (pair of six-panel folding screens, ink on paper)
Elephant and Whale, 1795. Recorded in Baron Kawasaki sale catalogue, Oct. 1928 (pair of six-panel folding screens; ink on paper)
Two Roosters and a Hen, 1796 (NO. 39)
Vegetables, 1796 (NO. 40).
Rooster and Hen, 1796. Private collection, Kagawa Prefecture (hanging scroll, ink on paper)
Fowl, 1796. Photograph of this work in Tokyo National Cultural Properties Research Institute (hanging scroll, ink on paper)
Fowl, 1796. Recorded in Katagiri sale catalogue, Oct. 1916 (six hanging scrolls, ink on paper)
Birds of Prey, 1796. Recorded in Kyoto 1927 (hanging scroll, ink on paper)
Carp, 1796. Recorded in Viscount Matsudaira sale catalogue (hanging scroll, ink on paper)
Portrait of Hoan Jōei, 1797 (NO. 41)
Fowl, 1797. Private collection, Hyōgo Prefecture (pair of six-panel folding screens, ink on paper)
Carp, 1798 (NO. 42)
Thirty-six Poets, 1798. Denver Art Museum (pair of six-panel folding screens, ink on paper)
Fushimi Ningyō, 1800. Shin'enkan Collection (hanging scroll, colors on silk)
Eagle, 1800. Shin'enkan Collection (hanging scroll, ink and light colors on silk)

In addition, Professor Kobayashi Tadashi has reported the existence of *Rooster and Hen under Paulownia Tree* (1798), which was a treasured possession of the Bunjin artist Kuwayama Gyokushū (1746–1799),[69] but it has not yet been seen by this writer.

43 *One Hundred Dogs*

Late 1790s

Colors on silk, hanging scroll
142.7 × 84.2 cm
Signature: *Painted by Beito, age eighty-six*

SEALS:
square intaglio: *Tō Jokin-in*
round relief: *Jakuchū koji*
rectangular relief: *Enlivened by his hand, his paintings are filled with a mysterious spirit.*
Private collection, Nagasaki Prefecture

In this unusual work, Jakuchū depicted fifty-nine puppies in various positions, playing happily together. The artist Sho Katsukan (?–1790), a member of the school of Shen Nan-p'in who was active in Edo, produced paintings of puppies that closely resemble this work, and it seems likely that Jakuchū studied and was inspired by such paintings by members of this school. The manner in which he executed the patterns of the fur and the shapes of the puppies—in ellipses and other free, abstract forms, with little resemblance to the markings and shapes of real animals—is characteristic of his special expressive means. All the puppies are essentially oval in form, even when depicted in an active pose; and almost all of them were arranged in a curvilinear sequence, starting in the lower right and moving toward the top in a meandering manner. This crowding together of animals may also be seen in one of the *Dōshoku Sai-e* works, *A Group of Roosters* (FIG. 33.16). A number of paintings of groups of cranes and deer whose compositions have the same sort of meandering sequence are reproduced in the *Kōrin Hyaku-zu* (*One Hundred Designs by Kōrin*, 1815)—which was compiled by Sakai Hōitsu (1761–1828), a member of the Rimpa school who worked in Edo;[70] works of this sort may well have influenced Jakuchū.

However, the prevailing mood in *One Hundred Dogs* is essentially different from that of the busy *Group of Roosters* and more like that of the polychrome pieces done in 1791 or 1792 (see list in NO. 42), which is noticeably more tranquil and subdued. In the present work, the sequence of the puppies' forms and the patterns of their fur have a strange, floating quality, but at the same time the frolicking dogs exhibit an infectious sense of playfulness—such as the puppy at the left that sits up alertly, staring directly at the viewer.

Although Jakuchū died when he was eighty-five, the signature on the painting gives his age as eighty-six. Despite the debilitated, somewhat tentative quality of the calligraphy, it is difficult to imagine that the signature could have been written by anybody but Jakuchū, so perhaps the "eighty-six" was simply an expression of his desire to live to that age (see also NO. 44).

In Japan, dogs are thought to bear their young in large numbers and to have an easy delivery; as a result, the animal has become deified as one of the gods who protect women in childbirth. Thus the intention behind the present painting may have been to bring good luck to the owner in the form of numerous and healthy progeny. Although this could well have been a motivation of the person who commissioned the work, it is not known how Jakuchū would have received this idea.

In the *Shōsai Hikki* (vol. 2) Hiraga Shōsai notes that Jakuchū's widowed sister and her child had come to live with the artist in his residence close to the main gate of the Sekihōji and that this circumstance was such that Jakuchū's sister might have been mistaken for his wife.[71] Thus, Jakuchū entered into a quasi-family life in his old age, assuming a new affection for children, as evidenced by a number of paintings depicting small figures—such as congenial families of chickens, happy *kasen* (poetical geniuses), and smiling Fushimi dolls—playing and enjoying themselves; he may have thought of these as his own symbolic offspring.

This painting was published in an auction catalogue in November 1916. The present owner acquired it in Tokyo.

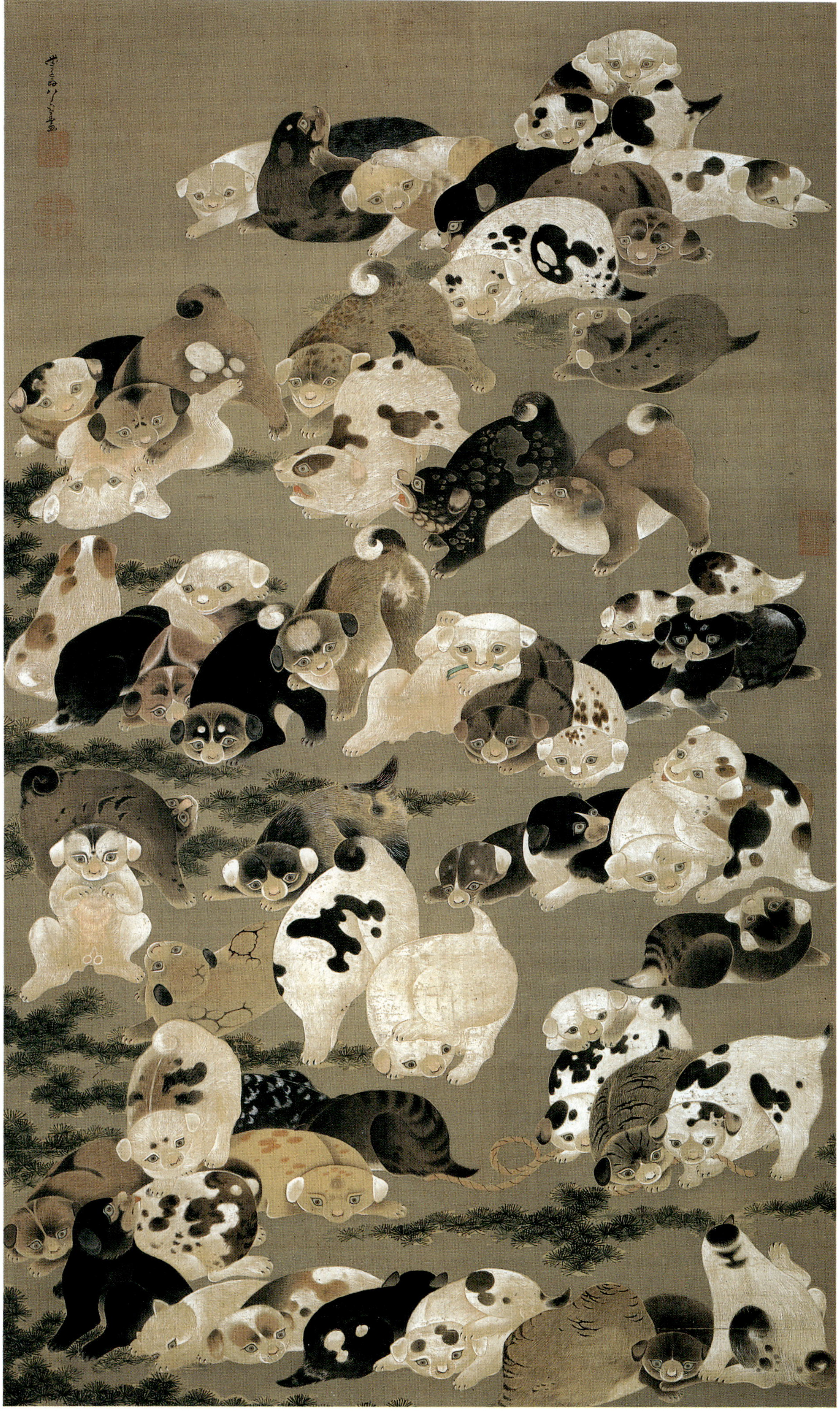

44 *Turtle*

c. 1799

Ink on paper, hanging scroll
111.3 × 28.8 cm
Inscription:
Old Man Beito, painted at the age of eighty-eight
Colophon: see below

SEALS:
square intaglio: *Tō Jokin-in*
round relief: *Jakuchū koji*
Rokuonji, Kyoto

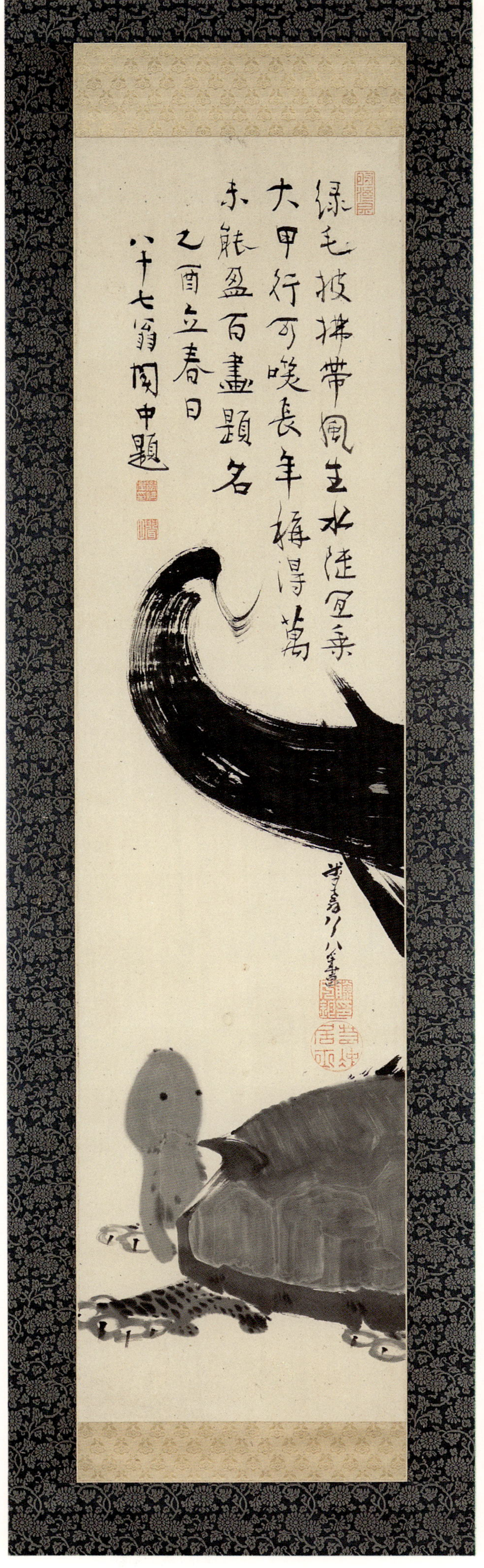

Although he died at the age of eighty-five, Jakuchū gave his age as eighty-eight on two works, this hanging scroll and a floral composition, originally done for the ceiling of the Kannondō of the Sekihōji and now preserved mainly in the Shingyōji in Kyoto. In written Japanese, the number eighty-eight resembles the character *kome* or *bei* (rice), and the celebration of a person's eighty-eighth birthday is therefore called *beiju*. No doubt Jakuchū aspired to live to this auspicious age, and as a consequence simply added a few years to his actual age. In Japanese, the word for "four," pronounced *shi*, is a homophone of the word for "death." Professor Tsuji Nobuo has suggested that, when Jakuchū was eighty-four years old, he may have added a few years to his age in order to avoid this inauspicious syllable.[72] If the inscription on *Vegetables* (No. 40) is correct, it seems likely that the ceiling paintings for the Kannondō were done when he was eighty-four, and Tsuji's suggestion seems to have more validity.

Like *Rooster and Blossoming Plum in Snow* (No. 13), *Turtle* follows one of Jakuchū's favorite compositional schemes. The rear half of the creature extends beyond the frame of the painting, and part of its long tail reappears at the top, slanting inward toward the center of the composition. Jakuchū rendered the raised head of the turtle in light ink tones, and the eyes and nostrils in dark spots. He executed the shell with a wide brush in individual, juxtaposed hexagonal shapes with a puddled effect along the borders. Jakuchū was not particularly adept at this technique, a shortcoming that may be ascribed to a decline in his brushwork as a result of his advanced age. However, the rough brush strokes delineating the body below the shell clearly show that meticulousness and detailed description were no longer the artist's primary concerns and that he had become interested mainly in directness of expression. He rendered the tail in thick, dark strokes characteristic of the monochrome style of works done when he was in his eighties, a feature that makes the viewer aware of the artist's vitality and his interest in transcending the limitations of realism.

Added after Jakuchū's death, the colophon was written by the noted Ōbaku monk Monchū Jōfuku (1739–1829), who studied the precepts of Sencha under Baisaō, literature under Daiten, and painting under Jakuchū; Monchū was also a friend of the painters Kakutei and Ike Taiga, and of the connoisseur and scholar Kimura Kenkadō. The first half of the colophon deals with the turtle, and the second half with the writer:

> The green moss that has accumulated on the aged creature bends in the wind and streams out behind. One might well ride on its broad carapace to cross a river. At this old age it would be laughable to boast of one's achievements. But I haven't yet inscribed colophons on one hundred paintings. Spring solstice, 1825, written by the old man Monchū, age eighty-seven.

45 *Portrait of Itō Jakuchū* by Kubota Beisen (1852–1906)

c. 1885

Colors on silk, hanging scroll
55.0 × 35.0 cm
Shōkokuji, Kyoto

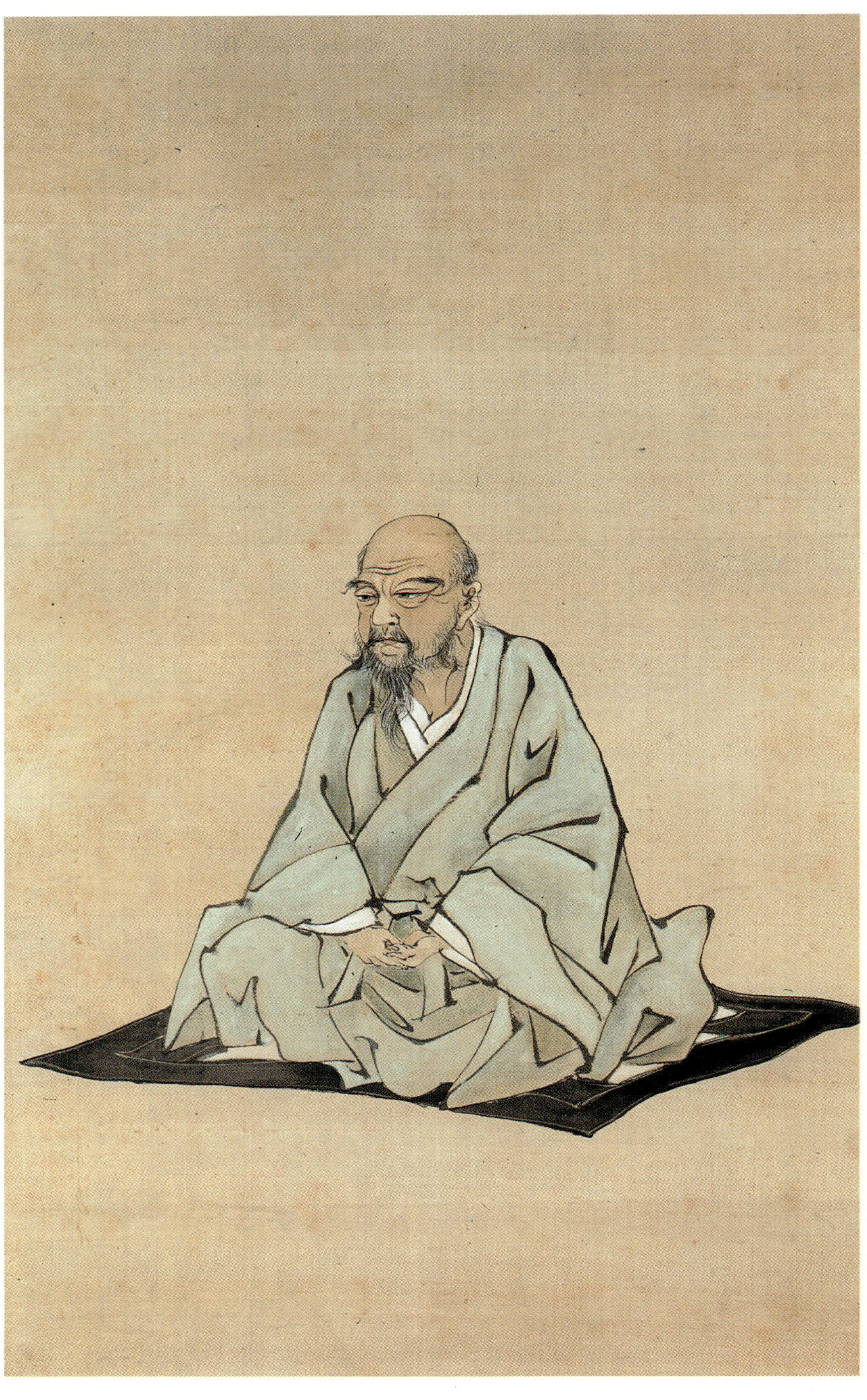

The only evidence regarding Jakuchū's physical appearance is a remark by Daiten in his "Ketsumei" (FIG. 3) that the artist "shaved his head."[73] There are no portraits from the period in which he lived, nor are there any other documentary records. It is perhaps best to imagine Jakuchū's appearance from his art, and the portraits shown here, painted many years after his death, must be regarded as no more than imaginative representations.

In 1885, Nakamura Sanshirō and Kawabata Yashichi of Kyoto, with the endorsement of the artist Kubota Beisen, carried out a memorial service at the Shōkokuji on the eighty-fifth anniversary of Jakuchū's death. On this occasion, not only the *Dōshoku Sai-e* scrolls (NO. 14), which were treasures of the Shōkokuji, but also dozens of other paintings by Jakuchū from various collections were displayed. (Apparently a catalogue of this event once existed, but it has not come to light). At this time, Beisen painted a portrait of Jakuchū after talking with a very elderly person who was quite knowledgeable about the past, and the portraitist donated this work to the Shōkokuji. A child born near the end of Jakuchū's life and still alive eighty-five years later would have been recalling the image of Jakuchū from an extremely distant memory. Thus there is considerable doubt as to how accurately this portrait, based at best on a tenuous recollection, conveys Jakuchū's appearance. Nevertheless, the firmly held body, bespeaking robust health, seems appropriate to the artist, whose creative activities continued for so many years.

Kubota Beisen lived in Kyoto, near the location of Jakuchū's ancestral home. One of his teachers, Suzuki Hyakunen (1825–1891), was a follower of the style of Kishi Ganku (1749–1838). Together with Kōno Bairei (1844–1895), he was instrumental in founding the Kyoto Prefectural School of Painting (the first public art school in Japan) in 1880. Beisen became a special correspondent for a newspaper company, providing pictorial coverage of such events as the Chicago World's Fair and the Sino-Japanese War. In his book

Beisen Gadan (1902), a collection of articles originally serialized in the newspaper, he touched on the subject of Jakuchū.[74]

Katō Eisen's portrait of Jakuchū is a copy of Beisen's work. The circumstances of its creation are recorded in the colophon:

> Portrait of Tobeian Jakuchū koji. The original version of this portrait was painted by Kubota Beisen-ō. In 1885, a memorial service was held at the Shōkokuji on the eighty-fifth anniversary of the death of Jakuchū koji. Beisen-ō himself questioned an old person from Kyoto, and as a consequence of this conversation he painted this picture, which he then donated to the Shōkokuji. In October of the present year the portrait was exhibited at the Kyoto Onshi Museum of Art.[75] I respectfully copied it. 1927, an autumn day. Copied and recorded by Eisen Katō Osamu.

The Kyoto Onshi Museum of Art, managed by the city of Kyoto, was the forerunner of the present-day Kyoto National Museum. Katō Osamu (1878–?), at the time a member of the art department of the museum also copied Beisen's portrait, innovatively using the plan of Jakuchū's stone images in the *Five Hundred Arhats* at the Sekihōji (see No. 27) for the lines of the garment. Katō donated his copy to the museum.

Katō, who studied under Kōno Bairei, used the name Eisen as his *gō*. He had been an employee of the Kyoto Onshi Museum since its earliest days as the Kyoto Imperial Museum and until 1943 was included among the artists listed in the *Nihon Bijutsu Nenkan* (*Year Book of Japanese Art*) compiled by the Tokyo National Cultural Properties Research Institute.[76] It is uncertain what became of him after the Second World War, but it is said that as late as 1949 he appeared from time to time at the museum.

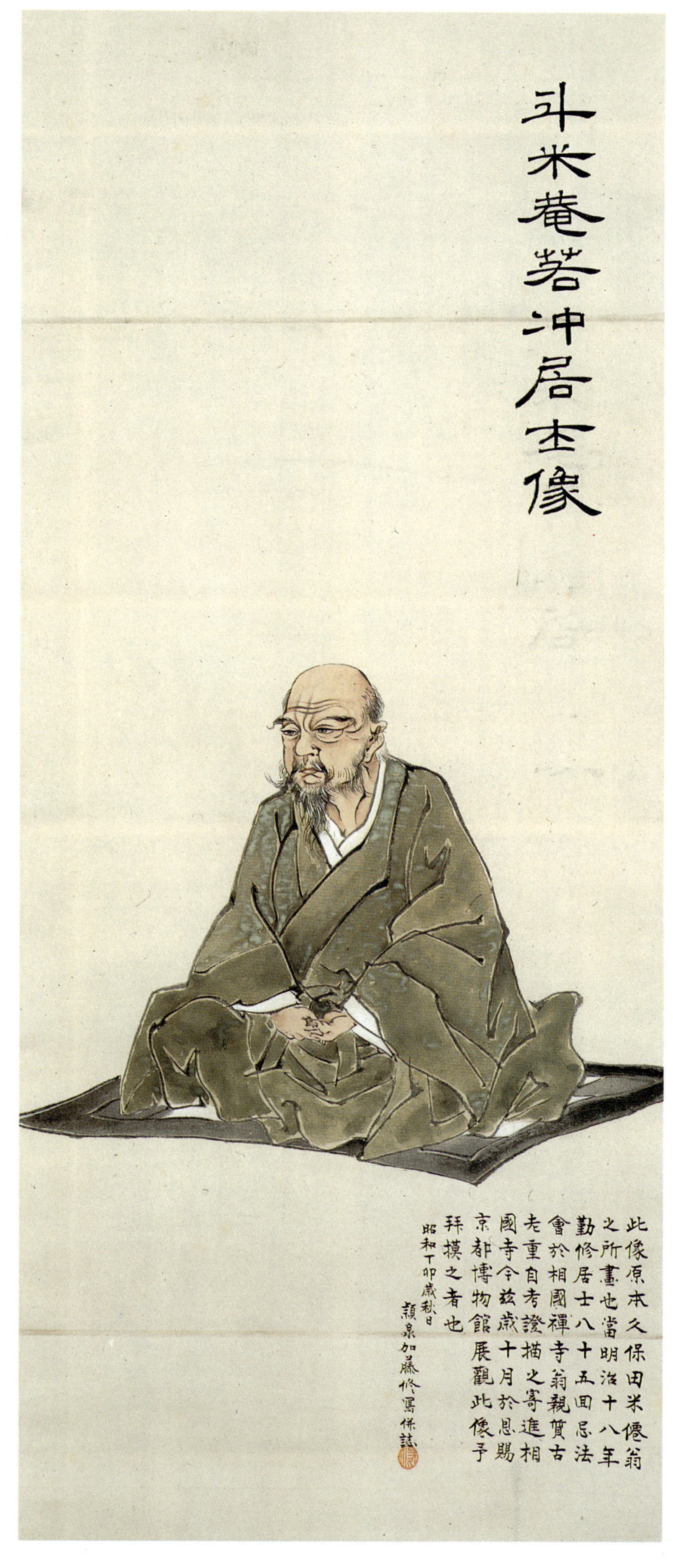

46 *Portrait of Itō Jakuchū* (copy) by Katō Eisen

1927

Colors on silk, hanging scroll
73.3 × 30.6 cm
Colophon: see above
Kyoto National Museum

Appendix
Chronology
Notes
Bibliography
Photograph Credits

APPENDIX

Selected Signatures, Seals and Inscriptions from Jakuchū's Paintings

No. 2 (Peonies)

No. 2 (Lilies)

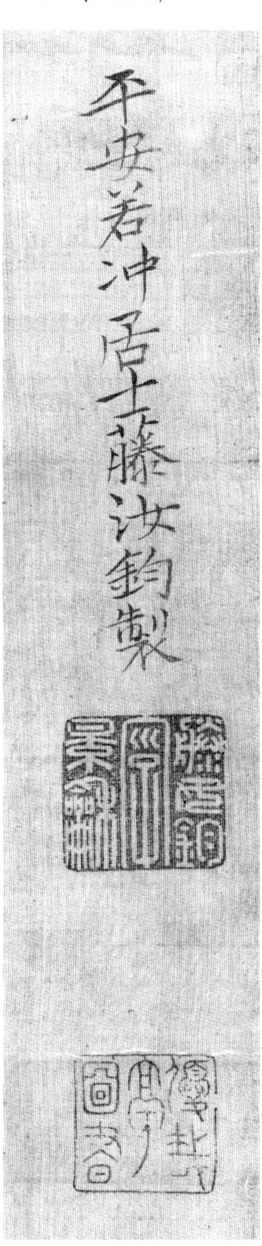

No. 5

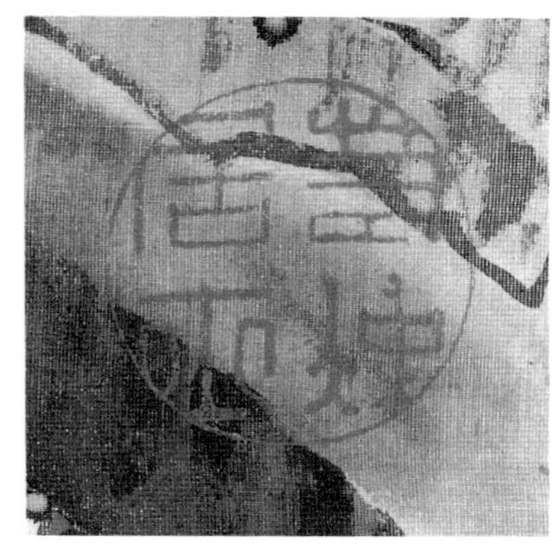

No. 6

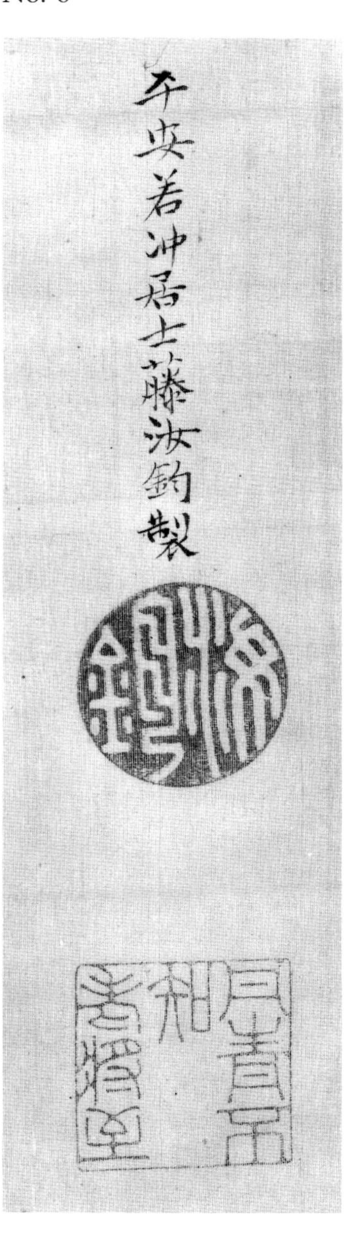

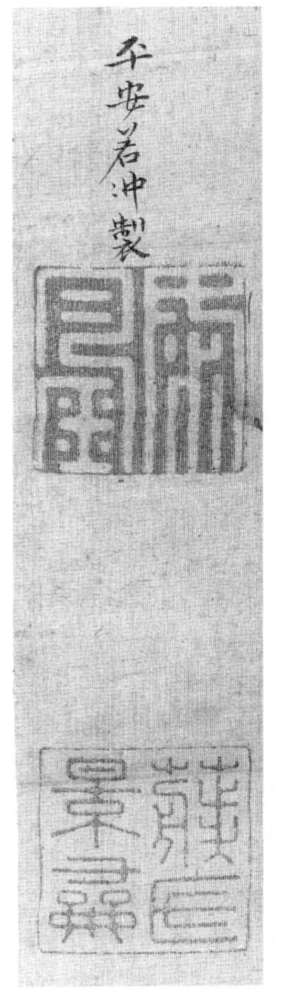

No. 8

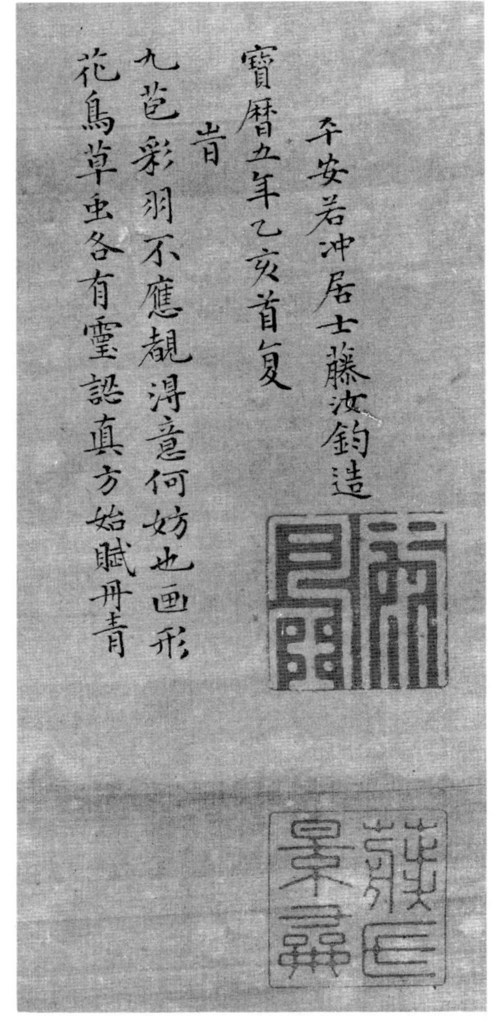

No. 9 (Right)

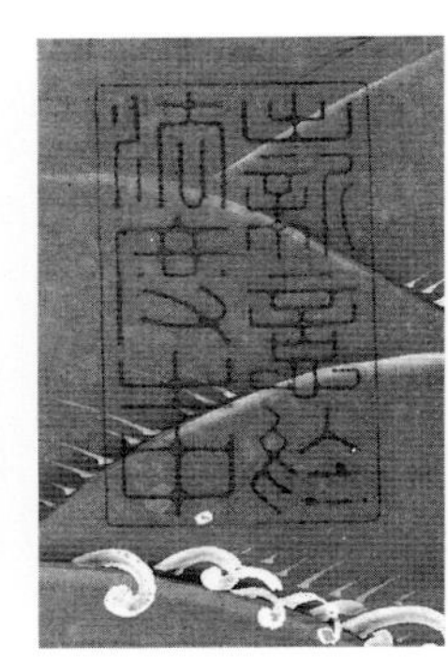

No. 9 (Left)

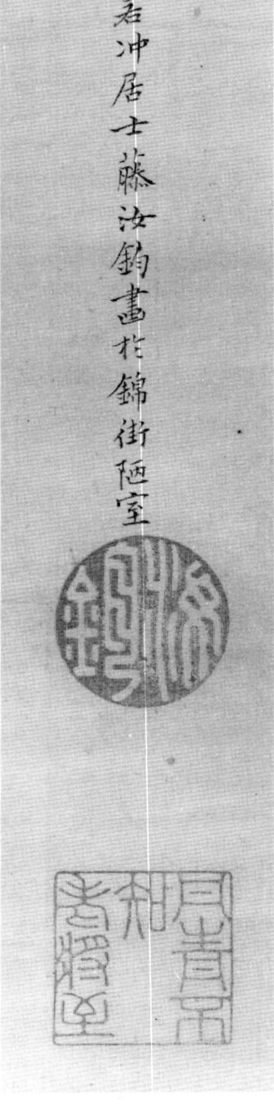

No. 13

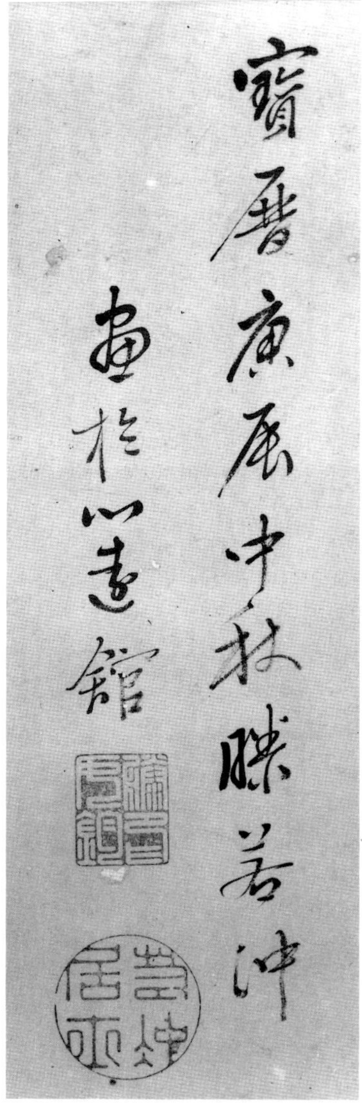

No. 17 (First screen)

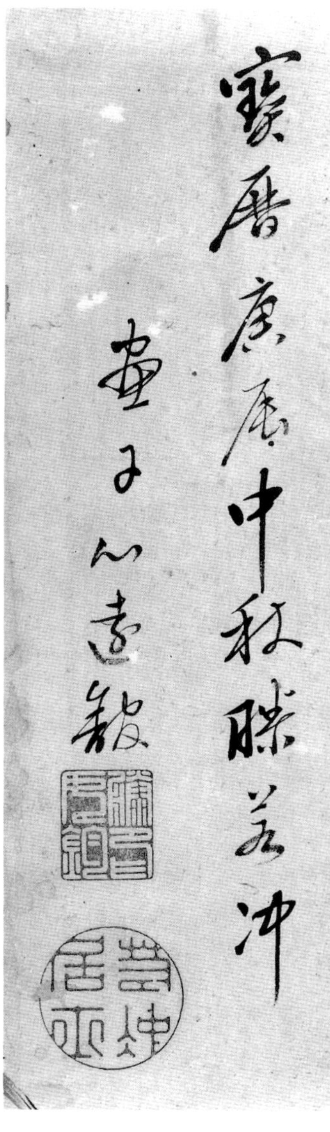

No. 17 (Second screen)

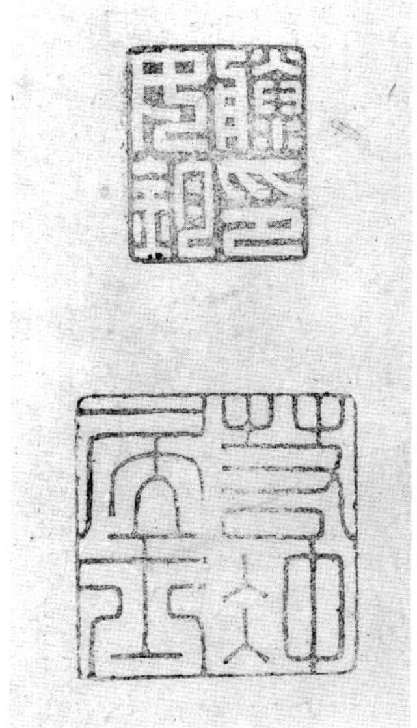

No. 22

No. 24 (Gama)

No. 24 (Tekkai)

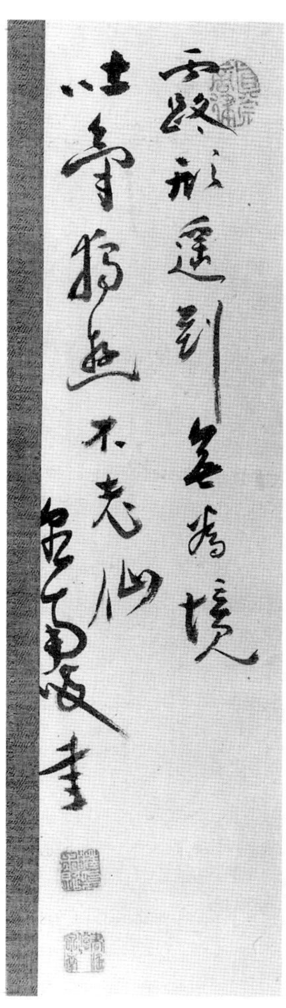

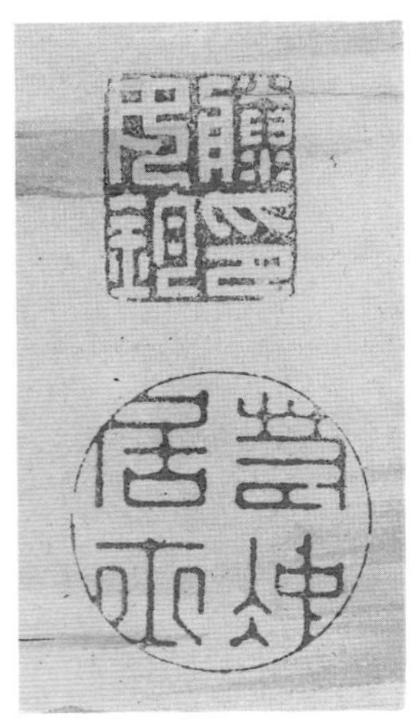
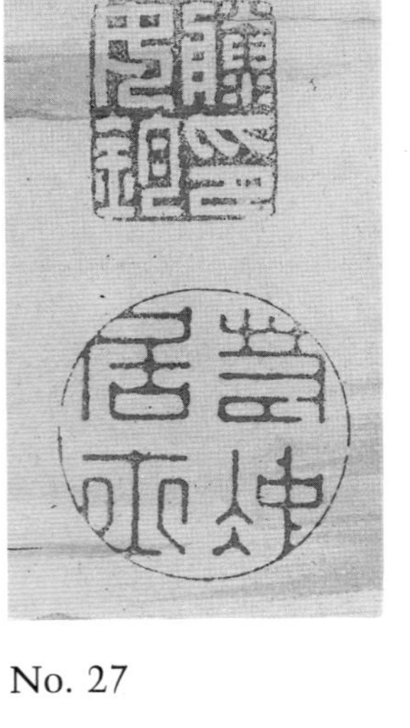

No. 27

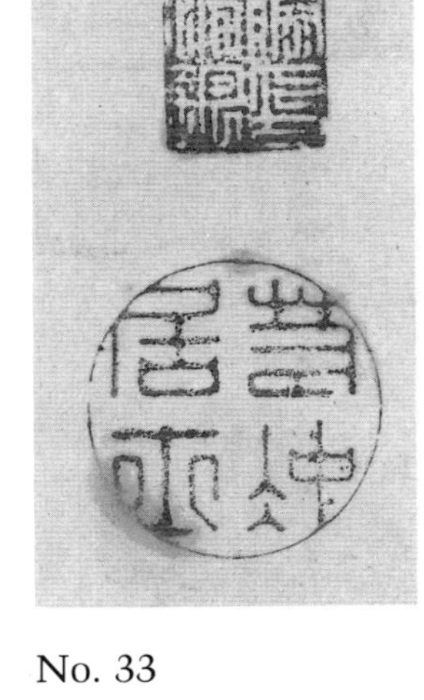
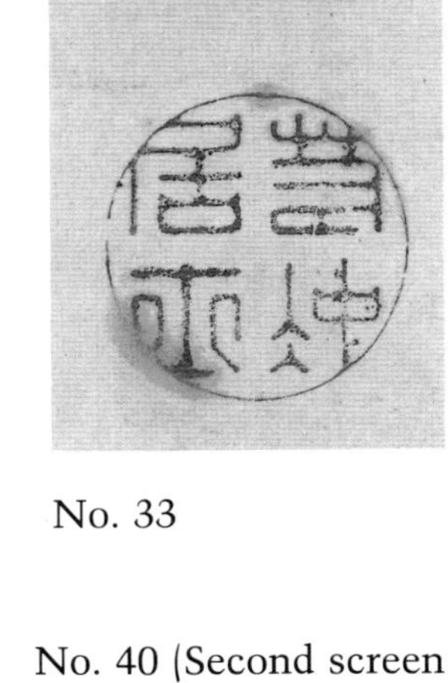

No. 33

No. 38

No. 39

No. 40 (First screen)

No. 40 (Second screen)

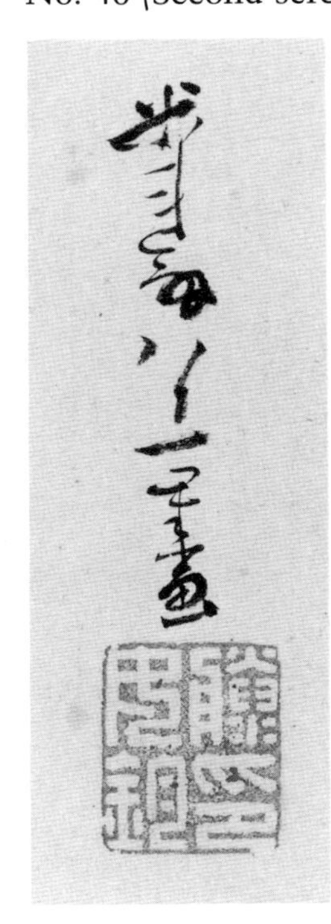

No. 41

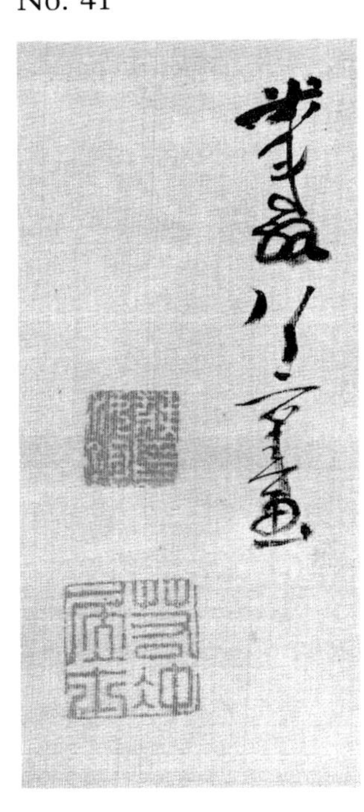

No. 42

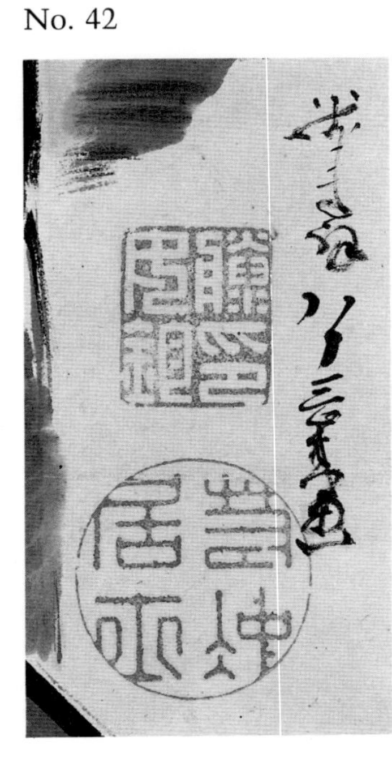

CHRONOLOGY

Japan

Nara (710–794)
Heian (794–1185)
Kamakura (1185–1336)
Northern and Southern Courts,
  Nambokucho (1336–1392)
Muromachi (1392–1568)
Momoyama (1568–1603)
Edo (1615–1868)

China

T'ang (618–907)
Five Dynasties (907–960)
Sung (960–1279)
  Northern Sung (960–1127)
  Southern Sung (1127–1279)
Yüan (Mongol) (1279–1368)
Ming (1368–1644)
Ch'ing (1644–1911)

Korea

United Silla (c. 668–935)
Koryŏ (918–1392)
Yi (1392–1910)

Biographical Events | *Works of Art* | *Historical Events*

Biographical Events

1716

(Shōtoku 6) Age 1. Eighth day of Second Month, Jakuchū is born. He is the first son of Itō Genzaemon (Sōsei), third-generation owner of Masugen, wholesale greengrocery in Kyoto. Jakuchū's given name is unknown. His mother's family name is Mutō; she is from Omi Province.

Works of Art

Historical Events

1716

(Shōtōku 6/Kyōhō 1). Ōgata Kōrin dies. Yosa Buson and Yokoi Nariari are born. Tokugawa Yoshimune, Eighth Shogun, takes office.

1717

(Kyōhō 2). Priest-painter Kokan dies. Nakayama Koyō is born.

1719

(Kyōhō 4). Daiten Kenjō and Tatebe Ryōtai are born.

1720

(Kyōhō 5). Second Month, Chinese painter I Fu-chiu (I Hai) comes to Japan; Twelfth Month, he returns to China. Ōoka Shumboku's *Ehon Tekagami* (see FIGS. 20, 21) is published.

1721

(Kyōhō 6). Chinese priest-painter Ta P'eng comes to Japan. Gyokusei Gessen and Ishida Yūtei are born.

1722

(Kyōhō 7). Kakutei Jōkō and Kō Fuyō are born.

1723

(Kyōhō 8). Ike Taiga is born.

1724

(Kyōhō 9). Kanō Eishuku dies. Kokan's *Jimbutsu Sōga* is published.

1728

(Kyōhō 13). Ogyu Sorai dies.

1730

(Kyōhō 15). I Fu-chiu comes to Japan again for one month. Sōga Shōhaku is born.

1731

(Kyōhō 16). Twelfth Month, Chinese painter Shen Nan-p'in arrives in Japan. Kumashiro Yūhi studies under him.

1732

(Kyōhō 17). Yamaguchi Sekkei dies.

1733

(Kyōhō 18). Shen Nan-p'in returns home to China. Maruyama Ōkyo is born.

Biographical Events *Works of Art* *Historical Events*

1734

(Kyōhō 19). Chinese painter Fei Han-yüan comes to Japan. Shumboku's *Ramma Zushiki* (FIG. 22) is published. Ryūmon Shōyū is born.

1735

(Kyōhō 20). Tachibana Morikuni compiles *Fusō Gafū*, based on woodblock edition of Chinese *Pa-chung Hua-p'u* (Japanese *Hasshū Gafū*).

1736

(Gembun 1). Kimura Kenkadō is born.

1737

(Gembun 2). Ike Taiga sees copy of *Pa-chung Hua-p'u* and takes up study of Bunjin painting.

1738

(Gembun 3) Age 23. Twenty-ninth day of Ninth Month, Jakuchū's father dies at age forty-two. Jakuchū takes over Masugen as fourth-generation Genzaemon.

1739

(Gembun 4). Kanō Eiryō and Monchū Jōfuku are born.

1740

(Gembun 5). Shumboku publishes *Gakō Senran* (see FIGS. 15, 16) in Osaka. Tachibana Morikuni publishes *Ehon Ōshukubai*, which incorporates section of *Chieh-tzu-yüan Hua-chüan.*

1743

(Kampo 3). Ōgata Kenzan dies.

1744

(Enkyō 1). Matsuoka Doan lectures in Kyoto on Chinese materia medica. Okada Beisanjin is born.

1745

(Enkyō 2). Tokugawa Ieshige, Ninth Shogun, takes office. Uragami Gyokudō and Hiraga Hakusan are born.

1746

(Enkyō 3). Shumboku's *Minchō Shiken* (*Minchō Seidō Gaen*; see FIG. 19) is published. Kakutei Jōkō introduces painting style of Shen Nan-p'in in Kyoto-Osaka region about this time. Kuwayama Gyokushū is born. Daiten becomes abbot of Jiun'an subtemple of Shōkukuji.

Biographical Events	*Works of Art*	*Historical Events*
		1748 (Kan'en 1). Kimura Kenkadō accompanies Yanagisawa Kien to visit Ike Taiga and becomes his student. Tachibana Morikuni dies. Satake Shozan is born. *Kaishien Gaden*, Japanese edition of the *Chieh-tzu-yüan Hua-chüan*, is published.
		1749 (Kan'en 2). Shumboku publishes *Wakan Meiga-en*.
		1750 (Kan'en 3). Tatebe Ryotai goes to Nagasaki and studies painting under Kumashiro Yūhi and Fei Han-yüan.
1751 (Kan'en 4) Age 36. Nineteenth day of Ninth Month, Jakuchū erects tombstone in his parents' honor in family temple (Hōzōji).		**1751** (Kan'en 4). Gion Nankai dies. Sakaki Hyakusen writes *Gemmei Gajin-ko* (*Painters of the Yüan and Ming Periods*). Shumboku publishes *Gashi Kaiyo*.
1752 (Hōreki 2) Age 37. Jakuchū's association with Daiten Kenjō begins about this time. Jakuchū has already begun to use the suffix *koji* after his name, signifying that he has taken the tonsure and become a Buddhist lay monk.	**1752** (Hōreki 2) Age 37. *White Fowl* (FIG. 31).	**1752** (Hōreki 2). Matsumura Goshun is born. Sakaki Hyakusen dies.
		1753 (Hōreki 3). Ono Ranzan opens school in Kyoto in which he lectures on Chinese materia medica.
		1754 (Hōreki 4). Nagasawa Rosetsu is born.
1755 (Hōreki 5) Age 40. Jakuchū passes on responsibility for operating Masugen to his brother Sōgan (Hakusai) and focuses his energies on painting.	**1755** (Hōreki 5) Age 40. *White Plum Blossoms and Moon* (FIG. 26); *Pair of Phoenixes and the Rising Sun*, (NO. 9); *Tiger* (FIG. 29).	**1755** (Hōreki 5). Shumboku paints compositions on sliding screens in abbot's quarters of Reiun'in in the Myōshinji. Ōoka Shunsen publishes *Ehon Fukujūsō*. Takada Keiho, Watanabe Shikō, Fukae Roshū, and Mochizuki Gyokusen die. Tachibana Yasukuni publishes *Noyama-gusa*.
1757 (Hōreki 7) Age 42. Jakuchū begins work on *Dōshoku Sai-e* project (NO. 14 and FIG. 33) in this or the following year.		
	1758 (Hōreki 8) Age 43. *Birds in a Blossoming Plum Tree* (FIG. 33.2) (*Dōshoku Sai-e* series no. 2).	**1758** (Hōreki 8). Maruyama Ōkyo begins to produce *megane-e* (Western-style perspective compositions) about this time. Daiten sees imported cockatoo at Imamiya shrine, Kyoto. Yanagisawa Kien dies.

Biographical Events

1759

(Hōreki 9) Age 44. Jakuchū is particularly productive during this year.

1760

(Hōreki 10) Age 45. Baisaō, viewing paintings from *Dōshoku Sai-e*, is deeply impressed by them and expresses his admiration for Jakuchū by presenting him with an inscription praising his abilities. Daiten writes *Tō Keiwa Gakanoki* about this time. Daiten, Mujū, Taiga, and Jakuchū go to outskirts of Kyoto to view plum blossoms in this or next year.

1764

(Meiwa 1) Age 49. Jakuchū travels to Shikoku, where he completes series of paintings on sliding screens in Kotohiragū shrine.

1765

(Meiwa 2) Age 50. Nineteenth day of Ninth Month, Jakuchū's youngest brother Sōjaku dies. Eleven days later Jakuchū presents Śākyamuni triptych, together with twenty-four of *Dōshoku Sai-e* paintings, to Shōkokuji. Eleventh day of Eleventh Month, Jakuchū erects tombstone for Sōjaku in Hōzōji. Twenty-eighth day of Twelfth Month, Jakuchū completes agreement with Shōkokuji so that annual religious services in his memory will be observed after his death.

Works of Art

1759

(Hōreki 9) Age 44. *Mandarin Ducks in Snow* (NO. 14.1); *Sparrows in Autumn* (FIG. 33.3); *Rooster, Sunflowers and Morning Glories* (FIG. 33.4); *Hydrangeas and Fowl* (NO. 14.2); and *Rooster and Hen* (FIG. 33.5) (*Dōshoku Sai-e* series nos. 3–7). Monochrome ink paintings on screens in Dai-shoin of Rokuonji, (NO. 16; FIGS. 41–44); inscription on painting of grape vines is written by the priest Suigan Joken of Tenryūji.

1760

(Hōreki 10) Age 45. *Flowers, Birds, and Vegetables* (pair of folding screens) (NO. 17).

1761

(Hōreki 11) Age 46. Six paintings from *Dōshoku Sai-e* (series NOS. 1, 8–12) are mentioned in *Tō Keiwa Gakanoki* (compiled by Daiten, 1760) and can therefore be presumed to predate spring 1761. These are *Herbaceous Peonies and Butterflies* (FIG. 33.1); *Blossoming Plum under the Moon* (FIG. 33.6); *White Peacock and Chrysanthemums under a Pine* (FIG. 33.7); *Rose Mallows and Fowl* (FIG. 33.8); *Pair of White Fowl and a Pine* (FIG. 33.9); and *Cockatoos in a Pine* (FIG. 33.10). *White Goose and Reeds* (FIG. 33.11; series no. 13) is completed in 1761, along with depiction of *Kanzan and Jittoku* with inscription by Tankei.

1763

(Hōreki 13) Age 48. Portrait of Baisaō Kō Yūgai is reproduced in *Baisaō Gego* (NOS. 18, 19).

1764

(Meiwa 1) Age 49. Polychrome paintings of plants and flowers on sliding screens (Oku-shoin, Jōdan-no-ma, of Kotohiragū shrine, Shikoku).

Historical Events

1759

(Hōreki 9). Hiraga Gennai holds conference on natural commodities and produce at Yūshima shrine, Edo. Daiten asks to be relieved of his duties as abbot at the Jiun'an subtemple of the Shōkokuji. Ryūmon Shōyū becomes abbot of Rokuonji. Hattori Nangaku dies.

1760

(Hōreki 10). Tokugawa Ieharu, Tenth Shogun, takes office. Toda Asahiyama holds conference on natural commodities and produce in Osaka. Hiraga Gennai goes to Kii Province to collect examples of shellfish. Noro Kaiseki visits Mampukuji. On observance of 100th anniversary of founding of Mampukuji, Taiga does screen paintings of *Five Hundred Arhats*.

1761

(Hōreki 11). Daiten's *Sakuhishu* is published.

1763

(Hōreki 13). Baisaō Kō Yūgai and Ōoka Shumboku die. Tani Bunchō is born.

1764

(Meiwa 1). Kanō Eihaku dies.

1765

(Meiwa 2). Hakuin dies. *Sō Shiseki Gafū* is published.

Biographical Events	Works of Art	Historical Events
1766 (Meiwa 3) Age 51. Commemorative funerary monument (*juzō*; FIG. 4), inscribed with Daiten's biographical tribute to Jakuchū ("Ketsumei"; FIG. 3), is erected in cemetery of Shō-ō'an subtemple of Shōkokuji.		**1766** (Meiwa 3). Yosa Buson paints folding screens *Poetical Gathering at the Orchid Pavilion* (inscription by priest Suigan Shōken; Tokyo National Museum).
1767 (Meiwa 4) Age 52. In spring, Jakuchū and Daiten take boating excursion on Yodo River. Nineteenth day of Ninth Month, third commemorative service for Sōjaku is held.	**1767** (Meiwa 4) Age 52. *Jōkyōshū* is completed.	**1767** (Meiwa 4). Aoki Mokubei is born.
1768 (Meiwa 5) Age 53. Tenth Month, Kohen Shōnin, bishop of Higashi Honganji and member of imperial family, asks authorities at Shōkokuji to show him *Dōshoku Sai-e* paintings, and he is permitted to borrow them. Jakuchū is ranked third among painters listed in *Heian Jimbutsushi*, after Ōnishi Suigetsu and Maruyama Ōkyo, and before Literati school artists Ike Taiga and Yosa Buson. Jakuchū's residence is given as "Takakura, Nishiki-koji-agaru-machi."	**1768** (Meiwa 5) Age 53. Two *taku-hanga* albums of bird-and-flower subjects, *Gempo Yōka* (FIG. 9) and *Soken Jō* (FIG. 8), are published.	**1768** (Meiwa 5). Ueda Akinari writes *Ugetsu Monogatari.*
1769 (Meiwa 6) Age 54. *Dōshoku Sai-e* scrolls and Śākyamuni triptych are displayed in abbot's quarters of Shōkokuji on occasion of annual "Kakusan" observances.		**1769** (Meiwa 6). Kanō Eiryō dies.
1770 (Meiwa 7) Age 55. Tenth Month, thirty-third memorial service for Jakuchū's father is held, and Jakuchū donates remaining six *Dōshoku Sai-e* scrolls to Shōkokuji by this year.		**1770** (Meiwa 7). Maruyama Ōkyo begins to produce *shasei-zu* (realistic representations) about this time. Tsukioka Settei publishes the *Kingyoku Gafū*.
	1771 (Meiwa 8) Age 56. *Kachō-zu* (NO. 26), set of *taku-hanga* bird-and-flower subjects, is published.	**1771** (Meiwa 8). Taiga and Buson collaborate in producing album *Jūben Jugi-chō*. Sugita Gempaku begins to translate *Kaitai Shinshō*, first treatise on Western medicine and anatomy to be translated into Japanese. Ōnishi Suigetsu dies.
		1772 (Meiwa 9). Fourth Month, Daiten resumes his duties as abbot of Jiun'an. Kumashiro Yūhi, student of Shen Nan-p'in, dies.
		1774 (An'ei 3). Tatebe Ryōtai and Ta-p'eng die.
1775 (An'ei 4) Age 60. In *Heian Jimbutsushi* Jakuchū is listed second, after Ōkyo, and still before Taiga and Buson.	**1775** (An'ei 4) Age 60. *Bamboo and Tiger* (NO. 28) and *Banana Plant* (NO. 29) are mentioned in Daiten's *Shōun Seikō*, published this year.	**1775** (An'ei 4). Daiten's *Shōun Seikō* and Kimura Kenkadō's *Kai-yose-no-ki* (*A Diary of Shell Studies*) are published.

Biographical Events

1776

(An'ei 5) Age 61. Jakuchū begins his stone sculpture project, *Five Hundred Arhats* (FIG. 11), at Sekihōji about this time.

1779

(An'ei 8) Age 64. Tenth day of Tenth Month, Jakuchū's mother dies at age eighty.

1782

(Temmei 2) Age 67. Rankings for painters in *Heian Jimbutsushi* remain same as in 1775. Jakuchū's address is given as "Takakura, Shijō-agaru-machi."

1783

(Temmei 3) Age 68. Prince Nikkō Jungōgū Kōjun, third son of Emperor Nakamikado, visits Shōkokuji in order to view *Dōshoku Sai-e* paintings and two depictions of cranes by Chinese painter Wen Cheng (FIG. 17).

1785

(Temmei 5) Age 70. Jakuchū has tombstone erected on behalf of his brother Sōgan (Hakusai) in cemetery of Hōzōji.

1786

(Temmei 6) Age 71. Passage devoted to *Five Hundred Arhats* is included in *Shūi Miyako Meisho Zue*, guidebook to noted locations in and around Kyoto.

Works of Art

1776

(An'ei 5) Age 61. *Monkeys in a Blossoming Peach Tree* (FIG. 13) with inscription by Hakujun, priest of Mampukuji, dated 1776, is finished before this year.

1782

(Temmei 2) Age 67. Painting of Fushimi dolls (NO. 33).

1783

(Temmei 3) Age 68. *Crabs*, with inscription by Yokoi Nariari.

Historical Events

1776

(An'ei 5). Obaku priest Hakujun and artist Ike Taiga die.

1777

(An'ei 6). Sakaki Hyakusen's *Genmeishin Shōga Jinmei-roku* (*Index of Calligraphers and Painters from the Yüan, Ming, and Ch'ing Periods*) is published.

1778

(An'ei 7). Satake Shozan writes *Gahō Kōryō*, treatise on Western-style painting. Nukina Kaioku is born.

1779

(An'ei 8). Daiten becomes 113th Bishop of Shōkokuji. Hiraga Gennai dies in prison.

1780

(An'ei 9). Chinese artists Fang Hsi-yüan and Ch'eng Ch'ih-ch'eng come to Nagasaki, and Watanabe Kazan and Tani Bunchō take calligraphy instruction from them. Nakayama Koyō dies.

1781

(Temmei 1). Sōga Shōhaku dies.

1783

(Temmei 3). Yosa Buson and Yokoi Nariari die. Shiba Kōkan produces copperplate prints.

1784

(Temmei 5). Kō Fuyō dies.

1785

(Temmei 5). Ōbaku priest Kakutei Jōkō, follower of Kumashiro Yūhi, and Satake Shozan die.

1786

(Temmei 6). Tokugawa Ienari, Eleventh Shogun, takes office. Tsukioka Settei, Ishida Yūtei, and Sō Shiseki die. Tanuma Okitsugu falls from power. Murata Shunkai comes to Kyoto, where he meets Minagawa Kien, Maruyama Ōkyo, Ban Kōkei, Ueda Akinari, and Kimura Kenkadō.

Biographical Events	Works of Art	Historical Events
1787 (Temmei 7) Age 72. Twenty-sixth day of Fourth Month, Imperial Prince Shinjin of Myōhōin inspects twelve paintings of fowl by Jakuchū and on following day commissions him to do set of paintings on sliding screens for Kyonoma (chamber) of Shinden. Fifth day of Fifth Month, Shinjin has sliding screens installed. Eighteenth day of Sixth Month, Shinjin allows four of Jakuchū's followers, together with seven people connected with Ōkyo, to view airing of paintings from Ryūka storehouse of Myōhōin.		**1787** (Temmei 7). Nagasawa Rosetsu paints sliding-screen compositions in Sōdōji, Muryōji, and Jōkyōji in Kii Province.
1788 (Temmei 8) Age 73. Last day of First Month, a disastrous fire breaks out on east bank of Kamo River, destroying much of Kyoto, including Imperial Palace, most of Shōkokuji, Nishiki area, and Jakuchū's residence. Jakuchū's paintings in Shōkokuji are saved. Tenth Month, Jakuchū twice visits Kimura Kenkadō in Osaka, along with Toda Tosaburō.		**1788** (Temmei 8). The Chinese painters Li Yung-yün, Chang Ch'iu-ku, and Fei Ch'ing-hu go to Nagasaki. Great fire levels most of Kyoto.
1790 (Kansei 2) Age 75. Jakuchū completes sets of screens for Saifukuji outside Osaka, and Kaihōji in Fushimi. He falls ill; twelfth and thirteenth days of Sixth Month, Daiten makes a special visit to Jakuchū's residence to inquire after his health. Illustrations of *Five Hundred Arhats* are published in *Sekitei Gadan* (see FIG. 12).	**1790** (Kansei 2) Age 75. *Cacti and Fowl* (FIG. 14) and *Lotus Pond* (NO. 35); and *Roosters and Hens* (NO. 36) are completed.	**1790** (Kansei 2). Fifth Month, "Kansei prohibitions," in which study of Western subjects is prohibited, are instituted. *Kinsei Kijin-den* (*Extraordinary Individuals of Recent Times*) published by Ban Kokei. Kimura Kenkadō is banished to Ise Province. Totoki Baigai goes to Nagasaki to study with Fei Ch'ing-hu. Kanō Eigaku is born.
1791 (Kansai 3) Age 76. As result of his impoverished circumstances, the Shōkokuji's agreement with Jakuchū (1765) to perform annual observances on his behalf is cancelled. Jakuchū lives in retreat in Sekihōji at this time.	**1791** (Kansei 3) Age 76. *Cockscomb and Mantis* (NO. 37) with inscriptions by Keishū Dorin of the Tenryūji.	
1792 (Kansei 4) Age 77. Second day of Sixth Month, Jakuchū's brother Sōgan dies at age seventy-four.	**1792** (Kansei 4) Age 77. *Vegetables and Insects* (handscroll); *Grapes, Rooster, and Hen* (hanging scroll; Metropolitan Museum of Art, New York); *Horse-beans and Insects* (hanging scroll; Satō 1987, pl. 117).	**1792** (Kansei 4). Minagawa Kien organizes "Higashiyama Shinshoga-ten" ("Exhibition of New Calligraphy and Painting Held in Higashiyama") in Kyoto. Daiten's *Hokuzen Bunsō* is published.
1793 (Kansei 5) Age 78. A passage in Hiraga Hakusan's *Shōsai Hikki* (vol. 2) deals with Jakuchū's circumstances in this year.		**1793** (Kansei 5). Kimura Kenkadō returns to Osaka. Watanabe Kazan is born. Daiten's *Hokuzen Shisō* is published.
1794 (Kansei 6) Age 79. Nineteenth day of Tenth Month, Hakusan calls on Jakuchū at his residence outside main gate of Sekihōji.	**1794** (Kansei 6) Age 79. *Weathered Skull* (NO. 38).	**1794** (Kansei 6). Ōkyo paints sliding-screen compositions at Kotohiragū shrine, Shikoku.

Biographical Events

1795

(Kansei 7) Age 80. Tenth Month, priest Hoan Jōei of Mampukuji writes an inscription on portrait of him done by Jakuchū (No. 41).

1799

(Kansei 11) Age 84. Jakuchū produces depictions of flowers, trees, and plants on ceiling of Kannondō of Sekihōji.

1800

(Kansei 12) Age 85. Eighth or Tenth day of Ninth Month, Jakuchū dies. He is buried in Sekihōji; twenty-seventh day of Tenth Month, the "forty-ninth day" memorial service is held on his behalf at Shōkokuji.

1830

(Bunsei 13). Extensive damage to *Five Hundred Arhats* as result of devastating earthquake.

1833

(Tempo 4). Descendant of the Itō family Seibō works to restore sculpture composition and has stone monument in shape of brush (with inscription by Nukina Kaioku) erected in Jakuchū's memory (FIG. 1).

Works of Art

1795

(Kansei 7) Age 80. *Cock on a Perch* (monochrome hanging scroll; Yamato Bunkakan; *Kokka* 944, pl. 4).

1796

(Kansei 8) Age 81. *Two Roosters and a Hen* (No. 39); *Vegetables* (No. 40); *Fowl* (monochrome hanging scroll; Yamato Bunkakan); *Hawk* (monochrome hanging scroll; Satō 1987, pl. 121).

1797

(Kansei 9) Age 82. *Portrait of Hoan Jōei* (No. 41); *Fowl* (pair of monochrome folding screens; private collection, Hyōgo Prefecture; Tsuji 1974, detail 25).

1798

(Kansei 10) Age 83. *Carp* (No. 42); *Thirty-six Poets* (pair of monochrome folding screens; Denver Art Museum).

1800

(Kansei 12) Age 85. *Fushimi Ningyō* (Shin'enkan Collection); *Eagle on a Cliff above Waves* (monochrome hanging scroll; FIG. 47).

Historical Events

1795

(Kansei 7). Fourteenth day of Seventh Month, Maruyama Ōkyo dies.

1796

(Kansei 8). Aoki Mokubei and Uragami Gyokudō visit Kimura Kenkadō.

1797

(Kansei 9). Rosetsu paints *ema* (votive painting) of Yamauba for Itsukushima shrine.

1799

(Kansei 11). Kuwayama Gyokushū and Nagasawa Rosetsu die.

1800

(Kansei 12). Ryūmon Shōyū dies. Publication of Matsudaira Sadanobu's *Shuko Jisshū* begins. Commemorative services honoring the twenty-fifth anniversary of Ike Taiga's death held at the Sōrinji.

1801

(Kyowa 1). Eighth day of Second Month, Daiten Kenjō dies.

1802

(Kyowa 2). Kimura Kenkadō dies.

1809

(Bunka 6). Gyokusei Gessen dies.

1811

(Bunka 8). Matsumura Goshun dies.

Biographical Events

1885

(Meiji 18). Commemorative religious services are held at Shōkokuji on occasion of eighty-fifth anniversary of Jakuchū's death. On basis of conversations with elderly person, Kubota Beisen paints portrait of Jakuchū (No. 45).

1889

(Meiji 22). December 30, *Dōshoku Sai-e* scrolls are presented to Imperial Household by Shōkokuji in return for donation of 10,000 yen.

1926

(Taisho 15). October, all thirty *Dōshoku Sai-e* paintings are exhibited to public at Tokyo Imperial Museum.

1927

(Showa 2). "Special Exhibition of the Paintings of Jakuchū" is held at Kyoto Museum.

1971

(Showa 46). September and October, "Special Exhibition of the Paintings of Jakuchū" is held at Tokyo National Museum.

NOTES

CHAPTER 2

1. All of the essential biographical references in the Japanese language to Jakuchū's life and artistic activities appear in Tsuji 1974, the most comprehensive study of the artist and his painting. This impressive publication has served as a fundamental source of information and inspiration in the preparation of this catalogue.

2. Although the proper name of the business was the Masuya, it was commonly referred to as the "Masugen," as it was the general practice among Japanese merchants to combine the first character of the firm's name (*masu*) with the first character of the traditional given name of the family head, in this case, Genzaemon.

3. For a brief account of the Nishiki market, see Takemura 1965, vol. 4, pp. 43–44.

4. Tsuji 1974, p. 241.

5. See Mori 1939; the passage is from Hiraga Hakusan, *Shōsai Hikki*, vol. 2, 1794. Hiraga (Ogawa) Hakusan was a minor official in the service of the Asano *daimyo* family of Hiroshima. He also achieved some note as a poet. Mori suggests that Hakusan probably came across a description of the incident and included it in his notes. The fact that the anecdote appears in a source compiled while Jakuchū was still alive (he was seventy-eight years old at the time) lends credence to the description, even though the incident itself would have occurred at least forty years earlier.

6. Daiten Kenjō was a noted specialist in the study of Chinese literature in Japan during the eighteenth century. As was the custom with men of learning and accomplishment, he went by a number of names. His *ji* (formal literary name) was Baisō; his various *gō* (artist's pseudonyms) were Daiten; Shōchu; Fusei-shujin; Tōko; Kounrokyo; Jibokusai; Hokuzen-shoin. He also used the *tsusho* (nickname) Chikujō. According to one tradition, he was the son of the Confucian scholar and physician Inabori Toan of Inawa (Izono?) in Omi; in another story he was the younger brother of Sono Dainagon Kikō, a member of nobility, and the Inabori family were his adoptive parents. His lifelong association with the Shōkokuji is reflected in his burial at the monastery.

7. In addition to the indoctrination and instruction he received from older monks in the Shōkokuji (at the time, among the foremost Rinzai monasteries in Japan), Daiten also was able to study Chinese literature and poetry under the learned monk Daichō, a member of the Ōbaku branch of Zen Buddhism. Daiten also received instruction in Confucian thought and literature from the scholar Uno Akakasu. Daiten's broad range of interests included not only Buddhist and Confucian studies, but also Japanese history, poetry, and literature. His extensive writings were widely published both during and after his lifetime.

8. Daiten's scholarly and artistic acquaintances included several influential members of the noble and military classes, as well as politicians, writers, and men of distinction such as Matsudaira Sadanobu, Masuyama Sessai, Katayama Hokkai, Akutagawa Tankyu, Takeda Bairyū, Kimura Kenkadō, Baisaō Kō Yūgai, and the painters Ike Taiga, Kō Fuyō, and Gessen-shonin.

9. Although there is a brief reference to Jakuchū's personality and attitude during his youth in this passage, it seems clear that it was based on some later conversation rather than direct observation by Daiten during Jakuchū's early years.

10. See the inscription on the white rooster and hen painting (see FIG. 31) that is dated Hōreki 2 (1752), when Jakuchū was thirty-seven years old.

11. This evocative phrase is, in turn, a part of a longer paradoxical observation:

    "What is most perfect seems somehow lacking
    Yet its function is unimpaired
    The greatest fullness is like a void
    But its function never fails
    The most straight appears crooked
    While ultimate skill seems somehow clumsy,
    And the greatest eloquence like stuttering
    Movement triumphs over cold, and inaction over heat
    Thus all under heaven is set straight through quietude."

    For a sampling of translations, see Paul Carus, *The Canon of Reason and Virtue*, Chicago: Open Court Publishing Co., 1913, pp. 45–46; Lionel Giles, *The Sayings of Lao-Tzu, Wisdom of the East* series, London: 1904, p. 45; and Arthur Waley, *The Way and Its Power*, London: Allen and Unwin, 1949, p. 198.

12. Tsuji 1974, p. 178 and footnote 6. The names (both of which include three of the four characters in the original phrase) are given in the Ōbaku Zen archival source *Ōbaku-shu Kanroku* as Jakuchū En'ei (d. 1808) and Jakuchū Joei.

13. Tsuji 1974, p. 241.

14. Satō 1987, p. 20.

15. Tsuji 1974, p. 241.

16. This location was proposed, on the basis of Daiten's description in the *Sakuhishu*, by Professor Akiyama Teruō in Akiyama 1926 and has been accepted by most scholars. It has been pointed out, however, that a brothel district was then situated nearby and that this would have made the area inappropriate for a studio-retreat. Another theory has it that the structure may actually have been located further to the west, in a more rural neighborhood close to the Mibudera temple.

17. See Tsuji 1974, pp. 189, 242.

18. Satō 1984, p. 19.

19. For the original text, see Tsuji 1974, p. 242.

20. The text of this inscription, known as the "Jakuchū koji Juzō Ketsumei," was included in the *Shōun Seikō*, published in 1775. See Tsuji 1974, p. 241.

21. Tsuji 1974, p. 186.

22. Satō 1987, p. 86.

23. Tsuji 1974, p. 187.

24. The author, Hiraga Hakusan (Shōsai), visited the Sekihōji in 1794.

25. See Tsuji 1974, pl. 49 and description.

26. See Satō 1987, pl. 15.

27. The Saifukuji, which belongs to the Nishi Honganji branch of Pure Land Buddhism, was at that time the tutelary temple of the Yoshino family, affluent wholesale merchants from the Unagidani neighborhood of Osaka, who dealt in Chinese materia medica and sold a distinctive ginseng patent medicine called Sanzōen, which was widely marketed in the provinces as well as in the region around Kyoto and Osaka. The business, founded in 1727, had flourished over the decades, and the lineal heads of the Yoshino family, distinguished by the use of the traditional firm name Goun, were all men of refined interests and accomplishment who associated with artists, men of letters, and arbiters of taste. Yoshino Kansai (also known as Yōsai), who commissioned Jakuchū to do the screens for the Saifukuji, is mentioned in the *Kyojitsu Ryūkō Hogen* (1794) as a rich merchant who appeared in amateur theatrical performances. The use of exotic and rare plants in the medicinal concoctions distributed by the Yoshino firm constituted part of their popular attraction (and, perhaps, something of their efficacy), and Jakuchū's inclusion of outsized, nonindigenous cacti in the screens may have been an oblique reference to this practice, as well as a more immediate reflection of the artist's own perennial interest in strange flora and unusual shapes.

28. Tsuji 1974, p. 190.

29. Earlier, during the late 1750s and 1760s, Jakuchū had utilized a similar distinctive name, "Beito-an" ("Hermitage of One *To* of Rice"—the name of his studio) in his signatures on paintings.

30. Tsuji 1974, p. 190.

31. Ibid.

32. Ibid., p. 191.

33. Ibid., p. 192.

CHAPTER 3

1. Tsuji 1974, p. 241.

2. Ibid.

3. Satō 1987, p. 20.

4. Asaoka 1904, vol. 2, pp. 1067–1068.

5. However, contradictory information elsewhere in the literature indicates that Shumboku perhaps did receive instruction from a Kanō teacher, whose identity is not given. The names of at least two Kanō painters, Shunsetsu and Eihaku, have been suggested, but the former is thought to have died in 1694, when Shumboku would have been only thirteen years of age, and the latter (who died in 1764 at the age of seventy-eight) was somewhat younger than Shumboku. Evidence of a working affiliation between Shumboku and Eihaku can be seen in the *Gakō Senran*, a six-volume *ehon* compiled by Shumboku and published in 1740; the final volume gives a genealogy of the Kanō school and the signatures and seals of its artists, along with an afterword by Eihaku, which is dated 1731. Eihaku was the son of Kanō Eikei (1662–1702), the fifth-generation head of the Kyoto line of the Kanō school, and son succeeded father as sixth-generation head.

6. Sets of sliding screens by Shumboku have been preserved in the abbot's quarters of two of the three subtemples of the Myōshinji, the Rei'un'in, and the Kobai'in. See Kyoto 1978, pp. 114–115.

7. Kenkadō's given name was Kimura Kōkyō; his *azana*, Seishuku; his familiar names, Kō and Kotarō; and his *gō*, Kenkadō and Sonsai. The family's prosperous sake factory, known as the Tsuboiya, was situated initially in the Minami-horie section of Osaka but was subsequently moved to Funaba, Gofuku-cho, close to the harbor. The area chosen for a garden at this new location had a stand of reeds, and this circumstance led to the choice of the studio name Kenkadō (Pavilion of the Reeds). As one might expect from a devoted sinophile like Kenkadō, his name had a Chinese origin; it had been used as a studio name by the Ming period poet and literary figure Lu Chieh, whose poems would have been available to Kenkadō in Chinese anthologies (Chien-chia T'ang is the Chinese equivalent of Kenkadō).

8. Kenkadō studied Chinese materia medica first under the Kyoto scholar Tsushima Jian and later under the scholar Ono Ranzan.

9. Kenkadō became friendly with Daiten at an early age as a result of their mutual interest in Chinese literature, for Kenkadō's teacher Katayama Hokkai was a follower of Daiten's teacher Uno Shishin. Kenkadō also became a close acquaintance of Daiten's student Monchū.

10. Despite the nature of the family business, Kenkadō did not drink sake. He was, however, an assiduous practitioner of Sencha (also referred to as Bunjin-cha, or Literati Tea) and one of Baisaō's most enthusiastic admirers. At the merchant's request, Jakuchū produced a lively portrait of the old priest, which stands as a tangible commemoration of their genial association. Kenkadō collected the tea utensils Baisaō had used and made careful drawings of them, which were subsequently copied by Aoki Shukuya and published in album form in 1823.

11. In 1789, when Kenkadō was fifty-four years old, he was singled out and accused by the authorities of illegally producing excessive quantities of sake. As punishment, his facilities and equipment were destroyed, the family business was terminated, and he was exiled to the Ise area, where his acquaintance Masuyama Masakata (an accomplished man of letters and a painter who used the *gō* Sessai) was the *daimyō* of the Nagashima fief. In the spring of 1793, Kenkadō was finally allowed to return to Osaka, where he established a firm that dealt in paper, inksticks, brushes, inkstones, and other materials for writers and artists, and this location became a center for artists and cultural connoisseurs in the region. He died in 1802 at the age of sixty-seven, and his friend Masuyama Sessai selected his funerary monument, had it inscribed with an appropriate inscription, and erected it.

12. Satō 1987, p. 20.

13. Tsuji 1974, p. 241.

14. Ibid., p. 226.

15. For a brief description of the symbolism and significance of the fabulous bird, see Weber 1923, vol. 1, p. 282.

16. The piece belongs to the Tokyo National University of Fine Arts and Music; Tokyo 1979, no. 147.

17. Ibid., no. 150. Phoenixes appear on the right screen, while peacocks are depicted on the left.

18. In addition to standing somewhat apart in style from the main body of Jakuchū's oeuvre, the piece also has two seals, neither of which appears elsewhere on the artist's works.

19. See Tokyo 1986, pl. 1. See also Ōoka Shumboku, *Wakan Meihitsu Ehon Tekagami*, vol. 4, pl. 22a, for a depiction of carp (attributed to Yamada Doan) based on Chinese pictorial tradition.

20. Tsuji 1974, pl. 41.

21. Yonezawa 1962, p. 148; collection of Takano Sugao, Tottori Prefecture.

22. "Ri Ichiwa-hitsu Goho Zukai," *Kokka* 442 (Jan. 1926):12.

23. Asaoka 1904, vol. 3, pp. 2224–2226.

24. Ibid., p. 2225.

25. Ibid., p. 2226.

26. Tsuji 1974, p. 227.

27. Ibid.

28. Evidence of the piece's fame can be seen in a sketch of it by Tani Bunchō that is reproduced in the *Shuko Jisshu*, compiled by Matsudaira Sadanobu.

29. *Kokka* 129 (Dec. 1900):160.

30. Tsuji 1974, p. 244.

31. Ibid., p. 231.

32. Ibid.

33. Kobayashi 1972b, p. 20ff.

34. See Tsuji 1974, p. 183.

35. See ibid., p. 241, for the text.

36. Akiyama 1926.

37. Ten of these extraordinary paintings have been generously lent by the Japanese Imperial Household for the exhibition to which this catalogue is a companion, and the reader will find more detailed information on their style, contents, and art-historical significance in the individual descriptive explanations for these pieces. In addition, the exhibition includes the monumental Buddhist triptych from the Shōkokuji that served as the central iconic focus in Jakuchū's grand conception (No. 15).

38. The funerary monument (*juzō*) commissioned by Jakuchū on his own behalf was erected in the Shō-ō'an subtemple of the Shōkokuji in the Eleventh Month of Meiwa 3 (1766), and Daiten's inscription ("Ketsumei") mentioned the artist as "the creator of thirty scrolls," suggesting the likelihood that all the scrolls were completed by this time (Satō 1987, p. 36). The last six paintings can be identified as a group because they have in common a small square intaglio seal reading *Tō-Jokin-in*, which Jakuchū used for the first time on these works.

39. Tsuji 1974, p. 183.

40. See Fontein and Hickman 1970 for an introduction to the subject.

41. Five pieces out of the first group of twelve depict various kinds of chickens, a subject that particularly interested Jakuchū during this period.

42. This is the fundamental thesis in a sermon delivered by the Buddha Śākyamuni entitled "Issai Shujō," or "The Fundamental Oneness of All Living Things."

43. The *Kundaikan Sōchōki* is a handbook of Chinese works of art, compiled in Japan toward the end of the fifteenth century. The author is unidentified, but the painters Nō'ami and Sō'ami both have been traditionally associated with the work. The earliest dated version is a manuscript from 1559 in the Tōhoku University Library. Although comments on individual painters are brief, the entries provide a survey of the Chinese artists (some of whom, such as Chang Ssu-kung, were unknown in China) known to the Japanese during the Muromachi period, as well as information about how Chinese artists and paintings were evaluated and ranked by Japanese connoisseurs. Various versions of the *Kundaikan Sōchōki* were circulated in manuscript form among Japanese enthusiasts until the early nineteenth century, when one version was finally published in the *Gunshō Ruijū*.

44. Tsuji 1974, p. 225.

45. For a selection of Koryō iconic paintings, see Kankoku 1986. A significant number of the extant Koryō pieces have been preserved in Japanese temples and shrines and, in more recent times, in public and private collections.

46. The Cleveland painting (Severance Fund 82.25) measures 217.8 × 112.7 cm; the Shōkokuji piece measures 210.3 × 111.3 cm.

47. For a stylistically related group, see the Amitabha triptych preserved in the Uesugi shrine in Japan; Lee 1981, pl. 12. The fact that no other Koryō iconic depictions of Śākyamuni have come to the attention of this writer further supports the assertion that the Cleveland painting is indeed the prototype.

48. At the same time, it was clearly not the artist's intention to create a literal facsimile, for he made no attempt to reproduce the signs of age present in the painting.

49. See Fontein and Hickman 1970, pp. 2–8. No other pieces that are clearly from the original set seem to have survived, but it is likely that they once belonged to a temple somewhere in Kyoto. Perhaps the three pieces in the Fujita Museum were the only survivors of the fire of 1788.

50. The same two seals, *Jakuchū koji* and *Tō-Jokin-in*, appear on both the Bodhisattva and the Arhat paintings, indicating that they were all produced during the same period. Jakuchū was then working at the Sekihōji, only a leisurely walk away from the Tōfukuji, where he must have had various opportunities to view the celebrated triptych. According to Asaoka 1904 (1970 ed., vol. 2, p. 631), Jakuchū's noted contemporary Sōga Shōhaku, an individualist painter, also created monochrome depictions of a Śākyamuni triptych and the sixteen Arhats. Unfortunately, these works do not appear to have been preserved.

51. The religious tradition of searching for enlightenment by pursuing in isolation such ascetic practices as abstinence, fasting, and prolonged meditation goes back to the origins of Buddhism, in India. This approach to enlightenment through the concentration of the devotee's own efforts and spiritual resources was a fundamental source of inspiration for Zen adepts in their arduous pursuit of *satori*. For a depiction of Śākyamuni undergoing austerities in the mountain wilderness, see the celebrated piece by Sōga Jasoku (d. 1473?) in Fontein and Hickman 1970, p. 126. It is likely that Jakuchū's retreat into the remote mountains of the Tamba region was inspired by this devotional tradition.

52. See Fontein and Hickman 1970, pp. 69–70.

53. The exact iconographic significance of the subject in Zen painting is still a matter of some disagreement among scholars. Canonical works such as the *Lalitavistara* describe how Śākyamuni was later nursed back to health and provided with new garments, and subsequently made a pilgrimage to Bodh Gaya, where he finally achieved Supreme Enlightenment. However, a consistent pictorial tradition in Zen painting that shows Śākyamuni returning from the mountains with certain of the bodily marks of the already enlightened Buddha—such as the *urna* (a white curl between the eyebrows), the *usnīsa* (a protuberance on top of the head symbolizing transcendent knowledge), and the halo—seem to indicate that Zen painters regarded Śākyamuni as having achieved enlightenment before his return from the mountains. Moreover, certain distinguishing pictorial features of the various versions of the *Shussan Shaka* (the Japanese name for the subject)—the stark background of rugged rock walls, rough trees, and foliage, and the diagonal line of the path leading out of the mountains—were abbreviated in later works or, as in the case of Jakuchū's piece, eliminated entirely. In addition, representations of the subject in early paintings consistently show the hems of Śākyamuni's garment blown forward by the wind, while later versions such as Jakuchū's often reverse this tradition.

54. It has been suggested that the painting was inspired by the inexpensive woodblock-printed folk icons produced for the popular market by anonymous workshop artists of the Ming and Ch'ing periods, presuming that Jakuchū simulated the essentially linear and often repetitive process of carving the blocks in his handling of the robes.

55. See Fontein and Hickman 1970, pp. 53–56, for a brief treatment of the subject.

56. Tsuji 1974, p. 233.

57. Ibid., p. 241.

58. During the Edo period, among both writers and artists there was a widespread interest in parodying the past. During the Hōreki (1751–1764) and Temmei (1781–1789) periods, this tendency was particularly strong in the Kamigata region, which includes Osaka, Kyoto, and surrounding areas. This phenomenon is likely to have been generally influential in motivating pieces such as that of Jakuchū.

59. For a typical representation and historical description, see Rosenfield and ten Grotenhuis 1979, p. 44.

60. See Shimizu n.d.

61. Reproduced in Sasaki 1980a, no. 10.

62. Both works are reproduced in Tokuriki et al. 1981.

63. The Chinese name *Hsüan p'u* (Japanese: Gempo) refers metaphorically to a legendary Taoist retreat in Tibet, and a temple by this name once stood in the Chinese capital of Ch'ang-an.

64. See Yamane 1978, pls. 61–66, item no. 111.

65. See Kobayashi 1982, p. 23; see p. 28, footnote 11, for the entire poem. The *Shōun Seiko* comprises poetry written by Daiten between 1759 and 1773.

66. Tsuji 1974, pl. 49.

67. A depiction of a similar section of cactus appears in Jakuchū's illustrated book the *Soken Jō*; see Tokuriki et al. 1981, pp. 86–87.

68. See Tsuji 1974, pl. 48.

69. For various examples of *chinsō*, see Fontein and Hickman 1970.

CATALOGUE

1. Morohashi 1984, vol. 1, pp. 503–504.

2. Satō 1983, p. 118.

3. Kobayashi and Nakamura 1984, pp. 50–52.

4. Takahashi 1986, p. 71.

5. Personal communication from Mr. Ariga Yoshitaka to Mr. Satō Yasuhiro.

6. Tsuji 1974, p. 195.

7. Kokka 1928, p. 237.

8. Suzuki 1963, pp. 37–39; Toda 1973a, pp. 248–249.

9. Tsuji 1974, pp. 20–28.

10. Kokka 1926, pp. 12–15.

11. Yonezawa 1962, pp. 148–151.

12. Otani et al. 1972, p. 448.

13. Hsüan-ho 1976, pp. 91–97.

14. Shufu-no-tomo-sha 1975, p. 43.

15. Tsuji 1974, p. 241.

16. Ibid.

17. Ibid.

18. Ibid.

19. Ibid., p. 242.

20. Ibid.

21. Ibid., p. 241.

22. Ibid., p. 194.

23. Fujita 1985, p. 230.

24. Ryūmon n.d., vol. 3.

25. Kobayashi 1971a, pp. 26–34.

26. Tsuji 1974, p. 241.

27. Toda 1988.

28. Tsuji 1974, p. 233.

29. Toda 1988.

30. Tanimura 1983, p. 89.

31. Takahashi 1983, pp. 25–45, 70–86; Kanō 1987a, pp. 22–36.

32. Kyoto 1927; Satō 1987, figs. 116, 117.

33. Mori et al. 1976, vol. 2, p. 519.

34. Sahashi 1984, vol. 2, pp. 25–68.

35. Kokka 1900, p. 160.

36. Asahina 1951, vol. 2, pp. 84–93.

37. Tsuji 1974, p. 241.

38. Aimi 1955, pp. 74–78.

39. Nakano and Kanō 1987, pp. 84–85.

40. Kobayashi 1982.

41. Shinshu 1968, vol. 12, p. 313.

42. Mori et al. 1980, vol. 9, pp. 195–196.

43. Sasaki 1980b, pp. 103–20.

44. Daiten 1775, vol. 5, pp. 17b–18a.

45. Satō 1983, p. 119.

46. Mr. Watanabe Akiyoshi has been of considerable help in clarifying a number of questions about this inscription.

47. Daiten 1775, vol. 5, p. 18b.

48. Kobayashi et al. 1973, p. 171.

49. Tsuji 1974, p. 195.

50. Kobayashi 1981, pp. 31–40.

51. Osaka 1933.

52. Shimizu n.d.

53. Tsuji 1974, p. 241.

54. Personal communication from Mr. Hayashi Susumu of the Yamato Bunkakan to Mr. Satō Yasuhiro.

55. Shimizu n.d.

56. Asahina 1951, vol. 3, pp. 198–211.

57. Otsuki et al. 1988, p. 489.

58. Ms. Beppu Setsuko has been of significant help in providing information on Fushimi dolls and in interpreting the inscription.

59. Mori et al. 1976, vol. 3, p. 484.

60. Myōhōin 1979, vol. 4, pp. 332–334.

61. Personal communication from Mr. Takeda Kōichi to Mr. Satō Yasuhiro.

62. Shōsai 1794, vol. 3.

63. Kokumin 1924, vol. 18, p. 37.

64. Myōhōin 1979, vol. 4, pp. 341–342.

65. Kobayashi 1972a.

66. Kyoto 1927; see also Satō 1987, fig. 116.

67. For the reading of the colophon and the significance of the Kanrodo, the author is grateful for the kind instruction of Mr. Hayashi Yukimitsu.

68. Morohashi 1984, vol. 7, p. 1217.

69. Kobayashi et al. 1973, p. 53.

70. Sakai 1815, fig. 39.

71. Shōsai 1794, vol. 2.

72. Tsuji 1974, p. 231.

73. Ibid., p. 241.

74. Beisen 1902, pp. 179–180.

75. The catalogue of this exhibition was Kyoto 1927.

76. Bijutsu 1947, p. 58.

BIBLIOGRAPHY

Acker 1954
Acker, William. *Some T'ang and Pre-T'ang Texts on Chinese Painting*. Leiden: Brill, 1954.

Addiss 1976
Addiss, Stephen. *Zenga and Nanga: Selections from the Kurt and Millie Gitter Collection*. New Orleans: New Orleans Museum of Art, 1976.

Addiss 1978
Addiss, Stephen. *Obaku: Zen Painting and Calligraphy*. Lawrence, KS: Helen Foresman Spencer Museum of Art, The University of Kansas, 1978.

Addiss 1978
Addiss, Stephen. "Obaku: The Art of Chinese Huang-Po Monks in Japan," *Oriental Art* n.s. 24, no. 4 (1978).

Aimi 1955
Aimi Kōu. "Jakuchū no Taku-hanga" ("Jakuchū's Rubbing Wood-block Prints"), *Geijutsu Shinchō* 6, no. 9 (Sept. 1955).

Aimi et al.
1958 Aimi Kōu et al. "Ryū Rikyō tokushū" (special issue on Yanagisawa Kien), *Yamato Bunka Kenkyū* 19–20 (1958).

Akiyama 1926
Akiyama Teruō. *Gyomotsu Jakuchū Dōshoku Sai-e Sei-ei*. Tokyo: Tokyo Imperial Museum, 1926.

Akiyama 1961
Akiyama, Terukazu. *Japanese Painting*. Lausanne: Skira, 1961.

Akiyama 1971
Akiyama Terukazu. "Jakuchū Kenkyū Yosetsu," *Museum* 245 (1971).

Akiyama et al. 1930
Akiyama Terukazu, Tanaka Ichimatsu, and Aimi Shige'ichi, eds. *Sogen Meigashu (Collection of Famous Sung and Yüan Paintings)*. 2 vols. Tokyo: Isseido, 1930.

Asahina 1951
Asahina Sogen (translator, annotator). *Hekigan Roku* (rev. ed.). Tokyo: Iwanami Shoten, 1951.

Asaoka 1904
Asaoka Okisada (1800–1856). *Koga Bikō (Handbook of Classical Painting)*. 3 vols. and index; rev. and enlarged by Ōta Kin as *Zotei Koga Bikō*, 1904. Tokyo: Shibunkaku, 1970.

Awakawa 1970
Awakawa, Yasuichi. *Zen Painting*. Trans. by John Bester. Tokyo: Kodansha, 1970.

de Bary 1969
de Bary, William Theodore, ed. *The Buddhist Tradition in India, China, and Japan*. New York: 1969.

Beisen 1902
Kubota Beisen. *Beisen Gadan*. Tokyo: Matsumura Sanshodo, 1902.

Bijutsu 1947
Bijutsu Kenkyujo (compilers). "Bijutsukan oyobi Bijutsu Kankeisha Meibo," in *Nihon Bijutsu Nenkan, Showa Juhachi-nen ban*. Tokyo: Zauho Kankokai, 1947.

Blofeld 1958
Blofeld, F. *The Zen Teaching of Huang Po on the Transmission of Mind*. London: 1958.

Blofield 1958
Blofield, John. *The Zen Teachings of Huang-po*. New York: 1958.

Blyth 1942
Blyth, R. H. *Zen in English Literature and Oriental Classics*. Tokyo: 1942; paperback ed. New York: 1960.

Brasch 1961
Brasch, Kurt. *Zenga (Zen Malerei)*. Tokyo: 1961.

Brinker 1973
Brinker, Helmut. "Shussan Shaka in Sung and Yuan Painting," *Ars Orientalis* 9 (1973): 21–40.

Brown 1924
Brown, L. N. *Block Printing and Book Illustration in Japan*. London: Routledge and Sons, 1924.

Bush 1971
Bush, Susan. *The Chinese Literati on Painting: Su Shih (1037–1101) to Tung Ch'i-ch'ang (1555–1636), Harvard Yenching Institute Series* 27. Cambridge, MA: Harvard University Press, 1971.

Cahill 1960
Cahill, James. "Confucian Elements in the Theory of Painting," in Arthur Wright, ed., *The Confucian Persuasion*: 115–140. Stanford: Stanford University Press, 1960.

Cahill 1971
Cahill, James, ed. *The Restless Landscape: Chinese Painting of the Late Ming Period*. Berkeley: University Art Museum, 1971.

Cahill 1972
Cahill, James. *Scholar Painters of Japan: The Nanga School*. New York: The Asia Society/New York Graphic Society, 1972.

Cahill 1978
Cahill, James. *Parting at the Shore: Chinese Painting of the Early and Middle Ming Dynasty, 1368–1580*. New York: Weatherhill, 1978.

Cahill 1982a
Cahill, James. *The Distant Mountains: Chinese Painting of the Late Ming Dynasty, 1570–1644*. New York: Weatherhill, 1982.

Cahill 1982b
Cahill, James. "Yosa Buson and Chinese Painting," in *International Symposium on the Conservation and Restoration of Cultural Property: Interregional Influences in East Asian Art History*: 245–263. Tokyo: Tokyo National Cultural Properties Research Institute, 1982.

Cahill 1983
Cahill, James. *Sakaki Hyakusen and Early Nanga Painting, Japan Research Monographs* 3. Berkeley: University of California Press, 1983.

Chang 1970
Chang, Aloysius. "The Chinese Community in Nagasaki." Ph.D. diss., St. John's University, 1970.

Chang and Sinclair 1945
Chang, Lily P., and Marjorie Sinclair. *The Poems of T'ao Ch'ien*. Honolulu: University of Hawaii Press, 1945.

Chang 1962
Chang Yen-yüan. *Li-tai Ming-hua Chi* (*Famous Paintings Through the Ages* [A.D. 847]) in Yang Chia-lo, ed., *I-shu Ts'ung-pien* 8, no. 58. Taipei: 1962.

Ch'en 1964
Ch'en, Kenneth K. S. *Buddhism in China: A Historical Survey*. Princeton: Princeton University Press, 1964.

Ch'iu 1951
Ch'iu, A. K'ai-ming. "The Chieh Tzu Yüan Hua Chuan," *Archives of the Chinese Art Society of America* 5 (1951): 55–69.

Chibbett 1977
Chibbett, David. *The History of Japanese Printing and Book Illustration*. Tokyo: Kodansha, 1977.

Collcutt 1975
Collcutt, Martin. "The Zen Monastic Institution in Medieval Japan." Ph.D. diss., Harvard University, 1975.

Daiten 1775
Daiten Kenjō. *Shōun Seikō*. Osaka: Tosaya Kibei, 1775.

Doi 1967a
Doi Tsugiyoshi. "Jakuchū—Saifukuji no Fusuma-e o chūshin ni" ("Jakuchū—Focusing on His Sliding-screen Paintings in the Saifukuji"), *Nihon no Bijutsu Kogei* (1967).

Doi 1967b
Doi Tsugiyoshi. *Jakuchū Tenjo-e* (*Jakuchū's Ceiling Paintings*). Tokyo: Maria Shobo, 1967.

Doi 1970
Doi Tsugiyoshi. *Kinsei Nihon kaiga no kenkyū* (*Research on Japanese Painting of the Early Modern Period*). Tokyo: Bijutsu Shuppansha, 1970.

Doi 1971
Doi Tsugiyoshi. "Shingyōji no Tenjo-e to Kompiragū no Shohekiga" ("The Shingyōji Ceiling Paintings and the Screen and Wall Paintings in the Kotohiragū"), *Museum* 245 (1971).

Doi 1980
Doi Tsugiyoshi. *Sanraku to Sansetsu, Nihon no Bijutsu* 172. Tokyo: Shibundō, 1980.

Doi 1981
Doi Tsugiyoshi. "Sanuki Kompiragū no Itō Jakuchū" ("Itō Jakuchū and the Kompiragū in Sanuki Province"), *Kokka* 1046 (Oct. 1981).

Dumoulin 1963
Dumoulin, Heinrich. *A History of Zen Buddhism*. Trans. by Paul Peachey. Boston: Beacon Press, 1963.

Ebara 1958
Ebara Taizō. "Buson to Hyakusen", in *Edo Bungei Kenkyū*. Tokyo: Kadokawa Shoten, 1958.

Fontein 1967
Fontein, Jan. *The Pilgrimage of Sudhana*. The Hague: Mouton, 1967.

Fontein and Hickman 1970
Fontein, Jan, and Money Hickman. *Zen Painting and Calligraphy*. Boston: Museum of Fine Arts, 1970.

Kinsei Zenrin 1974
Kinsei Zenrin Bokuseki (*Soto to Obaku*). Tokyo: 1974.

French et al. 1974
French, Calvin L., et al. *The Poet-painters: Buson and His Followers*. Ann Arbor: University of Michigan Museum of Art, 1974.

Fujikawa 1966
Fujikawa Hideo. *Edo Kōki no Shijintachi*. Tokyo: Mugi Shobō, 1966.

Fujita 1963
Fujita Tsuneo. *Kundaikan Sayū Chōki Shū (Collected Versions of the Kundaikan Sōchōki), Kokan Bijutsu-shiryō* 114. Tokyo: 1963. (Mimeographed; printed edition forthcoming.)

Fujita 1985
Fujita Keise, ed. *Kohan Bijutsu-shiryo Zokuhen*. Tokyo: Kohan Bijutsu-shiryo Zokuhen, 1985.

Furuta 1956
Furuta, S. "Nihon-zen no hattatsu" ("The Development of Japanese Zen"), in *Gendai Zen-kōza* 2: 49–81. Tokyo: 1956.

Graham 1988
Graham, Patricia. "A Heterodox Painting of Shussan Shaka in Late Tokugawa Japan." Unpublished manuscript, 1988.

Grilli 1970
Grilli, E. *The Art of the Japanese Screen*. New York and Tokyo: Walker/Weatherhill, 1970.

Haga 1956
Haga Kōshirō. *Chūsei Zenrin no Gakumon oyobi Bungaku ni Kansuru Kenkyū* (*A Study of the Learning and Literature in Medieval Zen Circles*). Tokyo: Nihon Gakujutsu Shinkōkai, 1956.

Hickman 1973a
Hickman, Money. "Paintings by Shohaku in the Museum of Fine Arts, Boston," in *Jakuchū, Shōhaku, Rosetsu* (*Suiboku Bijutsu Taikei* 14). Tokyo: Kodansha, 1973.

Hickman 1973b
Hickman, Money. "Sōga Shōhaku and the Museum of Fine Arts, Boston," *Ars Buddhica* 90 (Feb. 1973).

Hickman 1976
Hickman, Money. "The Paintings of Sōga Shōhaku." Ph.D. diss., Harvard University, 1976.

Hickman et al. 1977
Hickman, Money, Tsuji Nobuo, and Kono Motoaki. *Jakuchū, Shōhaku, Nihon Bijutsu Kaiga Zenshu* 23. Tokyo: Shueisha, 1977.

Hickman 1981
Hickman, Money. "On the Trail of Kume the Transcendent," *Bulletin of the Museum of Fine Arts, Boston* 79 (1981).

Hillier and Smith 1980
Hillier, J., and L. Smith. *Japanese Prints: 300 Years of Albums and Books*. London: British Museum, 1980.

Hisamatsu 1971
Hisamatsu Shin'ichi. *Zen and the Fine Arts*. Trans. by Gishin Tokiwa. Tokyo: Kodansha, 1971.

Hsüan-ho 1962
Hsüan-ho Hua-p'u (*Catalogue of Paintings in the Imperial Collection of the Hsüan-ho Era*; preface 1120), in Yang Chia-lo, ed., *I-shu Ts'ung-pien* 9, no. 65. Taipei: 1962.

Hsüan-ho 1976
Chung-hua Shu-hua Yen-chiu Tzu-liao She (compiler). *Hua-shih Ts'ung-shu* 1. Taipei: Wen-shih-che Press, 1976.

Hu 1932
Hu Shih. "Development of Zen Buddhism in China," *Social and Political Science Review* 15: 4 (1932).

Iijima 1957
Iijima Isamu. "Buson no Haiga ni Tsuite," *Museum* 78 (Sept. 1957).

Iijima 1980
Iijima Isamu. *Tanomura Chikuden, Nihon no Bijutsu* 165. Tokyo: Shibundō, 1980.

Ikkyū 1910
Ikkyū. "Gaikotsu" ("Skeleton"), in *Zenmon Hogoshū*, 6th ed. Tokyo: 1910.

Ima'eda 1952
Ima'eda Aishin. *Zenshū no Rekishi* (*A History of Zen Buddhism*). Tokyo: Shibundō, 1952.

Inazuka 1919
Inazuka Takeshi. "Goshun ni tsuite," *Kokka* 348 (May 1919): 349 (June 1919).

Inazuka 1920
Inazuka Takeshi. "Goshun Itsu Bun," *Kokka* 358 (March 1920): 359 (April 1920).

Ishizaki 1926
Ishizaki Kōkō. "Saifukuji no Jakuchū Fusuma-e" ("Jakuchū's Sliding-screen Paintings in the Saifukuji"), *Chuo Bijutsu* 126 (1926).

Kanazawa 1972
Kanazawa Hiroshi. *Shoki suibokuga* (*Ink wash Painting of the Early Period*), *Nihon no Bijutsu* 69. Tokyo: Shibundō, 1972.

Kanazawa 1979
Kanazawa Hiroshi. *Japanese Ink Painting: Early Zen Masterpieces.* Trans. by Barbara Ford. New York: Kodansha, 1979.

Kankoku 1986
Koryō Butsuga, Kankoku Bijutsu 2. Tokyo: Kodansha, 1986.

Kanō 1917
Kanō Ikkei (1599–1662). *Kōsoshū* (*Themes in Chinese Painting*; 1623), in Sakazaki Tan, ed., *Nihon Gadan Taikan*: 536–590. Tokyo: Mejiro Shoin, 1917.

Kanō 1926a
Kanō Einō (1634–1700). *Honchō Gashi* (*History of Japanese Painting*; 1678), in Sakazaki Tan, ed., *Nihon Garon Taikan* 2: 951–1017. Tokyo: Ars, 1926–1928.

Kanō 1926b
Kanō Einō (1634–1700). *Honcho Ga'in* (*Seals of Japanese Painters*; 1693), in Sakazaki Tan, ed., *Nihon Garon Taikan* 2: 1018–1054. Tokyo: Ars, 1926–1928.

Kanō 1926c
Kanō Ikkei (1599–1662). *Tansei Jakubokushu* (*Biographies of Japanese Painters*), in Sakazaki Tan, ed., *Nihon Garon Taikan* 2: 923–950. Tokyo: Ars, 1926–1928.

Kanō 1987a
Kanō Hiroyuki, "Edo Bunka no Nishi to Higashi—Jūhasseki no omoshirosa," *Hermes* 12 (Sept. 1987).

Kanō 1987b
Kanō Hiroyuki. *Sōga Shōhaku, Nihon no Bijutsu* 11. Tokyo: Shibundō, 1987.

Keene 1976
Keene, Donald. *World Within Walls: Japanese Literature of the Pre-Modern Era 1600–1867.* New York: Holt, Rinehart, and Winston, 1976.

Kobayashi 1971a
Kobayashi Tadashi. "Itō Jakuchū no Suibokuga ni tsuite—Rokuonji Shohekiga nado Zenki no Sakuhin o chūshin ni" ("On Itō Jakuchū's Monochrome Ink Paintings—Focusing on the Screen and Wall Paintings in the Rokuonji, and Other Early Works"), *Museum* 245 (Aug. 1971).

Kobayashi 1971b
Kobayashi Tadashi. *Jakuchū Tokubetsu Tenkan Zuroku* (*Catalogue of the Special Exhibition of Jakuchū's Paintings*). Tokyo: Tokyo National Museum, 1971.

Kobayashi 1972a
Kobayashi Tadashi. "Bannen-ki Jakuchū no Sakuhin; Suiboku Ryakuga o Chushin toshite" ("The Works of Itō Jakuchū in His Last Years—Chiefly with Reference to his Sketches in *Suiboku*"), *Kokka* 944 (March 1972): 11–19.

Kobayashi 1972b
Kobayashi Tadashi. "Sponge Gourd and Insects," *Kokka* 948 (Aug. 1972): 20–28.

Kobayashi 1981
Kobayashi Tadashi. "Itō Jakuchū Dokusō no Itsukaku Byoho ni tsuite" ("On Itō Jakuchū's Individual Manner of 'Abbreviated' Painting"), *Museum* 359 (Feb. 1981): 31–40.

Kobayashi 1982
Kobayashi Tadashi. "Itō Jakuchū no Hanga" ("Itō Jakuchū's Woodblock Prints"), *Museum* 377 (Aug. 1982): 20–28.

Kobayashi 1983a
Kobayashi Tadashi. *Edo Kaiga II (Koki)* (*Edo Painting II [late]*), *Nihon no Bijutsu* 210. Tokyo: Shibundō, 1983.

Kobayashi 1983b
Kobayashi Tadashi. *Edo kaigashi ron* (*Essays on the History of Edo Painting*). Tokyo: Ruri Shobō, 1983.

Kobayashi et al. 1973
Kobayashi Tadashi, Tsuji Nobuo, and Yamakawa Takeshi. *Jakuchū, Shōhaku, Rosetsu, Suiboku Bijutsu Taikei* 14. Tokyo: Kodansha, 1973.

Kobayashi and Nakamura 1984
Kobayashi Tadashi and Nakamura Tanio. "Yamagata de mitsukatta Jakuchū," *Geijutsu Shincho* 411 (March 1984).

Kokka 1900
"Jakuchū," *Kokka* 129 (Sept. 1900).

Kokka 1926
"Ri Ichiwa-hitsu Gohō-zukai" ("Picture of Five Phoenixes by Li I-hai [sic.]"), *Kokka* 422 (Jan. 1926): 12–15.

Kokka 1928
"Itō Jakuchū-hitsu Kannon zukai," *Kokka* 453 (Aug. 1928).

Kokumin 1924
Kokumin Tosho Kabushiki Kaisha (compilers). *Kōchū Kokka Taikei.* Tokyo: Kokumin Tosho Kabushiki Kaisha, 1924.

Kondo 1890
Kondo Tokutaro. *Jakuchū Gafū.* 1890.

Kono 1982
Kono Motoaki. *Kanō Tan'yū, Nihon no Bijutsu* 194. Tokyo: Shibundō, 1982.

Kundaikan 1933
Kundaikan Sayū Chōki (also known as *Kundaikan Sōchōki; A Fifteenth-Century Connoisseur's Manual of Chinese Art*), in *Gunsho Ruijū* 19: 648–670. Tokyo: Zoku Gunsho Ruijū Kanseikai, 1933.

Kyoto 1927
Tobeian Jakuchū Gasen. Kyoto: Kyoto Onshi Museum of Art/Benrido, 1927 (exhibition catalogue).

Kyoto 1939
Kyoto Hakubutsukan. *Nagasaki-ha: Shasei Nansō Meigasen.* Kyoto: Benrido, 1939.

Kyoto 1978
Kyoto no Edo-jidai Shoheki-ga. Kyoto: privately published, 1978.

Lee 1972
Lee, Sherman E. "Zen in Art: Art in Zen," *Cleveland Museum of Art Bulletin* 59 (1972): 238–259.

Lee 1981
Lee Tong-ju, ed. *Koryō Purhwa (Buddhist Paintings of the Koryō Period), Hanguk ui Mi* 7 *(Korean Beauty)*. Seoul: Chungang Ilbosa, 1981.

Lee and Ho 1968
Lee, Sherman E., and Wai-kam Ho. *Chinese Art Under the Mongols: The Yuan Dynasty (1279–368)*. Cleveland: Cleveland Museum of Art, 1968.

Matsumoto 1942
Matsumoto, B. *Daruma no Kenkyū (Studies on Bodhidharma)*. Tokyo: 1942.

Matsushita 1957
Matsushita Tadashi. *Edo Jidai no Shifū Shiron*. Tokyo: Meiji Shoin, 1957.

Matsushita 1974
Matsushita Takaaki. *Ink Painting, Arts of Japan* 7. Trans. and adapted by Martin Collcutt. New York: Weatherhill, 1974.

Matsushita 1983
Matsushita Takaaki. *Nihon suibokuga ronshū (Collection of Essays on Japanese Ink Wash Painting)*. Tokyo: Chūōkōron Bijutsu Shuppan, 1983.

Matsushita et al. 1976
Matsushita Takaaki et al. *Nihon Bijutsu Kaiga Zenshū (Collection of Japanese Painting)*. 25 vols. Tokyo: Shūeisha, 1976–1980.

Mitchell 1972
Mitchell, C. H. *The Illustrated Books of the Nanga, Maruyama, Shijō and Other Related Schools of Japan (A Biobibliography)*. Los Angeles: Dawson's Bookshop, 1972.

Miyajima 1984
Miyajima Shin'ichi. *Nagasawa Rosetsu, Nihon no Bijutsu* 218. Tokyo: Shibundō, 1984.

Miyajima n.d.
Miyajima Shin'ichi. "Santō ni okeru Nanpin Gafū no Denpan" ("The Transmission of the Nanpin Style to Three Major Cities"), *Yamato Bunka*.

Mizuo 1972
Mizuo, Hiroshi . *Edo Painting: Sōtatsu and Kōrin, Heibonsha Survey of Japanese Art* 18. Tokyo: Heibonsha, 1972.

Mori 1939
Mori Senzō. "Jakuchū Koroku," *Gasetsu* 29 (May 1939): 423–427.

Mori et al. 1976
Mori Senzō, et al., eds. *Kinsei Jimmei-roku Shusei*. Tokyo: Benseisha, 1976.

Mori et al. 1980
Mori Senzō et al., eds. *Zoku Nihon Zuihitsu Taisei*. Tokyo: Yoshikawa Kobunkan, 1980.

Morohashi 1984
Morohashi Tetsuji. *Dai Kanwa Jiten*. Tokyo: Daishuten Shoten, 1984.

Mote 1960
Mote, Frederick W. "Confucian Eremitism in the Yüan Period," in Arthur F. Wright, ed., *Confucianism and Chinese Civilization*: 202–240. Stanford: Stanford University Press, 1960.

Murayama 1918
Murayama Jungo. *Nanga Shū*. 3 vols. Tokyo: Kokka-sha, 1918.

Murase 1975
Murase Miyeko. *Japanese Art: Selections from the Mary and Jackson Burke Collection*. New York: Metropolitan Museum of Art, 1975.

Myōhōin 1979
Myōhōin-shi Kenkyūkai, eds. *Myōhoin Shiryō*. Tokyo: Yoshikawa Kobunkan, 1979.

Nagami 1927
Nagami Tokutaro. *Nagasaki no Bijutsu Shi*. Osaka: 1927.

Nagoya 1981
Owari no kaigashi Nanga (The Southern School in the Painting History of Owari). Nagoya: Nagoya Municipal Museum, 1981 (exhibition catalogue).

Nagoya 1984
Shirarezaru Nangaka Hyakusen (An Unknown Southern School Painter, Hyakusen). Nagoya: Nagoya Municipal Museum, 1984 (exhibition catalogue).

Nakamura 1966
Nakamura Yukihiko. *Kinsei Bungakuron Shu, Nihon Koten Bungaku Taikei* series. Tokyo: Iwanami Shoten, 1966.

Nakano and Kanō 1987
Nakano Mitsutoshi and Kanō Hiroyuki. "Chūmoku sareru Edo no Ehon"(dialogue), in Kanō Hiroyuki, *Sōga Shōhaku, Nihon no Bijutsu* 258. Tokyo: Shibundō, 1987.

Nakata 1950
Nakata Katsunosuke . *E-hon no Kenkyū*. Tokyo: Bijutsu Shuppansha, 1950.

Nishimura 1934
Nishimura Tadashi. *Ōbaku Gazō Shi*. Tokyo: 1934.

Nishimura 1972
Nishimura Tadashi. *Ōbaku Bunka*. Mampukuji, 1972.

Noma 1966
Noma Seiroku. *The Arts of Japan, Ancient and Medieval*. Trans. by J. M. Rosenfield. Tokyo: Kodansha, 1966.

Ogata 1971
Ogata Tomio, ed. *Rangaku to Nihon Bunka (Dutch Studies and Japanese Culture)*. Tokyo: Tokyo Daigaku Shuppankai, 1971.

Osaka 1933
Osaka Shōkō Kyokai, eds. *Rinkō Kinen Meika Hizōhin Ten'rankai Zuroku*. Osaka: Geiensha-Sankyusha, 1933.

Otani et al. 1972
Otani Tokuzō et al. *Buson-shu (A Collection of Buson), Koten Haibungaku Taikei (Library of Classic Literature)* 12. Tokyo: Shueisha, 1972.

Otsuki et al. 1988
Otsuki Mikio et al., eds. *Ōbaku Bunka Jimmei Jiten*. Kyoto: Shibunkaku, 1988.

Ozawa 1935
Ozawa Toshio. *Nagasaki Nempyō*. Nagasaki: Guroria Shobo, 1935.

Paine and Soper 1975
Paine, Robert Treat, and Alexander C. Soper. *The Art and Architecture of Japan* (rev. ed.). Baltimore: Penguin Books, 1975.

Papinot 1910
Papinot, E. *Historical and Geographical Dictionary of Japan*. Yokohama: Kelly and Walsh, 1910.

Ponsonby-Fane 1956
Ponsonby-Fane, R. A. B. *Kyoto—The Old Capital of Japan*. Kyoto: 1956.

Price
Price, Joe D. "Watakushi no Jakuchū Henreki" (My Jakuchū Pilgrimage"), *Geijutsu Shinchō* 22–23.

Roberts 1976
Roberts, L. P. *A Dictionary of Japanese Artists*. Tokyo and New York: Weatherhill, 1976.

Rosenfield 1979
Rosenfield, John M., ed. *Song of the Brush: Japanese Paintings from the Sanso Collection*. Seattle: Seattle Art Museum, 1979.

Rosenfield et al. 1973
Rosenfield, John M., Fumiko E. Cranston, and Edwin Cranston. *The Courtly Tradition in Japanese Art and Literature: Selections from the Hofer and Hyde Collections*. Cambridge, MA: Fogg Art Museum, Harvard University, 1973.

Rosenfield and Shimada 1970
Rosenfield, John M., and Shujiro Shimada. *Traditions of Japanese Art: Selections from the Kimiko and John Powers Collection*. Cambridge, MA: Fogg Art Museum, Harvard University, 1970.

Rosenfield and ten Grotenhuis 1979
Rosenfield, John M., and Elizabeth ten Grotenhuis. *Journey of the Three Jewels: Japanese Buddhist Paintings from Western Collections*. New York: The Asia Society, 1979.

Ryūmon n.d.
Ryūmon Shōyū. *Meiko Yoko*. Tokyo: National Diet Library.

Sahashi 1984
Sahashi Horyu. *Zenyaku Hekigan Roku*. Tokyo: Sanichi Shobo, 1984.

Saito 1912
Saito Ken. *Kanō-ha Taikan* (*General View of Works by the Kanō School*). 3 vols. Tokyo: Kanō-ha Taikan Hakkōjo, 1912–1914.

Saito 1931
Saito Ken. *Kanō-ha* (*Kanō School*), *Nihonga Taisei* 5–6. Tokyo: Tōhō Shoin, 1931.

Sakai 1815
Sakai Hōitsu, ed. *Hyaku-zu* (*One Hundred Pictures by Kōrin*). Vol.1. Edo: 1815. See also Tsuji Nobuo, "Hōitsu's *One Hundred Pictures by Korin* and Korin's Extant Works," in Yamane Yuzo, ed., *Korin School 1, Paintings of Rimpa* 3: 67-72. Tokyo: Nihon Keizai Shinbunsha, 1979.

Sakazaki 1917
Sakazaki Tan, ed. *Nihon Gadan Taikan* (*Collection of Japanese Painting Texts*). Tokyo: Mejiro Shoin, 1917.

Sakazaki 1926
Sakazaki Tan, ed. *Nihon Garon Taikan* (*Collection of Japanese Painting Texts*). 2 vols. Tokyo: Ars, 1926–1928.

Sakazaki 1980
Sakazaki Hiroshi, ed. *Nihon kaigaron taikei* (*Compendium on Japanese Painting Theory*). 5 vols. Tokyo: Meicho Fukyukai, 1980.

Saku 1943
Saku Misao, ed. *Kanshi Taikan*. Tokyo: Ida Shoten, 1943.

Sansom 1958
Sansom, George B. *A History of Japan*. 3 vols. Stanford: Stanford University Press, 1958–1963.

Sansom 1962
Sansom, George B. *Japan: A Short Cultural History* (rev. ed.). New York: Meredith Corporation, 1962.

Sasaki 1975
Sasaki Jōhei. *Yosa Buson, Nihon no Bijutsu* 109. Tokyo: Shibundō, 1975.

Sasaki 1979
Sasaki Jōhei. "Ike no Taiga—Sono seisaku katei ni kansuru ichi kosatsu" ("An Investigation into the Creative Process of Ike Taiga"), *Yamato Bunka* 65 (1979).

Sasaki 1980a
Sasaki Jōhei. *Ōkyo and the Maruyama-Shijō School of Japanese Painting*. Saint Louis: Saint Louis Art Museum, 1980.

Sasaki 1980b
Sasaki Jōhei. "The Paintings of Five Hundred Arhats on the Sliding Doors of Mampuku-ji, by Ike Taiga—Their Relation with the Original Scroll Paintings," *Ars Buddhica* 129 (March 1980): 103–120.

Sasaki 1980c
Sasaki Jōhei. *Uragami Gyokudō, Nihon no Bijutsu* 56. Tokyo: Shogakukan, 1980.

Sasaki 1981
Sasaki Jōhei. "Ōkyo kankei shiryo *Banshi* bassui" ("Selections from *Banshi* Relating to Ōkyo"), *Bijutsushi* 111 (1981).

Sasaki 1983
Sasaki Jōhei. *Edo Kaiga 1 (Zenki)* (*Edo Painting 1 [early]*), *Nihon no Bijutsu* 209. Tokyo: Shibundō, 1983.

Satō 1981
Satō Yasuhiro. "Jakuchū ni okeru Mosha no Igi" ("On the Significance of Jakuchū's Copies of Paintings"), *Museum* 364 (1981).

Satō 1983
Satō Yasuhiro. "Jakuchū no Tori," in *Bunga no Hana, Kiso no Tori, Kachōga no Sekai* (*Bird-and-flower Paintings of Japan*) 7. Tokyo: Gakushu Kenkyusha, 1983.

Satō 1987
Satō Yasuhiro. *Itō Jakuchū, Nihon no Bijutsu* 256. Tokyo: Shibundō, 1987.

Shiban 1972
Shiban (1626–1710). *Empō Dentōroku* (*Biographies of Japanese Zen Monks Compiled in the Empō Era*, 1673–1681), in *Dainihon Bukkyō Zensho* 70. Tokyo: Suzuki Gakujutsu Zaidan, 1972. (Also in *Dainihon Bukkyō Zensho* 2. Tokyo: Yuseido, 1931.)

Shimada 1961
Shimada Shujiro. "Concerning the I-p'in Style of Painting," trans. by James Cahill, *Oriental Art* 7 (1961): 66–74; 8(1962): 130–137; 10(1964): 19–26.

Shimizu n.d.
Shimizu Yoshiaki. "Multiple Commemorations: *The Vegetable Nehan* by Itō Jakuchū (1716–1800)." Unpublished research paper.

Shimizu and Wheelwright 1975
Shimizu Yoshiaki and Carolyn Wheelwright. *Japanese Ink Paintings*. Princeton: Princeton University Press, 1975.

Shimonaka 1956
Shimonaka Kunihiko, ed. *Shōdō Zenshū* (*Collected Works of Calligraphy*). 20 vols. Tokyo: Heibonsha, 1956–1960.

Shinshu 1968
Shinshū Kyoto Sōsho Hankokai, eds. *Shinshū Kyoto Sōsho*. Kyoto: Kodaisha, 1968.

Shōsai 1794
Hiraga Shōsai. *Shōsai Hikki* (1794). Tokyo: Tokyo University Library.

Shufu-no-tomo-sha 1975
Shufu-no-tomo-sha (compiler). *Baisaō Shusei*. Tokyo: Shufu-no-tomo-sha, 1975.

Siren 1956
Siren, Osvald. *Chinese Painting*. 7 vols. New York: The Ronald Press Co., 1956.

Sorimachi 1978
Sorimachi Shigeo. *Catalogue of Japanese Illustrated Books and Manuscripts in the Spencer Collection of the New York Public Library*. Tokyo: Kōbunsō, 1978.

Sugita 1969
Sugita Gempaku. *Dawn of Western Science in Japan* (*Rangaku Kotohajime*, 1815). Tokyo: Hokuseido, 1969.

Suzuki 1927
Suzuki, D. T. *Essays in Zen Buddhism*. Vol 1. London: 1927; new eds. London: 1949, 1958.

Suzuki 1933
Suzuki, D. T. *Essays in Zen Buddhism*. Vol 2. London: 1933; new eds. London: 1950, 1958.

Suzuki 1934
Suzuki, D. T. *Essays in Zen Buddhism*. Vol 3. London: 1934; new eds. London: 1953, 1958.

Suzuki 1938
Suzuki, D. T. *Zen Buddhism and Its Influence on Japanese Culture*. Kyoto: 1938; rev. 2nd ed. *Zen and Japanese Culture*, Bollingen series 64. Princeton: Princeton University Press, 1970.

Suzuki 1958
Suzuki Susumu. *Buson*. Tokyo: Nihon Keizai Shimbun, 1958.

Suzuki 1963
Suzuki Kei, "Budo-zu," *Kokka* 861 (Dec. 1963).

Takahashi 1983
Takahashi Hiromi. *Kyoto Geien no Nettowaku*. Tokyo: Pelican Press, 1983.

Takahashi 1986
Takahashi Hiromi. "Kien-shi Bunshu," in *Kinsei Jūka Bunshu Shusei* 9. Tokyo: Pelican Press, 1986.

Takeda 1967
Takeda Tsuneo. *Shōbyōga* (*Panel and Screen Painting*), *Genshoku Nihon no Bijutsu* 13. Tokyo: Shogakkan, 1967.

Takeda 1974
Takeda Tsuneo. *Kanō Eitoku*, *Nihon no Bijutsu* 94. Tokyo: Shibundō, 1974.

Takeda 1979
Takeda Kōichi. "Ike no Taiga no shiboku ni tsuite" ("Concerning Ike Taiga's Finger Painting"), *Tokyo Geijutsu Daigaku Bijutsu Gakubu kiyō* 14 (1979).

Takemura 1965
Takemura Shunsoku. *Shinsen Kyoto Meisho Zue*. Kyoto: Shirakawa Shoin, 1965.

Takeuchi 1983
Takeuchi, Melinda. "Ike Taiga: A Biographical Study," *Harvard Journal of Asiatic Studies* 43, no. 1 (1983): 141–186.

Takeuchi 1984
Takeuchi, Melinda. "Tradition, Innovation, and Realism in a Pair of Eighteenth-Century Japanese Landscape Screens," *The Register of the Spencer Museum of Art* 4, no. 1 (1984): 34–66.

Tanaka 1966
Tanaka Ichimatsu. *Nihon Kaigashi Ronshū* (*Collected Essays on the History of Japanese Painting*). Tokyo: Chūōkōron Bijutsu Shuppan, 1966.

Tanaka 1972
Tanaka Ichimatsu. *Japanese Ink Painting: Shūbun to Sesshū*. Trans. by Bruce Darling. New York: Weatherhill/Heibonsha, 1972.

Tanaka et al. 1973
Tanaka Ichimatsu et al. *Suiboku Bijutsu Taikei* (*Compendium of Ink Wash Painting*). 15 vols. and 2 supplements. Tokyo: Kodansha, 1973–1977.

Tanaka et al. 1966
Tanaka Ichimatsu, Do'i Tsugiyoshi, and Yamane Yuzo, eds. *Shohekiga Zenshu* (*Collected Works of Paintings on Sliding Doors and Folding Screens*). 10 vols. Tokyo: Bijutsu Shuppansha, 1966–1972.

Tanimura 1983
Tanimura Tameumi. "Baisaō Nempo," in *Baisaō*. Saga: Saga Prefectural Museum, 1983.

Thomas 1927
Thomas, E. J. *The Life of Buddha as Legend and History*. London: 1927; rev. ed. London: 1949; repr. London: 1952, 1956.

Toda 1931
Toda Kenji. *The Ryerson Collection of Japanese and Chinese Illustrated Books*. Chicago: Art Institute of Chicago, 1931.

Toda 1957
Toda Hiroaki. *Nihon Kambungaku Tsūshi*. Tokyo: Musashino Shoin, 1957.

Toda 1973a
Toda Teisuke. "Boku Budō-zu," in Suzuki Kei, ed., *Chūgoku Bijutsu* 2. Tokyo: Kodansha, 1973.

Toda 1973b
Toda Teisuke. *Mokkei, Gyokkan* (*Mu-ch'i, Yü-chien*), *Suiboku Bijutsu Taikei* 3. Tokyo: Kodansha, 1973.

Toda 1988
Toda Teisuke. "Bijutsu-shi ni okeru Nitchū Kankei (3); Nihon Bijutsu-shi no Kadai," *Shuppan Daijestu* 1255 (June 20, 1988).

Tokuriki et al. 1981
Tokuriki Tomikichiro et al. *Jakuchū no Takuhanga* (*The Rubbing or Intaglio Woodblock Prints of Jakuchū*). Tokyo: Ruri Shobo, 1981.

Tokyo 1965
Tokyo Kokuritsu Hakubutsukan. *Nihon no Bunjinga Ten Mokuroku*. Tokyo: Tokyo Hakubutsukan, 1965.

Tokyo 1979
Kanō-ha no Kaiga (*Painting of the Kanō School*). Tokyo: Tokyo National Museum, 1979 (exhibition catalogue).

Tokyo 1986
So Shiseki to sono Jidai (*So Shiseki and His Period*). Tokyo: Idabashi Ward Museum, 1986 (exhibition catalogue).

Tsuji 1966
Tsuji Nobuo. "Kanō Motonobu," *Bijutsu Kenkyū* 246, 249 (1966); 270, 271, 272 (1970).

Tsuji 1970
Tsuji Nobuo. *Kisō no Keifu* (*Lineages of Eccentrics*). Tokyo: Bijutsu Shuppansha, 1970.

Tsuji 1971
Tsuji Nobuo. "Jakuchū-hitsu *Dōshoku Sai-e* ni tsuite" ("On the *Dōshoku Sai-e* Paintings by Jakuchū"), *Museum* 245 (1971).

Tsuji 1972
Tsuji Nobuo. "Ise no Shōhaku ga—Matsuzakashi no ihin o chūshin to shite" ("Shōhaku Paintings in Ise, Focusing on Extant Works in Matsuzaka City"), *Kokka* 952 (1972): 21–40.

Tsuji 1974
Tsuji Nobuo. *Jakuchū*. Tokyo: Bijutsu Shuppansha, 1974.

Tsuji et al. 1983
Tsuji Nobuo et al. *Bunga no hana kisō no tori* (*The Flower of Elegance, the Bird of Eccentricity*), *Kachōga no Sekai* 7. Tokyo: Gakushū Kenkyūsha, 1983.

Tsuji et al. 1984
Tsuji Nobuo et al. *Edo Jidai no Bijutsu* (*The Arts of the Edo Period*). Tokyo: Yūhikaku, 1984.

Tsunoda et al. 1958
Tsunoda, Ryūsaku, William Theodore deBary, and Donald Keene. *Sources of Japanese Tradition*. 2 vols. New York: Columbia University Press, 1958.

Tsuruta 1970
Tsuruta Takehiko. "Nihon Garon Nempyō" ("A Chronology of Japanese Literature on Painting"), *Bunka* 33 (1970): 539–576.

Uemura 1936
Uemura Kankō, ed. *Gozan Bungaku Zenshū* (*Compilation of Literature of Gozan Monks*). 5 vols. Tokyo: Gozan Bungaku Zenshū Kankōkai, 1936.

Umezawa 1949
Umezawa Naganoki. *Nihon Nanga Shi*. Tokyo: 1949.

de Visser 1918
de Visser, M. W. "Arhats and Lohans in China and Japan," *Ostasiatische Zeitschrift* 7 (1918–1919); 9 (1920–1922); 10 (1923–1924).

de Visser 1923
de Visser, M. W. *The Arhats in China and Japan*. Berlin: 1923.

Washi'o 1947
Washi'o Junkei. *Nihon Zenshū-shi no Kenkyū* (*Study of the History of the Zen Sect in Japan*). Tokyo: Kyoten Shuppan Kabushiki Kaisha, 1947.

Watson 1968
Watson, Burton. "Some Remarks on the *Kanshi*," *Journal-Newsletter of the Association of Teachers of Japanese* 5, no. 2 (July 1968).

Weber 1923
Weber, V. F. *Ko-ji Ho-ten*. 2 vols. Paris: 1923.

Yamagishi 1966
Yamagishi Tokuhei. *Gozan Bungaku Shū, Edo Kanshi Shū, Nihon Koten Bungaku Taikei* series. Tokyo: Iwanami Shoten, 1966.

Yamakawa 1963
Yamakawa Takeshi. "Nanki ni okeru Nagasawa Rosetsu no sakuhin" ("Nagasawa Rosetsu's Paintings in Southern Kii"). *Kokka* 860 (1963).

Yamakawa et al. 1978
Yamakawa Takeshi et al. *Kachoga: kacho, sansui* (*Bird-and-Flower Painting: Bird and Flower, Landscape*), *Nihon Byobu-e Shusei* 8. Tokyo: Kodansha, 1978.

Yamane 1969
Yamane Yuzo. *Sōtatsu to Kōrin, Genshoku Nihon no Bijutsu* 14. Tokyo: Shogakkan, 1969.

Yamane 1978
Yamane Yuzo, ed. *Rimpa Kaiga Zenshu: Hoitsu Ha*. Tokyo: 1978.

Yampolsky 1971
Yampolsky, Philip. *The Zen Master Hakuin: Selected Writings*. New York: 1971.

Yonezawa 1962
Yonezawa Yoshiho. "Minga Hyakuchō-zu" ("A Ming Painting of One Hundred Birds"), *Kokka* 841 (April 1962): 148.

Yonezawa and Yoshizawa 1966
Yonezawa Yoshiho and Yoshizawa Chū. *Bunjinga* (*Literati Painting*), *Nihon no Bijutsu* 23. Tokyo: Heibonsha, 1966.

Yonezawa and Yoshizawa 1974
Yonezawa Yoshiho and Yoshizawa Chū. *Japanese Painting in the Literati Style, Heibonsha Survey of Japanese Art* 23. Trans. and adapted by Betty Iverson Monroe. New York: Heibonsha/Weatherhill, 1974.

Yoshizawa 1973
Yoshizawa Chū. *Ike no Taiga, Nihon no Bijutsu* 26. Tokyo: Shogakukan, 1973.

Yoshizawa 1977
Yoshizawa Chū. *Nihon Nanga Ronkō* (*Essays on Southern School Painting of Japan*). Tokyo: Kodansha, 1977.

Yoshizawa and Yamakawa 1969
Yoshizawa Chū and Yamakawa Takeshi. *Nanga to shaseiga* (*Southern School Painting and Naturalistic Painting*), *Genshoku Nihon no Bijutsu* 18. Tokyo: Shogakukan, 1969.

All photographs except those noted below are courtesy of the Agency for Cultural Affairs, Tokyo.

Los Angeles County Museum of Art, Shin'enkan Collection
Figs. 2, 29, 32, 34, 47, 48, 49, 53

Museum of Fine Arts, Boston
Figs. 36, 45
Hoyt Collection, Figs. 6, 7, 54
Asiatic Department, Figs. 15, 16 (Rare Book J6288.6/4742.2), 19 (Rare Book 20989), 20 (Rare Book 73269), 21 (Rare Book 73272), 22 (Rare Book 74123)
Bigelow Collection, Figs. 23, 38, 46

The Mary and Jackson Burke Collection
Fig. 26

The Cleveland Museum of Art, John L. Severance Fund
Fig. 35 (82.25)